Bedford Cultural Editions

Reading the West

An Anthology of Dime Westerns

EDITED BY

Bill Brown

University of Chicago

BEDFORD BOOKS   BOSTON   NEW YORK

For Bedford Books

President and Publisher: Charles H. Christensen
General Manager and Associate Publisher: Joan E. Feinberg
Managing Editor: Elizabeth M. Schaaf
Developmental Editor: John E. Sullivan III
Production Editor: Bridget Leahy
Copyeditor: Carol Trippel
Cover Design: Susan Pace

Library of Congress Catalog Card Number: 96–86764

1 0 9 8 7
f e d c b

For information, write: Bedford Books, 75 Arlington Street, Boston,
MA 02116 (617–426–7440)

ISBN: 0–312–13761–3 (paperback)
ISBN: 0–312–16373–8 (hardcover)

About the Series

The need to "historicize" literary texts — and even more to analyze the historical and cultural issues all texts embody — is now embraced by almost all teachers, scholars, critics, and theoreticians. But the question of how to teach such issues in the undergraduate classroom is still a difficult one. Teachers do not always have the historical information they need for a given text, and contextual documents and sources are not always readily available in the library — even if the teacher has the expertise (and students have the energy) to ferret them out. The Bedford Cultural Editions represent an effort to make available for the classroom the kinds of facts and documents that will enable teachers to use the latest historical approaches to textual analysis and cultural criticism. The best scholarly and theoretical work has gone well beyond the "new critical" practices of formalist analysis and close reading, and we offer here a practical classroom model of the ways that different kinds of issues can be engaged when texts are not thought of as islands unto themselves.

The impetus for the recent cultural and historical emphasis has come from many directions: the so-called new historicism of the late 1980s, the dominant historical versions of both feminism and Marxism, the cultural studies movement, and a sharply changed focus in older movements such as reader response, structuralism, deconstruction, and psychoanalytic theory. Emphases differ, of course, among schools and individuals, but what these movements and approaches have in common is a commitment to explore — and to have students in the classroom study interactively — texts in their full historical and cultural dimensions. The aim is to discover how older texts (and those from other traditions) differ from our own assumptions and expectations, and thus the focus in teaching falls on cultural and historical differences rather than on similarity or continuity.

Most of the volumes in this series supplement the primary text with a generous selection of historical documents. But other volumes — such as this one on the dime Western — are intended to provide teachers and students with longer texts that are important literary and cultural documents in their own right. Often these texts enrich and complicate the study of mass or popular culture and, furthermore, they reveal the interaction between the bestsellers and popular texts that modern scholars have too often neglected or reduced to stereotypes and the texts that have managed to secure canonical status. Not only does the dime Western tell us much about nineteenth-century attitudes toward race and gender, it also provides a new and important context for the examination of widely taught authors such as James Fenimore Cooper and Mark Twain. In many cases it was mass-market fiction that writers such as Stephen Crane, Frank Norris, and Theodore Dreiser learned from, adapted, and challenged.

All of the volumes contain a general introduction that provides students with information concerning the political, social, and intellectual contexts for the work as well as information concerning the material aspects of the text's creation, production, and distribution. There are also relevant illustrations, a chronology of important events, and, when helpful, an account of the reception history of the text. Finally, both the main work and any accompanying documents are carefully annotated to enable students to grasp the significance of historical references, literary allusions, and unfamiliar terms.

In developing this series, our goal has been to foreground the kinds of issues that typically engage teachers and students of literature and history now. We have not tried to move readers toward a particular ideological, political, or social position or to be exhaustive in our choice of contextual materials. Rather, our aim has been to be provocative — to enable teachers and students of literature to raise the most pressing political, economic, social, religious, intellectual, and artistic issues on a larger field than any single text can offer.

J. Paul Hunter, University of Chicago
William E. Cain, Wellesley College
Series Editors

About This Volume

Dime novels were not simply popular; they were written and marketed specifically for a mass audience and thus help us see the configurations of an emerging mass culture in America. Among the genres promoted by the new fiction factories of the 1860s, the Western instantly suggests how inextricable this culture is from nineteenth-century literary history. The dime Western originally appropriated the narrative paradigms established by the captivity narrative and by James Fenimore Cooper's *Leatherstocking Tales*; its popularity helped set the stage for the success of the regional fiction published by Bret Harte and Mark Twain, among others; and it became the object of censure for critics like William Dean Howells and of morbid humor for writers like Stephen Crane. By the close of the nineteenth century, the cheap thrills of the dime Western were regarded as an unavoidable topic in the nation's cultural history. This volume reintroduces the topic into the study of American literature.

I became interested in publishing a handful of dime Westerns because of an obvious irony. These texts, which are responsible for perpetrating, or at least perpetuating, so many stereotypes — of savage Indians, helpless maidens, and self-reliant desperadoes — have themselves routinely been reduced to a mere stereotype. Although the novels often remain unread, the dime Western is repeatedly cited to denote the sensationalist version of frontier adventure. While the mechanical practice of stereotyping (the printing process that perpetuates an impression of composed type) made mass-market fiction a possibility in the mid-nineteenth century, a figurative version of the practice is the mode by which the dime novel is now remembered. The fact that the first dime Western was written by a woman who integrates a sentimental tradition with that of the historical romance begins to blur the stereotype, as does the fact that the most stable (and stereotypical) characters disappear in the pages of disguise and performance in subsequent Western thrillers.

Reading dime novels is an indispensable means of studying American mythmaking and the rewriting of U.S. history. It is also a means of engaging with the history of the book, with working-class culture, with emergent mass culture, and thus with the dynamics (aesthetic, social, and political) between what we call "high" and "low" culture. Popular culture has been a staple component of the field of American studies, and literature courses wishing to include previously marginalized material often focus now on two or three popular texts, usually including Harriet Beecher Stowe's *Uncle Tom's Cabin* (1852). Recent work in American social and cultural history and in cultural studies and film studies suggests that the time has come for the dime novel to recirculate as an object of updated analysis — analysis that refuses to dismiss the Western just because it seems to be the already known American genre, if not familiar as the exploits of Deadwood Dick or the James Boys then familiar as the exploits of John Wayne or Clint Eastwood.

Studies of mass culture — and the dime Western marks a crucial transition from a *popular* culture of legend and folklore to a *mass* culture of mass-marketed fiction — once tended either to demonize mass culture's standardization of consumer desire or to celebrate its utopian expression of otherwise suppressed fantasies. By now, however, products of mass culture are generally recognized as satisfying emotional needs and registering sociopolitical pressures while formalizing both. Mass culture may provide imaginary resolutions to real social problems, but it can also prompt readers to imagine new social formations, and it can foster new affiliations (however virtual) between readers. My introduction emphasizes not only how the routinized modes of production and distribution are legible within the fiction itself, but also how the dime Western works to disrupt its own modernity, just as it disrupts a familiar ideology of the West. The headnotes and footnotes to the texts establish more precise historical and literary contexts for the individual novels and their authors.

Of the thousands of dime novels that were published in the second half of the nineteenth century, I have chosen texts from the predominant genre, the Western, that have more than arbitrary representative value: *Malaeska* and *Seth Jones*, both from 1860 (the year Irwin P. Beadle & Co. began to publish "dollar books for a dime"), suggest how the *Leatherstocking* tradition was reworked into a new format; *Deadwood Dick*, published in 1877 and often named the paradigmatic Western thriller, shows the radical transformation of the Western; and *Frank Reade*, from 1890, what we might call a "decadent" Western, is a text in which generic rivals — detective fiction, science fiction, and the Western — converge. Representative as I wish them to be, each novel also offers opportunities for exploring the margins of the genre, where moments of excess illuminate what the genre typically excludes. There is something incongruous, of course, in carefully selecting texts from a body of fiction that was read voluminously rather than selectively, and a selection can neither demonstrate the full power of plot and character formulas nor intimate (let alone replicate) the pleasure that readers took in sheer repetition. The four novels reprinted here should be read as invitations to further reading.

ACKNOWLEDGMENTS

I owe a particular debt to those readers of American popular fiction who (in very different ways) have made their object of analysis singularly compelling, in particular John Cawelti, Janice Radway, and Michael Denning. Charles Christensen, Joan Feinberg, Jay Fliegelman, and William Cain, along with several of my graduate and undergraduate students at the University of Chicago, encouraged me to pursue the idea of making dime Westerns more accessible in the classroom. The idea would not have materialized without the diligence and insight of Jon Sachs, who has helped me in every stage of the research and editing.

John Cawelti, Maureen Honey, Donald Pease, Richard Slotkin, and Jane Tompkins provided important readings of my introduction. With Miriam Hansen I had the pleasure of discussing the project as part of our ongoing discussion of mass culture and modernity, and I had the inestimable benefit of her cogent reading. And James Chandler (to whom I owe a future account of Walter Scott in American mass culture) read the manuscript with his typical patience and insight.

The special collections, interlibrary loan, and research staffs of the University of Chicago Library always responded calmly and quickly to my desperate pleas. The New York Public Library and the Library of Congress were models of generosity, as was the Division of Rare Books and Special Collections at the University Libraries of Northern Illinois University. There Jennifer Metras went considerably out of her way to find and secure illustrations from the Albert Johannsen Collection.

My editors at Bedford Books, Kathy Retan and John Sullivan, have been patient and astute in their attention to a project that became more challenging than it at first appeared. Carol Trippel deserves thanks for copyediting the manuscript, as do proofreaders Jocelyn Humelsine and Janet Cocker. Bridget Leahy and Elizabeth Schaaf ably guided the book through production.

A remarkable combination of wit, empathy, and critical savvy enables Diana Young to endure the mess I make when I work and to endure being the reader on whom I rely most. Fraser contributes to the mess, likes the pictures, and can hardly be bothered with the text.

Bill Brown
University of Chicago

Contents

Illustrations

Reading the West: Cultural and Historical Background

In Stephen Crane's short story "The Blue Hotel" (1898), the dime novel is stigmatized as the primary agent in a surreal tragedy. On his way West to find a job, a Swedish tailor from New York stops at a hotel in Fort Romper, Nebraska, and there, though playing an apparently friendly game of cards, he grows increasingly anxious. He can't overcome his fear of the American West. The other patrons respond knowingly. One suggests that "this man has been reading dime-novels, and he thinks he's right out in the middle of it — the shootin' and the stabbin' and all" (Crane 809). In the middle of the hell that the Swede creates for himself, his mounting panic transforms into nervous aggression. He gets drunk, provokes and wins a fist fight, wanders off to a saloon, and there, with his new-found bravado, accosts a professional gambler. The gambler responds with a knife. He stabs the Swede fatally. It seems as though, after all, the dime Western has revealed the truth, or created some new truth, about the "shootin' and stabbin'" in the West.

In the second half of the nineteenth century, to surmise that a "man has been reading dime-novels" was to imagine that he had been taken in by the sensational fiction, thriving from 1860 to 1900, that was dominated by stories of the nation's frontier. The term "dime novel" originally referred to pocket-sized, hundred-page books with woodcut illustrations on the paper covers but it came to designate any fiction selling between five and twenty-five cents. More

1

pointedly, it designated the action-packed adventure of capture and rescue, disguise and revelation, pursuit and escape, that was generally set in Western territory — be it the western New York of the mid-eighteenth century or the Wyoming of the late nineteenth century. In these frontier settings, law appears as a mere luxury, major and minor disputes are resolved violently, and the moral order is momentarily stabilized only by the superior strength and intelligence of a handsome, well-built hero. Violence was obviously part of the attraction. Edward Wheeler's *Wild Ivan, the Boy Claude Duval; or, The Brotherhood of Death* (1878) begins during a "wild, terrible night," with "a storm of fierce, shrieking, restless wind and pouring, beating rain." The human action begins no less terribly: "Blue Bob bent forward, and there was a piercing shriek of pain, a grating, crunching sound, after which the old ruffian leaped to his feet, holding aloft a severed finger from Alice La Rue's hand" (2–3). Wheeler and his fellow authors portrayed such excess as a part of everyday life in the remote regions of the continent; in his *Deadwood Dick, The Prince of the Road* (1877; see pp. 288–89), no card game ends without a violent confrontation.

Stephen Crane's story, read either as a psychological study of fear or as an existentialist study of man's fate, anticipates modernist modes of literary inquiry. But it does so only while deploying familiar elements of the nineteenth-century Western—the slang, the nervousness of the "tenderfoot" and the iciness of the gambler, the bravado of the cowboy, the staging of the hotel and the saloon scenes, the mounting tension of the card game interrupted by "three terrible words: 'You are cheating'!" (Crane 813). This use of the scenic details and emotional pitch of sensational fiction follows a pattern that typifies the relation between what we call high culture and popular culture. In its effort to attain some cultural legitimacy, the dime Western makes references to Mark Twain, to Shakespeare, to classical mythology. In his effort to attain some cultural currency, Crane appropriates elements of mass-market fiction.

But he also disavows the appropriated genre, distancing the story from that supposed source of moral danger. By the turn of the century, charges against the dime novel had become shrill and commonplace. Asserting its role as cultural authority in 1879, *The Atlantic Monthly* vilified the dime novel for its violence, describing "a hundred dead in two chapters only," and mocking the cover illustrations that "vie with one another in lurid horror and repulsiveness" (Bishop 386). Editors of the "blood-and-thunder" thrillers were called

"Satan's efficient agents" who were "destroying the young" (Comstock 242), distracting children in the schoolroom, increasing juvenile crime, and contaminating the morals of the working class. At more than one murder trial, the dime novel was named as the actual cause of the crime, the inspiration for the murderer (Bishop 383, Harvey 37). Such scapegoating, which typifies the use of popular culture to explain social failures, may indeed join the dime novel itself as an implicit subject of scorn in "The Blue Hotel." Both the dime novel and its social critics, it seems, sustain delusions — on the one hand, the idea that the West remains violent, and on the other, the idea that society's violence results from some sort of mass-cultural contamination.

In an effort to debunk such delusions, Crane abandoned the irony of his story when he wrote as a journalist. He soberly reported, in a piece titled "Galveston, Texas, in 1895," that the "radical differences between Eastern and Western life" amounted to a fiction maintained because of its "commercial value." By Crane's light, "an illustration of Galveston can easily be obtained in Maine" (Crane 706). Yet accounts of the West's actual disappearance, the waning of its essential difference, was hardly news; rather, the news had long been part and parcel of the West's appearance in print. In the *Leatherstocking Tales* (1823–1841), the sequence of novels that provides the first dime Westerns with both their plot structure and their iconography, James Fenimore Cooper details civilization's encroachment on the frontier while lamenting the disappearing wilderness. The artist and ethnographer George Catlin asks of the West, in 1859, "where is its location?" and concludes that "phantom like it flies before us as we travel" (110). And in his note to the reader, prefacing *The Virginian* (1902), Owen Wister asks of the "vanished world" about which he writes: "What is become of the horseman, the cowpuncher, the most romantic figure upon our soil?" (viii–ix). The commercial value of the West — for fiction and film — resides in the movement between proclaimed absence and textual presence, in the nostalgic portrayal of an image and era marked as passing if not passed.

In other words, while an authentic West is reported to be absent, its authenticity remains insistently present, to the point of being internalized within the visual and literary culture of the East — indeed, seemingly internal and central to America itself. More than anyone, Frederick Jackson Turner officially sanctioned the centrality of the Western frontier when he addressed the World's Congress of Historians at the Columbian Exposition, Chicago's celebrated World's Fair of 1893. Raised on the Wisconsin frontier and doing his first histori-cal research on the trading post, Turner asserted a material and socio-economic claim about the foundations of American character and American politics; he worked to refute the intellectual historians who understood the United States as the product of European philosophy and political theory. "The Significance of the Frontier in American History," ritualistically invoked to begin or conclude every account of the West, proposes an understanding of America based not on the nation's genealogical relation to older European nations but on the nation's relation to itself. Turner claimed that the frontier — the "meeting point between savagery and civilization" — had been the site where the nation experienced a "perennial rebirth" (32). The "re-turn to primitive conditions on a continually advancing frontier line" had been a means of escaping the economic, geographical, and social confines of civilization, just as it had been a "gate of escape from the bondage of the past" (32, 59). The fact of Westward expansion had produced the "American intellect," the "American character" of indi-vidualism and materialism, and the healthy resistance to government that made U.S. democracy functional (59).

Turner's proclamation was itself occasioned by the 1890 census, which described the disappearance of "unsettled area" in the United States. At the moment of being statistically erased, then, the frontier was rewritten by Turner as an originating and enduring fact of Amer-ican history. This is how so much history — meaning economic, social, and political history — gets suppressed within a totalizing image of the nation where one matter of fact assumes mythic propor-tion. In a country where one frontier had succeeded another — the Allegheny Mountains, the trans-Mississippi Valley, the Great Plains, the Far West — no frontier remained, yet it continued (and continues) to be a central object of national and nationalizing fascination. Whether or not the frontier as such was the constitutive feature of American identity and American democracy, the myth and rhetoric of the frontier, as Henry Nash Smith, Richard Slotkin, and others have shown, was central to the nation's political and social imagination. From a cultural historian's point of view, it is not the material fact of the frontier, but the image, idea, and ideology of the frontier, that shape a national and nationalist psyche.

When Turner centralized the nation's periphery, he helped to cen-tralize the violence by which that periphery had been extended as the United States fulfilled what the editor John O'Sullivan, in 1845, called the nation's "manifest destiny to overspread the continent allotted by Providence for the free development of our yearly multiplying millions"(5). The dime Western was the medium most responsible for disseminating that image of violence; it was the means of carrying a sensational, violent West with you while you rode on an elevated train in Manhattan or waited for the fighting to begin at Shiloh. While the frontier had offered actual escape from Eastern civilization (the Homestead Act of 1862 ceded 160 acres of government land to anyone who would cultivate it for five years), the dime novel offered imaginative escape from an increasingly urbanized East. The first dime novels, such as *Malaeska* (1860; see p. 53) and *Seth Jones* (1860; see p. 165), tell a story of America's past (the colonial and post-Revolutionary eras) in the tradition of the historical romance established by Sir Walter Scott, with the publication of *Waverly* in 1814, and Americanized by Cooper. But in subsequent dime fiction, often narrating the adventures of living legends like Jesse and Frank James, the action can take place in the present, or simply outside history, which is precisely why a Swedish tailor from New York can imagine that the West remains the scene of random violence. Cooper, like Scott before him, framed his novels with a grand historical overview of local events. At the outset of *The Prairie* (1827), he writes: "Much was said and written, at the time [1803], concerning the policy of adding the vast regions of Louisiana, to the already immense, and but half-tenanted territories of the United-States" (Cooper 887). Fifty years later, at the outset of *Deadwood Dick*, Edward Wheeler writes: "On the plains, midway between Cheyenne and the Black Hills, a train had halted for a noonday feed." In his effort to get to the action and sustain it, Wheeler does away with any introductory historical scheme, and as he renders scenes of confrontation, he often switches from the past to the present tense.

Moreover, in the absence of such a scheme, the narrative no longer seems national, as it always does in Cooper, but local, just as the forces shaping the plot are not social, but personal. The question will be how to wreak personal revenge, not how, within an unevenly modernizing society, to resolve the conflict between traditional custom and modern law. Cooper's effort to represent social change in its totality transforms into Wheeler's effort to sketch a series of incidents that become man-to-man conflicts. The writers who were developing the genre of the Western sketch and short story (among them, Bret Harte, Mark Twain, and Stephen Crane) isolated incidents from a historical trajectory to highlight causal and moral ambiguities. But the dime novelist eliminates all ambiguity in the denouement: the closing chapter typically consists of a series of revelations, and the abruptly disclosed information ensures that the foregoing plot makes complete emotional and moral, if not always logical, sense.

Among the many texts and images that constitute the American West, the dime Western is best understood as a subgeneric institution. It is neither a genre per se (like the novel, the romance, the epic) nor simply a subgenre (like the sentimental novel or the detective novel) but rather a subgenre that is inseparable from its systematic modes of production and distribution. Anticipating such products as the Harlequin romance, the soap opera, or superhero comics, the dime Western depended on an "institutional matrix," to use Janice Radway's term, within which a reading audience is organized and maintained (8). It is recognizable by its narrative structure (a set of plot formulas); it is recognizable by its basic lexicon and subject matter (ranging from the threatened innocence of the beautiful maiden to the ineptitude of the local and federal governments); and it is most recognizable by the standardized packaging.

The mode of distribution necessitated such recognizability. Originally selling their product at newsstands but eventually through mail order as well, the publishing houses sold not just novels but series — like *Beadle's Frontier Series*, *The Deadwood Dick Library*, or *The New York Detective Library* — that assured their readership familiar fare behind the enticing covers (see Figs. 1–7). Success depended on the fundamental reproducibility of scene, character, and action; on the diminishment of historical, political, and social specificity; on the next novel in the series being all but interchangeable with the novel in hand. This is hardly to say that the novels are in fact interchangeable, for authors clearly strived to produce novelty. In this respect, the randomness of the escalating violence in the Western can be understood as an effort to compensate for the regularity of the serial system.

From their first appearance dime novels were recognized as a new publishing "phenomenon," their "unprecedented" sales figures prompting the *North American Review,* in 1864, to caution that "a serious responsibility rests upon them," and to encourage general reflection: "Why these works are popular is a problem quite as much for the moralist and the student of national character as for the critic" (Everett 308). The moralists have certainly had their day, as have the students of national character; meanwhile, the popularity of the dime version of the West — the shootin' and the stabbin' — has sustained countless films, radio programs, TV shows, and computer games, to the point of making the Western the quintessential American

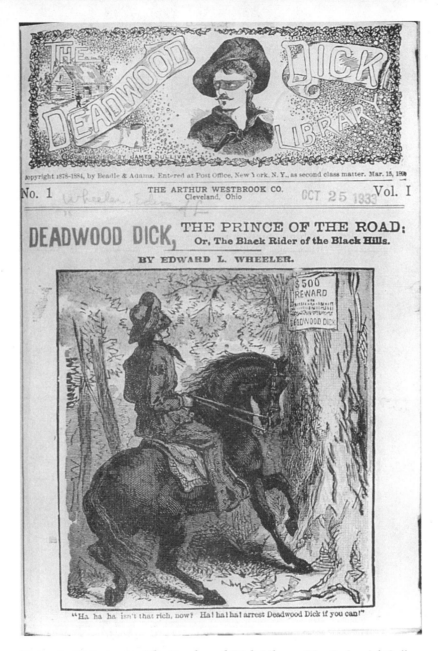

Figure 1. Paper cover, *The Deadwood Dick Library,* No. 1. Special Collections, University of Chicago Library.

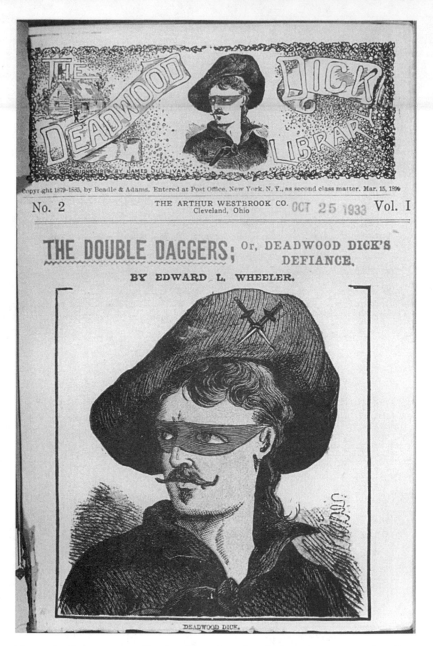

Figure 2. Paper cover, *The Deadwood Dick Library,* No. 2. Special Collections, University of Chicago Library.

No. 4   THE ARTHUR WESTBROOK CO.   Vol. I
Cleveland, Ohio

OCT 25 1933

BUFFALO BEN, The Prince of the Pistol;
Or, Deadwood Dick in Disguise.
A SEQUEL TO "THE DOUBLE DAGGERS."
BY EDWARD L. WHEELER,
AUTHOR OF "DEADWOOD DICK," "THE DOUBLE DAGGERS," ETC., ETC.

BUFFALO BEN.

Figure 3. Paper cover, *The Deadwood Dick Library,* No. 4. Special Collections, University of Chicago Library.

9

No. 5   THE ARTHUR WESTBROOK CO.   Vol. I
Cleveland, Ohio

OCT 25 1933

WILD IVAN, The Boy Claude Duval.

By Edward L. Wheeler,
AUTHOR OF
"DEADWOOD DICK."
ETC.

WILD IVAN.

Figure 4. Paper cover, *The Deadwood Dick Library,* No. 5. Special Collections, University of Chicago Library.

10

Figure 5. Paper cover, *The Deadwood Dick Library*, No. 15. Special Collections, University of Chicago Library.

Figure 6. Paper cover, *The Deadwood Dick Library,* No. 30. Special Collections, University of Chicago Library.

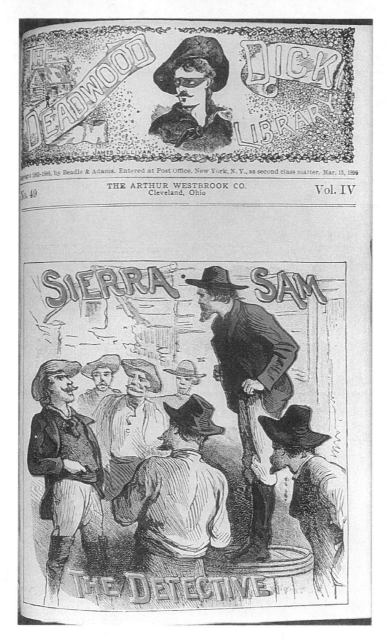

Figure 7. Paper cover, *The Deadwood Dick Library*, No. 49. Special Collections, University of Chicago Library.

genre. Still, we need to re-encounter the newness of the dime Western phenomenon or we risk rendering it legible only as the Western story we already know.

The dime Western is no less legible, however, as a phenomenon through which modernization infiltrated peoples' everyday lives — a phenomenon integral to the rapid reorganization of consumer culture that took hold in the second half of the nineteenth century. The subgeneric institution has rather less to do with its literary and ideological affiliates (from Cooper to Turner) and somewhat more to do with comparably momentous phenomena, such as the chain-store system, which deployed a new mode of distributing the same products to several different sites (by 1876, A&P had sixty-seven establishments); other mail-order enterprises, which recognized the attraction of shopping from home (by 1884, Montgomery Ward's catalogue was 240 pages); and the Five and Ten, which showed how profitable the sale of cheap goods could be (by 1895, Woolworth operated twenty-eight stores) (Boorstin, chs. 9–12).

For the Swede from New York in Stephen Crane's story, the dime Western expresses the sort of American violence that still reigned in Nebraska; but the dime novel also expresses a commitment to mass production, mass distribution, and mass consumption that took hold in the city from which the Swede has fled. The dime novel translated the material fact of the frontier into a literary image and simultaneously indoctrinated a national readership to the material fact of mass productivity. Moreover, it disengaged the story of the West from the story of the nation. Turner's frontier thesis, along with novels like Owen Wister's *The Virginian* and Theodore Roosevelt's history of the West, can thus be reread as efforts to repair the dime novel's damage to the Leatherstocking tradition and, in the name of official history and dominant culture, to reclaim the West from the pages of the Western. Phrased somewhat differently: though we can write a coherent history of the Western that begins by jumping quickly from Cooper's *The Pioneers* to Wister's *The Virginian*, it is by reading the mass market fiction between those novels that we begin to see how fragile that coherence was.

THE HOUSE OF BEADLE

The story of the dime Western as a subgeneric institution begins with the publishing house of Beadle ("Irwin Beadle and Company," later "Beadle and Company," then "Beadle and Adams"), which published over seven thousand novels between 1860 and 1897, when Arthur Westbrook purchased the company, retaining its name. In 1859, Irwin Beadle, who had worked several years as a bookbinder, and his brother Erastus Beadle, who had worked several years as a stereotyper, moved their new publishing firm from Buffalo to New York City, where they instantly succeeded in selling pocket-size (usually 6½ × 4¼ inch) handbooks: *Beadle's Dime Debater, Beadle's Dime Letter Writer, Beadle's Dime Book of Beauty, Beadle's Dime Book of Verses,* and *Beadle's Book of Dreams,* among others (see Figs. 8–11). On June 7 of the following year, deciding to continue the experiment with fiction, Beadle & Co. ran an advertisement in the *New York Tribune* that was soon to become famous in the annals of publishing:

BOOKS FOR THE MILLION!
A Dollar Book For A Dime!!
128 pages complete, only Ten Cents!!!
BEADLE'S DIME NOVELS NO. 1

MALAESKA;
the
Indian Wife Of The White Hunter
By Mrs. Ann S. Stephens
128 pages, 12 mo., Ready Saturday Morning, June 9

The publication was in fact a republication of the prize-winning novel that had appeared serially in *The Ladies' Companion* in 1839, written by a "Star of American Authors," as the publishers legitimately put it. Ann Sophia Stephens was a prolific and celebrated figure in the literary scenes of New England and New York; she was a professional writer and editor whose name alone was worth the $250 that the Beadles paid her for the rights to the volume. As a dime novel, *Malaeska* sold ten thousand copies in the first edition, twenty thousand in the second edition, and a reported three hundred thousand by the close of the century (Johannsen 31, Stern).

The exclamatory advertisement in the *Tribune* reveals more than a little about the origin and eventual history of the enterprise. By declaring their new novels to be "for the million," the Beadles worked to sell the books by selling their imagined popularity (foreshadowing the sale of modern "best sellers" as books that everybody should read because everybody is reading them). They go on to translate the fact of mass production into a populist fantasy by claiming to "provide"

BEADLE'S DIME

United States of America — One Dime

Book of Verses

COMPRISING

RHYMES, LINES AND MOTTOES,

FOR LOVERS AND FRIENDS;

VALENTINES, ALBUM PIECES. GIFT VERSES, BIRTHDAY
LINES, AND POETRY FOR BRIDALS, BIRTHS,
MOURNING, EPITAPHS, Etc.

NEW YORK:
BEADLE AND COMPANY, 118 WILLIAM ST.

Figure 8. Paper cover, *Beadle's Dime Book of Verses*. Courtesy of The Library of Congress.

16

BOOK OF DREAMS:

THEIR

ROMANCE AND MYSTERY,

WITH A COMPLETE

INTERPRETATION DICTIONARY.

COMPILED FROM THE

MOST ACCREDITED SOURCES FOR THE "DIME SERIES."

_____

NEW YORK:

BEADLE AND ADAMS, 98 WILLIAM ST.

The American News Company, New York.

Figure 9. Paper cover, *Beadle's Book of Dreams*. Courtesy of The Library of Congress.

STANDARD DIME PUBLICATIONS.

Speakers.

BEADLE AND ADAMS have now on their lists the following highly desirable and attractive text-books, prepared expressly for schools, families, etc. Each volume contains 100 large pages, printed from clear, open type, comprising the best collection of Dialogues, Dramas and Recitations, (burlesque, comic and otherwise.) The Dime Speakers for the season of 1882—as far as now issued—embrace twenty-four volumes, viz.:

1. American Speaker.	13. School Speaker.
2. National Speaker.	14. Ludicrous Speaker.
3. Patriotic Speaker.	15. Komikal Speaker.
4. Comic Speaker.	16. Youth's Speaker.
5. Elocutionist.	17. Eloquent Speaker.
6. Humorous Speaker.	18. Hail Columbia Speaker.
7. Standard Speaker.	er.
8. Stump Speaker.	19. Serio-Comic Speaker.
9. Juvenile Speaker.	20. Select Speaker.
10. Spread-Eagle Speaker	21. Funny Speaker.
11. Dime Debater.	22. Jolly Speaker.
12. Exhibition Speaker.	23. Dialect Speaker.

24. Dime Book of Recitations and Readings.

These books are replete with choice pieces for the School-room, the Exhibition, for Homes, etc. They are drawn from FRESH sources, and contain some of the choicest oratory of the times. 75 to 100 Declamations and Recitations in each book.

Dialogues.

The Dime Dialogues, each volume 100 pages, embrace twenty-nine books, viz.:

Dialogues No. One.	Dialogues No. Fifteen.
Dialogues No. Two.	Dialogues No. Sixteen.
Dialogues No. Three.	Dialogues No. Seventeen.
Dialogues No. Four.	Dialogues No. Eighteen
Dialogues No. Five.	Dialogues No. Nineteen.
Dialogues No. Six.	Dialogues No. Twenty.
Dialogues No. Seven.	Dialogues No. Twenty-one.
Dialogues No. Eight.	Dialogues No. Twenty-two.
Dialogues No. Nine.	Dialogues No. Twenty-three.
Dialogues No. Ten.	Dialogues No. Twenty-four.
Dialogues No. Eleven.	Dialogues No. Twenty-five.
Dialogues No. Twelve.	Dialogues No. Twenty-six.
Dialogues No. Thirteen.	Dialogues No. Twenty-seven.
Dialogues No. Fourteen	Dialogues No. Twenty-eight.

Dialogues No. Twenty-nine.

15 to 25 Dialogues and Dramas in each book.

These volumes have been prepared with especial reference to their *availability* in *all* school-rooms, They are adapted to schools with or without the furniture of a stage, and introduce a range of characters suited to scholars of every grade, both male and female. It is fair to assume that no volumes yet offered to schools, *at any price*, contain so many *available* and useful dialogues and dramas, serious and comic.

Dramas and Readings.

164 12m Pages. 20 Cents.

For Schools, Parlos, Entertainments and the Amateur Stage, comprising Original Minor Dramas, Comedy, Farce, Dress Pieces, Humorous Dialogue and Burlesque, by selected writers; and Recitations and Readings, new and standard, of the greatest celebrity and interest. Edited by Prof. A. M. Russell.

Figure 10. List of Beadle and Adams' Standard Dime Publications, from *Beadle's Book of Dreams*.

18

DIME HAND-BOOKS.

Young People's Series.

BEADLE'S DIME HAND-BOOKS FOR YOUNG PEOPLE cover a wide range of subjects, and are especially adapted to their end. They constitute at once the cheapest and most useful works yet put into the market for popular circulation.

Ladies' Letter-Writer.	Book of Games.
Gents' Letter-Writer.	Fortune-Teller.
Book of Etiquette.	Lovers' Casket.
Book of Verses.	Ball-room Companion.
Book of Dreams.	Book of Beauty.

Hand-Books of Games.

BEADLE'S DIME HAND-BOOKS OF GAMES AND POPULAR HAND-BOOKS cover a variety of subjects, and are especially adapted to their end.

Handbook of Summer Sports.

Book of Croquet.	Yachting and Rowing
Chess Instructor.	Riding and Driving.
Cricket and Football.	Book of Pedestrianism.
Guide to Swimming.	

Handbook of Winter Sports—Skating, etc.

Manuals for Housewives.

BEADLE'S DIME FAMILY SERIES aims to supply a class of text-books and manuals fitted for every person's use—the old and the young, the learned and the unlearned. They are of conceded value.

1. Cook Book.	4. Family Physician.
2. Recipe Book.	5. Dressmaking and Mil-
3. Housekeeper's Guide.	linery

Lives of Great Americans

Are presented complete and authentic biographies of many of the men who have added luster to the Republic by their lives and deeds. The series embraces:

I.—George Washington.	VII.—David Crockett.
II.—John Paul Jones.	VIII.—Israel Putnam.
III.—Mad Anthony Wayne	X.—Tecumseh.
IV.—Ethan Allen.	XI.—Abraham Lincoln.
V.—Marquis de Lafay-	XII.—Pontiac.
ette.	XIII.—Ulysses S. Grant.
VI.—Daniel Boone.	

The above publications for sale by all newsdealers or will be sent, post-paid, on receipt of price, by BEADLE & ADAMS, 98 WILLIAM ST., N. Y.

Figure 11. List of Beadle and Adams' Standard Dime Publications, from *Beadle's Book of Dreams.*

fiction for the millions at a time when, indeed, only a small portion of the remarkably literate U.S. population could afford to purchase books (let alone novels) regularly, since the standard working-class wage amounted to six dollars a week. As Erastus Beadle continued to explain the idea years later, other publishers, using thick paper, wide margins, and cloth covers, were "trying to see how little they could give their readers for a dollar or a dollar and a half," while he and his brother were trying to see how much they could give their readers for ten cents (quoted by Pearson 98).

While this quantifying rhetoric alone marks an obvious shift in attitude toward cultural production, it also signals more specific shifts in the history of reading and the history of the book. The materiality of the book, its status as an object, becomes inconsequential in deference to its status as an arresting image, a title and cover illustration. The act of reading becomes what we might call an act of genuine consumption (not of rereading and preservation) in which the product is digestible, disposable, and replaceable. While the reading of novels often continued to be a collective, familial affair, it could now emerge as a private indulgence, facilitated by the size of the books, which allowed them to be easily carried and hidden. The indulgence differentiates privacy from domesticity while it bridges the sphere of work and the sphere of the home. As George Putnam's pocket-size "Railroad Classics" of the 1850s had already made clear, reading was becoming a diversion for commuters (Zboray 192–93); not concentration and education, but distraction and sensation were soon to become hallmarks of the new American reading habit.

Such shifts, and the very success of the dime novel, were made possible by several technological transformations: the extremely cheap production of wood pulp paper, not perfected until the mid-1850s; the use of the steam-powered cylinder press, which drastically cut labor costs; the use of stereotyped plates, which eliminated the bulk of the reprinting costs for subsequent editions; and improvements in transportation, both interstate and intracity, which meant that novels could find their way to hundreds of newsstands (Zboray 188–94). The distributor for the Beadles, the American News Company, had a standing order for sixty thousand copies of any new novel (Pearson 46). The fit between the Beadles' experiment, the state of printing technology, and the reading market was so good that by the end of 1860 they faced competition from three other publishing houses, which offered their own series of dime fiction. More alarming, Okie, Dayton, & Jones suddenly announced the introduction of *People's*

Five Cent Novelettes, to which the Beadles responded by introducing *Half-Dime Novelettes* (Johannsen 36).

The rubric "dime novel" came to designate a variety of inexpensive publications, but the dime novel per se commanded the field of inexpensive fiction for a decade and a half, during which the house of Beadle commanded the most attention, publishing hundred-page books with salmon-colored wrappers and woodcut illustrations that were instantly recognizable at the newsstand. Sensationalist fiction and mass-market fiction weren't novelties in 1860, however. In the 1840s, Ned Buntline (Edward Z. C. Judson), an extraordinarily prolific writer who later wrote hundreds of novels for Beadle, published his own sensation sheet, *Ned Buntline's Own*, urban exposés (such as *The Mysteries and Miseries of New York*), and dollar sea adventures (such as *The Red Revenger*). Story papers, which printed both short stories and serialized novels (some later republished as dime novels), exploited both the U.S. government's failure to recognize international copyright and its postal rates for newspapers. When those rates were rescinded for story papers in 1843, the papers temporarily disappeared. The cheapest novels of the day were twelve-cent editions of foreign texts, which is why the Beadles take such care explaining, in their publisher's notice about *Malaeska*, that it "is American in all its features" (Monaghan 123–37, 157–67; Jones 1–15; see p. 59).

By repeatedly emphasizing that theirs was a series of "National and American Romances," of "Purely American Novels" written by Americans about America, the Beadles both differentiated their work from the republication of European fiction and coded their enterprise as a patriotic project, responding to the ongoing call for a national literature (expressed by the same journals, such as *Harper's New Monthly Magazine*, that continued to serialize fiction by English writers — William Thackeray, Charles Dickens, and Wilkie Collins). The dime novels themselves didn't shy away from literary jingoism. In *Buffalo Bill* (1886), Ned Buntline pauses to celebrate the romantic nature of his American subject: "Talk not to me of the Light Brigade, famed at Balakava — talk not to me of Lodi or Austerlitz. On a hundred fields in this, our dear native land, have charges been made and battles fought which were as far beyond them as light is superior to darkness" (305–06). While Buntline proclaimed the literary value of his subject, the publishers continued to assert the monetary value of their fiction. By using the dime itself as their trademark, they fused price and product under the sign of federal authority.

Such emphasis was merely part of the Beadles' effort to establish a reputation — what we now call a brand name — that in itself would sell products. They laid the blame for the dime novel's negative reputation at the feet of their competitors and frequently advertised their own policy, established by house editor Orville J. Victor: "We prohibit all things offensive to good taste, in expression or incident"; "We prohibit subjects or characters that carry an immoral *taint*"; "We require unquestioned originality"; "We require pronounced strength of plot and high dramatic interest of story" (Johannsen 4). The publishing house was trying to create consumer loyalty, an intimacy between reader and firm that assumed priority over the commodity itself.

Correspondingly, the advertisement for *Malaeska* names the novel as the initial number in a series, working to generate interest in an ongoing publishing project. The company multiplied and codified consumer choice by generating new series — *Beadle's Pocket Library*, *Beadle's Dime Library*, *Beadle's New Dime Novels*, *Beadle's New York Dime Library* (Fig. 12), and *Beadle's Half Dime Library* (Fig. 13) — a total of twenty-five, small in comparison to the number published by the house of Street and Smith and the house of Frank Tousey. Seriality (which included subseries, such as the Deadwood Dick novels within the *Half Dime Library*) played an overwhelming role in organizing and sustaining a readership. Lists of other novels in the series were printed in each book, and novels in a series made occasional reference to others. In a series like *The Deadwood Dick Library*, which began with the republication of several novels, the illusion of difference and development generates the desire to complete the series, the sense that the unread novel is the one that will fill up the lack in a larger story of Deadwood, and of the West, that the series is trying to tell.

This proliferation of series is the crucial aspect of the dime novel's promotion that is part of a history of promotional culture wherein manufacturers orchestrate consistency and change, the *effect* of stability and the *effect* of novelty. The Beadles went so far as to create a fictitious publisher (Frank Starr & Co.) for some of their series (see Figs. 14 and 15); and some authors were so prolific that their novels were published under several different pseudonyms. Conversely, the names of especially successful authors were appended to work that wasn't theirs; when Edward Wheeler died, the fact was suppressed, and the Deadwood Dick series continued for years, with Wheeler bylined as author. When a novel from one series appeared in another, often its title, cover illustration, and credited author changed (as did its length, if need be).

Vol. IV.   Complete In One Number.   *Beadle & Adams, Publishers,*   *No. 98 WILLIAM STREET, NEW YORK.*   Price, Ten Cents.   No. 41.

Gold Dan:

OR,

The White Savage of the Great Salt Lake.

BY ALBERT W. AIKEN.

AUTHOR OF "VELVET HAND," "OVERLAND KIT," "ROCKY MOUNTAIN ROB," "KENTUCK, THE SPORT," "INJUN DICK," ETC., ETC., ETC.

CHAPTER I.

THE CHIEF OF THE DANITES.

"By that lake whose gloomy shore
Sky-lark never warbled o'er—"

THE Great Salt Lake in the heart of the continent; that strange body of water within whose confines fish swim not, whose borders are incrusted with salty crystals, glistening, diamond-like, in the sun; whose dense, saline waters reject the human who essays to plunge beneath the wave; and of this wondrous lake, so strange, so wild,

we shall relate a story so terrible, so improbable, that even credulous man might refuse to believe such things could be, were not the pages of history already stained with the red story of the impartial historian.

We write of the days of the spring of '69, when the great overland road was rapidly approaching completion, and already the grading parties of both the Central and the Union Pacific railways were in strong force in the neighborhood of the town of Corinne, on Bear river, just to the north of the Great Salt Lake.

It is a lovely night in the month of April, and the clear heavens above are spangled with a myriad of stars, and these peaceful watchers looked down upon as strange a scene as they ever had beheld since the world was young.

In a secluded nook on Antelope island, the largest of the little group which dot the waters of the lake, burned a camp-fire, and around the flames were gathered a motley collection of men, twelve or fifteen in number.

One might search all the border, from the waters of the Missouri to the golden sands of the placid Pacific, and yet not find a dozen as desperate fellows.

All were armed to the teeth, with one exception, and he, with his plain black suit and clerical aspect, was a strange contrast to the rest.

These armed ruffians, so fierce of face and so lawless in aspect, were Danites—the "Destroying Angels" of the Mormon host, and the black-coated man was a Mormon elder.

After generations, when they read the record of the Danites, will wonder that such things could be in a Christian land, and think perhaps that the story is over-wrought, when in reality the half of the dark deeds done in the gloomy canyon and desolate wastes of Utah will never be revealed until the Judgment Day, when the murdered victims rise in accusing wrath.

Early in the existence of the Salt Lake settlement, the wily and unscrupulous leaders of this strange band of zealots saw that to crush opposition, awe the timid and overbear the bold, it was necessary to use the sword. A sentence in Genesis suggested the means: "Dan shall be a serpent by the way, an adder in the path, that biteth the horse's heels, so that his rider shall fall backward."

"WHOOP—YOW-YOW—WHOOP LA!" AND THE-MAN-FROM-RED-DOG EXECUTED A WAR-DANCE IN THE MIDDLE OF THE STREET.

Figure 12. Front page, *Beadle's New York Dime Library*, No. 41. Albert Johannsen Collection, Rare Books and Special Collections, Northern Illinois University Libraries.

23

BEADLE'S HALF DIME Library

$2.50 a year.   Entered at the Post Office at New York, N. Y., as Second Class Mail Matter.   Copyrighted in 1880 by BEADLE AND ADAMS.   March 16, 1880.

Vol. VI.   Single Number.   PUBLISHED WEEKLY BY BEADLE AND ADAMS, No. 98 WILLIAM STREET, NEW YORK.   Price, 5 Cents.   No. 138,

Blonde Bill; or, Deadwood Dick's Home Base.

BY EDWARD L. WHEELER,

AUTHOR OF "DEADWOOD DICK," "ROSEBUD ROB," "GILT-EDGED DICK," "BONANZA BILL," ETC., ETC.

" My name's Salamander Sam, pilgrims, ef ye don't know me, an' I've come down here ter sell this yere gal at auction, ter ther highest bidder. Sh.' my darter, is Dashing Dot, an' I opine ef I want ter sell her, that's my bizness. So, now, feller citizens, ef enny o' yer want 'er, jest give me a starting bid. How much do I hear, now? How much'll ye give fer her, loves—how much, now, hoss an' all? Durst ary man start 'er at any ― ―ter? Gal an' hoss! how much do I hee' now, for ther good will and fictures—sole right and title—how much, now?"

Figure 13. Front page, *Beadle's Half Dime Library,* No. 138. Albert Johannsen Collection, Rare Books and Special Collections, Northern Illinois University Libraries.

24

Figure 14. Paper cover, *Frank Starr's American Novels*, No. 44. Albert Johannsen Collection, Rare Books and Special Collections, Northern Illinois University Libraries.

Price, Ten Cents. Copyrighted 1877, by FRANK STARR & Co. Published on the 10th & 25th of every month. $2.25 a Year.

Vol. I. FRANK STARR & CO., PUBLISHERS, No. 4.
PLATT AND WILLIAM STS., NEW YORK.

The Kidnapper; Or, the Great Shanghai of the Northwest.

By Philip S. Warne, Author of "Tiger Dick," "A Hard Crowd," etc.

BEARING BLANCHE AWAY,

Figure 15. Paper cover, *Frank Starr's New York Library*, No. 4. Albert Johannsen Collection, Rare Books and Special Collections, Northern Illinois University Libraries.

As such observations suggest, the success of the dime novel depended not just on the efficient reproducibility of a single text but also on the ability to reproduce elements of plot and character. At its most extreme, at the house of Street and Smith, standardization went far beyond designated word length (70,000 or 35,000) to plot formulas, and to scene and character sketches, skeletons that were fleshed out by hack writers (Bold 1–18). Prentiss Ingraham, when pressed, reportedly wrote a novel in as few as twenty-four hours. In the Beadle factory on William Street, writers composed stories upstairs; below them, editors blue-penciled offensive language and excess words, artists produced illustrations, and typesetters set type; below them ran the presses. Authors were often able to assert themselves despite the restrictions, but once the system of the fiction factory was firmly in place, the novels tended to betray their mode of production in the very structure and rhythm of plot construction, deployed less to achieve narrative resolution than to sustain tension and generate as many dramatic scenes of confrontation as possible. In other words, plot became a means of producing successive theatrical tableaux. Instead of an integrated and progressive unfolding of events, distinct plots alternated until the denouement; the novel depended on a pattern of event and disclosure, with action in one chapter requiring a subsequent chapter's explanation, and with fragmentation and digression succeeded by hasty, retrospective reconstruction. The technology that produced the Western was completed by the narrative technology of the Western itself — a set of interchangeable parts, a standardized structure, and a regularized rhythm of crisis and resolution, event and explanation.

But the initial success of the dime novel enterprise lay not so much in efficient and inexpensive production, nor in scenic reproducibility, as in imaginative marketing. By the end of September 1860, the Beadles' promotional imagination extended beyond the topics of price and seriality, when they risked publishing a manuscript that had been humbly submitted by a twenty-year-old schoolteacher from Trenton, Edward Ellis. On the New York *Tribune*'s front page, in eye-catching half-inch letters, readers were repeatedly asked "Who is Seth Jones?" — a question that also appeared in posters tacked up around the city. In the words of Edward Ellis, "Everywhere you went this query met you. It glared at you in staring letters on the sidewalks. It came fluttering in to you on the little dodgers thrust by the handful into the Broadway stages."

New Yorkers next discovered that "Seth Jones is from New Hampshire"; that "Seth Jones understands the redskins"; that "Seth Jones takes an observation"; and "Seth Jones can't express himself."

The confusing assertions were meant to make Seth Jones the topic of citywide conversation. Then, as Ellis explains it, "big and little posters bearing a lithographic portrait of a stalwart, heroic looking hunter" were seen accompanied by the words "I am Seth Jones.'" The strategy generated sufficient consumer desire to sell an edition of sixty thousand copies in a few months. Not surprisingly, the Beadles celebrated "[s]uch a success [as] has rarely been witnessed in the history of our literature" in the pages of the *Tribune*, and *Seth Jones* established the model that would dominate the dime Western for a decade (Johannsen 1:32–36).

What the original question about Seth Jones never intimated was that he might be a fictional character from a novel. Such ambiguity was exploited again and again, as fact and fiction blended in dime biographies (of Kit Carson, Daniel Boone, David Crockett, Pontiac, Tecumseh, Jesse James, and Ulysses S. Grant), and dime novels capitalized on the already newsworthy (see Fig. 16). In 1876, in Deadwood, Dakota Territory, James ("Wild Bill") Hickok, a U.S. marshal who had become one of the country's most famous gunmen, was shot in the back and killed. By 1877, Edward Wheeler introduced the character of Deadwood Dick (a better shot than Hickok, who worked for himself). Sitting Bull, leader of Indian forces during the Sioux War of 1876–77, in which George Custer and his Seventh Cavalry were slain, showed up in the novel playing a bit part. Once Wheeler had established the figure of the virtuous outlaw, a notorious bandit like California's Joaquín Murieta was recast as a wronged vaquero seeking vengeance in Joseph Badger's *Joaquin, the Saddle King. A Romance of Murieta's First Fight* (1881).

Most famously, a Union soldier, army scout in the Plains Wars, and rider for the Pony Express, William F. Cody, was an object of local admiration who didn't attain national prominence until Ned Buntline met Cody in 1869 and began to sensationalize some biographical incidents into a series of articles and novelistic biographies of "Buffalo Bill." Thereafter, Buntline and Cody (and later Prentiss Ingraham and Cody) worked together on stage Westerns and dime Westerns (more than one hundred, many of which named Buffalo Bill as author). Cody fought again for the U.S. cavalry in 1876, and he performed his feat of taking *"the first scalp to avenge Custer"* on the battlefield, in the pages of books (like Ingraham's *Adventures of Buffalo Bill from Boyhood to Manhood* [1881]), and on the melodramatic stage. As Buffalo Bill's Wild West stage show toured nationally and internationally in the 1880s, he became a national icon; pitching

COMPLETE.   NO. 15.

BEADLE'S DIME
BIOGRAPHICAL LIBRARY

ULYSSES S. GRANT.

NEW YORK:
BEADLE AND COMPANY. 118 WILLIAM ST.
American News Company, 121 Nassau St.

Figure 16. Paper cover, *Beadle's Dime Biographical Library*, No. 15. Courtesy of The Library of Congress.

29

his show beside the Columbian Exposition in 1893, he repeatedly staged that confrontation between civilization and savagery that Turner identified as the central fact of the nation (see Slotkin 63–87). To capitalize on Cody's increased notoriety, *Beadle's Dime Library* published nine new Buffalo Bill novels, written by Ingraham, in the months before the opening of the Exposition (Leithead 1–2).

Reading examples of the dime Western, then, is a matter of witnessing not just how fact becomes fiction but also how popular culture becomes mass culture, how legend becomes mass-mediated memory. The dime novel exemplifies the way that the process of modernization does not so much eradicate local legend as it expropriates and redistributes it, reconstituting the folkloric as mail-order myth. This process is the culture industry's version of how, according to local-colorist writers like Hamlin Garland (in 1894), regionalist literature would precipitate a new national literature (Garland 29). If we suppose that the mass-produced myth effected some degree of national cohesion, then we should also suppose that both cohesion and alienation lay in the shared reading practice, the shared relation to consumer culture, and the newly shared pace and privacy of reading as an act of consumption. The material facts of the dime novel's production and distribution help us to appreciate the Western as a rationalization of the West that synchronized the realm of leisure in the rhythms of work and industry. The subgeneric institution contributed to what America's premier economist, Thorstein Veblen, described in 1904 as the "cultural incidence of the machine process," wherein the mechanization of modern industry infiltrates human consciousness (302–73).

CONFLICT AND CONCEALMENT

And yet the content of the dime Western works to violate the systematic, mechanistic character of its mass production. The heroic, self-reliant individual — unimpeded by urbanization, industrialization, and mechanization — appears center stage. The image, idea, and aura of the West offer an alternative to the rational dictates of modernity, while the fund of jargon, gesture, and attitude distinguishes the pragmatic American from the refined European: it favors anti-intellectual intuition, interrupts any class-coded system of taste in the name of authenticity, and hence protects America from what Theodore Roosevelt called the dangerous ease of "over-civilized man" (*The Strenuous Life* 7). In his own six-volume *The Winning of the West* (1889–96), the record of a "western conquest" that is "the crowning and greatest achievement of a series of mighty movements" (concluding with the 1804 expedition of Lewis and Clark), Roosevelt argues that in the "race-history" of the nation, the conflict with the Indian nations enabled a heterogeneous people to be "fused into one people" (*Winning* 1:40, 24, 40). In the logic of Roosevelt's epic, the confrontation enabled the settlers to understand themselves racially. The power of his story, at one with the Turner thesis, is the power of epic containment — the production of a history of national consolidation so monumental that it diminishes other events. In contrast, the dime novel makes visible the ways in which the narration of the West aestheticizes the genocidal foundation of the nation, turning conquest into a literary enterprise that screens out other violent episodes in the nation's history.

Cody and Carson, Hickok and James were Civil War soldiers whose postwar exploits seemed to perpetuate the military and paramilitary heroism of the prewar arena. Their literary careers insist on the priority of the East-West axis — over and against the North-South axis — to explain the nation, an insistence later sanctioned by Turner's conviction that "the slavery struggle . . . occupies its important place in American history because of its relation to westward expansion" (32). When, late in *Malaeska*, we confront the momentary appearance of slaves in colonial Manhattan, when a character in *Seth Jones* refers to the Indians as "them blasted Five Nation niggers" (p. 189), or when Jesse and Frank James fight vigilantes in a novel that D. W. Stevens entitles *The James Boys and the Ku Klux Klan* (1890) — we're reading residues of the racial tension and social crisis that the Western typically suppresses. The appeal of this suppression is inseparable from the fact that the dime novel first appeared in the year the Civil War erupted; by the succeeding June, the Union army was defeated at Bull Run.

For the Beadles, war became what we might call a crucial mode of distribution, pushing sales into the millions. As one early commentator put it, the "books were sent to the army in the field by cords, like unsawed firewood. Compact in form, they were easily made up into immense bales, and shipped on any kind of freight car, canal-boat or country wagon" (Jencks 109). As was the case with later wars, the publishing industry used the occasion to cultivate a specifically male audience for mass-market fiction. After the Beadles published *Malaeska*, they published six more of Ann Stephens's novels in the next four years, and several other women wrote for various firms. (Louisa May Alcott wrote pseudonymous thrillers for Loring's *Tales of the Day* and *Ten Cent Novelettes*.) But because of the popularity of the Western genre, the dime-novel enterprise increasingly became an enterprise of men writing for men about men. Although reformers claimed that this fiction was written for the "lower classes of society," or for "newsboys or bootblacks" (Bishop 389), it was also read by industrialists, bankers, and presidents, all of whom, it seems, were compelled by a unifying story of the West in the midst of the nation's actual North/South divide.

That story relied on a variety of popular genres. Captivity narratives, such as Mary Rowlandson's *Captivity and Restoration* (1676) and John Marrant's *Narrative of the Lord's Wonderful Healings* (1770), rivaled Scott's novels in popularity in the first decades of the nineteenth century. These accounts of being captured, tested, and degraded by Indians served as ethnographic accounts from "inside" Native American culture, and they centralized contact with the native culture as the paradigmatic personal and spiritual test. Pioneer biographies (authentic and inauthentic) of figures like Boone and Crockett, travelogues like Francis Parkman's immensely popular *Oregon Trail* (1847), and romantic histories of the European struggle over North America certified the sublimity of the frontier scene and its priority as the site where personal and national development could converge.

In his *Border Romances*, most popularly *The Yemassee* (1835), William Gilmore Simms followed Scott and Cooper in his account of the South Carolinian conflict between the Indians and the British. While Simms shared Cooper's ambivalent sentimentalization of Indian culture, Robert Montgomery Bird's *Nick of the Woods* (1837) vilified the Indians as reprobate savage beasts; and in the revenge plot, Nick's genocidal imagination, his passion to avenge his massacred family, transforms him into a no-less-savage figure. Among the antebellum novelists writing Western romances, Irish-born Mayne Reid most successfully managed to adapt to the dime-novel enterprise; he was paid the fee of $700 for *The White Squaw* (1868), a record that the Beadles made sure to advertise in the pages of the *Tribune*, just as they had advertised Reid's agreement to write for the house.

But as *Malaeska* and *Seth Jones* attest, it was Cooper's *Leatherstocking Tales*, beginning with *The Pioneers* (1823) and concluding with *The Deerslayer* (1841), that provided the dime Western with the structuring oppositions that give sense to the Western: the difference between personal morality and civil law, nature and domesticity, wilderness and civilization, transcended only in the figure of Natty Bumppo, "a fit subject to represent the better qualities of both conditions," both nature and culture, as Cooper himself explained it (2:491). Otherwise known as Leatherstocking, this frontiersman is a voluntary outsider who remains both uncorrupted by civilization and uncontaminated by his intimacy with the Indians. Mediating between wilderness and civilization while facilitating their contact in his role as scout, Leatherstocking bears witness to the displacement of the Indians, to his own displacement, and to the mercenary despoliation of the wilderness.

When Edward Ellis begins *Seth Jones* by writing, "As every one acquainted with our history must know, the war on the frontiers has been an almost interminable one" (see p. 176), he uses acquaintance as the precondition for reading the novel successfully. The brevity of the dime Western depends on a kind of cultural shorthand, legible thanks to the popularity of Cooper and his imitators. The elaborate transition from wilderness to civilization, for instance, can be condensed into the opening image of a woodman felling a gigantic oak; Jones's clothes can be described merely as dress "such as was in vogue on the frontiers at the time of which we write" (p. 173). Indeed, just as the "woodman, with characteristic penetration, [can] read the man before him at a glance," and just as the backwoodsman Jones can always decipher the faintest tracks in the wilderness, so too the reader of the novel is expected to transform gestural representations — such as the abrupt dialogue of the initial capture — into fully visualized scenes. The pages of later dime novels, like *Frank Reade, The Inventor, Chasing the James Boys With His Steam Team* (1890; see p. 359), can become mere dialogue because the staging has already been done by the novel's predecessors. This is how the Western produces what we might call its "mythology effect" — with the *presumption* that the West already exists as shared knowledge, with an absence of detail that insists on familiarity.

The compulsion to rewrite and reread the outlines of the same story is symptomatic of a mass readership continuing to work through the unresolved moral (though not political) question about the fate of the Native American population. The relentless dispossession of the Native American nations continued to be accompanied by guilt and nostalgia and by the hope, as Martin Van Buren had put it in his *Autobiography*, that the invading population of "unjustifiable aggressors" had become "guardians" and "benefactors" (quoted in

Rogin 137). The pages of the dime Western are replete with ethnic stereotypes — Irish, Dutch, German, Chinese, Mexican — but the stereotype of the Indian provokes obvious ambivalence (as it did in the eighteenth-century image of the Noble Savage). Despite the novel's account of Indian violence, *Malaeska* provides an inverse captivity narrative wherein an Indian woman suffers figurative captivity in Manhattan; the eponymous heroine, much like Leatherstocking, combines "all that was strong, picturesque, and imaginative in savage life, with the delicacy, sweetness, and refinement which follows in the train of civilization" (p. 124). And yet, although she assumes Leatherstocking's character, both gender and race prevent her from assuming his role.

Seth Jones presents "the horrors of Indian captivity" as a given, and asserts the mental superiority of the settlers (p. 188). Yet it is not the Mohawks themselves, but the Mohawks provoked by the British who threaten the Americans. And Haldidge, the Indian-hater whose wife and child were "tomahawked side by side, and weltering in each other's blood," and who has become a "terror to the savages," all but disappears from the story before the closing ceremonies, relegated to the margins of the plot (p. 209).

While the Buffalo Bill novels centralize the encounter with violent Indians, in *Deadwood Dick* such encounters become gratuitous. The Sioux may be named "infarnal critters" who, in the outset of the novel, have partially stripped, bound, and whipped a white woman, but they play no determining role in the plot, where "white savages" have assumed their role as the villains (p. 275). The Deadwood Dick series marks the moment in the dime novel's history when the Indians, however stereotyped, no longer function to unify the white population. When, in *Deadwood Dick's Claim; or, The Fairy Face of Faro Flats*, the outlaw hero fights in the name of granting a Crow Indian his land rights, the Western seems eager to compensate for the damage done in the history, and in the literary history, of the frontier's extension. In subsequent Deadwood Dick novels, the Indians join the ranks of the oppressed who need to be defended by the hero.

When, in the 1870s, white greed replaced Indian savagery as the most familiar source of villainy, we can sense how the genre had already produced a violent history that became an allegory for, and yet screened out, other histories of violence, from the racial violence of the Reconstruction era to the labor violence that finally stunned the nation in the great Railway Strike of 1877, when protests against wage cuts led to riots in Baltimore, Pittsburgh, Chicago, and St. Louis. *Deadwood Dick, The Prince of the Road; or, The Black Rider of the Black Hills* (1877; see p. 353) concludes with an elaborate account of how the orphan Ned Harris had been swindled out of his inheritance, how a corrupt legal system offered him no help, and how he has thus been forced to assume the role of Deadwood Dick, the persecuted bandit seeking vengeance. Cooper certainly prepared the way for such a plot by showing the insufficiency of civil law and vilifying the greed of advancing civilization, and Scott prepared the way for the bandit-hero in *Rob Roy*. The melodramatic stage, with plays like Dion Boucicault's *The Poor of New York* (1859), demonstrated how stories of the populist revenge against capitalist greed and government corruption could become popular hits. American popular culture and American mass culture thrive on antigovernment and antibusiness sentiment, which has helped to make the rhetoric of oppression and injustice all but universally available — not least to government officials and businessmen. Nonetheless, Michael Denning is certainly right to argue that the new outlaw figures, most prominently Deadwood Dick and Jesse James, contested the dominant ideology, the encroachment of advanced capitalism, and the moral codes that melodrama itself promoted (1–64).

Strikingly, in Wheeler's town of Deadwood an image of labor erupts into the typical adventure story where extraordinary exploits replace productive work as the source of respect and success. *Deadwood Dick* describes "the grinding, crushing rumble of ponderous machinery" at the Pocket Gulch Mines, with the "crusher in full operation," worked by "swarth-skinned red-men, whose faces declare them to be a remnant of the once great Ute tribe — now utilized to a better occupation than in the dark and bloody days of the past" (p. 326). The once great past has become a present characterized by the routine of mere occupation, by the pacification and assimilation of the violent Indian into the mainstream of production. The sensational novel later returns to this singular sensation — the sound of modern industry: "The day passed without incident in the mines. The work went steadily on, the sounds of the crusher making strange music for the mountain echoes to mock" (p. 343). In its elaborate reference to the industrial processes transforming the West, *Deadwood Dick* discloses the story of an efficient and modern economic advance that lies beneath the story of frontier adventurers. We might say that the dime novel here offers some sense of the very rhythm of its own industrial production.

Within the dime Western tradition, the Deadwood Dick novels from Beadle's *Half Dime Library* merit attention not just because of their enormous popularity, their responsibility for creating the image of the wild West, or their crystallization of the figure of the noble outlaw. Rather, Wheeler so exaggerates both the formula of the Western and elements foreign to it that the genre must abandon any lingering verisimilitude, just as it abandons any effort to write a story of the nation, and just as it discloses its participation in the industrial routine. For Orville Victor, the editor at Beadle, Wheeler's excesses were a trial. He constantly tried to curtail the incomprehensible dialect, the swearing, the violence, and the images of debauchery — the "metropolitan" saloon, "full of ribald songs and maudlin curses; full of foul atmospheres, impregnated with the fumes of vile whiskey, and worse tobacco, and full of sights and scenes, exciting and repulsive" (pp. 284–85). But those excesses seem minor in contrast to the way that Wheeler's novels, read within a trajectory of the dime Western, seem to unravel its most familiar, but nonetheless fragile, components.

IDENTITY AND DISGUISE

Like the racial bond that Theodore Roosevelt later asserts in his story of winning the West, the gender bond, and the difference between the male realm of adventure and a female world of domesticity, seems assiduously maintained by the Western only to end up compromised. While Cooper's Natty Bumppo remains single, Seth Jones ends up married in a novel that fuses the plots of adventure and romance. Indeed, the novel concludes with a triple wedding that asserts the priority of settler community, of civilization, over the ruggedness of frontier life. Characteristic of the Western paradigm, the effort to save a woman from villainous hands establishes a bond between Wild Bill Hickok and Buffalo Bill, which intensifies as *Buffalo Bill* progresses: "Mate, I loved you before better than I loved my own life — I don't know now how I can love you more" (Buntline 243). The priority of the affection between men is finally accompanied by paranoid misogyny when Wild Bill (prophetically) dreams of being murdered by the "traitorous beauty" Ruby Blazes and her friend Sal Perkins, both dressed in "male attire." But another triple marriage concludes the novel, ultimately reasserting the importance of domestic life as usual.

A Game of Gold; Or, Deadwood Dick's Big Strike ostentatiously establishes an all male scene. Told that "not one of the gentler sex was there in Big Bonanza, or had ever been there," we're then told that some "of the miners had families, but they were all boys, whose mothers were dead, or had deserted, and it left Big Bonanza literally a male town" (Wheeler, *A Game of Gold* 1). But this is also the novel where Wheeler reveals that Deadwood Dick has been "betrothed to Calamity Jane and married several times," not that such revelations spell the end of adventure (16). Indeed, Wheeler seems less concerned with managing the homosocial bond toward heterosexual domesticity and more concerned, as Calamity Jane's perpetual presence makes clear, with imagining a heterosocial sphere of lawless adventure.

In contrast, women serve a civilizing function in the Western fiction that reached the pages of the "journals of civilization." In Bret Harte's "A Passage in the Life of Mr. John Oakhurst" (1874), a professional gambler's interest in a pale woman quickly prompts him to change his habits; in Stephen Crane's "The Bride Comes to Yellow Sky," the mere presence of a new wife arrests a lifelong feud; and Owen Wister's *The Virginian* achieves closure by establishing the permanence of social accord with the image of marital accord between the cowboy and the New England schoolteacher who has introduced him to culture, from Shakespeare to Browning. In other Deadwood Dick novels, the relationship between Dick and Calamity Jane, who repeatedly rescues him, suggests the possibility of a relationship that is familiar and fraternal — not romantic — and neither maternal nor paternal. Although other women express an unprecedented erotic interest in the hero, Wheeler's female protagonists are most likely to ride horses and wield guns and to attract the female readership that the genre once seemed to exclude.

The power of such revision is no less compelling in the history of the dime Western's most stable stereotype — that of the male body itself. In Buntline's *Buffalo Bill*, Wild Bill Hickok is "six feet and one inch in height, straight as an ash, broad in shoulder, round and full in chest, slender in the waist, swelling out in muscular proportions at hips and thighs, with tapering limbs, small hands and feet, his form . . . a regular study," with his face "open and clean," with "regular features, the nose slightly aquiline." When Buntline goes on to write that the "same picture will do for Buffalo Bill," he makes it clear how the specificity serves in the name of stock generality (12–13).

Although reading the body thus seems a wholly adequate mode of reading character, such legibility was also confused by the element of disguise in *Seth Jones*, an element that Wheeler intensifies to a point where the Western reads like a masquerade. Not only is Deadwood Dick a masked marauder, but in several novels he disguises himself as other characters while other characters disguise themselves as him. Figuring out who everyone *is* is fundamental to the plot (indeed, at times, the very basis of the plot), but characters seem to disappear in an abyss of dissimulation.

The confrontations in *A Game of Gold; Or, Deadwood Dick's Big Strike* are typical. Accused by Dick, one character fulminates: "And you still dare to insinuate that I am not myself." He responds by quipping: "Oh! no. You are yourself, no doubt, but you are *not* Lola Bird." Himself accused of being a girl in disguise, Deadwood Dick asks, "What right have you to think that I am not what I appear?" His female interlocutor responds by saying, "Your whole appearance betrays femininity," to which Dick offers little in the way of retort: "Maybe I'd better adorn myself in feminine attire, if I'd make a better looking girl than I do a boy" (31–32). Stable as every character ultimately is (by being stabilized in the concluding chapter) Wheeler's novels nonetheless suggest how theatrical, rather than natural, gender is. More compellingly, though, because the masquerade establishes character as an abstract role that any "person" can play, these novels, at their most vertiginous, show how the artifice of the subgeneric institution could engender unexpected violations of the middle-class status quo.

While the dime Western persisted beyond the turn of the century (often in the form of recirculated titles from the past), its popularity waned in contrast to other genres, most notably detective fiction, which had produced its own heroes — Old Cap Collier, Old Sleuth, Old King Brady, Nick Carter — who rivaled Buffalo Bill and Deadwood Dick in popularity. The detective novel successfully transposed the frontier from the West to urban centers; at times it seemed to disguise the Western formula in the clothes of the big city. Of course, by the time Stephen Crane's Swede left New York, the violence in Eastern cities created far more national apprehension than the violence in the West. Still, the Western had always relied on elements of detection, and stories of the James Boys, for instance, appeared at their most violent in Frank Tousey's *New York Detective Library*, not in a Western series. Extraordinary horsemen and gunmen who fought for the South as guerrillas in the Civil War and who subsequently became nationally infamous for their bank and train robberies in the 1870s, the James brothers achieved iconic status as a force that could interrupt the success of capitalists (the bank) and the institutions of modernization (the train). Appearing in one series published by Street and Smith and in two published by Frank Tousey, Jesse and Frank James often found themselves chased by star detectives; *The New York Detective Library* was actually staging the intersection of two subgenres, which further intersect with the genre of science fiction in *Frank Reade, The Inventor, Chasing the James Boys With His Steam Team — A Thrilling Story From a Lost Diary* (1890). Science fiction (which amounted to adventures of invention) had entered the world of popular fiction at the hand of Edward Ellis, whose *The Huge Hunter; or, The Steam Man of the Prairies* was published by Beadle and Adams in 1869. Frank Reade, the boy inventor who became the protagonist of a series of novels beginning in the 1880s, was a fictionalized version of the irrepressible Thomas A. Edison, who captured the nation's imagination in the closing two decades of the century. The story of Frank Reade chasing the James Boys can be understood as an allegorical tale of basic conflicts between technology and the human body, reason and passion, manhood and boyhood; but the story also resolves those conflicts, not least by portraying the boy inventor as an action hero. In other words, the novel works to imagine how both technological invention and methodical detection can be coded as frontier pursuits rather than pursuits that would close Turner's "gate of escape from the bondage of the past" (59).

The novel also marks the cultivation of what finally became the dime Western's chief readership: adolescent boys. By 1896, Frank Meriwell, the phenomenally popular baseball hero created by Burt L. Standish (Gilbert Patten) for Street and Smith, demonstrated the possibilities of creating a new frontier in the realm of sport as well as a new frontier abroad, where the college sports star inserted himself in several paramilitary adventures in Latin America. While the dime sports novel can be read as a recoded Western, the Western as such was taken up by film and by mainstream fiction. Frank Norris, Owen Wister, and Zane Gray, among others, transformed the frontier, once again, into the setting for the historical novel and the Western romance.

The early history of motion pictures is inseparable from the Western genre. Thomas Edison filmed acts from Buffalo Bill's Wild West show in the 1890s; for Edison, Edwin S. Porter directed and photographed *The Great Train Robbery* in 1903, demonstrating the power of editing to produce melodramatic narrative. By 1920 the cinema had produced new Western heroes (Broncko Billy [Max Aronson], Tom Mix, William S. Hart), while the Western had attracted the most powerful producers and directors (Thomas Ince, D. W. Griffith, Cecil B. De Mille). The dime novel could hardly compete with the new medium's power to depict landscape and to generate sensationalistic thrills.

While writers like Max Brand and Louis L'Amour revived the sensationalism of the Western later in the century, Owen Wister's *The Virginian* (1902) demonstrated how elements of the genre could be reconfigured into "serious" fiction, as though the West's new historical centrality, certified by Turner and Roosevelt, required a less marginal (and marginalized) medium for its novelistic depiction. In his preface to the novel (which is dedicated to his Harvard classmate, Roosevelt), Wister describes it as a historical romance about Wyoming, 1874–1890, "a colony as wild as was Virginia one hundred years earlier" without "so many Chippendale settees" (vii). The Virginian himself, an Eastern cowboy who serves as a ranching foreman, suppresses a strike and protects the property of his boss. In other words, Wister manages to situate the classic outsider, the cowboy, within the managerial class as an insider protecting mainstream values.

It is from this historical moment, wherein Western adventure merely supports civilization and civility as they are, that the dime novel seems to tell us something about the recalcitrant possibilities of the West that we don't already know. After the century's turn, the hazards of reading dime novels — what seemed like a mortal hazard in Stephen Crane's story of the Swede — became a familiar joke. *Terrible Ted,* a short Vitagraph film from 1907, depends on its audience knowing both the Western formula and the formulaic accounts of its danger. In a Victorian parlor, a young boy hides a thriller within another book, falls asleep reading the adventure, and dreams of being a desperado, donning a cowboy hat and grasping two six-shooters. He chases the policemen out of the city, defends a stagecoach against robbery, and knifes a bear to protect an Indian maiden. He also escapes from other Indians, kills and scalps the enemy, and, playing cards in a saloon, shoots and kills the man he has caught cheating. Ultimately this magnificent outlaw-hero wakes to a good cuffing from his mother, and he leaves the room whimpering. The medium that was to catalyze a new interest in the Western thriller seems fully self-conscious of the inevitable cultural stakes involved. Like any joke, this short film may be said to express comically what are genuine anxieties; but more clearly, the joke expresses the dime novel's conventional promise of a challenge to cultural conventions, a challenge foreclosed by the reassertion of the West's integrating, unifying potency.

Chronology, 1860–1902: U.S. History, Culture, and Popular Publishing

1860

Election of Abraham Lincoln in November. In December, South Carolina secedes from the Union.

Nathaniel Hawthorne publishes *The Marble Faun*.

First dime novels published in numbered series by Irwin P. Beadle & Co. (changed to Beadle & Co. in October), New York. *Malaeska; The Indian Wife of the White Hunter* sells three hundred thousand copies in its first year, and *Seth Jones; or, the Captives of the Frontier* sells four hundred fifty thousand copies in its first year. Three hundred twenty-one novels, mostly frontier adventures, appear in *Beadle's Dime Novels* between 1860 and 1874, when the series is replaced by *New Dime Novels*.

1861

Formation of the Confederate States of America in February, with hostilities opening at Fort Sumter in April, and Union forces devastated at Bull Run, Virginia, in July. The scale of the fighting quickly fosters the mass manufacture of standardized arms and uniforms and of canned meat and milk. Elisha Graves Otis patents the steam-powered elevator. The first transcontinental telegraph message is received by Lincoln.

Linda Brent (Harriet Jacobs) recounts her experiences as a slave in *Incidents in the Life of a Slave Girl*. *The Atlantic Monthly* prints Rebecca Harding Davis's *Life in the Iron-Mills.* Already celebrated for the illustrative work in *Frank Leslie's Illustrated Weekly* (1855), Leslie begins publishing *Frank Leslie's Pictorial History of the American Civil War*, continuing for thirty-three numbers.

Orville J. Victor becomes the editor for Beadle publications and remains a powerful influence, known for his moral and literary standards, until 1898.

1862

The Homestead Act, signed by Lincoln in May, offers any settler 160 acres of government land in return for five years' cultivation of the acreage. Land grants benefit the railroads, above all, which ultimately receive close to two hundred million acres. In July, Lincoln authorizes the incorporation of the Union Pacific Company, and the Union and Pacific railways are charted. In August, a Sioux uprising reluctantly led by Chief Little Crow, responsible for the massacre of 800 whites in Minnesota, ends in defeat.

Henry David Thoreau dies on May 6. His lecture, "Walking," published as an essay, designates the West as the symbol both of "absolute freedom and wildness" and of "the path which we love to travel in the interior and ideal world." Theodore Winthrop publishes *John Brent*, a Western romance set in the Rockies.

1863

Lincoln issues the Emancipation Proclamation on January 1. He delivers the "Gettysburg Address" in November.

In April, William Bullock patents the continuous-roll printing press, able to print paper on both sides.

1864

Nevada admitted as a state in October. The Chivington Massacre on November 28, resulting in the deaths of nearly 500 Cheyenne Indians, concludes the hostilities that began with the mining rush to Colorado in 1861. Occurring after the Indian suit for peace, the massacre provokes other tribes to resist encroachment. The federal government grants ten square miles of the Yosemite Valley to the State of California as a public park.

The American News Company, formed in New York as a wholesale distributor of books, story papers, and other periodicals, assumes complete charge of distributing the dime novels published by Beadle. George Munro introduces *Munro's Ten Cent Novels*, for which Edward S. Ellis writes over ninety novels in the ensuing thirteen years. A. K. Loring publishes Horatio Alger Jr.'s *Frank's Campaign; or,*

What Boys Can Do on the Farm for their Camp, the first of the house's thirty-six Alger publications.

1865

Lincoln inaugurated for second term on March 4. General Lee surrenders at Appomattox on April 9, effectively concluding the war. Lincoln is assassinated on April 14. The Thirteenth Amendment, outlawing slavery, is ratified in December. The Sioux War along the western plains begins, provoked by the federal effort to construct highways through Indian hunting grounds, concluding in 1867 when the Congressional Peace Commission establishes the Black Hills Reservation, among others. In May, the first recorded train robbery occurs in Ohio.

Mark Twain publishes his first story, "Jim Smiley and His Jumping Frog" (later retitled "The Celebrated Jumping Frog of Calaveras County"). Walt Whitman publishes *Drum-Taps*. Francis Parkman publishes *Pioneers of France in the New World*.

1866

In the Fetterman Massacre, Captain J. Fetterman, outsmarted and outfought, loses all eighty-one of his troops trying to protect the Bozeman trail to the Montana gold mines. Western Union becomes the first effective monopoly, standardizing rates nationally.

Beadle publishes a shortened version of Twain's story of the jumping frog as *Jim Smiley's Frog* in the *Dime Book of Fun*.

1867

President Grant establishes a "Peace Policy" and a Peace Commission to convince all Indians to move to reservations. Nebraska is admitted as a state in March. Alaska is purchased from the Russians on October 18. Christopher Scholes builds the first typewriter. Granger movement begins in December in Washigton, D.C.

Parkman publishes *The Jesuits in North America*. Harper & Bros. introduces *Harper's Bazaar*, complementing *Harper's Weekly* (1857) and *Harper's New Monthly Magazine* (1850) with more affordable good reading. The *Monthly* publishes George Ward Nichols's account of "Wild Bill" Hickok from Springfield, Missouri. Munro begins publishing *The New York Fireside Companion* as a family paper.

1868

Louisa May Alcott publishes *Little Women*. *Overland Monthly* begins publication in San Francisco, with Bret Harte as editor, and publishes his "The Luck of Roaring Camp" in the second issue.

Beadle & Co. establishes Frank Starr & Co. as a subsidiary. Loring publishes Alger's *Ragged Dick; or, Street Life in New York*, which cements the rags-to-riches paradigm.

1869

On May 10, The Atlantic and Pacific coasts are connected by rail with the conjunction of the Union Pacific and Central Pacific Railroads at Promontory, Utah. The National Women's suffrage Association is formed in May, and Wyoming territory grants women's suffrage in December.

Harte publishes "Outcasts of Poker Flat" in the *Overland Monthly*. Harriet Beecher Stowe publishes *Old-town Folks*.

Ned Buntline (Edward Z. C. Judson) publishes the first Buffalo Bill dime novel, *Buffalo Bill, King of the Border Men*, in Street & Smith's *New York Weekly*. The front-page woodcut, supposedly modeled on Judson himself, establishes the buckskinned, knife-wielding image of William Cody.

1870

The construction of the Brooklyn Bridge begins on January 2. The Standard Oil Company is formed by John D. Rockefeller.

Harte publishes *The Luck of Roaring Camp, and Other Stories* and becomes internationally famous. Thomas Bailey Aldrich publishes *The Story of a Bad Boy*, fostering the fad for bad-boy literature.

Beadle enters the field of the story paper with the *Saturday Star Journal*, printing novels that would be published subsequently as books in one of the firm's series.

1871

The Indian Appropriation Act, passed on March 3, nullifies all previous treaties and designates Native Americans as national wards.

Whitman publishes *Democratic Vistas* and "A Passage to India." Edward Eggleston publishes *The Hoosier School Master*, which sells five hundred thousand copies. Bret Harte accepts *The Atlantic Monthly*'s $10,000 annual contract for a poem or story a month and becomes the nation's best-paid author.

1872

President Ulysses S. Grant signs an act that designates two million acres of northwestern Wyoming as Yellowstone National Park. Charles Loring Brace publishes *The Dangerous Classes of New York*.

Twain publishes *Roughing It*. D. Appleton & Company sells nearly a million of the richly illustrated sets of *Picturesque America: Or, The*

Land We Live In, distributed by subscription in forty-eight 50-cent monthly installments.

Beadle & Co. becomes Beadle & Adams. The first dime-novel detective appears in *Old Sleuth, the Detective; or, the Bay Ridge Mystery* in Munro's *New York Fireside Library.*

1873

Nevada silver rush. Financial panic in the East begins with the failure of Jay Cooke and Company on September 18 and ends with protracted depression.

Mary Mapes Dodge founds *St. Nicholas* magazine for children.

1874

The last great gold rush, to the Black Hills of South Dakota, following those to Montana (1862), Colorado (1859), Nevada (1858), and California (1849). In Custer City and Deadwood, the likes of Billy the Kid and Calamity Jane gain national attention. Women's Christian Temperance Union is organized.

1875

The Black Hills Reservation opened for prospectors.

Norman L. Munro, having departed from his brother's firm in 1873, begins publishing *The Boys Own Story Teller,* a series of novels with adolescent heroes.

1876

Central Park completed in New York. Machine for manufacturing barbed wire (invented in 1874) patented by Joseph Glidden, making cattle ranching more manageable by clearly dividing ranches, farms, and pastures; Glidden makes six hundred miles of wire daily by 1880. Alexander Graham Bell files for a patent for the telephone on February 14. General George Armstrong Custer and the 266 men of the seventh U.S. Cavalry are wiped out on June 25 at the Little Bighorn River in Montana by the Sioux under Sitting Bull. Colorado admitted as a state in August.

Frederick Whittaker publishes the *Complete Life of George A. Custer.* Twain publishes *Adventures of Tom Sawyer.*

The Pictorial Printing Company begins publishing the *Nickel Library,* the first 32-page octavo five-cent serial (monthly, then weekly), devoted to frontier adventures. The format dominates the field until the close of the century.

1877

Reconstruction ends in April with the withdrawal of federal troops from the South. Provoked by a cut in wages, the Great Strike leads to bloody conflicts in Baltimore, Pittsburgh, and Chicago in July. The Nez Percé Indians, refusing to surrender more reservation land (on behalf of gold interests in Idaho), make a fifteen hundred mile fighting withdrawal, through Yellowstone Park and toward Canada, pursued from June to October until Chief Joseph surrenders with a speech ("Hear me, my chiefs, I am tired; . . . I will fight no more, forever. . . .") that generates national sympathy for the plight of the Indian. The federal government removes the Nez Percé to Oklahoma.

Sarah Orne Jewett collects her local color sketches in *Deephaven*. Henry James publishes *The American*.

Beadle & Adams introduce the *Half Dime Library*, intended for boys, and *The Fireside Library*, intended for family reading. Frank Tousey begins publication of *New York Boys Weekly* and *The Young Men of America*, both with full-page cover illustrations.

1878

The Knights of Labor is established at a general assembly on January 1. The Greenback Labor Party, organized on February 22, argues for the free coinage of silver. Thomas Edison forms the first electric light company.

1879

On January 1, the federal government resumes specie payment for the first time since 1862. The Carlisle Indian School is founded at Carlisle, Pennsylvania.

George Washington Cable collects his French-dialect stories in *Old Creole Days*. Henry George publishes *Progress and Poverty*.

Beadle & Adams begin publishing the *Waverly Library* of romances for "young ladies."

1880

The National Farmer's Alliance organized in Chicago in April. The Chinese Exclusion Act, signed November 17, grants the U.S. government the right to regulate immigration.

Cable publishes *The Grandissimes*. Lew Wallace publishes *Ben-Hur*, which immediately becomes a best-seller. The American News Company, with thirty-two regional branches, distributes all the leading novel serials, story papers, and libraries, doing an annual business of more than fifteen million dollars — achieving a virtual monopoly.

1881

President Garfield shot July 2; dies September 19. Thomas Edison lights the Pearl Street neighborhood of lower Manhattan with a central power plant. The elevated railroad system is completed in New York City.

Helen Hunt Jackson publishes *A Century of Dishonor*, indicting the government's treatment of Native Americans. Henry James publishes *The Portrait of a Lady*. Joel Chandler Harris publishes *Uncle Remus: His Songs and His Sayings*.

1882

John D. Rockefeller reorganizes the Standard Oil Company in January as the nation's first major trust, monopolizing oil distribution throughout the country.

On April 3, Jesse James is assassinated. Chinese immigration is suspended in May by the Exclusion Act.

William Dean Howells publishes *A Modern Instance*.

Frank Tousey begins publishing the *New York Detective Library*.

1883

The Northern Pacific, the second transcontinental railroad, is completed. The railroads adopt standard time (adopted internationally in 1884). The Brooklyn Bridge is opened on May 24.

William Cody produces the first "Buffalo Bill's Wild West Show." Joseph Pulitzer purchases the New York *World*. Twain publishes *Life on the Mississippi*. *Ladies Home Journal* is founded, soon becoming the first U.S. magazine with a circulation of a half million.

Norman Munro transforms *The Boys Own Story Teller* into *Our Boys of New York*, a nickel biweekly magazine that runs serialized novels and draws the ire of reformers who believe that the adolescent criminal heroes will lead their readers to ruin.

1884

On August 26, Ottman Megenthaler patents the linotype automatic typesetting machine.

Twain publishes *Adventures of Huckleberry Finn*. Charles Egbert Craddock (Mary Noailles Murfree) collects her dialect stories in *In the Tennessee Mountains*. Helen Hunt Jackson publishes *Ramona*.

1885

First skeleton-frame skyscraper completed in Chicago. New York State establishes the 715,000-acre Adirondack Forest Preserve.

Howells publishes *The Rise of Silas Lapham.*

1886

A Chicago labor rally ends in the Haymarket Square Riot in May. Geronimo and the Apache surrender to General Nelson Miles in September; the Apache are resettled in Florida as prisoners, then in Oklahoma. American Federation of Labor organizes as a national trade union in December. Sears Roebuck founded.

Andrew Carnegie publishes *Triumphant Democracy.* Henry James publishes *The Bostonians* and *The Princess Casamassima.*

1887

The Dawes Severalty Act, passed on February 8, works to divide tribal lands into individually owned properties and thus diminish the power of tribal chiefs. Ransom Eli Olds introduces the first three-wheeled horseless carriage, followed by a gasoline-driven four-wheeled car in 1896.

Joseph Kirkland publishes *Zury: The Meanest Man in Spring County.*

1888

George Eastman markets his Kodak camera, inspiring a new mode of tourism. Edward Bellamy publishes *Looking Backward,* a best-selling technological utopia that inspires the creation of Bellamy societies throughout the country.

1889

Montana, South Dakota, North Dakota, and Washington admitted as states. Oklahoma opened for settlement. J. Walker Fewkes records Indian music and speech with the phonograph.

Theodore Roosevelt begins publishing the multivolume *Winning of the West.* Carnegie publishes his *Gospel of Wealth.*

Street & Smith, known since 1858 for the fiction published serially in *The New York Weekly* (including novels by Ned Buntline and Horatio Alger Jr.), enters the dime novel market with the *Log Cabin Library* (publishing sixty novels the first year) and the *Nugget Library* (novels selling for a nickel). Eventually publishing more than forty different novel series — among them the *Nick Carter Library*, the *Diamond Dick Library*, and *Tip Top Weekly* — Street & Smith quickly commands the field.

1890

Wyoming and Idaho admitted as states. Eleventh U.S. census shows that the frontier — defined as habitable area with fewer than two inhabitants per square mile — has disappeared. Eleven million acres of

Sioux territory, ceded to the United States in 1889, are opened for general settlement. Congress creates Sequoia and Yosemite national parks. A medicine man, Wavoka, inspires the Sioux to perform ghost dances in the effort to reassert themselves in the struggle against the white man; government efforts to suppress any possible uprising lead to the deaths of Sitting Bull and Big Foot. Sherman Antitrust Act passed in July.

Jacob Riis publishes *How the Other Half Lives*. William James publishes *Principles of Psychology*. William Dean Howells publishes *A Hazard of New Fortunes*.

1891

People's Party of the United States is formed on May 19 at a national convention in Cincinnati. On September 22, the president opens 900,000 acres of Indian land in Oklahoma for general settlement. Edison patents wireless telegraphy and a motion picture camera. Congress passes the International Copyright Act, protecting foreign authors from U.S. pirating.

Hamlin Garland publishes *Main-Travelled Roads*. Mary E. Wilkins Freeman publishes *A New England Nun and Other Stories*.

Street & Smith enters the field of science fiction with Philip Reade's *Tom Edison Jr., and His Air Yacht*.

1892

The Homestead, Pennsylvania, strike, provoked by reduced wages from the Carnegie Steel Company, prompts violent conflict with Pinkerton guards and the state militia. The Chinese Exclusion Act extends the prohibition of Chinese immigration for ten more years. The act is renewed for ten-year periods until World War II.

Mary Hallock Foote achieves national attention with *The Chosen Valley*, a Western written from a woman's point of view.

1893

World's Columbian Exposition in Chicago. Frederick Jackson Turner presents the paper "The Significance of the Frontier in American History." Financial panic in May, stock market crash in June, and ensuing depression are blamed on federal gold policy, which becomes the central topic of the presidential campaign in 1896.

Stephen Crane publishes *Maggie: A Girl of the Streets*. Abraham Cahan publishes *Yekl: A Tale of the New York Ghetto*.

1894

Provoked by diminished wages, the Pullman strikes begin in May, followed by the American Railway Union's general strike.

John Muir publishes *The Mountains of California*.

1895

A revolution against the Spanish government breaks out in Cuba in February. Joseph Pulitzer's New York *World* and William Randolph Hearst's New York *Journal* sensationalize the conflict and advocate U.S. intervention.

Stephen Crane publishes *The Red Badge of Courage*.

1896

Utah admitted as state. First U.S. moving pictures shown publicly in New York in April. In May, the Supreme Court upholds Louisiana's Jim Crow Car Law in the case of *Plessy v. Ferguson*.

Sarah Orne Jewett publishes *The Country of the Pointed Firs*.

Street & Smith begins publication of *Tip Top Weekly*, which soon achieves a circulation of one million.

1897

William McKinley is inaugurated president on March 4. U.S. gold rush to the Klondike (Canada) begins in June.

Richard Harding Davis publishes the best-selling *Soldiers of Fortune*.

1898

U.S. battleship *Maine* explodes in Havana harbor in February. In April, the United States declares war on Spain. With Colonel Theodore Roosevelt's "Rough Riders" helping to capture San Juan Hill, Cuba, and Commodore George Dewey achieving quick success at Manila Bay in the Philippines, the United States attains victory in August. Puerto Rico and Guam are ceded to the United States. The first professional football game is played in August. Roosevelt elected governor of New York state in November.

Assets of Beadle & Adams purchased by M. J. Ivers.

1899

United Mine Workers organize. Thorstein Veblen publishes *Theory of the Leisure Class*.

Kate Chopin publishes *The Awakening*. Charles Chesnutt publishes *The Conjure Woman*. Sutton Griggs publishes *Imperium in Imperio*.

1900

In September, the Wright brothers fly their first full-scale glider. William McKinley is re-elected president, with Roosevelt as vice president. Roosevelt publishes *The Strenuous Life*.

Theodore Dreiser publishes *Sister Carrie*. Frank Baum publishes *The Wonderful Wizard of Oz*.

1901

McKinley assassinated at the Pan-American Exposition in Buffalo, N.Y., in September. Roosevelt inaugurated president.

John Muir publishes *Our National Parks*. Booker T. Washington publishes *Up From Slavery*. Chesnutt publishes *The Marrow of Tradition*. Frank Norris publishes *The Octopus*.

1902

On June 28, Congress passes the Isthmian Canal Act to finance the building of the Panama Canal.

McClure's Magazine begins publishing Ida M. Tarbell's *History of the Standard Oil Company*, a muckraking exposé. Henry James publishes *The Wings of the Dove*. William James publishes *Varieties of Religious Experience*. Jacob Riis publishes *The Battle with the Slum*. Owen Wister publishes *The Virginian*, dedicated to his friend Theodore Roosevelt.

Frank Tousey furthers his command of the juvenile field of story papers and libraries by introducing several more publications, including the *Frank Reade Weekly* and the *Wild West Weekly*.

A Note on the Texts

Dime novels were frequently republished and sometimes radically altered — shortened, retitled, "cleaned up." With one exception, I have used the original dime or half-dime edition of a text. In the case of *Seth Jones* I accepted the few changes made for the 1877 edition (*Beadle's Half Dime Library* vol. 1, no. 8) that correct obvious errors from the 1860 edition (for example, "the shore on either hand was [changed from 'were'] perfectly outlined"). But I have generally preserved orthographic and grammatical peculiarities (whether apparently inadvertent or apparently intentional) because these contributed to a sense of an emerging American vernacular, and because idiosyncratic grammar and indecipherable dialect were often named in the dime novel's denunciation. I have nonetheless silently added some marks of punctuation (usually a missing period or quotation mark) and silently corrected what I read as obvious typesetting errors (for example, "But the old professor," instead of "But old the professor," "running" instead of "rnnning"). Where there was doubt, I preserved the original.

Malaeska; The Indian Wife of the White Hunter

Ann Sophia Stephens (1810–1886) serves as an outstanding example of the role women could play in the antebellum public sphere of letters. Editor of a journal published by her husband, *The Portland Magazine*, Mrs. Stephens soon worked independently, becoming the primary source of her family's income after she and her husband moved from Maine to New York in 1837. There, she assumed the role of editor and chief contributor for *The Ladies' Companion*, which soon increased its circulation from three thousand to seventeen thousand. She became an associate editor (along with Edgar Allan Poe) of *Graham's Magazine*, where her work appeared beside that of Nathaniel Hawthorne, Henry Wadsworth Longfellow, and James Fenimore Cooper; an editor of *Frank Leslie's Ladies Gazette of Fashion*; and, in 1856, the editor of *Mrs. Stephens' Illustrated New Monthly*, which merged two years later with *Peterson's Ladies National Magazine*. For these publications, her work served as a front-page attraction. Two of her bound novels, *Fashion and Famine* (1854) and *The Old Homestead* (1855), were best-sellers of the day; and one of her poems, "The Polish Boy," became a standard text in the postbellum Eclectic Readers, recited in schools throughout the country.

Declared to be not just "among the most prolific authors of the age" but also a "woman of great original genius" and the American heir of Sir Walter Scott, Mrs. Stephens enjoyed a notoriety that turned her two-year tour abroad (1850–1852) into a nationally publicized event (Stern 308, 312–13). She spent time with the likes of Charles Dickens and William

Makepeace Thackeray, Wilhelm Humboldt, and Maria Edgeworth. Mrs. Stephens was a frequent guest at the White House, and though, as an editor, she had maintained that "poetry, fiction, and the lighter branches of the sciences are woman's appropriate sphere," she seems to have had a considerable political influence in the Polk and Buchanan administrations (quoted by Stern 305). In short, Beadle & Co. took little risk when it paid this "Star of American Authors" $250 for the novel that had appeared as a three-part serial in *The Ladies' Companion* between February and April 1839.

While her two great successes had been urban melodramas, the Beadles chose to republish *Malaeska*, no doubt to establish the American emphasis of the series with a treatment of provincial New York in the manner of Cooper. Set in the Catskill Mountains and the valleys of the Hudson and Mohawk rivers, Malaeska's story occupies the landscape that was integral to American legend and romance by the 1830s, and not because of Cooper alone. Washington Irving set his two most famous tales, *Rip Van Winkle* and *The Legend of Sleepy Hollow*, in the Catskills; the local landscape inspired some of William Cullen Bryant's best poetry just as it inspired the Hudson River School of painting. Thomas Cole, leading spirit of this School, eventually took residence in the village of Catskill.

Mrs. Stephens frames her novel by invoking the familiar nineteenth-century trip up the Hudson, with the familiar stop at Catskill, at a time when the mountains already supported a resort industry — Catskill Mountain House, the region's best-known hotel, was built in 1823 and was famous for the panoramic views provided by its veranda, perched on a 1,400-foot drop. Malaeska's voyage to the mouth of the Mohawk River (at the Hudson) and on to Manhattan replicates a typical fur-trading route. Though the historical setting of the novel is vague, its events clearly take place when the Six Nations of the Iroquois still controlled the Mohawk Valley, sparsely settled by Dutch and English pioneers. As the close of the novel makes clear, however, it is not just the passing of the frontier but also the passing of old Manhattan that is the subject of Mrs. Stephens's nostalgia.

While Cooper grounds his plots in history — the surrender of Fort William Henry during the French and Indian wars (1755–63), for instance, in *The Last of the Mohicans* (1826) — Mrs. Stephens rather extracts her plot out of history to concentrate on the fate of her heroine in a sentimental tradition. The dime novel was to become a source of relentless violence, but it begins with the relentless "agony of sorrow." Chapter two closes with Malaeska digging a double grave for her father and her white husband; the story ends when her son, reunited with his mother after years, drowns himself, unable to bear the revelation that he is half Indian. In *Mary Derwent, A Tale of the Early Settlers* (1838), Mrs. Stephens told the story of a white woman's successful integration into a Shawnee tribe. In *Malaeska*, she tells the inverse story — of a "forlorn wanderer" (p. 94), an Indian woman denigrated by both the Dutch and the Indian populations, "the heart-broken victim of an unnatural marriage" (p. 163).

Miscegenation, suppressed by Cooper in *The Last of the Mohicans*, had been confronted by Lydia Maria Child in *Hobomok* (1824) and by Catherine Maria Sedgwick in *Hope Leslie* (1827). The *North American Review* called Child's depiction of love between a white woman and an Indian chief "revolting," but intermarriage was a fact of frontier history. Sir William Johnson, for one, who presided over the grand council at Fort Stanwix (1768) that established British peace and alliance with thirteen Indian tribes, had a Mohawk wife (whose brother, Joseph Brant, famously fought with the British during the Revolution). Effectively avoiding any treatment of intermarriage itself, Mrs. Stephens concentrates instead on the transcultural price of maternal devotion: "It was her woman's destiny, not the more certain because of her savage origin. Civilization does not always reverse this mournful picture of womanly self-abnegation" (p. 103).

This novel is not a simple reprint of its serialized predecessor. Mrs. Stephens complicated the plot, amplified the descriptive passages, added epigraphs to the chapters, and streamlined the punctuation, producing a far more substantial text to serve as the first "complete dollar book for a dime." The text published here reproduces the expanded novel published by Beadle in 1860.

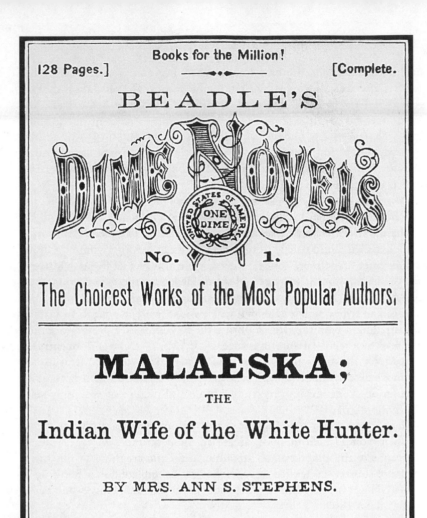

Figure 17. *Beadle's Dime Novels*, No. 1: The original title page of *Malaeska* (1860). Albert Johannsen Collection, Rare Books and Special Collections, Northern Illinois University Libraries.

PUBLISHER'S NOTICE

In presenting a new series of books before the public, the publishers of "BEADLE'S DIME NOVELS" have made every effort to obtain such works as are, in all respects, superior for ability, and faultless in taste and morals.

The extraordinary success which has attended their books of a domestic and utilitarian class, has induced the publishers to undertake the present series, which will be of a character that is certain to secure the approbation of all readers of sterling light-literature. The novel chosen to begin the list, is a proof of the high standard which the publishers have adapted. It is one of the best stories ever written by a lady universally acknowledged to be the most brilliant authoress of America, and can not fail to insure the success of the series, and amply sustain the reputation of the writer.

To usher in a work of MRS. STEPHENS, at this late day, with puffs, would indeed be a work of supererogation. Her name upon the title-page is enough to convince the reading public that the book is in every respect interesting and worthy. Its perusal will prove that in beauty of style, fervor of imagination, and construction of plot, it is quite equal to any of the numerous works which she has hitherto published, and which have been received with so much favor, that from the very commencement her literary career has been a succession of triumphs.

Neither pains nor expense will be spared to make the novels which succeed a fitting continuation to this brilliant commencement. The publishers intend to have a list of books issued with a style, and of a kind which will meet with the approval of the most refined and intelligent.

A series of the best productions of the best authors is now in a state of preparation, and will be issued from time to time, following "MALAESKA" in regular succession. There shall not be a line or a sentiment in any one of these books which may not be placed in the hands of a child, or be uninteresting to the grandmother of a family.

With no doubt of success, and a firm determination to deserve it, the publishers of the "DIME NOVELS" enter cheerfully upon this new enterprise.

NEW YORK, June, 1860

Figure 18. *Malaeska* reissued (1860) with a woodcut on the title page. Albert Johannsen Collection, Rare Books and Special Collections, Northern Illinois University Libraries.

NOTICE IN REISSUED EDITION

We take pleasure in introducing the reader to the following romance by Mrs. Ann S. Stephens. It is one of the most interesting and fascinating works of this eminent author. It is chosen as the initial volume of the Dime Novel series, from the chaste character of its delineations, from the interest which attaches to its fine pictures of border life and Indian adventure, and from the real romance of its incidents. It is American in all its features, pure in its tone, elevating in its sentiments; and may be referred to as a work representative of the series that is to follow — every volume of which will be of the highest order of merit, from the pens of authors whose intellectual and moral excellencies have already given the writers an enviable name, in this country and in Europe. By the publication of the series contemplated, it is hoped to reach all classes, old and young, male and female, in a manner at once to captivate and to enliven — to answer to the popular demand for works of romance, but also to instil a pure and elevating sentiment in the hearts and minds of the people.

BEADLE & CO.

New York,
June, 1860.

CHAPTER I

The brake hung low on the rifted rock
With sweet and holy dread;
The wild-flowers trembled to the shock
Of the red man's stealthy tread;
And all around fell a fitful gleam
Through the light and quivering spray,
While the noise of a restless mountain-stream
Rush'd out on the stilly day.

The traveler who has stopped at Catskill,[1] on his way up the Hudson, will remember that a creek of no insignificant breadth washes one side of the village, and that a heavy stone dwelling stands a little up from the water on a point of verdant meadow-land, which forms a lip of the stream, where it empties into the more majestic river. This farm-house is the only object that breaks the green and luxuriant beauty of the point, on that side, and its quiet and entire loneliness contrasts pleasantly with the bustling and crowded little village on the opposite body of land. There is much to attract attention to that dwelling. Besides occupying one of the most lovely sites on the river, it is remarkable for an appearance of old-fashioned comfort at variance with the pillared houses and rustic cottages which meet the eye everywhere on the banks of the Hudson. There are no flowers to fling fragrance about it, and but little of embellishment is manifest in its grounds; but it is surrounded by an abundance of thrifty fruit-trees; an extensive orchard sheds its rich foliage to the sunshine on the bank, and the sward is thick and heavy which slopes greenly from the front door down to the river's brink.

The interior of the house retains an air of substantial comfort which answers well to the promise conveyed without. The heavy furniture has grown old with its occupants; rich it has been in its time, and now it possesses the rare quality of fitness, and of being in harmony with surrounding things. Every thing about that house is in perfect keeping with the character and appearance of its owner. The occupant himself, is a fine stately farmer of the old class — shrewd, penetrating, and intelligent — one of those men who contrive to keep

---

[1] *Catskill:* Set in the valley of the Catskill Creek, Catskill (originally Catskill Landing) thrived because it was protected by inaccessible mountains to the west yet had waterway access to Albany and New York.

the heart green when the frost of age is chilling the blood and whitening upon the brow. He has already numbered more than the threescore years and ten allotted to man. His habits and the fashion of his attire are those of fifty years ago. He still clings to huge wood-fires, apples, and cider in the winter-season, and allows a bevy of fine cows to pasture on the rich grass in front of his dwelling in the summer. All the hospitable feeling of former years remains warm at his heart. He is indeed a fine specimen of the staunch old republican farmer of the last century, occupying the house which his father erected, and enjoying a fresh old age beneath the roof tree which shadowed his infancy.

During a sojourn in this vicinity last season, it was one of our greatest pleasures to spend an evening with the old gentleman, listening to legends of the Indians, reminiscences of the Revolution, and pithy remarks on the present age, with which he loved to entertain us, while we occasionally interrupted him by comparing knitting-work with the kind old lady, his wife, or by the praises of a sweet little grandchild, who would cling about his knees and play with the silver buckles on his shoes as he talked. That tall, stately old man, and the sweet child made a beautiful picture of "age at play with infancy," when the fire-light flickered over them, to the ancient family pictures, painted in Holland, hanging on the wall behind us, in the old-fashioned oval frames, which, with the heavy Dutch Bible, which lay on the stand, secured with hasps and brass hinges, ponderous as the fastenings of a prison-door, were family relics precious to the old gentleman from antiquity and association. Yes, the picture was pleasant to look upon; but there was pleasure in listening to his legends and stories. If the one here related is not exactly as he told it, he will not fail to recognize the beautiful young Indian girl, whom he described to us, in the character of Malaeska.

At the time of our story, the beautiful expanse of country which stretches from the foot of the Catskill mountains to the Hudson was one dense wilderness. The noble stream glided on in the solemn stillness of nature, shadowed with trees that had battled with storms for centuries, its surface as yet unbroken, save by the light prow of the Indian's canoe. The lofty rampart of mountains frowned against the sky as they do now, but rendered more gloomy by the thick growth of timber which clothed them at the base; they loomed up from the dense sea of foliage like the outposts of a darker world. Of all the cultivated acres which at the present day sustain thousands with their products, one little clearing alone smiled up from the heart of the wilderness. A few hundred acres had been cleared by a hardy band of settlers, and a cluster of log-houses was erected in the heart of the little valley which now contains Catskill village. Although in the neighborhood of a savage Indian tribe, the little band of pioneers remained unmolested in their humble occupations, gradually clearing the land around their settlement, and sustaining their families on the game which was found in abundance in the mountains. They held little intercourse with the Indians, but hitherto no act of hostility on either side had aroused discontent between the settler and the savages.

It was early in May, about a year after the first settlement of the whites, when some six or eight of the stoutest men started for the woods in search of game. A bear had been seen on the brink of the clearing at break of day, and while the greater number struck off in search of more humble game, three of the most resolute followed his trail, which led to the mountains.

The foremost of the three hunters was an Englishman of about forty, habited in a threadbare suit of blue broadcloth, with drab gaiters buttoned up to his knees, and a hat sadly shorn of its original nap. His hunting apparatus bespoke the peculiar care which all of his country so abundantly bestow on their implements of sport. The other two were much younger, and dressed in home-made cloth, over which were loose frocks manufactured from the refuse flax or swingled tow. Both were handsome, but different in the cast of their features. The character of the first might be read in his gay air and springy step, as he followed close to the Englishman, dashing away the brushwood with the muzzle of his gun, and detecting with a quick eye the broken twigs or disturbed leaves which betrayed the course of the hunted bear. There was also something characteristic in the wearing of his dress, in the fox-skin cap thrown carelessly on one side of his superb head, exposing a mass of short brown curls around the left ear and temple, and in the bosom of his coarse frock, thrown open so as to give free motion to a neck Apollo might have coveted. He was a hunter, who had occasionally visited the settlement of late, but spent whole weeks in the woods, professedly in collecting furs by his own efforts, or by purchase from the tribe of Indians encamped at the foot of the mountains.

The last was more sedate in his looks, and less buoyant in his air. There was an intellectual expression in his high, thoughtful brow, embrowned though it was by exposure. A depth of thought in his serious eye, and a graceful dignity in his carriage, bespoke him as one of those who hide deep feeling under an appearance of coldness and apathy. He had been a schoolmaster in the Bay State, from whence he had been drawn by the bright eyes and merry laugh of one Martha Fellows, a maiden of seventeen, whose father had moved to the settlement at Catskill the preceding summer, and to whom, report said, he was to be married whenever a minister, authorized to perform the ceremony, should find his way to the settlement.

The three hunters bent their way in a southwestern direction from the settlement, till the forest suddenly opened into a beautiful and secluded piece of meadow-land, known to this day by its Dutch title of "the Straka," which means, our aged friend informed us, a strip of land. The Straka lay before them of an oblong form, some eight or ten acres in expanse, with all its luxuriance of trees, grass, and flowers, bathed in the dew and sunshine of a warm summer's morning. It presented a lovely contrast to the dense wilderness from which the hunters emerged, and they halted for a moment beneath the boughs of a tall hickory to enjoy its delicious freshness. The surface of the inclosure was not exactly level, but down the whole length of it curved gently up from the middle, on either side, to the magnificent trees that hedged it in with a beautiful and leafy rampart. The margin was irregular; here and there a clump of trees shot down into the inclosure, and the clearing occasionally ran up into the forest in tiny glades and little grassy nooks, in which the sunlight slumbered like smiles on the face of a dreaming infant. On every side the trunks of huge trees shot up along the margin beneath their magnificent canopy of leaves, like the ivied columns of a ruin, or fell back in the misty perspective of the forest, scarcely discernible in its gloom of shadow. The heavy piles of foliage, which fell amid the boughs like a wealth of drapery flung in masses to the summer wind, was thrifty and ripe with the warm breath of August. No spirit of decay had as yet shed a gorgeous breath over its deep, rich green, but all was wet with dew, and kindled up by the sunlight to a thousand varying tints of the same color. A bright spring gushed from a swell of ground in the upper part of the inclosure, and the whole surface of the beautiful spot was covered with a vigorous growth of tall meadow-grass, which rose thicker and brighter and of a more delicate green down the middle, where the spring curved inward in a graceful rivulet, musical as the laugh of a child. As if called to life by the chime of a little brook, a host of white wild-flowers unfolded their starry blossoms along the margin, and clumps of swamp-lilies shed an azure hue along the grass.

Until that day, our hunters had ever found "the Straka" silent and untenanted, save by singing-birds, and wild deer which came down from the mountains to feed on its rich verdure; but now a dozen wreaths of smoke curled up from the trees at the northern extremity, and a camp of newly-erected wigwams might be seen through a vista in the wood. One or two were built even on the edge of the clearing; the grass was much trampled around them, and three or four half-naked Indian children lay rolling upon it, laughing, shouting, and flinging up their limbs in the pleasant morning air. One young Indian woman was also frolicking among them, tossing an infant in her arms, caroling and playing with it. Her laugh was musical as a bird song, and as she darted to and fro, now into the forest and then out into the sunshine, her long hair glowed like the wing of a raven, and her motion was graceful as an untamed gazelle. They could see that the child, too, was very beautiful, even from the distance at which they stood, and occasionally, as the wind swept toward them, his shout came ringing upon it like the gush of waters leaping from their fount.

"This is a little *too* bad," muttered the Englishman, fingering his gun-lock. "Can they find no spot to burrow in but 'the Straka?' St. George! but I have a mind to shoot the squaw and wring the neck of every red imp among them."

"Do it!" exclaimed Danforth, turning furiously upon him; "touch but a hair of her head, and by the Lord that made me, I will bespatter that tree with your brains!"

The Englishman dropped the stock of his musket hard to the ground, and a spot of fiery red flashed into his cheek at this savage burst of anger so uncalled for and so insolent. He gazed a moment on the frowning face of the young hunter, and then lifting his gun, turned carelessly away.

"Tut, man, have done with this," he said; "I did but jest. Come, we have lost the trail, and shall miss the game, too, if we tarry longer; come."

The Englishman shouldered his musket, as he spoke, and turned into the woods. Jones followed, but Danforth lingered behind.

"I must see what this means," he muttered, glancing after his companions, and then at the group of young Indians; "what can have brought them so near the settlement?"

He gave another quick glance toward the hunters, and then hurried across "the Straka" toward the wigwams. Jones and the Englishman had reached the little lake or pond, which lies about a mile south of "the Straka," when they were again joined by Danforth. His brow was unclouded, and he seemed anxious to do away the effect of his late violence by more than ordinary cheerfulness. Harmony was restored, and they again struck into the trail of the bear, and pursued toward the mountains.

Noon found our hunters deep in the ravines which cut into the ridge of the Catskill on which the Mountain House now stands. Occupied by the wild scenery which surrounded him, Jones became separated from his companions, and long before he was aware of it, they had proceeded far beyond the reach of his voice. When he became sensible of his situation, he found himself in a deep ravine sunk into the very heart of the mountains. A small stream crept along the rocky bottom, untouched by a single sun's ray, though it was now high noon. Every thing about him was wild and fearfully sublime, but the shadows were refreshing and cool, and the stream, rippling along its rocky bed, sent up a pleasant murmur as he passed. Gradually a soft, flowing sound, like the rush of a current of air through a labyrinth of leaves and blossoms, came gently to his ear. As he proceeded, it became more musical and liquid, swelled upon the ear gradually and with a richer burden of sound, till he knew that it was the rush and leap of waters at no great distance. The ravine had sunk deeper and deeper, and fragments of rock lay thickly in the bed of the stream. Arthur Jones paused, and looked about him bewildered, and yet with a lofty, poetical feeling at his heart, aroused by a sense of the glorious handiwork of the Almighty encompassing him. He stood within the heart of the mountain, and it seemed to heave and tremble beneath his feet with some unknown influence as he gazed. Precipices, and rocks piled on rocks were heaped to the sky on either side. Large forest-trees stood rooted in the wide clefts, and waved their heavy boughs abroad like torn banners streaming upon the air. A strip of the blue heavens arched gently over the whole, and that was beautiful. It smiled softly, and like a promise of love over that sunless ravine. Another step, and the waterfall was before him. It was sublime, but beautiful — oh, very beautiful — that little body of water, curling and foaming downward like a wreath of snow sifted from the clouds, breaking in a shower of spray over the shelf of rocks which stayed its progress, then leaping a second foaming mass, down, down, like a deluge of flowing light, another hundred feet to the shadowy depths of the ravine. A shower of sunlight played amid the foliage far overhead, and upon the top of the curving precipice where the waters made their first leap. As the hunter became more calm, he remarked how harmoniously the beautiful and sublime were blended in the scene. The precipices were rugged and frowning, but soft, rich mosses and patches of delicate white wild-flowers clung about them.

So profusely were those gentle flowers lavished upon the rocks, that it seemed as if the very spray drops were breaking into blossoms as they fell. The hunter's heart swelled with pleasure as he drank in the extreme beauty of the scene. He rested his gun against a fragment of rock, and sat down with his eyes fixed on the waterfall. As he gazed, it seemed as if the precipices were moving upward — upward to the very sky. He was pondering on this strange optical illusion, which has puzzled many a dizzy brain since, when the click of a gunlock struck sharply on his ear. He sprang to his feet. A bullet whistled by his head, cutting through the dark locks which curled in heavy masses above his temples, and as a sense of giddiness cleared from his brain, he saw a half-naked savage crouching upon the ledge of rocks which ran along the foot of the fall. The spray fell upon his bronzed shoulders and sprinkled the musket as he lifted it to discharge the other barrel. With the quickness of thought, Jones drew his musket to his eye and fired. The savage sent forth a fierce, wild yell of agony, and springing up with the bound of a wild animal, fell headlong from the shelf. Trembling with excitement, yet firm and courageous, the hunter reloaded his gun, and stood ready to sell his life as dearly as possible, for he believed that the ravine was full of concealed savages, who would fall upon him like a pack of wolves. But every thing remained quiet, and when he found that he was alone, a terrible consciousness of bloodshed came upon him. His knees trembled, his cheek burned, and, with an impulse of fierce excitement, he leaped over the intervening rocks and stood by the slain savage. He was lying with his face to the earth, quite dead; Jones drew forth his knife, and lifting the long, black hair, cut it away from the crown. With the trophy in his hand, he sprang across the ravine. The fearless spirit of a madness seemed upon him, for he rushed up the steep ascent, and plunged into the forest, apparently careless what direction he took. The sound of a musket stopped his aimless career. He listened, and bent his steps more calmly toward the eminence on which the Mountain House now stands. Here he found the Englishman with the carcass of a huge bear stretched at his feet, gazing on the glorious expanse of country, spread out like a map, hundreds of fathoms beneath him. His face was flushed, and the perspiration rolled freely from his forehead. Danforth stood beside him, also bearing traces of recent conflict.

"So you have come to claim a share of the meat," said the old hunter, as Jones approached. "It is brave to leave your skulking-place in the bushes, when the danger is over. Bless me, lad! what have you there?" he exclaimed, starting up and pointing to the scalp.

Jones related his encounter with the savage. The Englishman shook his head forebodingly.

"We shall have hot work for this job before the week is over," he said. "It was a foolish shot; but keep a good heart, my lad, for, hang me, if I should not have done the same thing if the red devil had sent a bullet so near my head. Come, we will go and bury the fellow the best way we can."

Jones led the way to the fall, but they found only a few scattered locks of black hair, and a pool of blood half washed from the rock by the spray. The body of the savage and his rifle had disappeared — how, it was in vain to conjecture.

One of the largest log-houses in the settlement had been appropriated as a kind of tavern, or place of meeting for the settlers when they returned from their hunting excursions. Here a store of spirits was kept, under the care of John Fellows and pretty Martha Fellows, his daughter, the maiden before mentioned. As the sun went down, the men who had gone to the woods in the morning, began to collect with their game. Two stags, raccoons and meaner game in abundance, were lying before the door, when the three hunters came in with the slain bear. They were greeted with a boisterous shout, and the hunters crowded eagerly forward to examine the prize; but when Jones cast the Indian's scalp on the pile, they looked in each other's faces with ominous silence, while the young hunter stood pale and collected before them. It was the first time that Indian life had been taken by any of their number, and they felt that in the shedding of red blood, the barriers of their protection were broken down.

"It is a bad business," said one of the elder settlers, waving his head and breaking the general silence. "There'll be no clear hunting in the woods after this; but how did it all come about, Jones? Let us know how you came by that scalp — did the varmint fire at you, or how was it?"

The hunters gathered around Jones, who was about to account for his possession of the scalp, when the door of the house was opened, and he happened to look into the little room thus exposed. It was scantily furnished with a few benches and stools; a bed was in one corner, and Martha Fellows, his promised wife, stood by a rough deal table, on which were two or three drinking-cups, a couple of half-empty bottles, with a pitcher of water, backed by a broken mug, filled to the fractured top with maple molasses. Nothing of the kind could have been more beautiful than pretty Martha as she bent forward, listening with rapt attention to the animated whisper of William Danforth, who stood by her, divested of his coarse frock, his cap lying on the table before him, and his athletic figure displayed to the best advantage by the roundabout buttoned closely over his bosom. A red silk handkerchief, tied like a scarf round his waist, gave a picturesque gracefulness to his costume, altogether in harmony with his fine proportions, and with the bold cast of his head, which certainly was a model of muscular beauty.

A flash of anger shot athwart Arthur Jones' forehead, and a strange jealous feeling came to his heart. He began a confused account of his adventure, but the Englishman interrupted him, and took it upon himself to gratify the clamorous curiosity of the hunters, leaving Jones at liberty to scrutinize each look and motion of his lady-love. He watched with a jealous feeling the blush as it deepened and glowed on her embrowned cheek; he saw the sparkling pleasure of her hazel eyes, and the pretty dimples gathering about her red lips, like spots of sunlight flickering through the leaves of a red rose, and his heart sickened with distrust. But when the handsome hunter laid his hand on hers and bent his head, till the short curls on his temples almost mingled with her glossy ringlets, the lover could bear the sight no more. Breaking from the little band of hunters, he stalked majestically into the house, and approaching the object of his uneasiness, exclaimed, "Martha Fellows," in a voice which caused the pretty culprit to snatch her hand from under the hunter's, and to overturn two empty tin cups in her fright.

"Sir," said Martha, recovering herself, and casting a mischievous glance at Danforth, which was reciprocated with interest.

Mr. Arthur Jones felt that he was making himself ridiculous, and suppressing his wrath, he finished his magnificent commencement: "Will you give me a drink of water?" At which Martha pointed with her little embrowned hand to the pitcher, saying:

"There it is;" then, turning her back to her lover, she cast another arch glance at Danforth, and taking his cap from the table, began to blow upon the yellow fur, and put it to her cheek, as if it had been a pet kitten she was caressing, and all for the laudable purpose of tormenting the man who loved her, and whom she loved better than any thing in existence. Jones turned on her a bitter contemptuous look, and raising the pitcher to his lips, left the room. In a few minutes the other hunters entered, and Jason Fellows, father to Martha, announced it as decided by the hunters, who had been holding a kind of council without, that Arthur Jones and William Danforth, as the two youngest members of the community, should be dispatched to the nearest settlement to request aid to protect them from the Indians, whose immediate attack they had good reason to fear.

Martha, on hearing the names of the emissaries mentioned, dropped the cup she had been filling.

"Oh, not him — not them, I mean — they will be overtaken and tomahawked by the way!" she exclaimed, turning to her father with a look of affright.

"Let Mr. Danforth remain," said Jones, advancing to the table; "I will undertake the mission alone."

Tears came into Martha's eyes, and she turned them reproachfully to her lover; but, full of his heroic resolution to be tomahawked and comfortably scalped on his own responsibility, he turned majestically without deigning to meet the tearful glance which was well calculated to mitigate his jealous wrath.

Danforth, on being applied to, requested permission to defer his answer till the morning, and the hunters left the house to divide the game, which had been forgotten in the general excitement.

Danforth, who had lingered to the last, took up his cap, and whispering good-night to Martha, left the house. The poor girl scarcely heeded his departure. Her eyes filled with tears, and seating herself on a settee which ran along one end of the room, she folded her arms on a board which served as a back, and burying her face upon them, wept violently.

As she remained in this position, she heard a familiar step on the floor. Her heart beat quick, fluttered a moment, and then settled to its regular pulsations again, for her lover had seated himself beside her. Martha wiped the tears from her eyes and remained quiet, for she knew that he had returned, and with that knowledge, the spirit of coquetry had revived; and when Jones, softened by her apparent sorrow, for he had seen her parting with Danforth — put his hand softly under her forehead and raised her face, the creature was laughing — laughing at his folly, as he thought.

"Martha, you are doing wrong — wrong to yourself and to me," said the disappointed lover, rising indignantly and taking his hat, with which he advanced to the door.

"Don't go," said Martha, turning her head till one cheek only rested on her arm, and casting a glance, half-repentant, half-comic, on her retreating lover; "don't go off so; if you do, you'll be very sorry for it."

Jones hesitated — she became very serious — the tears sprang to her eyes, and she looked exceedingly penitent. He returned to her side. Had he appealed to her feelings then — had he spoken of the pain she had given him in her encouragement of another, she would have acknowledged the fault with all proper humility; but he did no such thing — he was a common-sense man, and he resolved to end his first love-quarrel in a common-sense manner, as if common-sense ever had any thing to do with lovers' quarrels. "I will reason with her," he thought. "He will say I have made him very wretched, and I will tell him I am very sorry," *she* thought.

"Martha," he said, very deliberately, "why do I find you on terms of such familiarity with this Manhattan[2] fellow?"

Martha was disappointed. He spoke quite too calmly, and there was a sarcastic emphasis in the word "fellow," that roused her pride. The lips, which had just begun to quiver with repentance, worked themselves into a pouting fullness, till they resembled the rose-bud just as it bursts into leaves. Her rounded shoulder was turned pettishly toward her lover, with the air of a spoiled child, and she replied that "he was always finding fault."

Jones took her hand, and was proceeding in his sensible manner to convince her that she was wrong, and acted wildly, foolishly, and with a careless disregard to her own happiness.

As might be expected, the beautiful rustic snatched her hand away, turned her shoulder more decidedly on her lover, and bursting into tears, declared that she would thank him if he would stop scolding, and that she did not care if she never set eyes on him again.

He would have remonstrated; "Do listen to common-sense," he said, extending his hand to take hers.

"I hate common-sense!" she exclaimed, dashing away his hand; "I won't hear any more of your lecturing, — leave the house, and never speak to me again as long as you live."

Mr. Arthur Jones took up his hat, placed it deliberately on his head, and walked out of the house. With a heavy heart Martha

---

[2] *Manhattan:*   The seventeenth-century Dutch settlers of Manhattan Island founded New Amsterdam (renamed New York when the Dutch surrendered to the British in 1644). By the time of the Revolution, the island still consisted mostly of farm land and marsh land, but a population of 20,000 was crowded into the urban area of the island's southern tip. The Dutch were a distinct minority in the eighteenth century, but a wealthy and powerful one.

watched his slender form as it disappeared in the darkness, and then stole away to her bed in the garret.

"He will call in the morning before he starts; he won't have the heart to go away without saying one word, — I am sure he won't," she repeated to herself over and over again, as she lay sobbing and weeping penitent tears on her pillow that night.

When William left the log tavern, he struck into the woods, and took his course toward the Pond. There was a moon, but the sky was clouded, and the little light which struggled to the earth, was too faint to penetrate the thick foliage of the wilderness. Danforth must have been familiar with the track, for he found his way without difficulty through the wilderness, and never stopped till he came out on the northern brink of the Pond. He looked anxiously over the face of the little lake. The fitful moon had broken from a cloud, and was touching the tiny waves with beauty, while the broken, rocky shore encompassed it with shadow, like a frame-work of ebony. No speck was on its bosom; no sound was abroad, but the evening breeze as it rippled on the waters, and made a sweet whispering melody in the treetops.

Suddenly a light, as from a pine torch, was seen on a point of land jutting out from the opposite shore. Another and another flashed out, each bearing to a particular direction, and then a myriad of flames rose high and bright, illuminating the whole point, and shooting its fiery reflection, like a meteor, almost across the bosom of the waters.

"Yes, they are preparing for work," muttered Danforth, as he saw a crowd of painted warriors arrange themselves around the camp-fire, each with his firelock in his hand. There was a general movement. Dark faces flittered in quick succession between him and the blaze, as the warriors performed the heavy march, or war-dance, which usually preceded the going out of a hostile party.

Danforth left the shore, and striking out in an oblique direction, arrived, after half an hour of quick walking, at the Indian encampment. He threaded his way through the cluster of bark wigwams, till he came to one standing on the verge of the inclosure. It was of logs, and erected with a regard to comfort which the others wanted. The young hunter drew aside the mat which hung over the entrance, and looked in. A young Indian girl was sitting on a pile of furs at the opposite extremity. She wore no paint — her cheek was round and smooth, and large gazelle-like eyes gave a soft brilliancy to her countenance, beautiful beyond expression. Her dress was a robe of dark chintz, open at the throat, and confined at the waist by a narrow belt of wampum, which, with the bead bracelets on her naked arms, and the embroidered moccasins laced over her feet, was the only Indian ornament about her. Even her hair, which all of her tribe wore laden with ornaments, and hanging down the back, was braided and wreathed in raven bands over her smooth forehead. An infant, almost naked, was lying in her lap, throwing its unfettered limbs about, and lifting his little hands to his mother's mouth, as she rocked back and forth on her seat of skins, chanting, in a sweet, mellow voice, the burden of an Indian lullaby. As the form of the hunter darkened the entrance, the Indian girl started up with a look of affectionate joy, and laying her child on the pile of skins, advanced to meet him.

"Why did the white man leave his woman so many nights?" she said, in her broken English, hanging fondly about him; "the boy and his mother have listened long for the sound of his moccasins."

Danforth passed his arm around the waist of his Indian wife, and drawing her to him, bent his cheek to hers, as if that slight caress was sufficient answer to her gentle greeting, and so it was; her untutored heart, rich in its natural affections, had no aim, no object, but what centered in the love she bore her white husband. The feelings which in civilized life are scattered over a thousand objects, were, in her bosom, centered in one single being; he supplied the place of all the high aspirations — of all the passions and sentiments which are fostered into strength by society, and as her husband bowed his head to hers, the blood darkened her cheek, and her large, liquid eyes were flooded with delight.

"And what has Malaeska been doing since the boy's father went to the wood?" inquired Danforth, as she drew him to the couch where the child was lying half buried in the rich fur.

"Malaeska has been alone in the wigwam, watching the shadow of the big pine. When her heart grew sick, she looked in the boy's eyes and was glad," replied the Indian mother, laying the infant in his father's arms.

Danforth kissed the child, whose eyes certainly bore a striking resemblance to his own; and parting the straight, black hair from a forehead which scarcely bore a tinge of its mother's blood, muttered, "It's a pity the little fellow is not quite white."

The Indian mother took the child, and with a look of proud anguish, laid her finger on its cheek, which was rosy with English blood.

"Malaeska's father is a great chief — the boy will be a chief in her father's tribe; but Malaeska never thinks of that when she sees the white man's blood come into the boy's face." She turned mournfully to her seat again.

"He will make a brave chief," said Danforth, anxious to soften the effects of his inadvertent speech; "but tell me, Malaeska, why have the warriors kindled the council fire? I saw it blaze by the pond as I came by."

Malaeska could only inform that the body of a dead Indian had been brought to the encampment about dusk, and that it was supposed he had been shot by some of the whites from the settlement. She said that the chief had immediately called a council to deliberate on the best means of revenging their brother's death.

Danforth had feared this movement in the savages, and it was to mitigate their wrath that he sought the encampment at so late an hour. He had married the daughter of their chief, and, consequently, was a man of considerable importance in the tribe. But he felt that his utmost exertion might fail to draw them from their meditated vengeance, now that one of their number had been slain by the whites. Feeling the necessity of his immediate presence at the council, he left the wigwam and proceeded at a brisk walk to the brink of the Pond. He came out of the thick forest which fringed it a little above the point on which the Indians were collected. Their dance was over, and from the few guttural tones which reached him, Danforth knew that they were planning the death of some particular individuals, which was probably to precede their attack on the settlement. The council fire still streamed high in the air, reddening the waters and lighting up the trees and foreground with a beautiful effect, while the rocky point seemed of emerald pebbles, so brilliant was the reflection cast over it, and so distinctly did it display the painted forms of the savages as they sat in a circle round the blaze, each with his weapon lying idly by his side. The light lay full on the glittering wampum and feathery crest of one who was addressing them with more energy than is common to the Indian warrior.

Danforth was too far off to collect a distinct hearing of the discourse, but with a feeling of perfect security, he left the deep shadow in which he stood, and approached the council fire. As the light fell upon him, the Indians leaped to their feet, and a savage yell rent the air, as if a company of fiends had been disturbed in their orgies. Again and again was the fierce cry reiterated, till the woods resounded with the wild echo rudely summoned from the caves. As the young hunter stood lost in astonishment at the strange commotion, he was seized by the savages, and dragged before their chief, while the group around furiously demanded vengeance, quick and terrible, for the death of their slain brother. The truth flashed across the hunter's mind. It was his death they had been planning. It was he they supposed to be the slayer of the Indian. He remonstrated and declared himself guiltless of the red man's death. It was in vain. He had been seen on the mountain by one of the tribe, not five minutes before the dead body of the Indian was found. Almost in despair the hunter turned to the chief.

"Am I not your son — the father of a young chief — one of your own tribe?" he said, with appealing energy.

The saturnine face of the chief never changed, as he answered in his own language: "The red man has taken a rattlesnake to warm in his wigwam — the warriors shall crush his head!" and with a fierce grin, he pointed to the pile of resinous wood which the savages were heaping on the council fire.

Danforth looked round on the group preparing for his destruction. Every dusky face was lighted up with a demoniac thirst for blood, the hot flames quivering into the air, their gorgeous tins amalgamating and shooting upward like a spire of living rainbows, while a thousand fiery tongues, hissing and darting onward like vipers eager for their prey, licked the fresh pine-knots heaped for his death-pyre. It was a fearful sight, and the heart of the brave hunter quailed within him as he looked. With another wild whoop, the Indians seized their victim, and were about to strip him for the sacrifice. In their blind fury they tore him from the grasp of those who held him, and were too intent on divesting him of his clothes to remark that his limbs were free. But he was not forgetful. Collecting his strength for a last effort, he struck the nearest savage a blow in the chest, which sent him reeling among his followers, then taking advantage of the confusion, he tore off his cap, and springing forward with the bound of an uncaged tiger, plunged into the lake. A shout rent the air, and a score of dark heads broke the water in pursuit.

Fortunately, a cloud was over the moon, and the fugitive remained under the water till he reached the shadow thrown by the thickly-wooded bank, when, rising for a moment, he supported himself and hurled his cap out toward the center of the pond. The ruse succeeded, for the moon came out just at the instant, and with renewed shouts the savages turned in pursuit of the empty cap. Before they learned their mistake, Danforth had made considerable headway under the friendly bank, and took to the woods just as the shoal of Indians' heads entered the shadow in eager chase.

The fugitive stood for a moment on the brink of the forest, irresolute, for he knew not which course to take.

"I have it; they will never think of looking for me there," he exclaimed, dashing through the undergrowth and taking the direction toward "the Straka." The whoop of the pursuers smote his ear as they made the land. On, on he bounded with the swiftness of a hunted stag, through swamp and brushwood, and over rocks. He darted till he came in sight of his own wigwam. The sound of pursuit had died away, and he began to hope that the savages had taken the track which led to the settlement.

Breathless with exertion he entered the hut. The boy was asleep, but his mother was listening for the return of her husband.

"Malaeska," he said, catching her to his panting heart; "Malaeska, we must part; your tribe seek my life; the warriors are on my track now — now! Do you hear their shouts?" he added.

A wild whoop came from the woods below, and forcing back the arms she flung about him, he seized a war-club and stood ready for the attack.

Malaeska sprang to the door, and looked out with the air of a frightened doe. Darting back to the pile of furs, she laid the sleeping child on the bare earth, and motioning her husband to lie down, heaped the skins over his prostrate form; then taking the child in her arms, she stretched herself on the pile, and drawing a bear-skin over her, pretended to be asleep. She had scarcely composed herself, when three savages entered the wigwam. One bore a blazing pine-knot, with which he proceeded to search for the fugitive. While the others were busy among the scanty furniture, he approached the trembling wife, and after feeling about among the furs without effect, lifted the bear-skins which covered her; but her sweet face in apparent slumber, and the beautiful infant lying across her bosom, were all that rewarded his search. As if her beauty had power to tame the savage, he carefully replaced the covering over her person, and speaking to his companions, left the hut without attempting to disturb her further.

Malaeska remained in her feigned slumber till she heard the Indians take to the woods again. Then she arose and lifted the skins from off her husband, who was nearly suffocated under them. When he had regained his feet, she placed the war-club in his hand, and taking up the babe, led the way to the entrance of the hut. Danforth saw by the act, that she intended to desert her tribe and accompany him in his flight. He had never thought of introducing her as his wife among the whites, and now that circumstances made it necessary for him to part with her forever, or to take her among his people for shelter, a pang, such as he had never felt, came to his heart. His affections struggled powerfully with his pride. The picture of his disgrace — of the scorn with which his parents and sisters would receive the Indian wife and half-Indian child, presented itself before him, and he had not the moral courage to risk the degradation which her companionship would bring upon him. These conflicting thoughts flashed through his mind in an instant, and when his wife stopped at the door, and, looking anxiously in his face, beckoned him to follow, he said, sharply, for his conscience was ill at ease:

"Malaeska, I go alone; you and the boy must remain with your people."

His words had a withering effect on the poor Indian. Her form drooped, and she raised her eyes with a look so mingled with humiliation and reproach, that the hunter's heart thrilled painfully in his bosom. Slowly, and as if her soul and strength were paralyzed, she crept to her husband's feet, and sinking to her knees, held up the babe.

"Malaeska's breast will die, and the boy will have no one to feed him," she said.

That beautiful child — that young mother kneeling in her humiliation — those large dark eyes, dim with the intensity of her solicitude, and that voice so full of tender entreaty — the husband's heart could not withstand them. His bosom heaved, tears gathered in his eyes, and raising the Indian and her child of his bosom, he kissed them both again and again.

"Malaeska," he said, folding her close to his heart, "Malaeska, I must go now; but when seven suns have passed, I will come again; or, if the tribe still seek my life, take the child and come to the settlement. I shall be there."

The Indian woman bowed her head in humble submission.

"The white man is good. Malaeska will come," she said.

One more embrace, and the poor Indian wife was alone with her child.

Poor Martha Fellows arose early, and waited with nervous impatience for the appearance of her lover; but the morning passed, the hour of noon drew near, and he came not. The heart of the maiden grew heavy, and when her father came in to dine, her eyes were red with weeping, and a cloud of mingled sorrow and petulance darkened her handsome face. She longed to question her father about Jones, but he had twice replenished his brown earthen bowl with pudding and milk, before she could gather courage to speak.

"Have you seen Arthur Jones this morning?" she at length questioned, in a low, timid voice.

The answer she received, was quite sufficient punishment for all her coquettish folly of the previous night. Jones had left the settlement — left in anger with her, without a word of explanation — without even saying farewell. It really was hard. The little coquette had the heart-ache terribly, till he frightened it away by telling her of the adventure which Danforth had met with among the Indians, and of his departure with Arthur Jones in search of aid from the nearest settlement. The old man gloomily added, that the savages would doubtless burn the houses over their heads, and massacre every living being within them, long before the two brave fellows would return with men. Such, indeed, were the terrible fears of almost every one in the little neighborhood. Their apprehensions, however, were premature. Part of the Indian tribe had gone out on a hunting-party among the hills, and were ignorant of the fatal shot with which Jones had aroused the animosity of their brethren; while those who remained, were dispersed in a fruitless pursuit after Danforth.

On the afternoon of the fifth day after the departure of their emissaries, the whites began to see unequivocal symptoms of an attack; and now their fears did not deceive them. The hunting-party had returned to their encampment, and the detached parties were gathering around "the Straka." About dark, an Indian appeared in the skirts of the clearing, as if to spy out the position of the whites. Soon after, a shot was fired at the Englishman, before mentioned, as he returned from his work, which passed through the crown of his hat. That hostilities were commencing, was now beyond a doubt, and the males of the settlement met in solemn conclave, to devise measures for the defence of their wives and children. Their slender preparations were soon made; all were gathered around one of the largest houses in gloomy apprehension; the women and children within, and the men standing in front, sternly resolving to die in the defence of their loved ones. Suddenly there came up a sound from the wood, the trampling of many feet, and the crackling of brushwood, as if some large body of men were forcing a way through the tangled forest. The women bowed their pallid faces, and gathering their children in their arms, waited appalled for the attack. The men stood ready, each grasping his weapon, their faces pallid, and their eyes kindled with stern courage, as they heard the stifled groans of the loved objects cowering behind them for protection. The sound became nearer and more distinct; dark forms were seen dimly moving among the trees, and then a file of men came out into the clearing. They were whites, led on by William Danforth and Arthur Jones. The settlers uttered a boisterous shout, threw down their arms, and ran in a body to meet the new-comers. The women sprang to their feet, some weeping, others laughing in hysterical joy, and all embracing their children with frantic energy.

Never were there more welcome guests than the score of weary men who refreshed themselves in the various houses of the settlement that night. Sentinels were placed, and each settler returned to his dwelling, accompanied by three or four guests; every heart beat high, save one — Martha Fellows; she, poor girl, was sad among the general rejoicing; her lover had not spoken to her, though she lingered near his side in the crowd, and had once almost touched him. Instead of going directly to her father's house, as had been his custom, he accepted the Englishman's invitation, and departed to sleep in his dwelling.

Now this same Englishman had a niece residing with him, who was considered by some to be more beautiful than Martha herself. The humble maiden thought of Jones, and of the bright blue eyes of the English girl, till her heart burned with the very same jealous feelings she had so ridiculed in her lover.

"I will see him! I will see them both!" she exclaimed, starting up from the settle where she had remained, full of jealous anxiety, since the dispersing of the crowd; and unheeded by her father, who was relating his hunting exploits to the five strangers quartered on him, she dashed away her tears, threw a shawl over her head, and taking a cup, as an excuse for borrowing something, left the house.

The Englishman's dwelling stood on the outward verge of the clearing, just within the shadow of the forest. Martha had almost reached the entrance, when a dark form rushed from its covert in the brushwood, and rudely seizing her, darted back into the wilderness. The terrified girl uttered a fearful shriek; for the fierce eyes gazing down upon her, were those of a savage. She could not repeat the cry, for the wretch crushed her form to his naked chest with a grasp of iron, and winding his hand in her hair, was about to dash her to the ground. That moment a bullet whistled by her cheek. The Indian tightened his hold with spasmodic violence, staggered back, and fell to the ground, still girding her in his death-grasp; a moment he writhed in mortal agony — warm blood gushed over his victim — the heart under her struggled fiercely in its last throes; then the lifeless arms relaxed, and she lay fainting on a corpse.

CHAPTER II

He lay upon the trampled ground,
    She knelt beside him there,
While a crimson stream gush'd slowly
    'Neath the parting of his hair.
His head was on her bosom thrown —
    She sobb'd his Christian name —
He smiled, for still he knew her,
    And strove to do the same.

— Frank Lee Benedict[3]

"Oh, Arthur! Dear Arthur, I am glad it was you that saved me," whispered Martha, about an hour after her rescue, as she lay on the settle in her father's house, with Arthur Jones bending anxiously over her.

Jones dropped the hand he had been holding, and turned away with troubled features.

Martha looked at him, and her eyes were brimming with tears. "Jones," she said humbly and very affectionately, "Jones, I did wrong the other night, and I am sorry for it; will you forgive me?"

"I will — but never again — never, as I live," he replied, with a stern determination in his manner, accompanied by a look that humbled her to the heart. In after years, when Martha was Arthur Jones' wife, and when the stirrings of vanity would have led her to trifle with his feelings, she remembered that look, and dared not brave it a second time.

At sunrise, the next morning, an armed force went into the forest, composed of all who could be spared from the settlement, amounting to about thirty fighting-men. The Indians, encamped about "the Straka," more than doubled that number, yet the handful of brave whites resolved to offer them a decisive combat.

---

[3] *Frank Lee Benedict:* A poet and novelist, Frank Lee Benedict (1834–1910) began his literary career with publications in *Peterson's Ladies National Magazine*, coedited by Mrs. Stephens, who wrote the preface for Benedict's first book of poetry, *The Shadow Worshipper* (1857).

The little band was approaching the northeastern extremity of the Pond, when they halted for a moment to rest. The spot on which they stood was level, and thinly timbered. Some were sitting on the grass, and others leaning on their guns, consulting on their future movements, when a fiendish yell arose like the howl of a thousand wild beasts, and, as if the very earth had yawned to emit them, a band of warriors sprang up in appalling numbers, on the front and rear, and approaching them, three abreast, fired into the group with terrible slaughter.

The whites returned their fire, and the sounds of murderous strife were indeed horrible. Sternly arose the white man's shout amid the blazing of guns and the whizzing of tomahawks, as they flashed though the air on their message of blood. Above all burst out the war-whoop of the savages, sometimes rising hoarse, and like the growling of a thousand bears; then, as the barking of as many wolves, and again, sharpening to the shrill, unearthly cry of a tribe of wild-cats. Oh, it was fearful, that scene of slaughter. Heart to heart, and muzzle to muzzle, the white and red man battled in horrid strife. The trees above them drooped under a cloud of smoke, and their trunks were scarred with gashes, cut by the tomahawks which had missed their more deadly aim. The ground was burdened with the dead, and yet the strife raged fiercer and fiercer, till the going down of the sun.

In the midst of the fight was William Danforth. Many a dusky form bit the dust, and many a savage howl followed the discharge of his trusty gun. But at length it became foul with continued use, and he went to the brink of the Pond to wash it. He was stooping to the water, when the dark form of an Indian chief cast its shadow a few feet from him. He, too, had come down to clean his gun. The moment he had accomplished his purpose, he turned to the white man, who had been to him as a son, and drawing his muscular form up to its utmost height, uttered a defiance in the Indian tongue. Instantly the weapons of both were loaded and discharged. The tall form of the chief wavered unsteadily for a moment, and fell forward, half its length, into the Pond. He strove to rise. His hands dashed wildly on the crimson water, the blows grew fainter, and the chief was dead.

The setting sun fell brilliantly over the glittering raiment of the prostrate chief — his long, black hair streamed out upon the water, and the tiny waves rippled playfully among the gorgeous feathers which had been his savage crown. A little back on the green bank, lay Danforth, wounded unto death. He strove to creep to the battle-field, but the blood gushed afresh from his wounds, and he fell back upon the earth faint and in despair.

The savages retreated; the sounds of strife became more distant, and the poor youth was left alone with the body of the slain warrior. He made one more desperate effort, and secured the gun which had belonged to the chief; though faint with loss of blood, he loaded that as well as his own, and placing them beside him, resolved to defend the remnant of life, yet quivering at his heart, to the last moment. The sun went slowly down; the darkness fell like a veil over the lake, and there he lay, wounded and alone, in the solitude of the wilderness. Solemn and regretful were the thoughts of the forsaken man as that night of agony went by. Now his heart lingered with strange and terrible dread around the shadowy portals of eternity which were opening before him; again it turned with a strong feeling of self-condemnation to his Indian wife and the infant pledge of the great love, which had made him almost forsake kindred and people for their sakes.

The moon arose, and the dense shadow of a hemlock, beneath which he had fallen, lay within a few feet of him like the wing of a great bird, swayed slowly forward with an imperceptible and yet certain progress. The eyes of the dying man were fixed on the margin of the shadow with a keen, intense gaze. There was something terrible in its stealthy creeping and silent advance, and he strove to elude it as if it had been a living thing; but with every motion the blood gushed afresh from his heart, and he fell back upon the sod, his white teeth clenched with pain, and his hands clutched deep into the damp moss. Still his keen eyes glittered in the moonlight with the fevered workings of pain and imagination. The shadow on which they turned was to him no shadow but now a nest of serpents, creeping with their insidious coils toward him; and again, a pall — a black funereal pall, dragged forward by invisible spirits, and about to shut him out from the light forever. Slowly and surely it crept across his damp forehead and over his glowing eyes. His teeth unclenched, his hands relaxed, and a gentle smile broke over his pale lips, when he felt with what a cool and spirit-like touch it visited him. Just then a human shadow mingled with that of the tree, and the wail of a child broke on the still night air. The dying hunter struggled and strove to cry out, — "Malaeska — Ma — Ma — Mala — "

The poor Indian girl heard the voice, and with a cry, half of frenzied joy and half of fear, sprang to his side. She flung her child on the grass and lifted her dying husband to her heart, and kissed his damp forehead in a wild, eager agony of sorrow.

"Malaeska," said the young man, striving to wind his arms about her, "my poor girl, what will become of you? O God! who will take care of my boy?"

The Indian girl pushed back the damp hair from his forehead, and looked wildly down into his face. A shiver ran through her frame when she saw the cold, gray shadows of death gathering there; then her black eyes kindled, her beautiful lip curved to an expression more lofty than a smile, her small hand pointed to the West, and the wild religion of her race gushed up from her heart, a stream of living poetry.

"The hunting-ground of the Indian is yonder, among the purple clouds of the evening. The stars are very thick there, and the red light is heaped together like mountains in the heart of a forest. The sugar-maple gives its waters all the year round, and the breath of the deer is sweet, for it feeds on the golden spire-bush and the ripe berries. A lake of bright waters is there. The Indian's canoe flies over it like a bird high up in the morning. The West has rolled back its clouds, and a great chief has passed through. He will hold back the clouds that his white son may go up to the face of the Great Spirit. Malaeska and her boy will follow. The blood of the red man is high in her heart, and the way is open. The lake is deep, and the arrow sharp; death will come when Malaeska calls him. Love will make her voice sweet in the land of the Great Spirit; the white man will hear it, and call her to his bosom again!"

A faint, sad smile flitted over the dying hunter's face, and his voice was choked with a pain which was not death. "My poor girl," he said, feebly drawing her kindling face to his lips, "there is no great hunting-ground as you dream. The whites have another faith, and — O god! I have taken away her trust, and have none to give in return!"

The Indian's face drooped forward, the light of her wild, poetic faith had departed with the hunter's last words, and a feeling of cold desolation settled on her heart. He was dying on her bosom, and she knew not where he was going, nor that their parting might not be eternal.

The dying man's lips moved as if in prayer. "Forgive me, O Father of mercies! forgive me that I have left this poor girl in her heathen ignorance," he murmured, faintly, and his lips continued to move though there was no perceptible sound. After a few moments of exhaustion, he fixed his eyes on the Indian girl's face with a look of solemn and touching earnestness.

"Malaeska," he said, "talk not of putting yourself and the boy to death. That would be a sin and God would punish it. To meet me in another world, Malaeska, you must learn to love the white man's God, and wait patiently till he shall send you to me. Go not back to your tribe when I am dead. Down at the mouth of the great river are many whites; among them are my father and mother. Find your way to them, tell them how their son died, and beseech them to cherish you and the boy for his sake. Tell them how much he loved you, my poor girl. Tell them — I can not talk more. There is a girl at the settlement, one Martha Fellows; go to her. She knows of you, and has papers — a letter to my father. I did not expect this, but had prepared for it. Go to her — you will do this — promise, while I can understand."

Malaeska had not wept till now, but her voice was choked, and tears fell like rain over the dying man's face as she made the promise.

He tried to thank her, but the effort died away in a faint smile and a tremulous motion of the white lips — "Kiss me, Malaeska."

The request was faint as a breath of air, but Malaeska heard it. She flung herself on his bosom with a passionate burst of grief, and her lips clung to his as if they would have drawn him back from the very grave. She felt the cold lips moving beneath the despairing pressure of hers, and lifted her head.

"The boy, Malaeska; let me look on my son."

The child had crept to his mother's side, and crouching on his hands and knees, sat with his large black eyes filled with a strange awe, gazing on the white face of his father. Malaeska drew him closer, and with instinctive feelings he wound his arms round the neck, and nestled his face close to the ashy cheek of the dying man. There was a faint motion of the hands as if the father would have embraced his child, and then all was still. After a time, the child felt the cheek beneath his waxing hard and cold. He lifted his head and pored with breathless wonder over the face of his father's corpse. He looked up at his mother. She, too, was bending intently over the face of the dead, and her eyes were full of a wild, melancholy light. The child was bewildered. He passed his tiny hand once more over the cold face, and then crept away, buried his head in the folds of his mother's dress, and began to cry.

Morning dawned upon the little lake, quietly and still, as if nothing but the dews of heaven and the flowers of earth had ever tasted its freshness; yet all under the trees, the tender grass and the white blossoms, were crushed to the ground, stained and trampled in human blood. The delicious light broke, like a smile from heaven, over the still bosom of the waters, and flickered cheeringly through the dewy branches of the hemlock which shadowed the prostrate hunter. Bright dew-drops lay thickly on his dress, and gleamed, like a shower of seed pearls, in his rich, brown hair. The green moss on either side was soaked with a crimson stain, and the pale, leaden hue of dissolution had settled on his features. He was not alone; for on the same mossy couch lay the body of the slaughtered chief; the limbs were composed, as if on a bier — the hair wiped smooth, and the crescent of feathers, broken and wet, were arranged with care around his bronzed temples. A little way off, on a hillock, purple with flowers, lay a beautiful child, beckoning to the birds as they fluttered by — plucking up the flowers, and uttering his tiny shout of gladness, as if death and sorrow were not all around him. There, by the side of the dead hunter, sat Malaeska, the widow, her hands dropping nervously by her side, her long hair sweeping the moss, and her face bowed on her bosom, stupefied with the overwhelming poignancy of her grief. Thus she remained, motionless and lost in sorrow, till the day was at its noon. Her child, hungry and tired with play, had cried itself to sleep among the flowers; but the mother knew it not — her heart and all her faculties seemed closed as with a portal of ice.

That night when the moon was up, the Indian widow dug a grave, with her own hands, on the green margin of the lake. She laid her husband and her father side by side, and piled sods upon them. Then she lifted the wretched and hungry babe from the earth, and with a heavy heart, bent her way to "the Straka."

CHAPTER III

The sunset fell to the deep, deep stream,
  Ruddy as gold could be,
While russet brown and a crimson gleam
  Slept in each forest-tree;
But the heart of the Indian wife was sad
  As she urged her light canoe,
While her boy's young laugh rose high and glad
  When the wild birds o'er them flew.

Martha Fellows and her lover were alone in her father's cabin on the night after the Indian engagement. They were both paler than usual, and too anxious about the safety of their little village for any thing like happiness, or tranquil conversation. The old man had been stationed as sentinel on the verge of the clearing; and as the two sat together in silence, with hands interlocked, and gazing wistfully in each other's face, a rifle-shot cut sharply from the old man's station. They both started to their feet, and Martha clung shrieking to her lover. Jones forced her back to the settle — and, snatching his rifle, sprang to the door. There was a sound of approaching footsteps, and with it was mingled the voice of old Fellows, and the sweeter and more imperfect tones of a female, with the sobbing breath of a child. As Jones stood wondering at the strange sound, a remarkable group darkened the light which streamed from the cabin door. It was Fellows partly supporting and partly dragging forward a pale and terrified Indian girl. The light glittered upon her picturesque raiment, and revealed the dark, bright eyes of a child which was fastened to her back, and which clung to her neck silent with terror and exhaustion.

"Come along, you young porcupine! You skulking copper-colored little squaw, you! We shan't kill you, nor the little pappoose, neither; so you needn't shake so. Come along! There's Martha Fellows, if you can find enough of your darnationed queer English to tell her what you want."

As he spoke, the rough, but kind-hearted old man entered the hut, pushing the wretched Malaeska and her child before him.

"Martha! why what in the name of nature makes you look so white about the mouth? You needn't be afraid of this little varmint, no how. She's as harmless as a gartersnake. Come, see if you can find out what she wants of you. She can talk the drollest you ever heard. But I've scared away her senses, and she only stares at me like a shot deer."

When the Indian heard the name of the astonished girl, into whose presence she had been dragged, she withdrew from the old man's grasp and stole timidly toward the settle.

"The white man left papers with the maiden — Malaeska only wants the papers," she pleaded, placing her small palms beseechingly together.

Martha turned still more pale, and started to her feet. "It is true then," she said, almost wildly. "Poor Danforth is dead, and these forlorn creatures, his widow and child, have come to me at last. Oh! Jones, he was telling me of this the night you got so angry. I could not tell you why we were talking so much together; but I knew all the time that he had an Indian wife — it seemed as if he had a forewarning of his death, and must tell some one. The last time I saw him, he gave me a letter, sealed with black, and bade me seek his wife, and persuade her to carry it to his father, if he was killed in the fight. It is that letter she has come after; but how will she find her way to Manhattan?"

"Malaeska knows which way the waters run: she can find a path down the big river. Give her the papers that she may go!" pleaded the sad voice of the Indian.

"Tell us first," said Jones, addressing her kindly, "have the Indians left our neighborhood? Is there no danger of an attack?"

"The white man need not fear. When the great chief died, the smoke of his wigwam went out; and his people have gone beyond the mountains. Malaeska is alone."

There was wretchedness and touching pathos in the poor girl's speech, that affected the little group even to tears.

"No you ain't, by gracious!" exclaimed Fellows, dashing his hand across his eyes. "You shall stay and live with me, and help Matt, you shall — and that's the end on't. I'll make a farmer of the little pappoose. I'll bet a beaver-skin that he'll larn to gee and haw the oxen and hold plow afore half the Dutch boys that are springing up here as thick as clover-tops in a third year's clearing."

Malaeska did not perfectly understand the kind settler's proposition; but the tone and manner were kindly, and she knew that he wished to help her.

"When the boy's father was dying, he told Malaeska to go to his people, and they would tell her how to find the white man's God. Give her the papers, and she will go. Her heart will be full when she thinks of the kind words and the soft looks which the white chiefs and the bright-haired maiden have given her."

"She goes to fulfill a promise to the dead — we ought not to prevent her," said Jones.

Malaeska turned her eyes eagerly and gratefully upon him as he spoke, and Martha went to her bed and drew the letter, which had been intrusted to her care, from beneath the pillow. The Indian took it between her trembling hands, and pressing it with a gesture almost of idolatry to her lips, thrust it into her bosom.

"The white maiden is good! Farewell!" she turned toward the door as she spoke.

"Stay! It will take many days to reach Manhattan — take something to eat, or you will starve on the way," said Martha, compassionately.

"Malaeska has her bow and arrow, and she can use them; but she thanks the white maiden. A piece of bread for the boy — he has cried to his mother many times for food; but her bosom was full of tears, and she had none to give him."

Martha ran to the cupboard and brought forth a large fragment of bread and a cup of milk. When the child saw the food, he uttered a soft, hungry murmur, and his little fingers began to work eagerly on his mother's neck. Martha held the cup to his lips, and smiled through her tears to see how hungrily he swallowed, and with what a satisfied and pleased look his large, black eyes were turned up to hers as he drank. When the cup was withdrawn, the boy breathed a deep sigh of satisfaction, and let his head fall sleepily on his mother's shoulder; her large eyes seemed full of moonlight, and a gleam of pleasure shot athwart her sad features; she unbound a bracelet of wampum from her arm and placed it in Martha's hand. The next instant she was lost in the darkness without. The kind settler rushed out, and hallooed for her to come back; but her step was like that of a fawn, and while he was wandering fruitlessly around the settlement, she reached the margin of the creek; and, unmooring a canoe, which lay concealed in the sedge, placed herself in it, and shot round the point to the broad bosom of the Hudson.

Night and morning, for many successive days, that frail canoe glided down the current, amid the wild and beautiful scenery of the Highlands, and along the park-like shades of a more level country. There was something in the sublime and lofty handiwork of God which fell soothingly on the sad heart of the Indian. Her thoughts were continually dwelling on the words of her dead husband, ever picturing to themselves the land of spirits where he had promised that she should join him. The perpetual change of scenery, the sunshine playing with the foliage, and the dark, heavy masses of shadow, flung from the forests and the rocks on either hand, were continually exciting her untamed imagination to comparison with the heaven of her wild fancy. It seemed, at times, as if she had but to close her eyes and open them again to be in the presence of her lost one. There was something heavenly in the solemn, perpetual flow of the river, and in the music of the leaves as they rippled to the wind, that went to the poor widow's heart like the soft voice of a friend. After a day or two, the gloom which hung about her young brow, partially departed. Her cheek again dimpled to the happy laugh of her child, and when he nestled down to sleep in the furs at the bottom of the canoe, her soft, plaintive lullaby would steal over the waters like the song of a wild bird seeking in vain for its mate.

Malaeska never went on shore, except to gather wild fruit, and occasionally to kill a bird, which her true arrow seldom failed to bring down. She would strike a fire and prepare her game in some shady nook by the river side, while the canoe swung at its mooring, and her child played on the fresh grass, shouting at the cloud of summer insects that flashed by, and clapping his tiny hands at the humming-birds that came to rifle honey from the flowers that surrounded him.

The voyage was one of strange happiness to the widowed Indian. Never did Christian believe in the pages of Divine Writ with more of trust, than she placed in the dying promise of her husband, that she should meet him again in another world. His spirit seemed forever about her, and to her wild, free imagination, the passage down the magnificent stream seemed a material and glorious path to the white man's heaven. Filled with strange, sweet thoughts, she looked abroad on the mountains looming up from the banks of the river — on the forest-trees so various in their tints, and so rightly clothed, till she was inspired almost to forgetfulness of her affliction. She was young and healthy, and every thing about her was so lovely, so grand and changing, that her heart expanded to the sunshine like a flower which has been bowed down, but not crushed beneath the force of a storm. Part of each day she spent in a wild, dreamy state of imagination. Her mind was lulled to sweet musings by the gentle sounds that hovered in the air from morning till evening, and through the long night, when all was hushed save the deep flow of the river. Birds came out with their cheerful voices at dawn, and at midday she floated in the cool shadow of the hills, or shot into some cove for a few hours' rest. When the sunset shed its gorgeous dyes over the river — and the mountain ramparts, on either side, were crimson as with the tracks of contending armies — when the boy was asleep, and the silent stars came out to kindle up her night path, then a clear, bold melody gushed from the mother's lips like a song from the heart of a nightingale. Her eye kindled, her cheek grew warm, the dip of her paddle kept a liquid accompaniment to her rich, wild voice, as the canoe floated downward on waves that seemed rippling over a world of crushed blossoms, and were misty with the approach of evening.

Malaeska had been out many days, when the shady gables and the tall chimneys of Manhattan broke upon her view, surrounded by the sheen of its broad bay, and by the forest which covered the uninhabited part of the island. The poor Indian gazed upon it with an unstable but troublesome fear. She urged her canoe into a little cove on the Hoboken shore, and her heart grew heavy as the grave, as she pondered on the means of fulfilling her charge. She took the letter from her bosom; the tears started to her eyes, and she kissed it with a regretful sorrow, as if a friend were about to be rendered up from her affections forever. She took the child to her heart, and held him there till its throbbings grew audible, and the strength of her misgivings could not be restrained. After a time she became more calm. She lifted the child from her bosom, laved his hands and face in the stream, and brushed his black hair with her palm till it glowed like the neck of a raven. Then she girded his little crimson robe with a string of wampum, and after arranging her own attire, shot the canoe out of the cove and urged it slowly across the mouth of the river. Her eyes were full of tears all the way, and when the child murmured, and strove to comfort her with his infant caress, she sobbed aloud, and rowed steadily forward.

It was a strange sight to the phlegmatic inhabitants of Manhattan, when Malaeska passed through their streets in full costume, and with the proud, free tread of her race. Her hair hung in long braids down her back, each braid fastened at the end with a tuft of scarlet feathers. A coronet of the same bright plumage circled her small head, and her robe was gorgeous with beads, and fringed with porcupine quills. A bow of exquisite workmanship was in her hand, and a scarf of scarlet cloth bound the boy to her back. Nothing could be more strikingly beautiful than the child. His spirited head was continually turning from one strange object to another, and his bright, black eyes were brim-full of childish wonder. One little arm was flung around his young mother's neck, and its fellow rested on the feathered arrow-shafts which crowded the quiver slung against her left shoulder. The timid, anxious look of the mother, was in strong contrast with the eager gaze of the boy. She had caught much of the delicacy and refinement of civilized life from her husband, and her manner became startled and fawn-like beneath the rude gaze of the passers-by. The modest blood burned in her cheek, and the sweet, broken English trembled on her lips, when several persons, to whom she showed the letter passed by without answering her. She did not know that they were of another nation than her husband, and spoke another language than that which love had taught her. At length she accosted an aged man who could comprehend her imperfect language. He read the name on the letter, and saw that it was addressed to his master, John Danforth, the richest fur-trader in Manhattan. The old serving-man led the way to a large, irregular building, in the vicinity of what is now Hanover Square.[4] Malaeska followed with a lighter tread, and a heart relieved of its fear. She felt that she had

[4] *Hanover Square*:   In lower Manhattan, Hanover Square is located just south of the intersection of Water Street and Wall Street.

found a friend in the kind old man who was conducting her to the home of her husband's father.

The servant entered this dwelling and led the way to a low parlor, paneled with oak and lighted with small panes of thick, greenish glass. A series of Dutch tiles — some of them most exquisite in finish and design, surrounded the fire-place, and a coat-of-arms, elaborately carved in oak, stood out in strong relief from the paneling above. A carpet, at that time an uncommon luxury, covered a greater portion of the floor, and the furniture was rich in its material, and ponderous with heavy carved work. A tall, and rather hard-featured man sat in an arm-chair by one of the narrow windows, reading a file of papers which had just arrived in the last merchant-ship from London. A little distance from him, a slight and very thin lady of about fifty was occupied with household sewing; her work-box stood on a small table before her, and a book of common-prayer lay beside it. The servant had intended to announce his strange guests, but, fearful of losing sight of him, Malaeska followed close upon his footsteps, and before he was aware of it, stood within the room, holding her child by the hand.

"A woman, sir, — an Indian woman, with a letter," said the embarrassed servant, motioning his charge to draw back. But Malaeska had stepped close to the merchant, and was looking earnestly in his face when he raised his eyes from the papers. There was something cold in his severe gaze as he fixed it on her through his spectacles. The Indian felt chilled and repulsed; her heart was full, and she turned with a look of touching appeal to the lady. That face was one to which a child would have fled for comfort; it was tranquil and full of kindness. Malaeska's face brightened as she went up to her, and placed the letter in her hands without speaking a word; but the palpitation of her heart was visible through her heavy garments, and her hands shook as she relinquished the precious paper.

"The seal is black," said the lady, turning very pale as she gave the letter to her husband, "but it is *his* writing," she added, with a forced smile. "He could not have sent word himself, were he — ill." She hesitated at the last word, for, spite of herself, the thoughts of death lay heavily at her heart.

The merchant composed himself in his chair, settled his spectacles, and after another severe glance at the bearer, opened the letter. His wife kept her eyes fixed anxiously on his face as he read. She saw that his face grew pale, that his high, narrow forehead contracted, and that the stern mouth became still more rigid in its expression. She knew that some evil had befallen her son — her only son, and she grasped a chair for support; her lips were bloodless, and her eyes became keen with agonizing suspense. When her husband had read the letter through, she went close to him, but looked another way as she spoke. "Tell me! has any harm befallen my son?" Her voice was low and gentle, but husky with suspense.

Her husband did not answer, but his hand fell heavily upon his knee, and the letter rattled in his unsteady grasp; his eyes were fixed on his trembling wife with a look that chilled her to the heart. She attempted to withdraw the letter from his hand, but he clenched it the firmer.

"Let it alone — he is dead — murdered by the savages — why should you know more?"

The poor woman staggered back, and the fire of anxiety went out from her eyes.

"Can there be any thing worse than death — the death of the first-born of our youth — cut off in his proud manhood?" she murmured, in a low, broken voice.

"Yes, woman!" said the husband, almost fiercely; "there is a thing worse than death — disgrace!"

"Disgrace coupled with my son? You are his father, John. Do not slander him now that he is dead — before his mother, too." There was a faint, red spot then upon that mild woman's face, and her mouth curved proudly as she spoke. All that was stern in her nature had been aroused by the implied charge against the departed.

"Read, woman, read! Look on that accursed wretch and her child! They have enticed him into their savage haunts, and murdered him. Now they come to claim protection and reward for the foul deed."

Malaeska drew her child closer to her as she listened to this vehement language, and shrank slowly back to a corner of the room, where she crouched, like a frightened hare, looking wildly about, as if seeking some means to evade the vengeance which seemed to threaten her.

After the first storm of feeling, the old man buried his face in his hands and remained motionless, while the sobs of his wife, as she read her son's letter, alone broke the stillness of the room.

Malaeska felt those tears as an encouragement, and her own deep feelings taught her how to reach those of another. She drew timidly to the mourner and sank at her feet.

"Will the white woman look upon Malaeska?" she said, in a voice full of humility and touching earnestness. "She loved the young white chief, and when the shadows fell upon his soul, he said that his mother's heart would grow soft to the poor Indian woman who had slept in his bosom while she was very young. He said that her love would open to his boy like a flower to the sunshine. Will the white woman look upon the boy? He is like his father."

"He is, poor child, he is!" murmured the bereaved mother, looking on the boy through her tears — "like him, as he was when we were both young, and he the blessing of our hearts. Oh, John, do you remember his smile? — how his cheek would dimple when we kissed it! Look upon this poor, fatherless creature; they are all here again; the sunny eye and the broad forehead. Look upon him, John, for my sake — for the sake of our dead son, who prayed us with his last breath to love *his* son. Look upon him!"

The kind woman led the child to her husband as she spoke , and resting her arm on his shoulder, pressed her lips upon his swollen temples. The pride of his nature was touched. His bosom heaved, and tears gushed through his rigid fingers. He felt a little form draw close to his knee, and a tiny, soft hand strive with its feeble might to uncover his face. The voice of nature was strong within him. His hands dropped, and he pored with a troubled face over the uplifted features of the child.

Tears were in those young, bright eyes as they returned his grandfather's gaze, but when a softer expression came into the old man's face, a smile broke through them, and the little fellow lifted both his arms and clasped them over the bowed neck of his grandfather. There was a momentary struggle, and then the merchant folded the boy to his heart with a burst of strong feeling such as his iron nature had seldom known.

"He *is* like his father. Let the woman go back to her tribe; we will keep the boy."

Malaeska sprang forward, clasped her hands, and turned with an air of wild, heart-thrilling appeal to the lady.

"You will not send Malaeska from her child. No — no, white woman. Your boy has slept against your heart, and you have felt his voice in your ear, like the song of a young mocking-bird. You would not send the poor Indian back to the woods without her child. She has come to you from the forest, that she may learn the path to the white man's heaven, and see her husband again, and you will not show it her. Give the Indian woman her boy; her heart is growing very strong; she will not go back to the woods alone!"

As she spoke these words, with an air more energetic even than her speech, she snatched the child from his grandfather's arms, and stood like a lioness guarding her young, her lips writhing and her black eyes flashing fire, for the savage blood kindled in her veins at the thought of being separated from her son.

"Be quiet, girl, be quiet. If you go, the child shall go with you," said the gentle Mrs. Danforth. "Do not give way to this fiery spirit; no one will wrong you."

Malaeska dropped her air of defiance, and placing the child humbly at his grandfather's feet, drew back, and stood with her eyes cast down, and her hands clasped deprecatingly together, a posture of supplication in strong contrast with her late wild demeanor.

"Let them stay. Do not separate the mother and the child!" entreated the kind lady, anxious to soothe away the effect of her husband's violence. "The thoughts of a separation drives her wild, poor thing. *He* loved her; — why should we send her back to her savage haunts? Read this letter once more, my husband. You can not refuse the dying request of our first-born."

With gentle and persuasive words like these, the kind lady prevailed. Malaeska was allowed to remain in the house of her husband's father, but it was only as the nurse of her own son. She was not permitted to acknowledge herself as his mother; and it was given out that young Danforth had married in one of the new settlements — that the young couple had fallen victims to the savages, and that their infant son had been rescued by an Indian girl, who brought him to his grandfather. The story easily gained credit, and it was no matter of wonder that the old fur merchant soon became fondly attached to the little orphan, or that the preserver of his grandchild was made an object of grateful attention in his household.

CHAPTER IV

"Her heart is in the wild wood;
Her heart is not here.
Her heart is in the wild wood;
It was hunting the deer."

It would have been an unnatural thing, had that picturesque young mother abandoned the woods, and prisoned herself in a quaint old Dutch house, under the best circumstances. The wild bird, which has fluttered freely from its nest through a thousand forests, might as well be expected to love its cage, as this poor wild girl her new home, with its dreary stillness and its leaden regularity. But love was all-powerful in that wild heart. It had brought Malaeska from her forest home, separated her from her tribe in its hour of bitter defeat, and sent her a forlorn wanderer among strangers that regarded her almost with loathing.

The elder Danforth was a just man but hard as granite in his prejudices. An only son has been murdered by the savages to whom this poor young creature belonged. His blood — all of his being that might descend to posterity — had been mingled with the accursed race who had sacrificed him. Gladly would he have rent the two races asunder, in the very person of his grandchild, could the pure half of his being been thus preserved.

But he was a proud, childless old man, and there was something in the boy's eyes, in the brave lift of his head, and in his caressing manner, which filled the void in his heart, half with love and half with pain. He could no more separate the two passions in his own soul, than he could drain the savage blood from the little boy's veins.

But the house-mother, the gentle wife, could see nothing but her son's smile in that young face, nothing but his look in the large eyes, which, black in color, still possessed something of the azure light that had distinguished those of the father.

The boy was more cheerful and bird-like than his mother, for all her youth had gone out on the banks of the pond where her husband died. Always submissive, always gentle, she was nevertheless a melancholy woman. A bird which had followed its young out into strange lands, and caged it there, could not have hovered around it more hopelessly.

Nothing but her husband's dying wish would have kept Malaeska in Manhattan. She thought of her own people incessantly — of her broken, harassed tribe, desolated by the death of her father, and whose young chief she had carried off and given to strangers.

But shame dyed Malaeska's cheek as she thought of these things. What right had she, an Indian of the pure blood, to bring the grandchild of her father under the roof of his enemies? Why had she not taken the child in her arms and joined her people as they sang the death-chant for her father, "who," she murmured to herself again and again, "was a great chief," and retreated with them deep into the wilderness, to which they were driven, giving them a chief in her son?

But no! passion had been too strong in Malaeska's heart. The woman conquered the patriot; and the refinement which affection had given her, enslaved the wild nature without returning a compensation of love for the sacrifice. She pined for her people — all the more that they were in peril and sorrow. She longed for the shaded forest-paths, and the pretty lodge, with its couches of fur and its floor of blossoming turf. To her the very winds seemed chained among the city houses; and when she heard them sighing through the gables, it seemed to her that they were moaning for freedom, as she was in the solitude of her lonely life.

They had taken the child from her. A white nurse was found, who stepped in between the young heir and his mother, thrusting her ruthlessly aside. In this the old man was obstinate. The wild blood of the boy must be quenched; he must know nothing of the race from which his disgrace sprang. If the Indian woman remained under his roof, it must be as a menial, and on condition that all natural affection lay crushed within her — unexpressed, unguessed at by the household.

But Mrs. Danforth had compassion on the poor mother. She remembered the time when her own child had made all the pulses of her being thrill with love, which now took the form of a thousand tender regrets. She could not watch the lone Indian stealing off to her solitary room under the gable roof — a mother, yet childless — without throbs of womanly sorrow. She was far too good a wife to brave her husband's authority, but, with the cowardliness of a kind heart, she frequently managed to evade it. Sometimes in the night she would creep out of her prim chamber, and steal the boy from the side of his nurse, whom she bore on her own motherly bosom to the solitary bed of Malaeska.

As if Malaeska had a premonition of the kindliness, she was sure to be wide awake, thinking of her child, and ready to gush forth in murmurs of thankfulness for the joy of clasping her own son a moment to that lonely heart.

Then the grandmother would steal to her husband's side again, charging it upon her memory to awake before daylight, and carry the boy back to the stranger's bed, making her gentle charity a secret as if it had been a sin.

It was pitiful to see Malaeska haunting the footsteps of her boy all the day long. If he was taken into the garden, she was sure to be hovering around the old pear-trees, where she could sometimes unseen lure him from his play, and lavish kisses on his mouth as he laughed recklessly, and strove to abandon her for some bright flower or butterfly that crossed his path. This snatch of affection, this stealthy way of appeasing a hungry nature, was enough to drive a well-tutored woman mad; as for Malaeska, it was a marvel that she could tame her erratic nature into the abject position allotted her in that family. She had neither the occupation of a servant, nor the interests of an equal.

Forbidden to associate with the people in the kitchen, yet never welcomed in the formal parlor when its master was at home, she hovered around the halls and corners of the house, or hid herself away in the gable chambers, embroidering beautiful trifles on scraps of silk and fragments of bright cloth, with which she strove to bribe the woman who controlled her child, into forbearance and kindness.

But alas, poor woman! submission to the wishes of the dead was a terrible duty; her poor heart was breaking all the time; she had no hope, no life; the very glance of her eye was an appeal for mercy; her step, as it fell on the turf, was leaden with despondency — she had nothing on earth to live for.

This state of things arose when the child was a little boy; but as he grew older the bitterness of Malaeska's lot became more intense. The nurse who had supplanted her went away; for he was becoming a fine lad, and far removed from the need of woman's care. But this brought her no nearer to his affections. The Indian blood was strong in his young veins; he loved such play as brought activity and danger with it, and broke from the Indian woman's caresses with a sort of scorn, and she knew that the old grandfather's prejudice was taking root in his heart, and dared not utter a protest. She was forbidden to lavish tenderness on her son, or to call forth his in return, lest it might create suspicion of the relationship.

In his early boyhood, she could steal to his chamber at night, and give free indulgence to the wild tenderness of her nature; but after a time even the privilege of watching him in his sleep was denied to her. Once, when she broke the tired boy's rest by her caresses, he became petulant, and chided her for her obtrusiveness. The repulse went to her heart like iron. She had no power to plead; for her life, she dared not tell him the secret of that aching love which she felt — too cruelly felt — oppressed his boyhood; for that would be to expose the disgrace of blood which embittered the old man's pride.

She was his mother; yet her very existence in that house was held as a reproach. Every look that she dared to cast on her child, was watched jealously as a fault. Poor Malaeska! hers was a sad, sad life.

She had borne every thing for years, dreaming, poor thing, that the eternal cry that went up from her heart would be answered, as the boy grew older; but when he began to shrink proudly from her caresses, and question the love that was killing her, the despair which smoldered at her heart broke forth, and the forest blood spoke out with a power that not even a sacred memory of the dead could oppose. A wild idea seized upon her. She would no longer remain in the white man's house, like a bird beating its wings against the wires of a cage. The forests were wide and green as ever. Her people might yet be found. She would seek them in the wilderness. The boy should go with her, and become the chief of his tribe, as her father had been. That old man should not forever trample down her heart. There was a free life which she would find or die.

The boy's childish petulance had created this wild wish in his mother's heart. The least sign of repulsion drove her frantic. She began to thirst eagerly for her old free existence in the woods; but for the blood of her husband, which ran in the old man's veins, she would have given way to the savage hate of her people, against the household in which she had been so unhappy. As it was, she only panted to be away with her child, who must love her when no white man stood by to rebuke him. With her aroused energies the native reticence of her tribe came to her aid. The stealthy art of warfare against an enemy awoke. They should not know how wretched she was. Her plans must be securely made. Every step toward freedom should be carefully considered. These thoughts occupied Malaeska for days and weeks. She became active in her little chamber. The bow and sheaf of arrows that had given her the appearance of a young Diana when she came to Manhattan in her canoe, was taken down from the wall, newly strung, and the stone arrow-heads patiently sharpened. Her dress, with its gorgeous embroidery of fringe and wampum, was examined with care. She must return to her people as she had left them. The daughter of a chief — the mother of a chief — not a fragment of the white man's bounty should go with her to the forest.

Cautiously, and with something of native craft, Malaeska made her preparations. Down upon the shores of the Hudson, lived an old carpenter who made boats for a living. Malaeska had often seen him at his work, and her rude knowledge of his craft gave peculiar interest to the curiosity with which she regarded him. The Indian girl had long been an object of his especial interest, and the carpenter was flattered by her admiration of his work.

One day she came to his house with a look of eager watchfulness. Her step was hurried, her eye wild as a hawk's when its prey is near. The old man was finishing a fanciful little craft, of which he was proud beyond any thing. It was so light, so strong, so beautifully decorated with bands of red and white around the edge — no wonder the young woman's eyes brightened when she saw it.

"What would he take for the boat?" That was a droll question from her. Why he had built it to please his own fancy. A pair of oars would make it skim the water like a bird. He had built it with an eye to old Mr. Danforth, who had been down to look at his boats for that dark-eyed grandson, whom he seemed to worship. None of his boats were fanciful or light enough for the lad. So he had built this at a venture.

Malaeska's eyes kindled brighter and brighter. Yes, yes; she, too, was thinking of the young gentleman; she would bring him to look at the boat. Mrs. Danforth often trusted the boy out with her; if he would only tell the price, perhaps they might be able to bring the money, and give the boat a trial on the Hudson.

The old man laughed, glanced proudly at his handiwork, and named a price. It was not too much; Malaeska had double that amount in the embroidered pouch that hung in her little room at home — for the old gentleman had been liberal to her in every thing but kindness. She went home elated and eager; all was in readiness. The next day — oh, how her heart glowed as she thought of the next day!

CHAPTER V

Her boat is on the river,
    With the boy by her side;
With her bow and her quiver
    She stands in her pride.

The next afternoon old Mr. Danforth was absent from home. A municipal meeting, or something of that kind, was to be attended, and he was always prompt in the performance of public duties. The good housewife had not been well for some days. Malaeska, always a gentle nurse, attended her with unusual assiduity. There was some-thing evidently at work in the Indian woman's heart. Her lips were pale, her eyes full of pathetic trouble. After a time, when weariness made the old lady sleepy, Malaeska stole to the bedside, and kneeling down, kissed the withered hand that fell over the bed, with strange humility. This action was so light that the good lady did not heed it, but afterward it came to her like a dream, and as such she remembered this leave-taking of the poor mother.

William — for the lad was named after his father — was in a moody state that afternoon. He had no playfellows, for the indisposi-tion of his grandmother had shut all strangers from the house, so he went into the garden, and began to draw the outlines of a rude fortification from the white pebbles that paved the principal walk. He was interrupted in the work by a pair of orioles, that came dashing through the leaves of an old apple-tree in a far end of the garden, in full chase and pursuit, making the very air vibrate with their rapid motion.

After chasing each other up and down, to and fro in the clear sunshine, they were attracted by something in the distance, and darted off like a couple of golden arrows, sending back wild gushes of music in the start.

The boy had been watching them with his great eyes full of envious delight. Their riotous freedom charmed him; he felt chained and caged even in that spacious garden, full of golden fruit and bright flowers as it was. The native fire kindled in his frame.

"Oh, if I were only a bird, that could fly home when I pleased, and away to the woods again — the bright, beautiful woods that I can see across the river, but never must play in. How the birds love it though!"

The boy stopped speaking, for, like any other child kept to himself, he was talking over his thoughts aloud. But a shadow fell across the white pebbles on which he sat, and this it was which disturbed him.

It was the Indian woman, Malaeska, with a forced smile on her face and looking wildly strange. She seemed larger and more stately than when he had seen her last. In her hand she held a light bow tufted with yellow and crimson feathers. When she saw his eyes brighten at the sight of the bow, Malaeska took an arrow from the sheaf which she carried under her cloak, and fitted it to the string.

"See, this is what we learn in the woods."

The two birds were wheeling to and fro across the garden and out into the open space; their plumage flashed in the sunshine and gushes of musical triumph floated back as one shot ahead of the other. Malaeska lifted her bow with something of her old forest gracefulness — a faint twang of the bowstring — a sharp whiz of the arrow, one of the birds fluttered downward, with a sad little cry, and fell upon the ground, trembling like a broken poplar flower.

The boy started up — his eye brightened and his thin nostrils dilated, the savage instincts of his nature broke out in all his features.

"And you learned how to do this in the woods, Malaeska?" he said, eagerly.

"Yes; will you learn too?"

"Oh, yes — give hold here — quick — quick!"

"Not here; we learn these things in the woods; come with me, and I will show you all about it." Malaeska grew pale as she spoke, and trembled in all her limbs. What if the boy refused to go with her?

"What! over the river to the woods that look so bright and so brown when the nuts fall? Will you take me there, Malaeska?"

"Yes, over the river where it shines like silver."

"You will? oh my! — but how?"

"Hush! not so loud. In a beautiful little boat."

"With white sails, Malaeska?"

"No — with paddles."

"Ah, me! — but I can't make them go in the water; once grandfather let me try, but I had to give it up."

"But I can make them go."

"You! why, that isn't a woman's work."

"No, but everybody learns it in the woods."

"Can I?"

"Yes!"

"Then come along before grandfather comes to say we shan't; come along, I say; I want to shoot and run and live in the woods — come along, Malaeska. Quick, or somebody will shut the gate."

Malaeska looked warily around — on the windows of the house, through the thickets, and along the gravel walks. No one was in sight. She and her boy were all alone. She breathed heavily and lingered, thinking of the poor lady within.

"Come!" cried the boy, eagerly; "I want to go — come along to the woods."

"Yes, yes," whispered Malaeska, "to the woods — it is our home. There I shall be a mother once more."

With the steps of a young deer, starting for its covert, she left the garden. The boy kept bravely on with her, bounding forward with a laugh when her step was too rapid for him to keep up with it. Thus, in breathless haste, they passed through the town into the open country and along the rough banks of the river.

A little inlet, worn by the constant action of the water, ran up into the shore, which is now broken with wharves and bristling with masts. A clump of old forest-hemlocks bent over the waters, casting cool, green shadows upon it till the sun was far in the west.

In these shadows, rocking sleepily on the ripples, lay the pretty boat which Malaeska had purchased. A painted basket, such as the peaceful Indians sometimes sent to market, stood in the stern stored with bread; a tiger-skin, edged with crimson cloth, according to the Indian woman's fancy, lay along the bottom of the boat, and cushions of scarlet cloth, edged with an embroidery of beads, lay on the seat.

William Danforth broke into a shout when he saw the boat and its appointments.

"Are we going in this? May I learn to row, now — now?" With a leap he sprang into the little craft, and seizing the oars, called for her to come on, for he was in a hurry to begin.

Malaeska loosened the cable, and holding the end in her hand, sprang to the side of her child.

"Not yet, chief, not yet; give the oars to me a little while; when we can no longer see the steeples, you shall pull them," she said.

The boy gave up his place with an impatient toss of his head, which sent the black curls flying over his temples. But the boat shot out into the river with a velocity that took away his breath, and he sat down in the bow, laughing as the silver spray rained over him. With her face to the north, and her eyes flashing with the eager joy of escape, Malaeska dashed up the river; every plunge of the oars was a step toward freedom — every gleam of the sun struck her as a smile from the Great Spirit to whom her husband and father had gone.

When the sun went down, and the twilight came on, the little boat was far up the river. It had glided under the shadows of Weehawken,[5] and was skirting the western shore toward the Highlands, at that time crowned by an unbroken forest, and savage in the grandeur of wild nature.

Now Malaeska listened to the entreaties of her boy, and gave the oars into his small hands. No matter though the boat receded under his brave but imperfect efforts; once out of sight of the town, Malaeska had less fear, and smiled securely at the energy with which the little fellow beat the waters. He was indignant if she attempted to help him, and the next moment was sure to send a storm of rain over her in some more desperate effort to prove how capable he was of taking the labor from her hands.

Thus the night came on, soft and calm, wrapping the mother and child in a world of silvery moonbeams. The shadows which lay along the hills bounded their watery path with gloom. This made the boy sad, and he began to feel mournfully weary; but scenes like this were familiar with Malaeska, and her old nature rose high and free in this

[5] *Weehawken:* A township in what is now northeastern New Jersey (opposite Manhattan on the Hudson), Weehawken was the site of the duel in which Aaron Burr fatally wounded Alexander Hamilton in 1804.

solitude which included all that she had in the living world — her freedom and the son of her white husband.

"Malaeska," said the boy, creeping to her side, and laying his head on her lap, "Malaeska, I am tired — I want to go home."

"Home! but you have not seen the woods. Courage, my chief, and we will go on shore."

"But it is black — so black, and something is crying there — something that is sick or wants to get home like me."

"No, no, — it is only a whippowil singing to the night."

"A whippowil? Is that a little boy, Malaeska? Let us bring him into the boat."

"No, my child, it is only a bird."

"Poor bird!" sighed the boy; "how it wants to get home."

"No, it loves the woods. The bird would die if you took it from the shade of the trees," said Malaeska, striving to pacify the boy, who crept upward into her lap and laid his cheek against hers. She felt that he trembled, and that tears lay cold on his cheeks. "Don't, my William, but look up and see how many stars hang over us — the river is full of them."

"Oh, but grandfather will be missing me," pleaded the boy.

Malaeska felt herself chilled; she had taken the boy but not his memory; that went back to the opulent home he had left. With her at his side, and the beautiful universe around, he thought of the old man who had made her worse than a serf in his household — who had stolen away the human soul that God had given into her charge. The Indian woman grew sad to the very depths of her soul when the boy spoke of his grandfather.

"Come," she said, with mournful pathos, "now we will find an open place in the woods. You shall have a bed like the pretty flowers. I will build a fire, and you shall see it grow red among the branches."

The boy smiled in the moonlight.

"A fire out of doors! Yes, yes, let's go into the woods. Will the birds talk to us there?"

"The birds talk to us always when we get into the deep of the woods."

Malaeska urged her boat into a little inlet that ran up between two great rocks upon the shore, where it was sheltered and safe; then she took the tiger-skin and the cushions in her arms, and cautioning the boy to hold on to her dress, began to mount a little elevation where the trees were thin and the grass abundant, as she could tell from the odor of wild-flowers that came with the wind. A rock lay embedded in this rich forest-grass, and over it a huge white poplar spread its branches like a tent.

Upon this rock Malaeska enthroned the boy, talking to him all the time, as she struck sparks from a flint which she took from her basket, and began to kindle a fire from the dry sticks which lay around in abundance. When William saw the flames rise up high and clear, illuminating the beautiful space around, and shooting gleams of gold through the poplar's branches he grew brave again, and coming down from his eminence, began to gather brushwood that the fire might keep bright. Then Malaeska took a bottle of water and some bread, with fragments of dried beef, from her basket, and the boy came smiling from his work. He was no longer depressed by the dark, and the sight of food made him hungry.

How proudly the Indian mother broke the food and surrendered it to his eager appetite. The bright beauty of her face was something wonderful to look upon as she watched him by the firelight. For the first time, since he was a little infant, he really seemed to belong to her.

When he was satisfied with food, and she saw that his eyelids began to droop, Malaeska went to some rocks at a little distance, and tearing up the moss in great green fleeces, brought it to the place she had chosen under the poplar-tree, and heaped a soft couch for the child. Over this she spread the tiger-skin with its red border, and laid the crimson pillows whose fringes glittered in the firelight like gems around the couch of a prince.

To this picturesque bed Malaeska took the boy, and setting herself by his side, began to sing as she had done years ago under the roof of her wigwam. The lad was very weary, and fell asleep while her plaintive voice filled the air and was answered mournfully back by a nightbird deep in the blackness of the forest.

When certain that the lad was asleep, Malaeska lay down on the hard rock by his side, softly stealing one arm over him and sighing out her troubled joy as she pressed his lips with her timid kisses.

Thus the poor Indian sunk to a broken rest, as she had done all her life, piling up soft couches for those she loved, and taking the cold stone for herself. It was her woman's destiny, not the more certain because of her savage origin. Civilization does not always reverse this mournful picture of womanly self-abnegation.

When the morning came, the boy was aroused by a full chorus of singing-birds that fairly made the air vibrate with their melody. In and out through the branches rang their wild minstrelsy, till the sunshine came laughing through the greenness, giving warmth and pleasant light to the music. William sat up, rubbing his eyes, and wondering at the strange noises. Then he remembered where he was, and called aloud for Malaeska. She came from behind a clump of trees, carrying a partridge in her hand, pierced through the heart with her arrow. She flung the bird on the rock at William's feet, and kneeling down before him, kissed his feet, his hands, and the folds of his tunic, smoothing his hair and his garments with pathetic fondness.

"When shall we go home, Malaeska?" cried the lad, a little anxiously. "Grandfather will want us."

"This is the home for a young chief," replied the mother, looking around upon the pleasant sky and the forest-turf, enameled with wild-flowers. "What white man has a tent like this?"

The boy looked up and saw a world of golden tulip-blossoms starring the branches above him.

"It lets in the cold and the rain," he said, shaking the dew from his glossy hair. "I don't like the woods, Malaeska."

"But you will — oh yes, you will," answered the mother, with anxious cheerfulness; "see, I have shot a bird for your breakfast."

"A bird? and I am so hungry."

"And see here, what I have brought from the shore."

She took a little leaf-basket from a recess in the rocks, and held it up full of black raspberries with the dew glittering upon them.

The boy clapped his hands, laughing merrily. "Give me the raspberries — I will eat them all. Grandfather isn't here to stop me, so I will eat and eat till the basket is empty. After all, Malaeska, it is pleasant being in the woods — come, pour the berries on the moss, just here, and get another basketful while I eat these; but don't go far — I am afraid when you are out of sight. No, no, let me build the fire — see how I can make the sparks fly."

Down he came from the rock, forgetting his berries, and eager to distinguish himself among the brushwood, while Malaeska withdrew a little distance and prepared her game for roasting.

The boy was quick and full of intelligence; he had a fire blazing at once, and shouted back a challenge to the birds as its flames rose in the air, sending up wreaths of delicate blue smoke into the poplar branches, and curtaining the rocks with mist.

Directly the Indian woman came forward with her game, nicely dressed and pierced with a wooden skewer; to this she attached a piece of twine, which, being tied to a branch overhead, swung its burden gently to and fro before the fire.

While this rustic breakfast was in preparation, the boy went off in search of flowers or berries — any thing that he could find. He came back with a quantity of green wild cherries in his tunic, and a bird's nest, with three speckled eggs in it, which he had found under a tuft of fern leaves. A striped squirrel, that ran down a chestnut-limb, looked at him with such queer earnestness, that he shouted lustily to Malaeska, saying that he loved the beautiful woods and all the pretty things in it.

When he came back, Malaeska had thrown off her cloak, and crowned herself with a coronal of scarlet and green feathers, which rendered her savage dress complete, and made her an object of wondering admiration to the boy, as she moved in and out through the trees, and with her face all aglow with proud love.

While the partridge was swaying to and fro before the fire, Malaeska gathered a handful of chestnut-leaves and wove them together in a sort of mat; upon this cool nest she laid the bird, and carved it with a pretty poniard which William's father had given her in his first wooing; then she made a leaf-cup, and, going to a little spring which she had discovered, filled it with crystal water. So, upon the flowering turf, with wild birds serenading them, and the winds floating softly by, the mother and boy took their first regular meal in the forest. William was delighted; every thing was fresh and beautiful to him. He could scarcely contain his eagerness to be in action long enough to eat the delicate repast which Malaeska diversified with smiles and caresses. He wanted to shoot the birds that sang so sweetly in the branches, all unconscious that the act would inflict pain on the poor little songsters; he could not satisfy himself with gazing on the gorgeous raiment of his mother — it was something wonderful in his eyes.

At last the rustic meal was ended, and with his lips reddened by the juicy fruit, he started up, pleading for the bow and arrow.

Proud as a queen and fond as woman, Malaeska taught him how to place the arrow on the bowstring, and when to lift it gradually toward his face. He took to it naturally, the young rogue, and absolutely danced for joy when his first arrow leaped from his bow and went rifling through the poplar-leaves. How Malaeska loved this practice! how she triumphed in each graceful lift of his arm! how her heart leaped to the rich tumult of his shouts! He wanted to go off alone and try his skill among the squirrels, but Malaeska was afraid, and followed him step by step, happy and watchful. Every moment increased his skill; he would have exhausted the sheaf of arrows, but that Malaeska patiently searched for them after each shot, and thus secured constant amusement till he grew tired even of that rare sport.

Toward noon, Malaeska left him at rest on the tiger-skin, and went herself in search of game for the noonday meal; never had she breathed so freely, never had the woods seemed so like her home. A sense of profound peace stole over her. These groves were her world, and on the rock near by lay her other life — all that she had on earth to love. She was in no haste to find her tribe. What care had she for any thing while the boy was with her, and the forest so pleasant? What did she care for but his happiness?

It required but few efforts of her woodcraft to obtain game enough for another pleasant meal; so, with a light step, she returned to her fairy-like encampment. Tired with his play, the boy had fallen asleep on the rock. She saw the graceful repose of his limbs, and the sunshine shimmering softly through his black hair. Her step grew lighter; she was afraid of rustling a leaf, lest the noise might disturb him. Thus, softly and almost holding her breath, she drew nearer and nearer to the rock. All at once a faint grasping breath bespoke some terrible emotion — she stood motionless, rooted to the earth. A low rattle checked her first, and then she saw the shimmer of a serpent, coiled upon the very rock where her boy was laying. Her approach had aroused the reptile, and she could see him preparing to lance out. His first fling would be at the sleeping boy. The mother was frozen into marble; she dared not move — she could only stare at the snake with a wild glitter of the eye.

The stillness seemed to appease the creature. The noise of his rattle grew fainter, and his eyes sank like waning fire-sparks into the writhing folds that settled on the moss. But the child was disturbed by a sunbeam that slanted through the leaves overhead, and turned upon the tiger-skin. Instantly the rattle sounded sharp and clear, and out from the writhing folds shot the venomous head with its vicious eyes fixed on the boy. Malaeska had, even in her frozen state, some thought of saving her boy. With her cold hands she had fitted the arrow and lifted the bow, but as the serpent grew passive, the weapon dropped again; for he lay on the other side of the child, and to kill him she was obliged to shoot over that sleeping form. But the reptile crested himself again, and now with a quiver of horrible dread at her heart, but nerves strained like steel, she drew the bowstring, and, aiming at the head, which glittered like a jewel, just beyond her child, let the arrow fly. She went blind on the instant — darkness of death fell upon her brain; the coldness of death lay upon her heart; she listened for some cry — nothing but a sharp rustling of leaves and then profound stillness met her strained senses.

The time in which Malaeska was struck with darkness seemed an eternity to her, but it lasted only an instant, in fact; then her eyes opened wide in the agonized search, and terrible thrills shot through her frame. A laugh rang up through the trees, and then she saw her boy sitting up on the tiger-skin, his cheeks all rosy with sleep and dimpled with surprise, gazing down upon the headless rattlesnake that had uncoiled convulsively in its death-spasms, and lay quivering across his feet.

"Ha! ha!" he shouted, clapping his hands, "this is a famous fellow — prettier than the birds, prettier than the squirrels. Malaeska! Malaeska! see what this checkered thing is with no head, and rings on its tail."

Malaeska was so weak she could hardly stand, but, trembling in every limb, she staggered toward the rock, and seizing upon the still quivering snake, hurled it with a shuddering cry into the undergrowth.

Then she fell upon her knees and clasped the boy close, close to her bosom till he struggled and cried out that she was hurting him. But she could not let him go; it seemed as if the serpent would coil around him the moment her arms were loosened; she clung to his garments — she kissed his hands, his hair, and his flushed forehead with passionate energy.

He could not understand all this. Why did Malaeska breathe so hard, and shake so much? He wished she had not flung away the pretty creature which had crept to his bed while he slept, and looked so beautiful. But when she told how dangerous the reptile was, he began to be afraid, and questioned her with vague terror about the way she had killed him.

Some yards from the rock, Malaeska found her arrow on which the serpent's head was impaled, and she carried it with trembling exultation to the boy, who shrank away with new-born dread, and began to know what fear was.

CHAPTER VI

"Mid forests and meadow lands, though we may roam,
Be it ever so humble, there's no place like home;
    Home, home, sweet, sweet, home,
    There's no place like home;
    There's no place like home."

This event troubled Malaeska, and gathering up her little property, she unmoored the boat, and made progress up the river. The child was delighted with the change, and soon lost all unpleasant remembrance of the rattlesnake. But Malaeska was very careful in the selection of her encampment that afternoon, and kindled a bright fire before she spread the tiger-skin for William's bed, which she trusted would keep all venomous things away. They ate their supper under a huge white pine, that absorbed the firelight in its dusky branches, and made every thing gloomy around. As the darkness closed over them William grew silent, and by the heaviness of his features Malaeska saw that he was oppressed by thoughts of home. She had resolved not to tell him of the relationship which was constantly in her thoughts, till they should stand at the council-fires of the tribe, when the Indians should know him as their chief, and he recognize a mother in poor Malaeska.

Troubled by his sad look, the Indian woman sought for something in her stores that should cheer him. She found some seed-cakes, golden and sweet, which only brought tears into the child's eyes, for they reminded him of home and all its comforts.

"Malaeska," he said, "when shall we go back to grandfather and grandmother? I know they want to see us."

"No, no; we must not think about that," said Malaeska, anxiously.

"But I can't help it — how can I?" persisted the boy, mournfully.

"Don't — don't say you love them — I mean your grandfather — more than you love Malaeska. She would die for you."

"Yes; but I don't want you to die, only to go back home," he pleaded.

"We are going home — to our beautiful home in the woods, which I told you of."

"Dear me, I'm so tired of the woods."

"Tired of the woods?"

"Yes, I *am* tired. They are nice to play in, but it isn't home, no way. How far is it, Malaeska, to where grandfather lives?"

"I don't know — I don't want to know. We shall never — never go there again," said the Indian, passionately. "You are mine, all mine."

The boy struggled in her embrace restively.

"But I won't stay in the woods. I want to be in a real house, and sleep in a soft bed, and — and — there, now, it is going to rain; I hear it thunder. Oh, how I want to go home!"

There was in truth a storm mustering over them; the wind rose and moaned hoarsely through the pines. Malaeska was greatly distressed, and gathered the tired boy lovingly to her bosom for shelter.

"Have patience, William; nothing shall hurt you. Tomorrow we will row the boat all day. You shall pull the oars yourself."

"Shall I, though?" said the boy, brightening a little; "but will it be on the way home?"

"We shall go across the mountains where the Indians live. The brave warriors who will make William their king."

"But I don't want to be a king, Malaeska!"

"A chief — a great chief — who shall go to the war-path and fight battles."

"Ah, I should like that, with your pretty bow and arrow, Malaeska; wouldn't I shoot the wicked red-skins?"

"Ah, my boy, don't say that."

"Oh," said the child, shivering, "the wind is cold; how it sobs in the pine boughs. Don't you wish we were at home now?"

"Don't be afraid of the cold," said Malaeska, in a troubled voice; "see, I will wrap this cloak about you, and no rain can come through the fur blanket. We are brave, you and I — what do we care for a little thunder and rain — it makes me feel brave."

"But you don't care for home; you love the woods and the rain. The thunder and lightning makes your eyes bright, but I don't like it; so take me home, please, and then you may go to the woods; I won't tell."

"Oh, don't — don't. It breaks my heart," cried the poor mother. "Listen, William: the Indians — my people — the brave Indians want you for a chief. In a few years you shall lead them to war."

"But I hate the Indians."

"No, no."

"They are fierce and cruel."

"Not to you — not to you!"

"I won't live with the Indians!"

"They are a brave people — you shall be their chief."

"They killed my father."

"But I am of those people. I saved you and brought you among the white people."

"Yes, I know; grandmother told me that."

"And I belonged to the woods."

"Among the Indians?"

"Yes. Your father loved these Indians, William."

"Did he — but they killed him."

"But it was in battle."

"In fair battle, did you say that?"

"Yes, child. Your father was friendly with them, but they thought he had turned enemy. A great chief met him in the midst of the fight, and they killed each other. They fell and died together."

"Did you know this great chief, Malaeska?"

"He was my father," answered the Indian woman, hoarsely; "my own father."

"Your father and mine; how strange that they should hate each other," said the boy, thoughtfully.

"Not always," answered Malaeska, struggling against the tears that choked her words; "at one time they loved each other."

"Loved each other! that is strange; and did my father love you, Malaeska?"

White as death the poor woman turned; a hand was clenched under her dear-skin robe, and pressed hard against her heart; but she had promised to reveal nothing, and bravely kept her word.

The boy forgot his reckless question the moment it was asked, and did not heed her pale silence, for the storm was gathering darkly over them. Malaeska wrapped him in her cloak, and sheltered him with her person. The rain began to patter heavily overhead; but the pine-tree was thick with foliage, and no drops, as yet, could penetrate to the earth.

"See, my boy, we are safe from the rain; nothing can reach us here," she said, cheering his despondency. "I will heap piles of dry wood on the fire, and shelter you all night long."

She paused a moment, for flashes of blue lightning began to play fiercely through the thick foliage overhead, revealing depths of darkness that was enough to terrify a brave man. No wonder the boy shrank and trembled as it flashed and quivered over him.

Malaeska saw how frightened he was, and piled dry wood recklessly on the fire, hoping that its steady blaze would reassure him.

They were encamped on a spur of the Highlands that shot in a precipice over the stream, and the light of Malaeska's fire gleamed far and wide, casting a golden track far down the Hudson.

Four men, who were using a boat bravely against the storm, saw the light, and shouted eagerly to each other.

"Here she is; nothing but an Indian would keep up a fire like that. Pull steadily, and we have them."

They did pull steadily, and defying the storm, the boat made harbor under the cliff where Malaeska's fire still burned. Four men stole away from the boat, and crept stealthily up the hill, guided by the lightning and the gleaming fire above. The rain, beating among the branches, drowned their footsteps; and they spoke only in hoarse whispers, which were lost on the wind.

William had dropped asleep with tears on his thick eyelashes, which the strong firelight revealed to Malaeska, who regarded him with mournful affection. The cold wind chilled her through and through, but she did not feel it. So long as the boy slept comfortably she had no want.

I have said that the storm muffled all other sounds; and the four men who had left their boat at the foot of the cliff stood close by Malaeska before she had the least idea of their approach. Then a blacker shadow than fell from the pine, darkened the space around her, and looking suddenly up, she saw the stern face of old Mr. Danforth between her and the firelight.

Malaeska did not speak or cry aloud, but snatching the sleeping boy close to her heart, lifted her pale face to his, half-defiant, half-terrified.

"Take my grandson from the woman and bring him down to the boat," said the old man, addressing those that came with him.

"No, no, he is mine!" cried Malaeska, fiercely. "Nothing but the Great Spirit shall take him from me again!"

The sharp anguish in her voice awoke the boy. He struggled in her arms, and looking around, saw the old man.

"Grandfather, oh! grandfather, take me home. I do want to go home," he cried, stretching out his arms.

"Oh!" I have not the power of words to express the bitter anguish of that single exclamation, when it broke from the mother's pale lips. It was the cry of a heart that snapped its strongest fiber there and then. The boy wished to leave her. She had no strength after that, but allowed them to force him from her arms without a struggle. The rattlesnake had not paralyzed her so completely.

So they took the boy ruthlessly from her embrace, and carried him away. She followed after without a word of protest, and saw them lift him into the boat and push off, leaving her to the pitiless night. It was a cruel thing — bitterly cruel — but the poor woman was stupefied with the blow, and watched the boat with heavy eyes. All at once she heard the boy calling after her:

"Malaeska, come too. Malaeska — Malaeska!"

She heard the cry, and her icy heart swelled passionately. With the leap of a panther she sprang to her own boat, and dashed after her tormenters, pulling fiercely through the storm. But with all her desperate energy, she was not able to overtake those four powerful men. They were out of sight directly, and she drifted after them alone — all alone.

Malaeska never went back to Mr. Danforth's house again, but she built a lodge on the Weehawken shore, and supported herself by selling painted baskets and such embroideries as the Indians excel in. It was a lonely life, but sometimes she met her son in the streets of Manhattan, or sailing on the river, and this poor happiness kept her alive.

After a few months, the lad came to her lodge. His grandmother consented to the visit, for she still had compassion on the lone Indian, and would not let the youth go beyond sea without bidding her farewell. In all the bitter anguish of that parting Malaeska kept her faith, and smothering the great want of her soul, saw her son depart without putting forth the holy claim of her motherhood. One day Malaeska stood upon the shore and saw a white-sailed ship veer from her moorings and pass away with cruel swiftness toward the ocean, the broad, boundless ocean, that seemed to her like eternity.

CHAPTER VII

Alone in the forest, alone,
When the night is dark and late —
Alone on the waters, alone,
She drifts to her woman's fate.

Again Malaeska took to her boat and, all alone, began her mournful journey to the forest. After the fight at Catskill, her brethren had retreated into the interior. The great tribe, which gave its name to the richest intervale in New York State, was always munificent in its hospitality to less fortunate brethren, to whom its hunting-grounds were ever open. Malaeska knew that her people were mustered somewhere near the amber-colored falls of Genesee,[6] and she began her mournful voyage with vague longings to see them again, now that she had nothing but memories to live upon.

With a blanket in the bow of her boat, a few loaves of bread, and some meal in a coarse linen bag, she started up the river. The boat was battered and beginning to look old — half the gorgeous paint was worn from its sides, and the interior had been often washed by the tempests that beat over the little cove near her lodge where she had kept it moored. She made no attempt to remedy its desolate look. The tigerskin was left behind in her lodge. No crimson cushions ren-

[6] *Falls of Genesee:* The Genesee Falls are located on the Genesee river, fifty miles southeast of Buffalo.

dered the single seat tempting to sit upon. These fanciful comforts were intended for the boy — motherly love alone provided them; but now she had no care for things of this kind. A poor lone Indian woman, trampled on by the whites, deserted by her child, was going back to her kinsfolk for shelter. Why should she attempt to appear less desolate than she was?

Thus, dreary and abandoned, Malaeska sat in her boat, heavily urging it up the stream. She had few wants, but pulled at the oars all day long, keeping time to the slow movement with her voice, from which a low funeral chant swelled continually.

Sometimes she went ashore, and building a fire in the loneliness, cooked the fish she had speared or the bird her arrow had brought down; but these meals always reminded her of the few happy days spent, after the sylvan fashion, with her boy, and she would sit moaning over the untasted food till the very birds that hovered near would pause in their singing to look askance at her. So she relaxed in her monotonous toil but seldom, and generally slept in her little craft, with the current rippling around her, wrapped only in a coarse, gray blanket.

No one cared about her movements, and no one attempted to bring her back, or she might have been traced at intervals by some rock close to the shore, blackened with embers, where she had baked her corn-bread, or by the feathers of a bird which she had dressed, without caring to eat it.

Day after day — day after day, Malaeska kept on her watery path till she came to the mouth of the Mohawk.[7] There she rested a little, with a weary, heavy-hearted dread of pursuing her journey further. What if her people should reject her as a renegade? She had deserted them in their hour of deep trouble — fled from the grave of her father, their chief, and had carried his grandson away to her bitterest enemy, the white man.

Would the people of her tribe forgive this treason, and take her back? She scarcely cared; life had become so dreary, the whole world so dark, that the poor soul rather courted pain, and would have

---

[7] *The Mohawk:* North of Albany, the Mohawk River joins the Hudson. From the Hudson, the Mohawk leads directly west between the Catskills and the Adirondacks, creating a valley that extends between the Hudson Valley and the Great Lakes Plain, thus making it a crucial trading route for both the Indian and white populations. By 1760, Dutch and English settlements extended eighty miles west of Albany, but the Mohawk was still controlled by the tribes of the Iroquois, who made periodic raids on the settlers and resisted further encroachment.

smiled to know that death was near. Some vague ideas of religion, that the gentle grandmother of her son had taken pains to instill into that wild nature, kept her from self-destruction; but she counted the probabilities that the tribe might put her to death, with vague hope.

Weary days, and more weary nights, she spent upon the Mohawk, creeping along the shadows and seeking the gloomiest spots for her repose: under the wild grape-vines that bent down the young elms with their purple fruit — under the golden willows and dusky pines she sought rest, never caring for danger; for, what had she to care how death or pain presented itself, so long as she had no fear of either?

At last she drew up her boat under a shelving precipice, and making it safe, took to the wilderness with nothing but a little corn meal, her blanket, and bow. With the same heavy listlessness that had marked her entire progress, she threaded the forest-paths, knowing by the hacked trees that her tribe had passed that way. But her path was rough, and the encampment far off, and she had many a heavy mile to walk before it could be reached. Her moccasins were worn to tatters, and her dress, once so gorgeous, all rent and weather stained when she came in sight of the little prairie, hedged in by lordly forest-trees, in which her broken tribe had built their lodges.

Malaeska threw away her scant burden of food, and took a prouder bearing when she came in sight of those familiar lodges. In all her sorrow, she could not forget that she was the daughter of a great chief and a princess among the people whom she sought.

Thus, with an imperial tread, and eyes bright as the stars, she entered the encampment and sought the lodge which, by familiar signs, she knew to be that of the chief who had superseded her son.

It was near sunset, and many of the Indian women had gathered in front of this lodge, waiting for their lords to come forth; for there was a council within the lodge, and like the rest of their sex, the dusky sisterhood liked to be in the way of intelligence. Malaeska had changed greatly during the years that she had been absent among the whites. If the lightness and grace of youth were gone, a more imposing dignity came in their place. Habits of refinement had kept her complexion clear and her hair bright. She had left them a slender, spirited young creature; she returned a serious woman, but queenly withal.

The women regarded her first with surprise and then with kindling anger, for, after pausing to look at them without finding a familiar face, she walked on toward the lodge, and lifting the mat, stood within the opening in full view both of the warriors assembled there and the wrathful glances of the females on the outside.

When the Indians saw the entrance to their council darkened by a woman, dead silence fell upon them, followed by a fierce murmur that would have made a person who feared death tremble. Malaeska stood undismayed, surveying the savage group with a calm, regretful look; for, among the old men, she saw some that had been upon the war-path with her father. Turning to one of these warriors, she said:

"It is Malaeska, daughter of the Black Eagle."

A murmur of angry surprise ran through the lodge, and the women crowded together, menacing her with their glances.

"When my husband, the young white chief, died," continued Malaeska, "he told me to go down the great water and carry my son to his own people. The Indian wife obeys her chief."

A warrior, whom Malaeska knew as the friend of her father, arose with austere gravity, and spoke:

"It is many years since Malaeska took the young chief to his white fathers. The hemlock that was green has died at the top since then. Why does Malaeska come back to her people alone? Is the boy dead?"

Malaeska turned pale in the twilight, and her voice faltered.

"The boy is not dead — yet Malaeska is alone!" she answered plaintively.

"Has the woman made a white chief of the boy? Has he become the enemy of our people?" said another of the Indians, looking steadily at Malaeska.

Malaeska knew the voice and the look; it was that of a brave who, in his youth, had besought her to share his wigwam. A gleam of proud reproach came over her features, but she bent her head without answering.

Then the old chief spoke again. "Why does Malaeska come back to her tribe like a bird with its wings broken? Has the white chief driven her from his wigwam?"

Malaeska's voice broke out; the gentle pride of her character rose as the truth of her position presented itself.

"Malaeska obeyed the young chief, her husband, but her heart turned back to her own people. She tried to bring the boy into the forest again, but they followed her up the great river and took him away; Malaeska stands here alone."

Again the Indian spoke. "The daughter of the Black Eagle forsook her tribe when the death-song of her father was loud in the woods.

She comes back when the corn is ripe, but there is no wigwam open to her. When a woman of the tribe goes off to the enemy, she returns only to die. Have I said well?"

A guttural murmur of assent ran through the lodge. The women heard it from their place in the open air, and gathering fiercely around the door, cried out, "Give her to us! She has stolen our chief — she has disgraced her tribe. It is long since we have danced at the fire-festival."

The rabble of angry women came on with their taunts and menaces, attempting to seize Malaeska, who stood pale and still before them; but the chief, whom she had once rejected, stood up, and with a motion of his hands repulsed them.

"Let the women go back to their wigwams. The daughter of a great chief dies only by the hands of a chief. To the warrior of her tribe, whom she has wronged, her life belongs."

Malaeska lifted her sorrowful eyes to his face — how changed it was since the day he had asked her to share his lodge.

"And it is you that want my life?" she said.

"By the laws of the tribe it is mine," he answered. "Turn your face to the east — it is growing dark; the forest is deep; no one shall hear Malaeska's cries when the hatchet cleaves her forehead. Come!"

Malaeska turned in pale terror, and followed him. No one interfered with the chief, whom she had refused for a white man. Her life belonged to him. He had a right to choose the time and place of her execution. But the women expressed their disappointment in fiendish sneers, as she glided like a ghost through their ranks and disappeared in the blackness of the forest.

Not a word was spoken between her and the chief. Stern and silent he struck into a trail which she knew led to the river, for she had traveled over it the day before. Thus, in darkness and profound silence, she walked on all night till her limbs were so weary that she longed to call out and pray the chief to kill her then and there; but he kept on a little in advance, only turning now and then to be sure that she followed.

Once she ventured to ask him why he put off her death so long; but he pointed along the trail, and walked along without deigning a reply. During the day he took a handful of parched corn from his pouch and told her to eat; but for himself, through that long night and day, he never tasted a morsel.

Toward sunset they came out on the banks of the Mohawk, near the very spot where she had left her boat. The Indian paused here and looked steadily at his victim.

The blood grew cold in Malaeska's veins — death was terrible when it came so near. She cast one look of pathetic pleading on his face, then, folding her hands, stood before him, waiting for the moment.

"Malaeska!"

His voice was softened, his lips quivered as the name once so sweet to his heart passed through them.

"Malaeska, the river is broad and deep. The keel of your boat leaves no track. Go! the Great Spirit will light you with his stars. Here is corn and dried venison. Go in peace!"

She looked at him with her wild tender eyes; her lips began to tremble, her heart swelled with gentle sweetness, which was the grace of civilization. She took the red hand of the savage and kissed it reverently.

"Farewell," she said; "Malaeska has no words; her heart is full."

The savage began to tremble; a glow of the old passion came over him.

"Malaeska, my wigwam is empty; will you go back? It is my right to save or kill."

"*He* is yonder, in the great hunting-ground, waiting for Malaeska to come. Could she go blushing from another chief's wigwam?"

For one instant those savage features were convulsed; then they settled down into the cold gravity of his former expression, and he pointed to the boat.

She went down to the edge of the water, while he took the blanket from his shoulders and placed it in the boat. Then he pushed the little craft from its mooring, and motioned her to jump in; he forbore to touch her hand, or even look on her face, but saw her take up the oars and leave the shore without a word; but when she was out of sight, his head fell forward on his bosom, and he gradually sank to an attitude of profound grief.

While he sat upon a fragment of rock, with a rich sunset crimsoning the water at his feet, a canoe came down the river, urged by a white man, the only one who ever visited his tribe. This man was a missionary among the Indians, who held him in reverence as a great medicine chief, whose power of good was something to marvel at.

The chief beckoned to the missionary, who seemed in haste, but he drew near the shore. In a few brief but eloquent words the warrior spoke of Malaeska, of the terrible fate from which she had just been rescued, and of the forlorn life to which she must henceforth be consigned. There was something grand in this compassion that touched a thousand generous impulses in the missionary's heart. He was on his course down the river — for his duties lay with the Indians of many tribes — so he promised to overtake the lonely woman, to comfort and protect her from harm till she reached some settlement.

The good man kept his word. An hour after his canoe was attached to Malaeska's little craft by its slender cable, and he was conversing kindly with her of those things that interested his pure nature most.

Malaeska listened with meek and grateful attention. No flower ever opened to the sunshine more sweetly than her soul received the holy revelations of that good man. He had no time or place for teaching, but seized any opportunity that arose where a duty could be performed. His mission lay always where human souls required knowledge. So he never left the lonely woman till long after they had passed the mouth of the Mohawk, and were floating on the Hudson. When they came in sight of the Catskill range, Malaeska was seized with an irresistible longing to see the graves of her husband and father. What other place in the wide, wide world had she to look for? Where could she go, driven forth as she was by her own people, and by the father of her husband?

Surely among the inhabitants of the village she could sell such trifles as her inventive talent could create, and if any of the old lodges stood near "the Straka," that would be shelter enough.

With these thoughts in her mind, Malaeska took leave of the missionary with many a whispered blessing, and took her way to "the Straka." There she found an old lodge, through whose crevices the winds had whistled for many years; but she went diligently to work, gathering moss and turf with which this old home, connected with so many sweet and bitter associations, was rendered habitable again. Then she took possession, and proceeded to invent many objects of comfort and even taste, with which to beautify the spot she had consecrated with memories of her passionate youth, and its early, only love.

The woods were full of game, and wild fruits were abundant; so that it was a long, long time before Malaeska's residence in the neighborhood was known. She shrank from approaching a people who had treated her so cruelly, and so kept in utter loneliness so long as solitude was possible.

In all her life Malaeska retained but one vague hope, and that was for the return of her son from that far-off country to which the cruel whites had sent him. She had questioned the missionary earnestly about these lands, and had now a settled idea of their extent and distance across the ocean. The great waters no longer seemed like eternity to her, or absence so much like death. Some time she might see her child again; till then she would wait and pray to the white man's God.

CHAPTER VIII

Huzza, for the forests and hills!
Huzza, for the berries so blue!
Our baskets we'll cheerily fill,
    While the thickets are sparkling with dew.

Years before the scene of our story returns to Catskill, Arthur Jones and the pretty Martha Fellows had married and settled down in life. The kind-hearted old man died soon after the union, and left the pair inheritors of his little shop and of a respectable landed property. Arthur made an indulgent, good husband, and Martha soon became too much confined by the cares of a rising family, for any practice of the teasing coquetry which had characterized her girlhood. She seconded her husband in all his money-making projects; was an economical and thrifty housekeeper; never allowed her children to go barefooted, except in the very warmest weather; and, to use her own words, made a point of holding her head as high as any woman in the settlement.

If an uninterrupted course of prosperity could entitle a person to this privilege, Mrs. Jones certainly made no false claim to it. Every year added something to her husband's possessions. Several hundred acres of cleared land were purchased beside that which he inherited from his father-in-law; the humble shop gradually increased to a respectable variety-store, and a handsome frame-house occupied the site of the old log-cabin.

Besides all this, Mr. Jones was a justice of the peace and a dignitary in the village; and his wife, though a great deal stouter than when a girl, and the mother of six children, had lost none of her healthy good looks, and at the age of thirty-eight continued to be a very handsome woman indeed.

Thus was the family situated at the period when our story returns to them. One warm afternoon, in the depth of summer, Mrs. Jones was sitting in the porch of her dwelling occupied in mending a garment of home-made linen, which, from its size, evidently belonged to some one of her younger children. A cheese-press, with a rich heavy mass of curd compressed between the screws, occupied one side of the porch; and against it stood a small double flax-wheel, unbanded, and with a day's work yet unreeled from the spools. A hatchel and a pair of hand-cards, with a bunch of spools tied together by a tow string, lay in a corner, and high above, on rude wooden pegs, hung several enormous bunches of tow and linen yarn, the products of many weeks' hard labor.

Her children had gone into the woods after whortleberries, and the mother now and then laid down her work and stepped out to the greensward beyond the porch to watch their coming, not anxiously, but as one who feels restless and lost without her usual companions. After standing on the grass for awhile, shading her eyes with her hand and looking toward the woods, she at last returned to the porch, laid down her work, and entering the kitchen, filled the tea-kettle and began to make preparations for supper. She had drawn a long pine table to the middle of the floor, and was proceeding to spread it, when her eldest daughter came through the porch, with a basket of whortleberries on her arm. Her pretty face was flushed with walking, and a profusion of fair tresses flowed in some disorder from her pink sunbonnet, which was falling partly back from her head.

"Oh, mother, I have something strange to tell you," she said, setting down the basket with its load of ripe, blue fruit, and fanning herself with a bunch of chestnut-leaves gathered from the woods. "You know the old wigwam by 'the Straka?' Well, when we went by it, the brush, which used to choke up the door, was all cleared off; the crevices were filled with green moss and leaves, and a cloud of smoke was curling beautifully up from the roof among the trees. We could not tell what to make of it, and were afraid to look in at first; but finally I peeped through an opening in the logs, and as true as you are here, mother, there sat an Indian woman reading — reading, mother! Did you know that Indians could read? The inside of the wigwam was hung with straw matting, and there was a chest in it, and some tools, and a little shelf of books, and another with some earthern dishes and a china cup and saucer, sprigged with gold, standing upon it. I did not see any bed, but there was a pile of fresh, sweet fern in one corner, with a pair of clean sheets spread on it, which I suppose she sleeps on, and there certainly was a feather pillow lying at the top.

"Well, the Indian woman looked kind and harmless; so I made an excuse to go in, and ask for a cup to drink out of.

"As I went round to the other side of the wigwam, I saw that the smoke came up from a fire on the outside; a kettle was hanging in the flame, and several other pots and kettles stood on a little bench by the trunk of an oak-tree, close by. I must have made some noise, for the Indian woman was looking toward the door when I opened it, as if she were a little afraid, but when she saw who it was, I never saw any one smile so pleasantly; she gave me the china cup, and went with me out to the spring where the boys were playing.

"As I was drinking, my sleeve fell back, and she saw the little wampum bracelet which you gave me, you know, mother. She started and took hold of my arm, and stared in my face, as if she would have looked me through; at last she sat down on the grass by the spring, and asked me to sit down by her and tell her my name. When I told her, she seemed ready to cry with joy; tears came into her eyes, and she kissed my hand two or three times, as if I had been the best friend she ever had on earth.

"I told her that a poor Indian girl had given the bracelet to you, before you were married to my father. She asked a great many questions about it, and you.

"When I began to describe the Indian fight, and the chief's grave down by the lake, she sat perfectly still till I had done; then I looked in her face: great tears were rolling one by one down her cheeks, her hands were locked in her lap, and her eyes were fixed upon my face with a strange stare, as if she did not know what she was gazing so hard at. She looked in my face, in this way, more than a minute after I had done speaking.

"The boys stopped their play, for they had begun to dam up the spring, and stood with their hands full of turf, huddled together, and staring at the poor woman as if they had never seen a person cry before. She did not seem to mind them, but went into the wigwam again without speaking a word."

"And was that the last you saw of her?" inquired Mrs. Jones, who had become interested in her daughter's narration.

"Oh, no; she came out again just as we were going away from the spring. Her voice was more sweet and mournful than it had been, and her eyes looked heavy and troubled. She thanked me for the story I had told her, and gave me this pair of beautiful moccasins."

Mrs. Jones took the moccasins from her daughter's hand. They were of neatly dressed deer-skin, covered with beads and delicate needlework in silk.

"It is strange!" muttered Mrs. Jones; "one might almost think it possible. But nonsense; did not the old merchant send us word that the poor creature and her child were lost in the Highlands — that they died of hunger? Well, Sarah," she added, turning to her daughter, "is this all? What did the woman say when she gave you the moccasins? I don't wonder that you are pleased with them."

"She only told me to come again, and ———"

Here Sarah was interrupted by a troop of noisy boys, who came in a body through the porch, flourishing their straw hats and swinging their whortleberry baskets heavy with fruit, back and forth at each step.

"Hurra! hurra! Sarah's fallen in love with an old squaw. How do you do, Miss Jones? Oh, mother, I wish you coulda-seen her hugging and kissing the copper-skin — it was beautiful!"

Here the boisterous rogues set up a laugh that rang through the house, like the breaking up of a military muster.

"Mother, do make them be still; they have done nothing but tease and make fun of me all the way home," said the annoyed girl, half crying.

"How did the old squaw's lips taste, hey?" persisted the eldest boy, pulling his sister's sleeve, and looking with eyes full of saucy mischief up into her face. "Sweet as maple-sugar, wasn't it? Come, tell."

"Arthur — Arthur! you had better be quiet, if you know when you're well off!" exclaimed the mother, with a slight motion of the hand, which had a great deal of significant meaning to the mischievous group.

"Oh, don't — please, don't!" exclaimed the spoiled urchin, clapping his hands to his ears and running off to a corner, where he stood laughing in his mother's face. "I say, Sarah, was it sweet?"

"Arthur, don't let me speak to you again, I say," cried Mrs. Jones, making a step forward and doing her utmost to get up a frown, while her hand gave additional demonstration of its hostile intent.

"Well, then, make her tell me; you ought to cuff *her* ears for not answering a civil question — hadn't she, boys?"

There was something altogether too ludicrous in this impudent appeal, and in the look of demure mischief put on by the culprit. Mrs. Jones bit her lips and turned away, leaving the boy, as usual, victor of the field. "He isn't worth minding, Sarah," she said, evidently ashamed of her want of resolution; "come into the 'out-room,' I've something to tell you."

When the mother and daughter were alone, Mrs. Jones sat down and drew the young girl into her lap.

"Well, Sarah," she said, smoothing down the rich hair that lay against her bosom, "your father and I have been talking about you to-day. You are almost sixteen, and can spin your day's work with any girl in the settlement. Your father says that after you have learned to weave and make cheese, he will send you down to Manhattan to school."

"Oh, mother, did he say so? in real, real earnest?" cried the delighted girl, flinging her arms round her mother's neck and kissing her yet handsome mouth with joy at the information it had just conveyed. "When will he let me go? I can learn to weave and make cheese in a week."

"If you learn all that he thinks best for you to know in two years, it will be as much as we expect. Eighteen is quite young enough. If you are very smart at home, you shall go when you are eighteen."

"Two years is a long, long time," said the girl, in a tone of disappointment; "but then father is kind to let me go at all. I will run down to the store and thank him. But, mother," she added, turning back from the door, "was there really any harm in talking with the Indian woman? There was nothing about her that did not seem like the whites but her skin, and that was not so *very* dark."

"Harm? No child; how silly you are to let the boys tease you so."

"I will go and see her again, then — may I?"

"Certainly — but see; your father is coming to supper; run out and cut the bread. You must be very smart, now; remember the school."

During the time which intervened between Sarah Jones' sixteenth and eighteenth year, she was almost a daily visitor at the wigwam. The little footpath which led from the village to "the Straka," though scarcely discernible to others, became as familiar to her as the grounds about her father's house. If a day or two passed in which illness or some other cause prevented her usual visit, she was sure to receive some token of remembrance from the lone Indian woman. Now, it reached her in the form of a basket of ripe fruit, or a bunch of wild flowers, tied together with the taste of an artist; again, it was a cluster of grapes, with the purple bloom lying fresh upon them, or a young mocking-bird, with notes as sweet as the voice of a fountain, would reach her by the hands of some village boy.

These affectionate gifts could always be traced to the inhabitant of the wigwam, even though she did not, as was sometimes the case, present them in person.

There was something strange in the appearance of this Indian woman, which at first excited the wonder, and at length secured the respect of the settlers. Her language was pure and elegant, sometimes even poetical beyond their comprehension, and her sentiments correct in principle, and full of simplicity. When she appeared in the village with moccasins or pretty painted baskets for sale, her manner was apprehensive and timid as that of a child. She never sat down, and seldom entered any dwelling, preferring to sell her merchandise in the open air, and using as few words as possible in the transaction. She was never seen to be angry, and a sweet patient smile always hovered about her lips when she spoke. In her face there was more than the remains of beauty; the poetry of intellect and of warm, deep feeling, shed a loveliness over it seldom witnessed on the brow of a savage. In truth, Malaeska was a strange and incomprehensible being to the settlers. But she was so quiet, so timid and gentle, that they all loved her, bought her little wares, and supplied her wants as if she had been one of themselves.

There was something beautiful in the companionship which sprang up between the strange woman and Sarah Jones. The young girl was benefited by it in a manner which was little to be expected from an intercourse so singular and, seemingly, so unnatural. The mother was a kind-hearted worldly woman, strongly attached to her family, but utterly devoid of those fine susceptibilities which make at once the happiness and the misery of so many human beings. But all the elements of an intellectual, delicate, and high-souled woman slumbered in the bosom of her child. They beamed in the depths of her large blue eyes, broke over her pure white forehead, like perfume from the leaves of a lily, and made her small mouth eloquent with smiles and the beauty of unpolished thoughts.

At sixteen the character of the young girl had scarcely begun to develop itself; but when the time arrived when she was to be sent away to school, there remained little except mere accomplishments for her to learn. Her mind had become vigorous by a constant intercourse with the beautiful things of nature. All the latent properties of a warm, youthful heart, and of a superior intellect, had been gently called into action by the strange being who had gained such an ascendency over her feelings.

The Indian woman, who in herself combined all that was strong, picturesque, and imaginative in savage life, with the delicacy, sweetness, and refinement which follows in the train of civilization, had trod with her the wild beautiful scenery of the neighborhood. They had breathed the pure air of the mountain together, and watched the crimson and amber clouds of sunset melt into evening, when pure sweet thoughts came to their hearts naturally, as light shines from the bosom of the star.

It is strange that the pure and simple religion which lifts the soul up to God, should have been first taught to the beautiful young white from the lips of a savage, when inspired by the dying glory of a sunset

sky. Yet so it was; she had sat under preaching all her life, had imbibed creeds and shackled her spirit down with the opinions and traditions of other minds, nor dreamed that the love of God may sometimes kindle in the human heart, like fire flashing up from an
altar-stone; and again, may expand gradually to the influence of the
Divine Spirit, unfolding so gently that the soul itself scarcely knows
at what time it burst into flower — that every effect we make, for the
culture of the heart and the expanding of the intellect, is a step toward the attainment of religion, if nothing more.

When the pure simple faith of the Indian was revealed — when she
saw how beautifully high energies and lofty feelings were mingled with
the Christian meekness and enduring faith of her character, she began
to love goodness for its own exceeding beauty, and to cultivate those
qualities that struck her as so worthy in her wild-wood friend. Thus
Sarah attained refinement of the soul which no school could have given
her, and no superficial gloss could ever conceal or dim. This refinement
of principle and feeling lifted the young girl far out of her former
commonplace associations; and the gentle influence of her character
was felt not only in her father's household, but through all the
neighborhood.

CHAPTER IX

"She long'd for her mother's loving kiss,
  And her father's tender words,
And her little sister's joyous mirth,
  Like the song of summer birds.
Her heart went back to the olden home
  That her memory knew so well,
Till the veriest trifle of the past
  Swept o'er her like a spell."

Sarah Jones went to Manhattan at the appointed time, with a
small trunk of clothing and a large basket of provisions; for a sloop
in those days was a long time in coming down the Hudson, even with
a fair wind, and its approach to a settlement made more commotion
than the largest Atlantic steamer could produce at the present day. So

the good mother provided her pretty pilgrim with a lading of wonder-cakes, with biscuits, dried beef, and cheese, enough to keep a company of soldiers in full ration for days.

Besides all this plenteousness in the commissary department, the good lady brought out wonderful specimens of her own handiwork in the form of knit muffles, fine yarn stockings, and colored wristlets, that she had been years in knitting for Sarah's outfit when she should be called upon to undertake this perilous adventure into the great world.

Beyond all this, Sarah had keepsakes from the children, with a store of pretty bracelets and fancy baskets from Malaeska, who parted with her in tenderness and sorrow; for once more like a wild grape-vine, putting out its tendrils everywhere for support, she was cast to the earth again. After all, Sarah did not find the excitement of her journey so very interesting, and but for the presence of her father on the sloop, she would have been fairly homesick before the white sails of the sloop had rounded the Point. As it was, she grew thoughtful and almost sad as the somber magnificence of the scenery unrolled itself. A settlement here and there broke the forest with smiles of civilization, which she passed with a proud consciousness of seeing the world; but, altogether, she thought more of the rosy mother and riotous children at home than of new scenes or new people.

At last Manhattan, with its girdle of silver waters, its gables and its overhanging trees, met her eager look. Here was her destiny — here she was to be taught and polished into a marvel of gentility. The town was very beautiful, but after the first novelty gave way, she grew more lonely than ever; every thing was so strange — the winding streets, the gay stores, and the quaint houses, with their peaks and dormer windows, all seeming to her far too grand for comfort.

To one of these houses Arthur Jones conducted his daughter, followed by a porter who carried her trunk on one shoulder, while Jones took charge of the provision-basket, in person.

There was nothing in all this very wonderful, but people turned to look at the group with more than usual interest, as it passed, for Sarah had all her mother's fresh beauty, with nameless graces of refinement, which made her a very lovely young creature to look upon.

When so many buildings have been raised in a city, so many trees uprooted, and ponds filled up, it is impossible to give the localities that formerly existed; for all the rural landmarks are swept away. But, in the olden times, houses had breathing space for flowers around them in Manhattan, and a man of note gave his name to the house he resided in. The aristocratic portion of the town was around the Bowling Green[8] and back into the neighboring streets.

Somewhere in one of these streets, I can not tell the exact spot, for a little lake in the neighborhood disappeared soon after our story, and all the pretty points of the scene were destroyed with it — but somewhere, in one of the most respectable streets, stood a house with the number of gables and windows requisite to perfect gentility, and a large brass plate spread its glittering surface below the great brass knocker. This plate set forth, in bright, gold letters, the fact that Madame Monot, relict of Monsieur Monot who had so distinguished himself as leading teacher in one of the first female seminaries in Paris, could be found within, at the head of a select school for young ladies.

Sarah was overpowered by the breadth and brightness of this door-plate, and startled by the heavy reverberations of the knocker. There was something too solemn and grand about the entrance for perfect tranquillity.

Mr. Jones looked back at her, as he dropped the knocker, with a sort of tender self-complacency, for he expected that she would be rather taken aback by the splendor to which he was bringing her; but Sarah only trembled and grew timid; she would have given the world to turn and run away any distance so that in the end she reached home.

The door opened, at least the upper half, and they were admitted into a hall paved with little Dutch tiles, spotlessly clean, through which they were led into a parlor barren and prim in all its appointments, but which was evidently the grand reception-room of the establishment. Nothing could have been more desolate than the room, save that it was redeemed by two narrow windows which overlooked the angle of the green inclosure in which the house stood. This angle was separated by a low wall from what seemed a broad and spacious garden, well filled with fruit-trees and flowering shrubbery.

The spring was just putting forth its first buds, and Sarah forgot the chilliness within as she saw the branches of a young apple-tree, flushed with the first tender green, drooping over the wall. It reminded her pleasantly of the orchard at home.

The door opened, and, with a nervous start, Sarah arose with her father to receive the little Frenchwoman who came in with a fluttering courtesy, eager to do the honors of the establishment.

---

[8] *Bowling Green:* A popular lawn bowling locale with the original Dutch settlers, the Bowling Green occupied an area of lower Manhattan at the southernmost point of Broadway, near the Old Customs House.

Madame Monot took Sarah out of her father's hands with a graceful dash that left no room for appeal. "She knew it all — exactly what
the young lady required — what would best please her very respectable parents — there was no need of explanations — the young
lady was fresh as a rose — very charming — in a few months they
should see — that was all — Monsieur Jones need have no care about
his child — Madame would undertake to finish her education very
soon — music, of course — an instrument had just come from Europe
on purpose for the school — then French, nothing easier — Madame
could promise that the young lady should speak French beautifully
in one — two — three — four months, without doubt — Monsieur
Jones might retire very satisfied — his daughter should come back different — perfect, in fact."

With all this volubility, poor Jones was half talked, half courtesied
out of the house, without having uttered a single last word of
farewell, or held his daughter one moment against the honest heart
that yearned to carry her off again, despite his great ambition to see
her a lady.

Poor Sarah gazed after him till her eyes were blinded with unshed
tears; then she arose with a heavy heart and followed Madame to the
room which was henceforth to be her refuge from the most dreary
routine of duties that ever a poor girl was condemned to. It was a
comfort that the windows overlooked that beautiful garden. That
night, at a long, narrow table, set out with what the unsuspecting girl
at first considered the preliminaries of a meal, Sarah met the score of
young ladies who were to be her schoolmates. Fortunately she had no
appetite and did not mind the scant fare. Fifteen or twenty girls, some
furtively, others boldly, turning their eyes upon her, was enough to
frighten away the appetite of a less timid person.

Poor Sarah! of all the homesick school-girls that ever lived, she
was the most lonely. Madame's patronizing kindness only sufficed to
bring the tears into her eyes which she was struggling so bravely to
keep back.

But Sarah was courageous as well as sensitive. She came to Manhattan to study; no matter if her heart ached, the brain must work;
her father had made great sacrifices to give her six months at this ex-
pensive school; his money and kindness must not be thrown away.

Thus the brave girl reasoned, and, smothering the haunting wish
for home, she took up her tasks with energy.

Meantime Jones returned home with a heavy heart and a new assortment of spring goods, that threw every female heart in Catskill

into a flutter of excitement. Every hen's nest in the neighborhood was robbed before the eggs were cold, and its contents transported to the store. As for butter, there was a universal complaint of its scarcity on the home table, while Jones began to think seriously of falling a cent on the pound, it came in so abundantly.

CHAPTER X

'Twas a dear, old-fashion'd garden,
  Half sunshine and half shade,
Where all day long the birds and breeze
  A pleasant music made;
And hosts of bright and glowing flowers
  Their perfume shed around,
Till it was like a fairy haunt
  That knew no human sound.
                    — Frank Lee Benedict

It was a bright spring morning, the sky full of great fleecy clouds that chased each other over the clear blue, and a light wind stirring the trees until their opening buds sent forth a delicious fragrance, that was like a perfumed breath from the approaching summer.

Sarah Jones stood by the window of her little room, looking wistfully out into the neighboring garden, oppressed by a feeling of loneliness and home-sickness, which made her long to throw aside her books, relinquish her half-acquired accomplishments, and fly back to her quiet country home.

It seemed to her that one romp with her brothers through the old orchard, pelting each other with the falling buds, would be worth all the French and music she could learn in a score of years. The beat of her mother's lathe in the old-fashioned loom, would have been pleasanter music to her ear, than that of the pianoforte, which she had once thought so grand an affair; but since then she had spent so many weary hours over it, shed so many tears upon the cold white keys, which made her fingers ache worse than ever the spinning-wheel had done, that, like any other school-girl, she was almost inclined to regard the vaunted piano as an instrument of torture, invented expressly for her annoyance.

She was tired of thinking and acting by rule, and though Madame Monot was kind enough in her way, the discipline to which Sarah was forced to submit, was very irksome to the untrained country girl. She was tired of having regular hours for study — tired of walking out for a stated time in procession with the other girls — nobody daring to move with any thing like naturalness or freedom — and very often she felt almost inclined to write home and ask them to send for her.

It was in a restive, unhappy mood, like the one we have been describing, that she stood that morning at the window, when she ought to have been hard at work over the pile of books which lay neglected upon her little table.

That pretty garden which she looked down upon, was a sore temptation to her; and had Madame Monot known how it distracted Sarah's attention, there is every reason to believe that she would have been removed in all haste to the opposite side of the house, where, if she chose to idle at her casement, there would be nothing more entertaining than a hard brick wall to look at. Just then, the garden was more attractive than at any other season of the year. The spring sunshine had made the shorn turf like a green carpet, the trim flower-beds were already full of early blossoms, the row of apple-trees was one great mass of flowers, and the tall pear-tree in the corner was just beginning to lose its delicate white leaves, sprinkling them daintily over the grass, where they fluttered about like a host of tiny butterflies.

The old-fashioned stoop that opened from the side of the house into the garden, was covered with a wild grape-vine, that clambered up to the pointed Dutch gables, hung down over the narrow windows, and twined and tangled itself about as freely and luxuriantly as it could have done in its native forest.

Sarah watched the gardener as he went soberly about his various duties, and she envied him the privilege of wandering at will among the graveled walks, pausing under the trees and bending over the flower-beds.

Perhaps in these days, when nothing but scentless japonicas and rare foreign plants are considered endurable, that garden would be an ordinary affair enough, at which no well-trained boarding-school miss would condescend to look for an instant; but to Sarah Jones it was a perfect little paradise.

The lilac bushes nodded in the wind, shaking their purple and white plumes, like groups of soldiers on duty; great masses of snowballs stood up in the center of the beds; peonies, violets, lilies of the valley, tulips, syringas, and a host of other dear old-fashioned flowers, lined the walks; and, altogether, the garden was lovely enough to justify the poor girl's admiration. There she stood, quite forgetful of her duties; the clock in the hall struck its warning note — she did not even hear it; some one might at any moment enter and surprise her in the midst of her idleness and disobedience — she never once thought of it, so busily was she watching every thing in the garden.

The man finished his morning's work and went away, but Sarah did not move. A pair of robins had flown into the tall pear-tree, and were holding an animated conversation, interspersed with bursts and gushes of song. They flew from one tree to another, once hovering near the grape-vine, but returned to the pear-tree at last, sang, chirped, and danced about in frantic glee, and at last made it evident that they intended to build a nest in that very tree. Sarah could have clapped her hands with delight! It was just under her window — she could watch them constantly, study or no study. She worked herself into such a state of excitement at the thought, that Madame Monot would have been shocked out of her proprieties at seeing one of her pupils guilty of such folly.

The clock again struck — that time in such a sharp, reproving way, that it reached even Sarah's ear. She started, looked nervously round, and saw the heap of books upon the table.

"Oh, dear me," she sighed; "those tiresome lessons! I had forgotten all about them. Well, I will go to studying in a moment," she added, as if addressing her conscience or her fears. "Oh, that robin — how he does sing."

She forgot her books again, and just at that moment there was a new object of interest added to those which the garden already possessed.

The side door of the house opened, and an old gentleman stepped out upon the broad stoop, stood there for a few moments, evidently enjoying the morning air, then passed slowly down the steps into the garden, supporting himself by his stout cane, and walking with considerable care and difficulty, like any feeble old man.

Sarah had often seen him before, and she knew very well who he was. He was the owner of the house that the simple girl so coveted, and his name was Danforth.

She had learned every thing about him, as a school-girl is sure to do concerning any person or thing that strikes her fancy. He was very wealthy indeed, and had no family except his wife, the tidiest, darling old lady, who often walked in the garden herself, and always touched the flowers, as she passed, as if they had been pet children.

The venerable old pair had a grandson, but he was away in Europe, so they lived in their pleasant mansion quite alone, with the exception of a few domestics, who looked nearly as aged and respectable as their master and mistress.

Sarah had speculated a great deal about her neighbors. She did so long to know them, to be free to run around in their garden, and sit in the pleasant rooms that overlooked it, glimpses of which she had often obtained through the open windows, when the housemaid was putting things to rights.

Sarah thought that she might possibly be a little afraid of the old gentleman, he looked so stern; but his wife she longed to kiss and make friends with at once; she looked so gentle and kind, that even a bird could not have been afraid of her.

Sarah watched Mr. Danforth walk slowly down the principal garden-path, and seat himself in a little arbor overrun by a trumpet honeysuckle, which was not yet in blossom, although there were faint traces of red among the green leaves, which gave promise of an ample store of blossoms before many weeks.

He sat there some time, apparently enjoying the sunshine that stole in through the leaves. At length Sarah saw him rise, move toward the entrance, pause an instant, totter, then fall heavily upon the ground.

She did not wait even to think or cry out — every energy of her free, strong nature was aroused. She flew out of her room down the stairs, fortunately encountering neither teachers nor pupils, and hurried out of the street-door.

The garden was separated from Madame Monot's narrow yard by a low stone wall, along the top of which ran a picket fence. Sarah saw a step-ladder that had been used by a servant in washing windows; she seized it, dragged it to the wall, and sprang lightly from thence into the garden.

It seemed to her that she would never reach the spot where the poor gentleman was lying, although, in truth, scarcely three minutes had elapsed between the time that she saw him fall and reached the place where he lay.

Sarah stooped over him, raised his head, and knew at once what was the matter — he had been seized with apoplexy. She had seen her grandfather die with it, and recognized the symptoms at once. It was useless to think of carrying him; so she loosened his neckcloth, lifted his head upon the arbor seat, and darted toward the house, calling with all her might the name by which she had many times heard the gardener address the black cook.

"Eunice! Eunice!"

At her frantic summons, out from the kitchen rushed the old woman, followed by several of her satellites, all screaming at once to know what was the matter, and wild with astonishment at the sight of a stranger in the garden.

"Quick! quick!" cried Sarah. "Your master has been taken with a fit; come and carry him into the house. One of you run for a doctor."

"Oh, de laws! oh, dear! oh, dear!" resounded on every side; but Sarah directed them with so much energy that the women, aided by an old negro who had been roused by the disturbance, conveyed their master into the house, and laid him upon a bed in one of the lower rooms.

"Where is your mistress?" questioned Sarah.

"Oh, she's gwine out," sobbed the cook; "oh, my poor ole masser, my poor ole masser!"

"Have you sent for the doctor?"

"Yes, young miss, yes; he'll be here in a minit, bress yer pooty face."

Sarah busied herself over the insensible man, applying every remedy that she could remember of having seen her mother use when her grandfather was ill, and really did the very things that ought to have been done.

It was not long before the doctor arrived, bled his patient freely, praised Sarah's presence of mind, and very soon the old gentleman returned to consciousness.

Sarah heard one of the servants exclaim: "Oh, dar's missus! praise de Lord!"

A sudden feeling of shyness seized the girl, and she stole out of the room and went into the garden, determined to escape unseen. But before she reached the arbor she heard one of the servants calling after her.

"Young miss! young miss! Please to wait; ole missus wants to speak to you."

Sarah turned and walked toward the house, ready to burst into tears with timidity and excitement. But the lady whom she had so longed to know, came down the steps and moved toward her, holding out her hand. She was very pale, and shaking from head to foot; but she spoke with a certain calmness, which it was evident she would retain under the most trying circumstances.

"I can not thank you," she said; "if it had not been for you, I should never have seen my husband alive again."

Sarah began to sob, the old lady held out her arms, and the frightened girl actually fell into them. There they stood for a few moments, weeping in each other's embrace, and by those very tears establishing a closer intimacy than years of common intercourse would have done.

"How did you happen to see him fall?" asked the old lady.

"I was looking out of my window," replied Sarah, pointing to her open casement, "and when I saw it I ran over at once."

"You are a pupil of Madame Monot's, then?"

"Yes — and, oh my, I must go back! They will scold me dreadfully for being away so long."

"Do not be afraid," said Mrs. Danforth, keeping fast hold of her hand when she tried to break away. "I will make your excuses to Madame; come into the house. I can not let you go yet."

She led Sarah into the house, and seated her in an easy chair in the old-fashioned sitting-room.

"Wait here a few minutes, if you please, my dear. I must go to my husband."

She went away and left Sarah quite confused with the strangeness of the whole affair. Here she was, actually seated in the very apartment she had so desired to enter — the old lady she had so longed to know addressing her as if she had been a favorite child.

She peeped out of the window toward her late prison; every thing looked quiet there, as usual. She wondered what dreadful penance she would be made to undergo, and decided that even bread and water for two days would not be so great a hardship, when she had the incident of the morning to reflect upon.

She looked about the room, with its quaint furniture, every thing so tidy and elegant, looking as if a speck of dust had never by any accident settled in the apartment, and thinking it the prettiest place she had seen in her life.

Then she began to think about the poor sick man, and worked herself into a fever of anxiety to hear tidings concerning him. Just then a servant entered with a tray of refreshments, and set it on the table near her, saying:

"Please, miss, my missus says you must be hungry, 'cause it's your dinner-time."

"And how is your master?" Sarah asked.

"Bery comferble now; missee'll be here in a minit. Now please to eat sumfin."

Sarah was by no means loth to comply with the invitation, for the old cook had piled the tray with all sorts of delicacies, that presented a pleasing contrast to the plain fare she had been accustomed to of late.

By the time she had finished her repast Mrs. Danforth returned, looking more composed and relieved.

"The doctor gives me a great deal of encouragement," she said; "my husband is able to speak; by to-morrow he will thank you better than I can."

"Oh, no," stammered Sarah. "I don't want any thanks, please. I didn't think — I —— "

She fairly broke down, but Mrs. Danforth patted her hand and said, kindly:

"I understand. But at least you must let me love you very much."

Sarah felt her heart flutter and her cheeks glow. The blush and smile on that young face were a more fitting answer than words could have given.

"I have sent an explanation of your absence to Madame Monot," continued Mrs. Danforth, "and she has given you permission to spend the day with me; so you need have no fear of being blamed."

The thought of a whole day's freedom was exceedingly pleasant to Sarah, particularly when it was to be spent in that old house, which had always appeared as interesting to her as a story. It required but a short time for Mrs. Danforth and her to become well acquainted, and the old lady was charmed with her loveliness, and natural, graceful manners.

She insisted upon accompanying Mrs. Danforth into the sick room, and made herself so useful there, that the dear lady mentally wondered how she had ever got on without her.

When Sarah returned to her home that night, she felt that sense of relief which any one who has led a monotonous life for months must have experienced, when some sudden event has changed its whole current, and given a new coloring to things that before appeared tame and insignificant.

During the following days Sarah was a frequent visitor at Mr. Danforth's house, and after that, circumstances occurred which drew her into still more intimate companionship with her new friend.

One of Madame Monot's house-servants was taken ill with typhus fever, and most of the young ladies left the school for a few weeks. Mrs. Danforth insisted upon Sarah's making her home at their house during the interval, an invitation which she accepted with the utmost delight.

Mr. Danforth still lingered — could speak and move — but the favorable symptoms which at first presented themselves had entirely disappeared, and there was little hope given that he could do more than linger for a month or two longer. During that painful season Mrs. Danforth found in Sarah a sympathizing and consoling friend. The sick man himself became greatly attached to her, and could not bear that she should even leave his chamber.

The young girl was very happy in feeling herself thus prized and loved, and the quick weeks spent in that old house were perhaps among the happiest of her life, in spite of the saddening associations which surrounded her.

One morning while she was sitting with the old gentleman, who had grown so gentle and dependent that those who had known him in former years would scarcely have recognized him, Mrs. Danforth entered the room, bearing several letters in her hand.

"European letters, my dear," she said to her husband, and while she put on her glasses and seated herself to read them, Sarah stole out into the garden.

She had not been there long, enjoying the fresh loveliness of the day, before she heard Mrs. Danforth call her.

"Sarah, my dear; Sarah."

The girl went back to the door where the old lady stood.

"Share a little good news with me in the midst of all our trouble," she said; "my dear, my boy — my grandson — is coming home."

Sarah's first thought was one of regret — every thing would be so changed by the arrival of a stranger; but that was only a passing pang of selfishness; her next reflection was one of unalloyed delight, for the sake of that aged couple.

"I am very glad, dear madam; his coming will do his grandfather so much good."

"Yes, indeed; more than all the doctors in the world."

"When do you expect him?"

"Any day, now; he was to sail a few days after the ship that brought these letters, and as this vessel has been detained by an accident, he can not be far away."

"I am to go back to school to-day," said Sarah, regretfully.

"But you will be with us almost as much," replied Mrs. Danforth. "I have your mother's permission, and will go myself to speak with

Madame. You will run over every day to your lessons, but you will live here; we can not lose our pet so soon."

"You are very kind — oh, so kind," Sarah said, quite radiant at the thought of not being confined any longer in the dark old school-building.

"It is you who are good to us. But come, we will go over now; I must tell Madame Monot at once."

The explanations were duly made, and Sarah returned to her old routine of lessons; but her study-room was now the garden, or any place in Mr. Danforth's house that she fancied.

The old gentleman was better again; able to be wheeled out of doors into the sunshine; and there was nothing he liked so much as sitting in the garden, his wife knitting by his side, Sarah studying at his feet, and the robins singing in the pear-trees overhead, as if feeling it a sacred duty to pay their rent by morning advances of melody.

CHAPTER XI

A welcome to the homestead —
The gables and the trees
And welcome to the true hearts,
As the sunshine and the breeze.

One bright morning, several weeks after Mr. Danforth's attack, the three were seated in their favorite nook in the garden.

It was a holiday with Sarah; there were no lessons to study; no exercises to practice; no duty more irksome than that of reading the newspaper aloud to the old gentleman, who particularly fancied her fresh, happy voice.

Mrs. Danforth was occupied with her knitting, and Sarah sat at their feet upon a low stool, looking so much like a favorite young relative that it was no wonder if the old pair forgot that she was unconnected with them, save by the bonds of affection, and regarded her as being, in reality, as much a part of their family as they considered her in their hearts.

While they sat there, some sudden noise attracted Mrs. Danforth's attention; she rose and went into the house so quietly that the others scarcely noticed her departure.

It was not long before she came out again, walking very hastily for her, and with such a tremulous flutter in her manner, that Sarah regarded her in surprise.

"William!" she said to her husband, "William!"

He roused himself from the partial doze into which he had fallen, and looked up.

"Did you speak to me?" he asked.

"I have good news for you. Don't be agitated — it is all pleasant."

He struggled up from his seat, steadying his trembling hands upon his staff.

"My boy has come!" he exclaimed, louder and more clearly than he had spoken for weeks; "William, my boy!"

At the summons, a young man came out of the house and ran toward them. The old gentleman flung his arms about his neck and strained him close to his heart.

"My boy!" was all he could say; "my William!"

When they had all grown somewhat calmer, Mrs. Danforth called Sarah, who was standing at a little distance.

"I want you to know and thank this young lady, William," she said; "your grandfather and I owe her a great deal."

She gave him a brief account of the old gentleman's fall, and Sarah's presence of mind; but the girl's crimson cheeks warned her to pause.

"No words can repay such kindness," said the young man, as he relinquished her hand, over which he had bowed with the ceremonious respect of the time.

"It is I who owe a great deal to your grandparents," Sarah replied, a little tremulously, but trying to shake off the timidity which she felt beneath his dark eyes. "I was a regular prisoner, like any other school-girl, and they had the goodness to open the door and let me out."

"Then fidgety old Madame Monot had you in charge?" young Danforth said, laughing; "I can easily understand that it must be a relief to get occasionally where you are not obliged to wait and think by rule."

"There — there!" said the old lady; "William is encouraging insubordination already; you will be a bad counselor for Sarah."

Both she and her husband betrayed the utmost satisfaction at the frank and cordial conversation which went on between the young pair; and in an hour Sarah was as much at ease as if she had been gathering wild-flowers in her native woods.

Danforth gave them long and amusing accounts of his adventures, talked naturally and well of the countries he had visited, the notable places he had seen, and never had man three more attentive auditors.

That was a delightful day to Sarah; and as William Danforth had not lost, in his foreign wanderings, the freshness and enthusiasm pleasant in youth, it was full of enjoyment to him likewise.

There was something so innocent in Sarah's loveliness — something so unstudied in her graceful manner, that the very contrast she presented to the artificial women of the world with whom he had been of late familiar, gave her an additional charm in the eye of the young man.

Many times, while they talked, Mrs. Danforth glanced anxiously toward her husband; but his smile reassured her, and there stole over her pale face a light from within which told of some pleasant vision that had brightened the winter season of her heart, and illuminated it with a reflected light almost as beautiful as that which had flooded it in its spring-time, when her dreams were of her own future, and the aged, decrepit man by her side a stalwart youth, noble and brave as the boy in whom their past seemed once more to live.

"If Madame Monot happens to see me she will be shocked," Sarah said, laughingly. "She told me that she hoped I would improve my holiday by reading some French sermons that she gave me."

"And have you looked at them?" Danforth asked.

"I am afraid they are mislaid," she replied, mischievously.

"Not greatly to your annoyance, I fancy? I think if I had been obliged to learn French from old-fashioned sermons, it would have taken me a long time to acquire the language."

"I don't think much of French sermons," remarked Mrs. Danforth, with a doubtful shake of the head.

"Nor of the people," added her husband; "you never did like them, Therese."

She nodded assent, and young Danforth addressed Sarah in Madame Monot's much-vaunted language. She answered him hesitatingly, and they held a little chat, he laughing good-naturedly at her mistakes and assisting her to correct them, a proceeding which the old couple enjoyed as much as the young pair, so that a vast amount of quiet amusement grew out of the affair.

They spent the whole morning in the garden, and when Sarah went up to her room for a time to be alone with the new world of thought which had opened upon her, she felt as if she had known William Danforth half her life. She did not attempt to analyze her feelings; but they were very pleasant and filled her soul with a delicious restlessness like gushes of agony struggling from the heart of a song-bird. Perhaps Danforth made no more attempt than she to understand the emotions which had been aroused within him; but they were both very happy, careless as the young are sure to be, and so they went on toward the beautiful dream that brightens every life, and which spread before them in the nearing future.

And so the months rolled on, and that pleasant old Dutch house grew more and more like a paradise each day. Another and another quarter was added to Sarah's school-term. She saw the fruit swell from its blossoms into form till its golden and mellow ripeness filled the garden with fragrance. Then she saw the leaves drop from the trees and take a thousand gorgeous dyes from the frost. Still the old garden was a paradise. She saw those leaves grow crisp and sere, rustling to her step with mournful sighs, and giving themselves with shudders to the cold wind. Still the garden was paradise. She saw the snow fall, white and cold, over lawn and gravel-walk, bending down the evergreens and tender shrubs, while long, bright icicles hung along the gables or broke into fragments on the ground beneath. Sill the garden was paradise; for love has no season, and desolation is unknown where he exists, even though his sacred presence is unsuspected. Long before the promised period arrived, there was no falsehood in Madame Monot's assertion that her pupil should be perfect; for a lovelier or more graceful young creature than Sarah Jones could not well exist. How it would have been had she been entirely dependent on the school-teachers for her lessons, I can not pretend to say; but the pleasant studies which were so delicately aided in that old summer-house, while the old people sat by just out of ear-shot — as nice old people should on such occasions — were effective enough to build up half a dozen schools, if the progress of one pupil would suffice.

At such times old Mrs. Danforth would look up blandly from her work and remark in an innocent way to her husband, "That it was really beautiful to see how completely Sarah took to her lessons and how kindly William stayed at home to help her. Really," she thought, "traveling abroad did improve a person's disposition wonderfully. It gives a young man so much steadiness of character. There was William, now, who was so fond of excitement, and never could be persuaded to stay at home before, he could barely be driven across the threshold now."

The old man listened to these remarks with a keen look of the eye; he was asking himself the reason of this change in his grandson, and the answer brought a grim smile to his lips. The fair girl, who was now almost one of his household, had become so endeared to him that he could not bear the idea of even parting with her again, and the thought that the line of his name and property might yet persuade her to make the relationship closer still, had grown almost into a passion with the old man.

This state of things lasted only a few months. Before the leaves fell, a change came upon Mr. Danforth. He was for some time more listless and oppressed than usual, and seemed to be looking into the distance for some thought that had disturbed him. One day, without preliminaries, he began to talk with his wife about William's father, and, for the first time in years, mentioned his unhappy marriage.

"I have sometimes thought," said the lady, bending over her work to conceal the emotion that stirred her face, "I have sometimes thought that we should have told our grandson of all this years ago."

The old man's hands began to tremble on the top of his cane. His eyes grew troubled and he was a long time in answering.

"It is too late now — we must let the secret die with us. It would crush him forever. I was a proud man in those days," he said, at last; "proud and stubborn. God has smitten me, therefore, I sometimes think. The thought of that poor woman, whose child I took away, troubles me at nights. Tell me, Therese, if you know any thing about her. The day of my sickness I went to the lodge in Weehawken where she was last seen, hoping to find her, praying for time to make atonement; but the lodge was in ruins — no one could be found who even remembered her. It had cost me a great effort to go, and when the disappointment came, I fell beneath it. Tell me, Therese, if you have heard any thing of Malaeska?"

The good lady was silent; but she grew pale, and the work trembled in her hands.

"You will not speak?" said the old man, sharply.

"Yes," said the wife, gently laying down her work, and lifting her compassionate eyes to the keen face bending toward her, "I did hear, from some Indians that came to the fur-stations up the river, that an — that Malaeska went back to her tribe."

"There is something more," questioned the old man — "something you keep back."

The poor wife attempted to shake her head, but she could not, even by a motion, force herself to an untruth. So, dropping both hands in her lap, she shrunk away from his glance, and the tears began to roll down her cheeks.

"Speak!" said the old man, hoarsely.

She answered, in a voice low and hoarse as his own, "Malaeska went to her tribe; but they have cruel laws, and looking upon her as a traitor in giving her son to us, sent her into the woods with one who was chosen to kill her."

The old man did not speak, but his eyes opened wildly and he fell forward upon his face.

William and Sarah were coquetting, with her lessons, under the old pear-tree, between the French phrases; he had been whispering something sweeter than words ever sounded to her before in any language, and her cheeks were one flush of roses as his breath floated over them.

"Tell me — look at me — any thing to say that you have known this all along," he said, bending his flashing eyes on her face with a glance that made her tremble.

She attempted to look up, but failed in the effort. Like a rose that feels the sunshine too warmly, she drooped under the glow of her own blushes.

"Do speak," he pleaded.

"Yes," she answered, lifting her face with modest firmness to his, "Yes, I do love you."

As the words left her lips, a cry made them both start.

"It is grandmother's voice; he is ill again," said the young man.

They moved away, shocked by a sudden recoil of feelings. A moment brought them in sight of the old man, who lay prostrate on the earth. His wife was bending over him, striving to loosen his dress with her withered little hands.

"Oh, come," she pleaded, with a look of helpless distress; "help me untie this, or he will never breathe again."

It was all useless; the old man never did breathe again. A single blow had smitten him down. They bore him into the house, but the leaden weight of his body, the limp fall of his limbs, all revealed the mournful truth too plainly. It was death — sudden and terrible death.

If there is an object on earth calculated to call forth the best sympathies of humanity, it is an "old widow" — a woman who has spent the spring, noon, and autumn of life, till it verges into winter, with one man, the first love of her youth, the last love of her age — the spring-time when love is a passionate sentiment, the winter-time when it is august.

In old age men or women seldom resist trouble — it comes, and they bow to it. So it was with this widow: she uttered no complaints, gave way to no wild outbreak of sorrow — "she was lonesome — very lonesome without him," that was all her moan; but the raven threads that lay in the snow of her hair, were lost in the general whiteness before the funeral was over, and after that she began to bend a little, using his staff to lean on. It was mournful to see how fondly her little wrinkled hands would cling around the head, and the way she had of resting her delicate chin upon it, exactly as he had done.

But even his staff, the stout prop of his waning manhood, was not strong enough to keep that gentle old woman from the grave. She carried it to the last, but one day it stood unused by the bed, which was white and cold as the snow-drift through which they dug many feet before they could lay her by her husband's side.

CHAPTER XII

Put blossoms on the mantle-piece,
Throw sand upon the floor,
A guest is coming to the house,
That never came before.

Sarah Jones had been absent several months, when a rumor got abroad in the village, that the school-girl had made a proud conquest in Manhattan. It was said that Squire Jones had received letters from a wealthy merchant of that place, and that he was going down the river to conduct his daughter home, when a wedding would soon follow, and Sarah Jones be made a lady.

This report gained much of its probability from the demeanor of Mrs. Jones. Her port became more lofty when she appeared in the street, and she was continually throwing out insinuations and half-uttered hints, as if her heart were panting to unburden itself of some proud secret, which she was not yet at liberty to reveal.

When Jones actually started for Manhattan, and it was whispered that his wife had taken a dress-pattern of rich chintz from the store, for herself, and had bought each of the boys a new wool hat, conjecture became almost certainty; and it was asserted boldly, that Sarah Jones was coming home to be married to a man as rich as all out-doors, and that her mother was beginning to hold her head above common folks on the strength of it.

About three weeks after this report was known, Mrs. Jones, whose motions were watched with true village scrutiny, gave demonstrations of a thorough house-cleaning. An old woman, who went out to days' work, was called in to help, and there were symptoms of slaughter observable in the barn-yard one night after the turkeys and chickens had gone to roost; all of which kept the public mind in a state of pleasant excitement.

Early the next morning, after the barn-yard massacre, Mrs. Jones was certainly a very busy woman. All the morning was occupied in sprinkling white sand on the nicely-scoured floor of the out-room, or parlor, which she swept very expertly into a series of angular figures called herring-bones, with a new splint broom. After this, she filled the fire-place with branches of hemlock and white pine, wreathed a garland of asparagus, crimson with berries, around the little looking-glass, and dropping on one knee, was filling a large pitcher on the hearth from an armful of wild-flowers, which the boys had brought her from the woods, when the youngest son came hurrying up from the Point, to inform her that a sloop had just hove in sight and was making full sail up the river.

"Oh, dear, I shan't be half ready!" exclaimed the alarmed house-keeper, snatching up a handful of meadow-lilies, mottled so heavily with dark-crimson spots, that the golden bells seemed drooping beneath a weight of rubies and small garnet stones, and crowding them down into the pitcher amid the rosy spray of wild honeysuckle-blossoms, and branches of flowering dogwood.

"Here, Ned, give me the broom, quick! and don't shuffle over the sand so. There, now," she continued, gathering up the fragments of leaves and flowers from the hearth, and glancing hastily around the room, "I wonder if any thing else is wanting?"

Every thing seemed in order, even to her critical eye. The tea-table stood in one corner, its round top turned down and its polished surface reflecting the herring-bones drawn in the sand, with the distinctness of a mirror. The chairs were in their exact places, and the new crimson maroon cushions and valance decorated the settee, in all the brilliancy of their first gloss. Yes, nothing more was to be done, still the good woman passed her apron over the speckless table and flirted it across a chair or two, before she went out, quite determined that no stray speck of dust should disgrace her child on coming home.

Mrs. Jones closed the door, and hurried up to the square bedroom, to be certain that all was right there also. A patch-work quilt, pieced in what old ladies call "a rising sun," radiated in tints of red, green, and yellow, from the center of the bed down to the snow-white valances. A portion of the spotless homespun sheet was carefully turned over the upper edge of the quilt, the whole was surmounted by a pair of pillows, white as a pile of newly-drifted snow-flakes. A pot of roses, on the window-sill, shed a delicate reflection over the muslin curtains looped up on either side of the sash; and the fresh wind, as it swept through, scattered their fragrant breath deliciously through the little room.

Mrs. Jones gave a satisfied look and then hurried to the chamber prepared for her daughter, and began to array her comely person in the chintz dress, which had created such a sensation in the village. She had just encased her arms in the sleeves, when the door partly opened, and the old woman, who had been hired for a few days as "help," put her head through the opening. "I say, Miss Jones, I can't find nothin' to make the stuffin' out on."

"My goodness! isn't that turkey in the oven yet? I do believe, if I could be cut into a hundred pieces, it wouldn't be enough for this house. What do you come to me for? — don't you know enough to make a little stuffing, without my help?"

"Only give me enough to do it with, and if I don't, why, there don't nobody, that's all; but I've been a looking all over for some sausengers, and can't find none, nowhere."

"Sausages? Why, Mrs. Bates, you don't think that I would allow that fine turkey to be stuffed with sausages?"

"I don't know nothin' about it, but I tell you just what it is, Miss Jones, if you are a-growing so mighty partic'lar about your victuals, just cause your darter's a-coming home with a rich beau, you'd better cook 'em yourself; nobody craves the job," retorted the old woman, in her shrillest voice, shutting the door with a jar that shook the whole apartment.

"Now the cross old thing will go off just to spite me," muttered Mrs. Jones, trying to smother her vexation, and, opening the door, she called to the angry "help:"

"Why, Mrs. Bates, do come back, you did not stay to hear me out. Save the chickens' livers and chop them up with bread and butter; season it nicely, and, I dare say, you will be as well pleased with it as can be."

"Well, and if I du, what shall I season with — sage or summer-savory? I'm sure I'm willing to du my best," answered the partially mollified old woman.

"A little of both, Mrs. Bates — oh, dear! won't you come back and see if you can make my gown meet? There — do I look fit to be seen?"

"Now, what do you ask that for, Miss Jones? you know you look as neat as a new pin. This is a mighty purty calerco, ain't it, though?"

The squire's lady had not forgotten all the feelings of her younger days, and the old woman's compliment had its effect.

"I will send down to the store for some tea and molasses for you to take home to-night, Mrs. Bates, and — "

"Mother! mother!" shouted young Ned, bolting into the room, "the sloop has tacked, and is making for the creek. I see three people on the deck, and I'm almost sure father was one of them — they will be here in no time."

"Gracious me!" muttered the old woman, hurrying away to the kitchen.

Mrs. Jones smoothed down the folds of her new dress with both hands, as she ran down to the "out-room." She took her station in a stiff, high-backed chair by the window, with a look of consequential gentility, as if she had done nothing but sit still and receive company all her life.

After a few minutes' anxious watching, she saw her husband and daughter coming up from the creek, accompanied by a slight, dark, and remarkably graceful young man, elaborately, but not gayly dressed, for the fashion of the time, and betraying even in his air and walk peculiar traits of high-breeding and refinement. His head was slightly bent, and he seemed to be addressing the young lady who leaned on his arm.

The mother's heart beat high with mingled pride and affection, as she gazed on her beautiful daughter thus proudly escorted home. There was triumph in the thought, that almost every person in the village might witness the air of gallantry and homage with which she was regarded by the handsomest and richest merchant of Manhattan. She saw that her child looked eagerly toward the house as they approached, and that her step was rapid, as if impatient of the quiet progress of her companions. Pride was lost in the sweet thrill of maternal affection which shot through the mother's heart. She forgot all her plans, in the dear wish to hold her first-born once more to her bosom; and ran to the door, her face beaming with joy, her arms outstretched, and her lips trembling with the warmth of their own welcome.

The next moment her child was clinging about her, lavishing kisses on her handsome mouth, and checking her caresses to gaze up through the mist of tears and smiles which deluged her own sweet face, to the glad eyes that looked down so fondly upon her.

"Oh, mother! dear, dear mother, how glad I am to get home! Where are the boys? where is little Ned?" inquired the happy girl, rising from her mother's arms, and looking eagerly round for other objects of affectionate regard.

"Sarah, don't you intend to let me speak to your mother?" inquired the father, in a voice which told how truly his heart was in the scene.

Sarah withdrew from her mother's arms, blushing and smiling through her tears; the husband and wife shook hands half a dozen times over; Mrs. Jones asked him how he had been, what kind of a voyage he had made, how he liked Manhattan, and a dozen other questions, all in a breath; and then the stranger was introduced. Mrs. Jones forgot the dignified courtesy which she had intended to perpetrate on the entrance of her guest, and shook him heartily by the hand, as if she had been acquainted with him from his cradle.

When the happy group entered the parlor, they found Arthur, who had been raised to the dignity of storekeeper in the father's absence, ready to greet his parent and sister; and the younger children huddled together at the door which led to the kitchen, brimful of eager joy at the father's return, and yet too much afraid of the stranger to enter the room.

Altogether, it was as cordial, warm-hearted a reception as a man could reasonably wish on his return home; and, fortunately for Mrs. Jones, the warmth of her own natural feeling saved her the ridicule of trying to get up a genteel scene, for the edification of her future son-in-law.

About half an hour after the arrival of her friends, Mrs. Jones was passing from the kitchen, where she had seen the turkey placed in the oven, with his portly bosom rising above the rim of a dripping-pan, his legs tied together, and his wings tucked snugly over his back, when she met her husband in the passage.

"Well," said the wife, in a cautious voice, "has every thing turned out well — is he so awful rich as your letter said?"

"There is no doubt about that; he is as rich as a Jew, and as proud as a lord. I can tell you what, Sarah's made the best match in America, let the other be what it will," replied the squire, imitating the low tone of his questioner.

"What an eye he's got, hasn't he? I never saw any thing so black and piercing in my life. He's very handsome, too, only a little darkish — I don't wonder the girl took a fancy to him. I say, has any thing been said about the wedding?"

"It must be next week, at any rate, for he wants to go back to Manhattan in a few days; he and Sarah will manage it without our help, I dare say." Here Mr. and Mrs. Jones looked at each other and smiled.

"I say, squire, I want to ask you one question," interrupted Mrs. Bates, coming through the kitchen door and sidling up to the couple, "is that watch which the gentleman carries rale genuine gold, or on'y pinchbeck? I'd give any thing on 'arth to find out."

"I believe it's gold, Mrs. Bates."

"Now, du tell! What, rale Guinea gold? Now, if that don't beat all natur. I ruther guess Miss Sarah's feathered her nest this time, any how. Now, squire, du tell a body, when is the wedding to be? I won't tell a single 'arthly critter, if you'll on'y jest give me a hint."

"You must ask Sarah," replied Mr. Jones, following his wife into the parlor; "I never meddle with young folks' affairs."

"Now, did you ever?" muttered the old woman, when she found herself alone in the passage. "Never mind; if I don't find out afore I go home to-night, I lose my guess, that's all. I should just like to know what they're a talking about this minute."

Here the old woman crouched down and put her ear to the crevice under the parlor door; in a few moments she scrambled up and hurried off into the kitchen again, just in time to save herself from being pushed over by the opening door.

Sarah Jones returned home the same warm-hearted, intelligent girl as ever. She was a little more delicate in person, more quiet and graceful in her movements; and love had given depth of expression to her large blue eyes, a richer tone to her sweet voice, and had mellowed down the buoyant spirit of the girl to the softness and grace of womanhood. Thoroughly and trustfully had she given her young affections, and her person seemed imbued with gentleness from the fount of love, that gushed up so purely in her heart. She knew that she was loved in return — not as she loved, fervently, and in silence, but with the fire of a passionate nature; with the keen, intense feeling which mingles pain even with happiness, and makes sorrow sharp as the tooth of a serpent.

Proud, fastidious, and passionate was the object of her regard; his prejudices had been strengthened and his faults matured, in the lap of luxury and indulgence. He was high-spirited and generous to a fault, a true friend and a bitter enemy — one of those men who have lofty virtues and strong counterbalancing faults. But with all his heart and soul he loved the gentle girl to whom he was betrothed. In that he had been thoroughly unselfish and more than generous; but not the less proud. The prejudices of birth and station had been instilled into his nature, till they had become a part of it; yet he had unhesitatingly offered hand and fortune to the daughter of a plain country farmer.

In truth, his predominating pride might be seen in this, mingled with the powerful love which urged him to the proposal. He preferred bestowing wealth and station on the object of his choice, rather than receiving any worldly advantage from her. It gratified him that his love would be looked up to by its object, as the source from which all benefits must be derived. It was a feeling of refined selfishness; he would have been startled had any one told him so; and yet, a generous pride was at the bottom of all. He gloried in exalting his chosen one; while his affianced wife, and her family, were convinced that nothing could be more noble than his conduct, in thus selecting a humble and comparatively portionless girl to share his brilliant fortune.

On the afternoon of the second day after her return home, Sarah entered the parlor with her bonnet on and a shawl flung over her arm, prepared for a walk. Her lover was lying on the crimson cushions of the settee, with his fine eyes half-closed, and a book nearly falling from his listless hand.

"Come," said Sarah, taking the volume playfully from his hand, "I have come to persuade you to a long walk. Mother has introduced all her friends, now you must go and see mine — the dearest and best."

"Spare me," said the young man, half-rising, and brushing the raven hair from his forehead with a graceful motion of the hand; "I will go with *you* anywhere, but *do* excuse me these horrid introductions — I am overwhelmed with the hospitality of your neighborhood." He smiled, and attempted to regain the book as he spoke.

"Oh, but this is quite another kind of person; you never saw any thing at all like her — there is something picturesque and romantic about her. You like romance?"

"What is she, Dutch or English? I can't speak Dutch, and your own sweet English is enough for me. Come, take off that bonnet and let me read to you."

"No, no; *I* must visit the wigwam, if *you* will not."

"The wigwam, Miss Jones?" exclaimed the youth, starting up, his face changing its expression, and his large black eyes flashing on her with the glance of an eagle. "Am I to understand that your friend is an Indian?"

"Certainly, she *is* an Indian, but not a common one, I assure you."

"She *is* an Indian. Enough, *I* will *not* go; and I can only express my surprise at a request so extraordinary. I have no ambition to cultivate the copper-colored race, or to find my future wife seeking her friends in the woods."

The finely cut lip of the speaker curved with a smile of haughty contempt, and his manner was disturbed and irritable, beyond any thing the young girl had ever witnessed in him before. She turned pale at this violent burst of feeling, and it was more than a minute before she addressed him again.

"This violence seems unreasonable — why should my wish to visit a harmless, solitary fellow-being create so much opposition," she said, at last.

"Forgive me, if I have spoken harshly, dear Sarah," he answered, striving to subdue his irritation, but spite of his effort it blazed out again the next instant. "It is useless to strive against the feeling; I hate the whole race! If there is a thing I abhor on earth, it is a savage — a fierce, blood-thirsty wild beast in human form!"

There was something in the stern expression of his face which pained and startled the young girl who gazed on it; a brilliancy of the eye, and an expansion of the thin nostrils, which bespoke terrible passions when once excited to the full.

"This is a strange prejudice," she murmured, unconsciously, while her eyes sank from their gaze on his face.

"It is no prejudice, but a part of my nature," he retorted, sternly, pacing up and down the room. "An antipathy rooted in the cradle, which grew stronger and deeper with my manhood. I loved my grandfather, and from him I imbibed this early hate. His soul loathed the very name of Indian. When he met one of the prowling creatures in the highway, I have seen his lips writhe, his chest heave, and his face grow white, as if a wild beast had started up in his path. There was one in our family, an affectionate, timid creature, as the sun ever shone upon. I can remember loving her very dearly when I was a mere child, but my grandfather recoiled at the very sound of her name, and seemed to regard her presence as a curse, which for some reason he was compelled to endure. I could never imagine why he kept her. She was very kind to me, and I tried to find her out after my return from Europe, but you remember that my grandparents died suddenly during my absence, and no one could give me any information about her. Save that one being, there is not a savage, male or female, whom I should not rejoice to see exterminated from the face of the earth. Do not, I pray you, look so terribly shocked, my sweet girl; I acknowledge the feeling to be a prejudice too violent for adequate foundation; but it was grounded in my nature by one whom I respected and loved as my own life, and it will cling to my heart as long as there is a pulse left in it."

"I have no predilection for savages as a race," said Sarah, after a few moments' silence, gratified to find some shadow of reason for her lover's violence; "but you make one exception, may I not also be allowed a favorite especially as she is a white in education, feeling, every thing but color? You would not have me neglect one of the kindest, best friends I ever had on earth, because the tint of her skin is a shade darker than my own?"

Her voice was sweet and persuasive, a smile trembled on her lips, and she laid a hand gently on his arm as she spoke. He must have been a savage indeed, had he resisted her winning ways.

"I would have you forgive my violence and follow your own sweet impulses," he said, putting back the curls from her uplifted forehead, and drawing her to his bosom; "say you have forgiven me, dear, and then go where you will."

It was with gentle words like these, that he had won the love of that fair being; they fell upon her heart, after his late harshness, like dew to a thirsty violet. She raised her glistening eyes to his with a language more eloquent than words, and disengaging herself from his arms, glided softly out of the room.

These words could hardly be called a lovers' quarrel, and yet they parted with all the sweet feelings of reconciliation, warm at the heart of each.

CHAPTER XIII

By that forest-grave she mournful stood,
    While her soul went forth in prayer;
Her life was one long solitude,
    Which she offer'd, meekly, there.

Sarah pursued the foot-path, which she had so often trod through the forest, with a fawn-like lightness of step, and a heart that beat quicker at the sight of each familiar bush or forest-tree, which had formerly been the waymark of her route.

"Poor woman, she must have been very lonely," she murmured, more than once, when the golden blossoms of a spice-bush, or the tendrils of a vine trailing over the path, told how seldom it had been traveled of late, and her heart imperceptibly became saddened by the thoughts of her friend; spite of this, she stopped occasionally to witness the gambols of a gray squirrel among the tall branches, that swayed and rustled in the sunshine overhead, and smiled at her usual timidity, when, thus employed, a slender grass-snake crept across her foot and coiled itself up in the path like a chain of living emeralds; his small eyes glittering like sparks of fire, his tiny jaw open, and a sharp little tongue playing within like a red-hot needle cleft at the point. She forced herself to look upon the harmless reptile, without a fear which she knew to be childish, and turning aside, pursued her way to "the Straka."

To her disappointment, she found the wigwam empty, but a path was beaten along the edge of the woods, leading toward the Pond, which she had never observed before. She turned into it with a sort of indefinite expectation of meeting her friend; and after winding through the depths of the forest for nearly a mile, the notes of a wild, plaintive song rose and fell — a sad, sweet melody — on the still air.

A few steps onward brought the young girl to a small open space surrounded by young saplings and flowering shrubs; tall grass swept from a little mound which swelled up from the center, to the margin of the inclosure, and a magnificent hemlock shadowed the whole space with its drooping boughs.

A sensation of awe fell upon the heart of the young girl, for, as she gazed, the mound took the form of a grave. A large rose-tree, heavy with blossoms, drooped over the head, and the sheen of rippling waters broke through a clump of sweet-brier, which hedged it in from the lake.

Sarah remembered that the Indian chief's grave was on the very brink of the water, and that she had given a young rose-tree to Malaeska years ago, which must have shot up into the solitary bush standing before her, lavishing fragrance from its pure white flowers over the place of the dead.

This would have been enough to convince her that she stood by the warrior's grave, had the place been solitary, but at the foot of the hemlock, with her arms folded on her bosom and her calm face uplifted toward heaven, sat Malaeska. Her lips were slightly parted, and the song which Sarah had listened to afar off broke from them — a sad pleasant strain, that blended in harmony with the rippling waters and the gentle sway of the hemlock branches overhead.

Sarah remained motionless till the last note of the song died away on the lake, then she stepped forward into the inclosure. The Indian woman saw her and arose, while a beautiful expression of joy beamed over her face.

"The bird does not feel more joyful at the return of spring, when snows have covered the earth all winter, than does the poor Indian's heart at the sight of her child again," she said, taking the maiden's hand and kissing it with a graceful movement of mingled respect and affection. "Sit down, that I may hear the sound of your voice once more."

They sat down together at the foot of the hemlock.

"You have been lonely, my poor friend, and ill, I fear; how thin you have become during my absence," said Sarah, gazing on the changed features of her companion.

"I shall be happy again now," replied the Indian, with a faint sweet smile, "you will come to see me every day."

"Yes, while I remain at home, but — but — I'm going back again soon."

"You need not tell me more in words, I can read it in the tone of your voice, in the light of that modest eye, though the silken lash does droop over it like leaves around a wet violet — in the color coming and going on those cheeks; another is coming to take you from home," said the Indian, with a playful smile. "Did you think the lone woman could not read the signs of love — that she has never loved herself?"

"You?"

"Do not look so wild, but tell me of yourself. Are you to be married so *very* soon?"

"In four days."

"Then where will your home be?"

"In Manhattan."

There were a few moments of silence. Sarah sat gazing on the turf, with the warm blood mantling to her cheek, ashamed and yet eager to converse more fully on the subject which flooded her young heart with supreme content. The Indian continued motionless, lost in a train of sad thoughts conjured up by the last word uttered; at length she laid her hand on that of her companion, and spoke; her voice was sad, and tears stood in her eyes.

"In a few days you go from me again — oh, it is very wearisome to be always alone; the heart pines for something to love. I have been petting a little wren, that has built his nest under the eaves of my wig-

wam, since you went away; it was company for me, and will be
again. Do not look so pitiful, but tell me who is he that calls the red
blood to your cheek? What are his qualities? Does he love you as one
like you should be loved? Is he good, brave?"

"He says that he loves me," replied the young girl, blushing more
deeply, and a beautiful smile broke into her eyes as she raised them
for a moment to the Indian's face.

"And you?"

"I have neither experience nor standard to judge love by. If to
think of one from morning to night, be love — to feel his presence
color each thought even when he is far away — to know that he is
haunting your beautiful day-dreams, wandering with you through the
lovely places which fancy is continually presenting to one in solitude,
filling up each space and thought of your life, and yet in no way di-
minishing the affection which the heart bears to others, but increasing it rather — if to be made happy with the slightest trait of noble
feeling, proud in his virtues, and yet quick-sighted and doubly sensitive to all his faults, clinging to him in spite of those faults — if this
be love, then I do love with the whole strength of my being. They tell
me it is but a dream, which will pass away, but I do not believe it; for
in my bosom the first sweet flutter of awakened affection, has already
settled down to a deep feeling of contentment. My heart is full of
tranquillity, and, like that white rose which lies motionless in the sunshine burdened with the wealth of its own sweetness, it unfolds itself
day by day to a more pure and subdued state of enjoyment. This feeling may not be the love which men talk so freely of, but it can not
change — never — not even in death, unless William Danforth should
prove utterly unworthy!"

"William Danforth! Did I hear aright? Is William Danforth the
name of your affianced husband?" inquired the Indian, in a voice of
overwhelming surprise, starting up with sudden impetuosity and then
slowly sinking back to her seat again. "Tell me," she added, faintly,
and yet in a tone that thrilled to the heart, "has this boy—this young
gentleman, I mean — come of late from across the big waters?"

"He came from Europe a year since, on the death of his grandparents," was the reply.

"A year, a whole year!" murmured the Indian, clasping her hands
over her eyes with sudden energy. Her head sunk forward upon her
knees, and her whole frame shivered with a rush of strong feeling,
which was perfectly unaccountable to the almost terrified girl who
gazed upon her. "Father of Heaven, I thank thee! my eyes shall be-

hold him once more. O God, make me grateful!" These words, uttered so fervently, were muffled by the locked hands of the Indian woman, and Sarah could only distinguish that she was strongly excited by the mention of her lover's name.

"Have you ever known Mr. Danforth?" she inquired, when the agitation of the strange woman had a little subsided. The Indian did not answer, but raising her head, and brushing the tears from her eyes, she looked in the maiden's face with an expression of pathetic tenderness that touched her to the heart.

"And *you* are to be *his* wife? You, my bird of birds."

She fell upon the young girl's neck as she spoke, and wept like an infant; then, as if conscious of betraying too deep emotion, she lifted her head, and tried to compose herself; while Sarah sat gazing on her, agitated, bewildered, and utterly at loss to account for this sudden outbreak of feeling, in one habitually so subdued and calm in her demeanor. After sitting musingly and in silence several moments, the Indian again lifted her eyes; they were full of sorrowful meaning, yet there was an eager look about them which showed a degree of excitement yet unsubdued.

"Dead — are they both dead? his grandparents, I mean?" she said, earnestly.

"Yes, they are both dead; he told me so."

"And he — the young man — where is he now?"

"I left him at my father's house, not three hours since."

"Come, let us go."

The two arose, passed through the inclosure, and threaded the path toward the wigwam slowly and in silence. The maiden was lost in conjecture, and her companion seemed pondering in some hidden thought of deep moment. Now her face was sad and regretful in its look, again it lighted up a thrilling expression of eager and yearning tenderness.

The afternoon shadows were gathering over the forest, and being anxious to reach home before dark, Sarah refused to enter the wigwam when they reached it. The Indian went in for a moment, and returned with a slip of birch bark, on which a few words were lightly traced in pencil.

"Give this to the young man," she said, placing the bark in Sarah's hand; "and now good-night — good-night."

Sarah took the bark and turned with a hurried step to the forest track. She felt agitated, and as if something painful were about to happen. With a curiosity aroused by the Indian's strange manner, she examined the writing on the slip of bark in her hand; it was only a request that William Danforth would meet the writer at a place appointed, on the bank of the Catskill Creek, that evening. The scroll was signed, "Malaeska."

Malaeska! It was singular, but Sarah Jones had never learned the Indian's name before.

CHAPTER XIV

"Wild was her look, wild was her air,
Back from her shoulders stream'd the hair —
The locks, that wont her brow to shade,
Started erectly from her head;
Her figure seem'd to rise more high —
From her pale lips a frantic cry
Rang sharply through the moon's pale light —
And life to her was endless night."

The point of land, which we have described in the early part of this story, as hedging in the outlet of Catskill Creek, gently ascends from the juncture of the two streams and rolls upward into a broad and beautiful hill, which again sweeps off toward the mountains and down the margin of the Hudson in a vast plain, at the present day cut up into highly cultivated farms, and diversified by little eminences, groves, and one large tract of swamp-land. Along the southern margin of the creek the hill forms a lofty and picturesque bank, in some places dropping to the water in a sheer descent of forty or fifty feet, and others, sloping down in a more gradual but still abrupt fall, broken into little ravines, and thickly covered with a fine growth of young timber.

A foot-path winds up from the stone dwelling, which we have already described, along the upper verge of this bank to the level of the plain, terminating in a singular projection of earth which shoots out from the face of the bank some feet over the stream, taking the form of a huge serpent's head. This projection commands a fine view of the village, and is known to the inhabitants by the title of "Hoppy Nose," from a tradition attached to it. The foot-path, which terminates at this point, receives a melancholy interest from the constant presence of a singular being who has trod it regularly for years. Hour after hour, and day after day, through sunshine and storm, he is to be seen winding among the trees, or moving with a slow monotonous walk along this track, where it verges into the rich sward. Speechless he has been for years, not from inability, but from a settled unbroken habit of silence. He is perfectly gentle and inoffensive, and from his quiet bearing a slight observer might mistake him for a meditative philosopher, rather than a man slightly and harmlessly insane as a peculiar expression in his clear, blue eyes and his resolute silence must surely proclaim him to be.

But we are describing subsequent things, rather than the scenery as it existed at the time of our story. Then, the hillside and all the broad plain was a forest of heavy timbered land, but the bank of the creek was much in its present condition. The undergrowth throve a little more luxuriantly, and the "Hoppy Nose" shot out from it covered with a thick coating of grass, but shrubless, with the exception of two or three saplings and a few clumps of wild-flowers.

As the moon arose on the night after Sarah Jones' interview with the Indian woman, that singular being stood upon the "Hoppy Nose," waiting the appearance of young Danforth. More than once she went out to the extreme verge of the projection, looked eagerly up and down the stream, then back into the shadows again, with folded arms, continued her watch as before.

At length a slight sound came from the opposite side; she sprang forward, and supporting herself by a sapling, bent over the stream, with one foot just touching the verge of the projection, her lips slightly parted, and her left hand holding back the hair from her temples, eager to ascertain the nature of the sound. The sapling bent and almost snapped beneath her hold, but she remained motionless, her eyes shining in the moonlight with a strange, uncertain luster, and fixed keenly on the place whence the sound proceeded.

A canoe cut out into the river, and made toward the spot where she was standing.

"It is he!" broke from her parted lips, as the moonlight fell on the clear forehead and graceful form of a young man, who stood upright in the little shallop,[9] and drawing a deep breath, she settled back, folded her arms, and waited his approach.

The sapling had scarcely swayed back to its position, when the youth curved his canoe round to a hollow in the bank, and climbing along the ascent, he drew himself up the steep side of the "Hoppy Nose" by the brushwood, and sprang to the Indian woman's side.

---

[9]*Shallop:* Used in shallow water, a shallop is a small open boat fitted with oars, sails, or both.

"Malaeska," he said, extending his hand with a manner and voice of friendly recognition; "my good, kind nurse, believe me, I am rejoiced to have found you again."

Malaeska did not take his hand, but after an intense and eager gaze into his face, flung herself on his bosom, sobbing aloud, murmuring soft, broken words of endearment, and trembling all over with a rush of unconquerable tenderness.

The youth started back, and a frown gathered on his haughty forehead. His prejudices were offended, and he strove to put her from his bosom; even gratitude for all her goodness could not conquer the disgust with which he recoiled from the embrace of a savage.

"Malaeska," he said, almost sternly, attempting to unclasp her arms from his neck, "You forget — I am no longer a boy — be composed, and say what I can do for you?"

But she only clung to him the more passionately, and answered with an appeal that thrilled to his very heart.

"Put not your mother away — she has waited long — my son! my son!"

The youth did not comprehend the whole meaning of her words. They were more energetic and full of pathos than he had ever witnessed before; but she had been his nurse, and he had been long absent from her, and the strength of her attachment made him, for a moment, forgetful of her race. He was affected almost to tears.

"Malaeska," he said kindly, "I did not know till now how much you loved me. Yet it is not strange — I can remember when you were almost a mother to me."

"*Almost!*" she exclaimed, throwing back her head till the moonlight revealed her face. "Almost! William Danforth, as surely as there is a God to witness my words, you are my own son!"

The youth started, as if a dagger had been thrust to his heart. He forced the agitated woman from his bosom, and, bending forward, gazed sternly into her eyes.

"Woman, are you mad? Dare you assert this to *me*?"

He grasped her arm almost fiercely, and seemed as if tempted to offer some violence, for the insult her words had conveyed; but she lifted her eyes to his with a look of tenderness, in painful contrast with his almost insane gaze.

"Mad, my son?" she said, in a voice that thrilled with a sweet and broken earnestness on the still air. "It was a blessed madness — the madness of two warm young hearts that forgot every thing in the sweet impulse with which they clung together; it was madness which led your father to take the wild Indian girl to his bosom, when in the bloom of early girlhood. Mad! oh, I could go mad with very tenderness, when I think of the time when your little form was first placed in my arms; when my heart ached with love to feel your little hand upon my bosom, and your low murmur fill my ear. Oh, it was a sweet madness. I would die to know it again."

The youth had gradually relaxed his hold on her arm, and stood looking upon her as one in a dream, his arms dropping helpless as if they had been suddenly paralyzed; but when she again drew toward him, he was aroused to frenzy.

"Great God!" he almost shrieked, dashing his hand against his forehead. "No, no! it can not — I, an Indian? a half-blood? the grandson of my father's murderer? Woman, speak the truth; word for word, give me the accursed history of my disgrace. If I am your son, give me proof — proof, I say!"

When the poor woman saw the furious passion she had raised, she sunk back in silent terror, and it was several minutes before she could answer his wild appeal. When she did speak, it was gaspingly and in terror. She told him all — of his birth; his father's death; of her voyage to Manhattan; and of the cruel promise that had been wrung from her, to conceal the relationship between herself and her child. She spoke of her solitary life in the wigwam, of the yearning power which urged her mother's heart to claim the love of her only child, when that child appeared in her neighborhood. She asked not to be acknowledged as his parent, but only to live with him, even as a bond servant, if he willed it, so as to look upon his face and to claim his love in private, when none should be near to witness it.

He stood perfectly still, with his pale face bent to hers, listening to her quick gasping speech, till she had done. Then she could see that his face was convulsed in the moonlight, and that he trembled and grasped a sapling which stood near for support. His voice was that of one utterly overwhelmed and broken-hearted.

"Malaeska," he said, "unsay all this, if you would not see me die at your feet. I am young, and a world of happiness was before me. I was about to be married to one so gentle — so pure — I, an Indian — was about to give my stained hand to a lovely being of untainted blood. I, who was so proud of lifting her to my lofty station. Oh, Malaeska!" he exclaimed, vehemently grasping her hand with a clutch of iron, "say that this was a story — a sad, pitiful story got up to punish my pride; say but this, and I will give you all I have on earth — every farthing. I will love you better than a thousand sons.

Oh, if you have mercy, contradict the wretched falsehood!" His frame shook with agitation, and he gazed upon her as one pleading for his life.

When the wretched mother saw the hopeless misery which she had heaped upon her proud and sensitive child, she would have laid down her life could she have unsaid the tale which had wrought such agony, without bringing a stain of falsehood on her soul.

But words are fearful weapons, never to be checked when once put in motion. Like barbed arrows they enter the heart, and can not be withdrawn again, even by the hand that has shot them. Poisoned they are at times, with a venom that clings to the memory forever. Words are, indeed, fearful things! The poor Indian mother could not recall hers, but she tried to soothe the proud feelings which had been so terribly wounded.

"Why should my son scorn the race of his mother? The blood which she gave him from her heart was that of a brave and kingly line, warriors and chieftains, all——"

The youth interrupted her with a low, bitter laugh. The deep prejudices which had been instilled into his nature — pride, despair, every feeling which urges to madness and evil — were a fire in his heart.

"So I have a patent of nobility to gild my sable birthright, an ancestral line of dusky chiefs to boast of. I should have known this, when I offered my hand to that lovely girl. She little knew the dignity which awaited her union. Father of heaven, my heart will break — I am going mad!"

He looked wildly around as he spoke, and his eyes settled on the dark waters, flowing so tranquilly a few feet beneath him. Instantly he became calm, as one who had found an unexpected resource in his affliction. His face was perfectly colorless and gleamed like marble as he turned to his mother, who stood in a posture of deep humility and supplication a few paces off, for she dared not approach him again either with words of comfort or tenderness. All the sweet hopes which had of late been so warm in her heart, were utterly crushed. She was a heart-broken, wretched woman, without a hope on this side the grave. The young man drew close to her, and taking both her hands, looked sorrowfully into her face. His voice was tranquil and deep-toned, but a slight husky sound gave an unnatural solemnity to his words.

"Malaeska," he said, raising her hands toward heaven, "swear to me by the God whom we both worship, that you have told me nothing but the truth; I would have no doubt."

There was something sublime in his position, and in the solemn calmness which had settled upon him. The poor woman had been weeping, but the tears were checked in her eyes, and her pale lips ceased their quivering motion and became firm, as she looked up to the white face bending over her.

"As I hope to meet you, my son, before that God, I have spoken nothing but the truth."

"Malaeska!"

"Will you not call me mother?" said the meek woman, with touching pathos. "I know that I am an Indian, but your father loved me."

"Mother? Yes, God forbid that I should refuse to call you mother; I am afraid that I have often been harsh to you, but I did not know your claim on my love. Even now, I have been unkind."

"No, no, my son."

"I remember you were always meek and forgiving — you forgive me now, my poor mother?"

Malaeska could not speak, but she sank to her son's feet, and covered his hand with tears and kisses.

"There is one who will feel this more deeply than either of us. You will comfort her, Mala — mother, will you not?"

Malaeska rose slowly up, and looked into her son's face. She was terrified by his child-like gentleness; her breath came painfully. She knew not why it was, but a shudder ran through her frame, and her heart grew heavy, as if some terrible catastrophe were about to happen. The young man stepped a pace nearer the bank, and stood, motionless, gazing down into the water. Malaeska drew close to him, and laid her hand on his arm.

"My son, why do you stand thus? Why gaze so fearfully upon the water?"

He did not answer, but drew her to his bosom, and pressed his lips down upon her forehead. Tears sprang afresh to the mother's eyes, and her heart thrilled with an exquisite sensation, which was almost pain. It was the first time he had kissed her since his childhood. She trembled with mingled awe and tenderness as he released her from his embrace, and put her gently from the brink of the projection. The action had placed her back toward him. She turned — saw him clasp his hands high over his head, and spring into the air. There was a plunge; the deep rushing sound of waters flowing back to their place, and then a shriek, sharp and full of terrible agony, rung over the stream like the death-cry of a human being.

The cry broke from the wretched mother, as she tore off her outer garments and plunged after the self-murderer. Twice the moonlight fell upon her pallid face and her long hair, as it streamed out on the water. The third time another marble face rose to the surface, and with almost superhuman strength the mother bore up the lifeless body of her son with one arm, and with the other struggled to the shore. She carried him up the steep bank where, at another time, no woman could have clambered even without incumbrance, and laid him on the grass. She tore open his vest, and laid her hand upon the heart. It was cold and pulseless. She chafed his palms, rubbed his marble forehead, and stretching herself on his body, tried to breathe life into his marble lips from her own cold heart. It was in vain. When convinced of this, she ceased all exertion; her face fell forward to the earth, and, with a low sobbing breath, she lay motionless by the dead.

The villagers heard that fearful shriek, and rushed down to the stream. Boats were launched, and when their crews reached the "Hoppy Nose," it was to find two human beings lying upon it.

The next morning found a sorrowful household in Arthur Jones' dwelling. Mrs. Jones was in tears, and the children moved noiselessly around the house, and spoke in timid whispers, as if the dead could be aroused. In the "out-room" lay the body of William Danforth, shrouded in his winding-sheet. With her heavy eyes fixed on the marble features of her son, sat the wretched Indian mother. Until the evening before, her dark hair had retained the volume and gloss of youth, but now it fell back from her hollow temples profusely as ever, but perfectly gray. The frost of grief had changed it in a single night. Her features were sunken, and she sat by the dead, motionless and resigned. There was nothing of stubborn grief about her. She answered when spoken to, and was patient in her suffering; but all could see that it was but the tranquillity of a broken heart, mild in its utter desolation. When the villagers gathered for the funeral, Malaeska, in a few gentle words, told them of her relationship to the dead, and besought them to bury him by the side of his father.

The coffin was carried out, and a solemn train followed it through the forest. Women and children all went forth to the burial.

When the dead body of her affianced husband was brought home, Sarah Jones had been carried senseless to her chamber. The day wore on, the funeral procession passed forth, and she knew nothing of it. She was falling continually from one fainting fit to another, murmuring sorrowfully in her intervals of consciousness, and dropping gently away with the sad words on her lips, like a child mourning itself to sleep. Late in the night, after her lover's interment, she awoke to a consciousness of misfortune. She turned feebly upon her pillow, and prayed earnestly and with a faith which turned trustingly to God for strength. As the light dawned, a yearning wish awoke in her heart to visit the grave of her betrothed. She arose, dressed herself, and bent her way with feeble step toward the forest. Strength returned to her as she went forward. The dew lay heavily among the wild-flowers in her path, and a squirrel, which had made her walk cheerful two days before, was playing among the branches overhead. She remembered the happy feeling with which she had witnessed his gambols then, and covered her face as if a friend had attempted to comfort her.

The wigwam was desolate, and the path which led to the grave lay with the dew yet unbroken on its turf. The early sunshine was playing among the wet, heavy branches of the hemlock, when she reached the inclosure. A sweet fragrance was shed over the trampled grass from the white rose-tree which bent low beneath the weight of its pure blossoms. A shower of damp petals lay upon the chieftain's grave, and the green leaves quivered in the air as it sighed through them with a pleasant and cheering motion. But Sarah saw nothing but a newly-made grave, and stretched upon its fresh sods the form of a human being. A feeling of awe came over the maiden's heart. She moved reverently onward, feeling that she was in the sanctuary of the dead. The form was Malaeska's. One arm fell over the grave, and her long hair, in all its mournful change of color, had been swept back from her forehead, and lay tangled amid the rank grass. The sod on which her head rested was sprinkled over with tiny white blossoms. A handful lay crushed beneath her cheek, and sent up a faint odor over the marble face. Sarah bent down and touched the forehead. It was cold and hard, but a tranquil sweetness was there which told that the spirit had passed away without a struggle. Malaeska lay dead among the graves of her household, the heart-broken victim of an unnatural marriage.

Years passed on — the stern, relentless years that have at last swept away every visible trace which links the present with the past. The old house in Manhattan, where Sarah Jones had known so much happiness, which had been brightened for a little season by the sunshine of two young hearts, then darkened by the gloom of death, had long stood silent and untenanted.

After the death of William Danforth, there had been no relative in America to claim the estate left by his grandfather. In those days it took much time for tidings to cross the sea, and after they had reached England, there was such struggle and contention between those who claimed the property, that it was long before any actual settlement of it was made.

At last the old house was to be torn down, and its garden destroyed, to give place to a block of stores, the usual fate of every relic of old time in our restless city.

The day came upon which the solitary dwelling was to be demolished. The roof was torn off, the stout walls rudely pulled down, the timbers creaking as if suffering actual agony from their destruction; the grape-vine was buried beneath the fragments, the rose-bushes uprooted and thrown out upon the pavement to die, and in a few hours the only trace left of the once pleasant spot, was a shapeless mass of broken bricks and mortar, above which the swallows flew in wild circles, deploring the loss of their old nesting-places.

While that devastation was in progress, a lady stood upon the opposite side of the street, watching every blow with painful interest. She was many years past the bloom of youth, but the features had a loveliness almost saint-like from the holy resignation which illuminated them.

So when the work of ruin was complete, Sarah Jones stole quietly away, stilling the wave of anguish that surged over her heart from the past, and going back to her useful life, without a murmur against the Providence that had made it so lonely.

Seth Jones; or, The Captives
of the Frontier

Edward S. Ellis (1840–1916) became such a prolific author for the Beadle publishing house that he also published under the pseudonyms Lieutenant R. H. Jayne, Seelin Robbins, Captain R. M. Hawthorne, and James Fenimore Cooper Adams, among twenty others. *Seth Jones* (1860), for which the unknown, nineteen-year-old author received seventy-five dollars, eventually sold over a half million copies and was translated into eleven languages. The novel's unprecedented initial success — which the Beadles advertised to provoke something of a best-selling sensation — established the dime novel enterprise as profitable business and Ellis's fame as an author. Two months after *Seth Jones* reached the newsstands (in October), the publishers brought out Ellis's *Bill Biddon, Trapper; or, Life in the North-west*, soon followed by its sequel, *Nathan Todd; or, The Fate of the Sioux' Captive*, which secured Ellis's reputation as the new novelist of the frontier (in this case the frontier of the 1850s), pitting the frontiersman against the danger and deceit of an Indian population. Contracting with the house to write no fewer than four novels a year, he ended up writing fifty-three novels for the *Dime Novel* series (some reprinted in as many as six other series), and thirty-eight for the *Half Dime Library* that began in 1877.

Before Ellis became a writer, he was a teacher who enjoyed a legendary popularity with his students. A vice-principal while still in his teens, he eventually became the city-wide superintendent of the Trenton, New Jersey, schools. In his forties he gave up teaching to devote himself exclusively to writing, but dime novels were hardly his sole pre-occupation. He wrote textbooks in arithmetic, grammar, physiology, and mythology; a widely adopted *Eclectic Primary History of the United States* (1884); and the four-volume *Youth's History of the United States* (1887). Famous as a "historical" novelist, he was soon recognized as the country's foremost author of history books for a general audience. Along with his subsequent work on national history and biography, such as the six-volume *People's Standard History of the United States* (1898), the *History of Our Country* (1896), and *Dewey and Other Naval Commanders* (1899), he coauthored a ten-volume *Story of the Greatest Nations,* and co-edited a fifteen-volume *History of the German People.* Ellis was the inaugural editor of *Golden Days* (a juvenile weekly) and a regular contributor to several newspapers, most prominently the newly formed Trenton *Evening Times,* for which he wrote articles on politics and drew pen-and-ink portraits of legislators. Having become all but synonymous with the popularization of national history, Ellis was hired in 1915 by Edison and Co. to write a film scenario of U.S. history from the settling of Jamestown to the twentieth century.

By the time *Seth Jones* was published in 1860, the vast territory gained in the wake of the Mexican War (which would become California, Nevada, Utah, Arizona, New Mexico, and Colorado), along with the subsequent discovery of gold in California in 1848, had reasserted frontier conflict with Native Americans as a central topic in the national imagination. In *A Week on the Concord and Merrimack Rivers* (1849), Henry David Thoreau had recounted the captivity narrative of Hannah Dunstan; in *The Conspiracy of Pontiac* (1851), Francis Parkman had detailed the brutality of the Indian raids on the British in 1763; in *Hiawatha* (1855), Henry Wadsworth Longfellow had elegiacally portrayed the idyllic life of the Ojibway before the future "restless, struggling, toiling, striving" westward march of Christian civilization, "the unknown, crowded nations" (162). In *Seth Jones,* Ellis expresses little ambivalence toward the native population: not only does Jones "detest the whole cowardly race" (p. 256) but in the novel's most arresting scene he gets revenge for his torment by striking the "glittering blade" of a tomahawk "clean through the head" of an "unsuspecting savage" (p. 202).

While the Indian had inspired various representations in the antebellum period, Ellis clearly relies on the particular paradigm established by James Fenimore Cooper. *Seth Jones* demonstrated how the Leatherstocking model could be streamlined. In *The Pioneers* (1823) and its successors, Cooper integrates into his plot elaborate landscapes, Leatherstocking's philosophical musings that express his natural piety, and genre scenes of everyday life such as turkey shooting and sugar manufacturing. These details are excised from Ellis's action-packed story of capture and rescue.

With the device of disguise, Ellis could hastily resolve Cooper's central thematic tensions. Seth Jones's concluding revelation of himself as Eugene Morton — not the squeaky-voiced frontiersman but a deep-voiced gentleman — allows Ellis to conflate the frontier hero and the romantic hero. Cooper keeps these two types of heroes separate, the divide between nature and culture necessarily dividing the hero from the world of romance. Conflicts between civilization and wilderness, the law and a personal moral code, the outsider and the insider — these are resolved by being embodied in a single character, Seth Jones, who seems to undergo bodily transformation as he resumes his actual identity. In contrast, the elaborately dramatized authenticity of Cooper's Leatherstocking figure, Natty Bumppo, requires that the device of disguise be reserved for secondary characters.

Though Natty Bumppo may have been modeled after an actual frontiersman (David Shipman), and though Seth Jones may have been modeled after a fictional Yankee (Thomas Haliburton's Sam Slick), both clearly fulfill the type established by Daniel Boone (1734–1820). The Kentucky pioneer, trapper, rifleman, and Indian fighter — the proclaimed "first white man of the west" — spent six months as a Shawnee captive. Proclaimed to be a record of Boone's own account, John Filson's *The Discovery, Settlement, and Present State of Kentucke* (1784) initiated Boone's status as national hero; Lord Byron's treatment of Boone in canto eight of *Don Juan* (1823) established the international reputation of Boone as the quintessential American frontiersman. As a fictional Yankee, however, Jones attains some degree of historical specificity: the 1780s witnessed an influx of New Englanders into the plains of western New York. Locating his story in a "remote spot in western New York" in the 1780s (see p. 172), Ellis could elide the political crisis provoked by the newer frontiers — the ultimately unmanageable question of slavery's expansion — while capitalizing on the irrepressible literary fascination with the Indian.

The basic frontier plots of capture and rescue (or captivity and escape) had become so familiar to the U.S. audience in history, legend, and fiction that Ellis can casually switch between the two without transition, except to have Jones say, "With a few words, all will be plain to you" (p. 262). In what becomes a hallmark of the dime novel, though, more than a few words are needed to make the plot make sense. Ellis's readers weren't really reading for the plot, however; they were reading for the scenes of dramatic action.

The text published here is based on the original 1860 edition of the novel, but it incorporates a few of the corrections made for the 1877 edition in the *Half Dime Library*.

Figure 19. Paper cover of *Seth Jones* in *Beadle's American Sixpenny Library*, No. 1. 1861. (The London branch of Beadle & Co., which produced different printings, operated between 1861 and 1866.) Albert Johannsen Collection, Rare Books and Special Collections, Northern Illinois University Libraries.

Figure 20. Front page of *Seth Jones* in *Beadle's Half Dime Library*, No. 1104. 1900. By 1900, the publishing company was owned by M. J. Ivers. Albert Johannsen Collection, Rare Books and Special Collections, Northern Illinois University Libraries.

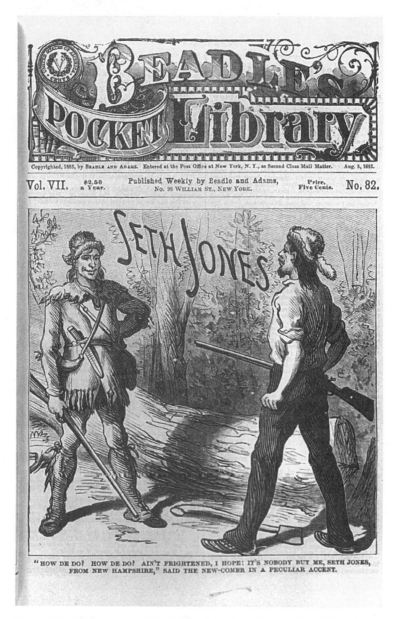

Copyrighted, 1885, by BEADLE AND ADAMS. Entered at the Post Office at New York, N. Y., as Second Class Mail Matter. Aug. 5, 1885.

Vol. VII. $2.50 a Year. Published Weekly by Beadle and Adams, No. 98 WILLIAM ST., NEW YORK. Price, Five Cents. No. 82.

SETH JONES

"HOW DE DO! HOW DE DO! AIN'T FRIGHTENED, I HOPE: IT'S NOBODY BUT ME, SETH JONES, FROM NEW HAMPSHIRE," SAID THE NEW-COMER IN A PECULIAR ACCENT.

Figure 21. Paper cover of *Seth Jones* in *Beadle's Pocket Library*, No. 82. 1885. Albert Johannsen Collection, Rare Books and Special Collections, Northern Illinois University Libraries.

CHAPTER I. THE STRANGER

The clear ring of an ax was echoing through the arches of a forest, three-quarters of a century ago; and an athletic man was swinging the instrument, burying its glittering blade deep in the heart of the mighty kings of the wood.

Alfred Haverland was an American, who, a number of years before, had emigrated from the more settled provinces in the East, to this then remote spot in western New York. Here, in the wilderness, he had reared a humble home, and, with his loving partner and a sister, laid the foundation for a settlement. True, this "settlement" was still small, consisting only of the persons mentioned, and a beautiful blue-eyed maiden, their daughter; but Haverland saw that the tide of emigration was rolling rapidly and surely to the west, and, ere many years, that villages and cities would take the place of the wild forest, while the Indians would be driven further on toward the setting sun.

The woodman was a splendid specimen of "nature's noblemen." His heavy coat lay upon a log a short distance away, and his swelling, ponderous chest was covered only by a close-fitting under-garment, with the collar thrown open, showing the glowing neck and heaving breast. Substantial pants met the strong moccasins which incased his feet. A small raccoon-skin cap rested on the back of his head, exposing his forehead, while his black hair swept around his shoulders. His features were regular, and strongly marked. The brow was rather heavy, the nose of the Roman cast, and the eyes of a glittering blackness. So he stood with one foot thrust forward; his muscles, moving and ridging as they were called into play, betrayed their formidable strength.

Still the flashing ax sunk deeper and deeper into the oak's red heart, until it had gone clean through and met the breach upon the opposite side. Then the grand old forest-king began to totter. Haverland stepped back and ran his eyes to the top, as he noticed it yielding. Slowly it leaned, increasing each second, until it rushed seemingly forward, and came down to the earth with a thundering crash and rebound. He stood a moment, his hot breath issuing like steam from his chest, and then moved forward toward its branches. At that instant his trained ear detected a suspicious sound, and dropping his ax, he caught up his rifle and stood on the defensive.

"How de do? How de do? Ain't frightened, I hope; it's nobody but me, Seth Jones, from New Hampshire," said the new-comer in a peculiar accent. As the woodman looked up he saw a curious specimen of the *genus homo* before him. He is what is termed a *Yankee,* being from New Hampshire; but he was such a person as is rarely met with, and yet which is too often described nowadays. He possessed a long, thin Roman nose, a small, twinkling gray eye, with a lithe, muscular frame, and long, dangling limbs. His feet were incased in well-fitting shoes, while the rest of his dress was such as was in vogue on the frontiers at the time of which we write. His voice was in that peculiar, uncertain state, which is sometimes seen when it is said to be "changing." When excited, it made sounds singular and unimaginable.

The woodman, with characteristic penetration, read the man before him at a glance. Changing his rifle to his left hand, he extended the other.

"Certainly not, my friend; but then, you know, these are times in which it behooves us all to use caution and prudence; and where one is placed in such a remote section as this it would be criminal to be careless, when more than one life is dependent upon me for support and protection."

"Very true, very true; you're right there, Mr. — ah! I declare I don't know your name."

"Haverland."

"You're right, as I said, Mr. Have-your-land, or Haverland, as the case may be. I tell *you* these *are* dubious times — no disputin' that, and I was considerably s'prised when I heard the ring of an ax down in these parts."

"And I was equally surprised to meet your visage when I looked up. Jones, I believe you said was your name?"

"Exactly — Seth Jones, from New Hampshire. The Joneses are a numerous family up there — rather too many of them for comfort — so I migrated. Mought be acquainted, perhaps?"

"No, I have no acquaintance to my knowledge in that section."

"Haven't, eh? Thought the Joneses were pretty generally known through the country. Some remarkable geniuses have sprung from the family. But what under the sun keeps you out in this heathen country? What brought you here?"

"Enterprise, sir; I was tired of the civilized portion of our country, and when such glorious fields were offered to the emigrant as are here spread before him, I considered it a duty to avail myself of them, and I have done so. And now, sir, be equally frank with me, and let me know what induced you to visit this perilous region when you had no reason to suppose that a settlement had yet been commenced by the whites. You look to me as if you were an Indian-hunter or scout."

"Wal, perhaps I am. At any rate I have been. I was a scout among the Green Mountain Boys, under Colonel Allen, and stayed with them till the Revolution was finished.[1] After that I went down on the farm and worked a while with the old man. Something occurred in our neighborhood that led me to think it was best for me to leave: I won't say what it was, but I will say it was no crime I committed. I stopped at the settlement down the river a few days, and then come to the conclusion to take a tramp in these parts."

"I am very glad you have come, for it isn't often we get sight of a white face. I hope you will take the welcome of a backwoodsman, and make your home with us as long a time as you can — remembering that the longer you stay the more welcome you will be."

"I shall probably stay till you git tired of me, at any rate," laughed the eccentric Seth Jones.

"As you are from the East, probably you can give information of the state of feeling among the Indians between that section and us. From your remarks, I should infer, however, that nothing very serious threatens."

"Don't know 'bout that," replied Seth, shaking his head and looking to the ground.

"Why so, my friend?"

"I tell you what, you, I heerd orful stories 'long the way. They say since this war, the darned red-coats have kept the Injins at work. Leastways, it's pretty sartin they are at work, anyhow."

"Are you sure?" asked the woodman, betraying an anxiety in his speech.

"Purty sure. There's a little settlement down here some miles, (I have forgot the name,) sot on by the imps and burned all up."

---

[1] *Green Mountain Boys; Colonel Allen:*   Organized in 1770 during the territorial disputes between New York and New Hampshire over the New Hampshire Grants (land grants that eventually became Vermont), the Green Mountain Boys were a military company led by the "colonel commandant" Ethan Allen. During the Revolution, the company fought for the patriot cause and was a crucial factor in the defeat of the British at the Battle of Bennington. Allen was captured during the war and became something of a national hero with his publication of *A Narrative of Col. Ethan Allen's Captivity* (1779).

"Is it possible? Reports have reached me during the past three or four months of the deadly hostility existing between the whites and reds, but I was glad to doubt it. Although I sometimes felt it was wrong."

"'Twas so; and if you vally that ar' wife of your bussum, and your little cherubims, (as I allow you've got,) you'd better be makin' tracks for safer quarters. Why, how have you stood it so long?"

"My conduct toward the Indians has ever been characterized by honesty and good-will upon my part, and they have ever evinced a friendly feeling toward me and my helpless ones. I place great reliance upon this state of feeling, in fact, my *only reliance.*"

"Just so; but I tell you, it won't do to trust an Injin. They're obstropertous. Go to put your finger on them, and they ain't thar. Jest so, by gracious."

"I fear there is too much truth in your suspicions," replied Haverland, in a saddened tone.

"I'm glad I've tumbled onto you, coz I begin to git skeerish, and I like to do a feller a good turn, and I'll stick to you, bein' I've found you."

"Thank you, friend, and let us now proceed homeward. I intended to spend the day in work, but your words have taken away all desire."

"Sorry to do it; but it's best, ain't it?"

"Certainly; it would have been wrong had you not warned me of impending danger. Let us go home."

So saying, Alfred drew on his coat, slung his rifle and ax over his shoulder, struck into a path in the forest, which he himself had worn, and with a thoughtful tread, made his way homeward. Close behind him followed his new-made friend.

CHAPTER II. THE DARK CLOUD

During the walk homeward, Haverland spoke but few words, although his loquacious friend kept up a continual unremitting stream of talk. The woodman's heart was too heavy to join him in his humorous, pointless words. Although dark and fearful suspicions had flitted before him, he had closed his eyes upon them until he could no longer shun them; they appeared at every turn, and now assumed a terrible certainty.

Although at the time to which we refer, the Revolutionary struggles of the colonies had closed, and their freedom was placed upon a firm basis, yet universal peace by no means reigned. Dark, sanguinary and bloody tragedies were constantly enacted upon the frontiers for a generation afterward. The mother country failing in her work of subjugation, continued to incite the Indians to revolting barbarities upon the unoffending inhabitants. They found them too-willing instruments, and, instigated by them, a protracted war was long maintained; and, when the inciting cause was removed, the savages still continued the unequal conflict. As every one acquainted with our history must know, the war on the frontiers has been an almost interminable one. As the tide of emigration has rolled westward, it has ever met that fiery counter-surge, and only overcome it by incessant battling and effort. And even now, as the distant shores of the Pacific are well-nigh reached, that resisting wave still gives forth its lurid flashes of conflict.

In a pleasant valley stood the humble home of Alfred Haverland. His own vigorous arm had cleared off a space on all sides so that his residence stood at some distance from the forest, which rolled away for miles. In the clearing still remained the stumps of the fallen trees, and in some places the rich virgin soil had been broken, and was giving signs of the exhaustless wealth it retained in its bosom, waiting only for the hand of man to bring it forth.

The house itself was such as are generally found in new settlements. A number of heavy logs, placed compactly together, with an opening for a door, and one for a window, were all that could attract attention from the outside. Within, were two apartments, the lower and upper. The former was used for all purposes except that of sleeping, which, of course, was done in the upper. In building it, Haverland had made little preparation for defense, as he fondly hoped it would never be needed for such, and it seemed to him that the idea of danger would ever be before him, should he construct it thus. And, besides, should he use his utmost skill in the purpose mentioned, he knew it would avail him little. He had no means of withstanding a protracted siege, and a handful of assailants could bring him to any terms.

As he stepped forth into the clearing, Ina, his daughter, caught sight of him, and bounded out the cabin to meet him.

"Oh, father! I am glad you have come back so soon, but dinner isn't ready. Did you think it was? I was just telling mother — "

She paused suddenly, as she caught sight of a stranger, and with her hand on her mouth, stood, fearing to approach, and afraid to yield to the impulse of turning and running into the house again.

"No, I didn't think dinner-time had come, but as I had a friend to visit me, I thought I could entertain him at home better than in the woods. But where is your kiss, dear?"

The father stooped, and touched his lips to the ruby ones of his blooming child, and taking her hand, moved forward toward the cabin.

"Whew! if that ain't a purty flower, then kick me!" exclaimed Seth Jones, in admiration. "Was she originated in these parts? Darter, I s'pose? Perhaps not, though?"

"Yes, she is my daughter, although she was not born in these parts."

"Dew tell. Darned if she ain't a beauty, and that makes what I said — "

The father motioned to him that the theme was forbidden, and they walked silently toward the house.

It was no wonder that Ina Haverland drew forth such encomiums from Seth Jones. She was, indeed, a beautiful creature. She had seen some fifteen or sixteen summers, several of which had been spent in the wilderness, which was now her home. She was rather small in stature, but graceful as a gazelle, free from the restraints which the conventionalities of life imposed on those of her age. She had dark hair, gathered in a roll behind, fine expressive blue eyes, a perfect Grecian nose, thin lips, and a full chin, rendering the profile perfectly straight from the forehead downward. Her face was oval, and her complexion almost too light for a full enjoyment of health. Her dress was a semi-civilized one, consisting of a short skirt, with leggins beautifully wrought, and a loose sack, similar to the ones worn at the present day. Her small feet were incased in tiny moccasins, elaborately wrought with beads and Indian ornaments, and a string of wampum hung around the neck.

She led the way toward the house, and the three entered.

Haverland introduced his friend to his sister and wife, as a man who had chanced down in this direction, and who would probably tarry a few days. But the quick eye of his wife caught the thoughtful expression upon her husband's face, and she felt there was something yet unrevealed — something deeper and more important that was to be disclosed. She, however, forbore questioning or hinting, knowing that he would communicate what was necessary when he deemed the proper time had come.

A commonplace conversation was maintained until the meal was prepared by the busy housewife, when they all gathered around the board. An earnest blessing was invoked upon the humble food, and it was partaken of in silence.

"Wife," said Haverland, tenderly, "I will depart awhile with this friend here, and you and Mary may busy yourselves as you think best till I return. Probably I will not be back until toward night. Take no anxiety upon my account."

"I will endeavor not to; but, dear husband, go not far from home, for strange fears have come over me since morning."

Even the usually staid and calm face of Mary betrayed an unusual expression of anxiety.

"Fear not, wife, I will not go far."

Haverland now stepped outside, where he saw Seth, all agape, gazing at Ina, as she passed to and fro in the house.

"By gracious, you, I'm goin' to fall in love with that gal. No 'bjections, hope?"

"No," answered Haverland, with a faint smile, "her heart is unfettered and I hope it will remain so for a long time."

"Oh! I don't mean to love her as you dew yer old woman — yer wife. I mean jest as I would my darter, yer know. She's too small to think about lovyers *yit*. Don't you let *sich* a thing git inter her head for five years or more."

"I'll try not to; but let us take a walk. I have something to say, which I would that they should not know for the present."

"All right — but jest hold on a minute."

At this juncture, Ina appeared with a small vessel, as if she intended bringing some water from some spring nigh at hand.

"Hold on a minute, gal, my beauty," said Seth, stepping forward, and reaching for the pail. "That's too big a load for you to carry."

"No, I have done it often, thank you, but it is no work for me."

"But jest let me fetch it *this* time, if only to show my good will, and my activity."

Ina laughingly yielded the vessel, and watched him as he took long, awkward strides toward the point where the path led into the forest.

"How far is it off?" he asked, turning round, as he reached the point mentioned.

"A short distance," answered Haverland; "the path leads to it."

Seth made some unintelligible answer, as he jerked his head back and disappeared.

This simple occurrence that we have just narrated, although trivial in itself, was one of the circumstances which often control important acts, and which seem to show that an all-wise Ruler orders them to suit his purposes, and to bring about good in the end. Seth Jones had no object other than a little amusement in his course, yet before he returned, he saw how fortunate it was.

He strode rapidly forward, and after passing a short distance, reached the spring. As he stooped, he was sure he heard a movement in the bushes beyond; and, as he was about to dip the vessel, he saw, in the smooth face of the water, a movement in the shrubbery. He had too much cunning and prudence to affect knowledge of it, and he filled the vessel without betraying any signs of suspicion. As he rose to the upright position, he gave an apparently careless sweep of his vision, and not twenty feet distant he saw the crouching forms of two Indians! As he turned his back, there was a peculiar, uncomfortable feeling, as he knew that it was the easiest matter in the world to receive one or two cold bullets. He, however, quickened his steps not in the least, and manifested no uneasiness, as he came to view in the clearing and laughingly handed the water to Ina.

"Come, let us go," said Haverland, moving toward the spring.

"Not that ar' way, by a long shot," said Seth, with a meaning shake of his head.

"Why not?"

"I'll tell you, purty soon."

"Let us to the river, then."

"That'll do, 'specially *as it ain't fur from your house!*"

Haverland looked searchingly at him, and saw there was a deep meaning behind those words, yet he said nothing, and led the way toward the river.

This stream was but a few hundred yards from the house, and flowed in a northerly and southerly direction. It was very smooth at this point, and not very wide, yet a mile or so further down it debouched into a large, broad, and deep river. The banks were lined, most of the distance, by close, impenetrable shrubbery, overarched by lofty trees, which were the edges of the almost interminable wilderness that then covered this part of the State, and of which great portions remain unto the present day.

Haverland moved to a spot where he had often stood and conversed with his wife, when they first entered the place. Resting his rifle upon the earth, and folding his arms over the muzzle, he turned around and looked Seth full in the face.

"What did you mean by telling me not to go *far from* the house?"

"Jest hol' on a bit," replied Seth, bending his ear as if to listen. Haverland watched him earnestly and he also heard something unusual — as if someone were rowing a canoe in the water. His companion then stepped down to the water's edge, and signaled for him to approach. Haverland did so and looked down the river. Some hundred yards off, he saw a canoe rapidly moving down-stream, impelled by the oars of three Indians.

"That is what I meant," said he, in a whisper, stepping back.

"Did you see them," asked Haverland.

"I reckon I did. They were at the spring watching for your gal to come, so that they mought run off with her."

CHAPTER III. THE DARK CLOUD BURSTS

"Are you certain?" asked Haverland, with a painful eagerness.

"As sure as I live!"

"How? when? where did you see them? Pray, answer quick, for I feel that the lives of precious ones stand in peril."

"The facts are few — they are. When I went down to the spring, I see'd them pesky varmints thar, and I knowed they war waitin' for your little booty, 'cause if they wa'n't, they'd have walloped me, thunderin' soon. I see'd 'em sneakin' 'round, and purtended as though I didn't s'picion nothin'. They've found I's about, and have gone down for more help. They'll be back here to-night with a whole pack. Fact, by gracious!"

"You speak truly; and as matters stand thus, it is time for *action*."

"Exactly so; and what is it you propose to dew?"

"As you have offered me such signal aid thus far, I must again ask you for advice."

"Pshaw! don't you know what to dew, man?"

"I have a plan, but I would hear yours first."

"Wal, I can give it purty soon. You know well enough you're in tight quarters, and the best thing you can do is to git away from here a leetle quicker nor no time. You know the settlements ain't more nor twenty miles off, and you'd better pack up and be off, and lose no time, neither."

"That was my plan, exactly. But hold! we must go by water, and will it not be best to wait and go by night, when we will have the darkness to protect us? We have just learned that the river contains enough enemies to frustrate our designs, should they be known. Yes, we must wait till night."

"You're right there; and, as there is no moon, we'll have a good chance, especially as we have to go down-stream instead of up. I tell *you*, the war *is* going on. When I left home, I had an idee things would be fixed so as to stop these infarnal red-skins from committin' on their depredations, although they looked might squally; but 'tain't no use, and it won't do to trust these critters."

Shortly after, Haverland turned and entered the house, followed by Seth. He called his wife and sister in, and explained, in a few words, the circumstances. It was but a realization of the fears entertained, and no time was lost in useless laments. Preparations were immediately made for the removal. The woodman owned a large boat, somewhat similar to the flatboats seen at this day upon the western waters. This was hauled in beneath the shrubbery which overhung the bank, and into this their things were placed. During the removal Seth remained along the river-bank, keeping watch of the stream, lest their enemies might return unawares.

The removal occupied most of the afternoon, and it was not until the shadows were lengthening across the river that the last article was placed on board. This completed, all seated themselves in the boat, and waited for the rapidly-approaching darkness, to glide out into the stream.

"It is hard," said Haverland, somewhat moodily, "to leave one's home after all the difficulty in rearing it is finished."

"Fact, by gracious!" added Seth, whom Mary eyed very closely, as if not satisfied with the fellow's ways and looks.

"But it is best, dear husband. Let us hope, now, that the war is ended, and that, as we have passed through as great dangers as those that now threaten us, the time is not far distant when we may return to this spot with safety."

"We can die but once," said Mary, abstractedly, "and I am ready for any fate."

Seth studied her face with a quick keen glance, then smiled, and said: "Oh, you look a-here now. I am captain here, by your leave, my dears, and I ain't goin' to allow any sick stomachs in this here crew." His sunny face seemed greatly to encourage the little band.

"I wouldn't fear to remain here now," said Ina bravely; "I am *sure* we soon may return. I *feel* it."

Haverland kissed his child, but made no further reply, and all relapsed into stillness, and ceased further conversation. There was something in the gathering gloom around, something in the peculiar situation in which they were placed, that imparted a despondency to all. The boat was still fastened to the shore, and the time for loosening it was close at hand. Mrs. Haverland had passed within the rude cabin, the door of which remained open, while Seth and the husband remained in the stern. Ina sat near at hand, and had fallen into the same silence that rested upon the others.

"Doesn't it look dark and awful, back there?" she asked, in a whisper, of Seth, pointing toward the shore.

"It does, somewhat, I think."

"And yet I wouldn't be afraid to go back to the house."

"You'd better stay in the boat, young 'un."

"You think I am *afraid,* do you?" she said, bounding out the boat to the shore.

"Ina! Ina! what do you mean?" asked the father, sternly.

"Oh, nothing; only I want to take a little run to ease my limbs."

"Come back here, instantly!"

"Yes — oh, father! quick! quick! come and take me!"

"Seize the oar and shove out!" commanded Seth, springing into the water and shoving the boat off.

"But, for God's sake, my child!"

"You can't help her — the Injins have got her. I see 'em; drop quick, they're goin' to fire! look out!"

At that instant there was a sharp crack of several rifles from the shore, and several tongues of fire flamed from the darkness, and the wild yell of a number of Indians pealed out in horrid strength.

Had it not been for Seth all would have been lost. He comprehended everything in an instant, and saved the others.

"Oh, father! mother! The Indians have got me!" came in agonized accents from the shore.

"Merciful God! must I see my child perish without heeding her cry?" groaned Haverland, in spirit.

"No, they won't hurt her, and we must take care of ourselves while we can. Don't stand up, for they can see you."

"Father, will you leave me?" came again in heartrending tones.

"Don't be scart, young 'un," called out Seth; "keep up a good heart. I'll git you ag'in ef you behave yourself. I will, as sure as I am

Seth Jones. Just keep up pluck, little one." The last words were shouted loudly, for the boat was fast gliding into the stream.

The mother had heard all, and said nothing. She comprehended it, and with a groan sunk back upon a seat. Mary's eyes flashed like a tigress at bay; and she did not cease to cast looks of indignation at Seth, for leaving the child to her horrid fate so coolly. But she said nothing — was as quiet and pale as a statue. Seth eyed her like a lynx; his eyeballs seemed like fire. But he was as cool as if at his ease perfectly; and he quickly made all feel that he was born for such appalling emergencies.

They were now in the center of the stream, and moving quite rapidly. The darkness was so great that the shores were now vailed from sight. And with hearts in as deep a gloom, the fugitives floated downward.

CHAPTER IV. THE LOST HOME AND A FOUND FRIEND

It was on the morning of the day which we have just seen close. As will be remembered, the air is clear and the day one of the most beautiful and pleasant of the year. The air was perfectly still, and had that peculiar, bracing sharpness which is only felt when it is in a perfect state of rest. It was such a morning as would make every healthy person feel that to merely *live* was pleasure.

That part of the State of New York in which the first scenes of this life-drama are laid, was a country at this time cut up and diversified by numerous streams — the greater number of comparatively small size, but a few of considerable magnitude. Skirting and between these were thousands of acres of thick, luxuriant forest, while in some places were plains of great extent entirely devoid of timber.

It was about the middle of the day referred to, that a single horseman was slowly skirting one of these open patches of country, a few miles distant from Haverland's home. A mere glance would have shown that he had come a great distance, and both he and the animal he bestrode were jaded and well-nigh worn out. He was a young man, some twenty or twenty-five years of age, attired in the costume of a hunter; and, although fatigued with his long ride, the watchfulness of his motions would have shown any one that he was no stranger to frontier life. He was rather prepossessing in appearance — had fine dark eyes, curly hair and whiskers, an expressive Roman nose, and small and finely-formed mouth. In front, a long, polished rifle rested across the saddle, ready for use at a second's warning. His horse's sides were steaming and foamy, and the animal made his way along with painfully evident weariness.

As the day waned, the traveler looked about him with more interest and eagerness. He carefully examined the streams he crossed, and the pieces of wood, as though searching for some landmark or habitation. At length he manifested a pleasure in what he saw, as though the signs were as he wished, and hurried the lagging steps of his animal.

"Yes," said he to himself, "the woodman's house cannot be far from this. I remember this stream, and that wood yonder. I shall then be able to reach it by night. Come, my good horse, go ahead with better spirits, for you are near your journey's end."

A short time after, he crossed a small stream that dashed and foamed over its rocky bed, and entered the broad tract which led to the clearing in front of Haverland's door. But although he had a tolerably correct idea of his situation, he had sadly miscalculated the distance. It was already dusk when he struck the stream several miles above where we have seen the fugitives take it. This river, or creek, he knew led directly by the cabin he was seeking, and he determined to keep it until he had reached his destination. His progress was now quite tardy, from being often obliged to pass around the thick undergrowth which lined the river; and, when he reached a point that he knew was a mile distant from Haverland's cabin, it was far in the night.

"Come, my good horse, we have had a longer tramp than I expected, but we are now very near the termination of our journey. Heigh! what does that mean?"

This last exclamation, or question, was caused by seeing directly ahead of him, a bright, lurid glare shoot high into the heavens.

"Can it be that the woodman's house is fired? Impossible! and yet, that is the precise spot. Heavens! something is wrong!"

Agitated by strong and painful emotions, Everard Graham (such was his name) now hurried his horse toward the spot from which the light emanated. In a short time he had proceeded as far as he dared with his horse, then dismounting, he tied him, and made his way cautiously forward on foot. The light was so strong that he found it necessary to pick his way with the greatest care.

A few moments sufficed to show him all.

He saw the house of Haverland, the one in which he expected to pass the night, but one mass of flame. And around it were a score of dark forms, leaping and dancing, and appearing, in the ghastly light, like fiends in a ghostly revel.

It was a ghastly and almost unearthly sight — the small cabin, crackling and roaring in one mass of living flame, throwing strange shadows across the clearing, and lighting up the edges of the forest with a brightness almost as great as the sun at noonday — the score of dusky beings, leaping and shouting in wild exultation, and the vast wilderness, shutting down like an ocean of darkness around.

Gradually the flames lessened, and the woods seemed to retreat into the gloom; the shouts of the savages ceased, and they, too, disappeared; and the building, which hitherto was a mass of crackling fire, was now a heap of slumbering coals and embers, which glowed with a hot redness in the darkness.

An hour or two afterward, a shadowy form could have been seen gliding stealthily and silently around the glowing ruins. He appeared like a specter as seen by the reflected light of the slumbering coals, or might have been taken for the shadow of some ruin of the building. At intervals he paused and listened as though he half expected to hear the footfall of some one, and then again continued his ghostly march around the ruins. Several times he stopped and peered into the embers, as though he supposed the whitened bones of some human being would greet his vision, and then he recoiled and stood as if in deep and painful thought. It was Everard Graham, searching for the remains of Haverland and his family.

"I see nothing," he said, musingly, "and it may be that they have escaped, or their bodies are now cooking in that heap of coals, and yet something tells me that they are not. And if it is not thus, what can have become of them? How could they have eluded the malignant vengeance of their savage foes? Who could have warned them? Ah, me! in spite of the unaccountable hope which I feel, my own sense tells me there are no grounds for it. Sad is the fate of the unprotected at this time."

"Fact, by gracious!"

Graham started as though he had been shot, and gazed around. A few yards off he could just discover the outlines of a man standing as if he were contemplating himself.

"And who are you?" he asked, "that appears upon this spot at such a time?"

"I am Seth Jones, from New Hampshire. Who mought be you that happens down in these parts at this pertickler time?"

"Who am I? I am Everard Graham, a friend of the man whose house is in ruins, and who, I fear, has been slaughtered with his family."

"Exactly so; but don't speak so loud. There mought be others about, you know. Jist let's step back here, where 'tain't likely we'll be observed."

The speaker retreated into the darkness, while Graham followed him. At first he had some slight misgivings, but the tones and voice of the stranger reassured him, and he followed him without distrust or hesitation.

"You say you're a friend of Haverland's, eh?" asked Seth, in a whisper.

"I am, sir; I was acquainted with him before he moved out in these parts. He was an intimate friend of my father's, and I promised to pay him a visit as soon as I could possibly do so, and I am here for that purpose."

"Jest so; but you took a rayther ticklish time for it, I reckon."

"So it seems; but, if I wished to wait till it would be perfectly safe, I am afraid my visit would never be made."

"Fact, by gracious!"

"But allow me to ask whether you know anything of the family?"

"I reckon that, perhaps, it mought be possible I do, seein' as how I've been around these times."

"Are they slain, or captives?"

"Neyther."

"Is it possible they have escaped?"

"Jest so. I helped 'em off myself."

"Thank heaven! Where are they?"

"Down the river, at one of the settlements."

"How far distant is it?"

"A dozen miles, p'raps, though it mought be more, and then ag'in it mightn't."

"Well let us then hasten to them, or, let me, at least, as I have nothing to detain me here."

"I'm willing," said Seth, moving forward, "but I forgot to tell you the darter's 'mong the Indians. I didn't think of that."

Graham started; for, perhaps, the shrewd reader has already suspected he had more than a passing interest in the fate of Ina. Visions of a fair, childish face *had* haunted him, and his perilous journey was owing much to their enchantment. He had played with her in childhood, and while they were yet children they had separated; but they had pledged their hearts to each other, and looked hopefully forward to a reunion in later years. Graham had dreamed of this meeting a long time; and, now that it was so cruelly thwarted, he felt agonized indeed. Years before, when still a boy, although quite a large one, he visited this section, and the memory of that visit had ever been a bright dream in the past. He mastered his emotion in a moment, with a strong effort, and asked his companion, calmly:

"What tribe has captured Ina?"

"Them infarnal Mohawks, I believe."[2]

"How long ago did it occur?"

"Only a few hours, as you can see by them coals there."

"Will you be kind enough to give me the particulars?"

"Sartinly."

And thereupon Seth proceeded to narrate the incidents given in the preceding chapter, adding, however, that the parents and sister were safe. He had accompanied them himself down to the settlement mentioned, where, leaving them, he had made all haste back again, and had arrived just in time to meet Graham. At first, he said, he mistook him for a savage, and as he was alone, he came very near shooting him; but, as he heard him communing with himself, he discovered at once that he was a white man.

"And what has brought you back here?" asked Graham, when he had finished.

"That's a pooty question to ax me, I swow! What has brought me back here? Why, the same thing, I cac'late as has brought you — to find out what is to be found out 'bout Ina, that purty darter."

"Ah — pardon me, friend, I am glad to hear it, and I am free to confess that that inducement has had more in bringing me here than anything else. From your starting alone to rescue her, I presume you entertained hopes of recovering her, and, as you, alone, entertained such hopes, I judge there is greater room for them, when another one joins you."

[2] *Mohawks:*   Circa 1570, the Mohawk, Oneida, Onondaga, Cayuga, and Seneca tribes formed the Five Nation Confederacy of the Iroquois, which subsequently monopolized the fur trade with the Europeans. The Mohawk were the easternmost population. When the Tuscarora joined the league it became known as the Six Nations Confederacy. The Revolution divided the Six Nations between allegiance to the English and the Continentals; the Mohawk became crucial British allies, wreaking severe damage on the New York frontier. After the war, many Mohawks left New York to occupy a Canadian reservation newly granted by the Crown. For Ellis's account of the Six Nations, see p. 188.

"Did I say, stranger, I 'spected to git that gal again?" asked Seth, in a low tone.

"You did not say so in words, it is true; but from *what* you said, I judged such was your intention. Was I mistaken?"

"No, sir; that's what I meant."

"I see no reason why we should not be friends, as we are both actuated by a desire to rescue an unfortunate one from the horrors of Indian captivity, and I trust, without that fact, we would find nothing distasteful in each other."

"Them's my sentiments, 'zactly. Give us your hand."

The two closed hands with a true friendly gripe, and could each have seen the other's face in the darkness, he would have beheld a radiant expression of friendship. They then retired further into the wood and continued the conversation.

We may mention in this place, that the Indians who had captured Ina were, as Seth had remarked, members of the Mohawk tribe. This tribe itself was a member of the "Five Nations," including with them the Seneca, the Cayuga, Onondaga, and Oneida tribes, which have become quite famous in history. They are known among the French as the *Iroquois,* and among the Dutch as *Maquas,* while at home they are called the *Mingoes,* or *Agamuschim,* signifying the *United People.* The Mohawks, or *Webingi,* first existed separately and alone. The Oneidas then joined them, and these, in turn, were followed by the Onondagas, Senecas, and Cayugas. In the beginning of the last century, the Tuscaroras of the South joined them, after which they took the name of the Six Nations. Of course, they were all united, and war made upon one tribe, was made upon all. They were truly a formidable confederation, and the Revolution testifies to what deeds they were sufficient when instigated by the British. During the predatory warfare which long existed upon the Old Frontier, the white settlers relied mainly upon stratagem to outwit their foes, and it was by this means alone that Seth Jones hoped to rescue Ina from their hands.

CHAPTER V. ON THE TRAIL, AND A SUDDEN DEPARTURE FROM IT BY SETH

"The Mohawks, you say, have then captured her?" remarked Graham, after a moment's pause.

"Yes; I know it's them."

"Did you get a glimpse of them?"

"I came up as soon as possible, and they were leaving at that moment. I saw one or two of them, and know'd it was them, sure 'nough. Howsumever, that don't make no difference, whether it's the Mohawks, Oneidas, or any of them blasted Five Nation niggers. They are all a set of skunks, and ere would just as lief run off with a man's gal as not. There ain't any difference atwixt 'em."

"I suppose not. The same difficulties would have to be surmounted in each case. The point is not whether one shall make an attempt at a rescue, but how shall it be done. I confess I am in a maze. The Mohawks are an exceedingly cunning people."

"That's a fact — that needn't be disputed."

"But then, you know, if we outwit them, we will not be the first whites who have done such a thing in their day!"

"That's a fact, too. Now, jest hold on a minute, while I think."

Graham ceased talking for a moment, while Seth remained as if in deep and anxious thought. Suddenly lifting up his head, he remarked:

"I have it."

"Have what? The plan which must be pursued by us?"

"I ca'c'late I have."

"Well, out with it."

"Why, it's this. We've got to git that gal, an' no mistake."

Despite the gloominess which had been upon Graham, he could not help laughing outright at the serious tone in which this was uttered.

"What are you laughing at?" indignantly demanded Seth.

"Why, I thought we had arrived at that conclusion long since."

"I didn't think of that; so we did. Howsumever, I've thort further — hey, what's that off yonder? 'Nuther building burning?"

Graham gazed in the direction indicated, and saw that day was breaking. This he remarked to his companion.

"Yes, so 'tis; and I'm glad of it, for we want some light on this subject."

In a short time, the sun appeared above the forest, and poured a flood of golden light over the woods and streams. Birds were singing their morning songs in every part of the wood, and everything wore as gay a look as though no deed of blood had been committed during the night. As soon as it was sufficiently light, Seth and Graham made their way toward the stream.

"As we shall shortly start," remarked the latter, "I will attend to my horse, which I brought with me. He is but a short distance away, and I will be back in a moment."

So saying, he departed in the wood. He found his horse completely worn out, asleep on the ground. He unloosened his fastening, and as there was abundant provender around in the shape of young and tender twigs and luxuriant grass, he removed the saddle and bridle, and concluded to allow him free scope of the wood until his return, trusting to the rather doubtful chances of ever recovering him again. This done, he returned to his companion.

He found Seth leaning upon his rifle and gazing meditatively into the silent stream flowing before him. Graham looked curiously at him a moment and then said:

"I am ready, Seth, if you are."

The individual addressed turned without a word and strode toward the clearing. When the ruins of the house were reached they both halted, and in an undertone he said:

"Hunt up the trail."

Each bent his head toward the ground and moved in a circle around the clearing. Suddenly Graham paused and proceeded quickly several yards in the wood, halted and exclaimed:

"Here it is, Seth."

The latter hastened to his side, and stooping a moment, and running his eye along the ground, both forward and backward, replied:

"This is the trail! They ain't very keerful 'bout it now, but I reckon it'll make us open our peepers wider to see it, after we get into the wood."

"Well, as the starting-point is now reached, we must perfect our arrangements. You must take the lead in following this up."

"Can't you?" asked Seth, looking up in his eyes.

"Not as well as you. From what little I have seen of you, I am sure you excel me in the knowledge of the forest. I have had some experience in fighting, but very little in tracing a foe through such a wilderness as this."

"Don't say? That's just where you an' I disagree. I was always the one to track the tories or red-coats for old Colonel Allen, and I remember one time — but I guess I won't go to telling stories now, being as I haven't much time; but I can say, though p'raps I oughtn't to, that I can foller any red-skin as far as he can go, and I don't care how much pains he takes to cover up his tracks. You see, if I undertake to foller this, I've got to keep my nose down to the ground, and won't be likely to see any danger we're running into; that'll have to be your business. You just hang close to my heels, and keep your eyes travelling all over."

"I'll endeavor to do my part, although I shall expect some aid from you."

"I may give some, as I can tell purty near 'bout when the imps have gone over the tracks I'm looking at. And now we must start. I promised Haverland that I wouldn't show myself again until I could tell him something about his darter, and I swow, I won't. Come ahead."

With these words, Seth started ahead on a rapid walk. He was slightly inclined forward, and his keen gray eye was bent with a searching look upon the ground. Graham followed him a few feet distant, with the barrel of his rifle resting in the hollow of his left arm, while the stock was held in his right, so to be ready at a moment's warning.

The signs that led Seth Jones forward were faint, and to an ordinary observer, invisible. The Indians, although they had little fears of pursuit, were yet too cunning and experienced to neglect any caution that would mislead what enemies might be disposed to follow them. They traveled in Indian file, each one stepping in the track of the one before him, so that, judging from the tracks made, it would appear that but a single savage had been journeying in these parts. Ina was compelled to walk in this manner, and more than once when she inadvertently made a misstep, a cruel blow warned her of her task.

Sometimes the leaves, as they lay, appeared perfectly devoid of the slightest depression or disturbance, yet, had one stooped and carefully scrutinized the ground, he would have seen the faint outlines of a moccasin defined upon it, or observed that a leaf had been displaced, or perhaps a slender twig had not yet recovered the position from which it had been forced by the passing of human feet. All these were trifling indications, it is true, yet they were unerring ones to the practiced eye of the hunter, and as plain as the footprints upon the dusty roads. Soon Seth paused, and raising his head, turned toward Graham.

"We are gaining on 'em."

"Ah — are we? Glad to hear it. When is it probable we shall overtake them!"

"Can't exactly say, but not for a considerable time yet. They are tramping at a purty good gait, and they only halted last night to rest Iny now and then. Darn 'em! she'll want rest, I ca'c'late, more'n once afore she's done with 'em."

"Can't you conjecture their number?"

"There's somewhere in the neighborhood of twenty of the best warriors of the Mohawks. I can tell that by their tracks."

"How is that? They make but a single one, do they?"

"Of course not, but I rayther ca'c'late they make that a little different, fur all that, from what one would. Are you hungry?"

"Not at all; I can stand it till noon, without the least inconvenience."

"So can I; keep a good look-out, and now ahead again."

With these words, Seth again plunged into the woods, and the two prosecuted their journey much as before. The sun was now high in the heavens, and its warm rays pierced the arches of the forest at many points, and there were golden patches of light scattered over the travelers' path. Several times they crossed small, sparkling streams, where sometimes could be seen signs of the pursued having slaked their thirst, and more than once the frightened deer bounded ahead, and paused and gazed in wonder at them, then leaped away again. Graham could hardly resist the temptation of bringing one of them down, especially as he began to feel a desire to taste them; but he too well knew the danger of risking a shot, when it might bring down their most mortal enemies in a moment upon them.

All at once Seth halted and raised his hand.

"What does this mean?" he asked, gazing off in a side direction from the trail.

"What is it!" queried Graham, approaching him.

"The trail divides here. They must have separated, though I can't see what has made them."

"Isn't it a stratagem of theirs to mislead pursuers?"

"I believe it is! Here, you follow the main trail, while I take the side one, and we'll soon see."

Graham did as directed, although it cost him considerable trouble to perform his part. It proved as they expected. In a short time, the two trails united again.

"We must look out for such things," remarked Seth. "I've got to watch the ground closer, and you must look out that I don't pitch heels over head into a nest of hornets."

They now proceeded cautiously and rapidly forward. About the middle of the afternoon, they halted beside a stream of considerable size. Seth produced a quantity of dried venison, which he had brought with him from the settlement, and of this they made a hearty meal. This done, they arose and again proceeded on their journey.

"See there!" said Seth, pointing to the middle of the stream. "Do you see that stone there? Notice how it is marked, and observe that print of a moccasin beside it. One of their number has slipped off of it. Let us be keerful."

He stepped into the water, and made his way carefully across, followed by Graham. When they stepped upon dry land again, the shades of evening were gathering over the forest, and already the birds had ceased their songs. There was, however, a bright moon — in fact, so bright, that they determined to keep up their pursuit.

The progress was now necessarily tardy, as it required the utmost straining of Seth's vision to keep the trail, and had it not been for the friendly openings in the wood, where it was as plain as at midday, they would have been compelled to abandon it altogether until the morning. Several times Graham was compelled to stand, while Seth, almost on his hands and knees, searched out the "signs." They came across no evidence of the Indians having encamped, and judged from this that they either intended reaching their tribe before doing so, or that they were somewhere in the vicinity. The latter was the most probable supposition, and prudence demanded them to be cautious and deliberate in their movements.

Suddenly Graham noticed the woods appeared to be growing thinner and lighter in front, as though an opening was at hand. He called the attention of Seth to this, who remarked that it was very probable. In a few moments they heard a noise as of flowing water, and immediately after stood upon the bank of a large creek, or more properly a river. The current was quite rapid, yet, without much hesitation, they plunged boldly in and swam across. The night being warm and moderate, they suffered little inconvenience from their wet and clinging clothes, as the exercise of walking kept them sufficiently warm.

As they ascended the bank, they stood upon a vast and treeless plain, over which the trail led.

"Must we cross this?" asked Graham.

"I don't see any other way. There ain't any chance to skirt it, 'cause it appears to run up and down about four thousand three hundred miles, while you can see the other side."

This was true — that is, the latter part of his assertion. The plain before them, from all appearances, was a prairie of great length, but comparatively narrow breadth. The dark line of the woods upon the opposite side could be plainly seen, but did not appear more than a good hour's walk away.

"I don't see any other way," repeated Seth, musingly, to himself. "It's got to be crossed, though it's a ticklish business, I swow!"

"Wouldn't it be better to wait until morning?" asked Graham.

"Why so?"

"We may walk into danger without seeing it, in the night."

"And how do you s'pose we're going to walk over here in daylight, without being targets for all the Injins that are a-mind to crack away at us?"

"Can we not pass around it?"

"Stars and garters! hain't I told you it reaches five thousand miles each way, and it would take us three years to get half-way round?"

"I was not aware that you had given me such interesting information, until just now; but, as such is the case, of course nothing is left for us but to move forward, without losing time talking."

"The trail goes purty straight," said Seth, turning and looking at the ground, "and I've no doubt it heads straight across to the other side. Hope so, 'cause it'll be convenient."

"You must help me keep watch," said Graham; "you will not need to watch the ground all the time, and you will need to keep a look-out elsewhere."

As might naturally be supposed, our two friends, although quite experienced backwoodsmen, had miscalculated the distance to the opposite side of the prairie. It was full midnight ere they reached its margin.

All was silent as death, as they cautiously and stealthily entered the wood again. Not a breath of wind stirred the boughs on the tree-tops, and the soft murmur of the river had long died away into silence. There were a few flying clouds that obscured the moon at intervals, and rendered its light uncertain and treacherous. Seth still pressed forward. They had gone a few hundred yards, when they heard voices! Cautiously and silently they picked their way, and soon saw the light of a fire reflected against the uppermost limbs of the trees. The fire itself was invisible, although it could not be far distant. Seth whispered for Graham to remain quiet, while he moved forward. He then stepped carefully ahead, and soon reached a massive embankment, up which on his hands and knees he crawled. He peered carefully over this, and saw, down in a sort of hollow, the whole Indian encampment! There were over twenty gathered around, most of whom were extended upon the ground asleep, while several sat listlessly smoking and gazing into the fire. Seth looked but a moment, as he knew there were watchful sentinels, and it was fortunate that he had not been discovered, as it was. Carefully retreating, he made his way down again to Graham.

"What's the news?" asked the latter.

"'Sh! not so loud. They're all there."

"*She* too?"

"I s'pose, though I didn't see her."

"What do you intend doing?"

"I don't know. We can't do nothin' to-night; it's too near morning. If we git her, we couldn't git a good 'nough start to give us a chance. We've got to wait till to-morrow night. There's a lot of 'em on the watch, too. We've got to lay low till daylight, and foller 'long behind 'em."

The two made their way off in a side direction, so as not to be likely to attract notice in the morning, should any of the savages take the back trail. Here they remained until daylight.

They heard the Indians, as soon as it was fully light, preparing their morning meal; and as they deemed they could see them without incurring great peril, they determined to obtain a glimpse of them, in order to assure themselves whether Ina was among them or not. Each had suspicion the company had separated, and that their trail had been overlooked in the darkness.

Accordingly, the two crept noiselessly to the top. There was a heavy, peculiar sort of brier growing on the summit of the embankment, which was fortunately so impenetrable as to effectually conceal their bodies. Seth pressed against this and peered over. His head just came above the undergrowth and he could plainly see all that was transpiring. Graham, with an unfortunate want of discretion, placed his arm on Seth's shoulder and *gazed over him!* Yet, singularly enough, neither was seen. Graham was just in the act of lowering his head, when the briers, which were so matted together as to hold the pressure against them like a woven band, gave way, and Seth rolled like a log down the embankment, directly among the savages!

CHAPTER VI. A RUN FOR LIFE

When the sad event just chronicled took place, and Seth made a rather unceremonious entrance into view of the savages, Graham felt that he too was in peril, and his life depended upon his own exertions. To have offered resistance would have been madness, as there were fully thirty Indians at hand. Flight was the only resource left, and without waiting to see the fate of Seth, our hero made a bound down the embankment, alighting at the bottom, and struck directly across the plain, toward the timber that lined the river. He had gained several hundred yards, when several prolonged yells told him that he was discovered, and was a flying fugitive. Casting his eye behind him, he saw five or six Indians already down the embankment and in full chase.

And now commenced a race for life and death. Graham was as fleet of foot as a deer, and as well trained and disciplined, but his pursuers numbered five of the swiftest runners of the Mohawk nation, and he feared he had at last found his match. Yet he was as skillful and cunning as he was sinewy and fleet of foot. The plain over which he was speeding was perfectly bare and naked for six or eight miles before him, while it stretched twice that distance on either hand before the slightest refuge was offered. Thus it will be seen that he took the only course which offered hope — a dead run for it, where the pursuers and pursued possessed equal advantages.

He was pretty certain that his pursuers possessed greater endurance than himself, and that in a long run he stood small chance of escape, while in a short race he believed he could distance any living Indian. So he determined to try the speed of his enemies.

As he heard their yells, he bounded forward almost at the top of his speed. The pursuers, however, maintained the same regular and rapid motion. Graham continued his exertions for about a half-mile, making such use of his arms and limbs as to give the impression that he was doing his utmost. Toward the latter part of the first mile, his speed began to slacken, and his dangling limbs and furtive glances behind him would have convinced any one that he was nigh exhausted.

But this was only a stratagem, and it succeeded as well as he could have wished. The Indians believed he had committed a common and fatal error — that of calling into play the uttermost strength and speed of which he was master at the outset, and that he was wearied out, while they themselves were just warming into the glow of the chase. Seeing this, they sent up a shout of exultation, and darted ahead at the top of their speed, each endeavoring to reach and tomahawk him before his companion.

But their surprise was unbounded when they saw the fugitive shoot ahead with the velocity of a racehorse, while his veins, too, were only filling with the hot blood of exertion. They saw this, and they saw, too, that should such speed continue long, he would be far beyond their reach, and all now ran as they never ran before.

We say Graham's stratagem succeeded. It did, and it gave him the knowledge he wished. It showed him that he had met his match! His pursuers, at least one or two of them, were nearly as fleet as was he; and, although he might distance them for a time, yet ere half the race was finished he would inevitably lose his vantage ground!

Could one have stood and gazed upon this race of life, he would have seen a thrilling scene. Far ahead, over a vast plain, a fugitive white man was flying, and his swift, steady gait showed that his limbs were well trained and were now put to their severest test. As his feet doubled with such quickness beneath him as to be almost invisible, the ground glided like a panorama from under them.

Behind were a half-dozen savages, their gleaming visages distorted with the passions of exultation, vengeance, and doubt, their garments flying in the wind, and their strength pressed to its utmost bounds. They were scattered at different distances from each other, and were spreading over the prairie, so as to cut off the fugitive's escape in every direction.

Two Indians maintained their places side by side, and it was evident that the pursuit would soon be left to them. The others were rapidly falling behind, and were already relaxing their exertions. Graham saw the state of things, and it thrilled him with hope. Could he not distance these also? Would they not leave him in such a case? And could he not escape ere he was compelled to give out from exhaustion?

"At any rate I will try, and God help me!" he uttered prayerfully, shooting ahead with almost superhuman velocity. He glanced back and saw his followers, and they seemed almost standing still, so rapidly did he leave them behind.

But as nature compelled him to again cease the terrific rate at which he was going, he saw his unwearied pursuers again recovering their lost ground. The parties now understood each other. The Indians saw his maneuvers, and avoided the trap, and kept on in the same unremitting, relentless speed, fully certain that this would sooner or later compel him to yield; while Graham knew that the only chance of prolonging the contest rested in his dropping into and continuing his ordinary speed.

They now sunk into the same steady and terribly monotonous run. Mile after mile flew beneath them, and still so exact and similar were their relative rates, that they were absolutely stationary with regard to each other! The two Indians now remained alone and they were untiring — they were determined to hold out to the end!

At last, Graham saw the friendly timber but a short distance from him. The trees seemed beckoning him to their friendly shelter, and, panting and gasping, he plunged in among them — plunged right ahead till he stood upon the bank of a large and rapidly-flowing stream.

When the Anglo-Saxon's body is pitted against that of the North American Indian, it sometimes yields; but when his mind takes the place of contestant, it *never* loses.

Graham gazed hurriedly around him, and in the space of a dozen seconds his faculties had wrought enough for a lifetime — wrought enough to save him.

Throwing his rifle aside, he waded carefully into the stream until he stood waist deep. Then sinking upon his face, he swam rapidly upward until he had gone a hundred yards. Here he struck out into the channel, swimming *up*-stream as well as *across* it, so as not to reach the bank at a lower point. The current was very swift, and required an exhausting outlay of his already fainting frame before he reached the opposite bank. Here he immediately sprung upon the shore, ran quickly a short distance down the stream, making his trail as plain as possible; and then springing into the stream, swam rapidly upward, remaining as close to the shore as possible, so as to avoid the resisting current. The reason of these singular movements will soon be plain.

The shore was lined thickly by overhanging bushes, and after swimming until he supposed it time for his pursuers to come up, he glided beneath their friendly shelter, and awaited the further development of things. Almost immediately after, both appeared upon the opposite bank, but at a point considerably lower down. Without hesitation, they sprung into the stream and swam across. As they landed, they commenced a search, and a yell announced the discovery of the trail. Instantly after, another yell proclaimed their disappointment, as they lost it in the river.

The savages supposed that the fugitive had again taken to the water, and had either drowned or reached the other side. At any rate, they had lost what they considered a certain prey, and with feelings of baffled malignity they sullenly swam back again, searched the other side an hour or so, and then took their way back to their companions.

CHAPTER VII. THE EXPERIENCE OF SETH

"By gracious! Stars and garters! &c.! &c.! This is a new way of introducing one's self!" exclaimed Seth, as he sprawled out among the savages around the council-fire.

The consternation of the Indians at this sudden apparition among them may well be imagined. The crackling of the undergrowth above had aroused them, yet the advent of Seth was so sudden and almost instantaneous that ere they could form a suspicion of the true nature of things, he was among them. Their habitual quickness of thought came to them at once. Graham was seen as he wheeled and fled, and as has been shown, a number sprung at once in pursuit, while a dozen leaped upon Seth, and as many tomahawks were raised.

"Now jest hold on," commanded Seth; "there ain't any need of being in a hurry. Plenty time to take my hair. Fact, by gracious."

His serio-comical manner arrested and amused his captors. They all paused and looked at him, as if expecting another outburst, while he contented himself with gazing at them with a look of scornful contempt. Seeing this, one sprung forward, and clenching his hair in a twist, hissed:

"Oh! cuss Yankee! we burn him!"

"If you know what's best, ole chap, you'll take yer paw off my head in a hurry. Ef you don't you mought find it rather convenient to."

The savage, as if to humor him, removed his hand and Seth's rifle, too. Seth gazed inquiringly at him a moment, and then, with an air of conscious superiority, said:

"I'll lend that to you awhile, provided you return it all right. Mind, you be keerful now, 'cause that ar' gun cost something down in New Hampshire."

From what has just been written, it will doubtless be suspected that Seth's conduct was a part which he was playing. When thrown into peril by the impatience of his companion, he saw at once that an attempt at flight was useless. Nothing was left but to submit to his misfortune with the best grace possible; and yet there was a way in which this submission could be effected which would result better for himself than otherwise. Had he offered resistance, or submitted despairingly, as many a man would have done, he would doubtless have been tomahawked instantly. So, with a readiness of thought which was astonishing, he assumed an air of reckless bravado. This, as we have shown, had the desired result thus far. How it succeeded after, will be seen in the remaining portion of this history.

Seth Jones was a man whose character could not be read in an hour, or day. It required a long companionship with him to discover the nicely-shaded points, and the characteristics which seemed in many cases so opposite. United with a genial, sportive humor and apparent frankness, he was yet far-seeing and cautious, and could read the motives of a man almost at a glance. With a countenance which seemed made expressly to vail his soul, his very looks were deceptive; and, when he chose to play a certain *role,* he could do it to perfection. Had any one seen him when the conversation above recorded took place, he would have unhesitatingly set him down as a natural-born idiot.

"How you like to burn, eh, Yankee?" asked a savage, stooping and grinning horribly in his face.

"I don't know; I never tried it," replied Seth, with as much *non-chalance* as though it was a dinner to which he was referring.

"E-e-e-e! you will try it, Yankee."

"Don't know yet; there are various opinions about that, p'raps. When the thing is did I mought believe it."

"You *sizzle* nice — nice meat — good for burn!" added another savage, grasping and feeling his arm.

"Just please do not pinch, my friend.'"

The savage closed his fingers like iron rods, and clenched the member till Seth thought it would be crushed. But, though the pain was excruciating, he manifested not the least feeling. The Indian tried again, and again, till he gave up and remarked, expressive of his admiration of the man's pluck:

"Good Yankee! stand pinch well."

"Oh! you wa'n't pinching me, was you? Sorry, I didn't know it. Try again, you mought p'raps do better."

The savage, however, retired, and another stepped forward and grasped the captive's hand.

"Soft, like squaw's hand — let me feel it," he remarked, shutting his own over it like a vise. Seth winced not in the least; but as the Indian in turn was about to relinquish his attempt at making sport for his comrades, Seth said:

"Your paws don't appear very horny," and closed over it with a terrific gripe. The savage stood like a martyr, till Seth felt the bones of his hand actually displacing, and yielding like an apple. He determined, as he had in reality suffered himself, to be revenged, and closed his fingers tighter and more rigid till the poor wretch sprung to his feet, and howled with pain!

"Oh! did I hurt you?" he asked, with apparent solicitude, as the savage's hand slid from his own with much the appearance of a wet glove. The discomfited Indian made no reply but retired amid the jeers of his comrades. Seth, without moving a muscle, seated himself deliberately upon the ground, and coolly asked a savage to lend him a pipe. It is known, that when an Indian sees such hardihood and power, as their captive had just evinced, he does not endeavor to conceal his admiration. Thus it was not strange that Seth's impudent request was complied with. One handed him a well-filled pipe, with a grin in which could be distinctly seen admiration, exultation, and anticipated revenge. From the looks of the others, it was plain they anticipated an immense deal of sport. Our present hero continued smoking, lazily watching the volumes of vapor, as they slowly rolled before and around him. His captors sat about him a moment, conversing in their own tongue (every word of which, we may remark, was perfectly understood by Seth), when one arose and stepped forward before him.

"White man strong; him pinch well, but me make him cry."

So saying he stooped, and removing the captive's cap, seized a long tuft of yellow hair which had its roots at the temple. A stab in the eye would not have caused an acuter twinge of pain; but, as he jerked it forth by the roots, Seth gave not the slightest indication save a stronger whiff at the pipe. The savages around did not suppress a murmur of admiration. Seeing no effect from this torture, the tormentor again stooped and caught another tuft that grew low upon the neck. Each single hair felt like the point of a needle thrust into the skin, and as it came forth, the Indians seated around noticed a livid paleness, like the track of a cloud, quickly flash over their captive's countenance. He looked up in his tormentor's eyes with an indescribable look. For a moment he fixed a gaze upon him, that, savage as he was, caused a strange shiver of dread to run through him.

To say that Seth cared nothing for these inflicted agonies would be absurd. Had the savage dreamed what a whirlwind of hate and revenge he had awakened by them he would not have attempted what he did. It was only by an almost unaccountable power that Seth controlled the horrible pains of both body and mind he suffered. He felt as though it was impossible to prevent himself from writhing on the ground in torment, and springing at his persecutor and tearing him limb from limb. But he had been schooled to Indian indignities, and bore them unflinchingly.

His temple had the appearance of white parchment, with innumerable bloody points in it, as the blood commenced oozing from the wound, and his neck seemed as though the skin had been scraped off! His momentary paleness had been caused by the sickening pain and the intensest passion. His look at the savage was *to remember him.* After the events which have just transpired they remained seated a moment in silence. At last one who appeared to be the leader, addressed, in an undertone, the Indian whom we have just seen retire from the post of tormentor. Seth, however, caught the words, and had he not, it is not probable he would have successfully undergone the last trying ordeal.

The same savage again stepped forward in the circle before the helpless captive, and removing the cap which had been replaced, clinched the long yellow locks in his left hand and threw the head backward. Then whipping out his scalping-knife, he flashed it around his head with the rapidity of lightning. The skin was not pierced, and it was only an artifice. Seth never took his eyes from the Indian during this awful minute.

The tormentor again retired. The savages were satisfied, but Seth was not. He handed his pipe back, replaced his cap, and rising to his feet, surveyed for a few seconds the group around. He then addressed the leader.

"Can the white man now try the red-man's courage?"

The voice sounded like another person's. Yet the chief noticed it not, and nodded assent to the request, while the looks of the others showed the eagerness and interest they felt in these dreadful proceedings.

The savage who had inflicted all this agony seated himself directly beside the chief. Seth stepped to him, and grasping his arm pressed moderately. The Indian gave a scornful grunt. Seth then stooped and gently took the tomahawk from his belt. He raised it slowly on high, bent down till his form was like the crouching panther ready to spring. The glittering blade was seen to flash as it circled through the air, and the next instant it crashed clean through the head of the unsuspecting savage!

CHAPTER VIII. AN UNEXPECTED MEETING

Wearied and exhausted, Graham crawled forth from the water, and lay down awhile to rest himself upon the soft, velvety carpet of grass. Here, overcome by the terrific strain which his system had undergone, he fell into a deep and lasting sleep. When he awoke, the day had far advanced, and the sun was already past the meridian. After fully awakening, and fervently thanking Heaven for his remarkable preservation and escape, he commenced debating with himself upon the best course for him to pursue. He was now alone in the great wilderness, and what step should he next take? Should he endeavor to hunt up his friend Haverland, or should he press on in the pursuit of the object which had led him thus far?

While these questions were yet unanswered, he mechanically cast his eye up the river, and started as he saw a small canoe coming around a bend quite a distance from him. He had just time to see that there were two beings in it, when prudence warned him to make himself invisible. He stepped behind the trunk of a massive king of the forest, and watched with eager interest the approach of the newcomers. The light canoe shot rapidly over the placid surface of the river, and in a few moments was abreast of him. He saw that the two occupants were white men, and he scanned their countenances with deep interest. The stronger of the two was seated in the center of the light vessel, and dipped the ashen blades deep into the water at every stroke. The other, seemingly an older man, was seated in the stern, and while he controlled the actions of the other, scanned either shore with the experienced eye of the frontiersman. Graham believed, though he knew he had been careful, that his presence was suspected, as the canoe, apparently without any intent of its occupants, sheered off toward the opposite shore. He remained concealed until it was directly abreast of him, when a sudden suspicion flashed over him that one of the men was Haverland, although it was so long since he had seen him that it was impossible to satisfy himself upon that point without a closer view. However, they were white men, and he determined to risk the probabilities of their being friends. In a subdued voice, without coming into view himself, he called to them. He knew he was heard, for the man at the oars halted a second, and glanced furtively toward the shore; but at a slight sign from the other he again bent to them, and they both continued, as though they suspected no danger.

"Hallo, my friends!" called he, in a louder tone, but still concealing himself. There was no notice, however, taken of him, save he fancied a quicker propulsion of the boat forward. He now stepped boldly forth and called:

"Do not be suspicious; I am a friend."

This brought them to a pause, while the one in the stern spoke:

"We are not satisfied of that: for what business have you here?"

"I might with equal justice put that question to you?"

"If you choose to give no answer, we can't wait to bandy words with you. Go ahead, Haverland."

"Hold! Is that Alfred Haverland with you?"

"Suppose it is? What is that to you?"

"He is the man whom, above all others, I wish to see. I am Everard Graham; and, perhaps he remembers the name." The woodman now turned toward the shore with a stare of wonder. A minute sufficed.

"It's he, Ned, sure enough."

With these words he turned the canoe toward shore. A few strokes sent it up against the bank, and he sprung out and grasped the hand of his young friend.

"Why, Graham, what in the name of the seven wonders has brought you here? I forgot — you *did* promise me a visit somewhere about this time, but so many other things have transpired as to make it slip my mind altogether. And I can assure you, I have had enough to break the heart of any ordinary mortal," he added, in a choking voice.

Explanations were then given; and the wonder, gratitude, and apprehension, that followed Graham's story, may be imagined. Before these were given, Haverland introduced his companion, Ned Haldidge.

"Seth promised to bring Ina back," said he, "but I could not bear to remain idle while he alone was searching for her. This good friend here, who has had much experience in border warfare, willingly joined me. I suppose you would like to see the mother; but if you did, you would see a well-nigh broken-hearted one, and I cannot bear to meet her until I have learned more of our darling daughter."

"And if them cowardly Mohawks don't rue the day they commenced their infernal work, then Ned Haldidge is mightily mistaken!" exclaimed that individual, warmly.

"I don't know," smiled Graham, "but that with our present number and present feelings, we might make an open attack upon them, especially as we have a friend in the camp."

"No, sir; that'll never do!" replied the hunter, with a shake of the head. "They can never be overcome in that way. We could have brought a dozen men with us who could have blown the cowards to atoms, but 'twouldn't do."

"You then rely wholly upon stratagem, eh?"

"Nothing else will do with *them* critters."

"And Heaven only knows whether that will," remarked Haverland, in a desponding tone.

"Ah! don't give way, Alf; wait till it's time."

"You must pardon any exhibition of weakness," said he, recovering himself. "Though I feel the strength of an army in these limbs of mine, yet I have the heart of a *father* in this bosom, and I can do any thing for the recovery of my darling daughter. Oh! I can hear her screams yet, as she was torn from us on that night."

Graham and Haldidge remained silent, respecting his deep and moving grief. Soon the father spoke again, and this time his voice and manner were changed.

"But why stand we here idle? Is there nothing for us to do? Are we to remain desponding, when a single effort may save her?"

"That's just what I've been thinking ever since we stopped here," replied Haldidge. "I don't see any use in waiting, especially when there *is* use in doing something."

"Let us depart, then. You will accompany us, of course, Graham?"

"Certainly; but I should like to inquire your intentions?" asked he, pausing on the bank a moment, as the others seated themselves.

"I should think you would remember we can have but *one* intention," answered Haverland, in a tone of slight rebuke.

"That is not exactly what I meant. Of course, I knew your ultimate intention, but I wished to inquire what course you intended to pursue."

"Oh, that's it!" replied Haldidge. "I've been considerable among the red-skins of this region, and know that they can be sooner reached by going down the river some distance further — several miles below this bend — and taking the land."

"But my experience tells me you are mistaken this time. Ina's captors are now at no great distance, and the shortest course to them, you will find, is a direct line from here, across the open prairie, the other side of the river."

"At any rate, we will cross to the opposite bank; so step in."

"Wait a minute. What does that mean?"

As Graham spoke, he pointed quickly up the river. From the position of the two within the boat, they could discern nothing.

"Jump ashore, quick, and pull the boat out of sight. There's something afoot, and you mustn't be seen," exclaimed Graham, excitedly, in an undertone, as he stooped and grasped the prow of the canoe. The men sprung ashore, and in an instant the vessel was hauled up out of sight, while the three made themselves invisible, and from their hiding-places eagerly watched the river.

The object which had arrested the attention of Graham was a second canoe, which was just making its appearance round the bend above, which had first brought his new friends to view. This latter one was of about the same size, and could be seen to hold either three or four persons. The dark-tufted heads of the occupants, rising like statues in the boat, showed unmistakably that they were Indians.

As it came nearer and nearer, Haldidge whispered there was a fourth person in the stern, *and she was a female.* Haverland and Graham breathed hard, for a wild hope filled the heart of each; but as the canoe came abreast of them, while they could plainly distinguish the features of the three savages, they could not gain a glimpse of the fourth person. She was covered by an Indian shawl, and her head was bowed low upon her bosom, as though in painful thought.

"Let us fire and send these three dogs to eternity," whispered Graham.

Haldidge raised his hand.

"'Twon't do; there may be others about, and if that other one is Ina, it may only be the means of her destruction. Alf, do you think that is her?"

"I can't tell — yes, by Heaven, 'tis her! Look! she has moved her shawl. Let us rescue her at once!" exclaimed the father, rising, and about to start.

"Hold!" imperatively and half angrily commanded Haldidge, "you will spoil all by your rashness. Don't you see it is near night? They are now below us, and we cannot get them in such a range as to insure us each of them. Wait till it is darker, and we will pursue them. I have a plan which I think cannot fail. Just restrain yourself a short time, and I will bring things about in a manner that will surprise them as much as it will you."

Haverland sunk down again beside the others. The night was now fast coming on, and in a few minutes the light birch canoe was shoved noiselessly into the water, and the three made ready for the race for life and death.

CHAPTER IX. THE CHASE

The night was even closer at hand than our friends suspected. In the forest, where the withdrawal of the sun was almost simultaneous with darkness, it came without much warning. The gloom was already settling over the water, and Haverland instantly shot the canoe from under the shrubbery out into the stream. There were rowlocks and oars for a second person, and Graham took up a couple of them and joined his labors with his friend, while Haldidge took the steering-oar. As they passed boldly into the channel, the canoe ahead was just disappearing around a bend below.

"Come, this won't do; we mustn't let them keep out of our sight," said Haverland, dipping his oars deep into the water.

A heavy darkness was fast settling over the river, and our friends noted another thing. A thick, peculiar fog, or mist, such as is often seen of summer nights, upon a sheet of water, was already beginning to envelop the bank and river. This, as will be evident, while it would allow the pursuers to approach the Indian canoe much closer than otherwise, still gave the latter a much greater chance of eluding them. Haldidge hardly knew whether to be pleased with this or not.

"It may help us in the beginning, boys, but we've got to hold on till it's fairly down on us. If the rascals catch a glimpse of us before, they'll give us the slip as sure as fate. Just lay on your oars a few minutes. We can float down with the current."

"I allow it's the best plan, although I am much in favor of dashing ahead, and ending the matter at once," remarked Graham, nervously handling his oars.

"And while I think of it," pursued Haldidge, "I don't see as it would do any hurt to muffle the oars."

Before starting they had abundantly provided themselves with means for this, and in a few moments a quantity of cloth was forced into the rowlocks, so as to be able to give full sweep to the oars without making enough noise to attract suspicion from the shore, unless an ear was listening more intently than usual.

By this time, too, the thick mist mentioned had enveloped the river in an impenetrable cloud, and they shot boldly into it. The light vessel flew as swiftly and noiselessly as a bird over the water. Haldidge understood every turn and eddy in the stream, and guided the canoe with unerring certainty around the sharp bends, and by the rocks whose black heads now and then shot backward within a few feet of their side.

In this way a mile was passed, when he raised his hand as a signal for them to cease efforts for a moment.

"Listen!" he uttered.

All did so, and faintly, yet distinctly and distantly, they heard the almost inaudible dip of oars, and the click of the rowlocks.

"Is that above or below?" asked Haverland, bending his head and intently listening.

"I think we have *passed* them, sure enough," replied Graham. The sound certainly appeared to come from above them, and all were constrained to believe that, rowing as swiftly and powerfully as they did, they must have swept by them in the darkness without suspecting their proximity.

"Can it be possible?" questioned Haldidge, wonderingly and doubtingly.

But such was the character of the river-banks at this point, that all had been deceived in listening to the sounds, and the Indians were all the time leaving them far behind. It was not until they heard unmistakably the sounds receding in the distance that they became conscious of the true state of matters. At that moment, as they were dying out, they all heard them plainly enough far below.

"We might have known it," said Haldidge, in vexation. "You've got to lay to it, to catch them now."

"But is there not danger of running afoul of them?"

"Not if we are careful. I think they will run in to shore, soon, and if so, it will be the eastern bank. I will hug that closely, and keep my ears open."

The two now bent to their oars and redoubled powers. They dipped the ashen blades deeply, and pulled until they bent dangerously, while the water parted in foam at the rushing prow, and spread away in a foamy pyramid behind.

The effect of this was soon apparent. The rattle of the oars ahead grew plainer and plainer at each stroke, and it was evident they were gaining finely. Haverland's arm was thrilled with tenfold power, as he felt that he was rushing to the rescue of his only darling child, and he only wished he might have the chance to spring upon her abductors and rend them limb from limb. Graham's heart beat faster as he reflected that, perhaps, in a few moments, he should be face to face with her who had hovered about his pillow, in visions, for many a night.

Haldidge sat perfectly cool and possessed. He had formed his plan and imparted it to the others; it was to pursue the canoe noiselessly until they were almost upon it, when the instant they were near enough to distinguish forms, they would fire upon the Indians, and dash ahead and rescue Ina at all hazards.

_____

This Haldidge, who has been introduced to notice in this chapter, was a middle-aged man, who ten years before had emigrated from the settlements along the Hudson, with a company which had formed the settlement from which he started, and where we saw Haverland and his wife and sister safely domiciled. He was a married man, and his cabin happened to be on the outskirts of the village. He joined and led the whites in several forays against the savages, when the latter became too troublesome; and in this way became a prominent object for the Indians' hatred. His residence became known to them, and one dark, stormy night a half-dozen made a descent upon it. By the merest chance, Haldidge was in the village at that time, and thus escaped their malignant revenge. Being disappointed of their principal prey, they cowardly vented their hatred upon his defenseless wife and child. When the father returned, he found them both tomahawked, side by side, and weltering in each other's blood. So silently had this onslaught been made that not a neighbor suspected anything wrong, and were horror-struck to find that such deadly peril had been so near their own doors. Haldidge took a fearful revenge upon the destroyers of his happiness. He succeeded, a couple of years afterward, in discovering them, and, before six months were over, shot them all. As may be supposed, his natural aversion to the race was intensified by this tragic occurrence, and had become so distinguished, that his name was a terror to the savages in that section. This will account for his readiness in accompanying Haverland upon his perilous expedition.

As was said, our friends were rapidly gaining upon the Indian canoe. At the rate at which they were going, they would be up to them in the course of half an hour. They were so close to the shore, as to see the dark line of the shrubbery along the bank, and several times an overhanging limb brushed over their heads. Suddenly Haldidge raised his hand again. All ceased rowing and listened. To their consternation not the slightest sound was heard. Graham leaned over, and placed his ear almost to the water, but detected nothing but the soft ripple of the stream against the roots and dipping branches along the shore.

"Can it be?" he asked, with a painful whisper, as he raised his head, "that we have been heard?"

"I do not think so," replied Haldidge, apparently in as much doubt as the rest.

"Then they have run in to shore, and departed."

"I fear that has been done."

"But we have kept so close to the shore, would we not have seen or heard the boat?"

"Provided they landed alone. They may have run in this very minute, and may not be more than a few yards off."

"If so, we must hear them yet, and it won't do to slide down upon them in the manner we are now going or we shall find ourselves in the same fix we expected to get them in."

"Very true, and a good suggestion," remarked Haldidge, and as he did so, he reached up and caught an overhanging limb, and held the canoe still.

"Now, boys, if you've got ears — "

"Sh! Look there!" interrupted Haverland, in an excited whisper.

Each turned his head and saw what appeared to be a common lighted candle floating upon the surface of the stream. It was a small point of light, which at intervals glowed with a fuller redness, and which for the time completely confounded our friends. On it came as noiselessly as death, gliding forward with such a smooth, regular motion as to show that it was certainly borne by the current.

"What in the name of — "

"Stop!" cried Haldidge; "that's the canoe we're after! It's the light of one of their pipes we see. Are your guns ready?"

"Yes," replied the two, just loud enough for him to hear.

"Make right toward it, then, and fire the instant you see your mark. Now!"

At the same instant he released his hold upon the limb, and they threw all their force upon their oars. The canoe bounded like a ball directly ahead, and seemed about to cut the other in twain. A minute after, the shadowy outlines of three forms could be dimly seen, and the avenging rifles were already raised, when the beacon-light was suddenly extinguished and the Indian canoe vanished as if by magic.

"It's one of their tricks!" excitedly exclaimed Haldidge. "Dash ahead! Curse them; they can't be far off."

The two dropped their rifles, and again seized the oars, and Haldidge sheered it abruptly up-stream, for he fancied they had turned in that direction. He bent his head forward, expecting each moment to see the forms of their enemies loom up to view in the mist, but he was mistaken; no savages greeted his anxious vision. He guided his boat in every direction — across the stream, up and down — but all to no purpose. They had surely lost their prey this time. The Indians had undoubtedly heard the pursuers — had muffled their own oars, and so proceeded as silently as they.

"Hold a minute!" commanded Haldidge.

As they rested, they listened deeply and intently.

"Do you hear anything?" he asked, leaning breathlessly forward. "There! Listen again."

They could distinguish the ripple of water, growing fainter and fainter each minute.

"They are below us again, and now for a trial of speed."

The two needed no more incentives, and for a time the canoe skimmed over the water with astonishing speed. The moon was now up, and there were patches in the stream, where the wind had blown away the fog, and being exposed to the light, were as clear as midday. Now and then they crossed such spots, sometimes but a few feet wide, and at others several rods. At these times the shore on either hand was perfectly outlined, and they glided over with a sort of instinctive terror, as they felt how easily a enemy might be concealed.

In crossing one of these, broader than usual, a glimpse of the Indian canoe showed itself, just disappearing upon the opposite shore. They were not more than a hundred yards apart, and they bounded toward it with great rapidity. The patches of light became more frequent, and the fog was evidently disappearing. Quite a breeze had arisen, which was fast sweeping it away. Haldidge kept close in to the eastern shore, feeling sure that their enemies would land upon this side!

Suddenly the whole mist lifted from the surface of the water in a volume, and rolled off toward the woods. The bright moon was reflected a long distance, and the pursuers gazed searchingly about, fully expecting to see their enemies not a dozen rods away. But they were again doomed to disappointment. Not a ripple disturbed the waters, except their own canoe. The moon was directly overhead, so that there was not a shadow cast along the banks, sufficient to conceal the slightest object. The Indians had evidently landed, and were far distant in the forest.

"It is no use," remarked Haverland, gloomily, "they are gone, and we might as well be too."

"It is a sore disappointment," said Graham.

"And as much so to me as to either of you," said Haldidge. "I have an old score against the infernal wretches that will take many years to wipe out. I hoped to do something toward it to-night, but have been prevented. There is no use of hoping more at this time; they have eluded us, that is self-evident, and we must try some other means. No doubt you are wearied of body as well as of mind, and don't fancy particularly this remaining out in the river here, a shot for any one who might possess the will; so let us go into shore, have a rest, and talk over things." Dispiritedly and gloomily the trio ran the canoe to the bank and landed.

CHAPTER X. A COUPLE OF INDIAN CAPTIVES

So sudden, so unexpected, so astonishing was the crash of Seth's tomahawk through the head of the doomed savage, that, for a moment after, not an Indian moved or spoke. The head was nearly cleft in twain (for an arm fired by consuming passion had driven it), and the brains were spattered over numbers of those seated around. Seth himself stood a second to satisfy himself the work was complete, when he turned, walked to his seat, sat down, coolly folded his arms and *commenced whistling*.

A second after, nearly every savage drew a deep breath, as if a load had been removed from his heart; then each looked at his neighbor, and in the scowling, ridged brows, the glittering eyes, the distorted visages, the strained breathing through the set teeth, could be read the fearful intention. Every face but that of the chieftain's was livid with fury. He alone sat perfectly unagitated. Three Indians arose, and, grasping their knives, stood before him waiting for the expected words.

"Touch him not," said he, with a shake of the head; "him no right here."

As the chief spoke, he tapped his forehead significantly with his finger, meaning that the prisoner was demented. The others believed the same, still it was hard to quell the pent-up fire which was scorching their breasts. But his word was law inviolate, and without a murmur, they seated themselves on the ground again.

Seth, although his eye appeared vacant and unmeaning, had noted all these movements with the keenness of the eagle. He knew that a word or sign from the chief would be sufficient to hack him to a thousand pieces. When he stood before his inhuman tormentor, with the keen tomahawk in his hand, the certainty of instant death or prolonged torture would not have prevented him from taking the savage vengeance he did. Now that it was over, he was himself again. His natural feelings came back, and with it the natural desire for life. The words of the chief convinced him that he was regarded as either insane or idiotic, and consequently as not deserving death. Still, although saved for the present, he ever stood in imminent peril. The fallen savage had living friends, who would seize the first opportunity to avenge his death. At any rate, let matters stand as they might, Seth felt that he was in hot quarters, and the safest course was to get out of them as soon as possible.

It was perhaps ten minutes after the horrid deed, that the savages commenced bestirring themselves. Several arose and carried their comrade to one side, while the others commenced preparations for taking up the day's march. At this moment the runners who had pursued Graham to the water's edge, returned, and the tragical occurrence was soon made known to them. A perfect battery of deadly, gleaming eyes were opened upon Seth, but he stood it unflinchingly. The Indians would have relished well the idea of venting their baffled vengeance upon the helpless captive in their hands; but the commanding presence of their chief restrained the slightest demonstration, and they contented themselves with meaning looks.

One thing did not escape Seth's notice from the first, and it was an occasion of wonder and speculation to him. Nothing could be seen of Ina. In fact, the appearance of things was such as to lead one to believe that the savages knew nothing of her. Could it be that he and Graham had been mistaken in the party? Could some other tribe have made off with her? Or, had they separated, and taken her in another direction? As he ruminated upon these questions, he became convinced that the last suggested the certain answer. They could not have mistaken the party, as they had never lost sight of the trail since taking it; and, moreover, he had noticed several slight occurrences, since his advent among them, that satisfied him, beyond a doubt, of the identity of the party with the one which had descended upon the home of the woodman. From the caution which the aggressors evinced in their flight, together with the haste with which it had been conducted, it was plain they had some fears of pursuit; and to guard their treasure, a number had left them at a favorable point, intending to join the main body where pursuit was not to be expected, or where the pursuers had been sufficiently misled to warrant it. As he reflected, Seth was satisfied that this was the only and true explanation of her non-appearance.

The preparations were soon completed, and the Indians commenced moving forward. If Seth had entertained any doubts of their intention relating to him, they were soon dispelled by his experience. It was not at all likely that he would be reserved as a prisoner, unless they intended to put him to some use. Accordingly he found himself loaded down with an enormous burden, consisting mostly of food, in the shape of deer's meat, which the savages had brought with them.

They buried their fallen comrade, without the ceremony and mourning which might be expected. The North American Indian rarely gives way to his emotions, except upon such occasions as the burial of one of their number, a "war-dance," or something similar, when the whole nest of devilish passions is allowed free vent. They indulged in no such ceremonies — if ceremonies they may be called — at this time. A comparatively shallow grave was dug, and into this the fallen one was placed in an upright position, his face turned toward the east. His rifle, knives, and all his clothing were buried with him.

The day was a suffocating one in August, and Seth's sufferings were truly great. He was naturally lithe, wiry, and capable of enduring prolonged exertion, but, unfortunately for him, the savages had become aware of this and loaded him accordingly. Most of the journey was through the forest where the arching tree-tops shut out the withering rays of the sun. Had they encountered any such open plains as the one passed over near their encampment, Seth would have never lived through it. As it was, his load nearly made him insensible to pain. A consuming thirst was ever tormenting him, although he found abundant means to slake it in the numberless rills which gurgled through the wilderness.

"How Yankee like it?" grinned a savage by his side, stooping and peering fiendishly into his face.

"First rate; goes nice. Say, you, s'posen you try it?"

"Ugh! walk faster," and a whack accompanied the word.

"Now I cac'late, I'm going to walk just about as fast as I durned please, and if you ain't a mind to wait, you can heave ahead. Fact, by gracious."

And Seth did not hasten his steps in the least. Toward noon he found he should be obliged to have a short rest or give out entirely. He knew it would be useless to ask, and consequently he determined to take it without asking. So, unloosing the cords which bound the pack to his back, he let it fall to the ground, and, seating himself upon it, again went to whistling.

"Go faster, Yankee — you no keep up!" exclaimed one, giving him a stunning blow.

"See here, you, p'raps you don't know who it mought be you insulted in that way. I'm Seth Jones, from New Hampshire, and consequently you'll be keerful of tetching me."

The savage addressed was upon the point of striking him insolently to the earth, when the chieftain interfered.

"No touch pale-face — him tired — rest a little."

Some unaccountable whim had possessed the savage, as this mercy was entirely unexpected by Seth, and he knew not how to account for it, unless it might be he was reserving him for some horrible torture.

The resting-spell was but a moment, however, and just as Seth had begun to really enjoy it, the chieftain gave orders for the replacement of the load. Seth felt disposed to tamper awhile, for the sake of prolonging his enjoyment, but, on second thought, concluded it the better plan not to cross the chief who had been so lenient to him thus far. So, with a considerable number of original remarks, and much disputation about the placing of the burden, he shouldered it at last and trudged forward.

Seth was right in his conjectures about Ina. Toward the latter part of the day, the three Indians who had been pursued by our other friends, rejoined the main party, bearing her with them. She noticed her companion in captivity at once, but no communication passed between them. A look of melancholy relief escaped her as she became assured that her parents were still safe, and that only she and her new friend were left to the sufferings and horrors of captivity. But there was enough in that to damp even such a young and hopeful spirit as was hers. Not death alone, but a fate from the sensuous captors far worse than death itself, was to be apprehended. In the future, there was but one Hand that could sustain and safely deliver them, and to that One she looked for deliverance.

CHAPTER XI. STILL IN PURSUIT

"It seems the devil himself is helping them imps!" remarked Haldidge, as they landed.

"But I trust Heaven is aiding us," added Haverland.

"Heaven will, if we help ourselves, and now as I'm in this scrape, I'm bound to see the end. Look for trail."

"It's poor work I'm thinking we'll make, groping in this moonlight," said Graham.

"While there's life there's hope. Scatter 'long the bank, and search every foot of land. I'll run upstream a ways, as I've an idea they landed not far off."

The hunter disappeared, with these words, and Graham and Haverland commenced their work in an opposite direction. The branches overhanging the water were carefully lifted up, and the muddy shore examined; the suspicious bending or parting of the undergrowth was followed by the minutest scrutiny and although the heavy darkness was against them, yet it would have required a most guarded trail to have escaped their vision. But their efforts were useless; no trail was detected; and convinced that the savages must have landed upon the opposite side, they turned to retrace their steps. As they did so, a low whistle from the hunter reached their ears.

"What does that mean?" asked Graham.

"He has discovered something. Let us hasten."

"What is it, Haldidge?" asked Haverland, as they reached the hunter.

"Here's their tracks as sure as I'm a sinner, and it's my private opine they ain't fur off neither."

"Shall we wait till daylight before we undertake to follow it?"

"I am much afraid we shall have to, as there may be signs which we might miss in this darkness. Day can't be far off."

"Several hours yet."

"Well, we will make ourselves comfortable until then."

With these words the trio seated themselves upon the earth, and kept up a low conversation until morning. As soon as the faint light appeared, they detected the Indian canoe a short distance up the bank, secreted beneath a heavy, overhanging mass of undergrowth. As it was during the summer season, their pursuit was continued at an early hour, so the savages could have had but a few hours' start at the most. With Ina they could not proceed very rapidly, and our friends were sanguine of overtaking them ere the day closed.

The only apprehension the pursuers felt was that the three savages, fully conscious now that their enemies were upon their trail, might hasten to rejoin the main body, and thus cut off all hope. They could not be many miles apart, and must have made some preparations for this contingency.

The trail to the hunter's eye was distinct and easily followed. He took the lead, striding rapidly forward, while Haverland and Graham were continually on the look-out for danger. Haverland was somewhat fearful that the savages, finding they could not avoid being overtaken, would halt and form an ambush into which the hunter would blindly lead them. The latter, however, although he appeared culpably rash and heedless, understood Indian tactics better; he knew no halt would be made until the savages were compelled to do so.

"Ah! — see here!" exclaimed Haldidge, suddenly pausing.

"What's the trouble?" queried Graham, stepping hastily forward with Haverland.

"Their camping-ground; that is all."

Before them were more visible signs of the trail than they had yet witnessed. A heap of ashes was upon the ground; and as Haverland kicked them apart, he discovered the embers still red and glowing. Sticks were broken and scattered around, and all the varied evidences of an Indian camp were to be seen.

"How long ago was this place vacated?" asked Graham.

"Not three hours."

"We must be close upon them."

"Rather, yes."

"Let us hasten forward, then."

"You see by these coals that they didn't start until daylight, and as that gal of yourn, Haverland, can't travel very fast, of course they've had to take their time."

"Very true; although disappointment has attended us thus far, I begin to feel a little of my natural hope return. I trust that this opportunity will not escape us."

"Ah! more signs yet," exclaimed Graham, who had been examining the ground for several yards around.

"What now?"

"That's a piece of her dress, is it not?"

And he held up a small, fluttering rag in his hands. The father eagerly took it, and examined it.

"Yes; that is Ina's; I hope no violence has placed it in our hands," and several involuntary tears coursed down his cheek at the illusion.

"I'm thinking she left it there on purpose to guide us," remarked Graham.

"She must have seen us, of course, and has done all she could to guide us."

"Very probable; but it strikes me rather forcibly that we are gaining nothing in particular by remaining here. Remember, the savages are *going* all the time."

Thus admonished, the three set rapidly forward again, the hunter taking the lead as before. The pursuit was kept up without halting until near noon. Conscious that they were rapidly gaining upon the fugitives, it was necessary to proceed with the extremest caution. The breaking of a twig, the falling of a leaf, startled and arrested their steps, and not a word was exchanged except in the most careful whisper. Haldidge was some dozen yards in advance, and the eyes of his companions were upon him, when they saw him suddenly pause and raise his hand as a signal for them to halt. They did so, and stooping downward, he commenced examining the leaves before him.

A moment sufficed. He turned and motioned his two companions forward.

"Just as I feared," he moodily exclaimed, in a half whisper.

"What's the matter?" asked Haverland, anxiously.

"*The two trails join here,*" he answered.

"Are you not mistaken?" asked Haverland, knowing that he was not, and yet catching at the faintest hope held out to him.

"No, sir; there's no mistake. Instead of three Indians, we've got over forty to follow up now."

"Shall we do it?"

"Shall we do it? Of course we shall; it's the only chance of ever getting a sight of Ina again."

"I know it, and yet the hope is so faint; they must know we are in pursuit, and what can we do against ten times our number?"

"No telling yet; come, strike ahead again."

With these words, the hunter turned and plunged deeper into the forest. Graham and Haverland silently followed, and in a few minutes the three were proceeding as carefully and silently as before through the dense wood.

As yet our friends had partaken of nothing, and began to experience the pangs of hunger; but, of course, in the present instance, these were disregarded. Somewhere near the middle of the afternoon, they came upon another spot where the savages had halted. Here, if Haverland and Graham had any lingering doubts of what the hunter had said, they were soon removed. It was plain that a large Indian party had halted upon this spot but a few hours before, and it was equally evident that they had taken no pains to conceal the traces they had made. If they had any suspicions of pursuit, they had no apprehensions of the consequences, as they were well aware of the disparity between the two forces, and scorned the whites.

This was gratifying on the other hand to the hunter. He knew well enough that as matters stood at present, he could hope for nothing except through his own cunning and stratagem; and, for this reason it was very probable that the Indians were satisfied no attempt would be made. They did not take into consideration that there was an enemy in their camp.

Considerable remains of the meal were discovered, and served to satisfy the wants of our friends for the present. The early time in the afternoon showed them that thus far they had gained quite rapidly upon the savages. It was the earnest wish of the three that they should come up to the Indian party by nightfall; but this expectation was doomed to a sudden disappointment; for in a few hours they reached a point where the trail *divided again.*

This was unaccountable even to the hunter, and for a few moments our friends stood perfectly non-plused. They had not looked for this, and knew not the slightest reason for it.

"This beats all creation!" remarked Haldidge, as he again examined the trail.

"Depend upon it, there is something meant in this," observed Haverland, with an air of deep concern.

"It is some stratagem of the imps which we must understand before going further."

"They must entertain different ideas of us from what we thought. You may safely believe that this is some plan to mislead us, and if there is ever a time when our wits shall be demanded it has now come."

During this fragmentary conversation, the hunter was minutely examining the trail. Graham and Haverland watched him a few seconds in silence, when the latter asked:

"Do you make anything of it?"

"Nothing more. The trail divides here; the main body proceeds onward in a direct line, while the minor trail leads off to the west. The division must have been very unequal, for as near as I can judge the smaller party does not number over three or four at the most. No efforts have been made to conceal their traces, and there is either a deep-laid scheme afloat, or they don't care a fig for us."

"Very probably both," remarked Graham. "They care enough for us to take good care to remain out of our reach, when they do not possess advantages over us, and have already shown their skill in not laying but in executing schemes."

"If we could only give that Seth Jones an inkling of our whereabouts and intentions, I should feel pretty sanguine again," said Haverland.

"Very likely if that Jones could give us an inkling of his whereabouts and experiences, you would lose a little of that expectation," rejoined the hunter, with a meaning emphasis.

"But this is a waste of time and words," said Graham; "let us lay our heads together and decide at once what is to be done. As for me, I'm in favor of following the smaller party."

"What give you that idea?" asked Haverland.

"I confess I cannot give much reason for the notion, but somehow or other it has struck me that Ina is with the smaller party."

"Hardly probable," returned Haverland.

"It don't seem so, I allow," remarked the hunter, "but queerly enough the same notion has got into my head."

"Of course you can then give some reason."

"I can give what appears to have a show of reason to me. I have been doing a big amount of thinking for the last few minutes, and have almost reached a conclusion. I believe that the gal is with the smaller party, and it is the wish of the savages that we shall follow the main body. We will thus be drawn into ambush, and all further trouble from us would be removed."

"It seems hardly probable that the savages would run such a risk of losing their captive when there is no occasion for it," remarked Haverland.

"It don't seem probable, but it ain't the first thing they've done (providing of course they've done it), that would make you open your eyes. I believe these Mohawks are certain we won't suspect they've let the gal go off with two or three of their number, when there were enough to watch her and keep her out of the hands of a dozen such as we are. Feeling certain of this, I say they have let her go; and being sure also that we'll tramp on after them, they have made arrangements some distance away from here to dispose of us."

"Sound reasoning, I admit, but here's something to offer on the other side," said Graham, producing another fluttering rag from a bush.

"How is that upon the other side of the question?" queried the hunter.

"If you will notice the bush from which I took this, you will see it is upon the trail of the larger party, and consequently Ina must have been with that party to have left it there."

"Just show me the exact twig from which you took it," quietly asked Haldidge. Graham led the way a few yards off and showed him the spot. The hunter stooped and carefully examined the bush.

"I'm now satisfied," said he, "that I was right. This rag was left there by a savage for the express purpose of misleading us. We must seek Ina in another direction."

"Haldidge," said Haverland, earnestly, "I place great reliance upon your skill and judgment, but it strikes me at this moment that you are acting capriciously against reason."

"There's but one way to decide it; will you agree to it?" asked the hunter, smilingly. The other two expressed their willingness, and he produced his hunting-knife. For fear that some of our readers may be apprehensive of the use to which he intended putting it, we will describe his *modus operandi* at once. Stepping back a pace or two, the hunter took the point of his knife between his thumb and fore-finger, and flung it over his head. As it fell to the earth again, the point was turned *directly toward the trail of the lesser party.*

"Just what I thought," remarked the hunter, with another quiet smile. The mooted question was now settled to the satisfaction of all, and our three friends turned unhesitatingly to the westward upon the trail of the smaller party.

How much sometimes hangs upon the slightest thread! How small is the point upon which great events often turn! The simple fact of the direction in which the blade of the hunting-knife remained when it fell, decided the fate of every character in this life-drama. Had it pointed to the northward, an hour later the three would have walked into an ambush intended for them, and every one would have been massacred. The hunter was right. Ina Haverland had gone with the smaller party.

CHAPTER XII. PENCILINGS BY THE WAY

We have said the hunter was right. By the accidental turning of the hunting-knife, he had not only saved his life, but his efforts had been turned in the right direction.

It must be confessed that Haverland himself had some misgivings about the course which they were taking. He could not believe that the savages were short-sighted enough to place a captive, who was secure in their possession, into the hands of one or two of their number, when they were conscious they were pursued. But the decision of the hunting-knife could not be appealed from, and in a moody silence he followed in the footsteps of the hunter.

It was now getting far along in the afternoon, and the pursued savages could be at no great distance. Their trail was plain, as no efforts had been made to conceal it; but, although Haldidge strove his utmost to detect signs of Ina's delicate moccasin, he failed entirely, and was compelled, in spite of the assurance which he manifested at the start, to take some misgivings to himself.

The hunter, notwithstanding the consummate cunning and skill he had shown thus far in tracing up the savages, had made one sad mistake. He had been misled altogether in the number of the smaller party. Instead of three or four Indians, there were six: he began to think he had undertaken a more difficult matter than he anticipated. Still, there was no time for halting or faltering, and he strode resolutely forward.

"Ah — some more signs," exclaimed he, stopping suddenly.

"What are they?" queried his companions, eagerly.

"Just notice this bush, if you please, and tell me what you make of it?"

The two friends did so, and saw that one of the branches of some sprouts of chestnut, growing round a stump, had been broken short off, and lay pointing toward the trail.

"I make it favorable. Ina has done this to guide us," said Haverland.

"My opinion exactly," added Graham.

"You are mistaken about one thing. *Ina did not do it.*"

"Did not do it?" exclaimed the others; "and who did then?"

"That's the question. I'm of the opinion that that white man you have told me about has done it."

"But it cannot be that he is with them too."

"Surely it is impossible that the Indians would allow *both* of their captives to be in charge of two or three of their number at the same time."

"As for two or three, there are six painted Mohawks ahead of us for that matter. I haven't detected the trail of the gal yet, but have discovered several times pretty convincing evidence that a white man is among them. If you will look at that stick again, you will see that it is not likely your gal broke it. In the first place I don't believe she is able; for notice how thick it is; and, if she could have done it, it would have taken so much time that she would have been prevented."

"Very probably Seth is among them, although it is singular, to say the least. Some unaccountable whim has take possession of the Indians."

"But you say you discern nothing of Ina's trail?" asked Graham.

"Not as yet."

"Do you think she is among them?"

"I do."

"Where is her trail, then?"

"Somewhere on the ground, I suppose."

"Well, why have we not seen it, then?"

"I suppose, because it has escaped our eyes."

"A good explanation," smiled Graham; "but if we have failed altogether thus far to detect it, is it probable that she is among them?"

"I think so. You must remember that these half-dozen Mohawks are walking promiscuously and not in Ingin file, as is generally their custom. It is very probable that the gal is in front, and what tracks her little moccasin might make would be entirely covered up with the big feet of the Ingins."

"I hope you are not mistaken," returned Haverland, in such a tone as to show that he still had his lingering doubts.

"That matter cannot be decided until we get a peep at the dusky cowards, and the only course is for us to push ahead."

"It strikes me that they can be at no great distance, and if we are going to come upon their camp-fire to-night, we have got to do it pretty soon."

"Come on, then."

With this, the hunter again strode forward, but with more stealth and caution than before. He saw in the different signs around them unmistakable proof that the Indians were at no great distance.

Just as the sun was setting, the trumvirate reached a small stream which dashed and foamed directly across their trail. They halted a moment to slake their thirst, and the hunter arose and moved forward again. But Graham made it a point to search at every halting-place for guiding signs, and he called out to his companions to wait a moment.

"Time is too precious," replied he, "and you won't find anything here."

"Won't find anything here, eh? Just come and look at this."

The hunter stepped back over the stones in the brook, and with Haverland approached Graham. The latter pointed to a broad, flat stone at his feet. Upon it was scratched, with some softer stone, the following words:

"Hurry forward. There are six Indians, and they have got Ina with them. They don't suspect you are following them, and are hurrying up for the village. I think we will camp two or three miles from here. Make the noise of the whippowil when you want to do the business, and I will understand.

"Yours, respectfully.
"Seth Jones."

"If I warn't afraid the imps would hear it, I would vote three cheers for that Jones," exclaimed Haldidge; "he's a trump, whoever he is."

"You may depend upon that," added Graham, "for what little I saw of him was sufficient to show me that."

"Let me see," repeated the hunter, again reading the writing upon the stone, "he says they will encamp two or three miles from here. The sun has now set, but we shall have light for over an hour yet, sufficient to guide us. It's best for us to be moving forward, as there is no time to spare."

"It beats my time how this Jones got into that crowd," said Graham, half to himself, as the three again moved forward.

"He's *there,* we know, and that is enough for the present; when we have the time to spare, we may speculate upon the matter. All ready?"

"Yes — but a moment. Haldidge, let us have some arrangement about the manner in which we are going to travel. Double caution is now necessary."

"I will keep my eyes upon the trail as I have done all along, and see that we don't walk into a hornet's nest with our eyes shut. You can help keep a look-out, while you, Graham, who have been so lucky thus far in stumbling upon what neither of us saw, will watch for more signs. Just as like as not, that Jones has been clever enough to give us some more good directions."

Each understanding his duty, now prepared to fulfill it. The progress was necessarily slow, from the extreme caution exercised.

The hunter had proceeded but a short distance when he noticed his shadow was cast upon the ground; and, looking up, he saw, to his regret, that the full moon was in the heavens. This was unfortunate for them; for, although it discovered the trail with as much certainty as in the day, and thus assisted them in the pursuit, yet the chances of their approach being made known to the Indians was almost certain.

"Hist!" suddenly called Graham, in a whisper.

"What's up now?" asked the hunter, turning stealthily around.

"Some more writing from Seth."

Haverland and Haldidge approached. Graham was stooping beside a flat stone endeavoring to decipher some characters upon it. The light of the moon, although quite strong, was hardly sufficient. By dint of patience and perseverance they succeeded in reading the following:

Figure 22. Illustration from the 1877 edition of *Seth Jones*. "Graham was stooping beside a flat stone, endeavoring to decipher some characters upon it." Albert Johannsen Collection, Rare Books and Special Collections, Northern Illinois University Libraries.

"Be *very* careful. The imps begin to suspect; they have seen me making signs, and are suspicious. They keep a close watch on the gal. Remember the signal when you come up with us. Yours, in haste, but nevertheless with great respect,

"Seth Jones, Esq."

It was now evident that they were in close proximity to the savages. After a moment's hurried debate, it was decided that Haldidge should walk at a greater distance ahead than heretofore, and communicate instantly with his companions upon discovering the camp.

Slowly, silently and cautiously the three moved forward. A half-hour later, Graham touched the shoulder of Haverland and pointed meaningly ahead. A red reflection was seen in the branches overhead; and as they stood in silence, the glimmer of a light was seen through the trees. The next instant the hunter stood beside them.

"We've come to them at last," he whispered; "see that your priming is all right, and make up your mind for hot work."

They had already done this, and were anxious for the contest to be decided. Their hearts beat high, as they realized how near the deadly conflict was, and even the hunter's breath was short and hurried. But there was no faltering or wavering, and they moved stealthily forward.

CHAPTER XIII. SOME EXPLANATIONS

The village of the Mohawks was at a considerable distance from the spot where had once stood the home of the woodman, and incumbered as they were with plunder, their progress was necessarily slow; besides, knowing full well that pursuit would be useless upon the part of the whites, their was no occasion to hasten their steps. When, however, Seth Jones' unceremonious entrance among them, together with the escape of his new companion and the subsequent report of the smaller party with Ina, was made known, the old chief began to have some misgivings about his fancied security. It occurred to him that there might be a large party of whites on the trail, and in such case, his greatest skill was required to retain the captives. And here was the trouble. If he was pursued — and upon that point there could be no doubt — his progress must be hastened. His pursuers would follow with the swiftness of vengeance. With the plunder in their possession, the thing was impossible, and he saw, at length, that stratagem must be resorted to.

He selected six of his bravest and fleetest warriors — two of whom had been Graham's most troublesome enemies in his fearful chase — and placed Ina in their charge, with instructions to make all haste to the Indian village. Before starting, it occurred to him that the best plan would be to send the white man also with them. Were he to remain with the larger party, in case of attack, his presence, he had reason to fear, would be their own destruction, while six savages fully armed and ever vigilant, could surely guard an unarmed idiot and a woman.

The chief, as stated, was satisfied he was pursued. Hence, if he could throw his pursuers off the scent, their discomfiture would be certain. He believed this could be done. The six savages with their charge parted from the larger party, and struck off rapidly in a direction diverging to the north. Their trail was so concealed as to give the impression that there were but three, and this deception we have seen misled the hunter. A piece of Ina's dress was purposely lodged upon a bush, in the rear of the larger party: and promiscuously and hopefully, the chief leisurely continued his way with his dusky followers.

After the parties had parted company, the smaller one hastened rapidly forward. Ina, in charge of a stalwart, athletic Indian, was kept to the front, the more effectually to conceal her trail, while Seth kept his position near the center of the file. He was allowed the free use of his hands, though, as has been remarked, he was deprived of his weapons. As they journeyed hastily forward, he made it a point to enlighten them as much as possible by his conversation, and certain original remarks.

"If you have no objection, I wouldn't mind knowing your idea in thus leaving the other Injins, eh?" he remarked, quizzically, to the savage in front. No reply being given, he continued:

"I s'pose you're thinking about that house you burnt down, and feeling bad — oh, you ain't, eh?" suddenly remarked Seth, as the Indian glared fiercely at him.

"It was a bad trick, I allow," he continued, "enough to make a fellur mad, I swow. That house, I shouldn't wonder now, took that Haverland a week to finish; 'twas an ugly piece of business — yes, sir."

At intervals the savages exchanged a word with each other, and once or twice one of them took the back trail, evidently to ascertain whether they had any pursuers. Finding they had not, they slackened their speed somewhat, as Ina had given signs of fatigue, and they believed there was really no occasion for hastening. But the weariness which the fair captive had endured, so increased, that long before the sun had reached its meridian, they halted for a half-hour's rest. This was at the crossing of a small, sparkling stream. As the sun was now quite hot, and the atmosphere thick and heavy, the rest in the cool shadows of the trees was doubly refreshing. Ina seated herself upon the cool moist earth, her captors preserving, singularly enough, a far more vigilant watch over her than over Seth Jones; but, for that matter, the latter was allowed no very special freedom. A couple of Indians again took the back trail, for prudent reasons, but met with nothing to excite their apprehensions.

In the meantime, Seth continued tumbling over the ground, occasionally giving vent to snatches of song, and now and then a sage remark. Without being noticed, he picked a small chalky pebble from the margin of the brook, and working his way to a large flat stone, executed, with many flourishes, the writing to which we referred in a preceding chapter. Although cleverly done, this latter act did not escape the eyes of the suspicious savages. One immediately arose, and walking to him, pointed down and gruffly asked:

"What that?"

"Read it fur yourself," replied Seth, innocently.

"What that?" repeated the savage, menacingly.

"A little flourishing I was executing, jist to pass away time."

"Ugh!" grunted the Indian, and, dipping his big foot in the brook, he irreverently swept it across the stone, completely wiping out Seth's beautiful chirography.

"Much obliged," said the latter; "saved me the trouble. I can write it on again when it gits dry."

But no opportunity was given, as a moment after the scouts returned, and the line of march was taken up. But Seth well knew he had accomplished all that could be desired. He had taken particular pains that the pebble should be flinty enough to scratch into the soft stone every word he wrote. Consequently the party had not been gone a half-hour when every letter came out as clear and distinct as before, despite the wet daub the indignant savage had given it.

Their progress for a time was quite rapid. Seth, somehow or other, was constantly pitching out of file, breaking down twigs along the way, stumbling against the stones which were not in the way, and, in spite of menaces and occasional blows from his captors, making the trail unnecessarily distinct and plain.

At noon another halt was made, and all partook of some food. Ina was sick at heart, and ate but a mouthful. An apprehension of her dreadful position came over her, and her soul reeled as she began picturing what was yet to come. Seth quarreled with two of his captors, because, he affirmed, they took more than their share of the dinner; and, take it all in all, affairs were getting into as interesting a state as one could well conceive.

The meal finished, they again set forward. From the whispered consultation of the savages, as well as the words which reached Seth's ears, and their utter disregard of Ina's painful fatigue, he began to believe that the Indians suspected that their stratagem had not misled their pursuers, and were apprehensive of pursuit. Finally, Seth became satisfied that such was the case, and when they halted, toward the middle of the afternoon, he again gave vent to his thoughts upon a friendly stone which offered itself, and this, again, received a fierce wipe from the foot of the same savage, and the words again came out to view, and accomplished all that their ardent author could have desired.

These acts of Seth settled the suspicions of his captors into a certainty, and a closer surveillance was kept upon their refractory captive. No further opportunities were given him, and as he himself had expected this turn of matters, there was no need of it upon his part. Although he had but little reason to hope it, he did hope and believe that Haverland and Graham were upon the trail, and he felt that if the words intended for their eyes could only reach them, the fate of Ina and himself was determined.

The moon being at its full, and shining in unclouded splendor upon the forest, so lightened the way that the savages continued their flight — as it may now be called — for an hour or two in the evening. They would have probably gone further, had it not been painfully evident that Ina was ready to give out. The old chief had given them imperative commands not to hasten her too much, and to rest when they saw she needed it. Accordingly, though they were brutal enough to insult her with menaces, they were of no avail, and, finally they came to a reluctant halt for the night.

It will be necessary to understand the situation of these savages and their captives, in order to comprehend the events that followed.

A fire was started, and just within the circle of this, half reclining upon the ground was Ina, with a heavy Indian shawl thrown around her. She had partaken of none of the food offered, and was already in a semi-unconscious state. On either side of her was seated a vigilant savage, well-armed and prepared for any emergency. Upon the opposite side was Seth, his feet firmly lashed together, while his hands were free. Two Indians were upon his right, and upon his left. The remaining one took his station about a hundred yards on the back-trail.

Here, lying flat on his face, he silently waited for the approach of the enemy.

CHAPTER XIV. IN THE ENEMY'S CAMP

The savages, after starting the fire, allowed it to smolder and die out, for fear of guiding their enemies. Now this was the most fortunate thing that could have happened for their pursuers; for, in the first place, it burned long enough to give them a perfect knowledge of the position of Ina and Seth; and, when its light could no longer be of any assistance, but would materially injure their hopes, the Indians were kind enough to let it fade entirely out.

Before giving the signal, the hunter deemed it best to ascertain the whereabouts of the savage missing at the camp-fire. Leaving his rifle in charge of Haverland, and cautioning them not to move, he crept stealthily forward. So silent and snakelike was his approach, that the savage lying directly in his path had not the slightest suspicion of his proximity. The first thing that attracted his attention was the *thought* that he heard a slight movement in front of him. Raising his head a few inches, he peered cautiously forward. Nothing meeting his keen vision he sunk back again.

The hunter and savage, both being on the ground, were in blank darkness, and although their forms, if standing on their feet, would have been plainly discernible, yet, under the thick shadows of the undergrowth, they might have touched each other without knowing it. The hunter, however, as he lay, caught the outlines of the savage's head against the fading light of the fire behind him, as he raised it. This gave him a knowledge of his position and determined his own mode of action.

Without the least notice, he slid slowly forward until he was so close that he could actually hear the Indian's breath. Then he purposely made a slight movement. The Indian raised his head, and was gradually coming to his feet, when the hunter bounded like a dark ball forward, clutched him by the throat, and bearing him like a giant to the earth, drove his hunting-knife again and again to the hilt in his heart. It was a fearful act, yet there was no hesitation upon the hunter's part. He felt that it must be done.

He loosened his gripe upon his victim's throat, when there was not a spark of life left. Then casting his body to one side, he made his way back to his companions. Here, in a few words, he explained what had taken place. It was evident that the Indians were so cautious and alarmed, that the most consummate skill was required, to accomplish the work in hand.

Suddenly an ingenious plan occurred to Graham. It was to dress himself in the fallen Indian's dress, walk boldly into the camp and be guided by circumstances. After a moment's consultation, it was acquiesced in by all. Haldidge made his way to where the savage lay, and hastily stripping him, returned with his garments. These Graham donned in a few moments, and was ready. It was agreed that he should walk leisurely among them, while Haverland and Haldidge would follow him, and remain nigh enough to be ready at a moment's warning. If discovered, he was to seize Ina and make off in the woods, while his two friends would rush forward, free Seth, and make an onslaught upon the others.

The fire was now so low, that Graham had little fear of exposing himself, unless compelled to hold a conversation. The savages started as he came to view, but fortunately said nothing, as they supposed it to be their comrade. Graham walked leisurely to the almost dead fire, and seated himself by Seth. The savages continued placidly smoking their pipes.

"Ugh!" grunted Graham, peering into Seth's face. The latter started slightly, looked up, and understood all in a moment. Seth pointed to his feet; Graham nodded.

"Say, you, you was clever enough to tie up my feet, and now just have the kindness to move 'em a little nearer the fire. Come, do, and I'll remember you in my will."

Graham mumbled something, and, stooping forward, he moved the feet slightly, dexterously cutting the thong at the same moment.

"Much obliged," said Seth; "that'll dew; needn't take no further trouble, you old painted heathen."

Graham felt that if he could now put Ina upon her guard, all that would be necessary was — to act. But this was hardly possible. While ruminating upon the next step to be taken, an Indian addressed him in the Indian tongue. Here was a dilemma, and Graham was already meditating upon making the onslaught at once, when the ready wit of Seth came to his aid. Disguising most completely his voice, the eccentric fellow replied in the Indian tongue. This slight stratagem was executed so perfectly that not a savage entertained the slightest suspicion that another than their dead comrade had spoken to them. Another question was put, but before Seth could reply, there came a startling cry of the whippowil close at hand. All the savages sprung to their feet, and one held his tomahawk, ready to brain the captive Ina, in case they could not retain her. Another leaped toward Seth, but his surprise was great, when the man in turn sprung nimbly to his feet, and this surprise became unbounded, when, doubling himself like a ball, Seth struck him with tremendous force in the stomach, knocking him instantly senseless. Quick as thought, Graham felled the savage standing over Ina, and seizing her in his arms, plunged into the woods, setting up a loud shout at the same instant. The scene now became desperate. Haldidge and Haverland, fired almost to madness, rushed forward, and the former added his own yells to those of the savages. Ten minutes after, not an Indian was in sight. Finding it impossible to withstand this terrible onslaught, they fled precipitately, carrying with them several desperate wounds in body and feelings.

No lives were lost on either side, and not a wound worth mentioning was received by the assailants. The rout was complete.

But there was still danger, as the routed Indians would make all haste to the main body, and would in turn pursue the whites. This Haldidge remarked, as he struck into the forest, and called upon the others not to lose sight of him. There was danger of this, indeed.

"By gracious! yew, Haverland, things begin to look up," exclaimed Seth.

"Thank God!" responded the father, with a trembling voice.

Ina, for a few moments after her recapture, was so bewildered as not to comprehend the true state of affairs. Finally, she realized that she was in the arms of friends.

"Am I safe? Where is father?" she asked.

"Here, my dearest child," answered the parent, pressing her to his heart.

"Is mother and aunty safe?"

"Yes, all — all are safe, I trust, now."

"And who are these with you?"

"This is Haldidge, a dear friend of ours, to whom, under Heaven, your rescue is owing, and — "

"Just hold on, Alf, now, if you please; that's plenty," interrupted the hunter.

"Of course I did not mean to leave out Seth here, and — "

"No, by gracious, it wouldn't do, especially when you recollect how nice it was me and Graham gave 'em the slip."

"You and who?" eagerly asked Ina.

"Me and Mr. Graham — that fellow standing there — the one that has come out here to marry you. Haven't you heard of him?"

Ina stepped forward and scrutinized the face before her.

"Don't you remember me?" asked Graham, pleasantly.

"Oh, is it you? I am *so* glad you are here," she repeated, placing both her hands in his and looking up into his face.

"Now, just see here," said Seth, stepping earnestly forward, "I 'bject to this. 'Cos why you haven't the time to go into the sparking business, and if you do, why, you'll be observed. I advise you to postpone it till you git home. What's the opinion of the audience?"

"Your suggestion is hardly necessary," laughed Graham. "The *business* you referred to shall most certainly be deferred until a more convenient season."

"It gives me great pleasure," remarked Haverland, "to witness this reunion of friends, and I thank God that my dear child, so nearly lost forever, has been restored to me; but there is another whose heart is nearly broken, who should not be kept waiting, and there is a long distance between us and perfect safety, which should be shortened as rapidly and quickly as possible."

"That's the idea," added Haldidge; "it won't do to consider yourself safe till you *are,* and that isn't yet."

"Just so exactly, and consequently all fall into line of march."

Our friends now set out on a rapid walk homeward. As has been remarked, there was yet a long distance to be passed, and even now, while surrounded by darkness, it was reckless to halt or lag upon the way. Haldidge, as well as Seth, resolved that they should not pause until it was evident that Ina needed rest. Both well knew that the Mohawks would not yield up their captives, as long as there was a chance to regain them.

Seth's only fear now was that they would be pursued and over-taken by some of the savages. That this apprehension was well-grounded, the events which we shall now record will plainly show.

CHAPTER XV. MANEUVERING AND SCHEMING

Through the entire night, with now and then an occasional halt of a few minutes each, the fugitives — for they may now be properly termed such — continued their journey. When day broke, they halted in a small valley through which a small sparkling stream made its way. On either side, it was surrounded by dark, overhanging forest-trees, and heavier undergrowth, through which none but the eagle eye of the hunter or savage could discover their retreat.

Seth, when they first halted, made off in the woods, and in the course of a half-hour returned with a large fowl. The feathers were plucked from this, a fire kindled, and in a few moments it was cooked. It furnished all with a hearty, substantial and nourishing breakfast — what all needed. After this a short consultation was held, when it was determined that they should halt for an hour or two. Several blankets were spread upon the greensward, as a bed for Ina, and in ten minutes she was sound asleep.

Our friends had decided upon making their homeward journey upon foot for several reasons, any of which was sufficient to influence them. In the first place, their course would be much shorter and more direct, and was really attended with less danger; and even if they desired to take to the river there was no means to do it.

"By gracious!" remarked Seth, after a few minutes' deep thought, "I feel, boys, as though we're to run into a scrape before we git home. I tell *yeou* I do."

"And I do, too," added Haldidge. "I don't know why it is, and yet I believe there is a reason for it. If there is any chance for them

Mohawks to play a game of *tit for tat,* they'll do it; you can make up your mind to that."

"Do you think the chance is given them?" queried Haverland.

"I am afraid we can't help it, any way we choose to fix it."

"What do you mean? What do you refer to!"

"You see, them Ingins can't help knowing the way we'll have to take to reach home, and what is to hinder them from getting ahead of us and giving us a little trouble?"

"Nothing at all, that's a fact. Our utmost vigilance will be required at every step. Don't you think, Seth, that one of us should act in the capacity of scout?"

"I *know* it; not only one, but two. As soon as we start, I shall shoot ahead and pilot you along, while one of you must flourish in the rear to announce any new visitors. This is the only way we can ever expect to move along with dignity."

"What course do you suppose the savages will take?" asked Graham.

"I guess they ain't in the neighborhood, though it's darned hard to tell where they are. You can make up your mind that they'll show themselves before we get any great distance ahead. They'll be dodging round in the woods till they find out where we are, and then they'll use their wits to draw us into ambush, and I can tell *yeou,* too, that 'cuter ones than we have walked right into the infarnal things."

An hour later, when preparations were making for resuming their journey, Ina awoke. She was greatly refreshed by the sleep thus obtained, and the others felt cheered and hopeful at the prospect of a rapid march for the day.

The burden and responsibility of this small band of adventurers naturally devolved upon Haldidge and Seth. Haverland, although a thorough hunter and woodsman, had but little or no experience in Indian warfare, and accordingly showed himself to be devoid of that suspicious watchfulness which makes up the success of the frontier ranger. As for Graham, he was suspicious enough, but he lacked also the great teacher — experience. Seth and Haldidge thus thrown together, rapidly consulted and determined in all cases the precautionary measures to be adopted. In the present instance, it was decided that Haldidge should linger some hundred yards in the rear, and use all the opportunities thus afforded of watching the actions or approach of their enemies. The same duty was imposed upon Seth at the front, with the additional certainty upon his part, that the entire safety of the company rested with him.

Haverland and Graham generally walked side by side, with Ina between them, and as watchful as though they had none but themselves to depend upon. They seldom indulged in conversation, except now and then to exchange a few words or inquiries.

As Seth Jones was well satisfied in his own mind that the post of danger was held by him, we will follow his adventures. After emerging from the valley, in which the whites had encamped, their way for a considerable distance led them through the unbroken forest, without hill or vale, and pretty thickly crowded with bushy, yielding undergrowth. Had a person chanced to cross the path of Seth, the only evidence he would have had of the presence of a human being would have been the snapping of a twig now and then, or the flitting of his form like a shadow from tree to tree, and perhaps the shrill, bird-like whistle as he signaled to those in the rear.

Through the forenoon, nothing occurred to excite suspicion upon his part, but at the period mentioned, he arrived at a point where his alarm was excited at once. The place offered such advantages for an Indian ambush, that he gave the signal for those behind to halt, and determined to make a thorough reconnoissance of the whole locality before passing through it. The spot referred to, had the appearance of having formerly been the bed of some large-sized lake, the waters of which having dried up years before, left a rich, productive soil, which was now covered over with the rankest undergrowth and vegetation. Not a tree of any size appeared. The hollow, or valley, was so much depressed that from the stand-point of Seth, he obtained a perfect view of the whole portion. It was about a third of a mile in breadth, and perhaps a couple of miles in length.

Seth stood a long time, running his eye over it, scanning every spot where it seemed likely an enemy might lurk. Hardly a point escaped his keen vision.

It was while he stood thus, eagerly scanning the valley, that his looks were suddenly attracted toward a point near the center of the valley, from which a faint, bluish wreath of smoke was curling upward. This puzzled our friend greatly. He possessed the curious, investigating habits so generally ascribed to his race, and his curiosity was wonderfully excited by this occurrence. That there was some design in it, not understood yet, he was well satisfied, and he determined that, before allowing those behind him to venture into the valley, he would gain all the knowledge possible of it. His first step was to take his own trail backward until he reached Haverland and Graham, to whom he imparted his intention. This done, he set forward again.

Having arrived at the point where he first discovered this suspicious appearance, he paused again for further consideration. The smoke was still visible, rising very slowly in the clear air, and making so slight an appearance that even his experienced eye searched a long time for it. Seth watched for awhile, until he felt that he could not understand the meaning of it without venturing into the valley. This conclusion arrived at, he hesitated no longer, but descended and entered at once the luxuriant growth.

When fairly within it, he made a *detour* to the right, so as to pass around the fire, and to avoid the path that one unsuspicious of danger would be apt to follow. As he made his way slowly and cautiously forward, he paused at intervals and listened intently. Sometimes he bent his ear to the ground and lay for minutes at a time. But as yet not the slightest sound had been heard. Finally he judged that he must be near the fire that had excited his apprehensions. The snapping of a burning ember guided him, and a few minutes later he stood within sight of it.

Here he met a sight that chilled him with horror!

Some wretched human being was bound to a tree and had been burned to death. He was painted black as death, his scalped head drooped forward, so that, from where Seth stood, it was impossible to distinguish his features; but he saw enough to make him shudder at the awful fate he had so narrowly escaped. Every vestige of flesh was burned off to the knees, and the bones, white and glistening, dangled to the crisp and blackened members above! The hands, tied behind, had passed through the fire unscathed, but every other part of the body was literally roasted! The smoke in reality was the smoke from this human body, and the stench, which was now horrible, had been noticed by Seth long before he suspected the cause.

"Heavens and earth!" he muttered to himself, "this is the first time I ever saw a person burned at the stake, and I hope in God it will be the last time. Can it be a *white man?*"

After some cautious maneuvering, he gained a point from which he could obtain a view of the face, and he experienced considerable relief when he discovered that it was not a white man. He was probably some unfortunate Indian, belonging to a hostile tribe, who had been captured by his enemies, and upon whom they had thus wreaked their vengeance. Whether he was a Mohawk, or the member of another tribe, it was impossible for Seth, under the circumstances, to tell. But what was singular and unaccountable to Seth was, that there appeared to be no other savages in the vicinity. He knew it was not their custom to leave a prisoner thus, and the very fact of their being absent upon the present occasion made him doubly cautious and suspicious.

It was while he stood meditating upon the terrible scene before him, that he was startled by the report of Haldidge's rifle. He was satisfied that it was his as it was from that direction, and he could not be mistaken in its report. He had noticed it during the conflict the night before as having a peculiar sound, entirely different from either his own or the savages'. This was a new source of wonder and perplexity. He was completely puzzled by the extraordinary turn affairs were taking. Some unusual cause must have discharged Haldidge's rifle. What it was he could only conjecture.

Still doubting and cautious, he determined to reconnoiter his own position before returning. Stooping almost to the earth, he made his way stealthily around the opposite side of the fire. Here he stretched out flat upon the earth, and bent his ear to the ground. A faint tremor was heard. He raised his head and heard the brushing of somebody through the wood. The next moment, five Mohawk warriors, in all the horrid panoply of war-paint, stepped into the open space in front of the Indian who had been burned at the stake.

The report of the rifle appeared to be the cause of the apprehension among them. They conversed earnestly, in a low tone at first, gesticulating violently, without noticing in the least the heart-sickening spectacle before them. Seth was satisfied that they had no suspicions of his own proximity, for they gradually spoke louder until he managed to hear the most of what they said. As he expected, it was the rifle report. They seemed to understand that it had not been discharged by one of their own numbers, and were afraid that their presence had been discovered. Seth learned further that there were at least a dozen Indians in the neighborhood, every one of whom was led thither by the one object.

Consequently he must have missed the others entirely in his movements, or else they were in the rear and had been discovered by Haldidge. That the latter was the case seemed more than probable. A collision in all probability had occurred between them and the hunter, and Seth felt that his presence was needed. Accordingly he turned to retrace his steps.

His presence was indeed required, for danger, dark and threatening, surrounded the little band of whites.

CHAPTER XVI. IN WHICH A HUNTER'S
NERVES ARE TESTED

In the morning when our friends started upon their day's march, Haldidge, as said, fell behind in order to guard against surprise from this direction. Although expecting as little as did Seth any demonstration from this quarter, still he was too much of a backwoodsman to allow himself to lose any of his usual suspicion and watchfulness. Sometimes he would take the back trail for a long distance, and then wander off to the right or left of it for perhaps a mile or more. By this means, he kept a continual watch, not only upon the trail itself, but upon the neighborhood for a long distance around it, and, in case of pursuit, made so many and conflicting tracks, that it could not but puzzle and delay their enemies.

Near noon, and at the very moment that Seth paused to take a survey of the suspicious valley-like depression, and when not more than a furlong in the rear, Haldidge caught sight of three Indians just ahead of him. They were sitting upon the ground, in perfect silence, and seemingly waiting for the approach of some one. The hunter found himself as much perplexed as was Seth to account for what he saw. Whether it was some stratagem to entrap himself or not, he could not tell, but, before venturing further, he made up his mind to gain a further knowledge of their intentions.

Haldidge had one formidable difficulty to contend with: the wood at this particular spot was open, and almost devoid of the protecting undergrowth, so that it was impossible to approach them closer without discovering himself to them. He noticed lying a short distance behind them a large, heavy log, apparently much decayed. In fact, this was so near them, that could he gain it, he could overhear everything said. He had a slight knowledge of the Mohawk tongue — not enough to converse in it — but still enough to understand the drift of a conversation. Accordingly he determined to reach the spot at all hazards.

Haldidge desired, if possible, to communicate with Haverland and warn him of the proximity of danger. To do this, it was necessary to make a long *detour,* and upon further consideration he decided not to attempt it. Lying flat upon his face, he worked himself toward the log mentioned, keeping it between himself and the Indians, and approaching it as silently and as steadily as a snake. So cautiously and carefully was it done, that it required at least twenty minutes to reach it, and all this time the Indians maintained the same unbroken silence. At length the concealment was reached, and the hunter noticed with pleasure that it was hollow. He lost no time in entering it, where, coiling himself up in as small a space as possible, he took himself to listening. As if to completely favor him, there was a small rent in the log, through which even the whispers of the savages could be heard, and which also admitted a thin ray of light.

Here Haldidge cramped himself up and listened intently. But not a word was exchanged between the Indians, who remained as motionless as statues. In the course of a few minutes he heard a footfall upon the leaves, and a second after several savages seated themselves upon the very log in which he had concealed himself! He judged that there were at least a half-dozen. Those whom he had first seen appeared to have risen, and, meeting the others, they had all seated themselves upon the log together.

They immediately commenced conversing in so low and guttural tones, that their deep base voices communicated their tremor to the log. Haldidge started as he soon learned that they were conversing about himself and the three fugitives. Of Seth they seemed to have no knowledge. He discovered that they had lain in ambush a short distance ahead to entrap Haverland, Graham, and Ina, and they were debating how he should be disposed of. They knew that he was acting in the capacity of scout and sentinel, and were fearful that he might detect the ambush, or at least escape it himself.

At this point, one of the Indians, probably impelled by some whim, stooped and looked into the log. Haldidge knew, by the darkness thus occasioned, that one of them was peering in it, and he scarcely breathed for a few seconds. But the face was removed, and the hollow being dark within — the small vent being on the opposite side of the hunter — the savage felt reassured and resumed the conversation.

But Haldidge was doomed to have a trial of his nerves, of which he had little dreamed. When he entered the log, it was head foremost, so that his feet were toward the opening, and his face was in the dim light beyond. He judged the rotten cavity extended several feet further back; but, as there was no necessity for entering further, he did not attempt to explore it. It was while he lay thus, his whole soul bent to the one act of listening, that he was startled by the deadly warning of a rattlesnake. He comprehended the truth in an instant. *There was one of these reptiles in the log beyond him!*

It is difficult to imagine a more fearful situation than the hunter's at this moment. He was literally environed by death; for it was at his head, his feet, and above him, and there was no escape below. He had just learned that his death was one of the objects of the Indians, so that to back out into their clutches would be nothing less than committing suicide. To remain where he was would be to disregard the second and last warning of the coiled snake. What was to be done? Manifestly nothing but to die like a man. Haldidge decided to risk the bite of the rattlesnake.

Despite himself, the hunter felt that the reptile was exerting its horrible fascination over him. Its small eyes, gleaming like tiny yet fiery stars, seemed to emit a magnetic ray — thin, pointed, and palpable, that pierced into his brain. There was a malignant subtlety — an irresistible magnetism. Now the small, glittering point of light seemed to recede, then to approach and expand, and then to wave and undulate all around him. Sometimes that bright, lightning-like ray would shiver and tremble, and then straighten out with metal-like rigidity, and insinuate itself into his very being, like the invisible point of a spear.

There was a desire on the part of Haldidge to shake off this influence, which wrapped him like a mantle. There was the desire, we say, and yet there was a languid listlessness — a repugnance to take the effort. The feeling was something similar to that produced by a powerful opiate, when we are first recovering from it. There was that dim consciousness — that indistinct knowledge of the outer world — that certainty that we can break the bond that holds us, by one vigorous effort, and yet the same sluggish indifference that prevents the attempt.

Haldidge drew his breath faintly and slowly, yielding more and more to that fatal, subtle influence. He knew he was charmed, and yet he couldn't help it. It was now impossible to shake off that weight which pressed him down like an incubus. That outer world — so to speak — had now receded, and he was in another, from which he could not return without help besides his own. He seemed to be moving, flitting, sinking, and rising, through the air, borne upward and downward, hither and thither, on a wing of fire. The spell was complete. That extraordinary power which instinct holds over reason — that wonderful superiority which a reptile sometimes shows he can exert over man, the snake now held over the hunter.

At this point, from some cause or other, one of the savages struck the log a violent blow with his hatchet. Haldidge heard it. He drew a long breath, closed his eyes, and when he reopened them, looked down at his hands upon which his chin had been resting.

The charm was broken! the hunter had shaken off the fatal spell!

Like the knocking at the gate in Macbeth;[3] which dispels the dark, awful world of gloom in which murderers have been moving and living, and ushers in our own world, with all its hurrying tide of human life and passions; so this blow of the Indian's tomahawk broke the subtle, magnetic spell of the serpent, and lifted the heavy mantle-like influence which wrapped Haldidge in its folds.

He looked downward and determined not to raise his eyes again, for he knew the same power would again rise above him. The serpent, seemingly conscious of its loss of influence, rattled once more, and prepared to strike. Haldidge stirred not a muscle; in fact, he had scarcely moved since entering the log. But the snake did not strike. The continued death-like stillness of the hunter evidently seemed to the reptile to be death itself. He coiled and uncoiled himself several times, and then lifting his head, crawled directly over his neck and body, and passed out of the log! Here he was killed by the Indians.

Now that the hunter was himself again, he prepared for further action. The Indians had arisen from the log and were at some distance. He could hear the mumbling of their voices, but could not distinguish their words. After awhile these ceased, and he heard no more.

Haldidge was now filled with apprehension for the others. He had enough faith in the power and cunning of Seth to feel pretty confident that he would neither lead any one into ambush or fall into one himself, let it be prepared as skillfully as it might be; but then he could know nothing of the Indians in the rear, who might surprise Haverland and Graham at any moment.

The hunter at length grew so restless and uneasy that he emerged from his hiding-place as rapidly and silently as possible. He looked cautiously around, but no savage was in sight. Filled with the most painful apprehensions, he hastened through the wood, avoiding the trail of his friends, however, and came finally in sight of them. Before making himself known, he concluded to reconnoiter the place. While doing so, he saw the head of an Indian rise slowly above a bush, and peer over at the unconscious whites. Without losing a moment, he raised his rifle, took a quick but sure aim, and fired. Then calling out to Haverland and Graham, he sprung for an instant into view.

"Make for cover," he shouted; "the Indians are upon us!"

In an instant every one of the whites was invisible.

---

[3] *Like the knocking at the gate of Macbeth:*   First heard in Act II, Scene 2 of Shakespeare's *Macbeth*, after Macbeth has murdered Duncan, the knocking at the gate is the subject of a morbid soliloquy spoken by the Porter at the outset of Scene 3.

Figure 23. Illustration from the 1877 edition of *Seth Jones*. "Without losing a moment, he raised his rifle, took a quick but sure aim, and fired." Albert Johannsen Collection, Rare Books and Special Collections, Northern Illinois University Libraries.

CHAPTER XVII. ENCOMPASSED BY DANGER

At the first warning of Haldidge, Haverland comprehended the threatened danger in an instant. Catching Ina in his arms, he sprung into the wood, sheltering himself behind a tree so quickly that Ina, till that moment, did not comprehend the meaning of the startling movements around her.

"What is it, father?" she whispered.

"Keep quiet, daughter, and don't move."

She said no more, but shrunk beneath his sheltering form, believing that his strong arm was capable of protecting her against any foe, however formidable.

Graham, at the alarm, had leaped toward Haldidge, and the two sheltered themselves within a few feet of each other. The shot of the hunter had been fatal, for that yell which the North American Indian, like an animal, gives when he receives his death-wound, was heard, and the fall had also reached his ears.

Minute after minute passed away and nothing further was heard of the savages. This silence was as full of meaning, and as dangerous as any open demonstration upon the part of the Indians. What new plan they might be concocting was a mystery to all but themselves. At length Graham ventured to speak:

"What do you suppose they're up to, Haldidge?"

"Hatching some devilish plot, I expect."

"It seems it requires a good while to do it."

"Don't get impatient; they'll show themselves in time."

"Have you any idea of their number?"

"There was something like a half-dozen prowling around."

"There is one less now, at any rate."

"I suppose so; but there's enough left to occasion a little trouble at least. Where did Alf go with the gal?"

"Off yonder, a short distance. Hadn't we better get closer together?"

"No; I don't know as there is any necessity for it. We're as safe, drawn up in this style, as in any other I can imagine."

"I am afraid, Haldidge, they will make an attempt to surround us. In such a case, wouldn't Haverland be in great peril?"

"They can't get around him without running their heads in range with our rifles, and Alf is a man who'll be pretty sure to discover such a trick without any help."

"Where can Seth be?"

"Not very far off; that shot of mine will be pretty sure to bring him."

"Haldidge, how was it that you discovered these Mohawks? Did you know of their presence before you fired?"

"Yes, long before. I've an idea they've been tracking you for an hour or two."

"Why, then, was their attack deferred?"

"They have made no attack, remember. I don't believe they had any such intention. There is an ambush somewhere ahead that they have laid, and it was their idea to walk you into that."

"What was their notion in watching us so closely?"

"They were hunting for me, for I heard them say as much, and, I suppose, in case you didn't walk into their trap, why, they were going to make the attack."

"Can it be that Seth has fallen into the snare?" asked Graham, in anxious tones.

"No, sir; such a thing can't be. He isn't such a fool as that amounts to. He is making himself generally useful; you can make up your mind to that. He is a smart chap, for all he is the most awkward, long-legged, gawky person I ever came across."

"I am puzzled to know who he is. It seems to me that he is only playing a part. Several times in conversing with him, he has used language such as none but a scholar and polished gentleman would use. At others and most of the time, he uses that ungainly mode of expression, which, in itself, is laughable. At any rate, whoever he may be, he is a friend, and the interest which he takes in the safety of Haverland and his family, is as efficient as it is singular."

"Maybe the interest is in Ina," said Haldidge, with a sly look.

"I understand you, but you are mistaken. He has assured me as much. No; there seems nothing of that feeling at all in him. He loves her as he would a child, but no more."

"How was it that he made that awkward tumble into the Indians' hands, when they gave you such a hard run for it?"

"That was all through my own blundering. He was cautious enough, but I became so impatient and careless that I precipitated him into the danger which would have been fatal to any one else. It was no fault of his."

"I am glad to hear it, for it seemed odd to me."

This conversation which we have recorded, it must not be supposed, was carried on in an ordinary tone, and with that earnestness which would have lessened their habitual caution. It was in whispers, and hardly once during its progress did the two look at each other. Sometimes they would not speak for several minutes, and then exchange but a single question and answer.

It was now toward the middle of the afternoon, and it became pretty evident that the night would have to be spent in this neighborhood.

"I do hope that Seth will make his appearance before dark," remarked Graham.

"Yes; I hope he will, for it will be dangerous when we can't see him."

"He must be aware of the threatened danger."

"Yes; I am pretty confident that he is not very distant."

"Hallo! what's that?" whispered Graham.

"Ah! keep quiet; there's something going on there."

A deathlike silence reigned for a few minutes; then a slight rustling was heard close by Haldidge, and as he turned his alarmed gaze toward it, the form of Seth Jones rose to his feet beside him.

"Where did you come from?" asked Graham in astonishment.

"I have been watching you. In a little trouble, eh?"

"We've found out we've got neighbors."

"They're not very nigh neighbors, leastways."

"What do you mean?"

"There isn't one in a quarter of a mile."

Haldidge and Graham looked at the speaker in astonishment.

"I tell *you*, it's so. Hallo, Haverland!" he called, stepping out from his concealment. "Come out here; there is nothing to be afraid of."

The manner of the speaker was singular, but the others well knew that he was not one to expose himself or others to danger, and accordingly all gathered around him.

"Are you not running great risk?" said Haverland, still experiencing some slight misgivings at stepping upon a spot which he well knew was so dangerous a short time before.

"No, sir; I reckon you needn't be at all skeerish, for if there was any danger of them Mohawks, I wouldn't be standing here."

"It's getting toward night, Seth, and we should make up our minds at once as to what we are going to do or how we are going to spend it."

"Can you shoot a gun?" asked Seth, suddenly, of Ina.

"I don't believe you can beat me," she answered, lightly.

"That is good."

So saying, he stepped into the bushes, where the dead body of the Indian was lying. Stooping over him, he removed the rifle from his rigid grasp, took his bullet-pouch and powder-horn and handed them to Ina.

"Now, there are five of us, all well armed," said he, "and if any of them infarnal Mohawks gets ahead of us, we all desarve red nightcaps for it."

"How are we to prevent it, when there seem to be ten times our number following us?" asked Haverland.

"The way on it is this 'ere: there is about a dozen trying to sarcumvent us. They're now ahead of us, and have laid an ambush for us. If we can pass that ambush we're safe as if we was home fair and sure. And there must be no *if* about it, for that ambush must be passed tonight."

CHAPTER XVIII. GETTING OUT OF THE WILDERNESS

Night, dark and gloomy, slowly settled over the forest. Nothing was heard save the dull soughing of the wind through the tree-tops, or the occasional howl of the wolf in the distance, or perhaps the near scream of the panther. Heavy, tumultuous clouds were wheeling through the sky, rendering the inky darkness doubly intense, and shrouding even the clearings in impenetrable gloom.

By and by, the distant rumbling of thunder came faintly through the air, and then a quivering fork of fire, like a stream of blood, trembling upon the edge of the dark storm-cloud for an instant. The heavy clouds, growing darker and more awful, poured forward until they seemed to concentrate in the western sky, where they towered aloft like some old embattled castle. The thunder grew heavier, until it sounded like the rolling of chariot-wheels over the courts of heaven, and the red streams of liquid fire streamed down the dark walls of the Storm Castle. Now and then the subtle element flamed out into a dazzling, instantaneous flash, and the bolt burst overhead.

"Keep close to me, and step light, for I tell *you* there's enough lightning."

Seth had thoroughly reconnoitered the valley to which we have referred, and had found, as he had expected, that there was an ambush laid for them. There was a sort of footpath, apparently worn by the passing of wild animals, which nearly crossed the valley. It was here that the Indians supposed the fugitives would be entrapped, until the death of a too daring member of their party led them to suspect that there intentions were discovered.

The little band was hours in crossing this valley. Seth with an almost inaudible "'sh!" would often pause, and they would stand for many anxious minutes listening intently for the dreaded danger. Then they would resume their march stepping with painful slowness.

It was at least three hours after the fugitives commenced this journey, and when Seth judged that he must be nearly through it, that he suddenly discovered he was walking in the very path he had striven so carefully to avoid. He was considerably startled at this and left at once.

"'Sh! down!" he whispered, turning his face behind him.

They were not ten feet from the path, when they all sunk quietly to the ground. Footsteps were now audible to all. The darkness was too profound to discern anything, but all heard their enemies almost near enough to touch them with the outstretched hand.

The situation of our friends was imminently perilous. The Mohawks were not passing along the path as at first supposed, but evidently searching it! Haldidge and Seth felt that they could not be aware of their proximity, and yet they knew a discovery was unavoidable.

Seth Jones rose to his feet so silently that even Haldidge who was within a foot of him, did not hear a rustle. He then touched Haverland's ear with his mouth and whispered:

"Scatter with the gal as quick as lightning, for they must find us out in a minute."

Haverland lifted Ina in his strong arms — she needed no caution — and stepped forward. It was impossible not to make some noise, when the wet bushes brushed against them. The savages heard it and started cautiously forward. They evidently suspected it was the fugitives, and had no suspicion that any one was lingering in the rear. The first warning Seth had was of a savage running plump against him.

"Beg your pardon, I didn't see you," exclaimed Seth, as each bounded backward. "Curse you," he muttered, "I only wish I could sight you for a minute."

Seth, Haldidge and Graham were now maneuvering against some five or six Indians. Had a bright flash of lightning illuminated the scene, just at this time, it is probable that all would have laughed outright at each other's attitudes and movements. The Indians, upon finding how near they were to their deadliest enemies, immediately bounded backward several yards, in order to avoid a too sudden collision with them. The three whites did precisely the same thing, each in his own characteristic way. Seth leaped to one side, crouched down in his usual panther-like manner, with his rifle in his left hand and his knife in his right, waiting until he could settle in his mind the precise spot upon which one of the savages was standing before making a lunge at him.

It would be tedious to narrate, the artifices and stratagem resorted to by these two opposing forces. Simon Kenton[4] and Daniel Boone once reached the opposite side of the Ohio river at the same moment, and at the same time became aware of the presence of another person upon the opposite side. These two old hunters and acquaintances reconnoitered for over *twenty-four hours*, before they discovered that they were friends. For nearly two hours, the Mohawks and the whites maneuvered with the most consummate skill against each other; now retreating and leading, dodging and eluding, each striving to lead the other into some trap that was as skillfully avoided, until, judging that

---

[4] *Simon Kenton:*   Appointed by Daniel Boone (1734–1820) as a scout, Simon Kenton (1755–1836) joined the settlement founded by Boone — Boonesborough, Kentucky — in 1775. Like Boone, he enjoyed notoriety as an Indian fighter.

Haverland was safe, Seth concluded to retreat himself. Accordingly, he cautiously withdrew, and ten minutes later found himself upon the outermost edge of the valley.

Ten minutes after Seth departed, Haldidge moved off, of course unknown to himself, in precisely the same direction. Graham soon adopted the same course. They all came out of the dangerous valley within twenty feet of each other. It took them some time before they came together; but, as each suspected the identity of the other, this did not require as long as it otherwise would.

"Now, boys," whispered Seth, "I cac'late we're out of the Valley of Death. Best give it a wide berth, is the private opinion of Seth Jones."

"But how about Haverland?" Graham asked.

"I think they must have come out near that point," replied the other.

"Let us move round them, and we've got to be spry, for daylight can't be far off, and I'm thinking as how them Ingins will find out that we've absconded; and, my gracious! won't they feel cheap?"

Just as the light of morning appeared in the east, they came upon Haverland, and resumed their journey. No halt was made for breakfast, for they were all too anxious to get forward on their way. In the course of an hour or so, they struck a sort of path, made by the passage of wild animals, which, besides being so hardened as to conceal their trail, was easily traveled.

Seth and Haldidge were too experienced woodsmen to relax their vigilance. They maintained the same duty as before, the former taking it upon himself to lead the way through the wilderness, and the latter to guard against danger from behind. The settlement toward which they were so anxiously hastening, was still several days distant, and to reach it, it was necessary to cross a river of considerable breadth. This river was reached by Seth at noon.

"By gracious! I forgot about this!" he exclaimed to himself. "Wonder if the gal can swim? If she can't how are we going to get her over? Put her on a chip, I s'pose, and let the breeze blow her across; the rest of us can swim, in course."

A few minutes later, our friends stood consulting upon the banks of the stream.

This consultation ended in active preparations for crossing on a raft. Hunting up material for constructing a raft now was the order of the hour. This was a work of extreme difficulty. They had no instruments except their hunting-knives, and these were little better than nothing. Large rotten limbs were broken from the trees, and placed together by Haverland, who took upon himself the task of lashing them with withes, while the others collected wood.

Haldidge went up the river, and Seth and Graham went down. Graham soon noticed a large, half-decayed log partly lying in the water. "Just the thing, exactly! Why, it's a raft itself. This will save further trouble. Let us launch it at once, and float it up to the spot," he exclaimed delightedly. The two approached it, stooped, and were in the very act of lifting it into the water, when Seth suddenly removed his shoulder, and arose to the upright position.

"Come, give us a lift," said Graham.

"Graham, I guess I wouldn't take the log, I don't think it will answer."

"Won't answer! Why not? In the name of common sense, give some reason."

"*Let that log alone! Do you understand?*"

Graham looked up, and started at the appearance of Seth. His eyes fairly scintillated, and he seemed ready to spring upon him, for daring to utter a word of dispute.

"Come along with me!" commanded Seth, in a voice hoarse with passion.

It wouldn't do to disregard that command; and, taking up his rifle, Graham lost no time in obeying it. But he wondered greatly whether Seth was suddenly become crazy or foolish. He followed him a short distance, and then hastened up beside him. Seeing that his face had recovered its usual expression, he gained courage and asked what he meant by such commands.

"Didn't you take notice that that log was holler?"

"I believe it was, although I did not examine it closely."

"Wal, if you *had* examined it closely, or even loosely, so that you took a peep into the log, you'd have seen a big Mohawk curled up there snug and nice!"

"Is it possible? How came you to see him?"

"The minute I see'd the log was holler, I had my s'picions that there might be something or other in it, and I made up my mind that we shouldn't try to lift it till I knowed how it was. When I come to look closer, I knowed thar was something sure enough, for the way the bark was scratched at the mouth showed that plain enough. It wouldn't do, you see, to stoop down and peep in, for like as not the red-skin would blaze away smack into my face. So I jest dropped my cap, and, as I stooped down to pick it up, I kind of slewed one eye 'round over my shoulder, and, as sure as blazes, I seen a big moccasin! I did, by gracious. I then proceeded to argufy the question; and, after considerable discussion, both in the affirmative and negative, I came unanimously to the conclusion that as I'd seen an Ingin's foot, if I'd foller it up, I'd be pretty sure to find the Ingin himself, and, moreover, also if there was *one* Ingin about, you could make up your mind that there are plenty more not far off. By gracious! if I hadn't looked a little ramparageous, you wouldn't have let go that log so very quick, eh?"

"No; you alarmed me considerably. But what is to be done?"

"The cowards are poking around the woods, fixing out some plan to ambush us again. They've no idea we've smelt the rat that's brewing in the bud, and they're too cowardly to show their faces until they find they've got to, or let us slip."

"Shall we tell Haverland?"

"No; I will let Haldidge know of it, if he hasn't found out already. The raft has got to be made, and we must keep on at it till it's finished, as though we knowed everything was right. Keep still, now, or Alf will notice our talking."

They were so close to the woodman that they changed their conversation.

"No material?" asked Haverland, looking up.

"It's rather scarce down where we've been," replied Graham.

"Sha'n't I help you?" asked Ina, looking up archly.

"I guess we won't need your help, as Haldidge seems to have enough already."

The hunter at this moment approached, bending under the weight of two heavy limbs. They were instantly lashed together, but it was found that the raft was much too weak and light, and more stuff was necessary before it would even float Ina. Accordingly, Haldidge plunged into the wood again. Seth walked beside him until they were a few yards away when he asked:

"Do you understand?"

"What?" asked the hunter, in astonishment.

"Over there," answered Seth, jerking his thumb over his shoulder, toward the log mentioned.

"Red-skins?"

"I rather guess so."

"I smelt them a while ago. You'd better go back and watch Alf. I'll get enough wood. Danger?"

"No; they'll try some game; look out for yourself."

With this Seth turned on his heel, and rejoined Haverland. Graham was a short distance away cutting withes, which the woodman was as busily using. As Seth came up he noticed Ina. She was sitting upon the ground a few feet from her father, and her attention seemed wholly absorbed with something down the stream. Seth watched her closely.

"Isn't that a log yonder?" she asked.

Seth looked in the direction indicated. With no small degree of astonishment, he saw the identical tree which he and Graham disputed over, afloat in the river. This awoke his apprehensions, and he signaled at once for Haldidge.

"What's the row?" asked the hunter, as he came up.

Seth gave his head a toss down-stream, by way of reply, and added:

"Don't let 'em see you're watching it, for it might scare 'em."

Nevertheless Haldidge turned square around and took a long, searching look at the suspicious object.

"What do you make of it?"

"Them Mohawks are the biggest fools I ever heard of, to think that such and old trick as *that* can amount to anything."

"What trick do you mean?" asked Haverland.

"Why, you see that log yonder, half-sunk in the water, that we are all looking at? Well, there are four or five Mohawks behind that, waiting for us to launch our raft."

"Maybe it's nothing more than a floating tree or log," said the woodman.

"Y-e-s," drawled the hunter, sarcastically, "*maybe* so; I s'pose a log would be very apt to float *up*-stream, wouldn't it?"

"Why is it approaching?" asked Graham.

"Not *very* fast," answered Seth, "for I guess it's hard work for them fellers to swim up-stream. Ah, by gracious! I understand the game. Look; don't you see it's further out than it was? They're going to get as near the middle as they can, and so close to us that when we undertake to cross, the current will carry us right down plump against 'em, when they'll rise up in their wrath and devour us. Fact, sure as you live!"

"We might as well understand matters at once," added Haldidge. "The plan of the Indians is undoubtedly the same as Seth suggests. In crossing, we cannot help drifting downward, and they are trying to locate themselves so as to make a collision between us. But they will make no attack until we are in the water. So you may keep at work upon the raft, Alf, without any fear, while Seth and I reconnoiter. Come, Graham, you may as well go along with us. Let us enter the woods separately at first, and we'll come together as soon as we can get out of sight. Act as though we didn't suspicion anything, and I'll wager my rifle here against your hat that we'll outwit the cowards after all."

The three entered the wood as proposed. After going a few yards they came together again.

"Now," whispered Seth, "by gracious, you will see fun. Follow close, boys, and keep shady."

Being now fairly within the wood, they proceeded in a direction parallel with the course of the river, using extreme caution, for it was more than probable that some of the Indian scouts were secreted in the wood. Keeping entirely away from the river until Seth judged they were below the suspicious log, they approached it. A reckless move, at this point, would have been fatal. Fortunately, there was a species of grass growing from the wood out to a considerable distance in the water. Through this they made their way much after the fashion of snakes. Seth, as usual, was in the front, and it struck Graham that he absolutely slid over the ground without any exertion on his part.

In a moment they were down to the river's brink. They now slowly raised their heads and peered over and through the grass out into the river. The log was a short distance above, and they had a perfect view of the side which was opposite to Haverland. Not a sign of an Indian was visible. The tree seemed anchored in the middle of the stream.

"There is something there," whispered Graham.

"'Sh! keep quiet and watch, and you'll see!" admonished Seth.

A moment more and the log, apparently without any human agency, slightly changed its position. As it did so, Graham saw something glisten on the top of it. He was at a loss to understand what it meant, and turned inquiringly toward Haldidge. The later had his keen eyes fixed upon it, and there was a grim, exalting smile upon his face. He motioned for Graham to preserve silence.

As our hero turned his gaze once more toward the river, he saw that the log was still further into the stream. Something like polished metal was seen glistening even brighter than before. He looked carefully, and in a moment he saw that there were several rifles resting upon the surface of it.

While gazing and wondering where the owners of these weapons could conceal themselves, the water suddenly seemed to part on the side of the log toward them, and the bronzed face of an Indian rose to view. Up, up it went, until the shoulders were out of the water, when he remained stationary for a moment, and peered over the log at Haverland. Seemingly satisfied, he quietly sunk down into the water again; but Graham noticed that he did not disappear beneath the surface, where he had hitherto kept himself, nestled in so close to the log that almost any one would have supposed that he was a part of it. His head resembled exactly a large black knot in the wood. Graham now noticed also that there were two protuberances, precisely like the first. The conclusion was certain. There were three fully-armed Mohawks concealed behind the log, who were doing their utmost to steal upon the fugitives.

"Just exactly one apiece, as sure as you live," exclaimed Seth, exultingly. "Get ready, each of you, for your man. Graham, take the one nearest this way; you the next one, Haldidge, and I'll pick off the last one in the genuine style. Get ready, quick, for I've got to hurrah over the way things is coming round."

The three pointed their deadly instruments toward the unsuspicious savages. Each took a long, deliberate and certain aim.

"Now, then, together — *fire!*"

Simultaneously the three rifles flashed, but that of Seth missed fire. The others sped true to their aim. Two yells of deathly agony broke upon the air, and one of the savages sprung his entire length out of the water, and then sunk like lead to the bottom. The other clung quivering to the log for a moment, and then loosening his hold, disappeared beneath the water.

"Thunder and blazes!" exclaimed Seth, springing to his feet, "hand me your rifle, Graham. Something is the matter with mine, and that other imp will get away. Quick! hand it here!"

He took the rifle and commenced loading it as rapidly as possible, keeping his eye upon the Indian, who now was swimming desperately for the other bank.

"Is yer iron loaded, Haldidge?" he asked.

"No; I've been watching you and that chap's doubling, to see who'll get the best, so long, that I didn't think of it."

"Load again, for s'posen this gun should miss fire, too, he'd get off then, sure. Wal, my stars! if he isn't coming out now!"

The Indian, as if scorning the danger, rose slowly from the water, and walked leisurely toward the shelter of the wood.

"Now, my fine fellar, see if you can dodge this?"

Seth once more aimed at the retreating Indian, and this time pulled the trigger; but, to his unutterable chagrin, the rifle flashed in the pan!

Before Haldidge could finish loading his gun, and before Seth could even reprime his, the Indian had disappeared in the wood.

"By the hokey-pokey! what's got into the guns?" exclaimed Seth, in a perfect fury. "That's *twice* I've been fooled. Worse'n two slaps in the face by a purty woman, I'll swow. Hallo! what's that?"

The discharge of a rifle across the river had sent the bullet so close to him as to whisk off a tuft of his long, sandy hair.

"By gracious; that was pretty well done," he exclaimed, scratching his head as though he was slightly wounded.

"Look out, for heaven's sake! Get down!" called Graham seizing him by the skirt of his hunting-dress, and jerking him downward.

"Don't know but what it *is* the best plan," replied the imperturbable Seth, going down on his knees in time to avoid another foul shot. "There are plenty of the imps about, ain't there?"

The firing so alarmed Haverland that he desisted from his work, and sought the shelter of the wood. By this time, too, the afternoon was so far advanced that darkness had already commenced settling over the stream and woods. Crossing on the raft was now out of the question, for it would have been nothing less than suicide to have attempted it, when their enemies had given them such convincing evidence of their skill in the use of the rifle, even at a greater distance than to the middle of the stream. But the river had to be crossed for all that, and the only course left was to shift their position to some other place, build a new raft, and make another attempt.

There was no excuse for further delay, and the party immediately set forward. The sky again gave signs of a storm. Several rumbles of thunder were heard, but the lightning was so distant as to be of neither benefit or use to them. The sky was filled with heavy, tumultuous clouds, which rendered the darkness perfectly intense and impenetrable; and as none of them understood a foot of the ground over which they were traveling, it may well be supposed that their progress was neither rapid nor particularly pleasant. The booming of the thunder continued, and shortly the rain commenced falling. The drops were of that big kind which are often formed in summer, and which rattle through the leaves like a shower of bullets.

"Can you look ahead, Seth?" asked Graham.

"In course I can. The darkness don't make no difference not at all to me. I can see just as well on a dark night as I can in daylight, and, what is more, I *do*. I should like to see me make a misstep or stumble — "

Further utterance was checked by the speaker pitching, with a loud splash, head-foremost over and into something.

"*You* hurt, Seth?" asked Graham, in alarm, yet half tempted to give way to the mirth that was convulsing those behind him.

"Hurt!" exclaimed the unfortunate one, scrambling to his feet; "I believe every bone in my body is broken in two; and by gracious! my head is cracked, and both legs put out of joint, the left arm broke above the elbow, and the right one severed completely!"

Notwithstanding these frightful injuries, the speaker was moving about with wonderful dexterity.

"My gracious! what do you suppose I've tumbled into?" he suddenly asked.

"Into a pitfall or a hole in the ground," replied Graham. "It's my opinion, too, that it will be very easy, with this noise we are making, to stumble into the Mohawks' hands."

"I should think you ought to know that I *didn't* fall," retorted Seth, angrily. "I happened to see sumthin', and I stepped forward to see if it would hold my weight. What are you laughing at, I should like to know?"

"What is it that you have stepped into?" asked Haverland.

"Why, it's nothing less than a *boat*, dragged up here by the varmints, I s'pose."

Such, indeed, was the case. There was a very large-sized canoe directly before them, and not a sign of the presence of others besides themselves. Not a more fortunate thing could have happened. Upon examination, the boat was found to be of unusual length and breadth, and amply sufficient to carry twenty men. It was quickly pushed back into the stream.

"Come, tumble in, and we'll set sail," said Seth.

The fugitives, without any hesitation, entered the boat, and Seth and Haldidge, lending their shoulders to it, shoved it into the river, and sprung in as it floated away.

CHAPTER XIX. DENOUEMENT

The whites found in a moment that they had committed a great mistake in launching as they did. In the first place, there was not an oar in the boat, and thus, not being able to "paddle their own canoe," they were also deprived of the ability to paddle one belonging to some one else. Besides this, the river was dark as Styx, and the whole sky and air were of the same inky blackness, and not one in the boat had the remotest idea of where they were going, whether it was to pitch over some falls, down some rapids, or into the bank.

"I'm going to set down and consider which is the biggest fool, Haldidge, you or me, in starting out in this canoe which we *borrowed* for a short time."

So saying, Seth made his way to the stern of the canoe, where he rested himself — not upon the bottom of it, as he expected, but upon something *soft*, which emitted a grunt audible to all, as he did so.

"My gracious! what's under me?" he exclaimed, reaching his hand down and feeling around in the dark. "A live Ingin, as sure as my name is Seth Jones. Ah, you copper-headed monkey!"

It was as he said. An Indian had stretched out on his back, with his feet dangling over the edge of the canoe, and Seth, without the faintest suspicion of his presence, had seated himself square upon his breast. As may be supposed, this was not relished at all by the startled savage, and he made several strenuous efforts to roll him off.

"Now, just lay still," commanded Seth, "for I've an idea that I can't find a more comfortable seat."

The savage was evidently so thoroughly frightened that he ceased his efforts and lay perfectly quiet and motionless.

"Have you got a real Indian here?" asked Haldidge, as he came up to Seth.

"To be sure I have; just feel under me, and see if I hain't."

"What are you going to do with him?"

"Nothing."

"Are you going to let him off? Let's pitch him overboard."

"No you won't Haldidge. I've two or three good reasons for not doing such a thing. In the first place, there ain't no need of it, the poor imp hasn't hurt us; and, for all I detest his whole cowardly race, I don't believe in killing them, except when they've done you some injury or are trying to. The most important reason, however, is that I don't want my seat disturbed."

"He is a cussed fool to let you sit on him that way. I'd give you a toss if I was in his place, that would send you overboard."

"Not if you knew what was best for you. Thunder!"

Perhaps the Indian understood the words of the hunter. At any rate, he made an attempt to carry out his suggestion, and well-nigh did it, too. Just as Seth gave vent to the exclamation recorded, he pitched headlong against Haverland, knocking him over upon his back, and falling upon him. At the same instant the savage sprung overboard, and swam rapidly away in the darkness.

"That's a mean trick," said Seth, as he recovered his sitting position. "I was just setting on him to keep the rain off. Jest like the ungrateful dog!"

The attention of all was now directed to the progress of the canoe. Drifting slowly onward through the darkness, no one knowing whither, their situation began to assume a terrible form. There was no power in their hands to guide it, and should they run into any of the trees which had caught in the bottom, or upon a rock, they would be instantly swamped. But there was no help for it, and each one seated and braced himself for the shock which might come at any instant.

It was while they were proceeding in this manner, that they all heard the bottom of the canoe grate over something, then tremble for a moment, and suddenly came to a stand-still. The stern swung rapidly round and commenced filling.

"Overboard, men, all of you! We're sinking!" commanded Haldidge.

Each sprung into the water, which was not more than two feet deep, and the canoe, thus lightened of its load, instantly freed itself, and floated off in the darkness.

"Don't move, till I take a few soundings," said Seth.

He naturally supposed that to reach the shore, he must take a direction at right-angles with the current. A few steps showed him that he was not in the river itself, but was walking in that portion which had overflowed its banks.

"Follow on, boys; we're right!" he called out.

Bushes and grass entangled their feet, and the branches overhead brushed their faces, as they toiled out of the water. A few moments and they were upon solid land again. The canoe had carried them safely across the river, so that this troublesome task was finished.

"Now, if we only had a fire," said Haverland.

"Yes; for Ina must be suffering."

"Oh! don't think of me!" replied the brave little girl, cheerfully.

Seth discovered with his customary shrewdness that the storm had been very slight in this section, and the wood was comparatively dry. By removing the leaves upon the surface of the ground, there were others beneath which were perfectly free from dampness. A quantity of these were thrown in a heap, a number of twigs found among them placed upon the top, and some larger branches placed upon these in turn. After great difficulty, Seth managed to catch a spark from his steel and tinder, and in a few moments they had a rousing, roaring, genial fire.

"That's fine," said Graham. "But won't it be dangerous, Seth?"

"Let it be, then; I'm bound to dry my skin to-night, if there's any vartue in fire."

But the Indians didn't choose to disturb them, although it was a rather reckless proceeding upon their part. It was more than probable, as Seth Jones remarked, that their pursuers had lost their trail, and would experience some difficulty in regaining and following it.

Morning at last broke upon the hungry, miserable, hopeful fugitives. As the light increased they looked about them and discovered that they had camped at the base of a large, heavily-wooded hill. It was also noticed that Haldidge, the hunter, was absent. While wondering at this, the report of his rifle was heard, and in a few moments he was seen descending the hill, bending under the weight of a half-grown dear. This was hastily dressed, several good-sized pieces skewered and cooked in the flame, and our friends made as hearty and substantial a meal as was ever made in this world.

"Before starting upon our journey again," said Haldidge, "I want you all to go to the top of the hill, here, with me, and see what a fine view we shall have."

"Oh! we've no time for views," replied Seth.

"I am afraid there is little spare time," added the woodman.

"But this is particularly fine, and I think you will be well pleased with it."

The hunter was so urgent that the others were finally obliged to consent. Accordingly they commenced the ascent, Haldidge leading them, and all anxiety, smiles and expectations.

"See how you like that view!" said he, pointing off to the west.

The fugitives gazed in the direction indicated. The prospect was one indeed which at that time pleased them more than could have other in the universe; for below them, about half a mile distant, was the very village toward which they had been so long making their way. It looked unusually beautiful that morning in the clear sunshine. A score of cabins nestled closely together, and the heavy smoke was lazily ascending from several chimneys while here and there a settler could be seen moving about. At one corner of the village stood the block-house, and the gaping mouth of its swivel shone in the morning sun like burnished silver. One or two small boats were visible in the water, their ashen paddles flashing brightly as they were dipped by strong and active hands. The river, down which the woodman and his wife and sister had escaped, flowed at the foot of the village, and its windings could be traced by the eye for miles. Here and there, scattered over the country, could be seen an enterprising settler's cabin, resembling in the distance a tiny beehive.

"You haven't told me how you are pleased with the landscape," said the hunter.

"Ah, Haldidge, you know better than to ask that question," replied Haverland, in a shaking voice. "Thank God that He has been so merciful to us!"

They now commenced descending the hill. Not a word was exchanged between them, for their hearts were too full of utterance. A strange spell seemed to have come over Seth Jones. At sight of the village, he had suddenly become thoughtful and silent, refusing even to answer a question. His head was bent down. Evidently his mind was engrossed upon some all-absorbing subject. Several times he sighed deeply, and pressed his hand to his heart, as though the tumultuous throbbing there pained him. The expression of his face was wonderfully changed. That quizzing, comical look was entirely gone, while wrinkles at the eyebrows and base of the nose could be seen no more. His face appeared to be positively handsome. It was a wonderful metamorphosis, and the question passed around unexpressed: "Is that Seth Jones?"

All at once, he seemed to become sensible that the eyes of others were upon him, and that he had forgotten himself. That old, peculiar expression came back to his face, and a few steps of the old straddling gait were taken, and Seth Jones was himself again!

The sentinels in the block-house had discovered and recognized the fugitives, and when they arrived at the palisade which surrounded the village, there were numbers waiting to receive them.

"I will see you all again!" said Haldidge, separating from the others and passing toward the upper end of the settlement.

After pausing a few moments to answer the inquiries of their friends, Haverland led the way toward the cabin where he had left his wife and sister. Here he found the good settlers had erected and presented him with a house. As he stepped softly to the door, intending to give his wife a playful surprise, she met him. With a low cry of joy, she sprung forward and was held in his arms, and the next instant she and Ina were clasped together and weeping.

"Thank Heaven! thank Heaven! Oh, my dear, dear child. I thought you lost forever."

Graham and Seth stood respectfully to one side for a few moments. The latter cleared his throat several times and brushed his arm across his forehead in a suspicious manner. As the mother regained herself, she turned and recognized Graham, and greeted him warmly.

"And you, too," she said, taking Seth's hand, and looking up into his face, "have been more than a friend to me. May Heaven reward you, for *we* never can."

"There! by gracious! don't say no more! boohoo! ahem! I believe I've caught a cold, being so exposed to the night air!"

But it was no use; the tears *would* come; and Seth for a few seconds, wept like a baby, yet smiled even through the tears. They all entered the house.

"Our first duty is to thank God for his mercy. Let us all do it," said the woman.

All sunk devoutly upon their knees, joining in fervent thanksgiving to the great Being who had shown his goodness to them in such a marvelous manner.

The settlers, with true politeness of heart, forbore to intrude until they judged the family were desirous of seeing them. After they had arisen from their knees, Mary, the sister of Haverland, entered. Graham chanced to glance at Seth, that moment, and was startled at the emotion he exhibited. He flushed scarlet, and trembled painfully, but, by a strong effort, recovered himself in time to greet her. She thanked him again, and began conversing, when she saw that he was embarrassed and ill at ease. A flash of suspicion crossed her fine, calm face, and it became pale and flushed by turns. What a riot emotion was making in her heart only she herself knew; her face soon became passive and pensive; and a pathos gleamed from her sad eyes which sent Seth quickly out of doors to commune with the mysteries of his own thoughts.

The cabin was crowded until near midnight with congratulating friends. Prominent among these, was the man who officiated in the capacity of minister for the settlement. He was a portly, genial, good-natured man, of the Methodist persuasion, and a preacher for the times — one who could plow, reap, chop wood, and lead the settlers against their foes, when he deemed it necessary, or preach and practice the gospel before them.

It was a glad — a happy reunion — a night that was long remembered.

Just one week after the reunion the little party was seated in Haverland's home, composed of Ina, Seth Jones, the woodman, Mrs. Haverland and Mary. Seth sat in one corner, conversing with Ina, while the other three were also together. There was a happy look upon each face. Even the sweet, melancholy beauty of Mary was lighted up by a smile. She was beautiful — queenly so. Her hair, black as night, was gathered behind, as if to restrain its tendency to curl; but, in spite of this, a refractory one was constantly intruding itself. A faint color was visible in her cheeks, and her blue eye had in it something of a gleam of the common joy and peace.

Seth had remained most of the time with the woodman. Several times he had asked Mary Haverland to walk with him, and yet upon each occasion, when about to start, he became painfully nervous, and begged to be excused. And then his language was so different at times. Often he would converse with words so polished and well-chosen, as to show unmistakably that he was a scholar. Perhaps the reader has noticed this discrepancy in his conversation. It attracted attention, and strengthened many in their belief that for some unknown reason he was playing a part.

At the present time there was a nervousness in his manner; and, although he was holding a playful conversation with Ina, his eyes were constantly wandering to the face of Mary Haverland.

"And so you and Graham are going to be married to-morrow night?" he asked.

"You know, Seth, that we are. How many times are you going to ask me?"

"Do you love him?" he asked, looking her steadily in the face.

"What a question! I have *always* loved him, and *always* will."

"That's right; then marry him, for if man ever loved woman, he loves you. And, Alf, while I think of it," he spoke in a louder tone, "what has that big, red-haired fellow been hanging around here so much for the last day or two?"

"You will have to ask Mary," laughed the woodman.

"Oh, I understand, there'll be two weddings to-morrow night, eh? That's so Mary?"

"Not that I know of; I have no expectation of becoming a wife for any one."

"Hain't, eh? Why, the man seems to love you. Why don't you marry him?"

"I am afraid Mary will never marry," Said Haverland. "She has rejected all offers, though many were from very desirable men."

"Queer! I never heard of such a case."

"Her love was buried long ago," replied Haverland, in a lower tone, to Seth.

After a moment's silence, Seth arose, took his chair, and seated himself beside her. She did not look at him, nor did any one else. He sat a moment; then whispered:

"Mary?"

She started. Her eyes flashed like meteors in his face a moment; then she turned as pale as death, and would have fallen from her chair, had not Seth caught her in his arms. Haverland looked up in amazement; the whole family were riveted in wonder. Seth looked up from the face of the fainting woman, and smiled as he said:

"She is mine forever!"

"Merciful Heaven! Eugene Morton!" exclaimed Haverland, starting to his feet.

"It is so!" said the one addressed.

"Have you risen from the dead?"

"I have risen to life, Alf, but have never been with the dead."

Instead of the weak, squeaking tone which had heretofore characterized his speech, was now a rich, mellow base, whose tones startled Mary into life again. She raised her head, but he who held her would not permit her to rise. He pressed her fervently to his bosom. The ecstasy of that moment, only the angels in Heaven could fathom.

Haldidge and Graham entered, and the man in his true character, arose to his feet — a tall, dignified, graceful, imposing person.

"Where is Seth?" asked Graham, not noticing the apparent stranger.

"Here is what you have heretofore supposed to be that individual," laughed the person before him, enjoying greatly their astonishment.

"Seth, truly, but not Seth, either," exclaimed they both, with astonishment written on their faces.

"With a few words," he commenced, "all will be plain to you. I need not tell you, dear friends, that my character, since my advent among you, has been an assumed one. Seth Jones is a myth, and to *my* knowledge, no such person ever existed. My real name is Eugene Morton. Ten years ago, Mary Haverland and I pledged our love to each other. We were to be married in one year; but, when a few months of that time had elapsed, the Revolutionary War broke out, and a call was made upon our little village, in New Hampshire, for volunteers. I had no desire nor right to refuse. Our little company proceeded to Massachusetts, where the war was then raging. In a skirmish, a few days after the battle of Bunker Hill, I was dangerously wounded, and was left with a farmer by the wayside. I sent word by one of my comrades to Mary, that I was disabled, but hoped to see her in a short time. The bearer of that message was probably killed, for it is certain my words never reached her, though a very different report did. We had a man in our company who was a lover of Mary's. Knowing of my misfortune, he sent her word that I was killed. When I rejoined my company, a few months after, I learned that this man had deserted. A suspicion that he had returned home impelled me to obtain leave of absence to visit my native place. I there learned that Haverland, with his wife and sister, had left the village for the West. One of my friends informed me that this deserter had gone with them, and, it was understood, would marry Mary. I could not doubt the truth of this report, and, for the time, I feared I should commit suicide. To soften this great sorrow, I returned at once, joined our company, and plunged into every battle that I possibly could. I often purposely exposed myself to danger, soliciting death rather than life. In the winter of 1776 I found myself under General Washington, at Trenton; I had crossed the Delaware with him, and, by the time it was fairly light, we were engaged in a desperate fight with the Hessians. In the very heat of the battle, the thought suddenly came to me that the story of Mary's marriage was untrue. Singularly enough, when the battle was over, I did not think any more of it. But in the midst of the following engagement, at Princeton, the same thought came to me again, and haunted me from that time until the close of the war. I determined to seek out Mary. All that I could learn was that Haverland had emigrated out this way. If she *had* married the deserter, I knew it was under a firm belief that I was dead. Consequently, I had no right to pain her by my presence. For this reason, I assumed a disguise. I discolored my now long-untamed hair. It so changed my whole appearance that I hardly knew myself. War had changed my youthful color into bronze, and sorrow had wrought its changes. It was not strange, then, that any old friend should not know me, particularly when I could so successfully personate the 'Green Mountain Boy,' in voice and manner. My identity was perfectly secure, I knew, from detection. I came to this section, and, after a long and persevering hunt, one day I found Haverland cutting in the wood. I introduced myself to him as Seth Jones. I found Mary. The report which had reached me of her marriage was false; she was still true to her first love. I should have made myself known then, had not the danger which threatened Haverland come upon him almost immediately. As his family were then tormented by the fate of Ina, I thought my recognition would only serve to embarrass and distract their actions. Besides, I felt some amusement in the part I was playing, and often enjoyed the speculation I created by giving you, as it were, a glimpse now and then into my real nature. I varied my actions and language on purpose to increase your wonder." He here paused and smiled, as if at the recollection of his numerous ludicrous escapades. He continued: "I have little more to add. I congratulate you, Graham, on the prize you have won. You are to be married to-morrow night. Mary, will you not marry me at the same time?"

"Yes," replied the radiant woman, placing her hands in his. "You have my hand now, as you've had my heart through all these long, sorrowing years."

Morton kissed her forehead tenderly.

"Now congratulate *me*," said he, with a beaming face.

And they gathered around him, and such shaking of hands, and such greetings, we venture to say were never seen before. Our friends experienced some difficulty at first in believing that Seth Jones was gone forever. They even felt some regrets that his pleasing, eccentric face had passed away; but they had gained in his place a handsome, noble-hearted man, of whom they were all proud.

The next day was spent in preparations for the great double wedding that was to take place that evening. Messengers were sent up and down the river, and back into the woods; there was not a settler within twenty miles who had not been invited. At nightfall the company began to collect. Some came in boats, some on horseback, and others on foot. A double wedding rarely took place in the backwoods, and this occasion was too full of romance to be slighted by any, old or young.

When the lights were produced in the woodman's house there was a motley assemblage without and within. You could have heard old and middle-aged men talking about the prospect of the crops, and looking up to the sky and wisely predicting the probabilities of a change in the weather, or discussing, in anxious tones, the state of feeling among the Indians along the frontier; you could have heard — as they would be termed nowadays — "gawky" young men as sagely discoursing upon the same subjects, venturing a playful thrust, now and then, at one of their number about some "Alminy," or "Sera, pheemy," sweetheart.

The woodman's house had been much enlarged for the occasion. A long shed, amply sufficient to contain all the guests, was built alongside and connecting with it. After participating in a bountiful meal in this, the tables were removed, and preparation made for the marriage.

A sudden hush fell upon the assemblage. All eyes turned toward the door, through which Eugene Morton and Edward Graham, each with his affianced leaning upon his arm, entered.

"Ain't they purty?"

"Don't they look bootiful?"

"Golly! if they ain't *some*, then there's no use in talking."

Such and similar were the whispered remarks of admiration at the couple. Mary Haverland was dressed in a plain, light-colored dress without any ornament, except a single white rose in her hair, which now fell in dark masses over her shoulders. Her beauty was of the true regal type. She was very happy, yet seemed as if in a world of her own.

Morton was clad in gray homespun, which well became his graceful form. His whole appearance was that of the *gentleman* which he was — a brave soldier, a true-hearted man.

Ina, a sweet young heroine, was fascinating. Her dress was of the purest white. Her curls clustered around her shoulders, and were confined at the temples by a simple wreath of blue violets. There was a contrast between Ina and Mary, and yet it would have been a difficult task to have judged which was the most beautiful — the pure, queenly, trusting woman, or the purity and innocence of the young maiden. Graham was a worthy participant in the drama and pleased all by his goodness and intelligence.

In a few moments, a portly gentleman, with a white neckcloth, and all aglow with smiles, entered the room. Morton and Mary arose and stood before him, and amid the most perfect silence the ceremony commenced. The questions were put and answered in a firm voice, audible to every one in the room.

"What God hath joined together let not man put asunder."

And every voice said "Amen!" as they reseated themselves.

Haldidge, who had stood as groomsman to Morton, now signaled with a quiet smile, for Graham to take his position. The young hero did, and Ina, blushing deeply, and leaning on the arm of her bridesmaid, followed, and the ceremony commenced.

While this was proceeding, an interesting affair was occurring at the opposite end of the room. A large, bony, red-faced young man sat holding and squeezing the hand of a bouncing, buxom girl, and indulging in several expressive remarks.

"I swow, if they don't look purty. Wonder how the gal feels?"

"Why, happy, of course," replied his companion.

"By jingo, I bet *he* does; I know *I* would."

"Would what?"

"Feel glorious if I was in *his* place."

"What! marrying Ina Haverland?"

"No — I mean — ahem! — why, somebody else — that is — yes, *somebody* else."

"Who else do you mean?" asked the girl, looking him steadily in the face.

"Why — ahem! — why, *you!* Darn it, now you know, don't you?"

"Sal, Don't talk so loud, Josiah, or they'll hear you."

"S'posen you was in her place, Sal, how would you feel?"

"Ain't you ashamed of yourself?" she asked reprovingly.

"No, darnation, I don't care. Say, Sal, how *would* you feel?"

"Do you mean if I was standing out there with you, and the minister talking to us?"

"Yes — yes; why don't you tell me?"

"You know well enough, Josiah, without asking me no such question."

Josiah commenced meditating. Some desperate scheme was evidently troubling him, for he scratched his head, and then his knees, and then laughed, and exclaimed to himself: "I'll do it, by George!" Then turning toward the girl, he said:

"Sal, let's you and I get married, won't you?"

"Why, Josiah!" and she hung her head and blushed charmingly.

"Come, Sal, the old folks won't care. Let's do it, won't you?"

"Oh, Josiah!" she continued, growing nervous and fidgety.

"Come, say quick, for the dominie is near done, and he'll go home. Say *yes*, Sal, do."

"Oh, dear! oh, my stars! — YES!"

"Good, by jingo! Hurry up there, Mr. Preacher."

At this point the good minister ceased his benediction upon the couples, and their friends commenced crowding around them. The minister started, not to go home, but to leave the room for a moment, when Josiah noticed it, and fearing that he was going, called out:

"Say, squire — you, dominie, I mean — just wait, won't you? Here's another job for you."

"Ah, I am glad to hear it," laughed the minister, turning round. "Are you the happy man?"

"Wel, I reckon so, and I calc'late as how Sal Clayton there is the happy gal."

All eyes were turned toward the speaker, and he stood their smiles unflinchingly. His face was of a fiery red, and a large flowing necktie hung disregarded over his breast.

"Go in, Josiah — that's you!" exclaimed several, patting him on the shoulder.

"Get out, all of you, till I'm through. Come up here, Sal; no use scroochin' now."

The females bore the blushing one forward, until she was near enough to Josiah to get hold of her hand.

"Now, go ahead, squire — you — minister, I mean, and don't be too thundering long about it, for I want to get married most terribly."

The company gave way and the two stepped forward and in a few moments were pronounced man and wife. When Josiah saluted his bride the smack was a telling one, and the congratulations of Morton and Graham were nothing to those which were showered upon the happy man.

Now the sport commenced. An old ranger suddenly made his appearance, bearing a violin under his arm — "a reg'lar old Cremony," as he termed it. The word was given to "make ready for the dance." The old folks disappeared and entered the house, where, with the minister, they indulged in conversation, story-telling, nuts, apples and cider.

The fiddler coiled himself up on the top of a box, and commenced twisting the screws on his instrument, and thumping the strings. The operation of "tuning" was evidently a painful one, for it was noticed that at each turn of the screw he shut one eye and twisted his mouth.

The violin was at length tuned, the bow was given two or three sweeps across a lump of resin; and then drawn across the strings, as if it said "attention!" As the couples were forming, the violinist slid partly down off the box, so that one foot could beat upon the sanded floor, and then, giving his head a jerk backward, struck up a reel that fairly set every heart dancing. The floor was immediately filled with the young folks. Tall, strapping fellows plunged around the room, like skeletons of India rubber, their legs bowed out, and sometimes tripping over each other. Rousing, solid girls bounded round, up and down, like pots of jelly, and "all went merry as a marriage-bell."

By and by the old folks made their appearances, "just to see the boys and girls enjoy themselves." The fiddler at this moment shot off on the "Devil's Dream." A timid elderly lady stepped up to him, and touching him softly on the shoulder, asked:

"Isn't that a profane tune?"

"No, it's Old Hundred with variations. Don't bother me," replied the performer, relieving his mouth of a quantity of tobacco juice at the same time.

"Supposing we try it for a moment, aunt Hannah," said the minister with a sly look.

The two stepped out upon the floor, the fiddler commenced another tune, and they disappeared in the whirling mass. In a few moments nearly all of the old folks, who had just come to "see them a minute," followed, and the way in which several elderly gentlemen and ladies executed some of the reels of a half-century's memory, was a lesson to the younger folks.

The company kept up their revelry until far beyond midnight. But by and by they commenced withdrawing. It was proposed by several to visit the different bridegrooms in bed, but, fortunately, the good taste of the others prevailed, and they departed quietly homeward.

Slumber, with the exception of the sentinels at the block-house, fell upon the village. Perhaps the Indians had no wish to break in upon such a happy settlement, for they made no demonstration through the night. Sweetly and peacefully they all slept; sweetly and peacefully they entered upon life's duties on the morrow; and sweetly and peacefully these happy settlers ascended and went down the hillside of life.

THE END.

Deadwood Dick, The Prince of the Road; or, The Black Rider of the Black Hills

Little is known of Edward L. Wheeler (1854?–1885?), who remained inconspicuous despite the unprecedented popularity of his hero, Deadwood Dick. His unabashed letterhead — *Studio of Edward L. Wheeler, Sensational Novelist, Philadelphia* — made it clear that he considered writing dime novels a perfectly reasonable profession (and an Eastern profession at that), uncharacterized by the exploits for which some of his fellow authors were famous. Colonel Prentiss Ingraham, for instance, one of Beadle's most prolific writers, fought for the Confederacy, for Juárez in Mexico, for Austria against Prussia, for Crete against Turkey, and for Cuban independence before returning to the United States, where he joined up with William Cody as a frontiersman and soon invented "Buffalo Bill." Wheeler, in contrast, was content to write of the West from his peaceful home in the East, never venturing so far as western Pennsylvania.

In 1877, Wheeler's first efforts in fiction resulted in the opening number not just of *Beadle's Half Dime Library* but also of *Starr's Ten Cent Pocket Library.* The latter, *Hurricane Nell, the Girl Dead-Shot; or, the Queen of the Saddle and Lasso,* makes it clear how he understood, as his predecessors rarely did, that poignant yet powerful women might be incorporated into the Western genre. His famous depictions of Calamity Jane — playing the wronged woman to Deadwood Dick's wronged man and demonstrating an intelligence and toughness no less than his — inspired a proliferation of sharp-shooting women (in and out of disguise as men) in the pages of subsequent Westerns. Wheeler himself devoted increasing attention to her in novels like *Deadwood Dick on Deck; or, Calamity Jane, the Heroine of Whoop-Up. A Story of Dakota* (1878), and he sustained an ongoing love interest between his hero and heroine throughout the series.

Though Wheeler hardly confined himself to their exploits (going on to write about Sierra Sam, Cyclone Kit, and Colorado Charlie as well as an assortment of New York detectives), he completed thirty-three Deadwood Dick novels between 1877 and 1884, establishing, with the exception of Buffalo Bill, the most successful serialized hero in the genre. Albert Johannsen, in his definitive history of the house of Beadle and Adams, was the first to suspect and to demonstrate that Wheeler's later works, including ninety-seven Deadwood Dick Jr. novels (1885–1897), were published pseudonymously, after Wheeler's death. Beadle's effort to suppress news of Wheeler's death while continuing to put his name on the work of staff writers is no doubt why so little information about the author remains.

Beadle's new half-dime series, introducing the quarto broadleaf format (which marked the end of the genuinely pocket-size novel), was specifically directed toward boys. This is one reason why moral reformers like Anthony Comstock and Thomas DeWitt Talmadge became increasingly outraged by popular fiction. Wheeler's Deadwood Dick was a new type of Western hero: the bandit, the vengeful outlaw who refuses to comply with what he understands to be a corrupt legal system, the outsider who remains on the margins of society as a "merry road-agent" with his fellow outsiders. The new hero, possessing none of the civility of a Natty Bumppo or a Seth Jones, was so popular that Street & Smith introduced *Diamond Dick* in 1878, and other publishing firms quickly added bandits of their own. Not only Deadwood Dick's status as a "grim and uncommunicative" rebel, though, but also Wheeler's details of the mining town — the drinking, the gambling, and the dancing women — transformed the Western into a subject of moral debate. The Beadle editors themselves struggled to curb Wheeler's language, characterization, and ubiquitous references to liquor.

Moreover, Wheeler was depicting rich capitalists as villains, easily manipulating the law, at a time when the nation had grown sensitive to the struggles between business and labor. The Knights of Labor was founded in 1869, the National Labor Reform Party formed in 1872, and labor tensions erupted in the Great Railway Strike of 1877, which President Rutherford B. Hayes suppressed by deploying federal troops, not without the cost of dozens of lives and millions of dollars. While subsequent

Deadwood Dick novels confront the labor struggle more explicitly, the first number can be read as an allegory of the violence required to resist the corruption of capital.

The unprecedented success of *Deadwood Dick, The Prince of the Road* no doubt resulted less from this socio-economic allegory (one finds the critique of business interests as far back as Cooper, after all) and more from the novel's engagement with the Black Hills gold rush that had captivated the national press. The dime Western owes a debt to the tradition of the historical romance, yet this is the moment when it romanticizes not history but current events. By federal treaty with the Sioux in 1868, the Black Hills of Dakota (a range of mountains spanning northeastern Wyoming and western South Dakota) became Indian territory. When General George A. Custer led a federal expedition into the hills in search of gold (prompted not least by the government's need to replenish funds spent during the Civil War), his report inspired thousands of prospectors toward what they imagined as the last mining frontier. The inevitable conflict with the Sioux led to the annihilation of Custer's Seventh Cavalry at the Battle of Little Bighorn in 1876 and ultimately to the subjugation of the Plains Indians. Wheeler's portrait of Sitting Bull is that of a figure still sought by the federal government in 1877 and still demonized in the press but soon to become the most internationally renowned Native American.

The text published here reproduces the original 1877 edition.

Copyrighted in 1877, by BEADLE AND ADAMS.

Vol. I.   Single Number.   BEADLE AND ADAMS, PUBLISHERS, No. 98 WILLIAM STREET, NEW YORK.   Price, 5 Cents.   No. 1

Deadwood Dick,

THE

PRINCE OF THE ROAD;

OR,

THE BLACK RIDER of the BLACK HILLS.

BY EDWARD L. WHEELER.

CHAPTER I.

FEARLESS FRANK TO THE RESCUE.

ON the plains, midway between Cheyenne and the Black Hills, a train had halted for a noonday feed. Not a railway train, mind you, but a line of those white-covered vehicles drawn by strong-limbed mules, which are most properly styled "prairie schooners."

There were four wagons of this type, and they had been drawn in a circle about a camp-fire, over which was roasting a savory haunch of venison. Around the camp-fire were grouped half a score of men, all rough, bearded, and grizzled, with one exception. This being a youth whose age one could have safely put at twenty, so perfectly developed of physique and intelligent of facial appearance. Frank, for there was something about him that was not handsome, and yet you would have been puzzled to tell what it was, for his countenance was strikingly handsome, and surely no form in the crowd was more noticeable for its grace, symmetry, and proportionate development. It would have taken a scholar to have studied out the secret.

He was of about medium stature, and as straight and square-shouldered as an athlete. His complexion was nut-brown, from long exposure to the sun; hair of hue of the raven's wing, and hanging in long, straight strands adown his back; eyes black and piercing as an eagle's; features well molded, with a firm, resolute mouth and prominent chin. He was an interesting specimen of young, healthy manhood, and, even though a youth in years, was one that could command respect, if not admiration, wheresoever he might choose to go.

One remarkable item about his personal appearance, apt to strike the beholder as being exceedingly strange and eccentric, was his costume—buckskin throughout, and that dyed to the brightest scarlet hue.

On being asked the cause of his odd freak of dress, when he had joined the train a few miles out from Cheyenne, the youth had laughingly replied:

"Why, you see, it is to attract buffalers, if we should meet any, out on the plains 'twixt this and the Hills."

He gave his name as Fearless Frank, and said he was aiming for the Hills; that if the party in question among them, he would extend to them his assistance as a hunter, guide, or whatever, until the destination was reached.

Seeing that he was well armed, and judging from external appearances that he would prove a valuable accessory, the miners were nothing loth in accepting his services.

Of the others grouped about the camp-fire only one is specially noticeable, for, as Mark Twain remarks, "the average of gold-diggers look alike." This person was a little, deformed old man; hump-backed, bow-legged, and white-haired, with cross eyes, a large mouth, a big head, set upon a slim, crane-like neck; blue eyes, and an immense brown beard, that flowed downward half-way to the belt about his waist, which contained a small arsenal of knives and revolvers. He hobbled about with a heavy crutch constantly under his left arm, and was certainly a pitiable sight to behold.

He too had joined the caravan after it had quitted Cheyenne, his advent taking place about an hour subsequent to that of Fearless Frank. His name he asserted was Nix—Geoffrey Walsingham Nix—and where he came from, and what he sought in the Black Hills, was simply a matter of conjecture among the miners, as he refused to talk on the subject of his past, present or future.

The train was under the command of an Irascible old plainsman who had served out his apprentice Charity Joe, which, considering his avaricious position, was the wrong handle on the wrong mar. Charity was the least of all Joe's redeeming characteristics; charity was the very thing he did not recognize, yet some wag had facetiously brand ed him Charity Joe, and the appellation had clun to him ever since. He was well advanced in years yet withal a good trafler and an expert guide, as th success of his many late expeditions into the Black Hills had evidenced.

Those who had heard of Joe's skill as a guide, in trusted themselves in his care, for, while the stage were stopped more or less on each trip, Charity Joe's train invariably went through all safe an sound. This was partly owing to his acquaintance with various bands of Indians, who were the chie cause of annoyance on the trip.

So far we see the train toward the land of gold without their having seen sight or sound of hostil red-skins, and Charity is just chuckling over his usu good luck:

"I tell ye what, fellers, we'¬ hed a fa'r sort uv a shake, ¬¬ fur, an' no mistake 'bout it Barrin' thar ain't no Sittin Bulls layin' in wait for us, be head yander, in ther mounta I'm of ther candid opinio we'll get through wi'out scrap in a ha'r."

"I hope so," said Fearles Frank, rolling over on the grass and gazing at the guide thoughtfully, "but I doubt it It seems to me that one bear of mere barbarity, lately than there was a month ago— all on account of the influx of ruffianly characters into the Black Hills!"

"Not all owing to that, chip py," interposed "General Nix, as he had immediately been christened by the min ers—"not all owing to that Thar's them gol danged cop per-colored guests uv ther gov ernment—they're kickin' up three pints uv ther rumpus more or less—consider'bly les of more than more o' less Take a passel uv them har bar ities an' sbet 'em up inter a prison for three or thirteen yeers, an' ye'd see w'at an impression et'd make, now. Thar'd be siveral less manay creea a week, an' ye wouldn't see a rufyan onc't a month W'y, gentlefellows, that'd nev yar been a ruffian, ef et hedn't been fer ther cussed Injun tribe—not one! Ther infarnal critters ar' ther instigators uv more devility nor a cat wit nine tails."

"Yes, we will admit that the¬ reds are not o' tainly oirgin," said Fearless Frank, with a quiet smile. "In fact I know of several who are far from being angels, myself. There is old Sitting Bull, for instance, and Lone Lion, Rain-in-the Face, and Horse-with-the-Red Eye, and so forth, and so forth!"

"Exactly. Every one o' 'em's a danged descendant o' ther old Satan, hisself."

"Layin' aside ther Injun subjeck," said Charity Joe, forking into the roasted veni son, "I move thet we take up a silent debate on 'ther

Ha! ha! ha! isn't that rich, now?   Ha! ha! ha! arrest Deadwood Dick if you can!

Figure 24. Front page of the opening number of *Beadle's Half Dime Library*. Courtesy of The Library of Congress.

CHAPTER I. FEARLESS FRANK TO THE RESCUE

On the plains, midway between Cheyenne and the Black Hills, a train had halted for a noonday feed.[1] Not a railway train, mind you, but a line of those white-covered vehicles drawn by strong-limbed mules, which are most properly styled "prairie schooners."

There were four wagons of this type, and they had been drawn in a circle about a camp-fire, over which was roasting a savory haunch of venison. Around the camp-fire were grouped half a score of men, all rough, bearded, and grizzled, with one exception. This being a youth whose age one could have safely put at twenty, so perfectly developed of physique and intelligent of facial appearance was he. There was something about him that was not handsome, and yet you would have been puzzled to tell what it was, for his countenance was strikingly handsome, and surely no form in the crowd was more noticeable for its grace, symmetry, and proportionate development. It would have taken a scholar to have studied out the secret.

He was of about medium stature, and as straight and square-shouldered as an athlete. His complexion was nut-brown, from long exposure to the sun; hair of hue of the raven's wing, and hanging in long, straight strands adown his back; eyes black and piercing as an eagle's; features well molded, with a firm, resolute mouth and prominent chin. He was an interesting specimen of young, healthy manhood, and, even though a youth in years, was one that could command respect, if not admiration, wheresoever he might choose to go.

One remarkable item about his personal appearance, apt to strike the beholder as being exceedingly strange and eccentric, was his costume — buck-skin throughout, and that dyed to the brightest scarlet hue.

On being asked the cause of his odd freak of dress, when he had joined the train a few miles out from Cheyenne, the youth had laughingly replied:

"Why, you see, it is to attract bufflers, if we should meet any, out on the plains 'twixt this and the Hills."

---

[1] *Black Hills*:   Sacred hunting ground of the Sioux Indians, the Black Hills became a site of conflict when a government expedition led by George Custer discovered gold in 1874. The Second Treaty of Laramie guaranteed Sioux rights to the remote mountain region. When miners entered the area and the Sioux, reluctant to sell either the land or mining rights, resisted the intrusion, the Black Hills War broke out in 1876, culminating in the Battle of Little Bighorn. [All notes are the Editor's unless otherwise identified.]

He gave his name as Fearless Frank, and said he was aiming for the Hills; that if the party in question would furnish him a place among them, he would extend to them his assistance as a hunter, guide, or whatever, until the destination was reached.

Seeing that he was well armed, and judging from external appearances that he would prove a valuable accessory, the miners were nothing loth in accepting his services.

Of the others grouped about the camp-fire, only one is specially noticeable, for, as Mark Twain remarks, "the average of gold-diggers look alike." This person was a little, deformed old man; humpbacked, bow-legged, and white-haired, with cross eyes, a large mouth, a big head, set upon a slim, crane-like neck; blue eyes, and an immense brown beard, that flowed downward half-way to the belt about his waist, which contained a small arsenal of knives and revolvers. He hobbled about with a heavy crutch constantly under his left arm, and was certainly a pitiable sight to behold.

He too had joined the caravan after it had quitted Cheyenne, his advent taking place about an hour subsequent to that of Fearless Frank. His name he asserted was Nix — Geoffrey Walsingham Nix — and where he came from, and what he sought in the Black Hills, was simply a matter of conjecture among the miners, as he refused to talk on the subject of his past, present or future.

The train was under the command of an irascible old plainsman who had served out his apprenticeship in the Kansas border war, and whose name was Charity Joe, which, considering his avaricious disposition, was the wrong handle on the wrong man. Charity was the least of all old Joe's redeeming characteristics; charity was the very thing he did not recognize, yet some wag had facetiously branded him Charity Joe, and the appellation had clung to him ever since. He was well advanced in years, yet withal a good trailer and an expert guide, as the success of his many late expeditions into the Black Hills had evidenced.

Those who had heard of Joe's skill as a guide, intrusted themselves in his care, for, while the stages were stopped more or less on each trip, Charity Joe's train invariably went through all safe and sound. This was partly owing to his acquaintance with various bands of Indians, who were the chief cause of annoyance on the trip.

So far we see the train toward the land of gold, without their having seen sight or sound of hostile red-skins, and Charity is just chuckling over his usual good luck:

"I tell ye what, fellers, we've hed a fa'r sort uv a shake, so fur, an' no mistake 'bout it. Barrin' thar ain't no Sittin' Bulls layin' in wait fer us, behead yander, in ther mounts, I'm of ther candid opinion we'll get through wi'out scrapin' a ha'r."

"I hope so," said Fearless Frank, rolling over on the grass and gazing at the guide, thoughtfully, "but I doubt it. It seems to me that one hears of more butchering, lately, than there was a month ago — all on account of the influx of ruffianly characters into the Black Hills!"

"Not all owing to that, chippy," interposed "General" Nix, as he had immediately been christened by the miners — "not all owing to that. Thar's them gol danged copper-colored guests uv ther government — they're kickin' up three pints uv the'r rumpus, more or less — consider'bly less of more than more o' less. Take a passel uv them barbarities an' shet 'em up inter a prison for three or thirteen yeers, an' ye'd see w'at an impression et'd make, now. Thar'd be siveral less massycrees a week, an' ye wouldn't see a rufyan onc't a month. W'y, gentlefellows, thar'd nevyar been a ruffian, ef et hedn't been fer ther cussed Injun tribe — not *one!* Ther infarnal critters ar' ther instignators uv more deviltry nor a cat wit nine tails."

"Yes, we will admit that the reds are not of saintly origin," said Fearless Frank, with a quiet smile. "In fact I know of several who are far from being angels, myself. There is old Sitting Bull, for instance, and Lone Lion, Rain-in-the-Face, and Horse-with-the-Red-Eye, and so forth, and so forth!"

"Exactly! Every one o' 'em's a danged descendent o' ther old Satan, hisself."

"Layin' aside ther Injun subjeck," said Charity Joe, forking into the roasted venison, "I move thet we take up a silent debate on the pecooliarities uv a deer's hind legs; so heer goes!"

He cut out a huge slice with his bowie, sprinkled it over with salt, and began to devour it by very large mouthfuls. All hands proceeded to follow his example, and the noonday meal was dispatched in silence. After each man had fully satisfied his appetite and the mules and Fearless Frank's horse had grazed until they were full as ticks, the order was given to hitch up, which was speedily done, and the caravan was soon in motion, toiling along like a diminutive serpent across the plain.

The afternoon was a mild, sunny one in early autumn, with a refreshing breeze perfumed with the delicate scent of after-harvest flowers wafting down from the cool regions of the Northwest, where lay the new El Dorado — the land of gold.

Fearless Frank bestrode a noble bay steed of fire and nerve, while old General Nix rode an extra mule that he had purchased of Charity

Joe. The remainder of the company rode in the wagons or "hoofed it," as best suited to their mood — walking sometimes being preferable to the rumbling and jolting of the heavy vehicles.

Steadily along through the afternoon sunlight the train wended its way, the teamsters alternately singing and cursing their mules, as they jogged along. Fearless Frank and the "General" rode several hundred yards in advance, both apparently engrossed in deepest thought, for neither spoke until, toward the close of the afternoon, Charity Joe called their attention to a series of low, faint cries brought down upon their hearing by the stiff northerly wind.

"'Pears to me as how them sound sorter human like," said the old guide, trotting along beside the young man's horse, as he made known the discovery. "Jes' listen, now, an' see if ye ain't uv ther same opinion!"

The youth did listen, and at the same time swept the plain with his eagle eyes, in search of the object from which the cries emanated. But nothing of animal life was visible in any direction beyond the train, and more was the mystery, since the cries sounded but a little way off.

"They *are* human cries!" exclaimed Fearless Frank, excitedly, "and come from some one in distress. Boys, we must investigate this matter."

"You can investigate all ye want," grunted Charity Joe, "but I hain't a-goin' ter stop ther train till dusk, squawk or no squawk. I jedge we won't get inter their Hills any too soon, as it ar'."

"You're an old fool!" retorted Frank, contemptuously. "I wouldn't be as mean as you for all the gold in the Black Hills country, say nothin' about that in California and Colorado."

He turned his horse's head toward the north, and rode away, followed, to the wonder of all, by the "General."

"You needn't; I do not want any of your wishes. I'm going to search for the person who makes them cries, an' ef you don't want to wait, why go to the deuce with your old train!"

"There ye err," shouted the guide; "I'm going ter Deadwood, instead uv ter the deuce."

"*Maybe* you will go to Deadwood, and then, again, maybe ye won't," answered back Fearless Frank.[2]

---

[2] *Deadwood*:   Gold was discovered in the Deadwood Gulch of the Black Hills in 1875, and during the gold rush of the following year, the town (originally the camp) of Deadwood swelled to a population of twenty-five thousand. Like other mining towns, it was known for its saloons, its gamblers, and its bawdy entertainments.

"More or less!" chimed in the general — "consider'bly more of less than less of more. Look out thet ther allies uv Sittin' Bull don't git ther *dead wood* on ye."

On marched the train — steadily on over the level, sandy plain, and Fearless Frank and his strange companion turned their attention to the cries that had been the means of separating them from the train. They had ceased now, altogether, and the two men were at a loss what to do.

"Guv a whoop, like a Government Injun," suggested "General" Nix; "an' thet'll let ther critter know thet we be friends a-comin'. Par'ps she'm g'in out ontirely, a-thinkin' as no one war a-comin' ter her resky!"

"She, you say?"

"Yas, she; fer I calkylate 'twern't no *he* as made them squawks. Sing out like a bellerin' bull, now an' et ar' more or less likely — consider'bly more of less 'n less of more — that she will respond!"

Fearless Frank laughed, and forming his hands into a trumpet he gave vent to a loud, ear-splitting "hello!" that made the prairies ring.

"Great whale uv Joner!" gasped the "General," holding his hands toward the region of his organs of hearing. "Holy Mother o' Mercy! don't do et ag'in b'yee — don' do et; ye've smashed my tinpanum ail inter flinders! Good heaven! ye hev got a bugle wus nor enny steam tooer frum heer tew Lowell."

"Hark!" said the youth, bending forward in a listening attitude.

The next instant silence prevailed, and the twain anxiously listened. Wafted down across the plain came in faint piteous accents the repetition of the cry they had first heard, only it was now much fainter. Evidently whoever was in distress was weakening rapidly. Soon the cries would be inaudible.

"It's straight ahead!" exclaimed Fearless Frank, at last. "Come along, and we'll soon see what the matter is!"

He put the spurs to his spirited animal, and the next instant was dashing wildly off over the sunlit plain. Bent on emulation, the "General" also used his heels with considerable vim, but alas! what dependence can be placed on a mule? The animal jolted, with a vicious nip back at the offending rider's legs, and refused to budge an inch.

On — on dashed the fearless youth, mounted on his noble steed, his eyes bent forward, in a sharp scrutiny of the plain ahead, his mind filled with wonder that the cries were now growing more distinct and yet not a first glimpse could he obtain of the source whence they emanated.

On — on — on; then suddenly he reins his steed back upon its haunches, just in time to avert a frightful plunge into one of those remarkable freaks of nature — the blind canal, or, in other words, a channel valley washed out by heavy rains. These the tourist will frequently encounter in the regions contiguous to the Black Hills.

Below him yawned an abrupt channel, a score or more of feet in depth, at the bottom of which was a dense chaparral thicket. The little valley thus nestled in the earth was about forty rods in width, and one would never have dreamed it existed, unless they chanced to ride to the brink, above.

Fearless Frank took in the situation at a glance, and not hearing the cries, he rightly conjectured that the one in distress had again become exhausted. That that person was in the thicket below seemed more than probable, and he immediately resolved to descend in search. Slipping from his saddle, he stepped forward to the very edge of the precipice and looked over. The next second the ground crumbled beneath his feet, and he was precipitated headlong into the valley. Fortunately he received no serious injuries, and in a moment was on his feet again, all right.

"A miss is as good as a mile," he muttered, brushing the dirt from his clothing. "Now, then, we will find out the secret of the racket in this thicket."

Glancing up to the brink above to see that his horse was standing quietly, he parted the shrubbery, and entered the thicket.

It required considerable pushing and tugging to get through the dense undergrowth, but at last his efforts were rewarded, and he stood in a small break or glade.

Stood there, to behold a sight that made the blood boil in his veins. Securely bound with her face toward a stake, was a young girl — a maiden of perhaps seventeen summers, whom, at a single glance, one might surmise was remarkably pretty.

She was stripped to the waist, and upon her snow-white back were numerous welts from which trickled diminutive rivulets of crimson. Her head was dropped against the stake to which she was bound, and she was evidently insensible.

With a cry of astonishment and indignation Fearless Frank leaped forward to sever her bonds, when like so many grim phantoms there filed out of the chaparral, and circled around him, a score

of hideously painted savages. One glance at the portly leader satisfied Frank as to his identity. It was the fiend incarnate — Sitting Bull![3]

CHAPTER II. DEADWOOD DICK, THE ROAD-AGENT

"**$500 Reward:** For the apprehension and arrest of a notorious
young desperado who hails to the name of Deadwood Dick. His present whereabouts are somewhat contiguous to the Black Hills. For further information, and so forth, apply immediately to
Hugh Vansevere,
"At Metropolitan Saloon, Deadwood City."

Thus read a notice posted up against a big pine tree, three miles
above Custer City, on the banks of French creek. It was a large placard tacked up in plain view of all passers-by who took the route
north through Custer gulch in order to reach the infant city of the
Northwest — Deadwood.

Deadwood! the scene of the most astonishing bustle and activity,
this year (1877.) The place where men are literally made rich and
poor in one day and night. Prior to 1877 the Black Hills have been
for a greater part undeveloped, but now, what a change! In Deadwood districts, every foot of available ground has been "claimed"
and staked out; the population has increased from fifteen to more
than twenty-five hundred souls.

The streets are swarming with constantly arriving new-comers; the
stores and saloons are literally crammed at all hours; dance-houses
and can-can dens exist; hundreds of eager, expectant, and hopeful
miners are working in the mines, and the harvest reaped by them is
not at all discouraging. All along the gulch are strung a profusion of

---

[3]*Sitting Bull:* Assuming the role of chief of the collective Sioux (Dakota) nation in
1867, Sitting Bull (Tatanka Yotanka, 1831?–1890), chief of the Hunkpapa division of
the Teton Sioux, refused to comply with government demands for Indian removal from
mining territory in 1876. He successfully inspired the defeats of General George Crook
in the Battle of the Rosebud and of General George Custer in the Battle of Little
Bighorn. Subsequent skirmishes and the annihilation of the buffalo subdued the Sioux,
many of whom surrendered, abandoning their hunting grounds and selling designated
mining sites. In 1877 Sitting Bull fled to Canada, where he was refused asylum. In
1885 he joined Buffalo Bill's Wild West show, gained national and international
renown for his bravery, and became the iconic defeated Indian hero. When in 1890 the
Ghost Dance movement seemed to be reinspiring Sioux resistance, the government
sought to arrest Sitting Bull; he was killed during the arrest.

cabins, tents and shanties, making Deadwood in reality a town of a dozen miles in length, though some enterprising individual has paired off a couple more infant cities above Deadwood proper, named respectively Elizabeth City and Ten Strike. The quartz formation in these neighborhoods is something extraordinary, and from late reports, under vigorous and earnest development are yielding beyond the most sanguine expectation.

The placer mines west of Camp Crook are being opened to very satisfactory results, and, in fact, from Custer City in the south, to Deadwood in the north, all is the scene of abundant enthusiasm and excitement.

A horseman riding north through Custer gulch, noticed the placard so prominently posted for public inspection, and with a low whistle, expressive of astonishment, wheeled his horse out of the stage road, and rode over to the foot of the tree in question, and ran his eyes over the few irregularly-written lines traced upon the notice.

He was a youth of an age somewhere between sixteen and twenty, trim and compactly built, with a preponderance of muscular development and animal spirits; broad and deep of chest, with square, iron-cast shoulders; limbs small yet like bars of steel, and with a grace of position in the saddle rarely equaled; he made a fine picture for an artist's brush or a poet's pen.

Only one thing marred the captivating beauty of the picture.

His form was clothed in a tight-fitting habit of buck-skin, which was colored a jetty black, and presented a striking contrast to anything one sees as a garment in the wild far West. And this was not all, either. A broad black hat was slouched down over his eyes; he wore a thick black vail over the upper portion of his face, through the eye-holes of which there gleamed a pair of orbs of piercing intensity, and his hands, large and knotted, were hidden in a pair of kid gloves of a light color.

The "Black Rider" he might have been justly termed, for his thoroughbred steed was as black as coal, but we have not seen fit to call him such — his name is Deadwood Dick, and let that suffice for the present.

It was just at the edge of evening that he stopped before, and proceeded to read the placard posted upon the tree in one of the loneliest portions of Custer's gulch.

Above and on either side rose to a stupendous hight the tree-fringed mountains in all their majestic grandeur.

In front and behind, running nearly north and south, lay the deep, dark chasm — a rift between mighty walls — Custer's gulch.

And over all began to hover the cloak of night, for the sun had already imparted its dying kiss on the mountain craters, and below, the gloom was thickening with rapid strides.

Slowly, over and over, Deadwood Dick, outlaw, road-agent and outcast, read the notice, and then a wild sardonic laugh burst from beneath his mask — a terrible, blood-curdling laugh, that made even the powerful animal he bestrode start and prick up its ears.

"Five hundred dollars reward for the apprehension and arrest of a notorious young desperado who hails to the name of Deadwood Dick! Ha! ha! ha! isn't that rich, now? Ha! ha! ha! *arrest* Deadwood Dick! Why, 'pon my word it is a sight for sore eyes. I was not aware that I had attained such a desperate notoriety as that document implies. They will make me out a murderer before they get through, I expect. Can't let me alone — everlastingly they must be punching after me, as if I was some obnoxious pestilence on the face of the earth. Never mind, though — let 'em keep on! Let them just continue their hounding game, and see which comes up on top when the bag's shook. If more than one of 'em don't get their fingers burned when they snatch Deadwood Dick bald-headed, why I'm a Spring creek sucker, that's all. Maybe I don't know who foots the bill in this reward business; oh, no; maybe I can't ride down to Deadwood and frighten three kind o' ideas out of this Mr. Hugh Vansevere, whoever he may be. Ha! ha! the fool that h'isted that notice didn't *know* Deadwood Dick, or he would never have placed his life in jeopardy by performing an act so uninteresting to the party in question. Hugh Vansevere; let me see — I don't think I've got that registered in my collection of appellatives. Perhaps he is a new tool in the employ of the old mechanic."

Darker and thicker grew the night shadows. The after-harvest moon rose up to a sufficient hight to send a silvery bolt of powerful light down into the silent gulch; like an image carved out of the night the horse and rider stood before the placard, motionless, silent.

The head of Deadwood Dick was bent, and he was buried in a deep reverie. A reverie that engrossed his whole attention for a long, long while; then the impatient pawing of his horse aroused him, and he sat once more erect in his saddle.

A last time his eyes wandered over the notice on the tree — a last time his terrible laugh made the mountains ring, and he guided his horse back into the rough, uneven stage-road, and galloped off up the gulch.

"I will go and see what this Hugh Vansevere looks like!" he said, applying the spurs to his horse. "I'll be dashed if I want him to be so numerous with my name, especially with five hundred dollars affixed thereto, as a reward."

Midnight.

Camp Crook, nestling down in one of the wildest gulch pockets of the Black Hills region — basking and sleeping in the flood of moonlight that emanates from the glowing ball up afar in heaven's blue vault, is suddenly and rudely aroused from her dreams.

There is a wild clatter of hoofs, a chorus of strange and varied voices swelling out in a wild mountain song, and up through the very heart of the diminutive city, where the gold-fever has dropped a few sanguine souls, dash a cavalcade of masked horsemen, attired in the picturesque garb of the mountaineer, and mounted on animals of superior speed and endurance.

At their head, looking weird and wonderful in his suit of black, rides he whom all have heard of — he whom some have seen, and he whom no one dare raise a hand against, in single combat — Deadwood Dick, Road-Agent Prince, and the one person whose name is in everybody's mouth.

Straight on through the single northerly street of the infant village ride the dauntless band, making weirdly beautiful music with their rollicking song, some of the voices being cultivated, and clear as the clarion note.

A few miners, wakened from their repose, jump out of bed, come to the door, and stare at the receding cavalcade in a dazed sort of way. Others, thinking that the noise is all resulting from an Indian attack, seize rifles or revolvers, as the case may be, and blaze away out of windows and loopholes at what ever may be in the way to receive their bullets.

But the road-agents only pause a moment in their song to send back a wild, sarcastic laugh; then they resume it, and merrily dash along up the gulch, the ringing of iron-shod hoofs beating a strange tatoo on the sound of the music.

Sleepily the miners crawl back to their respective couches; the moon smiles down on mother earth, and nature once more fans itself to sleep with the breath of a fragrant breeze.

Deadwood — magic city of the West!

Not dead, nor even sleeping, is this headquarters of the Black Hills population at midnight, twenty-four hours subsequent to the rush of the daring road-agents through Camp Crook.

Deadwood is just as lively and hilarious a place during the interval between sunset and sunrise as during the day. Saloons, dance-houses, and gambling dens keep open all night, and stores do not close until a late hour. At one, two and three o'clock in the morning the streets present as lively an appearance as at any period earlier in the evening. Fighting, shooting, stabbing and hideous swearing are features of the night; singing, drinking, dancing and gambling another.

Nightly the majority of the miners come in from such claims as are within a radius of from six to ten miles, and seldom is it that they go away without their "load." To be sure, there are some men in Deadwood who do not drink, but they are so few and scattering as to seem almost entirely a nonentity.

It was midnight, and Deadwood lay basking in a flood of mellow moonlight that cast long shadows from the pine forest on the peaks, and glinted upon the rapid, muddy waters of Whitewood creek, which rumbles noisily by the infant metropolis on its wild journey toward the south.

All the saloons and dance-houses are in full blast; shouts and maudlin yells rend the air. In front of one insignificant board, "ten-by-twenty," an old wretch is singing out lustily:

"Right this way, ye cum, pilgrims, ter ther great Black Hills Thee'ter; only costs ye four bits ter go in an' see ther tender sex, already a-kickin' in their striped stockin's; only four bits, recollect, ter see ther greatest show on earth, so heer's yer straight chance!"

But, why the use of yelling? Already the shanty is packed, and judging from the thundering screeches and clapping of hands, the entertainment is such as suits the depraved tastes of the ruffianly "bums" who have paid their "four bits," and gone in.

But look!

Madly out of Deadwood gulch, the abode of thousands of lurking shadows, dashes a horseman.

Straight through the main street of the noisy metropolis, he spurs, with hat off, and hair blowing backward in a jetty cloud.

On, on, followed by the eyes of scores curious to know the meaning of his haste — on, and at last he halts in front of a large board shanty, over whose doorway is the illuminated canvas sign: "Metropolitan Saloon, by Tom Young."

Evidently his approach is heard, for instantly out of the "Metropolitan" there swarms a crowd of miners, gamblers and bummers to see "what the row is."

"Is there a man among you, gentlemen, who bears the name of Hugh Vansevere?" asks the rider, who from his midnight dress we may judge is no other than Deadwood Dick.

"That is my handle, pilgrim!" and a tall, rough-looking customer of the Minnesotian order steps forward. "What mought yer lay be ag'in me?"

"A *sure* lay!" hisses the masked road-agent, sternly. "You are advertising for one Deadwood Dick, and he has come to pay you his respects!"

The next instant there is a flash, a pistol report, a fall and a groan, the clattering of iron-shod hoofs, and then, ere anyone scarcely dreams of it, *Deadwood Dick is gone!*

CHAPTER III. THE "CATTYMOUNT" — A QUARREL AND ITS RESULTS[4]

The "Metropolitan" saloon in Deadwood, one week subsequent to the events last narrated, was the scene of a larger "jamboree" than for many weeks before.

It was Saturday night, and up from the mines of Gold Run, Bobtail, Poor Man's Pocket, and Spearfish, and down from the Deadwood in miniature, Crook City, poured a swarm of rugged, grisly gold-diggers, the blear-eyed, used-up-looking "pilgrim," and the inevitable wary sharp, ever on the alert for a new buck to fleece.

The "Metropolitan" was then, as now, the headquarters of the Black Hills metropolis for arriving trains and stages, and as a natural consequence received a goodly share of the public patronage.

A well-stocked bar of liquors in Deadwood was *non est,* yet the saloon in question boasted the best to be had. Every bar has its clerk at a pair of tiny scales, and he is ever kept more than busy weighing out the shining dust that the toiling miner has obtained by the sweat of his brow. And if the deft-fingered clerk cannot put six ounces of dust in his own pouch of a night, it clearly shows that he is not long in the business.

Saturday night!

The saloon is full to overflowing — full of brawny, rough, and grisly men; full of ribald songs and maudlin curses; full of foul atmo-

---

[4] *Cattymount:* Cattymount (or catamount) is a name for the American cougar or any comparable wild cat.

spheres, impregnated with the fumes of vile whiskey, and worse tobacco, and full of sights and scenes, exciting and repulsive.

As we enter and work our way toward the center of the apartment, our attention is attracted by a coarse, brutal "tough," evidently just fresh in from the diggings; who, mounted on the summit of an empty whiskey cask, is exhorting in rough language, and in the tones of a bellowing bull, to an audience of admiring miners assembled at his feet, which, by the way, are not of the most diminutive pattern imaginable. We will listen:

"Feller coots and liquidarians, behold before ye a lineal descendant uv Cain and Abel. Ye'll reckolect, ef ye've ever bin ter campmeetin', that Abel got knocked out o' time by his cuzzin Cain, all becawse Abel war misproperly named, and warn't *able* when the crysis arriv ter defen' himsel' in an able manner.

"Hed he bin 'heeled' wi' a shipment uv Black Hills sixes, thet would hev en*abled* him to distinguish hisself fer superyer *a*bility. Now, as I sed before, I'm a lineal descendent uv ther notorious Ain and Cable, and I've lit down hyar among ye ter explain a few p'ints 'bout true blessedness and true cussedness.

"Oh! brethren, I tell ye I'm a snorter, I am, when I git a-goin' — a wild screechin' cattymount, right down frum ther sublime spheres up Starkey — ar' a regular epizootic uv religyun, sent down frum clouddum and scattered permiscously ter ther forty winds uv ther earth."

We pass the "cattymount," and presently come to a table at which a young and handsome "pilgrim," and a ferret-eyed sharp are engaged at cards. The first mentioned is a tall, robust fellow, somewhere in the neighborhood of twenty-three years of age, with clearcut features, dark lustrous eyes, and teeth of pearly whiteness. His hair is long and curling, and a soft brown mustache, waxed at the ends, is almost perfection itself.

Evidently he is of quick temperament, for he handles the cards with a swift, nervous dexterity that surprises even the professional sharp himself, who is a black, swarthy-looking customer, with "villain" plainly written in every lineament of his countenance; his eyes, hair, and a tremendous mustache that he occasionally strokes, are of a jetty black; did you ever notice it? — dark hair and complexion predominate among the gambling fraternity.

Perhaps this is owing to the condition of the souls of some of these characters.

The professional sharp in our case was no exception to the rule. He was attired in the hight of fashion, and the diamond cluster, inevitably to be found there, was on his shirt front; a jewel of wonderful size and brilliancy.

"Ah! curse the luck!" exclaimed the sharp, slapping down the cards; "you have won again, pilgrim, and I am five hundred out. By the gods, your luck is something astonishing!"

"*Luck!*" laughed the other, coolly; "well, no. I do not call it luck, for I never have luck. We'll call it chance!"

"Just as you say," growled the gambler, bringing forth a new pack. "Chance and luck are then twin companions. Will you continue longer, Mr. — "

"Redburn," finished the pilgrim.

"Ah! yes — Mr. Redburn, will you continue?"

"I will play as long as there is anything to play for," again finished Mr. R., twisting the waxed ends of his mustache calmly. "Maybe you have got your fill, eh?"

"No; I'll play all night to win back what I have lost."

A youth, attired in buck-skin, and apparently a couple of years younger than Redburn, came sauntering along at this juncture, and seeing an unoccupied chair at one end of the table (for Redburn and the gambler sat at the sides, facing each other), he took possession of it forthwith.

"Hello!" and the sharp swore roundly. "Who told *you* to mix in your lip, pilgrim?"

"Nobody, as I know of. Thought I'd squat right here, and watch your *sleeves!*" was the significant retort, and the youth laid a cocked six-shooter on the table in front of him.

"Go on, gentlemen; don't let me be the means of spoiling your fun."

The gambler uttered a curse, and dealt out the pasteboards.

The youth was watching him intently, with his sharp black eyes.

He was of medium hight, straight as an arrow, and clad in a loose-fitting costume. A broad sombrero was set jauntily upon the left side of his head, the hair of which had been cut close down to the scalp. His face — a pleasant, handsome, youthful face — was devoid of hirsute covering, he having evidently been recently handled by the barber.

The game between Mr. Redburn and the gambler progressed; the eyes of he whom we have just described were on the card sharp constantly.

The cards went down on the table in vigorous slaps, and at last Mr. Pilgrim Redburn raked in the stakes.

"Thunder 'n' Moses!" ejaculated the sharp, pulling out his watch
— an elegant affair, of pure gold, and studded with diamonds — and
laying it forcibly down upon the table.

"There! what will you plank on that!"

Redburn took up the time-piece, turned it over and over in his
hands, opened and shut it, gave a glance at the works, and then
handed it over to the youth, whom he instinctively felt was his friend.
Redburn had come from the East to dig gold, and therefore was a
stranger in Deadwood.

"What is its money value?" he asked, familiarizing his tone.
"Good, I suppose."

"Yes, perfectly good, and cheap at two hundred," was the unhesi-
tating reply. "Do you lack funds, stranger?"

"Oh! no. I am three hundred ahead of this cuss yet, and — "

"You'd better quit where you are!" said the other, decisively.
"You'll lose the next round, mark my word."

"Ha! ha!" laughed Redburn, who had begun to show symptoms
of recklessness. "I'll take my chances. Here, you gamin, I'll cover the
watch with two hundred dollars."

Without more ado, the stakes were planked, the cards dealt, and
the game began.

The youth, whom we will call Ned Harris, was not idle.

He took the revolvers from the table, changed his position so that
his face was just in the opposite direction of what it had been, and
commenced to pare his finger nails. The fingers were as white and
soft as any girl's. In his hand he also held a strangely-angled little
box, the sides of which were mirror-glass. Looking at his finger-nails
he also looked into the mirror, which gave a complete view of the
card-sharp, as he sat at the table.

Swiftly progressed the game, and no one could fail to see how it
was going by watching the cunning light in the gambler's eye. At last
the game-card went down, and next instant, after the sharp had
raked in his stakes, a cocked revolver in either hand of Ned Harris
covered the hearts of the two players.

"Hello!" gasped Redburn, quailing under the gaze of a cold steel
tube — "what's the row, now?"

"Draw your revolver!" commanded Harris, sternly, having an eye
on the card-sharp at the same time. "Come! don't be all night about it!"

Redburn obeyed; he had no other choice.

"Cock it and cover your man!"

"Who do you mean?"

"The cuss under my left-hand aim."

Again the "pilgrim" felt that he could not afford to do otherwise than obey.

So he took "squint" at the gambler's left breast after which Harris withdrew the siege of his left weapon, although he still covered the young Easterner the same. Quietly he moved around to where the card-sharp sat, white and trembling.

"Gentlemen!" he yelled, in a clear, ringing voice, "will some of you step this way a moment?"

A crowd gathered around in a moment: then the youth resumed:

"Feller-citizens, all of you know how to play cards, no doubt. What is the penalty of cheating, out here in the Hills?"

For a few seconds the room was wrapt in silence; then a chorus of voices gave answer, using a single word:

"Death!"

"Exactly," said Harris, calmly. "When a sharp hides cards in Chinaman fashion up his sleeve, I reckon that's what you call cheatin', don't you?"

"That's the size of it," assented each bystander, grimly.

Ned Harris pressed his pistol-muzzle against the gambler's forehead, inserted his fingers in each of the capacious sleeves, and a moment later laid several high cards upon the table.

A murmur of incredulity went through the crowd of spectators. Even "pilgrim" Redburn was astonished.

After removing the cards, Ned Harris turned and leveled his revolver at the head of the young man from the East.

"Your name?" he said, briefly, "is — "

"Harry Redburn."

"Very well. Harry Redburn, that gambler under cover of your pistol is guilty of a crime, punishable in the Black Hills by death. As you are his victim — or, rather, were to be — it only remains for you to aim straight and rid your country of an A No. 1 dead-beat and swindler!"

"Oh! no!" gasped Redburn, horrified at the thought of taking the life of a fellow-creature — "I cannot, I cannot!"

"You *can!*" said Harris, sternly; "go on — *you must salt that card-sharp, or I'll certainly salt you!*"

A deathlike silence followed.

"*One!*" said Harris, after a moment.

Redburn grew very pale, but not paler was he than the card-sharp just opposite. Redburn was no coward; neither was he accustomed to the desperate character of the population of the Hills. Should he shoot the tricky wretch before him, he knew he should be always calling himself a murderer. On the contrary, in the natural laws of Deadwood, such a murder would be classed justice.

"*Two!*" said Ned Harris, drawing his pistol-hammer back to full cock. "Come, pilgrim, are you going to shoot?"

Another silence; only the low breathing of the spectators could be heard.

"*Three!*"

Redburn raised his pistol and fired — blindly and carelessly, not knowing or caring whither went the compulsory death-dealing bullet.

There was a heavy fall, a groan of pain, as the gambler dropped over on the floor; then for the space of a few seconds all was the wildest confusion throughout the mammoth saloon.

Revolvers were in every hand, knives flashed in the glare of the lamplight, curses and threats were in scores of mouths, while some of the vast surging crowd cheered lustily.

At the table Harry Redburn still sat, as motionless as a statue, the revolver still held in his hand, his face white, his eyes staring.

There he remained, the center of general attraction, with a hundred pair of blazing eyes leveled at him from every side.

"Come!" said Ned Harris, in a low tone, tapping him on the shoulder — "come, pardner; let's git out of this, for times will be brisk soon. You've wounded one of the biggest card-devils in the Hills, and he'll be rearin' pretty quick. Look! d'ye see thet feller comin' yonder, who was preachin' from on top of the barrel, a bit ago? Well, that is Catamount Cass, an' he's a pard of Chet Diamond, the feller you salted, an' them fellers behind him are his gang. Come! follow me, Henry, and I'll nose our way out of here."

Redburn signified his readiness, and with a cocked six-shooter in either hand Ned Harris led the way.

CHAPTER IV. SAD ANITA — THE MINE
LOCATER — TROUBLE

Straight toward the door of the saloon he marched, the muzzles of the grim sixes clearing a path for him; for Ned Harris had become notorious in Deadwood for his coolness, courage and audacity. It had been said of him that he would "just es lief shute a man as ter look at 'im," and perhaps the speaker was not far from right.

Anyway, he led off through the savage-faced audience with a composure that was remarkable, and, strange to say, not a hand was raised to stop him until he came face to face with Catamount Cass and his gang; here was where the youth had expected molestation and hindrance, if anywhere.

Catamount Cass was a rough, illiterate "tough" of the mountain species, and possessed more brute courage than the general run of his type of men, and a bull-dog determination that made him all the more dangerous as an enemy.

Harry Redburn kept close at Ned Harris' heels, a cocked "six" in either hand ready for any emergency.

It took but a few moments before the two parties met the "Cattymount" throwing out his foot to block the path.

"Hello!" roared the "tough," folding his huge knotty arms across his partially bared breast; "ho! ho! whoa up thar, pilgrims! Don' ye go ter bein' so fast. Fo'kes 'harn't so much in a hurry now-'days as they uster war. Ter be sure ther Lord manyfactered this futstool in seven days; sumtimes I think he did, an' then, ag'in, my geological ijees convince me he didn't."

"What has that to do with us?" demanded Ned, sternly. "I opine ye'd better spread, some of you, if you don't want me to run a canyon through your midst. Preach to some other pilgrim than me; I'm in a hurry!"

"Haw! haw! Yas, I observe ye be; but if ye're my meat, an' I think prob'ble ye be, I ain't a-goin' fer ter let yer off so nice and easy. P'arps ye kin tell who fired the popgun, a minnit ago, w'at basted my ole pard?"

"I shall not take trouble to tell!" replied Ned, fingering the trigger of his left six uneasily. "Ef you want to know who salted Chet Diamond, the worst blackleg, trickster and card-player in Dakota, all you've got to do is to go and ask him!"

"Hold!" cried Harry Redburn, stepping out from behind Harris; "I'll hide behind no man's shoulder. *I* salted the gambler — if you call shooting salting — and I'm not afraid to repeat the action by salting a dozen more just of his particular style."

Ned Harris was surprised.

He had set Redburn down as a faint-hearted, dubious-couraged counter-jumper from the East; he saw now that there was something of him, after all.

"Come on, young man!" and the young miner stepped forward a pace; "are you with me?"

"To the ears!" replied Harris, grimly.

The next instant the twain leaped forward and broke the barrier, and mid the crack of pistol-shots and shouts of rage, they cleared the saloon. Once outside, Ned Harris led the way.

"Come along!" he said, dodging along the shadowy side of the street; "we'll have to scratch gravel, for them up-range 'toughs' will follow us, I reckon. They're a game gang, and 'hain't the most desirable kind of enemies one could wish for. I'll take you over to my coop, and you can lay low there until this jamboree blows over. You'll have to promise me one thing, however, ere I can admit you as a member of my household."

"Certainly. What is it?" and Harry Redburn redoubled his efforts in order to keep alongside his swift-footed guide.

"Promise me that you will divulge nothing, no matter what you may see or hear. Also that, should you fall in love with one who is a member of my family, you will forbear and not speak of love to her."

"It is a woman, then?"

"Yes — a young lady."

"I will promise; — how can I afford to do otherwise, under the existing circumstances. But, tell me, why did you force me to shoot that gambler?"

"He was a rascal, and cheated you."

"I know; but I did not want his life; I am averse to bloodshed."

"So I perceived, and that made me all the more determined you should salivate him. You'll find before you're in the Hills long that it won't do to take lip or lead from any one. A green pilgrim is the first to get salted; I illustrated how to serve 'em!"

Redburn's eyes sparkled. He was just beginning to see into the different phases of this wild exciting life.

"Good!" he exclaimed, warmly. "I have much to thank you for. Did I kill that card-sharp?"

"No; you simply perforated him in the right side. This way."

They had been running straight up the main street. Now they turned a corner and darted down one that was dark and deserted.

A moment later a trim boyish figure stepped before them, from out of the shadow of a new frame building; a hand of creamy whiteness was laid upon the arm of Ned Harris.

"This way, pilgrims," said a low musical voice, and at the same instant a gust of wind lifted the jaunty sombrero from the speaker's head, revealing a most wonderful wealth of long glossy hair; "the 'toughs' are after you, and you cannot find a better place to coop than in here." The soft hand drew Ned Harris inside the building, which was finished, but unoccupied, and Redburn followed, nothing loth to get into a place of safety. So far, Deadwood had not impressed him favorably as being the most peaceable city within the scope of a continent.

Into an inner room of the building they went, and the door was closed behind them. The apartment was small and smelled of green lumber. A table and a few chairs comprised the furniture; a dark lantern burned suspended from the ceiling by a wire. Redburn eyed the strange youth as he and Harris were handed seats.

Of medium height and symmetrically built; dressed in a carefully tanned costume of buck-skin, the vest being fringed with the fur of the mink; wearing a jaunty Spanish sombrero; boots on the dainty feet of patent leather, with tops reaching to the knees; a face slightly sun-burned, yet showing the traces of beauty that even excessive dissipation could not obliterate; eyes black and piercing; mouth firm, resolute, and devoid of sensual expression; hair of raven color and of remarkable length; — (such was the picture of the youth) as beheld by Redburn and Harris.

"You can remain here till you think it will be safe to again venture forth, gentlemen," and a smile — evidently a stranger there — broke out about the speaker's lips. "Good-evening!" "Good-evening!" nodded Harris, with a quizzical stare. The next moment the youth was gone.

"Who was that chap?" asked Redburn, not a little bewildered.

"That? — why that's Calamity Jane!"

"Calamity Jane? *What* a name."

"Yes, she's an odd one. Can ride like the wind, shoot like a sharp-shooter, and swear like a trooper. Is here, there and everywhere, seemingly all at one time. Owns this coop and two or three other lots in Deadwood; a herding ranch at Laramie, an interest in a paying placer claim near Elizabeth City, and the Lord only knows how much more."

"But it is not a *woman?*"

"Reckon 'tain't nothin' else."

"God forbid that a child of mine should ever become so debased and — "

"Hold! there are yet a few redeeming qualities about her. She was *ruined* —" and here a shade dark as a thunder-cloud passed over Ned Harris' face — "and set adrift upon the world, homeless and friendless; yet she has bravely fought her way through the storm, without asking anybody's assistance. True, she may not now have a heart; that was trampled upon, years ago, but her character has not suffered blemish since the day a foul wretch stole away her honor!"

"What is her real name?"

"I do not know; few in Deadwood do. It is said, however, that she comes of a Virginia City, Nevada, family of respectability and intelligence."

At this juncture there was a great hubbub outside, and instinctively the twain drew their revolvers, expecting that Catamount Cass and his toughs had discovered their retreat, and were about to make an attack. But soon the gang were heard to tramp away, making the night hideous with their hoarse yells.

"They'll pay a visit to every shanty in Deadwood," said Harris, with a grim smile, "and if they don't find us, which they won't, they'll h'ist more than a barrel of bug-juice over their defeat. Come, let's be going."

They left the building and once more emerged onto the darkened street, Ned taking the lead.

"Follow me, now," he said, tightening his belt, "and we'll get home before sunrise, after all."

He struck out up the gulch, or, rather, down it, for his course lay southward. Redburn followed, and in fifteen minutes the lights of Deadwood — magic city of the wilderness — were left behind. Harris led the way along the rugged mountain stage-road, that, after leaving Deadwood on its way to Camp Crook and Custer City in the south, runs alternately through deep, dark canyons and gorges, with an ease and rapidity that showed him to be well acquainted with the route. About three miles below Deadwood he struck a trail through a transverse canyon running north-west, through which flowed a small stream, known as Brown's creek. The bottom was level and smooth, and a brisk walk of a half-hour brought them to where a horse was tied to an alder sapling.

"You mount and ride on ahead until you come to the end of the canyon," said Harris, untying the horse. "I will follow on after you, and be there almost as soon as you."

Redburn would have offered some objections, but the other motioned for him to mount and be off, so he concluded it best to obey.

The animal was a fiery one, and soon carried him out of sight of Ned, whom he left standing in the yellow moonlight. Sooner than he expected the gorge came to an abrupt termination in the face of a stupendous wall of rock, and nothing remained to do but wait for young Harris.

He soon came, trotting leisurely up, only a trifle flushed in countenance.

"This way!" he said, and seizing the animal by the bit he led horse and rider into a black, gaping fissure in one side of the canyon, that had hitherto escaped Redburn's notice. It was a large, narrow, subterranean passage, barely large enough to admit the horse and rider. Redburn soon was forced to dismount and bring up the rear.

"How far do we journey in this shape?" he demanded, after what seemed to him a long while.

"No further," replied Ned, and the next instant they emerged into a small, circular pocket in the midst of the mountains — one of those beauteous flower-strewn valleys which are often found in the Black Hills.

This "pocket," as they are called, consisted of perhaps fifty acres, walled in on every side by rugged mountains as steep, and steeper, in some places, than a house-roof. On the western side Brown's creek had its source, and leaped merrily down from ledge to ledge into the valley, across which it flowed, sinking into the earth on the eastern side, only to bubble up again, in the canyon, with renewed strength.

The valley was one vast, indiscriminate bed of wild, fragrant flowers, whose volume of perfume was almost sickening when first greeting the nostrils. Every color and variety imaginable was here, all in the most perfect bloom. In the center of the valley stood a log-cabin, overgrown with clinging vines. There was a light in the window, and Harris pointed toward it, as, with young Redburn, he emerged from the fissure.

"There's my coop, pilgrim. There you will be safe for a time, at least." He unsaddled the horse and set it free to graze.

Then they set off down across the slope, arriving at the cabin in due time.

The door was open; a young woman, sweet, yet sad-faced, was seated upon the steps, fast asleep.

Redburn gave an involuntary cry of incredulity and admiration as his eyes rested upon the picture — upon the pure, sweet face, surrounded by a wealth of golden, glossy hair, and the sylph-like form, so perfect in every contour. But a charge of silence from Harris, made him mute.

The young man knelt by the side of the sleeping girl and imprinted a kiss upon the fresh, unpolluted lips, which caused the sleeping beauty to smile in her dreams.

A moment later, however, she opened her eyes and sprung to her feet with a startled scream.

"Oh, Ned!" she gasped, trembling, as she saw him, "how you frightened me. I had a dream — oh such a sweet dream! and I thought *he* came and kissed — "

Suddenly did she stop as, for the first time, her penetrating blue eyes rested upon Harry Blackburn.

A moment she gazed at him as in a sort of fascination; then, with a low cry, began to retreat, growing deathly pale. Ned Harris stepped quickly forward and supported her on his arm.

"Be calm, Anita," he said, in a gentle, reassuring tone. "This is a young gentleman whom I have brought here to our home for a few days until it will be safe for him to be seen in Deadwood. Mr. Redburn, I make you acquainted with Anita."

A courteous bow from Redburn, a slight inclination of Anita's head, and the introduction was made. A moment later the three entered the cabin, a model of neatness and primitive luxury.

"How is it that you are up so early, dear?" young Harris asked, as he unbuckled his belt and hung it upon a peg in the wall. "You are rarely as spry, eh?"

"Indeed! I have not been to bed at all," replied the girl, a weary smile wreathing her lips. "I was nervous, and feared something was going to happen, so I staid up."

"Your old plea — the presentiment of coming danger, I suppose," and the youth laughed, gayly. "But you need not fear. No one will invade our little Paradise, right away. What is your opinion of it, Redburn?"

"I should say not. I think this little mountain retreat is without equal," replied Harry, with enthusiasm. "The only wonder is how did you ever stumble into such a delightful place."

"Of that I will perhaps tell you, another time," said Harris, musingly.

Day soon dawned over the mountains, and the early morning sunlight fell with charming effect into the little "pocket," with its countless thousands of odorous flowers, and the little ivy-clad cabin nestling down among them all.

Sweet, sad-faced Anita prepared a sumptuous morning repast out of antelope-steak and the eggs of wild birds, with dainty side dishes of late summer berries, and a large luscious melon which had been grown on a cultivated patch, contiguous to the cabin.

Both Harris and his guest did ample justice to the meal, for they had neither eaten anything since the preceding noon. When they had finished, Ned arose from the table saying: "Pardner, I shall leave you here for a few days, during which time I shall probably be mostly away on business. Make yourself at home and see that Anita is properly protected; I will return in a week at the furthest; — perhaps in a day or two."

He took down his rifle and belt from the wall, buckled on the latter, and half an hour later left the "pocket." That was a day of days to Harry Redburn. He rambled about the picturesque little valley, romped on the luxuriant grass and gathered wild flowers alternately. At night he sat in the cabin door and listened to the cries of the night birds and the incessant hooting of the mountain owls (which by the way, are very abundant throughout the Black Hills.)

All efforts to engage Anita in conversation proved fruitless.

On the following day both were considerably astonished to perceive that there was a stranger in their Paradise; — a bow-legged, hump-backed, grisly little old fellow, who walked with a staff. He approached the cabin, and Redburn went out to find who he was.

"Gude-mornin'!" nodded General Nix, (for it was he) with a grin. "I jes' kim over inter this deestrict ter prospect fer gold. Don' seem ter recognize yer unkle, eh? boy; I'm Nix Walsingham Nix, Esquire geological surveyor an' mine-locater. I've located more nor forty thousan' mines in my day, more or less — ginerally a consider'ble more of less than less of more. I perdict frum ther geological formation o' this nest an' a dream I hed last night, thet thar's sum uv ther biggest veins right in this yere valley as ye'll find in ther Hills!"

"Humph! no gold here," replied Redburn, who had already learned from study and experience how to guess a fat strike. "It is out of the channel."

"No; et's right in the channel."

"Well, I'll not dispute you. How did you get into the valley?"

"Through ther pass," and the General chuckled approvingly. "See'd a feller kim down ther canyon, yesterday, so I nosed about ter find whar he kim from, that's how I got here; 'sides, I hed a dream about this place."

"Indeed!" Redburn was puzzled how to act under the circumstances. Just then there came a piercing scream from the direction of the cabin.

What could it mean? Was Nix an enemy, and was some one else of his gang attacking Anita?

Certainly she *was* in trouble!

CHAPTER V. SITTING BULL — THE FAIR CAPTIVE

Fearless Frank stepped back aghast, as he saw the inhuman chief of the Sioux — the cruel, grim-faced warrior, Sitting Bull; shrunk back, and laid his hand upon the butt of a revolver.

"Ha!" he articulated, "is that you, chief? You, and at such work as this?" There was stern reproach in the youth's tone, and certain it is that the Sioux warrior heard the words spoken.

"My friend, Scarlet Boy, is keen with the tongue," he said, frowning. "Let him put shackles upon it, before it leaps over the bounds of reason."

"I see no reason why I should not speak in behalf of yon suffering girl!" retorted the youth, fearlessly, "on whom you have been inflicting one of the most inhuman tortures Indian cunning could conceive. For shame, chief, that you should ever assent to such an act — lower yourself to the grade of a dog by such a dastard deed. For shame, I say!"

Instantly the form of the great warrior straightened up like an arrow, and his painted hand flew toward the pistols in his belt.

But the succeeding second he seemed to change his intention; his hand went out toward the youth in greeting:

"The Scarlet Boy is right," he said, with as much graveness as a red-skin can conceive. "Sitting Bull listens to his words as he would to those of a brother. Scarlet Boy is no stranger in the land of the Sioux; he is the friend of the great chief and his warriors. Once when the storm-gods were at war over the pine forest and picture rocks of the Hills; when the Great Spirit was sending fiery messengers down in vivid streaks from the skies, the Big Chief cast a thunderbolt in playfullness at the feet of Sitting Bull. The shock of the hand of the Great Spirit did not escape me; for hours I lay like one slain in battle. My warriors were in consternation; they ran hither and thither in affright, calling on the Manitou[5] to preserve their chief. You came, Scarlet Boy, in the midst of all the panic; — came, and though then

---

[5] *Manitou*: A manitou is a supernatural force that manifests in the form of a spirit or object.

but a stripling, you applied simple remedies that restored Sitting Bull to the arms of his warriors.[6]

"From that hour Sitting Bull was your friend — is your friend, now, and will be as long as the red-men exist as a tribe."

"Thank you, chief;" and Fearless Frank grasped the Indian's hand and wrung it warmly. "I believe you mean all you say. But I am surprised to find you engaged at such work as this. I have been told that Sitting Bull made war only on warriors — not on women."

An ugly frown darkened the savage's face — a frown wherein was depicted a number of slumbering passions.

"The pale-face girl is the last survivor of a train that the warriors of Sitting Bull attacked in Red Canyon. Sitting Bull lost many warriors; yon pale squaw shot down full a half-score before she could be captured; she belongs to the warriors of Sitting Bull, and not to the great chief himself."

"Yet you have the power to free her — to yield her up to me. Consider, chief; are you not enough my friend that you can afford to give me the pale-face girl? Surely, she has been tortured sufficiently to satisfy your braves' thirst for vengeance."

Sitting Bull was silent.

"What will the Scarlet Boy do with the fair maiden of his tribe?"

"Bear her to a place of safety, chief, and care for her until I can find her friends — probably she has friends in the East."

"It shall be as he says. Sitting Bull will withdraw his braves and Scarlet Boy can have the red-man's prize."

A friendly hand-shake between the youth and the Sioux chieftain, a word from the latter to the grim painted warriors, and the next instant the glade was cleared of the savages.

Fearless Frank then hastened to approach the insensible captive, and, with a couple sweeps of his knife, cut the bonds that held her to the torture-stake. Gently he laid her on the grass, and arranged about her half-nude form the garments Sitting Bull's warriors had torn off, and soon he had the satisfaction of seeing her once more clothed properly. It still remained for him to restore her to consciousness, and this promised to be no easy task, for she was in a dead swoon. She was even more beautiful of face and figure than one would have imagined at a first glance. Of a delicate blonde complexion, with

---

[6] *Restored Sitting Bull to the arms of his warriors:*   A fact. [Footnote in the original.]

pink-tinged cheeks, she made a very pretty picture, her face framed as it was in a wild disheveled cloud of auburn hair.

A hatful of cold water from a neighboring spring dashed into her upturned face; a continued chafing of the pure white soft hands; then there was a convulsive twitching of the features, a low moan, and the eyes opened and darted a glance of affright into the face of the Scarlet Boy.

"Fear not, miss;" and the youth gently supported her to a sitting position. "I am a friend, and your cruel captors have vamosed. Lucky I came along just as I did, or it's likely they'd have killed you."

"Oh! sir, how can I ever thank you for rescuing me from those merciless fiends!" and the maiden gave him a grateful glance. "They whipped me, terribly!"

"I know, lady — all because you defended yourself in Red Canyon."

"I suppose so: but how did you find out so much, and, also effect my release from the savages?"

Fearless Frank leaned up against the tree which had been used as the torture-stake, and related what is already known to the reader.

When he had finished, the rescued captive seized his hand between both her own, and thanked him warmly.

"Had it not been for you, sir, no one but our God knows what would have been my fate. Oh! sir, what can I do, more than to thank you a thousand times, to repay you for the great service you have rendered me?"

"Nothing, lady; nothing that I think of at present. Was it not my duty, while I had the power, to free you from the hands of those barbarians? Certainly it was, and I deserve no thanks. But tell me, what is your name, and were your friends all killed in the train from which you were taken?"

"I had no friends, sir, save a lady whose acquaintance I made on the journey out from Cheyenne. As to my name — you can call me Miss Terry."

"Mystery!" in blank amazement.

"Yes;" with a gay laugh — "Mystery, if you choose. My name is Alice Terry."

"Oh!" and the youth began to brighten. "Miss Terry, to be sure; Mystery! ha! ha! good joke. I shall call you the latter. Have you friends and relatives East?"

"No. I came West to meet my father, who is somewhere in the Black Hills."

"Do you know at what place?"

"I do not."

"I fear it will be a hard matter to find him, then. The Hills now have a floating population of about twenty-five thousand souls. Your father would be one to find out of that lot."

A smile came over the girl's face. "I should know papa among fifty thousand, if necessary;" she said, "although I have not seen him for years."

She failed to mention how many, or what peculiarities she would recognize him by. Was he blind, deaf or dumb?

Fearless Frank glanced around him, and saw that a path rugged and steep led up to the prairie above.

"Come," he said, offering his arm, "we will get up to the plains and go."

"Where to?" asked Miss Terry, rising with an effort. The welts across her back were swollen and painful.

"Deadwood is my destination. I can deviate my course, however, if it will accommodate you."

"Oh! no; you must not inconvenience yourself on my account. I am of little or no consequence, you know."

She leaned upon his arm, and they ascended the path to the plain above.

Frank's horse was grazing near by where the scarlet youth had taken his unceremonious tumble.

Off to the north-west a cloud of dust rose heavenward, and he rightly conjectured that it hid from view the chieftain, Sitting Bull, and his warriors.

His thoughts reverting to his companion, "General" Nix, and the train of Charity Joe, he glanced toward where he had last seen them.

Neither were to be seen, now. Probably Nix had rejoined the train, and it was out of eye-shot behind a swell in the plains.

"Were you looking for some one?" Alice asked, looking into her rescuer's face.

"Yes, I was with a train when I first heard your cries; I left the boys, and came to investigate. I guess they have gone on without me."

"How mean of them! Will we have to make the journey to the Hills alone?"

"Yes, unless we should providentially fall in with a train or be overtaken by a stage."

"Are you not afraid?"

"My cognomen is Fearless Frank, lady; you can draw conclusions from that."

He went and caught the horse, arranged a blanket in the saddle so that she could ride side-fashion, and assisted her to mount.

The sun was touching the lips of the horizon with a golden kiss: more time than Frank had supposed had elapsed since he left the train.

Far off toward the east shadows were hugging close behind the last lingering rays of sunlight; a couple of coyotes were sneaking into view a few rods away; birds were winging homeward; a perfume-laden breeze swept down from the Black Hills, and fanned the pink cheeks of Alice Terry into a vivid glow.

"We cannot go far," said Frank, thoughtfully, "before darkness will overtake us. Perhaps we had better remain in the canal, here, where there is both grass and water. In the morning we will take a fresh start."

The plan was adopted; they camped in the break, or "canal," where Alice had been tortured.

Out of his saddle-bags Frank brought forth crackers, biscuit and dried venison; these, with clear sparkling water from the spring in the chaparral made a meal good enough for anybody.

The night was warm; no fire was needed.

A blanket spread on the grass served as a resting-place for Alice; the strange youth in scarlet lay with his head resting against the side of his horse. The least movement of the animal, he said, would arouse him; he was keen of scent and quick to detect danger — meaning the horse.

The night passed away without incident; as early as four o'clock — when it is daylight on the plains — Fearless Frank was astir.

He found the rivulet flowing from the spring to abound with trout, and caught and dressed the morning meal.

Alice was awake by the time breakfast was ready. She bathed her face and hands in the stream, combed her long auburn hair through her fingers, and looked sweeter than on the previous night — at least, so thought Fearless Frank.

"The day promises to be delightful, does it not?" she remarked, as she seated herself to partake of the repast.

"Exactly. Autumn months are ever enjoyable in the West."

The meal dispatched, no delay was made in leaving the place.

Fearless Frank strode along beside his horse and its fair rider, chatting pleasantly, and at the same time making a close observation of his surroundings. He knew he was in parts frequented by both red and white savages, and it would do no harm to keep on one's guard.

They traveled all day and reached Sage creek at sunset.

Here they remained over night, taking an early start on the succeeding morning.

That day they made good progress, in consequence of Frank's purchase of a horse at Sage creek from some friendly Crow Indians, and darkness overtook them at the mouth of Red Canyon, where they went into camp.

By steady pushing they reached Rapid Creek the next night, for no halt was made at Custer City, and for the first time since leaving the torture-ground, camped with a miner's family. As yet no cabins or shanties had been erected here, canvas tents serving in the stead; to-day there are between fifty and a hundred wooden structures.

Alice was charmed with the wild grandeur of the mountain scenery — with the countless acres of blossoms and flowering shrubs — with the romantic and picturesque surroundings in general, and was very empathetic in her praises.

One day of rest was taken at Rapid Creek; then the twain pushed on, and when night again overtook them, they rode into the bustling, noisy, homely metropolis — Deadwood, magic city of the North-west.

CHAPTER VI. ONLY A SNAKE — LOCATING A MINE

Harry Redburn hurried off toward the cabin, which was some steps away. In Anita's scream there were both terror and affright.

Walsingham Nix, the hump-backed, bow-legged explorer and prospecter hobbled after him, using his staff for support.

He had heard the scream, but years' experience among the "gals" taught him that a feminine shriek rarely, if ever, meant anything.

Redburn arrived at the cabin in a few flying bounds and leaped into the kitchen.

There, crouched upon the floor in one corner, all in a little heap, pale, trembling and terrified, was Anita. Before her, squirming along over the sand-scrubbed floor, evidently disabled by a blow, was an enormous black-snake.

It was creeping away instead of toward Anita, leaving a faint trail of crimson in its wake; yet the young girl's face was blanched with fear.

"You screamed at that?" demanded Redburn, pointing to the coiling serpent.

"Ugh! yes; it is horrible."

"But, it is harmless. See: some one has given it a blow across the back, and it is disabled for harm."

Anita looked up into his handsome face, wonderingly.

"I guv et a rap across the spinal column, when I kim into the valley," said General Nix, thrusting his head in at the door, a ludicrous grin elongating his grisly features. "Twar a-goin' ter guv me a yard or so uv et's tongue, more or less — consider'bly less of more than more of less — so I jest salivated it across ther back, kerwhack!"

Anita screamed again as she saw the General, he was so rough and homely.

"Who are you?" she managed to articulate as Redburn assisted her to rise from the floor. "What are you doing here, where you were not invited?"

There was a degree of haughtiness in her tone that Redburn did not dream she possessed.

The "General" rubbed the end of his nose, chuckled audibly, then laughed, outright.

"I opine this ar' a free country, ain't it, marm, more or less? W'en a feller kerflummuxes rite down onter a payin' streek I opine he's goin' ter roost thar till he gits ready to vamoose, ain't he?"

"But, sir, my brother was the first to discover this spot and build us a home here, and he claims that all belongs to him."

"He do? more or less — consider'bly less of more than more uv less, eh? Yas, I kno' yer brother — leastways I ev seen him an' heerd heaps about him. Letters uv his name spell Ned Harris, not?"

"Yes, sir; but how can you know him? Few do, in Deadwood."

"Nevyer mind thet, my puss. Ole Walsingham Nix do kno' a few things yet, ef he ar' a hard old nut fer w'ich thar is not cra'kin'."

Anita looked at Redburn, doubtfully.

"Brother would be very angry if he were to return and find this man here. What would you advise?"

"I am of the opinion that he will have to vacate," replied Harry, decidedly.

"*Nix* cum-a-rouse!" disagreed the old prospecter. "I'm hayr, an' thar's no yearthly use o' denyin' *that*. Barrin' ye ar' a right peart-lookin' kid, stranger, allow me ter speculate that it would take a dozen, more or less — consider'bly less uv more than more o' less — ter put me out."

Redburn laughed heartily. The old fellow's bravado amused him. Anita however, was silent; she had dependence in her protector to arrange matters satisfactorily.

"That savors strongly of rebellion," Redburn observed, sitting down upon a lounge that stood hard by. "Besides, you have an advantage; I would not attack you; you are old and unfitted for combat; deformed and unable to do battle."

"Exactly!" the "General" confidently announced.

"What good can come of your remaining here?" demanded Anita.

"Sit down, marm, sit down, an' I'll perceed ter divest myself uv w'at little infermation I've got stored up in my noddle. Ye see, mum, my name's Walsingham Nix, at yer service — Walsingham bein' my great, great grandad's fronticepiece, while Nix war ther hind-wheeler, like nor w'at a he-mule ar' w'en hitched ter a 'schooner.' Ther Nix family were a great one, bet yer false teeth; originated about ther time Joner swallered the whale, down nigh Long Branch, and 've bin handed down frum time ter time till ye behold in me ther last survivin' pilgrim frum ther ancestral block. Thar was one remarkable pecooliarity about ther Nix family, frum root ter stump, an' ther war, they war nevyer known ter refuse a gift or an advantageous offer; in this respeck they bore a striking resemblance ter the immortell G'orge Washington. G'orge war innercent; he ked never tell a lie. So war our family; they never hed it in their hearts to say *Nix* to an offer uv a good feed or a decoction o' brandy.

"It war a disease — a hereditary affection uv ther hull combined system. The terrible malady attacked me w'en I war an infant prodigy, an' I've nevyer yit see'd thet time when I c'u'd resist the temptation an' coldly say 'nix' w'en a brother pilgrim volunteered ter make a liberal dispensation uv grub, terbarker, or bug-juice. Nix ar' a word thet causes sorrer an' suffering ter scores 'n' scores o' people, more or less — ginerally more uv less than less o' more — an' tharfore I nevyer feel it my duty, as a Christyun, ter set a bad example w'ich others may foller."

Redburn glanced toward Anita, a quizzical expression upon his genial face.

"I fail to see how that has any reference as to the cause of your stay among us," he observed, amused at the quaint lingo of the prospecter.

"Sart'in not, sart'in not! I had just begun ter git thar. I've only bin gi'in' ye a geological ijee uv ther Nix family's formation; I'll now perceed to illustrate more clearly, thr'u' veins an' channels hitherto unexplored, endin' up wi' a reg'lar hoss-car proposal."

Then the old fellow proceeded with a rambling "yarn," giving more guesses than actual information and continued on in this strain:

"So thar *war* gold. I went ter work an' swallered a pill o' opium, w'ich made me sleep, an' while I war snoozin' I dreampt about ther perzact place whar thet gold war secreted. It war in a little pocket beneath the bed of a spring frum which flowed a little creeklet.

"Next mornin', bright an' early, I shouldered pick, shuvyel an' pan, an' went for thet identical spring. To-day thet pocket, havin' been traced into a rich vein, is payin' as big or bigger nor any claim on Spring creek."[7]

Both Redburn and Anita were unconsciously becoming interested.

"And do you think there is gold here, in this flower-strewn pocket-valley?"

"I don't think it — I know it. I hed a dreem et war hayr in big quantities, so I h'isted my carcass this direction. Ter-nite I'll hev er-nuther nighthoss, an' thet'll tell me precisely where ther strike ar'."

Redburn drummed a tattoo on the arm of the lounge with his fingers; he was reflecting on what he had heard.

"You are willing to make terms, I suppose," he said, after a while, glancing at Anita to see if he was right. "You are aware, I believe, that we still hold possession above any one else."

"True enuff. Ye war first ter diskiver this place; ye orter hev yer say about it."

"Well, then, perhaps we can come to a bargain. You can state your prices for locating and opening up this mine, and we will consider."

"Wal, let me see. Ef the mine proves to be ekal ter the one thet I located on Spring creek, I'll rake in a third fer my share uv the divys. Ef 'tain't good's I expect, I'll take a quarter."

Redburn turned to Anita.

"From what little experience I have had, I think it is a fair offer. What is your view of the matter, and do you believe your brother will be satisfied?"

"Oh! yes, sir. It will surprise and please him, to return and find his Paradise has been turned into a gold-mine."

[7] *Spring creek*:   A fact. [Footnote in the original.]

"All right; then, we will go ahead and get things in shape. We will have to get tools, though, before we can accomplish much of anything."

"My brother has a miner's outfit here," said Anita. "That will save you a trip to Deadwood, for the present."

And so it was all satisfactorily arranged. During the remainder of the day the old "General" and Redburn wandered about through the flower-meadows of the pocket, here and there examining a little soil; now chipping rock among the rugged foothills, then "feeling" in the bed of the creek. But, not a sign of anything like gold was to be found, and when night called them to shelter, Redburn was pretty thoroughly convinced that Nix was an enormous "sell," and that he could put all the gold they would find in his eye. The "General," however, was confident of success, and told many doubtful yarns of former discoveries and exploits.

Anita prepared an evening meal that was both tempting and sumptuous, and all satisfied their appetites, after which Harry took down the guitar, suspended from the wall, tuned it up, and sung in a clear mellow voice a number of ballads, to which the "General," much to the surprise of both Redburn and Anita, lent a rich deep bass — a voice of superior culture.

The closing piece was a weird melody — the lament of a heart that was broken, love-blasted — and was rendered in a style worthy of a professional vocalist. The last mournful strains filled the cabin just as the last lingering rays of sunlight disappeared from the mountain top, and shadows came creeping down the rugged walls of rock to concentrate in the Flower Pocket, as Anita had named her valley home. Redburn rose from his seat at the window, and reached the instrument to its accustomed shelf, darting a glance toward sad Anita, a moment later. To his surprise he perceived that her head was bowed upon her arm that lay along the window-ledge — that she was weeping, softly, to herself.

Acting the gentlemanly part, the young miner motioned for Nix to follow him, and they both retired to the outside of the cabin to lounge on the grass and smoke, and thus Anita was left alone with her grief and such troubles as were the causes thereof.

Certain it was that she had a secret, but what it was Redburn could not guess.

About ten o'clock he and Nix re-entered the cabin and went to bed in a room allotted to them, off from the little parlor. Both went to sleep at once, and it was well along toward morning when Redburn was aroused by being rudely shaken by "General" Nix, who was up and dressed, and held a torch in his hand.

"Come! come!" he said in a husky whisper, and a glance convinced Harry that he was still asleep, although his eyes were wide open and staring.

Without a word the young man leaped from bed, donned his garments, and the old man then led the way out of the cabin.

In passing through the kitchen, Redburn saw that Anita was up and waiting.

"Come!" he said, seizing a hatchet and stake, "we are about to discover the gold-mine, and our fortunes;" with a merry laugh.

Then both followed in the wake of the sleep walker, and were led to near the center of the valley, which was but a few steps in the rear of the cabin. Here was a bed of sand washed there from an overflow of the stream, and at this the "General" pointed, as he came to a halt.

"There! *there* is the gold — millions of it deep down — twenty or thirty feet — in sand — easy to get! dig! DIG! DIG!"

Redburn marked the spot by driving the stake in the ground.

It now only remained to dig in the soil to verify the truth of the old man's fancy.

CHAPTER VII. DEADWOOD DICK ON THE ROAD

Rumbling noisily through the black canyon road to Deadwood, at an hour long past midnight, came the stage from Cheyenne, loaded down with passengers, and full five hours late, on account of a broken shaft, which had to be replaced on the road. There were six plunging, snarling horses attached, whom the veteran Jehu[8] on the box, managed with the skill of a circusman, and all the time the crack! snap! of his long-lashed gad made the night resound as like so many pistol reports.

The road was through a wild tortuous canyon, fringed with tall spectral pines, which occasionally admitted a bar of ghostly moonlight across the rough road over which the stage tore with wild recklessness.

Inside, the vehicle was crammed full to its utmost capacity, and therefrom emanated the strong fumes of whisky and tobacco smoke,

---

[8] *Jehu*: A "jehu" is a fast stage driver, the term being derived from Jehu (ninth century B.C.), a king of Israel famous for his military use of chariots.

and stronger language, over the delay and the terrible jolting of the conveyance.

In addition to those penned up inside, there were two passengers positioned on top, in the rear of the driver, where they clung to the trunk railings to keep from being jostled off.

One was an elderly man, tall in stature and noticeably portly, with a florid countenance, cold gray eyes, and hair and beard of brown, freely mixed with silvery threads. He was elegantly attired, his costume being of the finest cloth and of the very latest cut; boots patent leathers, and hat glossy as a mirror; diamonds gleamed and sparkled on his immaculate shirt-bosom, on his fingers and from the seal of a heavy gold chain across his vest front.

The other personage was a counterpart of the first in every particular, save that while one was more than a semi-centenarian in years, the other was barely twenty. The same faultless elegance in dress, the same elaborate display of jewels, and the same haughty, aristocratic bearing produced in one was mirrored in the other.

They were father and son.

"Confound such a road!" growled the younger man, as the stage bounced him about like a rubber ball. "For my part I wish I had remained at home, instead of coming out into this outlandish region. It is perfectly awful."

"Y-y-y-e-s!" chattered the elder between the jolts and jerks — "it is not what it should be, that's true. But have patience; ere long we will reach our destination, and — "

"Get shot like poor Vansevere did!" sneered the other. "I tell you, governor, this is a desperate game you are playing."

The old man smiled, grimly.

"Desperate or not, we must carry it through to the end. Vansevere was not the right kind of a man to set after the young scamp."

"How do you mean?"

"He was too rash — entirely too rash. Deadwood Dick is a daring whelp, and Vansevere's open offer of a reward for his apprehension only put the young tiger on his guard, and he will be more wary and watchful in the future."

This in a positive tone.

"Yes; he will be harder to trap than a fox who has lost a foot between jaws of steel. He will be revengeful too!"

"Bah! I fear him not, old as I am. He is but a boy in years, you remember, and will be easily managed."

"I hope so; I don't want my brains blown out, at least."

The stage rumbled on; the Jehu cursed and lashed his horses; the canyon grew deeper, narrower and darker, the grade slightly descending.

The moon seemed resting on the summit of a peak, hundreds of feet above, and staring down in surprise at the noisy stage.

Alexander Filmore (the elder passenger) succeeded in steadying himself long enough to ignite the end of a cigar in the bowl of Jehu's grimy pipe; then he watched the trees that flitted by. Clarence, his son, had smoked incessantly since leaving Camp Crook, and now threw away his half-used cheroot, and listened to the sighing of the spectral pines.

"The girl — what about her?" he asked, after some moments had elapsed.

"She will be as much in the way as the boy will."

"She? Well, we'll attend to her after we git him out of the way. He is the worst obstacle in our path, at present. Maybe when you see the girl you will take a fancy to her."

"Pish! I want no petticoats clinging to me — much less an ignorant backwoods clodhopper. She is probably a fit mate for an Indian chief."

"You are too rough on the tender sex, boy," and the elder Filmore gave vent to a disconnected laugh. "You must remember that your mother was a woman."

"Was she?" Clarence bit the end of his waxed mustache, and mused over his sire's startling announcement. "*You* recollect that I never saw her."

"D'ye carry poppin'-jays, pilgrims?" demanded Jehu, turning so suddenly upon the two passengers as to frighten them out of their wits.

"Popping-jays?" echoed Filmore, senior.

"Yas — shutin'-irons — rewolvers — patent perforatin' masheens."

"Yes, we are armed, if that is what you mean."

On dashed the stage through the echoing canyon — on plunged the snorting horses, excited to greater efforts by the frequent application of the cracking lash. The pines grew thicker, and the moonlight less often darted its rays down athwart the road.

"Hey!" yelled a rough voice from within the stage, "w'at d'ye drive so fast fer? Ye've jonced the senses clean out uv a score o' us."

"Go to blazes!" shouts back Jehu, giving an extra crack to his whip. "Who'n the name o' John Rodgers ar' drivin' this omnybust, pilgrim? — you or I?"

"You'll floor a hoss ef ye don' mind sharp!"

"Who'n thunder wants ye to pay fer et, ef I do?" rings back, tauntingly. "Reckon w'en Bill McGucken can't drive ther thru-ter-Deadwood stage as gude as ther average, he'll suspend bizness, or hire *you* ter steer in his place."

On, on rumbles the stage, down through a lower grade of the canyon, where no moonlight penetrates, and all is of Stygian darkness.

The two passengers on top of the stage shiver with dread, and even old Bill McGucken peers around him, a trifle suspiciously.

It is a wild spot, with the mountains rising on each side of the road to a stupendous hight, the towering pines moaning their sad, eternal requiem; the roar of the great wheels over the hardpan bottom; the snorting of the fractious lead-horses; the curses and the cracking of Jehu's whip; the ring of iron-shod hoofs — it is a place and moment conducive to fear, mute wonder, admiration.

"*Halt!*"

High above all other sounds now rings this cry, borne toward the advancing stage from the impenetrable space of gloom ahead, brought down in clear commanding tone wherein there is neither fear nor hesitation.

That one word has marvelous effect. It brings a gripe of iron into the hands of Jehu, and he jerks his snorting steeds back upon their haunches; it is instrumental in stopping the stage. (Who ever knew a Black Hills driver to offer to press on when challenged to halt in a wild dismal place?)

It sends a thrill of lonely horror through the veins of those to whose ears the cry is borne; it causes hands to fly to the butts of weapons, and hearts to beat faster.

"Halt!" Again the cry rings forth, reverberating in a hundred dissimilar echoes up the rugged mountain side.

The horses quiet down; Jehu sits like a carved statue on his box; the silence becomes painful to those within the stage — those who are trembling in a fever of excitement, and peering from the open windows with revolvers cocked for instant use.

The moon suddenly thrusts her golden head over the pinnacle of a hoary peak a thousand feet above, and lights up the gorge with a ghastly distinctness that enables the watchers to behold a black horseman blocking the path a few rods ahead.

"Silence! Listen!" Two words this time, in the same clear, commanding voice. A pause of a moment; then the stillness is broken by the ominous click! click! of a score of rifles; this alone announces that the stage is "covered."

Then the lone horseman rides leisurely down toward the stage, and Jehu recognizes him. It is Deadwood Dick, Prince of the Road!

Mounted upon his midnight steed, and clad in the weird suit of black, he makes an imposing spectacle as he comes fearlessly up. Well may he be bold and fearless, for no one dares to raise a hand against him, when the glistening barrels of twelve rifles protruding from each thicket that fringes the road threaten those within and without the stage.

Close up to the side of the coach rides the daring young outlaw, his piercing orbs peering out from the eye-holes in his black mask, one hand clasping the bridle-reins the other a nickel-plated seven-shooter drawn back at full cock.

"You do well to stop, Bill McGucken!" the road-agent, observes, reining in his steed. "I expected you hours ago, on time."

"Twarn't my fault, yer honor!" replies Jehu, meek as a lamb under the gaze of the other's popgun. "Ye see, we broke a pole this side o' Custer City, an' that set us behind several p'ints o' ther compass."

"What have you aboard to-night worth examining?"

"Nothin', yer honor. Only a stageful uv passengers, this trip."

"Bah! you are getting poor. Get down from off the box, there!"

The driver trembled, and hesitated.

"*Get* down!" again commanded the road-agent, leveling his revolver, "before I drop you."

In terror McGucken made haste to scramble to the ground, where he stood with his teeth chattering and knees knocking together in a manner pitiable to see.

"Ha, ha, ha!" That wild laugh of Deadwood Dick's made the welkin ring out a wierd chorus. "Bill McGucken, you should join the regular army, you are so brave. Ha, ha, ha!"

And the laugh was taken up by the road-knights, concealed in the thicket, and swelled into a wild, boisterous shout.

Poor McGucken trembled in his boots in abject terror, while those inside the coach were pretty well scared.

"Driver!" said the Prince of the Road, coolly, after the laugh, "go you to the passengers who grace this rickety shebang and take up a collection. You needn't cum to me wi' less'n five hundred ef ye don't want me to salt ye!"

Bowing humble obeisance, McGucken took off his hat, and made for the stage door.

"Gentlemen!" he plead, "there is need o' yer dutchin' out yer du-dads right liberal ef ye've enny purtic'lar anticypation an' desire ter git ter Deadwood ter-night. Dick, the Road-Agent, are law an' gospel heerabouts, I spec'late!"

"Durned a cent 'll I fork!" growled one old fellow, loud enough to be heard. "I ain't afeerd o' all the robber Dicks from here ter Jerusalum."

But when he saw the muzzle of the young road-agent's revolver gazing in through the window, he suddenly changed his mind, and laid a plethoric pocketbook into McGucken's already well-filled hat.

The time occupied in making the collection was short, and in a few moments the Jehu handed up his battered "plug" to the Prince of the Road for inspection.

Coolly Deadwood Dick went over the treasure, as if it were all rightfully his own; then he chucked hat and all into one of his saddle-bags, after which he turned his attention toward the stage. As he did so he saw for the first time the two passengers on top, and as he gazed at them a gleam of fire shot into his eyes and his hands nervously griped at his weapon.

"Alexander Filmore, you here!" he ejaculated, his voice betraying his surprise.

"Yes," replied the elder Filmore, coldly — "here to shoot you, you dastardly dog," and quickly raising a pistol, he took rapid and deadly aim, and fired.

CHAPTER VIII. NOT YET!

With a groan Deadwood Dick fell to the ground, blood spurting from a wound in his breast. The bullet of the elder Filmore had indeed struck home.

Loud then were the cries of rage and vengeance, as a score of masked men poured out from the thickets, and surrounded the stage.

"Shoot the accursed nigger!" cried one. "He's killed our leader, an' by all the saints in ther calendur he shall pay the penalty!"

"No! no!" yelled another, "we'll do no such a thing. He shall swing in mid-air!"

"Hey!" cried a third, rising from the side of the prostrate road-agent, "don' ye be so fast, boys. The capt'in still lives. He is not seriously wounded, even!"

A loud huzza went up from the score of throats, that caused a thousand echoing reverberations along the mountain side.

"Better let ther capt'in say what we shall do wi' yon cuss o' creashun!" suggested one who was apparently a leading spirit; "it's *his* funeral, ain't it?"

"Yas, yas, it's his funeral!"

"Then let him do ther undertakin'."

Robber Dick was accordingly supported to a sitting posture, and the blood that flowed freely from his wound was stanched. In the operation his mask became loosened and slipped to the ground, but so quickly did he snatch it up and replace it, that no one caught even a glimpse of his face.

In the meantime Clarence Filmore had discharged every load in his two six-shooters into the air. He had an object in doing this; he thought that the reports of fire-arms would reach Deadwood (which was only a short mile distant, around the bend), and arouse the military, who would come to his rescue.

Dick's wound dressed, he stood once more upon his feet, and glared up at the two men on the box. They were plainly revealed in the ghostly moonlight, and their features easily studied.

"Alexander Filmore!" the young road-agent said, a terrible depth of meaning in his voice, that the cowering wretch could but understand.

"Alexander Filmore, you have at last come out and shown your true colors. What a treacherous, double-dyed villain you are! Better so; better that you should take the matter into your own hands and face the music, than to employ *tools,* as you have done heretofore. I can fight a dozen enemies face to face better than one or two lurking in the bushes."

The elder Filmore uttered a savage curse.

"You triumph *now!*" he growled, biting his nether lip in vexation; "but it will not always be thus."

"Eh? think not? I think I shall have to *adopt* you for awhile. Boys, haul down the two, and bind them securely."

Accordingly, a rush was made upon the stage, and the two outside passengers. Down they were hauled, head over heels, and quickly secured by strong cords about the wrists and ankles.

This done, Deadwood Dick turned to Bill McGucken, who had ventured to clamber to the seat of the coach.

"Drive on, you cowardly lout — drive on. We've done with you for the present. But, remember, not a word of this to the population of Deadwood, if you intend to ever make another trip over this route. Now go!"

Jehu needed not the second invitation. He never was tardy in getting out of the way of danger; so he picked up the reins, gave an extra hard crack of the long whip, and away rolled the jolting stage through the black canyon, disappearing a moment later around the bend, beyond which lay Deadwood — magic city of the wilderness.

Then, out from the thicket the road-agents led their horses; the two prisoners were secured in the saddles in front of two brawny outlaws, and without delay the cavalcade moved down the gorge, weirdly illuminated by the mellow rays of the soaring moon.

Clarence Filmore had hoped that the report of his pistol-shots would reach Deadwood. If so, his wishes were fulfilled. The reports reached the barracks above Deadwood just as a horseman galloped up the — Major R———, just in from a carouse down at the "Met."

"Halloo!" he shouted, loudly. "To horse! there is trouble in the gorge. The Sioux, under Sitting Bull, are upon us!"

As the major's word was law at the barracks, in very short order the garrison was aroused, and headed by the major in person, a cavalcade of sleepy soldiers swept down the gorge toward the place whence had come the firing.

Wildly around the abrupt bend they dashed with yells of anticipated victory; then there was a frightful collision between the incoming stage and the outgoing cavalry; the shrieks and screams of horses, the curses and yells of wounded men; and a general pandemonium ensued.

The coach, passengers, horses and all was upset, and went rolling down a steep embankment.

Major R——— was precipitated headlong over the embankment, and in his downward flight probably saw more than one soaring comet. He struck head-first in a muddy run, and a sorrier-looking officer of the U. S. A. was never before seen in the Black Hills as he emerged from his bath, than the major. His ridiculous appearance went so far as to stay the general torrent of blasphemy and turn it into a channel of boisterous laughter.

No delay was made in putting things ship-shape again, and ere morning dawned Deadwood beheld the returned soldiers and wrecked stage with its sullen passengers within its precincts.

Dick and his men rode rapidly down the canyon, the two prisoners bringing up the rear under the escort of two masked guards.

These guards were brothers and Spanish-Mexicans at that.

The elder Filmore, a keen student of character, was not long in making out these Spaniards' true character, nor did their greedy glances toward his and his son's diamonds escape him.

"We want to get free!" he at last whispered, when none of those ahead were glancing back. "You will each receive a cool five hundred apiece if you will set us at liberty."

The two road-agents exchanged glances.

"It's a bargain!" returned one. "Stop your horses, and let the others go on!"

The main party were at this juncture riding swiftly down a steep grade.

The four horses were quietly reined in, and when the others were out of hearing, their noses were turned back up the canyon in the direction of Deadwood.

"This will be an unhealthy job for us!" said one of the brothers, "should we ever meet Dick again."

"Fear him not!" replied Alexander Filmore, with an oath. "If he ever crosses your path shoot him down like a dog, and I'll give you a thousand dollars for the work. The sooner he dies the better I'll be suited."

He spoke in a tone of strongest hate — deepest rancor.

CHAPTER IX. AT THE "MET"

A few nights subsequent to the events related in our last chapter, it becomes our duty to again visit the notorious "Metropolitan" saloon of Deadwood, to see what is going on there.

As usual everything around the place and in it is literally "red hot." The bars are constantly crowded, the gaming-tables are never empty and the floor is so full of surging humanity that the dance, formerly a chief attraction, has necessarily been suspended.

The influx of "pilgrims" into the Black Hills for the last few days has been something more than wonderful, every stage coming in overcharged with feverish passengers, and from two to a dozen trains arriving daily.

Of course Deadwood receives a larger share of all this immigration — nothing is more natural, for the young metropolis of the hills is *the* miner's rendezvous, being in the center of the best yielding locales.

Every person in Deadwood can tell you where the "Met" is, as it is general head-quarters.

We mount the mud-splashed steps and disappear behind the screen that stands in front of the door. Then the merry clink of glasses, snatches of ribald song, and loud curses from the polluted lips of some wretch who has lost heavily at the gaming-table, reach our hearing, while our gaze wanders over as motley a crowd as it has ever been our fortune to behold.

Men from the States — lawyers, doctors, speculators, adventurers, pilgrims, and dead-beats; men from the western side of the Missouri; grisly miners from Colorado; hunters and trappers from Idaho and Wyoming; card sharps from Denver and Fr'isco; pickpockets from St. Joe and bummers from Omaha — all are here, each one a part of a strange and on the whole a very undesirable community.

Although the dance has been suspended, that does not necessitate the discharge of the brazen-faced girls, and they may yet be seen here with the rest mingling freely among the crowd.

Seated at a table in a somewhat retired corner were two persons engaged at cards. One was a beardless youth attired in buck-skin, and armed with knife and pistols; the other a big, burly tough from the upper chain—grisly, bloated and repulsive. He, too, was nothing short of a walking arsenal, and it was plain to see that he was a desperate character.

The game was poker. The youth had won three straight games and now laid down the cards that ended the fourth in his favor.

"You're flaxed ag'in, pardner!" he said, with a light laugh, as he raked in the stakes. "This takes your all, eh?"

"Every darned bit!" said the "Cattymount" — fer it was he — with an oath. "You've peeled me to ther hide, an' no mistake. Salivated me' way out o' time, sure's thar ar' modesty in a bar-girl's tongue!"

The youth laughed. "You are not in luck to-night. Maybe your luck will return, if you keep on. Haven't you another V?"

"Nary another!"

"Where's your pard, that got salted the other night?"

"Who — Chet Diamond? Wal, hee's around heer, sum'ars, but I can't borry none off o' him. No; I've gotter quit straight off."

"I'll lend you ten to begin on," said the youth, and he laid an X in the ruffian's hands. "There, now, go ahead with your funeral. It's your deal."

The cards were dealt, and the game played, resulting in the favor of the "Cattymount." Another and another was played, and the tough won every time. Still the youth kept on, a quiet smile resting on his pleasant features, a twinkle in his coal-black eye. The youth, dear reader, you have met before.

He is not he, but instead — Calamity Jane. On goes the game, the burly "tough" winning all the time, his pile of tens steadily increasing in hight.

"Talk about Joner an' the ark, an' Noar an' ther whale!" he cries, slapping another X onto the pile with great enthusiasm; "I hed a grate, grate muther-in-law w'at played keerds wi' Noar inside o' thet eyedentical whale's stummick — played poker wi' w'alebones fer pokers. They were afterward landed at Plymouth rock, or sum uther big rock, an' fit together, side by side, in the rebellyuns."

"Indeed!" — with an amused laugh — "then you must have descended from a long line of respected ancestors."

"Auntsisters? Wa'al, I jest about reckon I do. I hev got ther blood o' Cain and Abel in my veins, boyee, an' ef I ken't raise the biggest kind o' Cane 'tain't because I ain't *able* — oh! no. Pace anuther-pilgrim?"

"I reckon. How much have ye got piled up thar in that heap!"

"Squar' ninety tens, my huckleberry, an' all won fa'r, you bet."

"Then it's the first time you ever won anything fair, Cass Diamond!" exclaimed a voice close at hand, and the two players looked up to see Ned Harris standing near by, with his hands clasped across his breast.

Calamity Jane nodded, indifferently. She had seen the young miner on several occasions; once she had been rendered an invaluable service when he rescued her from a brawl in which a dozen toughs had attacked her.

"Cattymount" Cass, brother of Chet Diamond, the Deadwood card-king, recognized him also, and with an oath, sprung to his feet.

"By all the Celestyals!" he ejaculated, jerking forth a six-shooter — "by all the roarin', screechin', shriekin', yowlin', squawkin', ringtailed, flat-futted cattymounts thet ever did ther forest aisles o' old Alaska traverse! *you* here, ye infernal smooth-faced varmint? *You* heer, arter all ye've did to ride ther cittyzens o' Deadwood inter rebellyun, ye leetle pigminian deputy uv ther devil? Hurra! hurra! boys; let's string him up ter ther nearest sapling!"

"Ha! ha!" laughed Harris, coolly, "hear the coward squeal for his pard's assistance. Dassen't stand on his own leather fer fear of gettin' salter fer all he's worth."

"You're a liar!" roared the "Cattymount" spreading himself about promiscuously, but the three words had scarcely left his lips when a blow from the fist of Ned Harris reached him under the left eye, and he went sprawling on the ground in a heap.

"Here! here!" roared a stranger, rushing in upon the scene, and hurling the crowd aside with a dexterity something wonderful. "What is the meaning of all this? Who knocked Cass Diamond down?"

"I had that honor!" coolly remarked Ned Harris, stepping boldly up and confronting the Deadwood card-king, for it was the notorious Chet Diamond who had asked the question. "I smacked him in the gob, Chet Diamond, for calling me a liar, and am ready to accommodate a few more, if there are any who wish to prefer the same charge!"

"Bully, Ned! and here's what will back you!" cried Calamity Jane, leaping to the miner's side, a cocked six in either white, shapely hand; "so sail in, pilgrims!"

Diamond cowered back, and swore furiously. The wound in his breast was yet sore and rankling, and he knew he owed it to the cool and calculating young miner whose name was an omen of terror among the "toughs" of Deadwood.

"Come on, you black-hearted ace thief!" shouted Calamity Jane, thrusting the muzzle of one of her plated revolvers forcibly under the gambler's prominent nose — "come on! slide in if you are after squar' up-an'-down fun. We'll greet you, best we know how, an' not charge you anything, either. See! I've got a couple full hands o' sixes — every one's a trump! Ain't ye got no aces hid up yer sleeves?"

The card sharp still cursed furiously, and backed away. He dare not reach for a weapon lest the dare-devil girl or young Harris (who now held a cocked pill-box in each hand), "should salt him on a full 'ay."

"Ha! ha! ha!" and the laugh of Calamity rung wildly through the great saloon — "Ha! ha! ha! here's a go! Who wants to buy a clipped-winged sharp?"

"Sold out right cheap!" added Ned, facetiously. "Clear the track and we'll take him out and boost him to a limb."

At this juncture some half a dozen of the gambler's gang came rushing up, headed by Catamount Cass, who had recovered from the effects of the blow from Harris' fist.

"At them! at 'em!" roared the "screechin' cattymount frum up nor'." "Rip, dig an' gouge 'em. Ho! ho! we'll see now who'll swing, *we* will! We'll l'arn who'll display his agility in mid-air, we will. At 'em, b'yees, at 'em. We'll hang 'em like they do hoss-thieves down at Cheyenne!"

Then followed a pitched battle in the bar-room of the "Metropolitan" saloon, such as probably never occurred there before, and never has since.

Revolvers flashed on every hand, knives clashed in deadly conflict; yells, wild, savage, and awful made a perfect pandemonium, to which was added a second edition in the shape of oaths, curses, and groans. Crack! whiz! bang! the bullets flew about like hailstones, and men fell to the reeking floor each terrible moment.

The two friends were not alone in the affray.

No sooner had Catamount Cass and his gang of "toughs" showed fight, than a company of miners sprung to Harris' side, and showed their willingness to fight it out on the square line.

Therefore, once the first shot was fired, it needed not a word to pitch the battle.

Fiercely waged the contest — now hand to hand — and loud rose the savage yells on the still night air.

One by one men fell on either side, their life-blood crimsoning the floor, their dying groans unheeded in the fearful melee.

Still unharmed, and fighting among the first, we see Ned Harris and his remarkable companion, Calamity Jane; both are black, and scarcely recognizable in the cloud of smoke that fills the bar-room. Harris is wounded in a dozen places and weak from loss of blood; yet he stands up bravely and fights mechanically.

Calamity Jane if she is wounded shows it not, but faces the music with as little apparent fear as any of those around her.

On wages the battle, even as furiously as in its beginning; the last shot has been fired; it is now knife to knife, and face to face.

Full as many of one side as the other have fallen, and lay strewn about under foot, unthought of, uncared for in the excitement of the desperate moment. Gallons of blood have made the floor slippery and reeking, so that it is difficult to retain one's footing.

At the head of the ruffians the Diamond brothers[9] still hold sway, fighting like madmen in their endeavors to win a victory. They cannot do less, for to back off in this critical moment means sure death to the weakening party.

But hark! what are these sounds?

The thunder of hoofs is heard outside; the rattle of musketry and sabers, and the next instant a company of soldiery, headed by Major R———, ride straight up into the saloon, firing right and left.

[9] *Diamond brothers:* Living characters. [Footnote in the original.]

"Come!" cried Calamity Jane, grasping Harris by the arm, and pulling him toward a side door, "it's time for us to slope now. It's every man for himself."

And only under her guidance was Ned able to escape, and save being killed and captured with the rest.

About noon of the succeeding day, two persons on horseback were coming along the north gulch leading into Deadwood, at an easy canter. They were the fearless Scarlet Boy, or as he is better known, Fearless Frank, and his lovely protege, Miss Terry. They had been for a morning ride over to a neighboring claim, and were just returning.

Since their arrival in Deadwood the youth had devoted a part of his time in a search for Alice's father, but all to no avail. None of the citizens of Deadwood or its surroundings had ever heard of such a person as Captain Walter Terry.

The young couple had become fast friends from their association, and Alice was improving in looks every day she stayed in the mountains.

"I feel hungry," observed Frank, as they rode along. "This life in the hills gives me a keen appetite. How is it with you, lady?"

"The same as with you, I guess. But look! Yonder comes a horseman toward us!"

It was even so. A horseman was galloping up the gulch — no other than our young friend, Ned Harris.

As the two parties approach, the faces of each of the youths grow deadly pale; there comes into their eyes an ominous glitter; their hands each clasp the butt of a revolver, and they gradually draw rein.

That they are enemies of old — that the fire of rancor burns in their hearts, and that this meeting is unexpected, is plain to see.

Now, that they have met, probably for the first time in months or years, it remains not to be doubted but a settlement must come between them — that their hate must result in satisfaction, whether in blood or not.

CHAPTER X. THE DUEL AND ITS RESULT

Belligerent were the glances exchanged between the two, as they sat there facing each other, each with a hand closed over the butt of a pistol; each as motionless as a carved statue.

Alice Terry had grown pale, too. She saw that friend and protector and the stranger were enemies, — that this meeting though purely accidental was not to end without trouble. Her lips grew set, her eyes flashed, and she reined her horse closer to that of the Scarlet Boy.

Ned Harris let a faint smile, of contempt and pity combined, come into relief on his lips, as he saw this action. Better ten male enemies than one female, he thought; but, then, women must not stand in the way now. No! nothing must block the path intervening between enmity and vengeance.

Harris was, if anything, the coolest of the three; but, after all, why should he not be? He had spent several years in society that seemed callous to fear, — that knew not what it was to be a Christian; where the utmost coolness was necessary to the preservation of life; where bravery was all, and education a dead letter. Fearless Frank, too, had seen all phases of rough western life, probably, but his temperament was more nervous and excitable, his passions tenfold harder to restrain. Still, he managed to exercise a cool exterior now, that equaled that of his opposite — his hated enemy. Mystery, as Frank habitually called the girl, did not offer to conceal her feelings. It was but natural that she should side with him to whom she owed her life, and the glances of scorn and indignation she shot at the young miner might have driven another man than him into a retreat.

Fearless Frank made no motion toward speech; he was determined that the young miner should open the quarrel, if a quarrel it was to be. But beneath his firm-set lips were clenched two rows of teeth, tightly, fiercely; while every nerve in the youth's body was drawn to its utmost tension.

Harris was wonderfully calm and at ease; only a gray pallor on his handsome face and a menacing fire in his piercing eyes told that he was in the least agitated.

"Justin McKenzie!"

Sternly rung out the words on the clear mountain air. Ned Harris had spoken, and the grayish pallor deepened on his countenance while the fire of rancor burned with stronger gleam in his eagle eye.

The effect on the scarlet youth was scarcely noticeable, more than that the lips grew more rigid and compressed, and the right hand clutched the pistol-butt more tightly. But no answer to the other's summons.

"Justin McKenzie!" again said the young miner, calmly, "do you recognize me?"

The Scarlet Boy bows his head slowly, his eyes watchful lest the other shall catch the drop on him.

"Justin McKenzie, you *do* recognize me, even after the elapse of two long weary years, during which I have sought for you faithfully, but failed to find you until this hour. We have at last met, and the time for settlement between you and me, Justin McKenzie, has arrived. Here in this out-of-the-way gorge, we will settle the grudge I hold against you — we will see who shall live and who shall die!"

Alice Terry uttered a terrified cry.

"Oh! no! no! you must not fight — you *must* not. It is bad — oh! so awful wicked!"

"Excuse me, lady, but you will have no voice in this matter;" and the miner's tone grew a trifle more severe. "Knew you the bitter wrong done me by this young devil with the smooth face and oily tongue — if you knew what a righteous cause I have to defend, you would say 'let the battle proceed.' I am not one to thirst for the blood of my fellow-men, but I *am* one that is ever ready to raise my hand and strike in the defense of women!"

Alice Terry secretly admired the stalwart young miner for this gallant speech.

Fearless Frank, his face paler than before, an expression of remorse combined with anguish about his countenance, and moisture standing in either eye, assumed his quasi-erect attitude as he answered:

"Edward Harris, if you will listen, I will say all I have to say in a very few words. You hate me because of a wrong I did you and yours, and you want my life for the forfeit. I shall not hinder you longer in your purpose. For two long years you have trailed and tracked me with the determination of a bloodhound, and I have evaded you, not that I was at all afraid of you, but because I did not wish to make you a murderer. I have come across your path at last; here let us settle, as you have said. See! I fold my arms across my breast. Take out your pistol, aim steadily, and fire twice at my breast. I have heard enough concerning your skill as a marksman to feel confident that you can kill me in two shots!"

Ned Harris flushed, angrily. He was surprised at the cool indifference and recklessness of the youth; he was angered that McKenzie should think *him* mean enough to take such a preposterous advantage.

"You are a fool!" he sneered, biting his lip with vexation. "Do you calculate I am a *murderer?*"

"I have no proof that you are or that you are *not!*" replied Fearless Frank, controlling his temper by a master effort. "You remember I have not kept a watch upon your actions."

"Be that as it may, I would be an accursed dog to take advantage of your insulting proposal. You must fight me the same as I shall fight you!"

"No, Ned Harris, I will do nothing of the kind. It is I who have wronged you and yours; you must take the offensive; I will play a silent hand."

"You refuse to fight me?"

"I *do* refuse to fight you, but do *not* refuse to give you satisfaction for what wrong you have suffered. Take my life, if you choose; it is yours. Take it, or forever after this consider our debt of hatred canceled, and let us be — "

"Friends? Never, Justin McKenzie, *never!* You forget the stain dyed by your hand that will never wash out!"

"No! no! God knows I do not forget!" and the youth's voice was hoarse with anguish. "Could it be undone, I would gladly undo the deed. But, tell me, Harris, about *her.* Does she still live?"

"*Live?* We-l-l, yes, if you can call staying living. Life is but a blank; better she had died ere she ever met you!"

"You speak truly; better she had died ere she met me."

Unconsciously the two had ridden closer to each other; had they forgotten themselves in recalling the past?

"She lives — may live on her lonely life for years to come," Harris resumed, thoughtfully, "but her life will be merely endurance."

"Will you tell me where — where I can go in secret and take but one look at her? If you will do this I will agree to meet you and give you your chance for satis — "

"No!" thundered Harris, growing suddenly furious, "*no!* a thousand times! I'd sooner see her in the burning depths of the bottomless pit than have you get within a hundred miles of her with your contaminating presence. She is safely hidden away, and that forever, from the companionship of our sex. So let her be till death claims her!"

"You are too hard on her!"

"And not hard enough on you, base villain that you are! Who is this young lady you have in your company — another of your victims?"

"Hold! Edward Harris; enough of your vile insinuations. This lady is one whom I rescued from Sitting Bull, the Sioux, and I am helping her to hunt a father who she says is somewhere in the Black Hills. Your language should at least be respectful!"

The rebuke stung young Harris to the quick, but he reined in his passion in a moment, and doffed his hat.

"Pardon me, miss, pardon me. It was ungentlemanly for me to speak as I did, but I was surprised at seeing one of your sex in company with this accomplished scamp, Justin McKenzie."

"My presence with him is, as he said, for the purpose of finding my father. He rescued me from the Indians, and has volunteered his services, for which I am very thankful. So far, sir, he has acted in a courteous and gentlemanly manner toward me!" said Alice Terry. "What he may have been heretofore concerns me not, as you must know."

"He is always that — smooth-tongued, until he has lured his victim to ruin!" retorted Ned, bitterly. "Beware of him, lady, for he is a rattlesnake in the disguise of a bright-winged butterfly."

Fearless Frank grew livid at this last thrust. Forbearance is virtue, sometimes, but not always. In his case the Scarlet Boy felt that he could bear the taunts of the miner no longer.

"You are a liar and a dastard!" he cried, fiercely. "Come on if you wish satisfaction, and I'll give it to you!"

"I am ready, always, sir. I challenged you first; you have no choice!" retorted Ned, as cool as ever, while his enemy was all trembling with excitement.

"Pistols, at fifty yards; to be fired until one or the other is dead!" was the prompt decision.

"Good! Young lady, you will necessarily have to act as second for both of us. If I drop, leave my body where I fall, and it will be picked up by friends. If he falls, I will ride on to Deadwood, and send you out help to carry him in."

Without delay the distance was guessed at, and each of the young men rode to position. Miss Terry, the beautiful second, took her place at one side of the gulch, midway between the antagonists, and when all was in readiness she counted:

"One!"

The right hands of the two youths were raised on a level, and the gleaming barrel of a pistol shone from each.

"Two!"

There was a sharp click! click! as the hammers of the weapons were pulled back at full cock. Each click meant danger or death.

Harris was very white; so was Fearless Frank, but not so much so as the young woman who was to give the signal.

"Three! *Fire!*" cried Alice, quickly; then, there was a flash, the report of two pistols, and Ned Harris fell to the ground without a groan.

McKenzie ran to his side, and bent over him.

"Poor fellow!" he murmured, rising, a few moments later — "poor Ned. *He is dead!*"

It was Harris' request to be left where he fell. Accordingly he was laid on the grass by the roadside, his horse tethered near by, and then, accompanied by Alice, Justin McKenzie set out to Deadwood.

CHAPTER XI. THE POCKET GULCH MINES — INVADERS OF THEM

We see fit to change the scene once more back to the pocket gulch — the home of the sweet, sad-faced Anita. The date is one month later — one long, eventful month since Justin McKenzie shot down Ned Harris under the noonday sun, a short distance above Deadwood.

Returning to the Flower Pocket by the route to the rugged transverse gulch, and thence through the gaping fissure, we find before us a scene — not of slumbering beauty, but of active industry and labor, such as was not here when we last looked into the flower-strewn paradise of the Hills.

The flowers are for the most part still intact, though occasionally you will come across a spot where the hand of man hath blighted their growth.

Where stood the little vine-wreathed cabin now may be seen a larger and more commodious log structure, which is but a continuation of the original.

A busy scene greets our gaze all around. Men are hurrying here and there through the valley — men not of the pale-face race, but of the red face; men, clad only to the waist, with remarkable muscular developments, and fleetness of foot.

Over the little creek which dashes far adown from pine-dressed mountain peaks, and trails its shining waters through the flowering land, is built another structure — of logs, strongly and carefully erected, and thatched by a master hand with bark and grass. From the roof projects a small smoke stack, from which emanates a steady cloud of smoke, curling lazily upward toward heaven's blue vault, and inside is heard the grinding, crushing rumble of ponderous machinery, and we rightly conjecture that it is a crusher in full operation. Across from the northern side of the gulch comes a steady string of mules in line, each pulling behind him a jack-sled (or, what is better known to the general reader as a stone-boat) heavily laden with huge quartz rocks. These are dumped in front of one of the large doorways of the crusher, and the "empties" return mechanically and disappear within a gaping fissure in the very mountain side — a sort of tunnel, which the hand of man, aided by that great and stronger arm — powder — has burrowed and blasted out.

All this is under the immediate management of the swarth-skinned red-men, whose faces declare them to be a remnant of the once great Ute tribe — now utilized to a better occupation than in the dark and bloody days of the past.

Near the crusher building is a large, stoutly-constructed windlass, worked by mule power, and every few moments there comes up to the surface from the depths of a shaft, a bucketful of rock and sand, which is dumped into a push-car, and from thence transferred to the line of sluice-boxes in the stream, where more half-clothed Utes are busily engaged in sifting golden particles from the rich sand.

What a transformation is all this since we left the Flower Pocket a little over a month ago! Now, everywhere within those majestic mountain-locked walls is bustle and excitement; then, the valley was sleeping away the calm, perfume-laden autumnal days, unconscious of the mines of wealth lying nestling in its bosom, and content and happy in its quietude and the adornments of nature's beauties.

Now, shouts, ringing halloos, angry curses at the obstinate mules, the rumbling of ponderous machinery, the clink of picks and reports of frequent blasts, the deadened sound of escaping steam, the barking of dogs, the whining of horses — all these sounds are now to be heard.

Then, the valley was peacefully at rest; the birds chimed in their exquisite music to the Æolian harplike music of the breeze through the branches of the mountain pines; the waters pouring adown from the stupendous peaks created an everlasting song of love and constancy; bees and humming-birds drank delicious draughts from the blushing lips of a million nodding flowers; the sun was more hazy and drowsy-looking; everything had an appearance of ethereal peace and happiness.

But, like a drama on the stage, a grand transformation had taken place; a beautiful dream had been changed into stern reality; quietude and slumber had fled at the bold approach of bustling industry and life. And all this transformation is due to whom?

The noonday sun shone down on all the busy scene with a glance of warmth and affection, and particularly did its rays center about two men, who, standing on the southern side of the valley, up in among the rugged foothills, were watching the living panorama with the keenest interest.

They were Harry Redburn and the queer old hump-backed, bow-legged little locater, "General" Walsingham Nix.

Redburn was now looking nearly as rough, unkempt and grizzled as any veteran miner, and for a fact, he actually had not waxed the ends of his fine mustache for over a week. But there was more of a healthy glow upon his face, a robustness about his form, and a light of satisfaction in his eye which told that the rough miner's life agreed with him exceedingly well.

The old "General" was all dirt, life and animation, and as full of his eccentricities as ever. He was a character seldom met with — ever full of a quaint humor and sociability, but never known to get mad, no matter how great the provocation might be.

His chance strike upon the spot where lay the gold of Flower Pocket embedded — if it could be called a chance, considering his dream — was the prelude to the opening up of one of the richest mining districts south of Deadwood.

We left them after Harry had driven a stake to mark the place which the somnambulist has pointed out as indicating the concealed mine.

On the succeeding day the two men set to work, and dug long and desperately to uncover the treasure, and after three days of incessant toil they were rewarded with success. A rich vein of gold, or, rather, a deposit of the valuable metal was found, it being formed in a deep, natural pocket and mixed alternately with sand and rock.

During the remaining four days of that week the two lucky miners took out enough gold to evidence their supposition that they had struck one of the richest fields in all the Black Hills country. Indeed, it seemed that there was no end to the depth of sand in the shaft, and as long as the sand held out the gold was likely to.

When, just in the flush of their early triumph, the old humpback was visited by another somnambulistic fit, and this time he discovered gold deposits in the northern mountain side, and prophesied that quartz rock which could be mined therefrom would more than repay the cost and trouble of opening up the vein and of transporting machinery to the gulch.

We need not go into detail of what followed; suffice it to say that immediate arrangements were made and executed toward developing this as yet unknown territory.

While Redburn set to work with two Ute Indians (transported to the gulch from Deadwood, under oath of secrecy by the "General") to blast into the mountain-side, and get at the gold-bearing quartz, the old locater in person set out for Cheyenne on the secret mission of procuring a portable crusher, boiler and engine, and such other implements as would be needed, and getting them safely into the gulch unknown to the roving population of the Hills country. And most wonderful to relate, he succeeded.

Two weeks after his departure, he returned with the machinery and two score of Ute Indians, whom he had sworn into his service, for, as a Ute rarely breaks his word, they were likely to prove valuable accessories to the plans of our two friends. Redburn had in the meantime blasted in until he came upon the quartz rock. Here he had to stop until the arrival of the machinery. He however busied himself in enlarging the cabin and building a curb to the shaft, which occupied his time until at last the "General" and his army returned.[10]

Now, we see these two successful men standing and gazing at the result of their joint labors, each financially happy; each growing rich as the day rolls away.

The miners are in a prosperous condition, and everything moves off with that ease and order that speaks of shrewd management and constant attention to business.

The gold taken from the shaft is much finer than that extracted from the quartz.

The quartz yielded about eighteen dollars to the ton, which the "General" declared to be as well as "a feller c'u'd expect, considerin' things, more or less!"

Therefore, it will be seen by those who have any knowledge whatever of gold mining that, after paying off the expenses, our friends were not doing so badly, after all.

"Yes, yes!" the "General" was remarking, as he gazed at the string of mules that alternately issued from and re-entered the fissure on the opposite side of the valley; "yes, yes, boyee, things ar' workin' as I like ter see 'em at last. The shaft 'll more'n pay expenses if she holds her head 'bove water, as I opine she will, an' w'at ar' squeezed out uv the quartz ar' cleer 'intment fer us."

"True; the shaft is more than paying off the hands," replied Redburn, seating himself upon a bowlder, and staring vacantly at the

---

[10] *Returned*: This crusher is said to have been the first introduced into the Black Hills. [Footnote in the original.]

dense column of smoke ejected from the smoke-stack in the roof of the crusher building.

"I was looking up accounts last evening, and after deducting what you paid for the machinery, and what wages are due the Utes, we have about a thousand dollars clear of all, to be divided between three of us."

"Exactly. Now, that's w'at I call fair to middling. Of course thar'll be more or less expense, heerafter, but et'll be a consider'ble less o' more than more o' less. Another munth 'll tell a larger finanshell tale, I opine."

"Right again, unless something happens more than we think for now. If we get through another month, however, without being nosed out, why we may consider ourselves all-fired lucky."

"Jes' so! Jes' so! but we'll hev ter take our chances. One natteral advantage, we kin shute 'em as fast as they come — "

"Ho!" Redburn interrupted, suddenly, leaping to his feet; "they say the devil's couriers are ever around when you are talking of them. Look! invaders already."

He pointed toward the east, where the passage led out the valley into the gorge beyond.

Out of this passage two persons on horseback had just issued, and now they came to a halt, evidently surprised at the scene which lay spread out before them.

No sooner did the "General" clap his eyes on the pair than he uttered a cry of astonishment, mingled with joy.

"It's thet scarlet chap, Fearless Frank!" he announced, hopping about like a pig on a hot griddle "w'at I war tellin' ye about; the same cuss w'at deserted Charity Joe's train, ter look fer sum critter w'at war screechin' fer help. I went wi' the lad fer a ways, but my jackass harpened to be more or less indispositioned — consider'bly more o' less than less o' more — an' so I made up my mind not ter continny on his route. Ther last I see'd o' the lad he disappeared over sum kind o' a precypice, an' calkylatin' as how he war done fer, I re-j'ined Charity Joseph, an' kim on."

"He has a female in his company!" said Redburn, watching the new-comer keenly.

"Yas, 'peers to me he has, an' et's more or less likely that et's the same critter he went to resky w'en he left Charity Joe's train!"

"What about him? We do not want him here; to let him return to Deadwood after what he has seen would be certain death to our interests."

"Yas, thar's more or less truth in them words o' yours, b'yee — consider'bly more o' less than less o' more. He ken't go back now, nohow we kin fix et. He's a right peart sort o' a kid, an' I think ef we was ter guv him a job, or talk reeson'ble ter him, then he'd consent to do the squar' thing by us."

Redburn frowned.

"He'll have to remain for a certain time, whether he wants to or not," he muttered, more savage than usual. It looked to him as if this was to be the signal of a general invasion. "Come! let's go and see what we can do."

They left the foothills, clambered down into the valley and worked their way toward where Fearless Frank and his companion sat in waiting.

As they did so, headed by a figure in black, who wore a mask as did all the rest, a band of horsemen rode out of the fissure into the valley. One glance and we recognize Deadwood Dick, Prince of the Road, and his band of road-agents!

CHAPTER XII. MAKING TERMS ALL AROUND

Old General Nix was the first to discover the new invasion.

"Gorra'mighty!" he ejaculated, flourishing his staff about excitedly, "d'ye mind them same w'at's tuk et inter the'r heads to invade our sancty sanctorum, up yander? Howly saints frum ther cullender! We shall be built up inter an entire city 'twixt this an' sunset, ef ther populatin' sect becum enny more numersome. Thar's a full fifty o' them sharks, more or less — consider'bly more o' less than less o' more — an' ef we hain't got ter hold a full hand in order to clean 'em out, why, ye can call me a cross-eyed, hair lipped hyeeny, that's all."

Redburn uttered an ejaculation as he saw the swarm of invaders that was perhaps more forcible than polite.

He did not like the looks of things at all. If Ned Harris were only here, he thought, he could throw the responsibility all off on his shoulders. But he was not; neither had he been seen or heard of since he had quitted the valley over a month ago. Where he was staying all this time was a problem that no one could solve — no one among our three friends.

The "General" had made inquiries in Deadwood, but elicited no information concerning the young miner. He had dropped entirely out of the magic city's notice, and might be dead or dying in some foreign clime, for all they knew. Anita worried and grew sadder each day at his non-return; it seemed to her that he was in distress, or worse, perhaps — dead. He had never stayed away so long before, she said, always returning from his trips every few days. What, then, could now be the reason of his prolonged absence?

Redburn foresaw trouble in the intrusion of the road-agents and Fearless Frank, although he knew not the character or calling of the former, and he resolved to make one bold stroke in defense of the mines.

"Go to the quartz mines as quickly as you can!" he said, addressing Nix, "and call every man to his arms. Then rally them out here, where I will be waiting with the remainder of our forces, and we will see what can be done. If it is to be a fight for our rights, a desperate fight it shall be."

The "General" hurried off with as much alacrity as was possible, with him, toward the quartz mine, while Redburn likewise made haste to visit the shaft and collect together his handful of men.

He passed the cabin on the way, and, seeing Anita seated in the doorway, he came to a momentary halt.

"You had better go inside and lock the doors and windows behind you," he said advisingly. "There are invaders in the gulch, and we must try and effect a settlement with them; so it is not desirable that they should see you."

"You are not going to fight them."

"Yes, if they will not come to reasonable terms, which I shall name. Why?"

"Oh! don't fight. You will get killed."

"Humph! what of that? Who would care if *I* were killed?"

"I would, for one, Mr. Redburn."

The miner's heart gave a great bound and he gazed into the pure white face of the girl, passionately. Was it possible that she had in her heart anything akin to love, for *him?* Already he had conceived a passing fancy for her, which might ripen into love, in time.

"Thanks!" he said, catching up her hand and pressing it to his lips. "Those words, few as they are, make me happy, Miss Anita. But, stop! I must away. Go inside, and keep shady until you see me again;" and so saying he hurried on.

In ten minutes' time two score of brawny, half-dressed Utes were rallied in the valley, and Redburn was at their head, accompanied by the "General."

"I will now go forward and hold parley," said Harry, as he wrapped a kerchief about the muzzle of his rifle-barrel. "If you see me fall, you can calculate that it's about time for you to sling in a chunk of your lip."

He had fallen into the habit of talking in an illiterate fashion, since his association with the "General."

"All right," assented the old locater; "ef they try ter salt ye, jes' giv' a squawk, an' we'll cum a-tearin' down ter yer resky at ther rate o' forty hours a mile, more or less — consider'bly more o' less than less o' more."

Redburn buckled his belt a hole tighter, looked to his two revolvers, and set out on his mission.

The road-agents had, in the mean time, circled off to the right of the fissure, and formed into a compact body, where they halted and watched the rallying of the savages in the valley.

Fearless Frank and his lovely companion remained where they had first halted, awaiting developments. They had stumbled into Paradise and were both surprised and bewildered.

Redburn approached them first. He was at loss how to open the confab, but the Scarlet Boy saved him the trouble.

"I presume I see in you one of the representatives of this concern," he said, doffing his hat, and showing his pearly teeth in a little smile, as the miner came up.

"You do," replied Redburn, bowing stiffly. "I am an owner or partner in this mining enterprise, which, until your sudden advent, has been a secret to the outside world."

"I believe you, pilgrim; for, though I am pretty thoroughly acquainted with the topography of the Black Hills country, I had not the least idea that such an enterprise existed in this part of the territory."

"No, I dare say not. But how is it that we are indebted to you for this intrusion? — for such we feel justified in calling it, under the existing circumstances."

"I did not intend to intrude, sir, nor do I now. In riding through the mountains we accidently stumbled into the fissure passage that leads to this gulch, and as there was nothing to hinder us, we came on through."

"True; I should have posted a strong guard in the pass. You have a female companion, I perceive; not your wife?"

"Oh, no! nor my sister, either. This is Miss Terry — an estimable young lady, who has come to the Black Hills in search of her father. Your name is — "

"Redburn — Harry Redburn; and yours, I am told, is Fearless Frank."

"Yes, that is the title I sail under. But how do you know aught of me?"

"I was told your name by a partner of mine. Now, then, concerning the present matter; what do you propose to do?"

"To do? Why, turn back, I suppose; I see nothing else to do."

Redburn leaned on his rifle and considered.

"Do you belong to that other crowd?"

"No, indeed;" Frank's face flushed, half angrily. "I thank my stars I am not quite so low down as that, yet. Do you know them? That's Deadwood Dick, the Prince of the Road, and his band of outlaws!"

"What — is it possible? The same gang whom the *Pioneer* is making such a splurge over, every week."

"The same. That fellow clad in black is Deadwood Dick, the leader."

"Humph! He in black; you in scarlet. Two contrasting colors."

"That is so. I had not thought of it before. But no significance is attached thereto."

"Perhaps not. Have you the least idea what brought them here?"

"The road-agents? I reckon I do. The military has been chasing them for the last two days. Probably they have come here for protection."

"Maybe so; or for plunder. Give me your decision, and I will go and see what they want."

"There is nothing for me to decide more than to take the back track."

Redburn shook his head, decidedly.

"You cannot go back!" he said, using positiveness in his argument; "that is, not for a while. You'd have all Deadwood down on us in a jiffy. I'll give you work in the shaft, at three dollars a day. You can accept that offer, or submit to confinement until I see fit to set you at liberty."

"And my companion, here — ?"

"I will place under the charge of Miss Anita for the present, where she will receive hospitable treatment."

Fearless Frank started as though he had been struck a violent blow; his face grew very white; his eyes dilated; he trembled in every joint.

"*Anita!*" he gasped — "*Anita!*"

"I believe that is what I said!" Redburn could not understand the youth's agitation. He knew that the sister of Ned Harris had a secret; was this Fearless Frank in any way connected with it, and if so, how?

"Do you know her?"

"Her other name is — "

"Harris — Anita Harris, in full. Do you know her, or aught of her?"

"I — I — I did, once!" was the slow reply. "Where is she; I want to see her?"

Redburn took a moment to consider.

Would it be best to permit a meeting between the two until he should be able to learn something more definite concerning the secret? If Ned Harris were here would he sanction such a meeting? No! something told the young miner that he would not: something warned him that it could result in no good to allow the scarlet youth an interview with sad, sweet-faced Anita.

"You cannot see her!" he at last said, decidedly. "There is a reason why you two should never meet again, and if you remain in the gulch, as you will be obliged to, for the present, you must give me your word of honor that you will not go near yonder cabin."

Fearless Frank had expected this; therefore he was not surprised. Neither did Redburn know how close he had shied his stone at the real truth.

"I promise," McKenzie said, after a moment's deliberation, "on my honor, that I will not approach the cabin, providing you will furnish me my meals and lodgings elsewhere. If Anita comes to me, what then?"

"I will see that she does not," Redburn answered, positively. Gradually he was assuming full control of things, in the absence of Harris, himself. "Miss Terry, you may ride down to yonder cabin, and tell Anita I sent you. Pilgrim, you can come along with me."

"No; I will accompany Alice as far as where your forces are stationed," said Frank, and then they rode down the slope, Redburn turning toward where the road-agents sat upon their horses in a compact body, with Deadwood Dick at their head.

As the miner drew nigh and came to a standstill, the Prince of the road rode forward to his side.

"Well — ?" he said, interrogatively, his voice heavy yet pleasant; "I suppose you desire to know what bizness we've got in your corn-field, eh, stranger?"

"That's about the dimensions of it, yes," replied Redburn, at once conceiving a liking for the young road-agent, in whom he thought he saw a true gentleman, in the disguise of a devil. "I came over to learn the object you have in view, in invading our little valley, if you have no objections in telling."

"Certainly not. As you may have guessed already, we are a band of road-agents, whose field of action we have lately confined to the Black

Hills country. I have the honor of being the leader, and you have doubt-less heard of me — Deadwood Dick, the 'Road-Agent Prince,' as the *Pioneer* persists in terming me. Just at present, things are rather sultry in the immediate vicinity of Deadwood, so far as we are concerned, and we sought this locality to escape a small army of the Deadwood mili-tary, who have been nosing around after us for the past week."

"Well — ?"

"Well, we happened to see a man and woman come this way, and believing that it must lead to somewhere or other, we followed, and here we are, out of the reach of the blue-coats, but, I take it, *in* the way of a party of secret miners. Is it not so?"

"No, not necessarily so, unless you put yourselves in the way. You wish to remain quartered here for the present?"

"If not contrary to your wishes, we should like to, yes."

"I have no objections to offer, providing you will agree to two points."

"And what are they, may I ask?"

"These. That you will camp at the mouth of the passage, and thus keep out any other intruders that may come; second, that you will keep your men to this side of the valley, and not interfere with any of our laborers."

"To which I eagerly agree. You shall experience no inconvenience from our presence here; you furnish us a haven of safety from the pursuing soldiers; we in return will extend you our aid in repelling a host of fortune-seekers who may any moment come down this way in swarms."

"Very well; that settles it, then. You keep your promise, and all will go well."

The two shook hands; then Redburn turned and strode back to dismiss his forces, while Dick and his men took up their position at the place where the fissure opened into the gulch. Here they made preparations to camp. Redburn, while returning to his men, heard a shout of joy, and looking up, saw, to his surprise, that the old "Gen-eral" and Alice Terry were locked in each other's arms, in a loving embrace.

CHAPTER XIII. AT THE CABIN

What did it mean?

Had the old hump-backed, bow-legged mine-locater gone crazy, or was he purposely insulting the beautiful maiden? Fearless Frank stood aside, apparently offering no objections to the hugging, and the Indians did likewise.

At least Miss Terry made no serious attempts to free herself from the "General's" bear-like embrace.

A few bounds brought Redburn to the spot, panting, breathless, perspiring. "What is the meaning of this disgraceful scene?" he demanded, angrily.

"Disgraceful!" The old "General" set Miss Terry down on her feet, after giving her a resounding smack, and turned to stare at the young miner, in astonishment. "Disgraceful! Waal, young man, ter tell the solid Old Testament truth, more or less — consider'bly less o' more 'n more o' less — I admire yer cheek, hard an' unblushin' as et ar'. Ye call my givin' this pretty piece o' feminine gander a squar', fatherly sort o' a hug, *disgraceful,* do ye? Think et's all out o' ther bounds o' propriety, do ye?"

"I look at it in that light, yes," Redburn replied.

"Haw! haw! haw!" and the General shook his fat sides with immoderate laughter. "Why, pilgrim-tender-fut, this 'ere hundred an' twenty-six pounds o' feminine gender b'longs to me — ter yours, truly, Walsingham Nix — an' I have a parfec' indervidual right ter hug an' kiss her as much as I please, wi'out brookin' enny interference frum you. Alice, dear, this ar' Harry Redburn, ginerall sup'intendent o' ther Flower Pocket gold-mines, an' 'bout as fair specimen as they make, nowadays. Mr. Redburn, I'll formerly present you to Miss Alice Terry, *my darter!*"

Redburn colored, and was not a little disconcerted on account of his blunder; but he rallied in a moment, and acknowledged the introduction with becoming grace and dignity.

"You must excuse my interference," he said, earnestly. "I saw the old 'General' here taking liberties that no stranger should take, and knowing nothing of the relationship existing between you, I was naturally inclined to think that he was either drunk or crazy; therefore I deemed it necessary to investigate. No offense, I hope."

"Of course not," and Alice smiled one of her sweetest smiles. "You did perfectly right and are deserving of no censure, whatever."

After a few moments of desultory conversation, Redburn took the "General" to one side, and spoke on the subject of Fearless Frank and Anita Harris — of his action in the matter, and so forth. Nix — or Terry, as the latter was evidently his real name — heartily coincided with his views, and both agreed that it was best not to let the Scarlet Boy come within range of Anita, or, at least, not till Ned Harris should return, when he could do as he chose.

Accordingly it was decided that Fearless Frank should be set to work in the quartz mine, that being the furthest from the cabin, and he could eat and sleep either in the mine or in the crusher building, whichever he liked best.

After settling this point the two men rejoined the others, and Frank was apprised of their decision. He made no remarks upon it, but it was plain to see that he was anything but satisfied. His wild spirit yearned for constant freedom.

The Utes were dismissed and sent back to their work; the "General" strolled off with McKenzie toward the quartz mine; it devolved upon Redburn to escort Alice to the cabin, which he did with pleasure, and gave her an introduction to sweet, sad-faced Anita, who awaited their coming in the open doorway.

The two girls greeted each other with warmth; it was apparent that they would become fast friends when they learned more of each other.

As for Redburn, he was secretly enamored with the "General's" pretty daughter; she was beautiful, and evidently accomplished, and her progenitor was financially well-to-do. What then was lacking to make her a fitting mate for any man? Redburn pondered deeply on this subject, as he left the girls together, and went out to see to his duties in the mines.

He found Terry and Fearless Frank in the quartz mine, looking at the swarthy-skinned miners; examining new projected slopes; suggesting easier methods for working out different lumps of gold-bearing rock. While the former's knowledge of practical mining was extended, the latter's was limited.

"I think thet thar ar' bigger prospects yet, in further," the old locater was saying. "I ain't much varsed on jeeological an' toppygraffical formation, myself, ye see; but then, it kinder 'peers to me thet this quartz vein ar' a-goin' to hold out fer a consider'ble time yet."

"Doubtless. More straight digging an' less slopes I should think would be practicable," McKenzie observed.

"I don't see it!" said Redburn, joining them. "Sloping and transversing discovers new veins, while line work soon plays out. I think things are working in excellent order at present."

They all made a tour of the mine which had been dug a considerable distance into the mountain. The quartz was ordinarily productive, and being rather loosely thrown together was blasted down without any extra trouble. After a short consultation, Redburn and the "General" concluded to place Frank over the Utes as superintendent and mine-boss, as they saw that he was not used to digging, blasting or any of the rough work connected with the mine, although he was clear-headed and inventive.

When tendered the position it was gratefully accepted by him, he expressing it his intention to work for the interest of his employers as long as he should stay in the gulch.

Night at last fell over the Flower Pocket gold-mines, and work ceased.

The Utes procured their own food — mainly consisting of fish from the little creek and deer and mountain birds that could be brought down at almost any hour from the neighboring crags — and slept in the open air. Redburn had McKenzie a comfortable bed made in the crusher-house, and sent him out a meal fit for a prince.

As yet, Anita knew nothing of the scarlet youth's identity; — scarcely knew, in fact, that he was in the valley.

At the cabin, the evening meal was dispatched with a general expression of cheerfulness about the board. Anita seemed less downcast than usual, and the vivacious Alice made life and merriment for all. She was witty where wit was proper, and sensible in an unusual degree.

Redburn was infatuated with her. He watched her with an expression of fondness in his eyes; he admired her every gesture and action; he saw something new to admire in her, each moment he was in her society.

When the evening meal was cleared away, he took down the guitar, and sung several ballads, the old "General" accompanying him with his rich deep bass, and Alice with her clear birdlike alto; and the sweet melody of the trio's voices called forth round after round of rapturous applause from the road-agents camped upon the slope, and from the Utes who were lounging here and there among the flower beds of the valley. But of the lot, Deadwood Dick was the only one bold enough to approach the cabin. He came sauntering along and halted on the threshold, nodding to the occupants of the little apartment with a nonchalance which was not assumed.

"Good-evening!" he said, tipping his sombrero, but taking care not to let the mask slip from his face. "I hope mine is not an intrusion. Hearing music, I was loth to stay away, for I am a great lover of music; — it is the one passion that appeals to my better nature."

He seated himself on the little stone step, and motioned for Redburn to proceed.

One of those inside the cabin had been strangely affected at the sight of Dick, and that person was Anita. She turned deathly pale, her eyes assumed an expression of affright, and she trembled violently, as she first saw him. The Prince of the Road, however, if he saw her, noticed not her agitation; in fact, he took not the second glance at her while he remained at the cabin. His eyes were almost constantly fastening upon the lovely face and form of Alice.

Thinking it best to humor one who might become either a powerful enemy or an influential friend, Redburn accordingly struck up a lively air, *a la banjo,* and in exact imitation of a minstrel, rendered "Gwine to Get a Home, Bymeby." And the thunders of *encore* that came from the outside listeners, showed how surely he had touched upon a pleasant chord. He followed that with several modern serio-comic songs, all of which were received well and heartily applauded.

"That recalls memories of good old times," said the road-agent, as he leaned back against the door-sil, and gazed at the mountains, grand, majestic, stupendous, and the starlit sky, azure, calm and serene. "Recalls the days of early boyhood, that were gay, pure, and happy. Ah! ho!"

He heaved a deep sigh, and his head dropped upon his breast.

A deathlike silence pervaded the cabin; that one heartfelt sigh aroused a sensation of pity in each of the four hearts that beat within the cabin walls.

That the road-agent was a gentleman in disguise, was not to be gainsayed; all felt that, despite his outlawed calling, he was deserving of a place among them, in his better moods.

As if to accord with his mood, Alice began a sweet birdlike song, full of tender pathos, and of quieting sympathy.

It was a quaint Scottish melody, — rich in its honeyed meaning, sweetly weird and pitiful; wonderfully soothing and nourishing to a weeping spirit.

Clear and flute-like the maiden's cultured voice swelled out on the still night air, and the mountain echoes caught up the strains and lent a wild peculiar accompaniment.

Deadwood Dick listened, with his head still bowed, and his hands clasped about one knee; — listened in a kind of fascination, until the last reverberations of the song had died out in a wailing echo; then he sprung abruptly to his feet, drew one hand wearily across the masked brow; raised his sombrero with a deft movement, and bowed himself out — out into the night, where the moon and stars looked down at him, perhaps with more lenience than on some.

Alice Terry rose from her seat, crossed over to the door, and gazed after the straight handsome form, until it had mingled with the other road-agents, who had camped upon the slope. Then she turned about, and sat down on the couch beside Anita.

"You are still, dear," she said, stroking the other's long, unconfined hair. "Are you lonely? If not why don't you say something?"

"I have nothing to say," replied Anita, a sad, sweet smile playing over her features. "I have been too much taken up with the music to think of talking."

"But, you are seldom talkative."

"So brother used to tell me. He said I had lost my heart, and tongue."

Redburn was drumming on the window-casing with his fingers; — a sort of lonely tattoo it was.

"You seemed to be much interested in the outlaw, Miss Terry," he observed, as if by chance the thought had just occurred to him, when, in reality, he was downright jealous. "Had you two ever met —"

"Certainly not, sir," and Alice flashed him an inquiring glance. "Why do you ask?"

"Oh! for no reason, in particular, only I fancied that song was meant especially for him."

Redburn, afterward, would have given a hundred dollars to have recalled those words, for the haughty, half-indignant look Alice gave him instantly showed him he was on the wrong track.

If he wished to court her favor, it must be in a different way, and he must not again give her a glimpse of his jealous nature.

"You spoke of a brother," said Alice, turning to Anita. "Does he live here with you?"

"Yes, when not away on business. He has now been absent for over a month."

"Indeed! Is he as sweet, sad, and silent as yourself?"

"Oh! no; Ned is unlike me; he is buoyant, cheerful, pleasant."

"Ned? What is his full name, dear?"

"Edward Harris."

Alice grew suddenly pale and speechless, as she remembered the handsome young miner whom Fearless Frank had slain in the duel, just outside of Deadwood. This, then, was his sister; and evidently she as yet knew nothing of his sad fate.

"Do you know aught concerning Edward Harris?" Redburn asked, seeing her agitation. Alice considered a moment.

"I do," she answered, at last. "This Fearless Frank, whom I came here with, had a duel with a man, just above Deadwood, whose name was Edward Harris!"

"My God; — and his fate — ?"

"He was instantly killed, and left lying where he dropped!"
There was a scream of agony, just here, and a heavy fall.
Anita had fainted!

CHAPTER XIV. THE TRANSIENT TRIUMPH

Redburn sprung from his seat, ran over to her side, and raised her
tenderly in his arms.

"Poor thing!" he murmured, gazing into her pale, still face, "the
shock was too much for her. No wonder she fainted." He laid her on
the couch; and kept off the others who crowded around.

"Bring cold water!" he ordered, "and I will soon have her out of
this fit."

Alice hastened to obey, and Anita's face and hands were bathed in
the cooling liquid until she began to show signs of returning consciousness.

"You may now give me the particulars of the affair," Redburn
said, rising and closing the door, for a chilly breeze was sweeping
into the cabin.

Alice proceeded to comply with his request by narrating what had
occurred and, as nearly as possible, what had been said. When she
had concluded, he gazed down for several moments thoughtfully into
the face of Anita. There was much yet that was beyond his powers of
comprehension — a knotty problem for which he saw no immediate
solution.

"What do you think about it, 'General'?" he asked, turning to the
mine-locater. "Have we sufficient evidence to hang this devil in
scarlet?"

"Hardly, boyee, hardly. 'Peers ter me, 'cordin' to ther gal's tell,
thet thar war a fair shake all around, an' as duelin' ar' more or less
ther fashun 'round these parts, — considera'bly more o' less 'n less o'
more — et ain't law-fell ter yank a critter up by ther throat!"

"I know it is not, according to the customs of this country of the
Black Hills; but, look at it. That fellow, who I am satisfied is a black-
hearted knave, has not only taken the life of poor Harris, but, very
probably, has given his sister her death-blow. The question is: should
he go unpunished in the face of all this evidence?"

"Yes. Let him go; *I* will be the one to punish him!"

It was Anita who spoke. She had partly arisen on the couch; her face
was streaked with water and slightly haggard; her hair blew unconfined

about her neck and shoulders; her eyes blazed with a wild, almost savage fire.

"Let him go!" she repeated, more of fierceness in her voice than Redburn had ever heard there, before. "He shall not escape my vengeance. Oh, my poor, poor dead brother!"

She flung herself back upon the couch, and gave herself up to a wild, passionate, uncontrollable outburst of tears and sobs — the wailings of a sorrowing heart. For a long time she continued to weep and sob violently; then came a lull, during which she fell asleep, from exhaustion — a deep sleep. Redburn and Alice then carried her into an adjoining room, where she was left under the latter's skillful care. Awhile later the cabin was wrapped in silence.

When morning sunlight next peeped down into the Flower Pocket, it found everything generally astir. Anita was up and pursuing her household duties, but she was calm, now, even sadder than before, making a strange contrast to blithe, gaysome Alice, who flitted about, here and there, like some bright-winged butterfly surrounded by a halo of perpetual sunshine.

Unknown to any one save themselves, two men were within the valley of the Flower Pocket gold-mines — there on business, and that business meant bloodshed. They were secreted in among the foot-hills on the western side of the flowering paradise, at a point where they were not observed, and at the same time were the observers of all that was going on in front of them.

How came they here, when the hand of Deadwood Dick guarded the only accessible entrance there was to the valley? The answer was: they came secretly through the pass on the night preceding the arrival of the road-agents, and had been lying in close concealment ever since.

The one was an elderly man of portly figure, and the other a young, dandyish fellow, evidently the elder's son, for they resembled each other in every feature. We make no difficulty in recognizing them as the same precious pair whom Outlaw Dick captured from the stage, only to lose them again through the treachery of two of his own band.

Both looked considerably the worse for wear, and the gaunt, hungry expression on their features, as the morning sunlight shone down upon them, declared in a language more adequate than words, that they were beginning to suffer the first pangs of starvation.

"We cannot hold out at this rate much longer!" the elder Filmore cried, as he watched the bustle in the valley below. "I'm as empty as a collapsed balloon, and what's more, we're in no prospects of immediate relief."

Filmore, the younger, groaned aloud in agony of spirit.

"Curse the Black Hills and all who have been fools enough to inhabit them, anyhow!" he growled, savagely; "just let me get back in the land of civilization again, and you can bet your bottom dollar I'll know enough to stay there."

"Bah! this little rough experience will do you good. If we only had a square meal or two and a basket of sherry, I should feel quite at home. Nothing but a fair prospect of increasing our individual finances would ever have lured me into this outlandish place. But money, you know, is the root of all —"

"Evil!" broke in the other, "and after three months' wild-goose-chase you are just as destitute of the desired root as you were at first."

"True, but we have at least discovered one of the shrubs at the bottom of which grows the root!"

"You refer to Deadwood Dick?"

"I do. He is here in the valley, and he must never leave it alive. While we have the chance we must strike the blow that will forever silence his tongue."

"Yes; but what about the girl? She will be just as much in the way, if not a good deal more so."

"We can manage her all right when the proper time arrives. Dick is our game, now."

"He may prove altogether too much game. But, now that we are counting eggs, how much of the 'lay' is to be mine, when this boy and girl are finished?" he queried.

"How much? Well, that depends upon circumstances. The girl *may* fall to you."

"The girl? Bah! I'd rather be excused."

The day passed without incident in the mines. The work went steadily on, the sounds of the crusher making strange music for the mountain echoes to mock.

Occasionally the crack of a rifle announced that either a road-agent or a Ute miner had risked a shot at a mountain sheep, bird, or deer. Generally their aim was attended with success, though sometimes they were unable to procure the slaughtered game.

Redburn, on account of his clear-headedness and business tact, had full charge of both mines, the "General" working under him in the shaft, and Fearless Frank in the quartz mine.

When questioned about his duel with Harris by Redburn, McKenzie had very little to say; he seemed pained when approached on the subject; would answer no questions concerning the past; was reserved and at times singularly haughty.

During the day Anita and Alice took a stroll through the valley, but the latter had been warned, and fought shy of the quartz mine; so there was no encounter between Anita and Fearless Frank.

Deadwood Dick joined them as they were returning to the cabin, loaded down with flowers — flowers of almost every color and perfume.

"This is a beautiful day," he remarked, pulling up a daisy, as he walked gracefully along. "One rarely sees so many beauties centered in one little valley like this — beautiful landscape and mountain scenery, beautiful flowers beneath smiling skies, and lovely women, the chief center of attraction among all."

"Indeed!" and Alice gave him a coquettish smile, "you are flattering, sir road-agent. You, at least are not beautiful, in that horrible black suit and villainous mask. You remind me of a picture I have seen somewhere of the devil in disguise; all that is lacking is the horns, tail and cloven-foot."

Dick broke out into a burst of laughter — it was one of those wild, terrible laughs of his, so peculiar to hear from one who was evidently young in years.

Both of the girls were terrified, and would have fled had he not detained them.

"Ha! ha!" he said, stepping in front of them, "do not be frightened; don't go, ladies. That's only the way I express my amusement at anything."

"Then, for mercy's sake, don't get amused again," said Alice, deprecatingly. "Why, dear me, I thought the Old Nick and all his couriers had pounced down upon us."

"Well, how do you know but what he has? *I* may be his Satanic majesty, or one of his envoys."

"I hardly think so; you are too much an earthly being for that. Come, now, take off that detestable mask and let me see what you look like."

"No, indeed! I would not remove this mask, except on conditions, for all the gold yon toiling miners are finding, which, I am satisfied, is no small amount."

"You spoke of conditions. What are they?"

"Some time, perhaps, I will tell you, lady, but not now. See! my men are signaling to me, and I must go. Adieu, ladies;" and in another moment he had wheeled, and was striding back toward camp.

In their concealment the two Filmores witnessed this meeting between Dick and the two girls.

"So there are females here, eh?" grunted the elder musingly. "From observation I should say that Prince Dick was a comparative stranger here."

"That is my opinion," groaned Clarence, his thoughts reverting to his empty stomach. "Did you hear that laugh a moment ago? It was more like the screech of a lunatic than anything else."

"Yes; he is a young tiger. There is no doubt of that in my mind."

"And we shall have to keep on the alert to take him. He came to the cabin last night. If he does to-night we can mount him!"

Before night the elder Filmore succeeded in capturing a wild goose that had strayed down with the stream from somewhere above. This was killed, dressed and half cooked by a brushwood fire which they hazarded in a fissure in the hillside wherein they had hidden. This fowl they almost ravenously devoured, and thus thoroughly satisfied their appetites. They now felt a great deal better, ready for the work in hand — of capturing and slaying the dare-devil Deadwood Dick.

As soon as it was dark they crept, like the prowling wolves they were, down into the valley, and positioned themselves midway between the cabin and the road-agent's camp, but several yards apart, with a lasso held above the grass between them, to serve as a "trip-up."

The sky had become overcast with dense black clouds, and the gloom in the valley was quite impenetrable. From their concealment the two Filmores could hear Redburn, Alice and the "General" singing up at the cabin, and it told them to be on their guard, as Dick might now come along at any moment.

Slowly the minutes dragged by, and both were growing impatient, when the firm tread of "the Prince" was heard swiftly approaching. Quickly the lasso was drawn taut. Dick, not dreaming of the trap, came boldly along, tripped, and went sprawling to the ground. The next instant his enemies were on him, each with a long murderous knife in hand.

CHAPTER XV. TO THE RESCUE!

The suddenness of the onslaught prevented Deadwood Dick from raising a hand to defend himself, and the two strong men pulled their combined weights upon him, had the effect to render him utterly helpless. He would have yelled to apprise his comrades of his fate, but Alexander Filmore, ready for the emergency, quickly thrust a cob of wood into his mouth, and bound it there with strong strings.

The young road-agent was a prisoner.

"Ha! ha!" leered the elder Filmore, peering down into the masked face — "ha! ha! my young eaglet; so I have you at last, have I? After repeated efforts to get you in my power, I have at last been rewarded with success, eh? Ha! ha! the terrible scourge of the Black Hills lies here at my feet, mine to do with as I shall see fit."

"Shall we settle him, and leave him lying here, where his gang can find him?" interrupted the younger Filmore, who, now that his blood was up, cared little what he did. "You give him one jab, and I will guarantee to finish him with the second!"

"No! no! boy; you are too hasty. Before we silence him, forever, we must ascertain, if possible, where the girl is."

"But, he'll never tell us."

"We have that yet to find out. It is my opinion that we can bring him to terms, somehow. Take hold, and we will carry him back to our hole in the hill."

Deadwood Dick was accordingly seized by the neck and heels, and borne swiftly and silently toward the western side of the gulch, up among the foothills, into the rift, where the plotters had lain concealed since their arrival. Here he was placed upon the ground in a sitting posture, and his two enemies crouched on either side of him, like beasts ready to spring upon their prey.

Below in the valley, the Utes had kindled one solitary fire, and this with a starlike gleam of light from the cabin window, was the only sign of life to be seen through the night's black shroud. The trio in the foothills were evidently quite alone.

Alexander Filmore broke the silence.

"Well, my gay Deadwood Dick, Prince of the Road, I suppose you wish to have the matter over with, as soon as possible."

The road-agent nodded.

"Better let him loose in the jaws," suggested Filmore the younger; "or how else shall we get from him what we must know? Take out his gag. I'll hold my six against his pulsometer. If he squawks, I'll silence him, sure as there is virtue in powder and ball!"

The elder, after some deliberation, acquiesced, and Dick was placed in possession of his speaking power, while the muzzle of young Filmore's revolver pressed against his breast, warned him to silence and obedience.

"Now," said the elder Filmore, "just you keep mum. If you try any trickery, it will only hasten your destruction, which is inevitable!"

Deadwood Dick gave a little laugh.

"You talk as if you were going to do something toward making me the center of funeralistic attraction."

"You'll find out, soon enough, young man. I have not pursued you so long, all for nothing, you may rest assured. Your death will be the only event that can atone for all the trouble you have given me, in the past."

"*Is* that so? Well, you seem to hold all the *trump* cards, and I reckon you ought to win, though I can't see into your inordinate thirst for *diamonds,* when *spades* will eventually triumph. Had I a *full hand* of *clubs,* I am not so sure but what I could *raise* you, *knaves* though you are!"

"I think not; when kings win, the game is virtually up. We hold altogether to high cards for you, at present, and *beg* as you may, we shall not *pass* you."

"Don't be too sure of it. The best trout often slips from the hook, when you are sanguine that you have at last been immoderately successful. But, enough of this cheap talk. Go on and say your say, in as few words as possible, for I am in a hurry."

Both Filmore, Sr., and Filmore, Jr., laughed at this — it sounded so ridiculously funny to hear a helpless prisoner talk of being in a hurry.

"Business must be passing!" leered the elder, savagely. "Don't be at all scared. We'll start you humming along the road to Jordan soon enough, if that's what you want. First, however, we desire you to inform us where we can find the girl, as we wish to make a clean sweep, while we are about it."

"Do you bathe your face in alum water?" abruptly asked the road-agent, staring at his captor, quizzically. "Do you?"

"Bathe in *alum*-water? Certainly not, sir. Why do you ask?"

"Because the hardness of you cheek is highly suggestive of the use of some similar application."

Alexander Filmore stared at his son a moment, at loss to comprehend; but, as it began to dawn upon him that he was the butt of a
hard hit, he uttered a frightful curse.

"My cheek and your character bear a close resemblance, then!" he
retorted, hotly. "Again I ask you, will you tell me where the girl is?"

"No! you must take me for an ornery mule, or some other kind of an
animal, if you think I would deliver her into *your* clutches. No! no! my
scheming knaves, I will not. Kill me if you like, but it will not accomplish
your villainous ends. She has all of the papers, and can not only put herself forward at the right time, but can have you arrested for my murder!"

"Bah! we can find her, as we have found you; so we will not trifle.
Clarence, get ready; and when I count one — two — three — pull the
trigger, and I'll finish him with my knife!"

"All right; go ahead; I'm ready!" replied the dutiful son.

Fearless Frank sat upon a bowlder in the mouth of the quartz
mine, listening to the strains of music that floated up to him from the
cabin out in the valley, and puffing moodily away at a grimy old pipe
he had purchased, together with some tobacco, from one of the Utes,
with whom he worked.

He had not gone down to the crusher-house for his supper; he did
not feel hungry, and was more contented here, in the mouth of the
mine, where he could command a view of all that was going on in the
valley. With his pipe for a companion he was as happy as he could
be, deprived as he was from association with the others of his color,
who had barred him out in the cold.

Once or twice during the day, on coming from within, to get a
breath of pure air, he had caught a glimpse of Anita as she flitted
about the cabin engaged at her household duties, and the yearning
expression that unconsciously stole into his dark eyes, spoke of a passion within his heart, that, though it might be slumbering, was not
extinct — was there all the same, in all its strength and ardor. Had he
been granted the privilege of meeting her, he might have displaced the
barrier that rose between them; but now, nothing remained for him
but to toil away until Redburn should see fit to send him away, back
into the world from which he came.

Would he want to go, when that time came? Hardly, he thought,
as he sat there and gazed into the quiet vale below him, so beautiful
even in darkness. There was no reason why he should go back again
adrift upon the bustling world.

He had no relative — no claims that pointed him to go thither; he was as free and unfettered as the wildest mountain eagle. He had no one to say where he should and where he should not go; he liked one place equally as well as another, providing there was plenty of provender and work within easy range; he had never thought of set- tling down, until now, when he had come to the Flower Pocket val- ley, and caught a glimpse of Anita — Anita whom he had not seen for years; on whom he had brought censure, reproach and —

A step among the rocks close at hand startled him from a reverie into which he had fallen, and caused him to spill the tobacco from his pipe.

A slight trim figure stood a few yards away, and he perceived that two extended hands clasped objects, whose glistening surface sug- gested that they were "sixes" or "sevens."

"Silence!" came in a clear, authoritative voice. "One word more than I ask you, and I'll blow your brains out. Now, what's your name?"

"Justin McKenzie's my name. Fearless Frank generally answers me the purpose of a nom de plume," was the reply.

"Very good," and the stranger drew near enough for the Scarlet Boy to perceive that he was clad in buck-skin; well armed; wore a Spanish sombrero, and hair long, down over the square shoulders. "I'm Calamity Jane."

If McKenzie uttered an ejaculation of surprise, it was not to be wondered at, for he had heard many stories, in Deadwood, concern- ing the "dare-devil gal dressed up in men's toggery."

"Calamity Jane?" he echoed, picking up his pipe. "Where in the world did *you* come from, and how did you get here, and what do you want, and — "

"One at a time, please. I came from Deadwood with Road-Agent Dick's party — unknown to them, understand you. That answers two questions. The third is, I want to be around when there's any fun going on; and it's lucky I'm here now. I guess Dick has just got layed out by two fellows in the valley below here, and they've slid off with him over among the foot-hills yonder. I want you to stub along after me, and lend the voices of your sixes, if need be. I'm going to set him at liberty!"

"I'm at your service," Frank quickly replied. Excitement was one of his passions; adventure was another.

"Are you well heeled?"

"I reckon. Always make it a point to be prepared for wild beasts and the like, you know."

"A good idea. Well, if you are ready, we'll slide. I don't want them toughs to get the drop on Dick if I can help it."

"Who are they?"

"Who — the toughs?"

"Yes; they that took the road-agent."

"I don't know 'm. Guess they're tender-foots — some former enemies of his, without doubt. They propose to quiz a secret about some girl out of him, and then knife him. We'll have to hurry or they'll get their work in ahead of us."

They left the mouth of the mine, and skurried down into the valley, through the dense shroud of gloom.

Calamity Jane led the way; she was both fleet of foot and cautious.

Let us look down on the foot-hill camp, and the two Filmores who are stationed on either side of their prisoner.

The younger presses the muzzle of his revolver against Deadwood Dick's heart; the elder holds a long gleaming knife upheld in his right hand.

"One!" he counts, savagely.

"Two!" — after a momentary pause. Another lapse of time, and then —

"Hold! gentlemen; that will do!" cries a clear ringing voice; and Calamity Jane and McKenzie, stepping out of the darkness, with four gleaming "sixes" in hand, confirm the pleasant assertion!

CHAPTER XVI. THE ROAD-AGENT'S
MERCY — CONCLUSION

Nevertheless, the gleaming blade of Alexander Filmore descended, and was buried in the fleshy part of Deadwood Dick's neck, making a wound, painful but not necessarily dangerous.

"You vile varmint," cried Calamity Jane, pulling the hammer of one of her revolvers back to full cock; "you cursed fool; don't you know that thet only seals yer own miserable fate?"

She took deliberate aim, but Dick interrupted her.

"Don't shoot, Jennie!" he gasped, the blood spurting from his wound; "this ain't none o' your funeral. Give three shrill whistles for my men, and they'll take care o' these hounds until I'm able to attend to 'em. Take me to the cab — "

He could not finish the sentence; a sickening stream of blood gushed from his mouth, and he fell back upon the ground insensible.

Fearless Frank gave the three shrill whistles, while Calamity Jane covered the two cowering wretches with her revolvers.

The distress signal was answered by a yell, and in a few seconds five road-agents came bounding up.

"Seize these two cusses, and guard 'em well!" Calamity said, grimly. "They are a precious pair, and in a few days, no doubt, you'll have the pleasure of attending their funerals. Your captain is wounded, but not dangerously, I hope. We will take him to the cabin, where there are light and skillful hands to dress his wounds. When he wants you, we will let you know. Be sure and guard these knaves well, now."

The men growled an assent, and after binding the captives' arms, hustled them off toward camp, in double quick time, muttering threats of vengeance. Fearless Frank and Calamity then carefully raised the stricken road-agent, and bore him to the cabin, where he was laid upon the couch. Of course, all was not excitement.

Redburn and Alice set to work to dress the bleeding wound, with Jane and the "General" looking on to see that nothing was left undone. Fearless Frank stood apart from the rest, his arms folded across his breast, a grave, half-doubtful expression upon his handsome, sun-browned features.

Anita was not in the room at the time, but she came in a moment later, and stood gazing about her in wondering surprise. Then, her eyes rested upon Fearless Frank for the first, and she grew deathly white; she trembled in every limb; a half-frightened, half-pitiful look came into her eyes.

The young man in scarlet was similarly effected. His cheeks blanched; his lips became firmly compressed; a mastering expression fell from his dark magnetic orbs.

There they stood, face to face, a picture of doubt; of indifferent respect, of opposite strong passions, subdued to control by a heavy hand.

None of the others noticed them; they were alone, confronting each other; trying to read the other's thoughts; the one penitent and craving forgiveness, the other cold almost to sternness, and yet not unwilling to forgive and forget.

Deadwood Dick's wound was quickly and skillfully dressed; it was not dangerous but was so exceedingly painful that the pangs soon brought him back to consciousness.

The moment he opened his eyes he saw Fearless Frank and Anita — perceived their position toward each other, and that it would require only a single word to bridge the chasm between them. A hard look came into his eyes as they gazed through the holes in the mask, then he gazed at Alice — sweet piquant Alice — and the hardness melted like snow before the spring sunshine.

"Thank God it was no deeper," he said, sitting upright, and rubbing the tips of his black-gloved fingers over the patches that covered the gash. "Although deucedly bothersome, it is not of much account."

To the surprise of all he sprung to his feet, and strode to the door. Here he stopped, and looked around for a few moments, sniffing at the cool mountain breeze, as a dog would. A single cedar tree stood by the cabin, its branches, bare and naked, stretching out like huge arms above the doorway. And it was at these the road-agent gazed, a savage gleam in his piercing black eyes.

After a few careful observations, he turned his face within the cabin.

"Justin McKenzie," he said, gazing at the young man, steadily, "I want you to do me a service. Go to my camp, and say to my men that I desire their presence here, together with the two prisoners, and a couple of stout lariats, with nooses at the end of them. Hurry, now!"

Fearless Frank started a trifle, for he seemed to recognize the voice; but the next instant he bowed assent, and left the cabin. When he was gone, Dick turned to Redburn.

"Have you a glass of water handy, Cap? This jab in the gullet makes me somewhat thirsty," he said.

Redburn nodded, and procured the drink; then a strange silence pervaded the cabin — a silence that no one seemed willing to break.

At last the tramp of many feet was heard, and a moment later the road-agents, with Fearless Frank at their head, reached the doorway, where they halted. The moment Deadwood Dick came forward, there was a wild, deafening cheer.

"Hurra! hurra! Deadwood Dick, Prince of the Road, still lives. Three long hearty cheers, lads, and a hummer!" cried Fearless Frank, and then the mountain echoes reverberated with a thousand discordant yells of hurrah.

The young road-agent responded with a nod, and then said:

"The prisoners; have you them there?"

"Here they are, Cap!" cried a score of voices, and the two Filmores were trotted out to the front, with ropes already about their necks. "Shall we h'ist 'em?"

"Not jest yet, boys: I have a few words to say, first."

Then turning half-about in the doorway, Deadwood Dick continued:

"Ladies and gentlemen, a little tragedy is about to take place here soon, and it becomes necessary that I should say a few words explaining what cause I have for hanging these two wretches whom you see here.

"Therefore, I will tell you a short story, and you will see that my cause is just, as we look at these things here in this delectable country of the Black Hills. To begin with:

"My name is, to you, *Edward Harris!*" and here the road-agent flung aside the black mask, revealing the smiling face of the young card-sharp. "I have another — my family name — but I do not use it, preferring Harris to it. Anita, yonder, is my sister."

"Several years ago, when we were children, living in one of the Eastern States, we were made orphans by the death of our parents, who were drowned while driving upon a frozen lake in company with my uncle, Alexander Filmore, and his son, Clarence — those are the parties yonder, and as God is my judge, I believe they are answerable for the death of our father and mother.

"Alexander Filmore was appointed guardian over us, and executor of our property, which amounted to somewhere in the neighborhood of fifty thousand dollars, my father having been for years extensively engaged in speculation, at which he was most always successful.

"From the day of their death we began to receive the most tyrannical treatment. We were whipped, kicked about, and kept in a half-starved condition. Twice when we were in bed, and, as he supposed, asleep, Alexander Filmore came to us and attempted to assassinate us, but my watchfulness was a match for his villainy, and we escaped death at his hands.

"Finding that this kind of life was unbearable, I appealed to our neighbors and even to the courts for protection, but my enemy was a man of great influence, and after many vain attempts, I found that I could not obtain a hearing; that nothing remained for me to do but to fight my own way. And I did fight it.

"Out of my father's safe I purloined a sum of money sufficient to defray our expenses for a while, then, taking Anita with me, I fled from the home of my youth. I came first to Fort Laramie,[11] where I spent a year in the service of a fur-trader.

---

[11] *Fort Laramie*:   A fur trading post and supply station for the Oregon Trail, Fort Laramie was appropriated by the U.S. government in 1849 to serve as campaign headquarters for conflicts with the Indians.

"My guardian, during that year, sent three men out to kill me, but they had the tables turned on them, and their bones lay bleaching even now on Laramie plains.

"During that year my sister met a gay, dashing young ranger, who hailed to the name of Justin McKenzie, and of course she fell in love with him. That was natural, as he was handsome, suave and gallant, and, more than all, reported tolerably well to-do.

"I made inquiries, and found that there was nothing against his moral character, so I made no objections to his paying his attentions to Anita.

"But one day a great surprise came.

"On returning from a buffalo-hunt of several days' duration I found my home deserted, and a letter from Anita stating that she had gone with McKenzie to Cheyenne to live; they were not married yet, but would be, soon.

"That aroused the hellish part of my passionate nature. I believed that McKenzie was leading her a life of dishonor, and it made my blood boil to even think of it. Death, I swore, should be his reward for this infidelity, and mounting my horse I set out in hot haste for Cheyenne.

"But I arrived there too late to accomplish my mission of vengeance.

"I found Anita and took her back to my home, a sad and sorrowing maiden; McKenzie I could not find; he had heard of my coming, and fled to escape my avenging hand. But over the head of my weeping sister, I swore a fearful oath of vengeance, and I have it yet to keep. I believe there had been some kind of sham marriage; Anita would never speak on the subject, so I had to guess at the terrible truth.

"And there's where you made an accursed mess of the whole affair!" cried McKenzie, stepping into the cabin, and leading Anita forward, by the hand. "Before God and man *I acknowledge Anita Harris to be my legally wedded wife.* Listen, Edward Harris, and I will explain. That day that you came to Cheyenne in pursuit of me, I'll acknowledge I committed an error — one that has caused me much trouble since. The case was this:

"I was the nearest of kin to a rich old fur-trader, who proposed to leave me all his property at his death; but he was a desperate woman-hater, and bound me to a promise that I would never marry.

"Tempted by the lust for gold, I yielded, and he drew up a will in my favor. This was before I met Anita here.

"When we went to Cheyenne, the old man was lying at the point of death; so I told Anita that we would not be married for a few days, until we saw how matters were going to shape. If he died, we would be married secretly, and she would return to your roof until I could get possession of my inheritance, when we would go to some other part of the country to live. If he recovered, I would marry her anyway, and let the old man go to Tophet with his money-bags. I see now how I was in the wrong.

"Well, that very day, before your arrival, the old man himself pounced down upon us, and cursed me up hill and down, for my treachery, and forthwith struck me out from his will. I immediately sent for a chaplain, and was married to Anita. I then went up to see the old man and find if I could not effect a compromise with him.

"He told me if I would go with him before Anita and swear that she was not legally my wife, and that I would never live with her, he would again alter his will in my favor.

"Knowing that that would make no difference, so far as the law was concerned, I sent Anita a note apprising her of what was coming, and stating that she had best return to you until the old man should die, when I would come for her. Subsequently I went before her in company with the old man and swore as I had promised to do, and when I departed she was weeping bitterly, but I naturally supposed it was sham grief. A month later, on his death-bed, the old trader showed me the letter I had sent her, and I realized that not only was my little game up, but that I had cheated myself out of a love that was true. I was left entirely out of the will, and ever since I have bitterly cursed the day that tempted me to try to win gold and love at the same time. Here, Edward Harris," and the young man drew a packet of papers from inside his pocket, "are two certificates of my marriage, one for Anita, and one for myself. You see now, that, although mine has been a grievous error, no dishonor is coupled with your sister's name."

Ned Harris took one of the documents and glanced over it, the expression on his face softening. A moment later he turned and grasped McKenzie's hand.

"God bless you, old boy!" he said, huskily. "I am the one who has erred, and if you have it in your heart to forgive me, try and do so. I do not expect much quarter in this world, you know. There is Anita; take her, if she will come to you, and may God shower his eternal blessings upon you both!"

McKenzie turned around with open arms, and Anita flew to his embrace with a low glad cry. There was not a dry eye in the room.

There was an impatient surging of the crowd outside; Dick saw that his men were longing for the sport ahead; so he resumed his story:

"There is not much more to add," he said, after a moment's thought. "I fled into the Black Hills when the first whispers of gold got afloat, and chancing upon this valley, I built us a home here, wherein to live away the rest of our lives.

"In time I organized the band of men you see around me, and took to the road. Of this my sister knew nothing. The Hills have been my haunt ever since, and during all this time you scheming knaves" — pointing to the prisoners — "have been constantly sending out men to murder me. The last tool, Hugh Vansevere by name, boldly posted up reward papers in the most frequented routes, and he went the same way as his predecessors. Seeing that nothing could be accomplished through aids, my enemies have at last come out to superintend my butchery in person; and but for the timely interference of Calamity Jane and Justin McKenzie, a short time since, I should have ere this been numbered with the dead. Now, I am inclined to be merciful to only those who have been merciful to me; therefore, I have decided that Alexander and Clarence Filmore shall pay the penalty of hanging, for their attempted crimes. Boys, *string 'em up!*"

So saying, Deadwood Dick stepped without the cabin, and closed the door behind him.

Redburn also shut down and curtained the windows, to keep out the horrible sight and sounds.

But, for all this, those inside could not help but hear the pleading cries of the doomed wretches, the tramp of heavy feet, the hushed babble of voices, and at last the terrible shout of, "Heave 'o! up they go!" which signaled the commencement of the victims' journey into mid-air.

Then there was a long blank pause; not a sound was heard, not a voice spoke, nor a foot moved. This silence was speedily broken, however, by two heavy falls, followed almost immediately by the tramp of feet.

Not till all was again quiet did Redburn venture to open the door and look out. All was dark and still.

The road-agents had gone, and left no sign of their work behind.

When morning dawned, they were seen to have recamped on the eastern slope, where the smoke of their camp-fires rose in graceful white columns through the clear transparent atmosphere.

During the day Dick met Alice Terry, as she was gathering flowers, a short distance from the cabin.

"Alice — Miss Terry," he said gravely, "I have come to ask you to be my wife. I love you, and want you for my own darling. Be mine,

Alice, and I will mend my ways, and settle down to an honest, straightforward life."

The beautiful girl looked up pityingly.

"No," she said, shaking her head, her tone kind and respectful, "I cannot love you, and never can be your wife, Mr. Harris."

"You love another?" he interrogated.

She did not answer, but the tell-tale blush that suffused her cheek did, for her.

"It is Redburn!" he said, positively. "Very well; give him my congratulations. See, Alice;" here the young road-agent took the crape mask from his bosom; "I now resume the wearing of this mask. Your refusal has decided my future. A merry road-agent I have been, and a merry road-agent I shall die. Now, good-by forever."

On the following morning it was discovered that the road-agents and their daring leader, together with the no less heroic Calamity Jane, had left the valley — gone; whither, no one knew.

About a month later, one day when Calamity Jane was watering her horse at the stream, two miles above Deadwood, the road-agent chief rode out of the chaparral and joined her.

He was still masked, well armed, and looking every inch a Prince of the Road.

"Jennie," he said, reining in his steed, "I am lonely and want a companion to keep me company through life. You have no one but yourself; our spirits and general temperament agree. Will you marry me and become my queen?"

"No!" said the girl, haughtily, sternly. "I have had all the *man* I care for. We can be friends, Dick; more we can never be!"

"Very well, Jennie; I rec'on it is destined that I shall live single. At any rate, I'll never take a refusal from another woman. Yes, gal, we'll be friends, if nothing more."

There is little more to add.

We might write at length, but choose a few words to end this o'er true romance of life in the Black Hills.

McKenzie and Anita were remarried in Deadwood, and at the same time Redburn led Alice Terry to the altar, which consummation the "General" avowed was "more or less of a good thing — consider'bly less o' more 'n' more o' less."

Through eastern lawyers, a settlement of the Harris affairs was effected, the whole of the property being turned over to Anita, thereby placing her and Fearless Frank above want for a lifetime.

Therefore they gave up their interest in the Flower Pocket mines to Redburn and the "General."

Calamity Jane is still in the Hills.

And grim and uncommunicative, there roams through the country of gold a youth in black, at the head of a bold lawless gang of road-riders, who, from his unequaled daring, has won and rightly deserves the name — Deadwood Dick, Prince of the Road.

THE END.

Frank Reade, The Inventor, Chasing the James Boys With His Steam Team

This anonymous account of Frank Reade, a boy inventor chasing Jesse and Frank James, marks the intersection of the three literary subgenres that would come to dominate popular fiction in the first half of the twentieth century: the Western, science fiction, and detective fiction. By 1890, Frank Reade was a well-known figure in the world of adolescent reading. A subsequent weekly, the *Frank Reade Library* (1892–1898), published by Frank Tousey, became the first science fiction serial. It printed close to two hundred stories about Frank Reade and his son, Frank Reade Jr., attributed to "Noname" and actually written by several house authors. Among these, the most notable was Luis Senarens (1865–1940), who earned two hundred dollars a week writing fiction at the age of sixteen and became known as the American Jules Verne (the French inventor of science fiction as we know it).

Edward S. Ellis's *The Steam Man of the Prairies* (1869), a Beadle publication reprinted under a variety of titles, introduced the idea of the boy inventor, and it clearly inspired *Frank Reade and His Steam Man of the Plains* (1876), written by Harry Enton (the pen name of Harold Cohen) and published in Tousey's *The Boys of New York Pocket Library* (and later in the *Frank Reade Library*). During the 1880s, in *Frank Tousey's Five Cent Wide Awake Library*, the young inventor could be found in Africa, Asia, Mexico, and in the "far west," making use of his innumerable inventions — the "air ship," the "electric boat," the "electric coach," the "electric air yacht" — to fight Aztecs, unruly natives, and

American Indians. The inventor fantasy, in other words, not only satisfied the adolescent longing for autonomy and fabulous individualistic
achievement; it also expressed a jingoistic and racist longing for imperial
conquest.

The success of the Frank Reade novels coincided with the national
celebrity of Thomas Alva Edison (1847–1931), who established his "invention factory" in Menlo Park, New Jersey, in 1876, invented the
phonograph in 1877, and instantly became America's favorite "wizard."
Having incorporated his own companies in 1889, he merged his Edison
General Electric Company with its largest rival to form General Electric
in 1892. To discover Frank Reade "chasing the James Boys with his
steam team" was to find this embodiment of American ingenuity confronting the no less celebrated rebels who, as bank and train robbers, became mythified as outlaws resisting the encroachment of technology,
modernization, and big money, an encroachment for which Edison
served as an obvious emblem.

By 1890, the James Boys had their own central place in the dime novel
as the fierce yet heroic outlaws who were misunderstood by society and
misrepresented by the law, somewhat in the manner of Deadwood Dick.
But the depiction of living outlaws sought by the federal government intensified the moral outrage over popular fiction: In 1883, the year following Jesse's murder and the year of Frank's trial in Missouri, Frank Tousey's
stories of the James Boys were suppressed by the postmaster general. Publication did not resume until 1889.

Though the dime Western typically moves all regional tensions to the
western frontier, stories of the James brothers brought the conflict between North and South back into view. Frank James fought as a "Border
Ruffian" during the dispute over Kansas in 1855–56, when proslavery
Missourians struggled to prevent the influx of antislavery settlers in order
to assure that Kansas would enter the Union as a slave state. Both Frank
and Jesse joined William C. Quantrill ("Charley Quantrell") as Confederate guerrillas during the war in an irregular band that recklessly robbed
and killed Union soldiers and sympathizers. After the war, the guerrilla
tactics of the James Gang, whose robberies were often savage massacres,
became an example of Southern lawlessness in the Northern press. At the
same time they were an illustration in the Southern press of how the war
was still being fought despite the disenfranchisement suffered during
Radical Reconstruction.

When the James brothers began to rob trains in 1873, they became
national criminals. And when the Pinkerton World-Wide Detective
Agency bombed the James house, succeeding only in killing a cousin and

permanently injuring Frank and Jesse's mother, the brothers were assured of their status as persecuted victims seeking vengeance. In 1881, the governor of Missouri offered a $10,000 reward for the James brothers, dead or alive, but the two remained sympathetic figures; in the same year, the first dime novel version of the James's story appeared.

Despite the competition from Street & Smith, Frank Tousey's *New York Detective Library* (1889–1897) was advertised as "The Only Library Containing the True Stories of the James Boys"; most were written by D. W. Stevens (John R. Musick), who had grown up in Missouri. The genre of the Western had often presented narratives of detection. James Fenimore Cooper's Natty Bumppo was also known as Hawkeye because of his detective powers; Seth Jones was especially adept at reading the slightest signs in the forest on his way to tracking the enemy; and Deadwood Dick became an outlaw detective, pursuing his own investigations to vindicate himself and others. With the appearance of the James brothers, however, the narrative of detection generally concluded with the criminals unapprehended, enabling the bandits to pursue further adventures in the next novel. Jesse and Frank achieved their stature in the *Detective Library* by defying "steam and telegraphs, improved detectives, and all modern ingenuities" (quoted by Slotkin, 138).

All this is to say that while *Frank Reade, The Inventor, Chasing the James Boys With His Steam Team* exemplifies popular fiction at its most formulaic — reduced to shoot-outs, predictable dialogue, and the display of technological marvels — it nonetheless entwines major strains of popular fiction before their distinction became a marketing necessity. Meanwhile, the novel shows how ironic the Wild West can be, since frontier adventure always depends on technological advance, from the completion of the Erie Canal in the 1820s to that of the transcontinental railway in the 1860s. That Frank Reade's "steel horses propelled by steam" might be understood as a figure for the "iron horse," the object of the James's scorn, seems obvious. In contrast, the elaborate introduction, in which the story itself is discovered as a lost manuscript, might be said to work at disguising a host of other technological advances (from the invention of the cylinder press to that of the stereotype) on which the Western depends .

The text published here, while following the only edition of the novel, standardizes the punctuation (by adding a few quotation marks and periods) where necessary to make sense of the text.

Figure 25. Front page of the *New York Detective Library*, No. 415. Courtesy of The Library of Congress.

PROLOGUE. A WONDERFUL FIND

Two men were walking through a dense wood in the western part of Missouri. The heavy forests there a few years ago were more common than at present, though there are even yet forests and prairies in which a person could be lost for whole days.

Both these men carried guns on their shoulders, and one had a dead turkey in his hand, the result of the forenoon's hunt.

"Ben," said the man who had the turkey, "were you ever here before."

"I don't know. The woods look strange."

"They are strange."

"I believe we are lost."

"Well, I know it."

Then the two stopped and gazed for a moment at each other.

"Things have come to a pretty pass, Bob," said the man called Ben.

"Why?"

"That we can't go out for a hunt without getting lost."

"It is a little hard on us, that's all true," Bob answered. "It will be harder if we can't find our way out. I'm getting hungry."

"We can eat the turkey."

Then both looked at the turkey. At last Ben said:

"Eat turkey without bread or salt, bah!"

"Oh, Ben, you may turn up your fine aristocratic nose at the turkey in that way, but let me just tell you right now, a few days on nothing will make even turkey without salt or bread good."

They both looked up at the sky, but it was so cloudy they could not see the sun.

The woods had very little underbrush, and the trees were scattering, so that a team could have traveled through it without much trouble.

"Hello, what's this — a road, isn't it?" said Ben.

"It's where there has been a road years ago," Bob answered.

"I don't believe it has been used for ten years."

"I wonder where it goes?"

"It goes to Specter Bend."

Then both paused and looked aghast at each other. People in the West still have some superstition, and Specter Bend is a place where once stood a small village. It was destroyed by the James Boys, every house burned down, and a report having got out that the Bend was haunted, since the last terrible crime it went by the name of Specter Bend.

The expression on the faces of the two men indicated that they had a wholesome dread of Spectre Bend.

"Bob, which end of the road goes to the bend?" Ben asked.

"I don't know, Ben."

"Which end shall we take?"

"I don't know."

"I tell you what let's do."

"What?"

"Take neither."

"And go off in the woods again?"

"Yes."

"And be lost?"

"Yes."

After a few moments Bob grew bolder, and with a laugh, said:

"Pshaw! I'm not afraid of ghosts."

"Neither am I."

"Come on."

"Which end are you goin' to take?"

"The right."

"The right might be the wrong."

"I don't believe it leads to Specter Bend."

They trudged along for half an hour, and the road seemed to lead them constantly into a wilder and more dreary part of the wood. At last Bob, who was before, stopped, and, turning to his companion, said:

"The day seems to grow darker every moment, and I be hanged if I believe this road has been traveled since Frank Reed drove his steam team along it when he drove out the James boys."

"I don't either, and I believe we are going right toward Specter Bend."

"Well, we've got to go somewhere."

"So we have."

"Let's go ahead."

The winds had drifted the dead leaves of several autumns over the road, until it was so dim that they scarce could make out that there had ever been a road there.

They waded through the dry leaves, kicking them about in showers.

At last Ben's boot struck something which had a metallic ring about it.

"Hello," he cried.

"What's the matter?"

"I've stubbed my toe."

"Are you hurt?"

"Well, it don't feel very good," Ben answered, sitting down on the road side.

"What did you stub it against?"

"I don't know."

"May be it was a stump?"

"No, it wasn't wood."

"May be a stone?"

"It sounded and felt like tin or iron."

"Where is it?"

"There among the leaves."

"Among the leaves?"

"Yes; hunt it out and see what it is for yourself," growled Ben, who was caressing his injured toe.

"Ha, ha, ha! I will see."

And Bob began raking away the dry leaves.

They heaped up about him, almost hiding him. At last he felt something. It was a hard, smooth substance evidently several inches square.

"Hello!" he cried.

"Have you got it?"

"Yes."

"What is it?"

"An iron box."

"Iron box?"

"As sure as you live."

"Pull it out."

"Here it is," and Bob held aloft an iron box about twelves inches long, eight inches wide and six inches deep.

"Great guns, what can it be?" cried Ben.

"It's a box."

"But what can it be for?"

"To hold things."

"Rats! You know what I mean. Is there anything in it?"

Ben had forgotten his injured toe in his anxiety to understand all about the box, and was now at the side of his companion examining it.

"Yes, it's got something in it," Bob answered, shaking the box.

"The outside is rusty."

"Yes."

"Can't you open it?"

"No, it's locked."

"Hello, what are those?"

"Where?"

"On the top lid. Letters, as I live."

"So they are letters."

"Can't you make them out."

"No, too dim and rusty."

"Wait, I'll fix it."

Ben went a little farther down the road to where there was a small round stone, which he took up and brought to Bob.

"Rub off the rust."

Bob took up the sand stone and did so.

In a few moments the letters came out.

"Can you see 'em now?" Ben asked.

"Yes."

"What do they spell?"

"F-r-a-n-k Frank — R-e-a-d-e, Reade."

"Frank Reade," cried Ben.

"That's it."

"Then by Jove! this is his box."

"You can depend on it."

"Ha, ha, ha, he lost it when he was here years ago and I'll — I'll wager it's full o' money."

"I shouldn't wonder."

Then the two men became jolly, and despite the fact that they were lost, they laughed and joked.

"Let's have it open."

"We must get to a house, where we can get a hammer to break the lock."

"All right; come on," and laughing and joking, they went, without any fear now of the ghosts of Specter Bend.

"It's been a long time since Frank Reade was in this country with his steam team, chasing the James Boys, and he lost this box then," Ben reasoned. "I'll warrant that it's full of money. Frank Reade made millions out of his steam team, and this box is stuffed full of green-backs."

Thus feeding each other's fancies, they continued to journey and talk about their prospects of a speedy fortune and what they would do with the money when they got it.

At last they came to a house, and with a meat ax, a pair of tongs, and a hatchet assailed the lock.

It stubbornly resisted their efforts for some time, until Bob in his rash anxiety struck it a blow with the ax which shattered the padlock and the lid flew open.

To their amazement and chagrin, not a dollar appeared before them.

Nothing but a thick, leather-back book.

For a few moments their disappointment was so great that neither touched the book. Ben at last picked it up, and turning to the title page of the book, saw written in a plain, bold hand:

FRANK READE'S DIARY.

CONTAINING A FULL ACCOUNT OF CHASING THE
JAMES BOYS WITH HIS STEAM TEAM.

The closely written pages of the last diary were as follows:

CHAPTER I. THE AGENT OF THREE RAILROADS

My name is Frank Reade and my home is in New York. By nature I am an inventor.

I once invented a steam man with which myself and a party of friends traversed the plains and had a world of adventures and hair-breadth escapes. I gave the steam man to a cousin named Charley Garse and he became careless with it and it blew up, nearly killing him and a negro named Pomp. My next invention was a steam horse which likewise proved a wonderful success.

The third invention was a steam team with which I traversed the West and had just returned home. I now found myself growing famous.

I could scarce pick up a newspaper anywhere that I did not see some mention of my wonderful invention, though I did all in my power to keep the public from knowing anything about it.

Had I seen fit to have put my inventions on exhibition I could, I believe, have made more money than Barnum ever made. But I kept them in my workshop under lock and key and but very few friends ever saw them.

I should have stated that I am a practical machinist, and have devoted my life to inventions.

But it will be necessary here to describe my steam team as they stood in the shed.

They are two steeds of metal, united by a metallic harness. They are harnessed to a large wagon, greatly resembling an oblong box. The wagon box was spacious, capable of holding a number of people and a large quantity of baggage.

The wheels were large and set far apart to give firmness to the vehicle when in motion. A thorough trial had proved that my team could go in double harness. They were connected on the same plan as my steam horse. Each belly contained a boiler and steam chest, the valves for examination and regulation were on the haunches, the furnaces in the advance of the bellies, the doors being in their chests and the flues run up through the ears while the steam escaped by means of the nostrils.

It required great skill and practice to drive them, for as the power was equally divided, it had to be equally let on to get a uniform motion. If the reins which controlled the levers were not pulled evenly, then more power would be let on in one horse than in the other, and the unequal motion would rack the machinery to pieces. The steam power being independent gave one the ability to run around in a circle, by putting on more power in one animal than in the other, which of course did not matter for a few seconds, although to do that required some very nice skill, and practice alone could acquire it.

I could by reversing the power make the horses back, and as each iron hoof was provided with steel spikes, there was no danger of their slipping.

The body of the wagon was high, and when one would kneel in it, the sides, which were of iron, formed a bullet-proof breastwork. At the rear I had mounted a small four pound rifled cannon. I also had some rifles of my own invention, with globe sights, capable in the hands of an expert marksman of hitting a man's hat two miles away.

One, by reading this accurate description of my machinery, will at once discover that my steam team and armament was formidable.

One night I was sitting in my library reading an evening paper. On the desk at my side were some drawings and plans of my own, for I am never long idle.

There came a rap at my door.

"Come in," I said.

The door opened and a gentleman of fifty entered.

His evenly trimmed beard, dress and manner at once indicated that he was a business man.

"I beg pardon," he said, "but I wanted to see Mr. Reade."

"Frank Reade?" I asked.

"Yes, sir."

"I am Frank Reade."

"But Frank Reade, the inventor."

"I am Frank Reade, the inventor."

"What!"

"I assure you I am Frank Reade."

"But I expected to see a much older man."

I smiled, for I now understood why he was so slow in believing me.

"One does not have to live to be a hundred years old to make a good invention in this fast age," I answered.

Fearing that this man was only one of those bores who come daily to see my inventions and talk about them, I was slow to ask him to be seated.

"I am Nathan Bristoe, of Chicago," he began slowly and carefully, as though he was measuring and weighing every word before he uttered it.

"Oh, Mr. Nathan Bristoe, I am very glad to have met you!"

But I wasn't. One has to tell a fib sometimes in order to be polite.

"I came to see you on a matter of business, Mr. Reade."

"Oh, well, if that is it, pray be seated," I interrupted.

Mr. Bristoe, slow of speech as he was, was quick in his perception, and I thought a smile flitted over his face as he took the proffered seat.

"I am from Chicago," he said.

"Yes, sir."

"I am agent for three great railroads."

"Is it possible?"

"The Chicago and Alton, the Missouri Pacific and the Illinois Central."

"Yes, sir."

"All three of these roads run through Missouri."

"Yes, sir."

"And all three roads have been more or less injured by the great banditti known as the James Boys."

"I have heard of them."

"So has everybody. In fact, a more desperate band of ruffians never lived."

"I presume you are right, Mr. Bristoe."

"Well, we have determined to exterminate the banditti."

"That is a good motive," I said, beginning to wonder how I could personally be interested in the matter.

"We have tried detectives and sheriffs," Mr. Reade, until we find them of no avail. Timberlake has done his best, Wicher lost his life and Carl Greene, one of Pinkerton's best and shrewdest detectives,[1] a man who has never failed in any other undertaking, has failed in this."

"Yes, sir."

All this I had read in the papers.

"Now, Mr. Reade, we want to engage you."

"Me?"

"Yes, you and your steam team. We want to engage you to take your steam team and hunt down the James Boys. Jesse James rides a black horse called Siroc, with supernatural powers. Frank's bay Jim Malone, is equally as swift and untiring. Your steel horses propelled by steam, may run them down, but no other horses can."

"I am quite sure that my steam team will outrun even Siroc and Jim Malone," I answered.

"I am too."

"And I think I can capture or at least break up the band."

"Well, sir, I am here to make a bargain with you."

"What do you propose to pay?"

"What will you take?"

One question was thus answered by another to make the matter more evasive. I saw at once that in order to succeed I must come right down to business; I said:

"Mr. Bristoe, I will not work for a reward."

"How then will you work?"

---

[1] *Pinkerton, . . . detectives*: The first national investigative organization, the Pinkerton Detective Agency, was begun in 1850 by Allen Pinkerton (1819–1884), Chicago's first police detective, and E. H. Rucker, a Chicago attorney. The agency disclosed a plot to assassinate Lincoln in 1861, and conducted intelligence work for the Union during the Civil War. After the war, Pinkerton's men, concentrating on railroad robberies, expended massive efforts to pursue the James gang. They subsequently worked to suppress union organization and labor unrest, most famously during the "Homestead Massacre" in 1892, where the Carnegie Steel Company employed the detectives to battle striking workers, seven of whom died.

"By the month."

"The month?"

"Yes."

"How much?"

"For one thousand dollars per month and two assistants whom I shall select, I will undertake it."

"Two."

"Yes, I want two New York detectives."

"Well, will you pay them?"

"Not much."

"What will they cost?"

"Perhaps another thousand."

"Will you agree that the entire salary shall not exceed two thousand?"

"I will not exceed two thousand, but remember it must be two thousand dollars for any month or part of a month. If we only work one day in the month and capture or break up the gang we must have a full month's pay."

"And how about expenses?"

I laughed as I noticed how careful and close the agent was.

"Mr. Bristoe, you represent three wealthy corporations. Three powerful railroads, all with millions at their back, and there is no need in being parsimonius. I am risking my life and a machine which represents my life's work. You should pay expenses."

He soon saw that it was no use to endeavor to beat me down, and he finally consented.

"All right, consider the contract made, and here is one month's pay in advance."

"That is business," I casually remarked, as he counted out the money.

After I had counted it he shook hands with me and "hoped I would get through all right, Mr. Reade. You are a man of wonderful nerve, I have heard, but all your former adventures are but babies compared to this. The James Boys are desperate men in a desperate cause."

"And will come to a desperate end," I interrupted.

He laughed and replied:

"I hope so. Well, I have to catch the early morning train, so I must go. Good-by."

"Good-by, Mr. Bristoe, and I will be on my way in a week's time."

He was gone. I knew my men, and next day secured two of the best detectives in New York. One was the well known George Brass, and the other a no less personage than Bob Buttons. Both were personal acquaintances and friends, jolly, good natured fellows, and brave as lions. With them, I felt quite sure that I should at least make it quite warm for the James Boys.

CHAPTER II. A SAD STORY — DISCOVERED

Two weeks later found us in Missouri. I secured George and Bob, whom I sometimes jokingly called my Brass Buttons. Notwithstanding their rather odd names, they were genial souled fellows and just the men I wanted.

The steam team was flying down a road. People crowded the doors and windows of the farmhouses we passed — though there were very few of them — as if they thought a demon from the lower region had escaped.

I don't know how many poor negroes we frightened, but I never saw poor black fellows run so in my life. And who can blame them, for those mettled steeds flying along the road were certainly a very scarey object?

"Hello! what's that?" asked George Brass.

"Where?" I asked.

He pointed across a point of timber which came down a ridge, extending far into the ravine.

"Why, that's smoke," Buttons answered.

"Of course it's smoke, but what I would like to know is what is burning."

"The prairie?"

"Not at this time of the year, Bob."

"Well, then, what is it?"

"Houses."

"Houses! Why do you say houses?"

"Simply because there is too much smoke for one house."

I was sitting in the seat and had the reins in my hands.

"Boys," I said, "I am going to find out."

"That's right."

"Go ahead, Reade."

"Crush on more steam."

I did so. The metal horses gave fearful snorts, emitting fire and smoke from ears and nostrils, and their well-regulated machinery began to play.

Faster and faster we flew. The clatter of heavy iron hoofs on the road, and the cloud of dust which rolled behind us was simply terrible. Onward and onward we flew, like the wind. The wagon jostled and jolted and bounced.

I looked back and saw that my companions had about all they could do to hold their places in their seats.

"Talk about jolting," yelled Brass, "if this doesn't beat any I ever heard of, I don't know the meaning of the word."

I laughed, and shouted back to him:

"It's nothing, Brass, after you get used to it," and cracked on more steam.

"About the time I get used to it I'll be dead," roared Brass.

But we were rounding the bit of timber, and I could see a long distance down the valley. There was a long, level stretch of road for several miles, and I put on more steam, and my vehicle flew over the ground. Away we sped like the wind.

The rumbling thunder of wheels, the loud clatter of horses' feet, all made a tremendous roar, like an approaching storm, while behind us there rose on the air a vast cloud of dust.

The road was leveler, however, and my two companions ventured to stand up and look at the grand sight, the steam team flying along the road at the speed of a lightning express.

"Ho, look," cried Brass.

"Where?"

He pointed off at the right in an angle of forty-five degrees, and there I saw a sight which at once fired my soul. There only a few hours before had stood a peaceful quiet little village.

But now it was ablaze or in smoking ruins. Women and children could be seen on the hill among the woods, crying and wringing their hands in an agony of despair.

I pulled the whistle valve and my steam steeds gave forth ear splitting screams, as we darted into the ruined village.

The whistles were the first the horrified people had of our approach, and not knowing what those strange monsters could be, some of them took fright and fled away from the spot.

We slackened our speed as we approached.

A few dark bodies could be seen lying on the grass up among the hills, which we afterward learned were bodies of those slain or badly hurt in the fight which took plack a short while before our arrival.

I halted my Steam Team near the ruins and called to a woman who stood near gazing at us as if she thought we had come from another world.

Surely the ships of Columbus caused no more wonder among the natives of the West Indies than did my Steam Team.

"Come here!" I cried.

She screamed and fled.

"They are afraid of us," said Brass.

"I shouldn't wonder," said Buttons.

I sprang to the ground and advanced toward an old white-haired man.

He had a slight wound on the side of his head which had probably been received during the skirmish.

The old fellow was rather shy at first, but after a few moments he grew more talkative.

"Who did this?" I asked, pointing to the ruins.

"The James Boys."

"Could you not defend yourselves?"

"We did, but see."

He pointed to the hillside, on which stretched several dark and silent forms, the fruits of resistance.

"How many were they?"

"The James Boys?"

"Yes."

"Twenty."

"So many!"

"Yes, the band is greatly recruited. You might say that every one of Quantrell's old guard[2] has joined them."

"Well, what caused this terrible attack on you?" I asked.

The work had evidently been one of revenge rather than plunder. What could those poor people have to excite the cupidity of Frank and Jesse James. Those gentlemen seldom bothered with people of low degree. It was a fat bank vault or a railway train which they preferred to rob.

The old man rubbed his hand over his wounded forehead, as if he was in great pain, and answered:

"They hate us."

"You mean Jesse and Frank?"

---

[2] *Quantrell's old guard:*   William Clarke Quantrill (1827–1865) was a school-teacher who became a guerrilla leader during the Civil War. His guard kept Kansas and Missouri terror-stricken by robbing mail coaches and destroying communities of supposed Union sympathy. Members of the guard were declared outlaws by Union authorities in 1862 and were not granted the amnesty extended to veterans of the Confederate Army. Quantrill was fatally wounded during a shoot-out with federal forces.

"Yes, and the whole band."

"Why do they hate you?"

"Well, you see, we refused to shelter Jesse. Only a few weeks ago Jesse ventured to ride out on some other horse besides Siroc. Well, Timberlake got after him, and he was easily run down. He abandoned his horse about a mile above here and came in the town on foot. We suspected him, and that night all gathered around him and took him in, and handed him over to Timberlake."

"They never forgave us."

"And Jesse was a prisoner?"

"Yes."

"Is he yet?"

"No — they could not hold him. He got away from them, and then the band swore vengeance on us. To-day while we were not thinkin' at all about 'em, they all at once swooped right down on us. We fought 'em, fought like men and they fought like furies. But we were surprised and what could we do? Nothin'," and the old man pressed a handkerchief to his bleeding head.

"Which way did the James Boys go?" I asked.

He silently pointed to a road leading off to westward.

"In that course?"

He nodded.

"And how many did you say there were of them?"

"Twenty. I counted 'em."

I said no more, but went back to my steam team, where Brass and Buttons were waiting in no little anxiety.

"Well, what did you learn?" Brass asked, his eyes flashing with excitement.

I never saw just another such a fellow as George Brass. I believe he loved a fight of any kind more dearly than he loved the best-cooked dinner when he was hungry.

"It is the James Boys."

"Are they near?" he cried.

"Yes."

"Hooray!"

We were about to take our places and start, when a curly-haired young fellow came up. He was bare headed and his face flushed with excitement.

"Say mister," he called.

"What will you have?" I asked.

"Are you going after 'em?"

"The James boys?"

"Yes."

"I am."

"Can I go?"

I hesitated and he began to plead:

"Oh do let me go. I saw you coming when you were away off and I know that you fellows can outrun even Siroc and Jim Malone."

Then he pointed upon the hill where we could see some dark, mangled objects lying in the grass under the trees.

"Just look up there," he added. "I have a brother and a father lyin' in the grass there, and — oh, I want to go."

"Jump in."

He did so.

"Clear the track," I cried.

The whistle blew and the steam turned on.

Slowly at first the strong, iron-limbed steeds began to move. Slowly at first, and then faster and faster.

The wheels whizzed over the ground, and the people whom we passed gazed at us in amazement and wonder.

A herd of cattle were grazing in the valley below.

I touched the valve rein. Toot, went the whistle, and away scampered the cattle in every direction, giving vent to snorts of terror.

Along the road we flew at an even, yet a terrible pace, for I was determined to overtake the villains and make them pay for their atrocious work.

"Crack on more steam," said Brass.

"Brass is anxious for a fight," said Buttons.

"You are right, I am."

"So am I," cried the man whom we had taken with us.

I made no answer for my whole attention was given to the steam team which was speeding like a whirl wind.

There was not a moment to lose I knew, and I saw that to drive the steam team would require a skill which I flatter myself I alone possessed.

Down a road we thundered and up a grade.

"What is your name?" asked Buttons.

"My name's Jack Cravens."

"You look as if you were craving a little vengeance," began Buttons, when Brass interrupted him with a howl of revenge.

"Oh, Buttons, don't — this is serious enough now, without any of your wretched puns."

"Well, what's a fellow to do before we come up with 'em?"

"Look to you rifles."

"They're in trim."

"Say, you men," put in Jack Cravens.

"What?" asked Brass.

"You've got such a wonderful running machine as this is. I would think you ought to have some extra good guns."

"We have one that will hit the bull's eye every pop at two miles."

"Will it?"

"Yes."

"Let me have it."

"Are you a good shot?"

"I'll not miss with that gun."

"But it has a globe or telescope sight."

"So much the better. Please let me have it."

"What do you say, Frank?"

"He can try it," I answered.

"All right."

At this moment I caught sight of a score of mounted men riding away across the hill.

"Look! look! look! the game is sighted," I cried.

"Where?"

"On our right."

"Correct," answered Brass. "Now Jack take a look at them and see if we are right."

Jack stood up in the wagon as we sped along the ground, and cried:

"Yes, yes, it is they."

"Hurrah — hurrah — hur —— ," began Brass:

"Silence!" I shouted at him.

"Why?"

"Do you want to let them know we are right on their heels."

"Oho, they'll know by the snort of the metal horses," and Brass laughed.

Brass always laughed when going into a fight. I never saw a more plucky fellow. I sometimes thought he lacked discretion.

"Where is the gun?" said Jack.

"Here it is."

"Is it loaded?"

"Yes."

"Show him how to use it," I said to Brass.

Brass then explained to the young man the peculiarities of the gun.
I now gave my whole attention to the James Boys and their band
of outlaws.

Jesse and Frank James had heard of my wonderful machine, for I
had been all through Kansas with it only the summer before, and broken up a fearful nest of outlaws.

I could not hear them, but by aid of the field-glass, which I raised
to my eyes, I saw their faces.

Jesse and Frank turned deathly white. Here were a pair of horses
which even Siroc and Jim Malone could not outrun.

Jesse pointed to the hill across on their right. I knew that he was
announcing that they were discovered.

They galloped across the valley to the left to head us off, and
began to ascend a hill. I was not quite sure what their plan was,
whether they intended to fight or run.

But a few moments elapsed, during which time I put on a little
more power, and we went thundering along toward them. Then Jack
Cravens cried:

"I see him — I see the man who killed my brother."

"Where?" asked Brass.

"On one of the horses."

"Then bring him down."

"Are we near enough?"

"Yes, we are less than two miles."

"Will the gun hold up?"

"Yes. Put on the globe-sight, and with it hold her on the spot."

"I'll do it."

Brass showed him, and he put up the globe-sights of the gun.

The James Boys and their band having discovered us, all were flying like the wind up the hill.

"Ha, ha, ha, ha!" roared Jack Cravens, "now brother, you'll be revenged," and he had his gun leveled on one of the flying horsemen.

CHAPTER III. SIROC MEETS HIS MATCH

Crack!

Sharp and keen rang out the report of the rifle on the air.

A little puff of smoke, but I was watching the result. Would Young
Cravens know how to handle the gun?

Yes.

I could not have made a better shot myself. One of the horsemen reeled and fell from the saddle and the others fled for life.

Being near the brow of the hill they disappeared very quickly.

"Now crack on all power, Frank Reade, and bring us up alongside them," cried the anxious Brass. "Oh, do so, I want to get to close quarters."

"You may be made to cry for quarters."

"Buttons, if you don't stop your puns you'll unfit me for duty."

"Ha, ha, ha, old fellow, you will see the time you prefer puns to grins."

"Oh, mercy, he's got rhyming now, what other misfortune will befall us?"

I was paying but little heed to their sallies of wit. I was glad to hear it though, for one who can keep his wits on such trying circumstances, would be sure to be brave in a fight.

As we reached the top of the hill we once more came in sight of them.

We were much nearer than before, and I asked:

"Have you got the rifle loaded again?"

"No."

"Load it."

"Hand it to me," said Brass.

Brass put a charge in the rifle and leveled it at one of the banditti.

"Aim high," I cried. But I was giving too much attention to the steam team, for we were now going over a very rough part of the country.

I suppose Brass heard me, but at the moment he fired the wheel struck one of those hard tussocks or ant hills, so common on western prairies, and gave a tremendous jolt.

Bang!

I was watching the shot. He missed the man, but down went the horse dead.

"Hold up!"

The James Boys sounded a whistle, which we could hear, and a moment later every member of the band had wheeled about.

"They are going to fight," said Buttons.

Buttons was as brave a detective as lives, but he had learned enough of the James Boys to know that they were expert shots, and that we would have a slim show against twenty of them.

I was not slow of comprehending the situation myself, and holding the team well in hand by one of those graceful curves which I always pride myself in, brought them about in a half circle before the James Boys was aware of my intent, and was in full flight.

"Forward!" roared Jesse James.

We could even hear his hoarse voice shouting every word of command to his men. I have heard many a voice that was terrible, but I am sure that I never heard such a voice as Jesse James'. I have met many desperadoes, but never such as the great Missouri bandits.

"I'll fix him!" roared Brass, and he sprang to the small swivel or cannon.

"Brass!" I screamed.

"Well, what?"

"What are you going to do?"

"Fire the cannon."

"It's no use."

"Why?"

"The ground is too rough, and the wagon jolts too much."

"I can hit his horse, if I don't hit Jesse."

"Hit Siroc!" I cried, and although I knew that my whole attention was required to watch the team, I could not but look back at the noble animal.

"Yes."

"Not for worlds."

"Why, Frank Reade?"

"Because I am going to capture that horse."

"Oh, well, if that's your plan, we can't use an uncertain gun."

"Oh, I want to fight!" roared Buttons.

"So do I," roared Jack Cravens.

"Why not stop, Frank, and let 'em come up close enough," said George Brass.

The James Boys were in the lead, and the others coming on like the wind at their heels.

They showed no fear nor indication of halting, but pressed on like madmen.

They were enraged at the loss of one of their number, and seeing we were only four, were determined to overhaul and kill and scalp us, as they sometimes did people whom they hated.

"Stop, Frank, and let us give them a fight. This wagon is bullet proof."

"I have a better plan," said I.

"What is it?"

"Keep out of their range and use our long range rifle."

"Good."

"Now don't shoot at Frank or Jesse James."

"Why?" Brass asked.

"You might hit Siroc or Jim Malone, and I want to capture those horses alive and unharmed."

"Very well."

I then slowed up a little while Jack Cravens pulled away at one of the bandits with the rifle, and brought him down.

Three or four like shots began to open the eyes of our pursuers, and they came to a halt.

"They have stopped," cried Brass.

"All right, we'll stop too," I said, and I brought the steam team to a standstill.

"Brass, you might throw more coal in the furnaces, and you Buttons see that we have an abundance of water."

Both sprang out and proceeded to follow my directions. Buttons succeeded and Brass had only a few more shovels full to put in when Cravens looking back at the pursuers cried:

"They come, they come!"

"What?"

"See, they come."

I looked back and saw the James Boys with all their terrible band at their heels coming down at us at full speed.

"Brass," I cried.

"What?"

"Inside, quick."

"All right, let me shut this door."

"Hurry, they are coming."

The James Boys had seen two get out of the wagon, and supposing that something was wrong with the machinery, determined to charge down on us and make us all captives.

"Hurry, Brass, hurry."

"The confounded thing won't catch."

Crack! went Craven's rifle.

"Close it, quick!"

"They are coming like the wind," roared Buttons, seizing a Winchester[3] and opening fire.

"Hurry, Brass!"

---

[3] *Winchester*:   Patented in 1859 by Oliver Winchester, the Winchester is a repeating rifle that gave the North a considerable advantage during the Civil War.

"I can't shut it."

"What's the matter?"

"I don't know."

The James Boys were now so near that I could hear the roar of their horses' hoofs, and knowing how well those horsemen rode, and what desperate fighters they were, I understood that there was no time to be lost.

Quick as a flash I sprang from my seat to the ground and ran with all speed to the furnace. The catch had sprung a little owing to the heat, and I struck it a blow with my hammer, sending the door closed with a crash.

"Inside — quick!"

The cracking of the rifles and pistols of Buttons and Cravens now made the air resound with echoes.

I sprang upon the seat, and seizing the reins, threw on the power.

The steam team sprang forward at a bound. But the James Boys were on us.

"Down — down!" I cried.

"I have you now!" roared Jesse.

Brass and Buttons understood me and dropped beneath the iron side, but Cravens either did not comprehend or was too rash to obey.

The steam team could not bound away at full speed, and the excellent horses of the James Boys kept up with us for some time.

"Down, down," I roared to the rash young fellow.

I should state, perhaps that I was no longer in the seat, but down in the great bullet-proof box where from a pair of holes I could watch the road ahead and guide the steam team.

The James Boys were pouring in a perfect rain of bullets, and poor Cravens who, in his eagerness to be revenged, had leaped upon the side of the box, went over, as I afterward learned, pierced by a score of bullets.

Their bullets rattled like hail against the sides of our vehicle and the metal steeds.

Neither of us dared show our heads, but Brass and Buttons both fired at random and their shots went wild.

I now had the steam team going at a rate of speed which soon began to distance all the horses save one.

That horse was Jesse James' famous Siroc.

Like a meteor that dark wonder flew along over the ground, keeping well abreast of the steam team. Jesse had emptied his pistols, and so great was the rate of speed at which he flew over the ground that even that veteran rider had not an opportunity to reload his revolver.

I could see him from a narrow opening under the seat. I could see the noble animal straining every nerve to outstrip the steam horses. Jesse James had, perhaps, never ridden even Siroc at such a wonderful rate of speed. I doubt if he had ever known before the wonderful powers of that very wonderful horse.

Siroc had met his match.

Never before had the gallant steed found a horse he could not distance, but lo, here was an iron horse that was proving entirely too much for him.

Down the long level stretch of prairie we flew.

"Frank," cried Brass.

"What?" I asked.

"There is Jesse James on Siroc."

"Yes."

"Right alongside."

"I see him."

"Hadn't I better shoot him?"

"Can you do so without endangering the horse?"

"Yes."

"Then do it."

"My gun's not loaded."

"Use a pistol."

"All empty. Hand me one of yours."

"I have already given you my pistols," I said.

I now saw that Jesse's weapons were empty, too, and resolved to again mount the seat and drive side by side with him.

In a moment I had climbed to my place.

We were far ahead of the other pursuers.

"Surrender, Jesse," I cried on regaining my seat.

"Never," was the defiant answer.

"Then you will be run down."

"Fool, you have come West with your infamous machine to capture the James Boys, take that for your pains."

He aimed a blow at me with the butt of his pistol, but I was quick enough to catch the blow on an iron rod that I carried by the seat in front of me. It was the only available weapon at that time, and I seized it and turned aside the blow which he aimed at me.

"Look out Jesse!" cried I, and I aimed a downward blow at his head. The rod, which went down at his head, he dodged, and partly caught on his arm.

His pistol was knocked from his hand.

"Furies seize you," he roared.

"Surrender!" cried I.

"Never!"

"Whack!"

I struck at him again, and this he partially dodged. The blow only fell on his hip, but produced a roar of pain.

Jesse snatched one of his empty revolvers from his belt, snapped it at me, and then hurled the pistol at my head.

I tried to dodge it, but did not altogether succeed, as it struck me a severe blow on the shoulder and bounced off against the side of my head, and stunned me so that I reeled and for a moment or two came near falling.

As I clung to the side of the seat, I heard Brass cry:

"Buttons."

And Buttons yelled:

"Brass."

"He's killed Frank."

"No, he hasn't."

"Yes, he has."

"No, he hasn't."

"Yes, he has."

"Catch him or he will fall off."

Then it occurred to Brass to save me from a fall which, beneath one of the iron wheels, would have been like plunging beneath the grinding car of jaugernaut.

Brass caught me, and as he shook me up in my seat again he shouted:

"Frank! Frank!"

"What?" I answered.

"Are you dead? Speak. Tell me if you are dead."

"If I were dead I could not speak," I answered.

"Then you are not dead."

"No."

"Bad hurt?"

"I think not."

"Where did he hit you?"

"Oh my head, I guess. That very important member feels about as large as an ordinary sized hogshead," I answered.

"But you are all right?"

Brass was evincing great anxiety.

"Yes, I am all right?"

"Good! I would not have you killed or hurt for anything. We want to never give up until we have cleaned up the gang of infamous outlaws."

"Where is he?" I asked, looking about.

"Who?"

"Jesse James."

"By Jove he's fallen back."

I had not been giving much attention to the steam team for the last few moments and it had been speeding along at a tremendous rate.

In fact my hands as I fell having jerked the reins put on full power and we were now going at a dangerous rate.

Siroc had met his match and Jesse James finding it was useless to follow further, slackened his speed and waited for his band which was far behind.

CHAPTER IV. PROFESSOR DRYDUST

"Whew! Well this has been a pretty good heat," said Brass, as the steam team came to a standstill and we all stood looking back at the outlaws, now so far in the rear that it would be impossible for them to do us any harm.

"Are you seriously hurt, Frank?" asked Buttons.

"No."

"Your head is bleeding."

"Where?"

"On the left side."

I now put my hand up to the left side of my head, and just behind the ear the blood was flowing quite freely.

"Well I never dreamed of this."

"Wait a moment," said Brass, "and I'll stop it. I always carry court plaster and everything for an accident."

Brass was sort of a rude surgeon, and in a short time had my wound very well dressed.

"What are they doing now?" Buttons asked.

"Who?"

"The James Boys."

We all looked back.

"They are consulting."

"Yes."

"It's about us."

"What are they going to do about us?"

"Well, I know what they would like to do," Brass put in.

"So do I," said Buttons.

I sat listening to the two detectives and rubbing my head.

"Buttons, it's a shame we haven't got a dozen fellows."

"Half a dozen more would answer."

"Yes."

"But why not turn the cannon on them?"

"The very thing. We can hit one or two, or maybe more with our cannon."

Both turned toward the gun, but I, seeing their intention, cried:

"Hold!"

"Why?"

"Don't use the cannon."

They looked sad and disappointed.

"We must not hurt either Siroc or Jim Malone," I answered. "I am more determined now than ever to capture the horses unharmed, if such a thing is at all possible."

"I don't know that it is."

"I think it is."

"We can outrun 'em, that's sure, but then they can turn quicker."

Brass was a little disappointed.

"Do you know if Cravens was mortally wounded?" I asked, for I did not at this time know that he was dead.

"I guess he is," said Brass.

"He was foolish," added Buttons.

"Yes, it was rank folly for him to stand up on the side of the wagon as he did when they were blazing away at us like so many million fiends."

"Of course it was, but I guess Jack was excited."

"We'll excite the James Boys yet," I said.

"Let us try a shot with the cannon, Frank."

"Not now. The time for the use of heavy ordinance has not yet come."

I had turned about in the seat, for I had fixed my seat so it would revolve and was watching the James Boys.

"Aha, see, they are retiring," cried Brass.

"Yes, they go back sadder but wiser men," answered Buttons.

"They won't want to run afoul of Frank Reade's steam team soon again."

"No, they'll not try to run the team down any way."

The James Boys were all huddled together talking very earnestly, and really they made such a tempting shot for our cannon that I could hardly refrain from trying them one.

But I resolved to adhere to my original plan, which was if possible to capture the two horses alive.

"Where is the long range rifle?" I asked.

"Lost," said Brass.

"Lost!" I cried.

"Yes."

"Where?"

"Jack had it when he fell."

"And it's out there on the prairie," said I.

"I suppose so."

"Well, we must find it."

"May be they have picked it up," suggested Buttons.

"If they have not, we must not allow a stone to go unturned until we have found it."

"You are right, we won't."

The James Boys held a conference for a few moments, and then all wheeled about and retreated at a brisk trot.

"On the retreat, ha, ha, ha," laughed Brass. "They don't find it very comfortable pursuing the Steam Team."

"I knew they'd get enough of it," answered Buttons.

I now seized the reins, put on a small part of the power, and the vehicle began to move.

Slowly at first, the metal steeds snorting fire and smoke at every step, and the wheels crushing and killing the green grass and wild buttercups and daisies.

"What are you going to do now, Frank," asked Brass.

"Follow."

"Follow them?"

"Yes, we will harass them, cut them off, and run them down, one at a time, until we have the last one of them, and then will quit."

"A good idea."

"But it won't do to stop to fire up when we are so close to them," said Buttons. "Especially it won't do to send Brass to do the firing."

"Firing," growled Brass. "It was the old door that wouldn't close."

"Frank closed it."

"Yes, with a sledge hammer."

We gracefully rounded to, and came up directly in the wake of the James Boys, and not over two miles away.

They saw our maneuver, and clapping spurs to their horses, galloped over the hill, and were soon out of sight.

"There, we've lost them," cried Brass.

"Only for the time being," I answered. "Let them go for awhile."

"You won't give them up, Frank."

"No," and I laughed.

We went at a lively rate over the prairie drawing nearer and nearer to the spot where we had first encountered the James Boys.

"Brass, Buttons," I cried, "look for him. Keep your eyes on the ground."

"Look for who?" asked Brass.

"For Jack, of course."

"Oh, yes, you want the rifle."

"We do, and we want to give him decent burial."

"That's so."

Away we clattered over the prairie startling the Jack rabbits and coyotes from their lairs and crushing many an unfortunate prairie rattlesnake beneath the wheels of our vehicle.

"There he is," cried Brass.

"Where?"

"There!"

He pointed toward an object on our left.

I ran the Steam Team close up to it and came to a halt.

Both Brass and Buttons sprang out but I thought it better to remain in the seat and keep my eyes opened for the James Boys or some of their myrmidons might be lurking near.

I had a great dread of some of them getting possession of the team, for we would have been as helpless without the Steam Team as a tortoise without his shell.

The detective went to the body and raised it from the ground.

"Do you see the gun?" I asked.

"No."

"Is it gone?"

"Yes."

"Then they took it."

"Great suds!" groaned Brass, "now they will be raking us two miles away."

"No, they can't!" cried Buttons.

"Why not? They've got the gun, and I'd like to know why they can't, when they are among the best marksmen in the world," Brass returned.

"Because they have no cartridges for it."

"Was the gun loaded when he fell?" I asked.

"No," said Buttons.

"Are you quite sure?"

"I am, because he had just fired it before he fell."

"And he had no cartridges?"

"No. He only fired cartridges just as I handed 'em to him."

"Then we are safe," I said. "They can't use the gun."

We had some shovels and spades and spare boards. So we made a grave and buried the brave young fellow.

"Now to avenge him," said Brass.

"That's the ticket," roared Buttons, as the last shovel of earth had been thrown over our late acquaintance.

"Come every one and get aboard," I said, "for we must be moving."

"All right, here we are."

The tools were put away and the men sprang to their places.

Once more I mounted the box and seizing the rein, gave it a steady pull.

With a snort, the steam horses stepped forward with that fearless, tireless, firm gait, which only a steed of iron can go.

As the wagon went skimming over the prairie at a rate of speed that was wonderful, we all kept a sharp look out for the James Boys. They had disappeared in the woods. The timber was their safety, for we could not pursue them where the trees grew very close together, and it seemed as if those trees in the forest where they had escaped could not have grown closer together.

"What are you going to do, Frank?" Brass asked.

"Skirt along the woods until we find they have left them."

"Let's throw a few shots from the gun into them."

"Oh, no."

"We might drive 'em out."

"And we might kill either Siroc or Jim Malone."

"Confound the horses. I believe they'll be the salvation of the James Boys yet."

"They have been many times," I answered.

"Well, let Frank have his way," said Buttons.

We had run along within about five hundred yards of the woods for about three miles, when suddenly we saw a sight that was both thrilling and ridiculous.

To our surprise we saw a man mounted on a mule, spur out from a cluster of trees, and dash away as though pursued by Old Nick.[4]

---

[4] *Old Nick*:   In the nineteenth century, Old Nick was a vernacular nickname for the devil.

And though the latter personage was not after him, half a dozen of the outlaws were, which certainly made it about as bad.

The mule, fortunately for the rider, had a good start, for though he might have been a very sure footed, sweet-tempered, patient animal, he was not noted for his speed.

"See, he comes," cried Brass.

"They come."

"They all come."

"Here goes to help the party on the mule," cried Brass, and raising his Winchester, he hit one of the pursuers.

"I guess he's a little sick after that."

"Now for another." Buttons blazed away and missed.

"What's the matter, Buttons?" asked Brass.

"I don't know."

"Try another shot."

Crack!

He missed again.

"Keep cool, all of you, and you'll have your hands full yet."

The pursuers were gaining on the mule every moment. The animal was about a quarter of a mile away from the grove when the foremost of the pursuers caught up with it, and grasped the bridle rein.

With a scream such as only a frightened or enraged mule can utter, that animal sent his heels out with such force as to hurl the horse and rider ten or twenty feet away, and flung his own rider over his head.

At this very moment of victory the mule ran away, leaving his rider prostrate on the ground.

"Hurrah!" yelled Brass.

"Hurrah!" cried Buttons.

"Hurrah!" we all three roared.

And with a united cheer from those who rode behind, the steam team came dashing up to the spot, Brass and Buttons firing their rifles as rapidly as they could all the time.

The James boys saw us coming, and, having had a taste of our skill, they wheeled their horses about and fled like the wind. Brass got in one shot, however. He hit his man too, for we could see him hanging to the saddle as his horse thundered away as though he was bad hurt.

The man whose horse had been kicked down by the mule managed to get up with the beast, and they rode away as rapidly as they could go.

I brought the steam team to a standstill.

"Brass!" I called.

"Yes, sir."

"Get out."

"All right."

He sprang to the ground.

"Find the man who rode the mule."

"I will if I can."

"Hadn't I better help?"

"No, we'll risk but one out this time."

I sounded my whistle, tested the steam cocks, and satisfied myself that we had an abundance of steam.

"Here he is," cried Brass.

"Hurt?"

"I believe the old chap's neck's broke," Brass answered.

He was lifting the fallen man to his feet when that individual responded:

"I beg your pardon, gentlemen, I beg your pardon, but I am quite comfortable here."

"Are you?"

"Oh, yes, but — What has happened?" he said, as though puzzled. He was on his feet now, and I never saw a more laughable-looking personage. He was tall, thin and cadaverous. He was about forty-five or fifty years of age, and a very sober, sedate-looking fellow, with a body like a lath, a face like a hatchet, and a mouth like a slit cut across the face, while his iron-gray hair reached down below his shoulders.

His clothes were what might be called clerical cut, and very much worn.

"Who are you," I asked, as this tall ungainly looking personage was marched up to the wagon.

"Ah, I beg your pardon, sir, but I am Prof. Roderick Drydust, and my mission in this part of the moral vineyard is to teach the young idea how to shoot."

"Well, my friend," said Buttons in his quaint dry humorous way, "I don't know but that you were teaching some of the James Boys to shoot."

"That's a wretched pun," put in Brass.

Prof. Drydust carefully brushed his almost thread bare garments and looking at me said:

"I am Prof. Drydust, sir, and — and — let me see, have I lost it?" He began feeling about in his pockets for something.

"Have I lost it, if I have I am a ruined man."

"What is it, your pocket-book?"

"Oh no, money can be replaced but that never."

"A letter of introduction?"

"No."

"Instructions?"

"No, I could get new ones, but this — oh this could not be replaced. Ah, here it is," and a smile which was positively hideous came over the professor's face.

"What is it?"

"My journal."

He drew forth from an inside pocket an old book, one which had been considerably worn by long wear and use.

"What is that?" I asked.

"My journal, sir, the most important document in the world, I beg your pardon, your ten thousand pardons my dear — young friend, but don't you keep a journal?"

"Yes, I keep a diary."

"Oh, the same thing, sir, the same thing."

Notwithstanding we were in momentary danger of being attacked by the very men who had come so nearly taking his life, he whipped out his pencil and asked:

"What is your name?"

"Frank Reade."

"Frank Reade," he repeated, writing it down. "Where are you from?"

"New York."

"Well, well," and he wrote, reading as he wrote: "On this day I met Mr. Frank Reade, of New York, under very peculiar circumstances, which are as follows."

"Hold on," said I.

"Wait — wait until I write the circumstances in my journal."

"We have no time for the circumstances, Professor Drydust."

"Why?"

"The James Boys are not ——"

"The James Boys — oh, yes, I must not forget to write that down in my journal."

"Look here, Professor Drydust, if you want to get away with your scalp on your head you had better come aboard this wagon."

"But, Mr. Reade — Mr. Reade, I have just now a brilliant thought. Please let me jot it down before it escapes my memory."

"The James Boys will be jotting you down."

"Go off and leave him."

"Inside, quick!" I cried. "We are going to get under way."

He realized his danger at last, and with his precious journal in his hand, climbed into the wagon.

I applied the power and away we went skimming over the prairie as a swift sailing yacht might over a smooth sea with a favorable breeze.

"Well, well, I must remark that you certainly have a very wonderful invention," cried Professor Drydust, watching the steam team as it thundered along over the ground. "I believe I will write a full description of it in my journal."

CHAPTER V. THE STEAM TEAM TO THE RESCUE

I am a very patient sort of a fellow generally. I can stand an ordinary bore, but that Professor Drydust made me very tired about his journal.

He was the most complete monomaniac on the subject of keeping a journal it has ever been my painful duty to see.

"I want to talk to you about my journal," he said, climbing up on the seat by my side.

"What do you want to say?" I answered.

"I am glad to know you keep one."

"Yes, I do, but in these troublesome times, I find very little time to talk about it."

"Well, perhaps you do. Yet what a pleasure it is to have it to refer to in after years."

"I suppose so."

"And mine — oh, what a journal mine is! It contains my brightest thought. Did you never have a brilliant idea flashing in your brain in the still watches of the night? I do and then I rise at once and record them in my journal. Many a man, who is too lazy to get out of bed, would just lay there and allow those brilliant ideas to effervesce ——"

"There they are again," cried Brass, cutting short the long-winded lecture of Professor Drydust.

Crack!

The distant report of a rifle rang out on the air, and a ball came whizzing through the air.

It passed a few inches above our heads, and Professor Drydust shrinking back cried:

"Why, what was that?"

"A bullet."

"Now do you suppose they shot at me?"

"I don't know, it looks very much like it."

His face grew more grave, more serious and cadaverous than before, and clutching my arm he said:

"Mr. Reade, Mr. Reade!"

"Well, sir, don't hold my arms, because I have these steam horses to hold and they are about all I can manage," I said.

"Well, I have a request to make of you."

"What is it?"

"Should I fall I want you to ——"

"Look after your wife and children?" I asked.

"No, I have never burdened myself with a wife and children."

"Then what is your request?"

"That you save my journal."

There was no time for all this nonsense, and I knew it.

The James Boys and band, now to the number of forty or more, hung like a cloud on our left, and some of them had long range guns.

As every man on the frontier is a marksman these fellows, of course, were dangerous shots.

"Frank, they have been reinforced," called Brass.

"How many do you make out?" I asked, now giving my attention to the steam team which was galloping away beautifully over the prairie.

"There are forty at least."

"Crack!"

"Crack!"

"Crack!"

Three shots came whizzing through the air, and one struck against the tail gate of the wagon, with a ring.

"That's cutting close," cried Drydust.

"You had better get down in there."

"Where?"

"Where the others are."

"But you?"

"I am used to it. I have to take my chances," I answered. I did not tell him so, but really I would about as soon be exposed to the raking shot of the enemy as to his harangue about his journal.

"Frank, crack on more steam."

"Are they coming after us?" I asked.

"Yes — keep to the right well up the slope, for, see, they are trying to head us off. To drive us down into that ditch."

I turned the powerful heads of my metal steeds up a sloping hill, and put on full speed.

Away we flew.

The iron hoofs, armed with steel spikes, cut the turf, and sent it flying into our wagon.

"Hold on to your places," I cried. "We are going to run at full power now."

The motive of the enemy was quite plain.

They had only to make a short cut around a hill so as to get to the bridge ahead of us, and then we would be at their mercy.

But I had a plan which I believed would work.

We could outrun them, I knew, and the steam team did bravely.

The roar and thunder of the river ahead of us could be heard, and now we are in full view of the great covered bridge. I saw the James Boys, Jesse and Frank, ahead only five or six hundred yards away.

They gave us a volley.

"Don't fire back," I cried.

"Why?"

"Wait until they are closer."

"Can we make it?"

"With ease."

"Won't they pursue us beyond the bridge?"

"No."

"Why?"

"Wait and you will learn."

And they did learn what my plan was.

Like a tremendous whirlwind we sped along the ground toward the bridge, and as we went over it with a rumbling like thunder, making every timber of the covered bridge strain, I suddenly pulled open an under grate and let two great heaps of blazing coals fall upon the bridge.

They ignited in a moment.

"What did you do that for," cried Brass, as we thundered across the bridge and began climbing the hill on the other side.

"Look back and see."

"Why, the bridge is on fire."

"So it is."

"They can't follow us. I have burned the bridge behind us," I cried.

"Ha, that's a good idea, a splendid idea, one worthy of preservation, and I will put that down in my journal," cried Professor Drydust.

"Where are you going now, Frank?" asked Brass.

"I don't know."

We ran up on the hill, and then, making a graceful curve, I brought the steam team like a four-in-hand around, and we all gazed back at the burning bridge.

The wood was very dry, and it ignited like a tinder box. In a moment the whole thing was in a blaze.

"What a smoke," said Brass.

"Yes."

"Do you see the James Boys, Buttons?" Brass asked.

"No."

"What's that moving on the other side the river?"

"A man on a horse."

"You can't see it plain."

"No, the smoke is too thick."

"Don't it burn!"

"Looks as if the blaze would touch the sky."

"So it does."

"How high they leap!"

"They do."

"There goes the bridge."

"Oh, what a crash!"

"The water has swallowed up the smoking ruins."

While they were talking of the burning bridge Professor Drydust was busily engaged writing in his journal.

"What are you writing?" Brass asked.

"I am writing a description of the burning."

"Are you?"

"Yes."

"How far have you got."

"To the crash."

"Well, go on."

"I guess we will all go on," I remarked.

"Why not wait and watch it awhile longer?" asked Brass.

"Look at the sun and you will see that it is time for us to be hunting a camping-place."

I turned to the team and opened the valves.

We went rapidly over the hill and struck a large, well-traveled road.

For an hour we sped along. When I became assured we were at a safe distance from the James Boys I began to look about for a suitable place for camping.

The sun had nearly set, and the night would soon be upon us.

Suddenly we came in sight of some plowed fields, and a little further on was a house. It had now grown dusk, and as the steam team thundered along the road, stamping and puffing great volumes of smoke and sparks, it looked very much like a demon escaped from the lower regions I have no doubt.

Suddenly we heard a scream ahead.

The scream came from the house to which we were approaching. It was from a girl.

"What's the matter?" we heard the mother ask.

"The steam mill has broke loose, and is coming right up the road."

"Oh, what nonsense!"

"It's so."

"Hush!"

"Come and see for yourself."

"I'll box your ears, Katy, for saying anything of the kind."

At this I touched the whistle cord, and the steam horses gave forth a scream, which would to the woman in the house seem to confirm the girl's story.

"Laws of massy!" we heard her exclaim.

Then she ran to the door, gave one glance at the fiery monster thundering up to her very door, and cried:

"Oh, law, we are undone — it's Old Nick himself!" and she sank down helpless in the door.

"It is not Old Nick, madame," I answered, stopping the team and slipping from my seat on the box.

I ran to her, and seeing she had fainted from fright, called to the girl to bring me some water.

She did so, and in a moment the woman began to recover her consciousness.

"Don't be alarmed, madame," I said, "for we are only people like yourselves and I assure you we won't harm you."

"But your horses, what kind of horses have you?" she asked.

I laughed.

"Our horses are of iron," I answered.

"See, they eat fire."

"They are like locomotives."

She recovered rapidly and went out to see the wonders which stood at their gate.

The farmer came home from his work in the field and was amazed at seeing the Steam Team.

"We would like to stay at your house over night," I explained.

"Well, I reckin ye kin. Don't want ter put yer horses in the barn I guess."

I appreciated his joke and laughed as I answered.

"No but we will run the team into your lot."

"All right — I'll open the big gate."

"He did so and we ran the Steam Team into the house lot and left it with the heads of the steam horses toward the gate.

We remained all night at the farm house and next morning were at breakfast when a man on horseback galloped up to the door gate and called out:

"Hello, Grierson?"

"Hello, Shoemaker!"

Grierson, our farmer, got up from the table and went out to the front gate.

"What's the matter?" he asked.

No doubt he then saw by the face of his friend and neighbor that something had gone wrong.

We were near enough to hear even at the table, for in this house, like many houses on the frontier, the front room answered for both kitchen and parlor.

"The James Boys, fully forty strong, have crossed the river," said the man on horseback.

"Have they?"

"They have."

"When?"

"This morning at sunrise."

"I thought the bridge was burned?"

"So it was," answered the man on horseback, "but they forded the river. Swam their horses over."

"What are they going to do?"

"They intend to attack Raytown. There's no doubt about it."

"Do you think so?"

"I know it. They were moving that way, and I have rode everywhere to rouse all the people I can. We don't want another scene like Shopville was yesterday."

"No, we don't."

"Grierson, have you a gun?"

"Yes."

"A good one?"

"Pretty fair."

"Rifle?"

"Yes."

"Pistols?"

"One revolver."

"Won't you fight?"

"I never backed out yet," cried the brave farmer.

"Well, mount your horse and ride to Raytown. Take your gun and all the pistols ye've got. We won't have a minute to lose."

"Where are you goin'?"

"Goin' up here to git old man Lutes and his four sons and three sons-in-law, with their guns and dogs and horses, and we will just naturally make it so hot for the James Boys they won't cross over into Kansas again soon."

I did not know until this assertion was made that we were in the State of Kansas, but it seems that we had entered the prairie state on crossing the river.

The horseman galloped away and Grierson turned about and started to the house.

"Brass, you and Buttons fire up," I cried.

"What are we to do?"

"The steam team goes to the rescue."

"Hurrah."

"Aye, very enthusiastic, I will put that down in my journal."

Brass and Buttons were out in a moment and had the fires started anew in the furnaces of the steam team.

"Now, sir, are you going to the rescue of that town?" I asked of the farmer.

"Yes."

"So am I."

"Shake."

"Have you arms?"

"Here they are."

He took down an old army rifle and a revolver.

"I'll saddle up."

"No, get in the wagon."

"Ah, yes, sir, the wagon, it is a wonderful wagon," interposed Drydust, "and I have here a fine description of it in my journal."

"Never mind that now," I said, "come on."

He took up his weapons and followed me to the barn, where we found everything in readiness.

The hiss of escaping steam told that we had on a good head of that article.

"Is all ready, Brass?" I asked.

"Yes."

"How is the water?"

"Boiler's full."

"And coal?"

"Plenty for some time yet."

"All aboard."

"Here we are."

Everybody climbed upon the wagon.

The farmer's boy opened the gate.

As I took my place on the driver's seat, I heard a voice say behind me:

"This will be a wonderful day of adventure, all of which I shall record in my journal."

I glanced back behind me and beheld Professor Drydust sitting with others in the wagon.

"I wish we could leave that old fool and his journal, too, behind," said Brass, who had taken a dislike to Drydust.

"The gate's open," said the small boy, who was anxious to see the steam team go thundering down the road.

"All ready, clear the track!" I cried and put on the power. The steam team bolted out into the road, and we went thundering along at a speed unknown to living horses.

"The steam team to the rescue!" cried Brass, growing enthusiastic.

CHAPTER VI. THE STEAM TEAM CAPTURED

We saw men and boys everywhere, armed with almost every kind of a conceivable weapon, hastening toward the threatened village.

Never since the first shots fired at Leexington[5] roused sons of liberty in North America has there been such a turn out to fight a foe.

We stopped two or three times and picked up some fellows along the way who were armed with rifles and double-barreled shotguns.

---

[5] *Leexington*:   Lexington, Massachusetts, was the site of the opening engagement of the American Revolution on April 19, 1775.

"Great gosh!" I heard one boy cry as we came thundering up the road, "jist look thar!"

"What ist it?" asked another.

"A train o' kears broke loose and running through the country!"

"It's old Nick!" cried another.

"Frank," cried Brass, "do you see the town?"

I was sitting higher than the others, being on the seat.

"No."

"We can't be far."

"How far are we?" I asked of one of the farmers.

"'Bout four miles."

"Which way is it?"

"Don't yer see thet air hill?"

He pointed to a hill covered with trees and underbrush.

"Yes," I answered.

"Wall, it's erround that. Now look whar the big road bends erround that, and when we git erround it we'll be in sight o' ther town."

"Will we?"

"Yes."

Then I cracked on more steam.

We could hear a noise off to the right three or four miles.

Men could be seen everywhere on horseback and on foot, running toward the threatened town.

Partly from excitement and partly to escape the ceaseless hurangue of Prof. Drydust expatiating on the virtues of his great journal, Brass stood up behind me clinging to the seat.

"Frank," he said.

"What, Brass."

"If we get in a scrimmage, and any one has to go under I do hope it will be him."

"Who?"

"That Prof. Drydust."

"Why?" I asked laughing.

"I am tired being bored with his journal."

"Well, Brass, the chances for a lively skirmish are quite flattering."

"Do you think so?"

"I do."

"These fellows mean fight."

"Yes, and the James Boys are not to be backed down. Where did they get so many men?"

"Their ranks are always recruited," the detective answered. "I have heard it said that Jesse and Frank James could almost at any time muster a hundred men to battle."

"I believe it."

"Hark! What's that?"

"The village church bells are ringing," I answered.

"Yes, you are right."

"What does it mean?"

"Alarm."

"The James Boys have been sighted."

"Hark?"

"Aye, do you hear that yell?"

"Yes."

"And shots?"

"I hear them."

"Put on more steam."

I now let the power on to the full capacity which I dared, and the road being broad and level, we flew along at a rate of speed which almost took our breath away.

I cast a glance behind me at the farmers in the wagon, and I never saw a more terrified-looking set of wretches in all my life.

"Gosh! we'll be capsized and slung across the State!" roared one fellow.

"Don't be afraid," Buttons answered. "He knows how fast to run it."

"Yes, yes, gentlemen, a very remarkable machine indeed — a remarkable machine," said Professor Drydust. "I have a full account of it in my journal, which I will read to you by and by, as soon as we get a little leisure."

We sped like lightning around the tree-covered mound, and in a few moments were in full view of a pretty little village, all frame houses, neat, clean, white, and pretty.

The excited populace were running hither and thither in every direction.

Women were screaming, men were seizing guns.

A body of horsemen, forty or fifty in number, were approaching the village from the west, while we were coming in from the north.

I saw at once that we would not have time to reach the village before the horsemen, as they were fully a quarter of a mile nearer, and I cried:

"Brass, Buttons!"

"What?"

"What?" both cried.

"Work the gun."

"The cannon?"

"Yes," and I began swinging the team around so as to bring the tail-end of the wagon to the village.

"Why, do you mean to fire it?"

"Yes."

"You might hit Siroc or Jim Malone," said Brass somewhat sarcastically, for the reader will remember that this had all along been my excuse for not using the cannon.

"Never mind that now," I answered. "Better lose both Siroc and Jim Malone than a single human life."

Having brought the steam team about stern to the town, I reversed the engines and we began backing into the town.

We could back almost as rapidly, though not quite, as we could go forward, and it required much more skill to run backward than forward.

"Hurry up!" I cried, as I heard another yell from the banditti, and a sprinkle of shots began to sing out on the air.

"Slow up a little, Frank!" cried Brass, who was sighting the gun. I did so.

"Take sure aim."

The steam team was almost stopped and Brass, at last having sighted it, cried:

"Fire!"

Buttons jerked the cord.

I had turned about to watch the effect of the shot.

The two pound ball went whizzing across the west end of the village, clipped off a top rail from a fence, and down went one of the banditti horse and all rolling in the road.

"Reload quick!" I shouted.

Then I suddenly changed the power. The steam team bounded forward with a suddenness which almost unseated everybody and again I wheeled them about, and we were thundering down on the village.

The sharp boom of the swivel gun caused everybody at the village to turn their eyes toward us.

Then when fire-vomiting horses were seen drawing a curious-looking wagon, everybody screamed and took flight.

As for the James boys, they seemed paralyzed at our appearance.

At least we thought so then, but we were, ere long, to learn that as far as Frank and Jessie James were concerned, they had no dread of us.

The entire body of bandits wheeled about and beat a precipitate retreat.

I ran the steam team into the village, and in a short speech assured the people we were their friends, and had come to defend them against the banditti.

Everybody crowded forward to see the wonderful steam team, and nearly all had heard of it before, but had believed all along that it was not a reality.

As I concluded a wild cheer went up from the crowd. Someone proposed three cheers for Frank Reade and his steam team, and three cheers were given in such lusty tones as made the welkin ring.

The echoes of those cheers had not ceased to reverberate when a tall, ungainly-looking figure, which had been sitting in the bottom of the wagon, struggled to his feet and mounted on the side of the wagon-box.

"Ladies and gentlemen, quite pertinent to the issue indeed are those ringing cheers, and I will write that down in my journal."

"Oh, sit down," roared Brass.

"Very appropriate."

"Don't you hear?"

"A good word, yes. I'll just jot down that thought in my journal also."

Brass was so exasperated at the old fellow that he seized the tails of his faded coat and pulled him back into his seat.

"Now sit down."

Everybody laughed.

I joined them. I could not help it.

As for Professor Drydust, he was so intent on catching some brilliant thought on the fly and jotting it down in his journal that he never ceased to write.

The villagers were very grateful to us for having saved their pretty little town, and would insist on giving us a banquet, which they did.

Everything that one could wish for was brought to us, and we feasted like kings.

Next day we took our departure. Nothing more had been seen of the James Boys, and the villagers hoped they would never hear of them again, but we cautioned them to beware of the outlaws and under no circumstances to allow themselves to be taken unawares.

Our steam team was hissing and impatient to go.

I climbed to my seat and Brass and Buttons were in places, the former crying:

"Go ahead, Frank," when suddenly a tall, angular looking figure at this moment appeared and leaped on the vehicle.

Under his left arm he carried a book and had a pencil in his hand.

"Are you going with us?" cried Brass.

"Why yes, why not, my dear anxious friend. You are unsophisticated."

"Well, why are you going?"

"To pick up incidents of travel, I assure you."

"You had better stay behind."

"Oh no, I could not. I say, friend, do you keep a journal?"

"No."

"Well, you should, you will find it wonderful convenient. Now your friend there, Mr. Reade, keeps an excellent diary; I saw him writing in it last night and I know that it is a good one."

I had the reins and opened the valves.

The steam team started up. Then the crowds shouted, I blew the whistle and away we went like the wind.

The forenoon was passed without any adventure worth narrating. Professor Drydust had been very quiet.

We noticed that he had brought an excellent rifle with him and a brace of revolvers.

When asked why he had brought them he answered:

"Verily, a man must needs defend himself. Now, that's a good maxim, a golden text for a Sunday school lesson. I must write that down in my journal," and he hastily wrote.

We were on a vast prairie. The James Boys having crossed over the line into Kansas, would be easy chasing for us, we thought. But had they gone back into Missouri, or would we find them still in Kansas?

The prairie in this part of the country is interspersed with vast groves of trees everywhere, and in some places the groves were large and so dense that one could not see any distance in them.

The team was halted near a lovely spring of clear cold water, and we all got out.

"Oh, what a delightful spot," remarked Professor Drydust, opening his journal and looking about in admiration. "I really must write a description of it."

"Frank," said Brass.

"Well, what, Brass?"

"Is there no way to get rid of this old crank?"

"No."

"Then I almost wish for another attack from the James Boys."

"Why?"

"In the hope he might be killed."

Buttons laughed and remarked:

"It would do no good, Brass."

"Why, Buttons?"

"That old fellow can't be killed by a bullet."

"Well, then, let's turn the cannon on him."

The old professor was the meanwhile walking about near the grove. He had taken his rifle with him, he said, to shoot some game.

"Now, let him get off a few hundred rods," Brass whispered. "And then we'll all get in the wagon, and pull out and leave him."

I laughed at the plan and told Brass we could not afford to be so cruel.

"Hello!" called Buttons.

"What's the matter," I asked.

"I see a deer!"

"Where?"

"Over the hill."

He pointed across a ridge which was partly covered with grass and partly with bushes.

Now the hunting desire was quite strong in all of us, and at my suggestion we all seized rifles and started out to stalk the game.

"Be careful, keep low," I said.

We crouched low as we ran a long distance up the hillside. Had I been less excited, I would have been more cautious and at least left one with the steam team.

But every body wanted a shot at that deer, and I had it not in my heart to command any to stay.

"Where is the deer, Buttons?" I asked.

"Don't you see it!"

"Where?"

"There is the head just over the hill."

"Yes, I see it now."

"So do I," cried Brass.

"There it goes."

We could only see the head and horns of a stag as it moved slowly out of sight around a thicket.

But our blood was up, and we determined to have that stag.

"Come this way," I cried.

"To the left?" asked Brass.

"Yes. Keep well under the hill and out of sight. Keep low, so he can't see you."

"Frank!"

"What, Brass?"

"We are out of sight of the Team."

"Yes."

"We ought to keep it in sight."

"It won't run away," Buttons laughed.

"And we can't take it with us," I added.

"No."

"We'll not be gone long."

"Now, be careful."

"Yes."

"We're not far."

We ran around the hill, holding our guns ready.

"We will come up to windward and tumble right in on the deer," said I.

"Yes, Yes."

We were all eagerness.

Everybody wanted to be first to see the deer.

With rifles cocked, and at our shoulders, we ran up the hill, and reached the spot where the deer had last been seen.

Here a sight met our gaze that might have appalled stouter hearts than ours.

"What was it?" methinks I hear the readers of this diary ask.

It was a deer's head and skin stuck on a pole and the end of the pole in the ground.

So natural and life-like did it appear, that Brass came very nearly to firing at it before he discovered that it was not a deer, and only an effigy of one.

"What does this mean?" I asked.

"Frank," said Brass, panting so he could hardly talk.

"What!"

"It's a trick — a blamed mean trick."

"All is not right," put in Buttons.

"I am convinced of that myself," I returned. "Come, let us get back to our steam team."

"All right."

We all ran and tore our way through the bushes over the brow of the hill, until we were in sight of the valley below where we had left the steam team.

Here a sight met our gaze that almost froze our blood and filled us with chagrin.

The steam team was smoking and snorting. Two horses were tied behind it, and the steam team was going, leading the horses behind.

"Who is that?" cried Brass. "I see two men in the wagon."

"It's Frank and Jesse James!" I cried, pausing for a single moment to level my field glass on them.

"They have stolen the steam team," roared Brass.

"Captured our team!" and poor Buttons wrung his hands in agony as he saw them going faster and faster.

Already the horses tied on behind had to go in a gallop to keep up with the steam horses.

"Why, really that is a very extraordinary occurrence," said a familiar voice and Prof. Drydust who had been taking a quiet nap on the ground rose to his feet. "Quite an extraordinary occurrence. The steam team captured! Let me write that down in my journal."

CHAPTER VII. JESSE AND FRANK

Almost beside himself at losing our steam team, Brass could stand no more from the taunting professor, and he yelled:

"I'll put you out of the way."

Click, click!

He had actually raised his rifle, and though he afterward declared it was only his intention to frighten him, I have always been of the opinion that he really would have shot him.

But the old professor was really too busily engaged on his journal to realize any danger.

"Brass, come on," I cried, "we have no time to waste with him."

"I half believe he is in with them," roared Brass.

"See, there are only two men near the steam team. The other members of the band are gone away, I am now quite certain."

"Those two are Frank and Jesse James."

"Yes."

"Have you ever seen them?"

"I have," I answered.

"And you know them?"

"Yes."

We were all three running toward the steam team as rapidly as we could.

Jesse James' portly form could be seen sitting on the seat, and he had the reins in his hands.

He had hardly got the hang of the thing yet, and was running it badly.

"Come on, boys," I cried, "he won't run it far until we shall have them."

"Why," roared Brass, "they are going faster than we can."

"But he don't know how to manage it."

"No, he don't."

A whistle sounded.

"It was blown by mistake," I cried. "He don't know how to manage it."

"See, he lets more power on one horse than the other."

"Ha, there will be a balk."

"They are slowing up."

We were greatly encouraged at this. Somehow we had no thought of danger, save the danger of losing our steam team, and we ran at the top of our speed toward the steam team, which was certainly running slower.

Siroc and Jim Malone had no trouble in keeping up, and in fact they went around on the opposite side of the wagon seeming to have no fear of the steam horses.

In our mad haste we did not observe what Frank James was about.

Jesse sat on the seat a conspicuous figure, and I was thinking very strongly about trying a shot at him when a wreath of white smoke suddenly curled up from the wagon, and a two-pound cannon ball came whizzing so close to my head that for a moment I staggered and hardly knew whether my head was blown off my shoulders or not.

I staggered, and in a moment Brass was at my side.

"Frank, are you hit?" he cried.

"Where are you struck?" Buttons asked.

"I don't know."

I shook my head.

"Look, Brass, where is he hit?"

"On the head."

I shook my head.

"No, his head's whole."

Figure 26. Illustration of the Steam Team from *Frank Reade*. "Jesse sat on the seat a conspicuous figure, and I was thinking very strongly about trying a shot at him, when suddenly a two-pound cannon ball came whizzing close to my head." Courtesy of The Library of Congress.

"Then where did it strike him?"

"I am not hit at all," I answered.

"Didn't the ball strike you?"

"No."

"Good."

"We are all right now."

"There are only two of them," I cried, "and they are in rifle range, can't you bring them down?"

"How about Siroc?"

"Never mind Siroc."

"Both fired."

"Ha, see them dodge."

"The James Boys have learned the value of those bullet proof sides," I answered.

"But we can keep 'em down."

"Yes."

"Fire again!"

Three shots rang out.

"Now, boys, every time you catch sight of a head pull away at it! I am going to the team."

By this time the Steam Team had almost come to a standstill. It was in reality going at a slow walk.

"We'll do it, Frank," Brass said.

"You are both good shots."

"You bet we are."

"And your sixteen-shot rifles will enable you to shoot without having to reload."

"Trust us," put in Buttons.

My position, I knew, was a very dangerous one, but I resolved to do my very best. I have ran many narrow risks in my life, and have at last come to the conclusion that the safest plan is always the boldest. I did on this occasion what might seem rash.

I ran right toward the Steam Team.

Jesse and Frank James were both within that metal-sided wagon, both cool, and both desperate shots. I knew this, and I knew that I was unprotected out on the prairie.

But I had two faithful marksmen.

"Shoot at every head that peeps over the side!" had been my order, and I knew that order would be fulfilled to the letter.

I ran nearer and nearer. Soon something dark began to appear over the rim of the wagon bed.

Crack!

A shot rung out behind.

Down went the dark something, and I could have sworn the bullet had bored it through.

But a few paces were between me and my coveted steam team.

But what means this?

The team suddenly quickens its pace.

Can it be that Jesse James had found out the secret of running the steam team, and keeping his head below the bed.

I ran at the top of my speed, and by putting forth my utmost strength was soon near enough to lay my hand on the side of the wagon above one of the wheels.

"Frank Reade — Frank Reade," cried a chuckling, exulting voice inside.

"Jesse James, I'll have you yet."

"Ha, ha, this a splendid invention of yours, Frank Reade."

"Villain, give it up."

"We are in no hurry."

Then I tried to get a sight of one of them, but both kept close.

I looked back at my companions.

Brass and Buttons were running their best to catch up with the vehicle.

A wild and desperate plan now entered my mind.

The situation was desperate, and it required a desperate remedy.

My wagon was so constructed that the top of the bed came out over the wheels.

The hubs were protected by flat pieces of steel extending out over them, and my plan was to cling to the underside of the wagon and work my way around until I got on the opposite side where the horses were, mount one of them, cut both loose, and shoot down both of the James Boys.

The steam team was now going at a rate of speed which required all my strength and speed to keep up with them. I ran as I had never run before nor since.

I had no way to communicate my plans and designs to my companions.

They were both coming after us as rapidly as they could. I held to the wagon with one hand and turning, I waved my rifle in the air and dropped it. Of course I could not use it in this enterprise, and I dropped it, beckoning them to pick it up and bring it with them.

A wild shout was my only answer.

I was now ready for my very desperate adventure.

I leaped upon the side of the wagon, clinging under the sides by small handles which I had placed under there.

It was as much as my life was worth, for a single slip or misstep and I would fall to the ground and be crushed to death beneath those ponderous wheels.

But I have always been noted as an athlete. I have a steady nerve, a true eye and am very sure footed.

I clung on like grim death, for the speed was increasing every moment, and now Siroc and Jim Malone had all they could do to keep up to the steam team.

"Jess!" I heard Frank call.

"Ay, ay!" Jesse answered.

"Are you getting the hang of it?"

"Yes."

"Is it hard to control?"

"No."

"Difficult to understand?"

"It's very simple."

"A wonderful machine, isn't it, Jesse?"

"You are right, Frank James; it is certainly the most wonderful piece of machinery that has ever been made."

"What will we do with it, now that we have got it?"

"We will have to wreck it, unless we use it to run down trains."

"We can't do it, Jess."

"No."

"I think the thing will be almost useless to use."

"I tell you what we can do."

"What?"

"Take it to our rendezvous."

"Our hiding-place?"

"Yes."

"Could we get it in?"

"The cavern?"

"Yes."

"Of course."

"It's larger than our horses."

"We can take it to pieces."

"So we can."

"Oho! so this is your plan," thought I, as I clung to the underneath side of the wagon, holding on for dear life. "I will, in all probability, spoil your very neat little game."

Then I glanced back at my companions.

We were leaving them so far behind that they looked like specks on the prairie.

Jesse James at this moment said:

"Frank, look over the side and see if you can see them."

Frank was in a moment gazing over the very side of the wagon under which I was clinging for dear life.

"Do you see them?"

"I see two."

"Only two?"

"That's all."

"Where is Frank Reade?"

"He is not one of them."

"Been thrown down or run over."

"I guess that's so, for one man carries two guns."

"Are they still running this way?"

"Yes."

"But we are out of range, are we not?"

"Yes."

"Then I'll mount the seat."

"Jess, can you manage it down there?"

"Yes. He's got a pair of windows here through which I can see."

"He fixed that to screen himself from our bullets."

"Yes."

"Ha, ha, ha, and we've got it."

"Fools build houses, and wise men live in them."

"And you mean also to say that fools invent machinery, and wise men use it."

"That's it, exactly."

"Ha, ha, ha!"

I felt no little chagrin at this. Jesse and Frank James were adding insult to my injury, and I was almost furious with rage.

But I did not lose my presence of mind.

I try to manage, whatever may happen, to keep my senses about me.

I made several efforts to get around on the other side, but found it utterly impossible. A bat gifted with the powers of flying and sticking to nothing, could not have performed that quite impossible feat while the vehicle was plunging along over the uneven ground at a rate of speed that was amazing.

"Jess," said Frank.

"Well."

"Can you see from where you are?"

"Yes."

"Can you see the horses?"

"No."

"Well, you'd better slow up."

"I had forgotten Siroc and Jim Malone."

"Poor fellows, they can't keep pace with Frank Reade's metal steeds."

"No."

The team began to slow up, and as it did so, I began to have some hope. If they would only come to a standstill but for a moment, I might slip around on the other side and mount one of the horses.

Oh, to be once astride of Siroc, many a horse jockey would give a fortune for that privilege, and no horse jockey ever more strongly desired that pleasure than did I at that moment.

"Take your seat, Jesse."

"All right."

"The coast is clear."

I could hear Jesse James climbing up from the front part of the vehicle to my seat.

Though the steam team was not running so fast as it had been, the great wheels were still revolving at a tremendous rate, and it would have been dangerous to attempt to climb around the rear end of the vehicle.

"The coast is clear," I heard Jesse say.

"Do you see any of them?"

"Not a soul."

"Nor I."

"We have left all out of sight."

Then came a short silence, and Jesse said:

"Frank, we can use this after all."

"How?"

"To bring off Louisa."

"Louisa Allen, the heiress?"

"Yes."

"Jess are you going to persist in that mad notion?"

"What mad notion!"

"Marrying Louisa Allen."

"Yes, why not?"

"She is Bob Allen's daughter."

"I know it."

"And she is very rich."

"What of that," laughed Jesse. "Don't I need a rich wife?"

"But she don't know."

"Don't know what?"

"Don't know that we are robbers."

"Ha, ha, ha, no I suppose not, we are not going around just now telling people that we are lifting purses on the highway, robbing stage coaches, banks and railway trains, and sacking cities."

"No, and when she finds out."

"Needn't ever find it out."

"But she will," said Frank.

"How."

"In some way. In a hundred ways which I can't begin to enumerate."

"Well, Frank, I've made up my mind."

"You have?"

"Yer."

"For sure?"

"For sure."

"Then it's not worth while to try to change you, Jesse, for when your mind is made up it is made up."

"Yes, you are right."

"But I wish you would give this mad idea up."

"What mad idea?"

"Marriage."

"How about Annie Ralston," laughed Jesse.

"Why, I have kept nothing concealed."

"Does she know you are a robber?"

"Yes."

"And will she marry you, a bandit?"

"Yes."

"Well, Frank, she is an extraordinary woman."

CHAPTER VIII. IN THE MUD

"Can it be possible," I thought, "that the James Boys have their love affairs."

In fact, I was so much interested in their conversation that I had almost forgotten my own critical position.

Though Jesse had slacked up the speed of the Steam Team, it was still running so fast that the horses, Siroc and Jim Malone, had to go at a gallop.

Seeing that my original plan was sure to fail, I was debating in my own mind whether I had better hang on to the rings or hand holds I had or let go and fall to the ground.

While the fall would have given me a considerable jolt, I have no doubt I could have thrown myself far enough out from the wheels to have escaped being crushed.

But I became interested in what the bandits were saying, and though I had to strain every nerve to do it, I clung on to the rings with all the powers I had.

I was growing very tired, my hands and feet were almost exhausted, but I reasoned that if I could but hold on until night I would be near when they stopped and might capture Jesse and Frank alone and single-handed.

True, it was a desperate scheme, but I was hard driven, and willing to take desperate chances. Besides, I wanted to hear what Jesse and Frank James had to say among themselves. They supposed they were alone, and would of course talk freely to each other.

"Yes, Jesse, Annie Ralston is a remarkable woman," Frank answered.

"She is. You say she knows that you are an outlaw?"

"Yes."

"And yet she does not reject you?"

"No."

"She must indeed be a grand girl."

"She is. Oh, Annie is a noble girl."

"But, Frank, how about the old man Ralston."

"He will object."

"Of course — I heard that he had forbidden you to come to the house."

At this Frank James laughed and said:

"Who ever heard of a lover heeding such a command?"

"Well, Frank, you'll get along all right. But now how about the Winston affair?"

"The train we are to rob?"

"Yes."

"Well, let's do it."

"Can't we with this machine?"

"How?"

"Run down the train!"

"Jesse, are you watching which way we are going?"

"Of course."

"Seems to me we are out of the road."

It was now growing late. The sun had set, and we would soon have it quite dark.

"Sun has set, Frank."

"Yes — where are we going to stop to-night?"

"I don't know."

"I suppose we can camp anywhere with this rig."

"It's going slower."

"What's the matter, Jess?"

"I don't know. I've put on all the power I can."

"The machinery must be wrong."

"Seems like the thing was about run down."

"That's just it."

"What's just it?"

"It's about run down."

Jesse and Frank were now both at the seat, watching the metal steeds stepping slowly yet with dignity over the ground.

Siroc and Jim Malone could now keep up with perfect ease, and occasionally they made short halts to pick the grass that grew in abundance all along the way.

"What do you mean by being run down?" Frank James at last asked.

"I mean that we are about out of steam. Our fire has run out."

"Is that so?"

"Yes."

"Well, let's stop and fire up."

It was growing dark so rapidly that all the landscape was now enwrapt in the sable cloak of night.

"Let us go down into the low lands," said Jesse. "I think I can throw on a little more power, and as it is down grade we will make it!"

"All right."

Jesse had learned a little something about managing the machine, though he was as yet an unsafe driver. He turned the vehicle a little to the right, clapped on all the power, and it sped down grade at a rate of speed which put Jim Malone and Siroc to their swiftest gallop.

"Now," I thought, "my trial has come. Soon I will be pitted against both Jesse and Frank James, two of the worst men who ever handled a pistol."

"It goes at a good rate now," said Frank.

"Yes, but it is only because it is down grade. I doubt if we have enough steam to go up a hill."

"You ought to know, Jesse; you have been an engineer."

"Yes; if I had never been an engineer I could not have run this thing."

"It must be very complicated."

"It is."

On we thundered.

Soon I felt the grass and marshy bushes come swishing by me.

The wheels began to sink, and I could hear the feet of the horses and the feet of the metal steeds splashing in the water.

"Hello!" cried Jesse.

"What's the matter?"

"Mud."

"Are we in mud?"

"In a swamp."

"There."

The steam team came to a standstill.

"We're stuck."

"Stalled!"

Then a few moments more of silence, and Frank said:

"How are we to get out of this?"

Jesse was silent for a long time, and then be said:

"I don't know, Frank, but really I have almost come to the conclusion that it don't make no difference anyway."

"What don't make any difference anyway?"

"Whether we get out of here or not?"

"Oh, we don't want to be stuck here in the mud all the time."

"No, nor are we going to be. But this thing is our worst enemy. If we can get it stuck in the mud, all right."

"I see."

"Good idea, ain't it?"

"Yes."

"Well, shall we go now?"

"Why not make our night out in this wagon?"

"In the wagon?"

"Yes."

"Well, why not?"

After a few moments' silence Jesse James said:

"It will be a pity, though, to leave Siroc and Jim Malone in the mud and water all night."

"Well, it will."

"What'll we do with them?"

There was another interval of silence, broken at last by Jesse James saying:

"I believe we'll have to take them out on the hill."

"A good idea."

"But do we dare?"

"Dare what?"

"Sleep so far away from our horses. This thing is powerless."

"Yes, so it is."

Then they both seemed to be pondering on the question.

At last Frank cried:

"But we've got no pursuers near. The boys have gone back into Missouri and everybody will think we went with them unless Frank Reade and his men ——"

At this Jesse laughed:

"They are fifty miles behind."

"Then we'll risk our horses up on the hill."

From this moment my plan of action was clear. I would steal Siroc, go back, hunt my companions and we would capture Frank and Jesse while they slept.

It was a wild, desperate scheme; but I like desperate chances.

The James Boys seemed to entertain no fear whatever of any possible harm. They evidently thought that no one was within miles.

My hands and feet were growing numbed, with the long strain upon them; and I knew I could not hold on to it much longer.

At last Jesse and Frank sprung on their horses and rode away up the hill.

It was now dark, quite dark, and I let go my hold after releasing my foot from the ring and fell partly on the grass and partly in the muddy water.

A kind of a coarse marsh grass grew on this bottom land, and in places the tussocks were above the water and mud.

Fortunately my fall was noiseless, or the quick ears of the James Boys might have heard it.

I lay perfectly still for several moments, then was beginning to consider how I was to get out of there, when I heard Frank and Jesse returning, after having left their horses in the grove above.

"We'll get our feet wet crossing the lagoon," said Frank.

"No we won't."

"Why, it's all water."

"Here is a ship that is above the water."

"How the mischief did we run so far into the mud before we found out what we were doing?" Frank asked.

"The thing was under headway," said Jesse, "and couldn't be stopped."

"Well, it's stopped now."

"Yes."

"And it will never go on, for I don't believe there is any power that can get that machine out of the mud."

"It is certainly stuck fast enough for the time being at least."

"They'll never get it out."

This thought troubled me not a little.

How was I to get my wonderful machine out of the mud?

"Follow me right along this strip of high land, Frank," Jesse said. "Keep well to the right and you will come right up at the right side of the steam team."

"All right."

"It's easy enough, isn't it?"

"Yes."

They were coming nearer; they were right at the wagon, and when they halted by the side of it, I could not but tremble. I had my revolver in my hand, but I hardly dared trust it in the darkness. For a moment the wild plan of assaulting both myself entered my mind. But my soul revolted at the idea of killing, unless absolutely compelled to do so, and I resolved to adopt the safer plan of going for my two companions.

"Well, here we are," said Jesse at last, and they climbed in the wagon.

"I am tired," Frank answered, as he climbed in also.

"I am hungry."

"So am I."

"Have we nothing to eat?"

"Not a bite. I am hungry enough to eat some of those croaking toads out there in the pond."

"So could I."

"But what can't be cured must be endured."

Then a short silence ensued, broken at last by Jesse saying:

"Maybe those fellows have some grub in this car?"

"That's it. Frank Reade is too good a traveler to go without an ample supply of grub."

"I know it."

"Jess, light your lantern and make search."

In a few moments I could catch the occasional gleam of a lantern as it flashed over the sides of the car.

"Now is my time," I thought. "While they are engaged in hunting for something to eat I will get out of here."

I began crawling as noiseless as a shadow over the ground.

Slowly and cautiously, fearing that an accidental dip or splash in the water would betray me, or that an unlucky flash of Jesse's lantern might make me the target for the unerring aim of the James Boys. It seemed that I had gone miles before I reached the solid shore, but at last I made it.

Then I rose to my feet and looked back. Whereas I had before been horrified at the great distance, I was now alarmed at the steam team being so near.

It seemed that I could put out my hand, and almost touch the captured machine.

I sighed as I thought that my property and my pride was now in possession of an enemy, and made a mental resolution that I would have it back if it was in the power of human kind to get it back.

I did not wait long by the brink of the marsh, but crept away up the hillside as rapidly as I dared in the direction of the horses.

Then as I went toward them another fear came to my heart. This fear was produced by hearing an uneasy sniff of the air.

Siroc and Jim Malone had winded me, and in order to succeed I must get, as the sailors say, to leeward, or where the wind blew from them to me.

I made a short half circuit, and thus came to the proper point, when I began again to advance.

There was danger yet.

Siroc and Jim Malone owned but one master each, and a stranger might be resented with bites, kicks and squeals.

I was right in my conjectures, for when I suddenly came along, Jesse's famous horse began neighing and kicking like a mad beast.

"Hello, do you hear that, Jess?" cried Frank.

"Yes, there's trouble there."

"They don't neigh for nothing."

"Come on."

There was not a moment to lose. I am a skilled horseman, and, despite Siroc's wild squeals and kicks, I leaped on his back and went speeding away like the wind.

I took the trouble to cut Jim Malone's halter, and the poor beast, frightened and confused, followed Siroc for two miles before he discovered his mistake, and then, suddenly stopping, he turned about and trotted back to the James Boys.

Mine was an unwilling steed, but by my superior management I managed to keep him in the right course, and went thundering over the prairie more rapidly than I ever rode before on the back of a horse.

It was nearly midnight when a light in the distance attracted my attention.

I rode cautiously toward it. I was not long in making it out to be a camp-fire, and I could see one or more tall figures moving about sometimes between me and the light.

I cautiously approached the light, and when I was near enough to see distinctly, I made out three men sitting, standing or walking about the camp-fire.

One was Brass, one was Buttons, and the third tall, angular, ungainly personage, with long hair and hatchet face, there could be no doubt about being the professor.

A mule was grazing near. A sheepskin saddle and a rope bridle were near the tall, lean, cadaverous man.

I recognized the mule as the very animal which had thrown the professor off his back when we rescued him from the James Boys.

"Well, my friends," the professor was saying in his sanctimonious way, "it is a very sad affair. Indeed, it is very sad. I have been very much grieved over the singular taking off of Mr. Reade, who is a very estimable young man, and I have written my thoughts down in my journal. Mr. Reade had many good qualities and among his best points is that he keeps a diary."

"I don't believe Frank is dead," said Brass.

"Chances are against him," sighed Buttons.

"What mad freak possessed him to cling as he did to the side of the wagon in which the James Boys were."

I wanted to hear no more, but urging Siroc into the circle of the camp-fire light, I cried:

"Well, here I am!"

They all started to their feet, each with an exclamation of wonder, and Brass came very near to shooting me before he made out who I was.

"It's I, my real self," I explained. "Don't be alarmed. I will not harm you."

"Where have you been?" asked Brass.

"Taking a ride with the James Boys."

"Where is the steam team?"

"In the mud."

CHAPTER IX. A FRIENDLY FLASH

Then I explained in as few words as possible the condition in which I had left the steam team.

"And they captured it and run it in the mud," said Professor Dry dust, slowly, writing the event in his journal.

"Yes."

"Well, Frank, if they know of your escape we'll either not find them there or they will be waiting for a fight," said Buttons.

"I think you are right."

"We want a fight," put in Brass.

"Well, boys, what shall we do?" I asked. "Let's go on to-night."

"To-night?"

"Yes."

"Well, I am willing."

"How far is it?" asked Buttons.

"I think twenty miles."

"Great guns — a twenty mile tramp."

"We have the horse and can take it time about riding."

"And my mule, gentlemen, my mule, remember."

"Professor Drydust, how did you get your mule?"

"Oh, Jerry is a most noble animal, and I knew he would follow me. You could hardly lose him from me."

"And has he followed you all the time?"

"Yes, sir. He's been ever near."

"What say you to making an immediate move on the enemy," I asked.

"All right — we'll do it."

In a moment we were all ready for breaking camp.

I was somewhat rested and offered Brass my horse while Buttons mounted the wall.

"Now we'll move rapidly as Napoleon always did, and strike them in a mass."

We hurried over the ground as rapidly as we could, and for two hours traveled in silence.

Then we changed.

It was long after daylight before we came in full view of the steam team. There it still stood stuck in the mud.

"How are we to get it out," said Brass.

At this moment there came a shot from a distant grove, and a bullet grazed my cheek.

"The James Boys," I cried.

I was mounted on Siroc when the shot was fired, and that animal became almost ungovernable.

"Hold him steady," said the professor.

"Frank, get down," cried Brass.

"Yes, you make too good a shot up there."

I realized what was said, when a moment later two bullets passed through my hat and another cut a round hole through the collar of my coat.

After a fourth had plowed a little furrow in my shoulder I dismounted.

A wild shrill whistle rang out on the air. The whistle is far beyond my powers of description. It was half whistle and half cry, and had a most peculiar effect on Siroc.

Before we could comprehend that it was the call of a beloved master for his horse, Siroc had squatted to the earth, given one tremendous bound which snapped the rein I held in my hand and was away.

Tossing his head and kicking up his heels, he squealed with delight and flew at the speed of the wind to the grove where his master was.

"Ha, ha, ha, ha!" rang out a wild demoniac laugh. "You thought to steal my Siroc from me, did you?"

"Well, did you ever?"

"Not in my day."

"It's remarkable."

"Beats anything I ever saw."

These were some of the expressions uttered by Buttons and Brass. Even Professor Drydust was for a moment held speechless and silent in wonder. At last, however, he regained his speech, and, dipping his pencil between his lips, he said:

"A wonderful horse, truly a very wonderful horse. I must write that down in my journal."

"Down, all of you, and be ready for a charge," I cried, as soon as I could speak. My brave lads obeyed me, and with cocked rifles we all three crouched on the grass ready to send death to the James Boys.

I should have stated that Brass had secured my rifle which I had dropped and brought it to the camp for me.

The professor finished recording some gem of thought which had come to his mind, and then putting the precious document carefully away in a capacious inside pocket he seized his long barreled rifle and lay down on the grass by the side of us.

But the James Boys had no notion of fighting us it seemed. They knew perhaps that our long range guns gave us an advantage, for Jesse and Frank seldom burdened themselves with rifles. They were too large and clumsy to suit their purposes.

"There they come!" cried Brass.

They rode out on the top of the hill and waving their hats at us galloped away.

"Well, now may I be hung for a traitor for treason and spoils, if I don't think that a shabby trick," cried Brass.

"They are gone," said I.

"Yes, and left us in the mud."

"Stuck fast."

I arose and watched them as they galloped away until they became two specks in the horizon.

Then we turned to the Steam Team.

"How are we going to get out of the swamp," Buttons asked.

"That's a question."

"Boys let's fire up, get up steam and try to pull through," I suggested.

We went down to the machine and found the metal steeds in mud and water far above their knees and the wheels had sunk several inches in the soft earth.

"Now, lads, I'll try to put on steam enough to move it, but I am afraid that it is useless."

I built a fire in each furnace and in a few moments we had the steam hissing. When the boilers had about all they could bear I turned it on. Slow at first, but more and more until the legs and feet of the metal horses began to move.

I put on more power.

The vehicle moved, but only deeper in the mud. The feet and legs splashed and kicked and kicked and floundered until I was convinced that it was useless to put any more power on and turned off the steam.

"We'll never get out that way," I said.

At this moment we heard a shout or a report like a pistol on the hill.

"Get up, buck, woa, haw, yer blamed rascal."

The shout was the yell of a driver of a long team of oxen, and the report his whip.

"There's a bull whacker," cried Brass.

"How many yoke of cattle has he?"

"Eight."

A new thought came to my mind.

"He must pull us out," I cried, and leaping from the wagon I ran up the hill, shouting:

"Hold, mister. Say, stop your team, won't you?"

"Woa there, Bright 'n Ned. Woa, Buck 'n Beny. Why, howdy mister, wots ther matter?" asked the bull whacker.

"We are stuck."

"Stalled?"

"Yes."

"What kind av a blamed rig 'av yer got, any way," he asked, as he fixed his amazed eyes on the steam team.

"That is a steam team," I explained.

"A what?"

"A steam team."

"Great Scott, yer don't tell me. Why, it's er smokin'. Looks like er ditched locomotive."

"It is stuck in the mud; we want to engage your eight yoke of steers to pull it out."

He scratched his head and said:

"Well, I don't believe I kin."

"Oh, yes, try. I'll give you twenty-five dollars."

"'Taint money as iz botherin' uv me, mistur, but I'm afeerd my oxen ain't strong ernuff, but there's two more teams er commin' an' with them we'll hev twenty four yoke, then mebbe we kin make it."

"How far are they away?"

"Be hyar in a hour ef yer kin wait."

"We will have to wait, and I will give all three of you twenty-five dollars each to get us out."

The fellow gave utterance to a loud whistle, and said it was 'most a month's wages right slap down. Then he unyoked his cattle and allowed them to rest and feed on the grass.

We passed the time as well as we could until the other teams came up.

A few minutes were given them to let their cattle rest.

A bountiful supply of log chains were among the teams, and they soon had a long string of twenty-four yoke of oxen hitched to the Steam Team. Forty-eight great, stout, sturdy beasts, were ready to pull the massive vehicle.

"Frank, they may break it," suggested Brass.

"I think not, and besides it is our only hope."

"Hadn't you better get up steam and help back it out?"

It was a good idea. This would prevent the steam horses having legs broken.

They had the oxen hitched to the rear end of the car or wagon, and the long string of cattle extended up over the top of the hill.

When all were ready, I took my place on the seat, and reversing the power, set the machinery in motion.

"Get up!"

"Hoo ay!"

"Whack!"

"Crack!"

"Crack!"

It was a lively scene. The drivers were cracking their whips, and Brass, Buttons and the professor, each with a stick, was belaboring the oxen.

Never had I seen such a sight.

Forty-eight stout oxen, straining every nerve, and the log chains creaking to their utmost.

"Go on, get up!"

"Get up!"

Some of the cattle were down on their knees and others had their toes stuck in the ground, heaving.

The legs and feet of the steam horses were moving, and, to my great joy, I saw the great wheels begin to roll.

"She comes! she comes!" yelled Brass, almost beside himself in his transports of joy.

"Hooray!" cried Buttons, equally elated, while the professor, in his joy, proceeded to write it down in his journal.

There were great clods of mud hanging to the wheels, showing how deeply they had been imbedded.

"Get up!"

"Go on!"

"Heave to it, my beauties!" yelled the bull-whackers, making the air resound with reverberating echoes of whips.

We were now out on solid ground, and I signaled the men to stop.

"Come, get here quick and clean off the mud so we can travel," I called out to my companions.

By the time I had counted out the money to each of the happy teamsters, the wheels and feet of the metal steeds were scraped clean of mud.

"Is anything broken?" Brass asked.

"No, I believe not. I can't tell until we try it. All aboard!"

In a moment every one was on board.

Then I seized the reins and threw open the valves.

With shouts the metal horses began to step off.

"All is right," I cried, and in a few moments we were flying away across the prairie at lightning speed, leaving the three amazed teamsters gazing after us.

"Have you noticed how late it is?" asked Brass.

"No, it's cloudy."

"You are right, and it's going to rain."

I took out my watch, and discovered to my amazement it was five o'clock.

"What, is it possible we have spent the entire day here at this?" I asked.

"I guess it is."

"Well, where will we camp?"

That was a question we found it not easy to settle. We allowed our horses to run on, hoping to come to some house.

But night came on, and we had reached no place yet. The James Boys had destroyed our provisions, and we were hungry.

"I'll turn on the electric headlights," I said, "and we'll travel, even if it is night."

Then I touched the spring, but to my amazement all was darkness yet.

The team was rushing on in the darkness at a tremendous rate.

"Why don't you turn it on?" Brass cried.

"It won't turn."

"Broke?"

"Out of order some way."

Then I tried again with some effect.

"How dark it is," cried Buttons.

"Yes."

The thunder rolled above us, and the lightning at this moment flushed.

Great Heaven! how I started. There right before us was a precipice fully two hundred feet deep, revealed by the friendly flash.

I reversed my engine, put on the brakes, and stopped when on the very verge of the precipice.

CHAPTER X. PROFESSOR DRYDUST HAS SOME DIVERSION

The lightning's flash was gone, and we were enveloped in total darkness, save the dull glow from the furnace.

For a moment a horrified silence held us all dumb.

So near to death — and such an awful death it would have been! — was enough to freeze us to silence.

The first to regain his speech was Brass, and he, in a tone that was as calm and unconcerned as if he had not been on the brink of an awful death, said:

"I wonder if you couldn't back out of this, Frank? I don't believe I would try to go any further."

I laughed. I could not help it, for he was so droll and cool that it was impossible for me to restrain my risibles.[6]

"I don't believe I'll try it, Brass."

"Well, I wonder if we can back?" put in Buttons.

At this moment another voice put in, which I recognized full well. It said:

"Most extraordinary affair indeed! A very thrilling adventure, and but for the friendly flash of lightning we might all have been dashed to death. I regret that it is too dark to record the event in my journal."

I put on the power with reversed engines, and in a few moments the great iron legs of the horses began pushing backward.

Oh, horror! I felt one slip. Something was loosened, and a moment later I heard a great booming sound like a clap of thunder, as a bowlder, loosened from its base, went rolling with a peal like thunder down to the awful blackness and depths below.

But the engines were working, and the metal steed made a tremendous effort and righted himself.

One inclined to be superstitious would almost think that the steam team was gifted with powers of reason.

We were in a few moments at a safe distance, and then I stopped.

"What are you going to do now, Frank?" asked Brass.

"I am going to see what is wrong with our head-lights."

"A good idea."

"Brass, light a lantern."

"By George, why haven't I thought of this before?"

"Yes, and I can finish my journal."

"Confound your journal!"

"Oh, dear — oh, dear! Now Mr. Reade wouldn't say that."

The lantern was lighted, and I climbed out of the car. By the aid of the powerful lantern, I could see how nearly we had been on the brink of destruction, and I shuddered.

Where one iron foot had been the embankment was broken away and gone.

It was my policy to treat the matter as lightly as possible, so I said nothing and assumed the jocose air of Brass.

---

[6] *Risibles*:   Risibles are the muscles used during laughter.

"If we had gone any further we would have needed a flying machine," I said to my companions.

"We would have taken a tumble in lieu of one," answered Brass.

I went to the front rigging, and opening some of the head gearing of the metal horses discovered that the wire by which the electric head lights were attached had slipped and failed to make any connection.

In a moment's time I had it back in place and we were all right.

The wire had no doubt slipped while we were backing and pulling out of the mud.

"Have you got it all right?" asked Brass.

"Yes."

"Suppose I turn on the head light?"

"You may."

"Well, here goes."

And the two powerful lights which steamed far out into the darkness lighting up the awful abyss beyond streamed out before us.

"All right, it works all right now," cried Brass.

"Ah, it's all right."

Then I ran back and climbed aboard, taking the reins in my hands.

"Ah, it is beautiful, beautiful indeed," cried the eccentric professor. "Please hold the lantern so I can see, Mr. Brass, and I'll give a description of it in my journal."

"Can't you find some other diversion?" asked Brass.

"Diversion, Mr. Brass, why yes, that's a good word and now I'll write that down in my book."

"Oh never mind, I think you might have some other amusement."

"Yes, so do I, and now as I come to think of it, diversion is what I want most; I am sadly in need of diversion."

"That is what we are seeking ourselves."

"I trust we will find it."

"The James Boys are our chief diversion, and I believe we can spare some of it with you."

"Quite generous."

I had backed the team several rods away from the dangerous precipice and starting out in a circuit we was soon turned out of the dangerous path thundering through grass and hazel bushes.

There was no danger now of running down a precipice for our powerful head lights threw out a light, far, far ahead of us.

At last we came into a sort of a dim road but it was sufficient to suit our purposes and we went thundering along it at a rapid rate of speed.

Along we sped, the metal steeds tireless and no doubt looking terrible to one who was unacquainted with them.

As we were being whirled along at such a tremendous rate of speed, I could not help thinking of the conversation I had overheard between Frank and Jesse James, and to myself I kept asking:

"Who is Louisa Allen, the daughter of Bob Allen, and who is this Annie Ralston?"

Brass and Buttons were really both as much in the dark in regard to the matter as I, I knew, for neither had ever been in Missouri or Kansas before.

Suddenly a lucky thought entered my head.

Maybe the professor knew.

Slowing up the team a little, I called:

"Professor!"

No answer.

"Professor Drydust!"

I thought I heard him snore.

"The old chap's asleep," answered Brass.

"Wake him."

"No, let him sleep, for now we have some peace from his abominable journal."

"But I want to ask him some important questions!"

"All right, if you say it."

Then he shook the professor, saying:

"Wake up, you old rascal."

"Oh, ah, eh! What'll you have, gentlemen — a new thought ——"

"No — the boss wants to talk with you."

"Talk with me?"

"Yes."

"What does he want to say?"

"Are you awake?" I called.

"Yes, sir."

"Come over here in the seat at my side."

"Oh, yes, I guess he wants me to read my journal to while away the tedious hours as we glide along. Quite an intelligent young man, and he knows how to pass the time to an advantage too."

"I beg pardon," I said.

"Eh!"

"We won't need that."

"What?"

"The journal."

"Won't need the journal?"

"I assure you not."

"You may be mistaken."

"I simply want to ask you a few questions, that is all."

"A few questions? Well, I may need my journal."

"You will not."

"What do you want to ask?"

"Have you lived long in Missouri?"

"Twelve years, sir. I can tell the very day I came there by referring to ——"

"No, you need not," I interrupted, as he began turning over the leaves in his journal. "I only want you to approximate, you need not go to the trouble of ascertaining the very day. Have you been much in Kansas?"

"Yes, sir. My duty as a teacher of the young has taken me in many places in the country."

"So you are pretty well acquainted in both States?"

"I am."

"Now, I want to ask you about some people."

"Who?"

"Do you know Ralston?"

"Colonel Ralston?"

"I suppose so. Has he a daughter?"

"Oh, yes."

"What's her name?"

"Annie, Annie Ralston."

"Annie Ralston is one of the people I am inquiring about."

"Well, she is the romantic young girl who has fallen in love with Frank James. Her father has driven Frank from the house, and threatens to arrest him if he comes near the house again."

"Does she know he is a robber?"

"Yes."

"Well, then, we'll let her go. If she will go to destruction there is no help for her."

"That's just what I say. I've got it in my ——"

"But there is another person I want to inquire about."

"Who?"

"Allen."

"I know a number of Allens."

"Do you know Bob Allen?"

"Of Kansas?"

"I don't know which State he lives in, but it must be either in Missouri or Kansas."

"Guess it is Kansas."

"Do you know a Bob Allen?"

"Yes."

"Has he a daughter?"

"Three."

"Do you know their names?"

"Well, I should. They all three were my pupils. Yes, sir, all three attended school to me and I know them."

"Well, give me their names."

"Isabella, Araminta and Louisa."

"Which is youngest?"

"Louisa."

"How old is she?"

"Not over seventeen."

"Is Bob Allen very rich?"

"Rich?"

"Yes."

"Why, he is worth millions. He is the great cattle king of the West."

"Then I am on the right track."

"What do you mean?"

"How near does Allen live to the Missouri line?"

"Within a dozen miles."

"It's he."

"Who?"

"I mean she."

"What do you mean, Mr. Reade?"

"Are the Allens your friends?"

"Yes."

"Well, they are in great danger, especially the young girl Louisa."

"Why, my dear sir, that is alarming. What — what do you mean. Pray, let me record the fact in my journal, so it will not be forgotten."

"No, it will not be forgotten."

"Then what are we to do?"

"This is a very delicate matter, Professor Drydust, and you must leave the matter somewhat in my hands."

"What is it?"

"Well, to begin with, you see Miss Louisa has been wofully deceived."

"Deceived?"

"Yes."

"By whom?"

"Jesse W. James."

"Oh, you mistake. She has not the honor of that gentleman's acquaintance."

"I beg your pardon. She has. She knows him not by his real name, but by an assumed name."

"Is that so?"

"It certainly is."

"Who is your informant?"

"Jesse W. James himself."

"What, have you been talking to him?"

"No."

"How did he tell you, then?"

"He did not tell me. While I was clinging to the side of the wagon, when the steam team was captured by the James Boys, I heard him tell Frank James that he was going to marry Louisa."

"What?"

"It is true!"

"Why, she don't know him."

"No, not as Jesse James, for he has done all his courting under another name."

"Well, he's a villain, that's what I have to say of him, and I shall write him down as such."

"Can you direct us to Allen's house?" I interrupted, for I did not care to hear any further harangue about his abominable journal.

"I am, as soon as it is daylight."

"That will do then, you may go back to your nap. I don't care to talk with you any more for awhile."

He went back to his place and was soon asleep.

He was puzzled what to do. It had begun to rain and we were in the open country. We came at last to a wooded road.

Ere long our head lights showed us a field.

A little further and we came to an old log house which had been abandoned. The fences had been taken down from around it and it had been occupied by hogs.

The swine were sneaking away as we came in sight.

There was a long high porch or shed, for it was built on the old Virginia style of houses, and we ran in under this to pass the night.

As we stopped Professor Drydust yawned, and looking about, rubbed his eyes and growled:

"Oh, oh, I wish I could have some kind of diversion."

"Diversion?" cried Brass.

"Yes."

"What kind of diversion?"

"Anything to stir up my stagnant blood."

"This cold rain makes you chilly."

"Slightly."

"If the James Boys gang should be near, you might have some diversion."

"Oh, would I?"

"Very likely."

"I wish they were."

The words were scarce out of his mouth ere:

Crack! went a pistol, and a ball whizzed close to the professor's head.

"Hello!" yelled the professor.

A wild yell put an end to anything further he might have uttered.

"The James Boys!" I cried, and turned off the electric headlights.

Crack!

Crack!

The shots were poured in on us.

"Out with the lights, Brass! Put out the lantern!" I shouted. "See, we are being made the target for their broadside."

"All right."

In a moment the lights were put out, and then commenced one of the most stubborn fights I have ever witnessed.

The banditti in full force charged us so close that we could see their faces by the flash of their pistols. We had some double-barreled shotguns and poured our fire in on them.

Then went at them with revolvers and drove them back.

During a temporary lull in the fight Brass, who even in the midst of danger seemed bubbling over with mischief, turned to Professor Drydust and asked:

"Are you getting all the diversion you want?"

CHAPTER XI. THE STEAM TEAM LOST

The storm raged with the fight. The rain poured in torrents, and the pistol balls of the banditti rained all about us like hail.

It was so dark that we could scarcely see. I was crouching behind the corner of the house when, from the whiz of bullets from behind, I was convinced that they had outflanked us.

"Brass!" I called.

"Here!"

"Are you hit?"

"No."

"Where is Buttons?"

"Here."

It was too dark to see my companions and I could only ascertain that they were living by calling to them. I was about to ask for Professor Drydust when a voice which could not be mistaken, said:

"Quite an extraordinary conflict, indeed. Now, if it was only light enough for one to see I would record the memorable events which are now transpiring, in my journal."

Soon after, the flash of a rifle, followed by a yell from one of our enemies, convinced us that Prof. Drydust was doing anything else than writing.

Drydust was a study for me. I never met with a more puzzling character in all my life.

He seemed a fool at times, but he was far from being an idiot. He was brave as a lion, comical as a clown, and shrewd as the shrewdest.

For some time I had come to entertain a suspicion that his journal business was all a humbug, done for effect.

"Frank!" a voice whispered.

It was Brass. I recognized his voice.

"What is it, Brass?"

"I — I have discovered something."

"What?"

"They are making an attack on the Steam Team."

"Are they?"

"Yes."

"Well, Brass, I've got a new plan now."

"What is that?"

"Watch from this corner; I'm going to turn the lights on."

He understood what I meant.

"All right, Frank, I'll load both barrels of the shotgun almost fit to burst."

I then crept away in the darkness. It was so dark that we could see nothing, and fired only at the flash of pistols or sounds. Several bullets had whizzed from the backs and sides of the metal steeds, and I knew that the James Boys were under the impression that we were in the wagon.

To approach the steam team was dangerous.

But I managed to reach the step, and quick as lightning I leaped up into the wagon.

I lay down just as a volley of shots fired at very close quarters flew over and against the wagon.

Then I began feeling about for the knob to throw on the head-lights.

I found it, and touched it.

In a moment a great brilliant light was thrown out far across the field, over the fence and into the road.

We could see the James Boys band in considerable numbers massed to charge upon us.

The dazzling light thrown so suddenly in their faces blinded them, and they threw their hands up to their eyes.

"Now, boys, let them have it," I cried.

Oh, what a yell, and oh, what a volley.

We all fired, and poured in a deadly rain of bullets until they were glad to get out of our way and run for their lives.

They mounted horses, and flew for life.

We knew that some of them were hit, and Buttons, who was of a very sanguine as well as enthusiastic temperament, vowed that he saw some of them lying on the ground badly hurt.

"Frank," said Brass, coming over to my side.

"Well, what, Brass?"

"Hadn't we better be going?"

"I don't know."

"They have retreated, but it will not be far. How is the steam?"

"Low."

"I'll fire up."

At this moment we heard the voices of Jesse and Frank James rallying their men in the distance.

"Hurry, Brass."

"Aye, aye."

Brass was an excellent fireman, and he soon had the steam hissing from the boilers.

"All aboard," I whispered, turning off the light and seizing the reins.

"Aye aye," Brass whispered.

"Are we all aboard?"

"Yes."

It was too dark to see, and I was so intently listening to the rally-ing bandits that I did not hear them as they came aboard.

"All here," Buttons answered.

I reversed and put on a little steam.

"Brass," I called.

"Aye, aye, sir."

"Light the lantern and hold it over the back part of the wagon."

"All right."

He did so.

"Now keep a close watch, and if you see danger ahead, or rather behind, let me know," for we were backing out of our dangerous position.

"All right."

"Won't they see the light," whispered Buttons.

"No, the steam team is between them and the light."

It had ceased raining, but the roads were muddy and slippery. The steam horses were so skillfully made that they raised and put down their feet softly when moving slow.

Backward, slowly backward step by step, we moved every moment, increasing the distance between our enemies, and they knowing nothing about it.

In this way we moved backward over a hill and came to a small level bit of ground covered with grass only.

Here I gracefully swung my team around and throwing on the electric light, which lit up the road ahead of us, went flying away from our enemies.

We ran about ten miles and then came to a halt. We concluded that it would be best to remain on the prairie all night.

So we left one on guard and the others fell asleep.

We were very tired and hungry.

When morning came we saw a little town about five miles away and put our metal horses in motion heading for it. It was not long until we reached it, when we bought and stored away provisions enough to last us several days, perhaps a week or two.

Everybody turned out to see the wonderful steam team. All had heard of it, and everybody wanted to see it.

We remained only an hour in town, and then according to the opinion of Professor Drydust, an opinion which he took great pains to record in his journal, we started off in a south eastern direction as the most direct course to Bob Allens.

When it grew late, we came to a halt for dinner.

I had been sleeping, and the driving had been intrusted to Buttons.

Buttons, perhaps, knew less about the machine than any one in our party.

Even Professor Drydust, who would insist on being with us, had some idea of machinery, and he soon learned how to manage the steam team, as the management of it was quite easy, for it was not at all complicated.

When we stopped, Buttons had steam up to the very highest pitch.

"Buttons, what do you mean?" I asked.

"I don't know why you ask me that," he answered.

"Why have you got the fire up so strong?"

"To keep the machine going."

"Well, you've got entirely too much steam on."

"I thought it was about right."

"You'll blow us up one of these days."

"Well, I don't know much about it," he answered.

He need not have said that, for any one could see at a glance that he didn't.

"Well, don't put on any more coal. Let the steam die down a little."

"I will."

We had halted near a lonely little grove, and there was a stream of fine cold water boiling out of the stones near. What a lovely place to camp it was.

"Boys, get out; we will all stretch our limbs on the ground," I said.

"All right. I am glad of that," cried Brass.

"My legs are growing round like barrel hoops," growled the professor, as he leaped out on the ground.

"Come, be lively, Brass, spread the cloth," said I. "I will go up on the hill and take a look about to see if the enemy are in sight."

"All right."

"I'll help you," said Drydust.

"Come on, old fellow."

"You'll think I'm not such a bad fellow after all," remarked Drydust, with an effort to conciliate Brass, whom he had come to look upon as a sort of general enemy.

"No, if you would quit talking about your journal."

"Now Mr. Brass, let me argue the point with you. Don't you think that a journal is a pretty good thing after all?"

"Yes, but when one makes it a hobby, it becomes a bore."

I had gone but a few paces up the hill when I saw that the steam was pretty high and turning to Buttons, I said:

"Go and raise the gage and let the steam escape, Buttons. We have too much on."

"All right, I will," he answered.

Then I turned about and went on up the hill.

Reaching the crest I raised my field glasses and swept the horizon far around, but could see no one save a few hunters away to the south about six miles from us.

I was still gazing around in every direction when suddenly I heard a wild yell in the direction of our little camp accompanied by a sudden hissing and snorting.

I wheeled about and the sight was one well calculated to fill any one with amazement if not fear.

The Steam Team was acting strangely.

It seemed that Buttons had made a mistake, and instead of opening the escape valve, he had started the machinery. The horses had lunged forward under the powerful pressure of steam and Buttons who was standing with one foot on the hub guard of the fore wheel, and leaning forward for the purpose of opening the valve lost his hold and fell back upon the ground.

The steam team leaped forward at incredible speed.

I saw the danger and shouted:

"Brass, Brass, stop them!"

Brass was kneeling down spreading out a cloth on which to put our dinner, and Prof. Drydust was at his side.

"Be quick!" I yelled.

They both started to their feet in a moment, and Brass ran away after the runaways, while Prof. Drydust put his hands to his side, and with his old plug hat well on the back of his head, leaned backward and cried:

"Woa!"

Notwithstanding our position was a decidedly critical one the professor cut such a comical figure that I roared with laughter. I could not help it.

Brass was running at full speed, but what could he do against steam legs and muscles of steel?

"It's no use, Brass!" I called, for I saw he could not catch them.

I ran down to where Buttons lay, just where he had been thrown.

I raised him in my arms and asked:

"Are you hurt?"

There was no answer.

"Buttons — Buttons, can't you speak? Won't you speak?"

But Buttons was still silent.

I raised him higher and laid him on the grass.

Drydust, who had not as completely lost his presence of mind as I thought, now came up with a tin cup of water, which he dashed on the face of the insensible man.

He had only had the breath knocked out of his body, and really had no very severe injuries. In a few moments he was all right again.

"Well, he's alive, Mr. Reade; he's not dead!" cried Drydust.

I was now giving all my attention to the runaways. Like the wind they were speeding across the prairie, and I expected every moment to see them fall and kick themselves to pieces.

But they kept on.

Sometimes one horse struck an ant knoll, which caused it to halt a little, shoving the other ahead, and this caused the machine to turn a little.

I was glad of this, for I saw that they were liable soon to get turned apart, and might come toward us again or run around in a circle.

"It's no use," said Brass, returning to us and shaking his head ruefully; "the thing is running away, and there is not a man or beast able to keep up with or overtake it."

"It has on a full head of steam."

"Yes."

"Maybe it will get stuck again," said Professor Drydust.

"No danger of such good luck," said Brass, who was very angry at Buttons.

"It was all Buttons' fault," he growled.

"Never mind ——" I began.

"But I do mind."

"Never mind, I say. Buttons could not help it."

"I tell you he could. If Buttons had given the attention to the steam team he ought to have done he would not have allowed it to have on such a bursting head of steam as it did, and then an idiot who doesn't know the distance between an escape valve and a power valve ought to never be allowed to run an engine."

"No; hush. He was hurt, and is just coming to his senses," I said.

We could see the steam team like a speck flying over the prairie. Now it disappears, and we see it no more, but above the horizon a cloud of smoke tells us where it is.

"There, he's all right now. Ain't you all right, Mr. Buttons?" we heard the professor say.

"Yes."

"Well, Mr. Reade, what about your steam team?"

"It has run away," I said, pointing across the prairie, where, far in the distance, could be seen the column of smoke rising. "There is where the steam team disappeared," I said.

"Oh, I am so sorry," began Buttons.

"That won't do any good," said the professor, who seemed to have suddenly been changed into quite a different man.

"What are we to do?"

"Why, follow it up. Even a steam horse will run itself down after a while."

Brass, who was not a little astonished at the earnest manner of the professor, and who had not believed him capable of anything save writing in his journal, turned to the quaint old fellow and said:

"Had n't you better write it down in your journal, or did you leave that valuable document in the wagon."

The professor smiled and said:

"I never intrust so precious a document as my journal out of my sight."

"Don't you?"

"No, but we have not time now even to record the thoughts that breathe and words that burn within us. Let us after the wild fiery horses."

In a few moments we had shouldered our rifles and were hurrying away over the prairie.

"How far will it go before the steam gives out?" asked Brass.

"That is owing to circumstances."

"Well, about how far?"

"A hundred miles," I answered and we hurried on in our hopeless search after the lost steam team. Even the smoke had now disappeared.

CHAPTER XII. PROF. DRYDUST AS A MARKSMAN

"All hope is gone," sighed Buttons, who was in deep despair over the loss of the steam team.

"No, it's not," urged the professor.

"What hope have we?"

"A hundred hopes."

"But the steam team which ran away — disappeared over the hill and is now out of sight. Not even the smoke can be seen," sighed Buttons.

"There are a thousand ways it might stop."

"Tell me one."

"Stick in the mud."

"Yes."

"Upset."

"Not probable."

"Run against a tree."

"That's probable."

"It might be ditched."

"Yes."

"Or stick in a badger hole."

"That's true."

"Now, Mr. Buttons, I have suggested some of the thousand ways, but my breath is entirely too precious for me to give all of them. You must yourself think of the others."

"Well, I haven't time."

"Neither have I."

"It was lucky we put the guns out on the grass," said Brass.

"Yes, we may be run down by the banditti at any moment," I answered.

We traveled on for some time, eating the cold provisions which we had spread out for a luncheon, and we walked.

Prof. Drydust's long legs stood him in good need, as with his old battered hat on his head he took the lead.

"Mr. Reade," he suddenly said.

"Well, professor?"

"I see the smoke again."

"So do I," said Brass.

"And I," put in Buttons.

"She has stopped," added Brass.

I now raised my field glass and took a long and careful survey of the prairie.

Yes, there, far in the distance, could be seen the smoke of the vanished steam team.

"What do you believe about it, Mr. Reade?" asked the professor.

"It is not going away from us," I answered. "I fear it has upset, burst the boiler or ——"

"But, Mr. Reade," interrupted the professor, "if the boiler had burst, would there be any smoke?"

"There are two boilers," I answered. "One might explode and the other remain intact, in which case there might be smoke."

"Yes, so I see."

We traveled on for a few moments, when Brass said:

"It seems to me that that smoke is getting plainer."

"Seems to me that way," said Buttons.

"Yes, and nearer."

"Of course it's nearer, Brass, for we are going toward it."

"But we are not going rapid enough to make it get so much nearer ——"

"By jove!" cried Buttons, "she's coming this way."

"Oh, impossible," said Brass. "Coming this way, nonsense."

"But see for yourself; that smoke and steam is a great deal nearer than it was."

"Of course."

"Hold!" cried the professor. "I have a theory."

"What is it?" Brass asked.

"By some means the machine, and a wonderful machine it is, has got turned around, and is coming back on the back track."

"But that machine, when not guided by some hand, will go right ahead in one straight direction," answered Brass.

"Sure enough, such is the tendency if it has no outward opposition. But who can say what obstructions the steam team has met with in its mad career. Something may have turned it completely about and is sending it this way, or rather it is sending itself this way."

"There is no doubt," I now said, "but that it is coming back this way, though, what is the occasion of its coming, I can't pretend to say. It is possible that it might have got turned around."

On in its wild flight came the steam team. The smoke grew plainer, and at last a speck appeared on the plain.

It grew larger.

"That is what it is," said Brass. "It is the steam team, and no mistake."

"Let us board her," cried Buttons.

"Well, I doubt if the thing stops for us."

"Stop it."

"How?"

"Well ——"

Buttons raised his hand and scratched his head. When a man gets puzzled for an answer, he usually resorts to scratching his head, as though scratching his head would help him to think.

"Yes," I put in at this moment. "I want to ask you, Buttons, how you are going to stop it?"

"As it is coming this way, gentlemen," said Professor Drydust, "and as it will certainly be here before long, I see no occasion why we should go to meet it. Let us save our strength."

"He is wise," I answered. "Let us all sit down and wait."

We sat down.

"We won't have to wait long, I am thinking," cried Brass.

"No, she's coming at a two-forty rate," put in Buttons.

"Mr. Reade," said Professor Drydust, taking his journal from his capacious coat pocket, "did you save your diary?"

"Yes."

"Hadn't we better record the brilliant thoughts which flit through our minds."

"I am thinking we had as well."

"All right."

I had my diary in my pocket, for a wonder, for I usually keep it in a sheet iron box which is water-tight, so that in case it should get lost, it will be as dry and in as good condition fifty years hence as when first completed.

"It is coming fast," I heard Brass say.

I looked up, and now saw the steam team coming directly toward us.

"Buttons, did you ever hear the story of the phantom ship?" Brass asked.

"No."

"That thing puts me in mind of it."

"What is a phantom ship?"

"A ghost ship."

"Nonsense. I don't believe it."

"Neither do I, but it's a nice little story, anyway."

"Well, tell it."

"Oh, you don't want to hear it."

"Yes, I do."

"Said you didn't believe in ghosts."

"Maybe I don't, but that don't prevent me from wanting to hear something about them."

"Do you want to hear real bad?"

"Yes."

"Well, let me see. I'll tell you."

"Go ahead."

"The phantom ship was a ship called the Flying Dutchman, and the captain, who was a man somewhat addicted to hot punch and swearing, got mad at the wind one day because it wouldn't blow to suit him and carry his vessel around Cape of Good Hope; and it is said he used some pretty strong language. He talked in such strong terms and used such adjectives that the atmosphere grew blue, and was a very strong odor of brimstone ——"

"He was using brimstone talk, I guess."

"Well, the bards report that about the case."

"Go on. I don't want to interrupt you."

"Are you interested?"

"I am not quite asleep."

"Well the captain said he would go around the cape or weather the cape if he beat about those seas until the day of judgment."

"Did he do it."

"No."

"What did he do."

"Why, he had no sooner made that terrible oath than he saw in the skies great red letters which said, 'Doomed!' Then they all turned to ghosts."

"Who?"

"The captain and crew."

"Captain and crew."

"Yes, from that moment they were only shadows."

"And the ship?"

"It turned to a ghost too."

"Oh, nonsense."

"It's a fact."

"Why, before you commenced you said the story wasn't true."

"It's a fact, as a part of the story. According to the way the story is told, it turned to a shadow, and it's never seen except just before a storm. Then the wind whistles through its ghostly rigging, and whatever ship sees it sinks. It's always trying to round the cape but it never does."

"Why don't it?"

"It can't."

"Why can't it?"

"The punishment on captain and crew is that it must beat about those seas until the day of judgment."

"So she still beats?"

"Yes."

"Well, here comes our gallant bark."

The steam team was now so near we could hear the loud puffing and snorting of the horses of metal.

I rose to my feet and cried:

"Professor, put up your journal, here she comes."

The steam team thundered on like a pair of mad chargers.

"Woa, woa, woa!" yelled the professor waving his journal before them. "Head 'em off, stop 'em."

In his excitement the old fellow could hardly believe the metal horses were not alive and would not obey him to stop.

I laughed.

"You can't stop the machine!" I cried. "It's no use to try."

"Why, what ails the fools?"

"Steam is up."

He was directly before them, and for fear the steam team might run over him, I pulled him away, and the wonderful machine went thundering on.

Brass made a leap at the wagon as it passed, but failed to catch on.

The steam was going at a very rapid rate, but I was convinced from the manner in which it puffed along up the hill, that the steam was running low.

Brass, who had an excellent idea of machinery was of the same opinion.

"The steam is getting low," he said, "though she runs at a pretty good rate yet."

"Yes."

"How long can she keep that up?"

"I can't say."

"Not many hours?"

"No, but they may run many miles yet."

"Oh, for another mud hole!" sighed Buttons.

But the steam team disappeared in the south, and we followed on after it.

I was more hopeful now, for if it merely ran itself down without any accident, we could follow on its track and find it without any difficulty.

I took the lead and the others followed.

Going over the hill we saw before us three solitary trees standing on the plain. Those lone trees were like so many solitary sentinels.

Scarce had we discovered them ere we heard a yell on our left.

"Look!" cried Buttons.

"The James Boys!"

There were seven horsemen armed with rifles and revolvers, and all came galloping down toward us.

I saw at a glance that our only hope of escape lay in reaching cover of the lone trees.

"To the trees!" I shouted.

"Aye, aye!"

Away we flew.

Again did the professor's long legs stand him in good play.

He flew along at some distance ahead of me, and gaining the trees first sprang behind one of them.

Crack!

Crack!

A pair of rifles rang out in our rear.

Whiz!

Zip!

Bullets came frightfully close to my ears.

One struck the ground just at my side and sent the dust in my face.

"Shoot, Drydust. Why don't you shoot?" cried Brass.

"I am an accurate marksman," said Drydust, "and I never draw trigger until I am sure of my game."

"Well, here we are," said I as we all reached the lone trees and came to a halt.

Bang!

Whiz!

A bullet ripped off a piece of bark just above my head.

"Oh, how I wish I had my long-range rifle that we lost," I said.

"I do too," put in Brass.

Buttons was too badly blown to shoot accurately, but he was quick and nervous and would not wait.

He blazed away and missed.

"There, Buttons, you are a shot gone," said Brass.

"What's the odds?"

"Well, gentlemen, lead is plentiful, very plentiful," put in Professor Drydust, who was taking matters quite cool. "It is more plentiful than the reputation of a good marksman."

"So you are not going to play the part of a bad marksman, eh?" said Brass, who was examining his gun to assure himself it was all right.

"No. Now ye never saw me shoot, did you?"

"No."

"Well, when you do ——"

"What then?"

"When you do, you'll hear something drop."

"Ha, ha, ha!"

Brass laughed, and the old fellow compressed his lips and winked a humorous wink.

Brass blazed away and missed.

I fired and wounded a man, though the distance was too great yet to make shooting accurate.

"Now just watch some one do it scientifically," cried the professor.

He laid his gun against the side of a tree and took a deliberate aim.

For a few moments all was silence. Then his finger touched the trigger.

Crack!

Sharp and keen rang out the report. Then without shout or groan one of the horsemen fell limp and lifeless to the ground, and lay weltering in his blood.

"That's the way to do; now the next thing is to record it in my journal. Now, boys, let me give you a bit of advice, and that is always record all important incidents in your journal."

"Yes. It's a good idea," I answered. "Then you have them for future reference."

"Hello, they are going off," cried Brass.

"Got enough of this."

"So it seems."

"They are picking up the fellow the professor hit and are carrying him away."

"By the way he lies across the horse I guess he is done fur."

"So it seems."

"They are going."

"What does it mean?"

"It means they have got enough of my skill. They don't care to risk another shot from Prof. Drydust the marksman," and with a quiet chuckle the old man reloaded his rifle.

CHAPTER XIII. UNHINGED

"Well, that little event is over," said Brass; "suppose we be moving."

"No, it's not over," cried the professor.

"Not over."

"No."

"Why not? They are in full flight."

"Yes, but it is not over until the principal events have been recorded in my ——"

"Go ahead."

Brass threw himself on the ground at the foot of the tree very much like a man who is resigned to his fate.

The professor then began to carefully write down the chief incidents in the conflict.

When he had finished and I had also recorded them in my diary, I called all to come on.

"We'll be going now," I said.

"All right."

All day we traveled in the track of the steam team, and when night came had seen nothing of it. But we camped for the night, and after partaking of some cold provisions which we had had the foresight to put in our pockets, placed a guard, and the others went to sleep on the ground.

Buttons was the first guard.

We had scarce got to sleep, when he came to me and whispered:

"Wake up."

I am not a heavy sleeper, and in a moment my eyes were open.

"What is it?" I asked.

"I don't know."

"Is there danger?"

"I don't know."

"What did you wake me for?"

"I think it would be better for us if we were all awake."

"Well — wake the others — but no, hold ——"

"Well?"

"Have you seen anything?"

"Yes."

"A ghost?"

"I don't know."

"What was it like?"

"There was something moving through the grass, and it had eyes like fire."

Buttons had never been on the prairie before, for I had engaged him a raw New Yorker unaccustomed to prairie life.

"Well, Buttons, don't be alarmed."

"I want to shoot it."

"You may."

"Thought I'd better wake you first."

"That's all right."

"Hadn't I better wake the others?"

"Your gun will wake them. Where was it?"

He pointed off to the south where the ground was a little higher.

"Is your gun loaded?"

"Gun loaded! What a question, as if I did not always keep my gun loaded."

"Well, I didn't know."

"Well, I do."

Then he took two or three steps and sat down on the ground, his gun across his knees.

I threw on a few more buffalo chips to make the fire brighter, for I had an idea what it was that had alarmed him.[7] It blazed up and from the hill above I saw a something creeping, cautiously creeping along the ground.

It didn't make any noise and seemed like a shadow.

From the position I had I saw a pair of bright and shining orbs. They gleamed like living coals of fire and I knew what it was.

Slowly and cautiously it advanced.

Sometimes it dipped down below the grass so that it could not be seen at all.

At last I saw Buttons raise his rifle to his shoulder.

His eye glanced along the barrel a moment, and then —

Crack!

A flash of fire, ringing echoes, and something very like a whine was heard, then a spasmodic kicking in the grass.

"What — what — what's the matter?" roared Brass.

"What's up?" shouted the professor.

"Nothing is up. Something went down!" cried Buttons.

"What?"

"I don't know."

"Who fired that shot?"

"I did."

"At what?"

"I don't know."

"And hit it, too!" I cried.

Then I explained:

---

[7] *Buffalo chips*:   Buffalo chips were pieces of dried manure used as fuel for fires.

"It was a coyote — a prairie wolf — sneaking up here to steal some food."

This proved to be correct, for we found the wolf with a bullet through his brain.

"That's a wretched poor excuse for waking a fellow!" growled Brass.

"I had no wish to wake you," Buttons responded. "All I wanted was to shoot the wolf."

"Couldn't you do it without making so much noise?"

"Blame the gun, not me."

"Well, you've killed your coyote; now let us have no more disturbance."

"Go to sleep, all of you," said I. "I will remain on guard for two or three hours."

The night passed without any other adventure worthy of note.

Next morning, at early dawn, we were again on our journey after the steam team.

The trail was easily followed, for the grass and weeds were broken down, and the road cut up in a dozen places. I was now pretty confident that we should come on to the machine before nightfall.

We came to some houses where a small settlement had pushed its way out on the frontier, and found a plowed field across which the team had sped, tearing its way through a wire fence.

I saw a man gazing ruefully at the trial made by the passage of my great invention.

He was an ignorant frontier farmer, and when I asked:

"Did you see a steam team pass this way?" actually did not know to what I alluded.

"I saw suthin' strange," he growled, "but I guess it war old nick."

"What was it like?"

"A pair o' the biggest hosses, with silver on 'em, I ever seed. They snorted fire, un' jist look wot they done."

And he pointed to his shattered fence and newly hoed corn trampled down by the steam team.

"When did you see them?"

The old fellow looked up at the sun, and turned his eyes first in one direction and then the other. At last he said:

"Wall, guess it war wall on inter the shank o' the evenin', mister. Wife an' I hed jist sot down to eat our supper w'en I heerd a kind uv a screechin' an' jinglin' uv chains. Then I looked at wife, an' wife she jist looked at me. She turns kinder white, an' so did I. Wall, I got up an' went ter the winder an' looked out."

"'Great Scott!' sez I.

"'Wot's ther matter?' sez she.

"'It air Old Nick?'

"'Where?'

"'Comin' right across the prairie.'

"'Lem me see.'

"'Come ter the door.'

"Well, we both ran ter the door an' looked out.

"Blest ef thar didn't come them air fire snortin' horses and jist plunge whack through the fence as though them air wires what u'd turn a Texas steer war rotten twine. An' they went across my corn a-slingin' the dirt on young corn right an' left. They smashed out on t'other side an' went snortin' on. Thar war some dry grass t'other side an' it sot it all on fire, and sich a burnin' and sich a time yer never seed.

"Well, stranger, the thing, wotever it war, war gone," and he pointed on the trail, which was now plain enough to be seen.

We had got about all the information from him we could and pressed on.

Next we met a boy.

"Did you see horses of fire," I asked, "pulling a wagon?"

"Wall, I did."

"When?"

"Last night."

"Did they scare you?"

"Skeer me. Wall now mister, I'll say this ere much ter you. I'm not usually very easy skeered, yer know. I've fi't Injuns and all them things. Shot a painter once down on Painter crick, and fit more rattle snakes 'n ye could shake a stick at in er week, but I'm blamed if that air thing didn't jist take the starch out o' me."

"What did you do?" asked Brass.

"Do! goodness! why I jist ran and ran."

"Home?"

"Home, no; I didn't know whar I war goin' till I found myself away out on Injun Crick."

"You didn't?"

"Nary bit."

"Have you been home since?"

"No."

"Where are you going now?"

"Wall, I thort I'd jist sneak back hum, yer know, an' see if the blamed thing war gone."

We went on, and the boy, I suppose, went home.

From all we could learn, in answer to our inquiries, the Steam Team ran down into some low lands, and we would probably find it fast in the mud, or, what I most feared, in some creek.

Fortunately for the safety of my wonderful invention there were few creeks in this part of the country, and it was possible that it might run until the steam was exhausted before it would run into one.

It was nearly dusk when we came upon a party of farmers who were armed with rifles and pistols.

"Hold on thar, stranger," said one of them.

"Who are you?" I asked.

"I am the constable in this 'ere deestrict."

"Oh, are you?"

"Guess I am. I war elected the constable."

"What do you want with us, Mr. Constable?"

"Guess we're goin' to hev a scrimmage."

"A fight?"

"That's it."

"With whom?"

"Dun know 'em, stranger, but they air hoss-thieves."

I turned to Brass and whispered:

"Maybe it's the James Boys."

"I'll bet it is."

"I suppose they want us to help them."

"Yes."

Then I turned to the constable and said:

"Well, my friend, what do you want with us?"

"I want you ter help us."

"Capture the horse-thieves?"

"Captur' or kill 'em, it's erbout all ther same thing ter us. Ye look like fellers wot ain't afeered o' powder."

"We have all been in conflicts, and are not afraid of powder," I answered. "Where are your horse-thieves?"

"Down in the old stun' house."

"Where?"

"Down under the hill."

"How far away?"

"'Bout a mile."

And he pointed off to our left. I discovered by the course indicated by his finger that the house would not take us a great distance out of our way.

"Boys, we'll go," I said.

"All right," all assessed.

"Now how do you know they are in that old stone house?"

"Oh, bekase we've got 'em hemmed up thar."

"Have you?"

"Yes."

"How long since?"

"Since mornin'."

"And have you a guard around the house?"

"Yes."

"You are quite sure?"

"I know it."

"And they have not got out?"

"No, an' we can't git in. Ef it warn't fur ther big door, yer know, we mought git in, but we can't unhinge that."

"We'll agree to unhinge it for you."

"Good. Come on."

Then we hurried down to the hill.

"Now look out, you fellers wot don't know anything erbout it. D'yer see that ar place whar ther road turns down the hill an' yer kin see some white clay and dust?"

"Yes, we see it."

"Wall, sir, right thar's whar ye'll hev trouble."

"How?"

"They've got their guns sighted on it, an' when yer git thar they'll begin ter pour in hot shot."

"How'd we do to avoid their raking fire?"

"Rakin' fire — yas, that's what I call it. Why, run. 'Tain't twenty jumps, yer know, until yer out o' sight o' them in the bushes, an' ef a feller's quick ernuff he'll git out o' danger afore he kin be hit."

"Bear that in mind," said I to the men.

"Wait a moment, Mr. Reade, I deem it necessary to record this in my journal."

"Oh, wait until we get over," said Brass.

"Well now, Mr. Brass, that might all do very well if I ever got over, but perhaps I might never pass yon history spot."

Then with his pencil he wrote, speaking aloud as he did so:

"Very remarkable adventure — we are going to unhinge a door. We are going just now to jump over a spot where bullets are to rain."

"If we jump right lively it is reported that we may get over safely, but the chances of being killed just now are quite good. I don't know that I can write any more in this journal until I get over that bald spot of ground, and then I may not feel like it."

"Well, have you done?" I asked.

"I've finished," he said.

"Who will be first to make the jump?"

"I will," said Brass.

"Go in a hurry when you start."

"I will — good-bye!"

He turned about and shook hands with all of us, and then holding his rifle in his hand ran at full speed up the barren spot and made a tremendous leap. He touched the ground only to make another spring and was quickly over.

Crack!

Crack!

Two shots cut up the dust behind him.

It would be more dangerous for the next and the next.

So I called on a volunteer.

Prof. Drydust, with his face as solemn as ever, said he would try it.

Holding his rifle, he ran up the barren spot and leaped half way across at one bound.

Half a dozen shots rang out as he fled, and one of them chipped a corner off his beloved journal, which so enraged the professor that he vowed he would be revenged.

I went next and a bullet cut a small place on the stock of my rifle.

It was not long before we all got over, and beyond a small scratch on one of the farmer's shoulders no man was hurt.

"How many are in the house?" I asked.

There was a difference of opinion on that.

"I doubt thar air but five," the constable answered, "though some on 'em say thar air ten."

"Ten?"

"Yes."

"Well, how many men have you here?"

"Sixteen now'n all, besides you 'uns."

We four would make twenty.

I then informed the farmer that we had traveled all day without food, and he sent a boy off to the house for some food for us.

We sat down among some bushes and waited for the boy to bring us our food. It came at last, and we made a hearty meal.

By this time the sun had set, and it was growing quite dark.

"Now, boys, the first thing to do is to unhinge the door."

"Can it be done?" asked Brass.

"I think so."

"How?"

"Well, I am not prepared just yet to state how, but I am going to reconnoiter just as soon as it is a little darker."

"Don't do it, Frank," said Brass.

"Why?"

"It's too dangerous."

"Ha, ha, old boy, nothing is too dangerous when it comes to capturing the James Boys."

"Oh, yes, if you want to die, you know, you couldn't die in a better cause," said the professor. "Now," he added, a moment later, "that is a brilliant thought, and I will just record it in my journal."

And then he wrote it down.

As soon as it was quite dark I began crawling up to the door.

The house was up on the hillside, and the hillside was covered with bushes and trees and stones. Slowly and cautiously I wound my way serpent-like about among the bushes and stones and trees until I was at the front great porch and halted.

I could now hear the men inside talking.

I crawled up to the great door and began feeling in my pocket for a steel bit and small brace. Being an inventor and machinist as well, I have formed the habit of carrying some small tools in my pocket.

These tools which I carried were exceedingly hard and sharp.

I drove a small chisel in the door facing.

Then I took the gimlet and bored under the hinge. All this made some noise, it is true, but inside they never heard it, for they were talking and making no little noise.

As silently as was possible I scooped out some wood above and below the hinge.

Then I slipped the chisel under it and pushed up the wire which fastened the two hinges together until I had actually drawn it out.

The top hinge I served the same way.

It was risky business, it was true, for I had to stand almost against the door. Had they suspected I was outside there, they would have poured a volley on me.

But the dangerous and by all odds the most difficult task I had ever attempted, was accomplished. The door was unhinged, but stood yet in its place.

How was I to get it down?

CHAPTER XIV. THE STEAM TEAM FOUND

A lucky thought at last came to me. I had, among other things in my pocket, a screw with a ring on the end, and I bored the screw into the door. Then I fastened a strong bit of twine-cord to the ring and crawled away with the string, unwinding as I went.

Slowly and cautiously down the slope, and every moment exposed to a shot from within.

A voice speaking within the house now attracted my attention, and I came to a halt and listened.

"It won't be long," said one.

"Are they coming?"

"Yes."

"How do you know?"

"It's time."

"Time for them to come?"

"Yes."

"You can't set a time for Jesse James to come."

"Well, we can cut our way out just whenever we want to."

"They have reinforcements."

"I know it."

"I wonder who they are?"

"I don't know."

"It can't be that terrible Frank Reade?"

"Frank Reade! No; he travels around in a steam wagon."

"But did you hear about his steam team?"

"No — what of it?"

"It was seen running away."

"When?"

"Didn't Dick Little tell you of it?"

"No. Is Dick here?"

"Yes, down in the cellar making hand grenades."

"What did Dick say?"

"Dick said he saw a great smoke coming over the prairie yesterday, and soon saw it was the steam team. Then he rode his horse into a thicket to hide, for Frank Reade and his two detectives are dead shots."

"Yes, and that old long haired professor sends a bullet entirely too straight to be comfortable."

"He can."

"But go on, and tell us all about what he saw."

"Well, you see, the thicket in which Dick was hiding was a sort of upland, you know, and he could see down into the wagon as it passed under him."

"And did he?"

"Yes."

"What did he see?"

"There wasn't a soul in or about the steam team. It was just running away of its own accord."

Then I heard a prolonged whistle, and some one asked:

"What had become of all of them?"

"That no one knows," was the answer. "They had all gone. Dick is certain they were not in the steam wagon nor about it."

I waited to hear no more, but crept on down the hill, playing out the cord until I reached my companions under the hill.

"Frank, Frank, is it you?" asked Brass.

"Yes."

"All right?"

"I am all right," I answered.

"What have you done?"

"Unhinged the door," I answered. "Now get all the men ready for a charge, and I will pull it down, and we will go in on them at a charge."

"All right; we will have them ready in a few moments."

While Brass and Buttons, assisted by the constable, were getting the storming party ready for a charge, I heard in the distance the thunder of horses' feet.

"What does that mean?" I asked of Professor Drydust, who was at my side.

"It means horsemen are coming."

"Yes, and a few of them at that," I answered.

Then I remembered the conversation I had overheard in the house, and I knew now what it meant.

"It is the James Boys coming with reinforcements, professor," I said.

"Maybe."

Then there was no time for delay.

"Hurry up! everybody be ready to storm before reinforcements come!" I shouted. "Now, ready! One — two — three!"

I gave the cord a pull; with a crash the door fell. There was a volley, a rush, another volley, fire and smoke, groans and falling bodies.

Men scattered in every direction, seeking shelter from the rain of death about them. I tried to rally them and partly succeeded, when suddenly there burst on us, like a mighty avalanche, a body of horsemen.

Shooting right and left and yelling like demons.

Men were knocked down and trampled on by the horses. I saw in a moment that all was lost, and seizing Brass by the hand I ran with him back down the hill.

When I reached the foot of the hill I looked back. Some one was coming.

"Who comes there?" I cried.

"Me."

The voice was familiar, and I had no trouble in recognizing the tall, lank form of the professor, who was dragging after him a no less personage than Buttons.

"Is Buttons hurt?" I asked.

"No," he answered.

"Is Brass hurt?" asked Buttons.

"No," Brass answered.

"Well, boys, the jig is up, so far as storming that stone house is concerned," I said.

"Yes, and the jig is almost up with us," cried Buttons.

"I would suggest, Mr. Reade," said the professor, "that we are not as safe here as sheep in the fold."

"No, and we will get out of here just as soon as we can," I answered.

"The sooner the better," returned Brass.

"I would like to kill a dozen or two of those fellows before I go," said Buttons.

"Yes, but they might object," returned Brass.

"Very well put in," returned the professor.

"Suppose we put out," added Buttons.

We ran down the creek bank for a few rods and were about to cross on the other side, when on looking up I discovered a sentry sitting there on his horse with a Winchester rifle.

"It won't do," I whispered.

Then we ran through the thicket trying to make our way back up to the house.

We gained a grassy mound about a fourth of a mile from the stone house and here paused to look back. Ah, what a scene of desolation and destruction was behind us.

The constant crackling of fire-arms was accompanied by the yells of victims.

"Oh, how they are shooting down the poor wretches," sighed Brass.

"So they are," answered Buttons.

"It would have been our fate but for the wonderful forethought and sagacity of Mr. Reade," put in Professor Drydust. "Really I must devote a whole page of my journal to him."

"We are not out of the woods yet," I returned. "Let us go to the house back on the road."

"The little farm-house we passed?" asked Brass.

"Yes, it can't be far from here."

"No, it's not. The house is just over the hill."

We again started running over the hill, and had gained the crest, when Buttons cried:

"Stop!"

"What's the matter, Buttons?"

"Look there."

We all paused and gazed in the direction indicated by the finger of Buttons. It certainly was a sight well calculated to curdle the blood of the beholder. The bright flames were leaping up the sides of the house, and licking the roof.

"They are ahead of us, boys," I said.

"Yes."

"What'll we do?"

"There's but one way left."

"What is that?"

"Let us get down to the wheat field and crawl through it."

"All right, Frank, lead the way," answered Brass.

"We must all keep together."

"We know that."

"Come on, then."

Down the hill we descended, and hurried into the wheat field.
Then we began crawling through it.

The wheat was tall, and concealed us.

At last we were on the other side.

"Here is a hill," said Brass.

"So much the better," I answered.

"Why?"

"On the other side we will be out of sight of them."

"That's so."

"Then let's get on the other side of it just as quickly as possible."

We were not long in getting over the hill into the ravine below, and
were quite sure we had not been discovered by any of the James Boys.

"Oh, if we only had the steam team," sighed Brass, "we could
then defy them."

"Yes, but we haven't got it," I answered.

"And they haven't got it," put in the professor. "That's a mite of
consolation to our poor aching hearts."

"They wouldn't have sense enough to run it, even if they had it,"
said Brass.

"I don't know. Jesse James was making a good stagger at it," returned Buttons.

"He ran it in the mud."

"That was because he did not know how to turn on the electric
light, and was not able to see his way without it," I returned.

"Suppose he would learn the next time."

"Yes, he would. We all profit by our mistakes," I answered.

"Now that's a good word — an excellent word. I will just write
that down in my journal ——"

"Not now," returned Brass.

"Well, then, just as soon as an occasion presents itself I will."

We had not gone far before I discovered a dark object sweeping
over the prairie. My eyes are very keen, and I can see an object a long
distance away, even in the night.

"I see something," I said.

"What is it?" asked the professor.

"Yes, your eyes are keen as a hawk's. Look again, Frank, and tell
us what it is that you see."

I had my field glass, but unfortunately it was not a night glass, and
did me but very little good.

"I can't make it out just now," I answered, "but we will soon
know."

"Why?"

"It is coming this way, and coming very rapidly."

"Can't you guess what it is?"

"I would hardly dare venture a guess," I answered, "but if I was to do so, I would say that it was a man on horseback."

"A man on horseback?"

"Yes."

"Then, boys, let's lay for him."

"Hold on, Brass."

"Why hold on, are there more?"

"No, but ——"

"Then what harm can it be in shooting down one of the James Boys' banditti?"

"None, if it was one."

"Isn't it one?"

"We don't exactly know yet," I answered.

"We'll find out soon, for I am itching to leave one of them on the grass."

"It will be too dark to tell, so let us lay low and capture him."

This plan was agreed upon by all, and we consequently lay down in the grass until the horseman came up.

He was riding from an opposite direction from the stone house, but I believed, nevertheless, that he was one of the James Boys' gang.

He came up until he was almost on us, and then I sprang up from the grass and caught his bridle rein.

In a moment the others were all around him and had dragged him from the saddle.

But he proved to be only a belated farmer, and he was frightened almost out of his wits by our sudden assault.

From him we learned that a wonderful team of horses had run into a wood not over twenty miles away, and that they had not been seen to come out.

He said the horses snorted fire and drew a wide, heavy wagon after them.

"Do you think the team is in that wood yet?" I asked.

"I believe so."

"It's ours," said Brass.

"Yes."

"Yer team?" cried the amazed farmer. "Do yer hosses snort fire like that?"

"Yes."

"Great gosh! Please lem me go hum, won't yer?"

We let him go and set out to find the steam team.

Next morning at sunrise we came upon the forest and then we pursued our way into it, following the track until we came upon the steam team.

CHAPTER XV. UP AND AWAY

The steam team was about half way in the forest.

It had by some marvelous coincidence or circumstance run against no tree or stone that would injure it, and was whole.

Not a thing was broken. Not a cog had slipped.

"Well, this is luck!" cried Brass. "How did it stop?"

"It just ran down — that was all," I answered. "Steam gave out."

"Nothing broke?" asked Buttons.

"Not a thing."

"How lucky."

"Well, yes."

"A most remarkable incident. I shall have to make a note of that in ——"

"Hurry out — now gather up some dry wood and let's have a fire," I interrupted.

"All right — all right," cried Brass.

"There is no time for anything until we get fire up."

Prof. Drydust saw the point, and putting up his journal with a sigh, busied himself with the others in gathering up dry sticks to start the fires. I examined the furnaces.

Our coal supply was good yet, but the water was about all exhausted, and while Brass gathered some kindling wood, I set Drydust and Buttons to carrying water from a spring to fill the boilers and water tank.

Fortunately the spring was not a great distance away.

I was busy arranging everything, rubbing and polishing the machinery so that there might not be a particle of rust or dirt on any of it. More machinery rusts out than ever wears out.

In fact, if engines were only taken care of, and run as they should be, a good one would last ten generations. This has always been my theory.

Buttons and Drydust were gone for water, Brass was in the wood picking up dry sticks here and there and I was alone at the machine, when I heard a footstep near.

Supposing that it was either Brass or Buttons, I went on with my rubbing and polishing without looking up.

"Hello!" said a strange voice at my side.

I started up, and was amazed to find a stranger standing within four paces of me.

"How are you?" he said, with a smile.

The stranger was a man about forty-five, with a pleasant face and dark beard.

He looked more like a business man than a farmer, though he wore the broad-brimmed hat and heavy boots of the cow-boy.

In his hand he carried the short quirt used by cattlemen.

"Who are you?" I asked.

"I am Bill Parker. Have you ever heard of me?"

"No."

"Well, I am."

"Do you live about here?"

"My cattle ranch is not over ten miles away."

"Where are you going?"

I did not know what else to say, and in fact I did not at all like the appearance of the stranger, though I could not say that there was anything about him to warrant my suspicions.

"I was just out hunting some strays from my herd."

"Yes, sir."

"A fine machine there."

"It is."

"Yours?"

"Yes."

"You must be Mr. Frank Reade?"

"I am."

"I am glad to meet a man who has made such a wonderful reputation as an inventor. Why, sir, your name is known far and near. Wherever I go I hear Frank Reade, the inventor, spoken of, and if I pick up a newspaper I read in it only accounts of Frank Reade."

I blushed modestly, and bowed under the compliment which he had paid me.

"And so this is the wonderful steam team?"

"Yes."

"I heard you were in the West."

"I have been here some time, sir."

"Ah, may I ask on what mission you are on now?"

"That is a secret, sir."

"Oh, is it? May I look at the team?"

"Certainly."

"Thank you."

I did not like the appearance of the fellow one bit, and I dared not say so. I followed him around, as he looked at the team, explained every part of it to him, and took care that he touched no part of it.

"Confound those fellows, why don't they come on?" I mentally asked myself, as I kept one eye on my invention and one on the man who had paid me this unexpected visit.

"Where have I seen him before?" I thought. His features or his voice were not altogether new to me. I had heard him speak at some other time, or I had seen his face.

This was strange, exceedingly strange, yet I could not call to mind where I had seen or heard him.

"I say, Mr. Reade, I've heard it hinted what your business in Missouri and Kansas was."

"Have you?"

"Yes."

"What are those hints?"

"People hint that you have come to Missouri for the purpose of hunting down the James Boys."

"Is that the rumor?"

"Yes."

"You will be kind enough to inform the people that they do not know what they are talking about."

"Do you say that is not your mission?"

"I do not say anything about it."

"Silence is an affirmative."

"Not always."

I never felt an eye pierce me so like a knife as did his. I met his gaze, but it tried my nerves and self-possession about as completely as they were ever tried before.

"You don't say so," he said somewhat impudently.

"I do, and furthermore, Mr. Bill Parker, if such is your name, the matter is none of your business."

His face flushed a moment, and he answered:

"I don't know now, I don't know. I will see about that."

"Will you?"

"Yes."

"Now, as you have made so free as to question into and even doubt my motives, I want to tell you something."

"What?"

"I doubt your name being Bill Parker, and you are no cattle king."

His face paled and flushed alternately, and his breath came hard and quick. After a moment of silence, he said:

"If I am not Bill Parker, who am I?"

"Jesse James himself, for all I know."

"What! you know me?"

I started back, now dumfounded with amazement, for now I knew him.

"You are Jesse James."

His hand went toward his belt, and he snatched a pistol. My last moment had well nigh come, I knew, but with a mad desperation I hurled the wrench I carried in my hand at him and knocked the pistol out of his hand.

With a wild yell he sprang at me.

I struck him with my fist.

Though he partially parried the blow with his left arm, it somewhat stunned him. He gave me an ugly rap as he staggered and then we clenched.

"Frank Reade!" he hissed, through his teeth, as we struggled up and down for the mastery, "I will kill you!"

"I have no doubt you would, you miserable wretch, if you could, but I intend choking you to death."

He made several frantic efforts to get a weapon, but as rapidly as he drew one I managed to kick it out of his hand.

We dealt each other furious blows, that were raising great welts on our heads, but as yet neither had got in a good square knock down.

For several moments we had fought and clung to each other with wonderful tenacity, and had tumbled and scuffled all over the ground. At last, from sheer exhaustion, we paused, and clinging to each other so that neither could get an advantage over the other, we gazed in each other's eyes.

"Frank Reade, I am going to kill you!" he hissed, hoarse with rage and exhaustion.

"If you can."

"I can."

"Why don't they come?" I mentally asked myself a hundred times in that brief struggle. Surely Brass, or Buttons, or Drydust should come to my relief.

Any of them were within call and all I would have to do would be to raise my voice and call them. But I was out of breath, and besides my whole attention was given to Jesse James.

If I made any call, or my whole mind and energies were for a moment diverted from him, I felt sure that he would in some way get the advantage of me.

So all through the conflict, which had been most terrible, I had been as silent as the tomb.

"Jesse James, you will have to surrender to me."

"Ha, ha, ha," laughed the burly ruffian. "You are not enough for a breakfast scuffle for me."

"I know I am not as large as you are."

"No, nor as strong."

"Perhaps not, but you know the battle is not always for the strong nor the race for the swift."

"I'll be strong and swift enough for you. I will teach you not to come meddling with my affairs, you infernal interloper."

"You thief."

"Thief I am, but not a meddler."

"I meddle only when in the protection of society."

It was my design to delay the struggle as long as possible, for if I could only hold out a few moments longer, I was quite sure that some one of my three companions would come to my aid.

"What's society to you away back there in New York?" growled Jesse James. "What do you care for us here?"

"Everything."

"It's a lie. The railroads and express companies care, and you come because they hire you to come. That's all there is to it."

I made no answer, and Jesse, after waiting for a few moments, added:

"Yes, it's blood money that brings you here. It's blood money — you are hired to kill me just as men are hired to shoot wolves," and his face grew blacker and he gnashed his teeth more fiercely as he glared at me.

"Jesse James, you are not a suitable judge of such matters."

"I am not?"

"No."

"I have been hounded and hunted year after year for the last fifteen years. Every man's hand is against me. Everybody hates me and I hate everybody for hating me."

"Who began this?"

"Who began it?" he cried, hoarse with rage.

"Yes, who began it but you? Had you never offended any law, no law's minions would ever have been on your trail."

"Well, there is no need to delay this longer," he cried. "Your companions will be returning soon and then I will be at a disadvantage. There will be two to one; let us get to it at once. Let us fight to the death, for I tell you that I am going to kill you. Yes, kill you sure, ha, ha, ha!"

With demoniacal fury he hurled himself on me. He had a decided advantage in weight and strength, but I was most agile of the two, though Jesse James was as active as an acrobat.

I managed to keep him at bay for a few moments, and but for an unforeseen event I would have conquered him.

But at the most interesting moment of the proceedings I accidentally stepped on the wrench which lay on the ground at my feet, and my foot slipped.

I had been clutching at his throat, and it was telling on his strength.

Jesse's face grew black and his knees were tottering. Only a few seconds longer and I would have triumphed over him, but at this unlucky moment, just on the verge of victory, so slight an incident as the slipping of my foot a single inch caused me to lose my hold on his throat, and in a second he had recovered.

Whack!

A blow staggered me.

He had turned the tables now, and had me by the throat, and oh, how wildly, how furiously I struggled to regain the advantage I had over him, but in vain.

"I'll kill you now — I'll kill you!" hissed Jesse James.

Everything swam about me, and my eyes grew dim, and I knew that consciousness was slipping away. At this moment I heard the voices of some of my companions talking as they returned. They were too far away for me to catch a word they said, and they were walking very slowly, or seemed to be walking slowly, and talking in an unconcerned way, which led me to believe they either did not know or care anything of what became of me. They had no idea that I was at that moment engaged in a terrible life and death struggle with the bandit.

I could hear Jesse chuckling when he found me sinking.

I clung to both his arms to prevent his using a pistol, but my strength was going so fast that I too knew it would soon be over.

My senses were slipping away.

They were coming, but would not be in time to save me.

Then suddenly I heard something which sounded very much like the explosion of a bomb, and I felt a sense of great relief.

"Frank, Frank," said Buttons, holding me up. "Are you dead?"

I opened my eyes and found Buttons bending over me, while Professor Drydust was chasing a melody.

"Frank, it was a close rub."

"Yes, very."

"But you are all right?"

"Yes. Buttons?"

"What?"

"Where is Brass?"

"Hasn't come with the wood yet."

"Well, you are the slowest fellows I ever saw."

"No, we are not."

"I have had what to me seemed a seven years' fight with Jesse James."

"Jesse James?"

"Yes, Jesse James."

"That man wasn't Jesse James."

"He was."

"Great guns. I would have shot him dead in his tracks if I had known that."

"Did you have a chance?"

"Could have done it easily, old boy. I came right up behind him while you and he were fighting, and I struck him a whack that broke the charm, and sent him flying away through the woods. Had I known it was Jesse James I would have pulled out my revolver and shot him dead in his tracks."

"Buttons?"

"Yes."

"You have lost the golden opportunity of your life."

"I guess I have."

Brass came up a few moments later with the wood.

He was amazed to learn that Jesse James had been here during his absence.

"Well, if that fellow is lurking around here we can't get away any too soon," he said.

"Fire up, Brass. Put in the water, Buttons. Where is Drydust?"

"Here I am."

"Did you catch up with him?"

"No, verily, he runs as if he was all springs."

In a few moments we had the steam up.

By this time I was fully recovered, and cried:

"All get in."

"Aye aye," and the three faithful fellows climbed into the wagon, and I took my place on the seat.

"Now, away!"

"Up and away," cried Brass, as the Steam Team began moving through the wood.

CHAPTER XVI. STORMING THE STONE HOUSE

"Is it all right?" asked Brass.

"Yes."

"Nothing broken?"

"No."

"Nothing lost?"

"Not a thing, as I have yet discovered."

"Try the headlights and see if they are all O. K. We don't want to run into another such a scrape as we did that night."

"We didn't run into it, Brass," put in Buttons, "we only got on the edge of it."

"Hello!"

"What's the matter, Brass?" I asked.

"Buttons is recovering his wit. The sign is a good one."

"Rather."

"There is a better sign," said Buttons.

"What?"

"Recovering the Steam Team."

"Yes, we will all agree with you in that."

"Well, Frank, where are you going now?" asked Brass, as we ran out of the wood and emerged on the prairie.

"I don't know exactly," I answered. "I want to find Jesse James now."

"You found him a bit ago."

"Yes — but under unfavorable circumstances."

"Frank, you have a black eye."

I had been conscious all the while of one of my eyes growing larger.

Jesse had struck me several blows on the face, and they were nearly all telling, as well as swelling, blows. My chief satisfaction was that I had given him a few.

I stopped the steam team and turning about raised the lid of a small box which I used as a medicine chest.

"What are you going to do?" asked Brass.

"I need some repairs," I answered. "I am going to be my own surgeon."

"Oh, by the way, Mr. Reade, I have just finished recording the principal events in my journal, and I wish to be your surgeon. I — I am skilled in the craft."

"I don't need a surgeon very bad. They are only scratches," I answered.

But he would insist on binding up my wounds, and I found him quite handy with the scissors and sticking plaster. He succeeded very well, and proved to be quite an efficient surgeon.

When he had got my wounds all bound up he said:

"Now, sir, I'll warrant that you will be able for duty. Let me advise you, however, before we proceed to any new adventures to have in your diary everything recorded that has transpired, for there have been some very remarkable adventures this day."

"We had better discuss what we are to do," said I.

"Well, we will. Now, gentlemen, the meeting is called to order, and we are open for business. What is the pleasure of this meeting?" said Professor Drydust.

"To capture or kill the James Boys," answered Brass.

"Do you put that as a motion?"

"Yes."

"A second to it."

"We all second it and it's carried without a vote," interrupted Buttons.

I laughed at the coolness and drollness of my companions, and said:

"It's all well enough, my friends, to make motions and pass resolutions about the James Boys, but they don't care a fig for all the resolutions we may pass."

"No."

"What will we do? What plan will we adopt to capture them?" I asked.

"Let's see. Better find them the first thing," put in Buttons.

"The humor of that fellow is just getting to be excruciating," put in Brass.

For a few moments a silence reigned over the group.

At last it was broken by myself.

"Boys," I said, "I believe we had as well go back to the stone house."

"Do you think so?"

"Yes."

"Why?"

"I don't know, but I have an impression that the James Boys are lingering about it yet."

"Well, we were there," growled Prof. Drydust, "and we couldn't effect anything."

"We didn't have that," said I.

"What?"

I pointed to the cannon.

"Oh, yes. I see now."

"That's the very thing," said Brass. "We can blow the old stone house down."

"We'll batter down the walls," put in Buttons.

"I wish we were there now."

"I don't care to be there unless the James Boys are there. Then we can just play about on the prairie and send balls into the old house at long range. They may charge on us. If they do we can retreat."

"Yes, faster than their horses can come."

"Let's go at once."

"Well, Mr. Reade, what assurance have we that we will find the James Boys there when we get there?" asked Professor Drydust.

"None."

"Then why go?"

"What assurance have we of finding them anywhere we may go?" I asked.

"None."

"Well, then, we might as well go there as anywhere."

"That's so."

"Then let's go."

"Hold on a moment, let us consider."

"What?"

"How did Jesse James come here, and what was his object in doing so?"

"Well, that's worthy of considering."

"Did you see his horse?" asked Buttons.

"I did not," I answered.

"I did."

"Did you, professor?"

"I did."

"Where — when?"

"Well, you know where we came upon you fighting for life?"

"Yes — well, no, I don't know much about it; fact is, I have a faint recollection of almost going under about that time."

"Well, I guess you did," said Drydust. "You had a decidedly gone under look."

"Did I?"

"Yes."

"Well, go ahead."

"Well, Mr. Buttons here struck one terrific blow, a part of which landed on Jesse's head and sent him spinning away twenty steps and made him drop his knife, which he was going to stick in you. Then he ran ——"

"Oh, yes, we know all about that. Come down to the horse," said I, impatiently.

"There wasn't any need of going back to the birth of Adam, anyway," growled Brass.

"Well, I chased him, and —— But hold on, I've got it all written down in my journal. Now let me turn to it and read it to you in order to avoid all mistakes. Ah, I tell you, my friends, there is nothing like keeping a journal. Keep a journal and record every event that ——"

"Please spare us a lecture, professor," I said, "Read or tell us about the horse."

"Here, I've got it. This is the very page." And he read:

"And when I had chased him three hundred and twenty-two steps — by exact measurement, for being a very accurate man I counted them off myself — I came in sight of a horse. It was a large, black horse, and the stranger so pugilistically inclined was mounting.

"'Hold,' said I. 'Hold, will you. Stop until I know your name.'

"But he kept on mounting until he mounted.

"'Leave your card if you haven't time to give your name,' was my next suggestion, all of which was scrupulously unheeded; and wheeling his black horse about, the stranger of pugilistic tendencies galloped away, disappearing from sight over the brow of a most romantically situated hill, down which the tawny blue vault of heaven kissed the verdant earth ——"

"Hold!" yelled Brass, "that will do! We know now that Jesse James had Siroc with him, mounted him and rode away. That was enough, professor. You might have spared us the tawny blue vault of heaven kissing the verdant earth."

The professor gazed at him with an injured air and slowly put up his journal.

"Well, boys, we had as well go back to the old stone house anyway," said I. "It can't be any worse."

"No."

"Then here goes."

I drew the reins opening the valves and away we went.

The steam horses galloped over the prairie as merrily as if they were real living steeds and out for exercise.

I could see a long distance ahead of me and no one was in sight.

The sun went down with us a few miles from the river on which the stone house was situated.

"Let us camp until morning," said Brass.

"The moon will rise at midnight," I answered, "and we will take advantage of the moonlight to get near the enemy."

"That's a good thought, and as all good thoughts are liable to be lost, I will record it in my journal."

We had scarcely got settled in camp before two horsemen rode up to us. On inquiring as to who they were, they answered that they were farmers.

"Do you live near Wolf Branch?" I asked.

"Yes."

"Where?"

"Just a little beyond it."

"Well, what are ther people doing?"

"They are all hidin' or lookin' for the James Boys. Where are you fellers goin'?" he asked.

"We are on our way to New York."

"Goin' all the way in that air machine?"

"Yes."

"How long will it take yer?"

"Four or five days."

"Will ye git there so soon?"

"I mean if we were to run right through. We may have to stop on the way."

"Yes, I see."

They hung about for an hour and went off.

"I don't like those fellows," said Brass to me.

"Nor I."

"You didn't fool 'em one bit."

"No, I know I didn't."

"They know just as well as can be that we are going to the old stone house and there is no need of trying to deceive them."

"I guess not. Well, we'll double our guard, Brass, and as soon as the moon is well up we'll be moving."

Buttons and the professor remained on duty until a short time after midnight, and then Brass and I were awakened.

The low fires in the boilers were replenished, and we soon had the engines going.

Buttons and the professor lay down to sleep and we started the team.

At early dawn we came upon a man who looked as if he had slept for a year in a straw pile.

His face had a wild, haggard look about it, and it was some time before we recognized him. He was the constable who had summoned us to aid in capturing the James Boys in the old stone house.

"Where are you going?" I asked, as soon as I recognized him.

"Runnin' away."

"From whom?"

"The James Boys!"

"The James Boys! Where are they?" I asked.

"Back at the old stun house. They air all there."

"What have they been doing?"

"Killin', burnin' and stealin'," he answered. "Oh, sir, ye ort ter see that country. What a country it is! All tore up everywhere. Houses burnt, country ruined, people running away."

"What is about the old stone house that they stay there?"

"What! didn't ye never hear erbout it?"

"About what?"

"The gold."

"No."

"Wall, then, yer can't understand anything at all about it, kin yer?"

"I guess not."

"I'll tell yer."

"Do so. Please lighten my understanding."

"All right, here goes. Durin' the war — or ruther before the war, a rich old feller came out here, yer know, from France ur some sich a place and he was as rich as all git out.

"They say't he had barrels o' money, and when Quantrell's band found it out, they determined to come and take his gold. He found it out and buried his gold somewhar, every cent on it, and no un knew but hisself an' son.

"Then Quantrell came, and with him came Jesse and Frank James, who war guerrıllas then, and guerrıllas war just as bad as the robbers air now. Wall, they killed the old man and his hull family, and no one war ever able ter find the gold, so it's not been found to this day."

"Is that what Jesse and Frank James are here for now?"

"Yes. They came and took up their abode in the old house, and air diggin' the old yard all ter pieces ter find it."

"Have they succeeded?"

"Guess not. They air thar yit."

"When did you see them last?"

"Jist at daylight. I am runnin' away from 'em now."

"Are you?"

"Yes."

"Come and go back with us."

"And be killed? Oh, no!"

"But you will not be killed."

"Jesse and Frank both hate me and would like ter shoot me."

"They can't catch us. This is my steam team."

"Oh, air it? Is it what ran through here bustin' down fences and houses t'other day? Some thort it war Old Nick broke loose and snortin' erround. Some said it must be a comet got loose."

"It was only my steam team got loose. Come, get in now, and we'll be going."

He climbed in the wagon and we set off.

As we went flying over the ridge, the roof of the stone house could be seen.

We could see a score of men about it.

Some were standing, some sitting and some lying on the ground. Some held horses and some were seated in their saddles.

There was no question about their being the James Boys.

"Brass — Buttons!"

"Yes."

"Yes," both answered.

"Get the cannon ready."

"All right."

"We are going to storm the old stone house."

"Hurrah for that!"

I brought the steam team about with the rear of the wagon toward the house, and began slowly backing.

Figure 27. Illustration of the Steam Team from *Frank Reade.* "I brought the steam team about with the rear of the wagon toward the house, and began slowly backing. 'They see us now.' 'Ay, they do, and by jingo they are all getting on their feet. We have them all round now.'" Courtesy of The Library of Congress.

"They see us now."

"Ay, they do, and by jingo they are all getting on their feet. We have them all round now."

"We'll rouse them a little better soon."

"Are you ready, Brass?"

"Yes."

"Let them have it."

"Send the bullet at the crowd?" he asked.

"No — the house."

"All right."

He sighted a moment and cried:

"Ready — fire!"

Boom!

The shot scarce caused the wagon to tremble, so firmly was it made.

The ball crashed in at a window, and the banditti hurried out.

Twenty-five or thirty were now gathered about the house.

We re-loaded and fired again.

We were too far away for their rifles to reach us, and continued slowly backing and storming the old stone house with two-pound balls.

CHAPTER XVII. DELUSION

One shot struck the tall brick chimney of the stone house near the roof with such force as to send the bricks flying in every direction.

"That's a fine shot," I cried, watching the effect the flying bricks had on the crowd below.

"Remarkable, very remarkable, indeed," said the professor. "I will just record that in my journal."

"No need of that," said Brass.

But the old fellow was writing away.

"I say, mister, yer going ter hev all ye kin do," cried the constable.

"Why?"

"Don't yer see it's boots and saddles?" answered the constable, who had been a cavalry man during the late war.

"You mean they are mounting?"

"That's just it."

"Well, we all know just what that means. So, boys, look out."

"You look out for us," answered Brass.

"I will. Can't you give the old house another shot?"

"Better aim at them."

"No, the house."

"But there isn't a soul in the house."

"Aim at the house anyway," said I.

And they leveled the cannon and once more trained it on the house and fired.

Boom went the shot and I could see that a hole was knocked right through the wall of the old building.

Jesse James could be seen mounted on Siroc giving orders to his men.

Although I could not hear a word he uttered I could read his designs and knew exactly what he was saying. He was directing his men to deploy in a long line, to go in two parties to try to flank us.

All were to ride slowly until they were almost upon us and then to charge at full speed right upon us and not stop until they had brought us down, no matter how many of their men fell.

All this was as clear as daylight to me and I resolved not to be caught in the net Mr. Jesse James was so carefully spreading for me.

"Boys, load all the guns," said I.

"They are loaded," said Brass.

"And revolvers, too?"

"Yes."

"Put every one at the back part of the wagon."

"Why, Frank, you are not going to fight at close quarters, are you?"

"No."

"Then why small arms?"

"Keep them by in case we should need them."

"All right."

"I say, Mr. Reade," said the constable.

"What?"

"It's one o' two things now."

"Explain yourself."

"It's run or fight."

"I think it will be both."

"Frank, don't let 'em get too close," said Brass.

"Trust everything to me, Brass."

"Of course."

"Here they come."

"They ride slow, though."

"Very slow."

"How many are they, Brass?"

"I counted twenty-six."

"Very nearly the full band," said I.

"I guess, Mister Reade, 'at they've got a few fellers more in that air gang o' thieves in the band," said the constable.

"Do you mean recruits?"

"Yes."

"Frank!"

"Well?"

"How is the steam?"

"There is an abundance."

"How far would it run us?"

"Two hundred miles at a rapid race."

"Good."

"Don't have any fears. The steam will do its duty."

"See how deliberately they come," put in Buttons, looking back at the banditti, who were riding slowly forward, on their horses, at a walk

"They are taking their time, that is certain."

Professor Drydust had been sitting in the bottom of the wagon-bed gazing back at the approaching enemy, but saying nothing. At last he said:

"Gentlemen, I am losing too much time. I should be even now recording the very brilliant thoughts which go, like so many race horses, coursing through my brain. Aye, Mr. Brass, if I could only convert you into keeping a journal, I would be delighted."

"Well, it wouldn't delight me at all."

"Why?"

"I don't want nothing to do with keeping journals. We'll have enough to-day to do to keep out of the way of the James Boys."

"Brass."

"Well, sir?"

"You might try another shot."

"At the house?"

"No, the men. You have punished the old house enough for a while."

"All right."

"Is the cannon loaded?"

"It is."

"Train it, and as soon as you fire, we'll start up."

He trained the gun a moment and cried:

"Fire!"

Buttons pulled the cord.

"Boom!"

The smoke for a second hid them from view, but when it cleared away we saw a man and horse struggling down on the ground.

I now started the team.

Jesse saw that their only show was to press right on at once, and I heard him shout:

"Charge."

"Here they come," cried Brass.

"Get your guns."

"We are running slow yet."

"We'll go faster soon."

The steam team was not going faster than a swift trot, and the banditti were coming at full speed.

I knew that in a moment I could outstrip them, for what could horses of flesh and blood do against horses of iron and steel?

"Get your guns," I cried.

"We have got them."

"Be ready to give them a broadside when I give the word."

"What? You ain't going to stop?"

"Yes."

"Why?"

"You can shoot better at a standstill."

"Yes, but see they are separating. They intend to flank us."

"They'll be very sick of that."

Jesse at the head of one squad came up at a run, and Frank with the other half on our right.

"Fire!"

A volley of shots answered the command, and I was quite sure I saw some men dropping from their saddles as leaves falling in autumn.

Frank James and the other half of the band were coming down on our right like the wind.

I saw that there was no time for dallying, and quickly clapped on all the steam necessary, and we flew away amid a shower of balls.

"Down! down!" I shouted, on seeing that we were going to be exposed to a raking fire from the enemy.

Immediately everybody was down in the bottom of the wagon. I managed the team and kept below the seat.

The ring of bullets against the iron rim and whizzing of leaden messengers above us made us quite glad that we were out of reach of them.

When we were beyond reach of their shots I once more rose to the seat and looked back at the banditti.

They had halted and were gathered together in a group.

"Now is your time, Brass," I said.

"Why, what to do?"

"While they are thus grouped let us have a shot from your long tom."

"All right. Come, Buttons."

"The gun is not loaded, is it?"

"No."

"Well, load it."

They drew out from the iron chest beneath the heavy gun a package of ammunition, and proceeded to reload the cannon.

In a few moments they had it ready and sent a shot booming right into the group.

Such scattering and dismay can better be imagined than described.

I saw Jesse and Frank James trying hard to rally the flying outlaws, but all in vain. They were disheartened.

In a moment I had the steam team again in motion, and coming around went thundering after them.

They fled.

We ran near enough to wound two, but they got away.

In a few moments the prairie was cleared of the wretches, and we again turned toward the old stone house.

"Look out, Frank!" cried Brass. "Go carefully, for they are not all gone away from there yet."

"How do you know?" I asked.

"I can see them."

"Where?"

"One just now poked his head out of the window."

"All right. If they are going to make that a fort, we'll soon make them sick of it."

We ran up to within a quarter of a mile of the house and then I brought the steam team around, stern to the old building, and backed up a few rods nearer to the top of the hill.

"What are you going to do, Frank?" asked Brass.

"We'll lay siege."

"Cannonade them?"

"That's it. Go in now."

"All right."

They swabbed the little cannon, put in a cast iron ball, and sent it crashing into the stone wall.

We had both leaden and iron balls for our cannon, but against a stone wall the iron bullets would be most effective.

For the next half hour we continued to blaze away at the old stone house. A corner fell out, and we poured in a few leaden shots into the breach thus made.

"They can't stand it. See, they are coming out."

Half a dozen men, among whom we had little trouble in making out Frank and Jesse James, come out of the house last and went to their horses.

We had by this time backed up to the edge of the bluff, and reloading the cannon sent a ball whizzing at them, killing a horse.

Then we opened with small arms, and hit one fellow in the jaw.

"Frank Reade," roared Jesse James, shaking his fist at me, "I will be even with you yet for this."

Great as the distance was, his strong, terrible voice could be distinctly heard by every one of us.

The wind set toward us, however, which no doubt accounted for us hearing it.

He wheeled about with his men at his heels and galloped away.

We fired another shot at them, but by this time they were so far away that the ball only dug up the dirt behind them.

"Well, what now, Frank?" asked Brass.

"We'll go down to the old stone house."

"All right."

We had to run up the ridge almost two miles before we found a place where we could descend with the team.

Here we found a gentle slope, and the road wound down the hill so as to make the descent or ascent quite easy.

"I don't suppose, Mr. Reade, that there is a possibility of us getting down in a place here where we can't get out."

"Hardly possible," I answered. "I can drive the steam team almost anywhere that any kind of a team can go."

We ran down to the house and halted. The steam team was left with a guard of two, under some oaks, while the others began skirmishing about, so as to ascertain if the James Boys and their gang were gone.

Not one could be found, either dead or living.

Two dead horses, one below the house, and one on the hill above, were all we could find that gave any proof that they had ever been there.

We found some blood among the stones and debris in the house, but nothing to show whether we had killed any of their gang.

"I wonder what they did with their dead?" asked Brass.

"Guess they didn't have any."

"If they didn't I was one of the most deluded mortals that ever walked this mundane earth," said Brass.

"I guess it was a delusion," said Buttons. "I believe you trained the artillery."

"Yes."

"Well, that accounts for it."

"For what?"

"There being no dead."

"Why, you needn't boast, I can beat you shooting the very best day you ever saw in your life."

"Never mind boasting of your marksmanship, either of you," I put in.

"Yes, you had better keep a journal," added the professor, who was squatted under a tree, easily engaged in writing in his journal.

Brass smiled.

"Now let's look about the place a little and see what they have been doing," said I.

We left the team and all save the old professor engaged in going about the premises to see what they had been doing.

Never was Gardner's Island so completely dug to pieces by men seeking after the buried treasures of Captain Kidd than were the grounds about the old stone house.[8]

Holes of every depth were found, and the place had the appearance of a newly plowed field.

They had at last given over finding the treasure, and, as we afterward learned, were on the point of leaving the stone house when we came upon them.

"They didn't find it," said Brass.

"I guess not," put in Buttons. "I don't see why they didn't, though, for it seems to me as if every available part of the ground has been dug up."

"D'yer see that air tree?" asked the constable, pointing to an old oak.

"Yes."

"Wall, on that air limb which comes out a bit war hung the old man an' boy."

"Where were they buried?"

"At foot of it fust, but some o' their friends came an' dug 'em up."

"Perhaps they dug up the treasure, too?" I said.

"No, didn't."

"How do you know?"

"They said they didn't."

"That may have been done to throw you all off your guard."

"Why?"

"They might have had some fears at the time of going across the country with the treasure."

"Wall, I dun know erbout that, but them fellers war putty clusly watched, lemme tell yer, and ef they tuk erway any treasure nobody ever knowed it."

---

[8] *Gardner's Island*:   £ 14,000 of Captain Kidd's treasure was discovered on Gardiner's Island (just east of Long Island) after William Kidd was hanged in London, May 23, 1701, for piracy and murder.

"What would have been done if it had been known they had the treasure?"

"Boys talked o' a divvy."

"Perhaps that was the reason they smuggled it out of the country."

"But they didn't do no diggin'."

"Didn't do any digging?"

"No."

"Not a bit?"

"None, except ter dig up them bodies, an' come across ther country ter the depot."

We had been half an hour searching about among the ruins of the old house, and Professor Drydust had been sitting busily engaged in writing his journal.

"I want to find that treasure," said Brass.

"So do I," put in Buttons.

"Well, you can't," I answered.

"We haven't tried," said Brass. "Now, my theory about such things is just this. It will be much more easy to find it now than it was before."

"Why?"

"Simply because they have dug over more than one-half of the ground, and all we'll have to do will be to finish up the work."

"Well, boys, I don't believe we can spare the time."

"Why, there is a big treasure here. It would be worth much more to us than all the reward any three railroads will ever pay us for capturing the James Boys."

"But the treasure is not sure."

"Capturing the James Boys don't seem a dead certainty."

"I know that, but you forget ——"

"Forget what?"

"We are not working on a contingency. We are paid a salary."

"Well, yes, I guess that is certain," said Brass.

"Quite certain."

"But the treasure would be more."

"Of course it would, but while we are wasting our time here we are neglecting the very business on which we came, and doing an injustice to our employers."

Brass looked puzzled for a few moments, and then said:

"Well, well, I don't want to do that, but you might give us an hour or two. Five minutes more work might lay bare the treasure."

"Go ahead," said I with a laugh. "I want an hour to write up my diary, so I will give you that length of time to dig in the dirt."

"Look here, Frank ——"

"Well, what will I see?"

"Me."

"Oh, you are no pretty object."

"But I want to give you some advice."

"What?"

"Don't lose your head over your diary as that old fellow has over his journal," and he gave a significant nod toward the professor.

I laughed, and said I thought there was really no danger.

"I don't know. It breaks out bad sometimes, you know."

I went away and left them. Brass, Buttons and the constable had gathered up some tools, some picks and shovels, and went to work digging away in the places which the others had failed to touch.

"Well, professor, how are you getting along with your journal?" I asked.

"Very well," he answered. "I have recorded almost everything. True, a few brilliant thoughts which were born of danger and excitement have escaped me, but they are few. Most of them have been recorded in my journal."

"I think I will bring up my diary while those fellows are digging."

"For what are they digging, Mr. Reade?"

"For the gold and treasure."

"What gold and treasure?"

"The gold and treasure of the rich old man who was murdered about here during the war by Quantrell."

"What, digging for that treasure?"

"Yes."

"It's a delusion."

"What?"

"A delusion, sir. I repeat and reiterate most forcibly and emphatically, sir, that the whole thing is a delusion."

"A delusion?"

"Yes, a delusion and a snare. The treasure is a delusion."

CHAPTER XVIII. CONFUSION

I had been so long led to believe that there had been a buried treasure there about that house that I was hard to convince there was not.

"Professor?" said I.

"Yes, sir."

"Do you know anything of this affair?"

"All about it."

"Were you a relative?"

"No."

"A friend of the deceased?"

"No."

"Then how did you learn?"

"By means I do not care to reveal," he answered.

"What became of the treasure?"

The thin, cadaverous face brightened into a smile as he said:

"There never was any."

"What!"

"Never was any."

"Never any treasure?"

"No."

"But why was he killed?"

"It was reported that the old man had run off from his country to defraud his creditors, and that he had brought millions of dollars with him."

"But it wasn't so. They had only money enough to build that big stone house. It was all they had."

"And why were they killed for their treasure, which you say they never had?"

"They were killed because it was believed by all that they had an abundance of treasure. It was all a false report," said the professor.

"Well, there is no need of having those fellows wasting their energies!"

"Not the least, it's not there."

"Did you ever investigate the matter?"

"Yes."

"Thoroughly?"

"Thoroughly, quite thoroughly."

"And you are fully convinced?"

"Yes."

"Well, if you are fully convinced on the matter, we will give up any further thought of buried gold. But they had as well continue to amuse themselves as not while we are finishing our diaries."

"Ah, yes, it won't hurt them very badly."

"Not at all."

"Well, I want to ask you a few questions, professor, in regard to Mr. Allen and his daughter."

"All right — you haven't forgot them amid all we have gone through?"

"No."

"And you will make an attempt to rescue her?"

"Yes."

"All right."

"How far are we from there?"

"Well, it's — it must be — let me see — I don't know for certain, but it must be seventy-five miles from here there."

"So far?"

"Yes."

"Well, we can make it in a day easily enough."

"But, Mr. Reade, that's a very delicate mission you are going on, do you know it?"

"Yes."

"How are you going to manage it?"

"Don't know."

"Any plans?"

"Only a general outline."

"What is it?"

"It is that we must, at all hazards, warn them."

"Yes, you are right."

"And we must save the girl."

"Yes."

"Will they believe us?"

"I don't know."

"How is Allen?"

"Rich."

"But his disposition?"

"Quick-tempered."

"Reasonable?"

"Yes."

"We can manage him — but the girl?"

"She is pretty."

"Very?"

"Yes."

"Reasonable?"

"Quite a sensible girl."

"Then I think we will have but little trouble in convincing her," I said.

Then I proceeded to write out my dairy and completed everything in a few moments.

"Now I'll go and tell the boys to come on."

"All right, Mr. Reade. I will just get in the wagon and finish my journal."

He went to the wagon while I went to where they were still hard at work.

"Boys," I said.

"Yes," said Brass.

"We'll be going now. You have been playing here long enough."

Brass leaned on his spade and wiped the perspiration from his face.

"We haven't found it yet, Frank," he said.

"You haven't and you won't."

"Oh, yes; we've only got a little more digging to do, and we'll have the entire yard dug up."

"Then you won't find it."

"Oh, yes, we're bound to."

"No."

"It's here somewhere."

"No, it's not."

"Why? Has it been taken away?"

"It never was here," I answered.

"What do you mean, Frank?"

"Just what I say. The treasure which you are seeking was never buried here."

"Where was it buried?"

"Nowhere."

"Then where is it?"

"There never was any treasure. The old man whom Quantrell murdered for his money never had any money."

"Oh, how do you know that?"

"The professor there knows all about it. He has investigated everything, and assures me there was not a cent of money. The old fellow was insolvent, and came out to these backwoods to avoid his creditors, so you see it is utterly useless for you to dig any longer."

"I guess you are right if that's the state of affairs," and Brass threw down the shovel in disgust.

I called Buttons and told him the same thing.

Buttons looked aghast as he dropped his pick, and turning to Brass, said:

"Brass, you're a fool."

"I guess so," said Brass.

"And I am too," added Buttons.

They then gave up the idea of any further search for the treasure, and decided to go to the wagon.

"Guess I won't go any furder," said the constable. "Reckon the James Boys won't come er botherin' around here any more, an' I'll jist gather up some o' ther boys wot's erround here, and make things hot for 'em if they come back. Seems ter me that most of our fellers hev run off, an' there ain't much chance o' getting 'em back soon. This hull country seems ter hev gone ter the dogs, that are all thar is erbout it."

We left the poor fellow in his almost ruined country and took our departure.

"Now, professor, you must be our pilot."

"I'll steer you through," said the professor.

We were speeding over the prairie, along a beautiful road, when Brass suddenly climbed over into the seat at my side.

"Frank, I want to talk with you," he said, in a low tone. In fact he spoke so low that I could scarcely hear him, as the wagon and steam horses made considerable noise.

"Well, what do you want to talk about?"

"Him."

A nod backward accompanied his answer.

"You mean the professor?"

"Yes."

"What about him?"

"I've been studying him a long time, and I've finally come to the conclusion that he isn't what he pretends to be."

"That he is not a professor?"

"No."

"Then you think he is deceiving us?"

"It's just possible, Frank."

"Well, he is a shrewd fellow."

"Yes, and brave."

"Well, what do you think he is, Brass?"

He answered my question by asking another.

"Did you ever see his journal?"

"No."

"Well, I haven't, either."

"But we have heard him read extracts."

"Maybe they were what was in the journal and maybe they were not."

"That might all be true. I admit that the professor has never sub-mitted his journal to me, as much as he has read it, and as much as he has talked about it."

"Well, there is something mysterious about him. He shoots too well and has too good a knowledge of criminals and things to be a professor."

"I have thought that."

"Did you ever think?"

"Think what?"

"That he might be fooling us."

"Yes."

"That he might be a ——"

I didn't catch the last word, so I said:

"Please repeat? I didn't get that last word."

"That he might be a detective."

"Well, I have thought almost everything possible to think about him."

"And you have thought that, of course?"

"Yes."

"Well, I wish I only knew it for certain."

"We will have to wait and let time determine," I answered. "He is a shrewd one, and we must not let him outwit us. That wonderful journal of his may after all be an elaborate note-book."

"Just what I thought."

"And now, Brass?"

"Well?"

"There is another thing about this to consider."

"What is that?"

"After all, he may be deceiving us about the treasure."

"That is just what I had thought."

"It may be that there is a buried treasure there, and he is employed to find it. And it may be that he has been all these years looking for it."

"Yes, that is true."

"Well, now, go back and say nothing that will lead him to suspect us."

"I won't."

"And say nothing to Buttons."

"I won't, but Buttons has his suspicions, I'll warrant."

"I hope he won't give the professor reason to suppose he has any suspicions."

"No, he won't."

And then Brass went back, leaving me alone.

We had not run many miles ere night came on us.

We reached a small village shortly after dark, and almost ran the people out of the town as we came puffing and rolling into the village.

"Great goodness, it's a horse on fire," screamed one woman.

"Look at that now. Ef thar hain't a wagon pulled by steam horses."

"Oh, it must be the chariot o' fire come fur ter carry me up," cried one pious old woman.

A darky got frightened and ran away down an Indian creek, where he plunged in and almost drowned himself.

But we managed after a bit to convince them that we were only common mortals of this earth, and that we would do them no harm.

When they were sure we were only ordinary mortals, they became more pacified and gathered in great crowds about us to inspect our wonderful machine, which they pronounced marvelous.

We fared well.

Everything we wanted within their power was given us without money and without price.

"Ain't you'ns the fellers wot chased the James Boys out o' the country?" said one old man.

"Yes."

"Wall, we thort so. We've been up in arms here for three or four days on account o' 'em. Blame 'em. They burnt Micasia and robbed so many towns that we're a leetle mite skittish about 'em."

"We will drive them away if they come while we are here. They won't dare tackle the steam team," I asserted.

"That's all right, an' now yer kin hev anything yer want here thet we'ns hev got."

We remained until morning and once more set out on our journey.

The roads in this part of the country, the extreme eastern part of Kansas, are very fine.

Trees grew along them in abundance, and there were beautiful farms. I found more civilization here than I had expected.

Only a few years before I had come to this part of the country on a tour of adventure and found it a wilderness, but now it was nearly all cultivated.

The plowman in the field paused and leaned on his plow as he watched the strange phenomenon speeding along the road at the speed of a lightning express. Then next the housewife stood in the door looking at us as she shaded her eyes with her hands. The watch dog barked until overcome by fright and ran under the house, where he continued to growl and bark most furiously.

We passed on, and at evening were in sight of a great farm and an immense cattle ranch.

It was large. Exceedingly large. There were hundreds of acres in the farm, and thousands in the cattle ranch or range, as it is sometimes called.

Great fields of wild grass had been fenced off, on which cattle were grazing in herds of hundreds and thousands.

The large farm-house or home residence of the owner and proprietor of this great range stood upon a hill. It was a large substantial building of stone.

The Kansas gray stone is of a very fine quality and I was struck with the beauty of the house.

"Who lives there?" I asked of Prof. Drydust when we were a mile or so away.

"Mr. Allen."

"Mr. Robert Allen?"

"Yes, sir, Bob Allen."

"The father of Louisa Allen?"

"Yes, sir."

"There is where we are going?" I asked.

I thought I saw a shade of confusion come over the face of Prof. Drydust.

"Yes, yes — but to be sure, let me examine my journal."

He turned the leaves of his journal, and his pale, thin, hatchet-face seemed alternately to flush and pale as though he were at a loss what to do.

"Yes — ahem — here it is. This is the place where we were to find the Mr. Allen."

"Yes, and it was his daughter ——"

"Yes, yes, yes — his daughter."

"She was the young lady whom you used to teach?"

"Ah, yes, yes — let me see. Let me look at my journal. Now I really do believe I made a mistake — yes, sir, a very serious mistake."

"What?"

"I was not her preceptor."

"Not her preceptor?"

"No."

"But I thought you said you were?"

"I — I was mistaken. I was at the house several times, but not in the capacity of a preceptor."

"What then?"

"Let me consult my journal."

The professor was growing more and more confused every moment.

I could not understand the cause of his confusion, and I glanced at Brass, who winked.

Brass' wink seemed to say:

"It's just as I suspected."

And I thought it was all just as I suspected.

"Well, well, well, what a singular affair. Why, I have called there in a dozen different vocations, once as a book-agent."

"It's a wonder they did not kill you," growled Brass.

"Ah, well, they do not treat book-agents here like they do in New York. You see they are not quite so plentiful."

"No, I suppose not. What capacity did you call in next?" I asked.

"Oh, I have been there in various capacities, one way and another. I have sold goods there — a peddler, in other words. I was there seeking a job as herder."

"A likely looking cowboy you would make, I am thinking," Brass growled.

I gave Brass a look that silenced him.

"Then I went there as a farm-hand, as a surveyor, local preacher, music teacher, hunting stray cattle, peddling lightning rods, and carrying the mail. In fact, Mr. Reade, I have traveled over this country in so many different capacities that I find it almost impossible for me to attempt to enumerate all of them."

"Then they know you?"

"The people?"

"The people at the house."

"Yes."

"Well, you must introduce us."

"Yes."

"Now we must get on the right side of the farmer and cattle king, and the first stroke of policy will be completed," said I.

"Yes."

But I fancied that all through I could see that the professor was covered with confusion.

Two cowboys in the employ of Mr. Allen came galloping up toward us, and seeing the steam team, drew rein.

We came on cautiously, for we noticed that they carried pistols in their belts, and looked very much as if they would as soon shoot the strange animal as not.

Their ponies snorted and turned aside, bucking as only a professional mustang can buck.

We rode leisurely on, paying no heed whatever to them.

At last one of them yelled:

"Say, what air you, anyway?"

We all laughed at his odd manner, but Buttons, whose ready wit came to his aid, answered:

"We are a little Kansas cyclone killer."

"I believe ye, yes, I believe ye."

As he evinced a disposition to be talkative, I checked the steam team, and allowed him to spur his frightened pony alongside.

"Wall, stranger, yer got the slickest way o' travelin' I've seed in a long time."

"Rather convenient."

"Whar yer goin'?"

"To Mr. Allen's."

"Ah, the boss?"

"Do you work for Mr. Allen?"

"Yes."

"Is he at home?"

"Yes."

"Well, we want to see him."

"Guess ye'll find him at the house."

"Much obliged to you; good-day, boys — good-day."

"Good-bye ter yer, and I guess ye'll stun ther boss."

We ran down the road to the great old house, which, in that country, was a palace in elegance.

The cattle king came to the front gate to see what it was.

"Are you Mr. Allen?" I asked, alighting.

"Yes, sir."

"We have come to see you."

"Whom have I the pleasure of seeing?"

"You, perhaps, know Professor Drydust?"

"No, I don't."

By this time Professor Drydust, very ill at ease and covered with confusion, had alighted.

"Oh! ah, perhaps you remember me," he began.

"No, I don't," answered Mr. Allen.

"I was at your house."

"When?"

"Several times."

"I must a been away."

"I was a book agent."

Mr. Allen fixed his sharp, keen eyes on the confused professor for a moment and said:

"I don't remember you."

"I — I — didn't I teach your daughter?"

"No."

"Your daughter, Miss Louisa?"

"Never."

"Well, then I helped the cowboys. No, no! I sold goods here. Hang it, I was here in some capacity, and I know it," cried the confused professor.

"Perhaps you was, but I have no recollection in the matter," said Mr. Allen politely.

CHAPTER XIX. MISCONSTRUCTION

Seeing that the professor would get no further with his bungling manner, I now interposed.

"Mr. Allen, I am Frank Reade, of New York, the inventor."

"Yes, sir, I've heard of you."

"I have come to see you on a matter of great concern to yourself. Perhaps it is best, however, that I defer explanation until we are alone."

The face of the cattle king grew a little pale, and he said:

"Very well; come in, gentlemen. Won't you run your steam team inside the barn, or do you prefer to leave it there?"

I told Brass to run it in the barn, and he did so, while I entered the house with Mr. Allen.

"If you wish it, we will go to my room right at once," said Mr. Allen, "and we'll talk on the matter about which you wished to converse."

"Very well, Mr. Allen."

He conducted me up to his room, and when we were alone he said:

"Now you can proceed, for we are alone."

"Well, Mr. Allen, to begin with, I am in the West on a strange mission, one attended with great danger. It is nothing more or less than the capture of the James Boys."

"It is a mission full of danger, I have no doubt. I never saw one of the gang that I know of, but they are terrible."

"I beg your pardon, Mr. Allen, for unless I very much mistake you have seen one."

"I."

"Yes you."

"When, where and who?"

"I can't give you the time. The place was at your own house, and the person whom you saw was the chief of the banditti, Jesse James himself."

"Impossible."

"It's true."

"How do you know?"

"Wait and I will tell you. I came west with my steam team, for as I have stated, the purpose of capturing the James Boys. One day they captured the steam team, when we were but a few rods away from it, and I ran and caught the wagon without their seeing me. I clung on the underneath side of the wagon and while there I heard a conversation between Jesse James and his brother Frank. It was to this purport. Jesse James had gone under an assumed name — I am not quite certain of the name he gave though I know it was assumed — been a frequent visitor at your house, was quite intimate with your daughter and was engaged to her."

"Why — why, there must be some mistake. You have misconstrued what he said."

"I have not. You have misconstrued your daughter's lover."

"Has she one?"

"Yes."

"What is his name?"

"Charley Howard."

"Where does he live?"

"At Independence, Missouri."

"Well, do you know he lives there?"

"Yes."

"How do you know it?"

"He says so."

"No one else?"

"No."

"Mr. Allen, I will wager my life that he is a fraud. He is Jesse James himself."

"Well, I — I — I can't believe it."

"Will you do me the favor to send for your daughter? This is a delicate matter, I know, but I think it best to come to an understanding."

"All right."

Mr. Allen was very reasonable, after all, and under the circumstances quite easy to manage. More easily managed than I had at first expected.

In a few moments he brought Miss Louisa Allen, who was a beautiful brunette, of about eighteen, with large dark eyes and a beautiful face and form.

"This is Mr. Frank Reade, Louisa, and he has come with a strange story."

"What is it?" she asked, growing pale.

I felt that it was almost cruel to tell her, but there was no other help for it, and I began and told her all.

"It must be Charley, papa," she said.

"Do you know him? Do you know any of his people, where he lives, and what he does for a living?"

"Only what he says."

"What does he say?"

"Sometimes he is in Kansas City and sometimes in Independence. But he takes long journeys somewhere, I don't know where."

"My daughter," said the cattle king, "I greatly fear that it is true."

"I do, too, papa, and I will give him his walking papers when he comes again."

"When do you expect him?" I asked.

"To-morrow evening."

"Please don't do that, Miss Allen," said I. "Let us be near. Let us see him, and if you have no objection we will take him in custody."

"I will. I will be glad to aid you to bring such a scoundrel as Jesse James to justice."

"Louisa," said her father.

"Well?"

"Do you care nothing for him?"

"Nothing, father. Now that he has deceived me I hate him."

"Let me explain, Miss Allen," I said.

"Proceed, sir."

"Jesse James is a very bad, bold, desperate man, and we may have to resort to desperate means in effecting his arrest."

"Do it then."

"Are you very brave?"

"I am."

"Will you dare risk it?"

"Arrest him right in my presence, and I will know then that it is done," she answered.

My plans were quickly arranged. I determined to send the steam team away, and consequently when we had had supper I called all aboard, and we ran away a few miles, leaving our wonderful machine in charge of Buttons at the ranch of a cattleman whom Mr. Allen assured us we could trust.

Then the professor, Brass and I returned after dark on foot, and reached the house of Mr. Allen about an hour before daylight.

The cattle king was waiting for us, and admitted us himself.

"None of the servants know a thing about it. No one but myself and daughter will know that you are here."

"Brass, that girl is brave," I whispered when we were alone.

"She has the grit, and she is as pretty as a picture," he answered.

"You are right; she is very pretty."

"Well, we've got nothing to do but wait here," said the professor when we had reached our room, "until night. We might employ our time on our journals."

I smiled, and Brass winked. As soon as he had an opportunity he took me aside, and in a whisper said:

"He don't write as much as he pretends in that journal."

"He is a great mystery to me, Brass."

"To me, too."

"I believe more than ever that he is a detective."

"Did you ever see his journal?"

"No."

"Or ask him to let you see it?"

"No."

"Do so."

"Why?"

"I'll wager a dinner at Delmonico's when we go back that he won't let you."

"I believe you, but I'll try."

So I approached the professor and said:

"Professor Drydust, I would like to look over your journal."

He raised his eyes and gave me an astonished glance, while a confused flush swept over his face.

After a moment he said:

"I — I beg pardon, really I — but you see, you must know that you will place a wrong construction upon it. Don't you know."

"I think not."

"I can't show you my journal just yet. Wait until I have it filled out, then there can be no misconstruction."

I said no more. I was now more than ever convinced that we had put a misconstruction on him.

We slept most of the day, and when evening came were conducted to the rear parlor, where, through a crack in the folding doors, we could see any one in the parlor.

At sundown Mr. Allen reported to us a horseman coming, whom he avowed to be none other than Mr. Charley Howard himself.

I told the boys to be patient, keep cool, and we would soon have the great bandit king, Jesse James, in our power.

Miss Allen was in the parlor to receive him, and the Delilah who betrayed Samson was not more lovely than she.

We heard the tramp of horse's feet, and knew that Siroc was at the front gate.

A quick, firm step told that Jesse James was approaching the house.

I told Brass to seize the knob of the door on his right, and Drydust to take the knob of the door on his left, and at a given signal from me they were to jerk the door open, and I was to leap out on Jesse James, demanding his surrender, they, of course, to follow.

It was a well-laid plan, and with any other man would have been a success. But Jesse James possessed ears unusually keen, and when I gave the signal to throw open the doors he heard me.

One door caught for a single fatal instant, and the bandit was on his feet, a pistol in each hand.

"You have betrayed me, girl?" he roared, and one cocked revolver was aimed at Miss Allen's breast and the other at me.

"Hold!" he shouted. "A single step, a single movement, and I will send the girl and you, Frank Reade, to eternity."

I would not have hesitated a single moment on my own account, but how dared I endanger the life of Miss Allen?

"Stop!" I cried.

"I see through your game," said Jesse James. "This is a very cleverly-laid trap to catch me, but you haven't done it yet. You know I will never be taken alive; I have sworn to that. Why should I be taken alive to be hanged — yes, slowly hanged — choked to death by slow torture? I — I would much prefer to die. Now if you will let me go out unharmed from the house I will spare you and the girl, for though I hate a traitoress as she has proved, I can't kill her."

"Don't anybody hesitate on my account," said Louisa.

"Brave girl," said Jesse. "I honor you."

At this moment Drydust, evidently seeing an opportunity, with a yell made a leap at Jesse.

"Bang!"

A cloud of smoke.

Crash! window-sash, glass and all went as the bandit leaped through it.

"Who is hit?" cried I, as I heard a groan. The smoke lay too thick for me to make out who had been struck down.

But in a moment it cleared away.

"Brass, are you hurt?"

"No."

"Go quick — shoot him down!"

Brass ran out, and a few moments later there came the rapid discharge of fire-arms.

The whole family, servants and all, came rushing in the parlor. I ran to Miss Allen and asked:

"Are you hurt?"

"No," she answered. "Look at him."

It was Prof. Drydust. He was sinking, and before I could catch him had fallen to the floor.

Brass came in to report that Jesse had mounted Siroc and made good his escape.

"What! is Drydust hit?" he cried, seeing me holding the dying man in my arms.

"Yes," he gasped, "I am killed. In a few minutes I'll be a dead man. But I want to say something."

"What? Speak quick, for you haven't many minutes."

"You have put a misconstruction on me."

"I know it," I said. "You are not Prof. Drydust."

"No."

"You are a detective?"

"I am not."

"What are you?"

"The only relative of the men who were hanged by Quantrell at the stone house," he gasped.

His breath came hard, and I knew the struggle would soon be over.

CHAPTER XX. CONCLUSION

"Lay him on the sofa," said Mr. Allen. "He will be better there."
Brass and I took him up gently and laid him down upon the sofa.

As soon as we had laid him down the servant brought the wounded man some water, and Mr. Allen got him a glass of wine. Then he revived a little, and I asked:

"Why are you here, if you are a relative of that man?"

"Seeking the treasure."

"The treasure?"

"Yes."

"I thought you said there was none."

"But there was — there is, and I feared your men would find it. The key to the treasure was in sight when we were there. They had turned it out of the ground, and I, fearing that some of you might discover it, determined to get you all away before you saw the key. I have spent years here looking for that treasure. I knew there was a key. A letter came to me before they were killed, telling me all, and — and I tried to find it. Just as the key was found I — I — well, it makes no difference now."

His breath came quick, and his sentences thick and voice almost inarticulate.

At last he said:

"It's all over now. I give and bequeath the treasure to Frank Reade ——"

"Where is it? How can I find it?" I asked.

He turned his dying eyes, already grown glassy, upon me, and in a tone of voice that was sinking, scarce above a whisper, gasped:

"Read my journal."

He was gone. Dead.

For a long time we stood gazing on the mysterious man, who, despite his odd ways, was brave and generous at the end.

"Well, it's all over," said Mr. Allen, at last.

I now bent over him and took from his pocket his journal, in which he had kept a record of his past events.

It was not a regular diary, as daily incidents were not recorded, but more like a note-book of events, and without dates.

"Can you find what he meant by the key?" asked Brass.

"There must be an explanation in there somewhere?"

"No doubt."

"Well, read it through. That treasure will be our fortune."

"You don't feel, after all, that you are such a fool, do you, Brass?"

"No, and I knew it all the time."

I continued turning page after page, reading strangely disconnected accounts of the professor, who had been living a peculiar sort of life. His journal was by no means an autobiography. It was merely notes, something like this:

"I went in sight of the stone house to-day, and looked all over it. I went down and examined the ground, but I could not find the keystone."

Another page:

"I have almost a notion to go to digging anyway, although I was cautioned not to try it until the stone had been found."

A little further and I read:

"This is the twelfth year I have looked for that keystone and not been able to find it."

"Then we are as far at sea as he was," said Brass, when I had read this.

"No, we are not."

"Why are we not?"

"He told me the keystone was found, and said, read the journal."

"Who found the keystone?"

"I don't know. He said it had been turned up, and by reading the journal and the cypher in it it might readily be found."

"Well, read it."

I turned page after page as quickly as I could, and at last said:

"Here it is."

"The cypher?"

"No; that's on the first page."

"What, then?"

"About the keystone."

"Who found it?"

"A man named Brass."

"What?" roared Brass.

"Listen and I will read."

And I read:

"Now, having driven the James Boys away, Frank Reade approached the old stone house which he had been storming. I trembled when I saw that the James Boys had been digging all over the yard for the treasure. Then Brass and Buttons, with the constable, decided to finish digging up the yard. Though I never believed the treasure was buried in the yard, I never knew to a certainty, and consequently I fear it might be. I was anxious to get away, but dared not evince my anxiety. While sitting at the root of a tree I saw the fellow named Brass throw out a stone. It was a stone with a smooth surface on which were some letters cut.

"He threw it right at the foot of the blasted oak and without pretending to see it I saw that the stone had the key cut on it for finding the treasure which my uncle had buried.

"I trembled now for fear it would be discovered. But it was not. They did not see that strange letters and numbers were on the stone, Mr. Reade came to me and said they were hunting for the treasure and I told him there was no treasure. He believed me and we went away. As soon as they are gone I will go back, find the stone and dig my uncle's millions and go to Paris."

This then was the great secret. We buried the professor, as we still called him, and bade Mr. Allen adieu. He thanked us and offered to reward us, but we accepted nothing.

When we went to Buttons and told him all, he was amazed. We set out at once for the stone house and found the keystone. It read S. W. cor. — house — 42 rods — and 6 links to a stone. Dig 8 ft. We had a surveyor's chain and measured the distance, dug three feet and unearthed three millions of dollars in gold, which I will divide with my companions. We have decided to set out to-night for New York.

EDITOR'S NOTE: The Diary ends with the above and we have the information of Frank Reade's further attempt to capture the James Boys. We learned that he and two detectives, Buttons and Brass, were very rich from money found out West.

THE END.

Selected Bibliography

The Bibliography is divided into two parts, "Works Cited" and "Suggestions for Further Reading." The first part contains all primary and secondary works quoted or discussed in the Introduction or Headnotes. The second part is a selective list of materials that will be of use to the student wishing to know more about the history and cultural context of the dime Western. It is subdivided into four broad categories: "Bibliographies, Reference Works, and Collections," "The West: History and Myth," "The West and the Western," and "Popular Culture and Mass Culture: Theory and History."

WORKS CITED

Allen, Ethan. *A Narrative of Col. Ethan Allen's Captivity.* 1779. 4th ed., with notes. Burlington (VT): C. Goodrich, 1846.

Badger, Joseph. *Joaquin, the Saddle King. A Romance of Murieta's First Fight.* New York: Beadle and Adams, 1881.

Bird, Robert Montgomery. *Nick of the Woods.* 1837. New York: NCUP, 1967.

Bishop, W. H. "Story-Paper Literature." *Atlantic* 44 (Sept. 1879): 383–93.

Bold, Christine. *Selling the Wild West: Popular Western Fiction, 1860–1960.* Bloomington: Indiana UP, 1987.

Boorstin, Daniel J. *The Americans: The Democratic Experience*. New York: Vintage, 1974.

Boucicault, Dion. *The Poor of New York*. New York: S. French, 1857.

Buntline, Ned. (Edward Z. C. Judson.) *Buffalo Bill*. New York: Ogilvie, 1886.

———. *The Mysteries and Miseries of New York: A Story of Real Life*. New York: E. Z. C. Judson, 1848.

———. *The Red Revenger; or, the Pirate King of the Floridas: a Romance of the Gulf and its Islands*. Boston: F. Gleason, 1847.

Byron, Lord. *Don Juan*. 1819–24. New York: Penguin, 1973.

Catlin, George. *Letters and Notes on the Manners, Customs, and Condition of the North American Indians*. Philadelphia, 1859.

Comstock, Anthony. *Traps for the Young*. 1882. Cambridge: Harvard UP, 1967.

Cooper, James Fenimore. *The Leatherstocking Tales*. 2 vols. New York: Library of America, 1985.

Crane, Stephen. *Prose and Poetry*. Ed. J. C. Levenson. New York: Library of America, 1984.

Denning, Michael. *Mechanic Accents: Dime Novels and Working-Class Culture in America*. New York: Verso, 1987.

Ellis, Edward. *Bill Biddon, Trapper; or, Life in the North-west*. New York: Beadle, 1860.

———. *Nathan Todd; or, The Fate of the Sioux' Captive*. New York: Beadle, 1861.

———. *Dewey and Other Naval Commanders*. New York: Havendon, 1899.

———. *Ecclectic Primary History of the United States*. New York: American Book, 1884.

———. *A History of Our Country*. Boston: Lee and Shephard, 1898.

———. *The People's Standard History of the United States, from the Landing of the Norsmen to the Present Time*. 5 vols. New York: Woodfall, 1896–97.

———. *The Steam Man of the Prairies*. New York: American Novel, 1869. Rpt. as *The Huge Hunter; or, The Steam Man of the Prairies*. New York: Beadle and Adams, 1870.

———. *The Youth's History of the United States, from the Discovery of America by the Northmen, to the Present Time*. 4 vols. New York: Cassell, 1887–89.

——— and Charles F. Harne. *The Story of the Greatest Nations, from the Dawn of History to the Twentieth Century; a Comprehensive History*. 10 vols. New York: Niglutsch, 1906.

——— and Augustus R. Keller, eds. *History of the German People, from the First Authentic Annals to the Present Time*. New York: International Historical Society, 1916.

Enton, Harry. *Frank Reade and his Steam Man of the Plains.* New York: Frank Tousey, 1876.

Everett, William. "Beadle's Dime Books." *North American Review* 24 (1864): 303–09.

Filson, John. *The Discovery, Settlement, and Present State of Kentucke.* Wilmington (Del.), 1784. University Microfilms, American Culture series no. 200.

Garland, Hamlin. *Crumbling Idols.* 1894. Ann Arbor: Edwards Bros., 1952.

Harte, Bret. *Selected Stories and Sketches.* Ed. David Wyatt. New York: Oxford UP, 1995.

Harvey, Charles M. "The Dime Novel in American Life." *Atlantic* 100 (July 1907): 37–45.

Ingraham, Prentiss. *Adventures of Buffalo Bill from Boyhood to Manhood.* New York: Beadle and Adams, 1881.

Jencks, Geroge C. "Dime Novel Makers." *The Bookman* 20 (Oct. 1904): 108–14.

Johannsen, Albert. *The House of Beadle and Adams and Its Dime and Nickel Novels. The Story of a Vanished Literature.* 2 vols. Norman: U of Oklahoma P, 1950.

Leithead, Edward J. "Buffalo Bill Item." *Dime Novel Roundup* 61 (April 15, 1938): 1–2.

Longfellow, Henry Wadsworth. "The Song of Hiawatha." *The Complete Poetical Works of Henry Wadsworth Longfellow.* Boston: Houghton, 1893, 113–64.

Marrant, John. *A Narrative of the Lord's Wonderful Dealings with John Marrant, a Black, Taken Down from his Own Relation, arranged, corrected and published, By the Rev. Mr. Aldridge.* Rpt. in *Held Captive by Natives: Selected Narratives, 1642–1836.* Rev. ed. Ed. Richard Van Der Beets. Knoxville: U of Tennessee P, 1994, 177–201.

Monaghan, Jay. *The Great Rascal: The Life and Adventures of Ned Buntline.* Boston: Little, 1952.

O'Sullivan, J. L. "Annexation." *The United States Magazine, and Democratic Review* 17 (1845): 5–10.

Parkman, Francis. *The Conspiracy of Pontiac and the Indian War after the Conquest of Canada.* 2 vols. Lincoln: U of Nebraska P, 1994.

———. *The Oregon Trail.* 1847. New York: Viking Penguin, 1985.

Pearson, Edmund. *Dime Novels; or, Following an Old Trail in Popular Literature.* Boston: Little, 1929.

Radway, Janice A. *Reading the Romance: Women, Patriarchy and Popular Literature.* Chapel Hill: U of North Carolina P, 1984.

Reid, Mayne. *The White Squaw.* New York: Beadle and Adams, 1868.

Rogin, Michael. *Ronald Reagan, the Movie, and Other Episodes in Political Demonology*. Berkeley: U of California P, 1987.

Roosevelt, Theodore. *The Winning of the West*. 6 vols. 1889–1896. New York: Putnam, 1900.

———. *The Strenuous Life: Essays and Addresses*. New York: Century Co., 1901.

Rowlandson, Mary. *The Soveraignty and Goodness of God, Together with the Faithfulness of His Promises Displayed; Being a Narrative of the Captivity and Restauration of Mrs. Mary Rowlandson*. 1676. Rpt. in *Held Captive by Natives: Selected Narratives, 1642–1836*. Rev. ed. Ed. Richard Van Der Beets. Knoxville: U of Tennessee P, 1994, 41–90.

Scott, Walter. *Rob Roy*. 1817. New York: Viking Penguin, 1995.

———. *Waverly*. 1814. New York: Viking Penguin, 1981.

Simms, William Gilmore. *The Yemassee. A Romance of Carolina*. 1835. New York: NCUP, 1964.

Slotkin, Richard. *Gunfighter Nation: The Myth of the Frontier in Twentieth-Century America*. New York: Harper, 1992.

Stern, Madeleine B. "Ann S. Stephens: Author of the First Beadle Dime Novel, 1860." *Bulletin of the New York Public Library* 64 (1960): 303–22.

Stevens, D. W. [Musick, John Roy.] *The James Boys and the Ku Klux Klan*. New York: Frank Tousey, 1881.

Terrible Ted. Vitagraph. 1907.

Thoreau, Henry. *A Week on the Concord and Merrimack Rivers*. 1849. New York: Penguin, 1997.

Turner, Frederick Jackson. "The Significance of the Frontier in American History." 1893. Rpt. in *Rereading Frederick Jackson Turner*. Ed. John Mack Faragher. New York: Holt, 1994.

Veblen, Thorstein. *The Theory of Business Enterprise*. 1904. New York: Scribner's, 1927.

Wheeler, Edward. *Deadwood Dick on Deck; or, Calamity Jane, the Heroine of Whoop-Up. A Story of Dakota*. New York: Beadle and Adams, 1878.

———. *Deadwood Dick's Claim; or, The Fairy Face of Faro Flats*. New York: Beadle and Adams, 1884.

———. *A Game of Gold; or, Deadwood Dick's Big Strike*. New York: Beadle and Adams, 1878. Rpt. Cleveland: Arthur Westbrook, 1899.

———. *Hurricane Nell, the Girl Dead-Shot; or, the Queen of the Saddle and Lasso*. New York: Frank Starr, 1877.

———. *Wild Ivan, The Boy Claude Duval*. New York: Beadle and Adams, 1878. Rpt. Cleveland: Arthur Westbrook, 1899.

Wister, Owen. *The Virginian: A Horseman of the Plains*. New York: Macmillan, 1902.

Zboray, Ronald J. "Antebellum Reading and the Ironies of Technological Innovation." *Reading in America: Literature and Social
History.* Ed. Cathy N. Davidson. Baltimore: Johns Hopkins UP,
1989.

SUGGESTIONS FOR FURTHER READING

Bibliographies, Reference Works, and Collections

Bragin, Charles. *Bibliography: Dime Novels 1860–1964.* Brooklyn:
Charles Bragin, 1964.
Etulain, Richard W., and N. Jill Howard. *A Bibliographic Guide to
the Study of Western American Literature.* Albuquerque: U of
New Mexico P, 1995.
Dime Novel Round-Up (1953–); originally *Reckless Ralph's Dime
Novel Round-Up* (1931–1953). [A journal devoted to the history
of dime and half-dime publications.]
Dime Novels, Escape Fiction of the Nineteenth Century. Ann Arbor:
University Microfilms Int'l, 1980. [A bound catalog of a seven-
unit index to microfilmed dime novels.]
Johannsen, Albert. *The House of Beadle and Adams and Its Dime
and Nickel Novels: The Story of a Vanished Literature.* 2 vols.
Norman: U of Oklahoma P, 1950.
———. *The Nickel Library.* Fall River, MA: Edward T. Le Blan,
1959.
Lamar, Howard R. *The Reader's Encyclopedia of the American
West.* New York: Crowell, 1977.
The Oxford History of the American West. New York: Oxford UP,
1994.
Stern, Madeleine B. *Imprints on History: Book Publishers and Amer-
ican Frontiers.* Bloomington: Indiana UP, 1956.
———, ed. *Publishers for Mass Entertainment in Nineteenth Century
America.* Boston: G. K. Hall, 1980.
Tebbel, John. *A History of Book Publishing in the United States.*
4 vols. New York: Bowker, 1981.
Tuska, Jon, and Vicki Piekarski, eds. *Encyclopedia of Frontier and
Western Fiction.* New York: McGraw-Hill, 1983.

Many libraries hold dime novels in their special collections. The
following provide particularly important resources:

University of Arkansas Library (Fayetteville)
Bowling Green State University Library (Bowling Green, Ohio)
Brandeis University, Goldfarb Library (Waltham, MA)

Huntington Library (San Marino, California)
Library of Congress (Washington, D.C.)
New Mexico State University Library (Las Cruces)
New York Public Library
New York University, Elmer Holmes Bobst Library
Northern Illinois University, Founders Memorial Library
   (De Kalb)
Oberlin College Library (Oberlin, Ohio)
University of Minnesota Libraries, George H. Hess Collection
   (St. Paul)
University of Rochester, Rush Rhees Library (Rochester, NY)
University of South Florida (Tampa)
Yale University Libraries (New Haven, CT)

The West: History and Myth

Billington, Ray Allen, and Martin Ridge. *Western Expansion: A History of the American Frontier.* 5th ed. New York: Macmillan, 1992.

Boorstin, Daniel J. *The Americans: The Democratic Experience.* New York: Vintage, 1974.

Bowman, Isaiah. *The Pioneer Fringe.* New York: American Geographical Society, 1931.

Cronon, William, George Miles, and Jay Gitlin, eds. *Under an Open Sky: Rethinking America's Western Past.* New York: Norton, 1992.

Drinnon, Richard. *Facing West: The Metaphysics of Indian-Hating and Empire Building.* New York: NAL, 1980.

Faragher, John Mack. *Daniel Boone: The Life and Legend of an American Pioneer.* New York: Holt, 1992.

Kolodny, Annette. *The Land Before Her: Fantasy and Experience of the American Frontiers, 1630–1860.* Chapel Hill: U of North Carolina P, 1984.

———. *The Lay of the Land: Metaphor as Experience and History in American Life and Letters.* Chapel Hill: U of North Carolina P, 1975.

Limerick, Patricia Nelson, Clyde A. Milner III, and Charles E. Rankin, eds. *Trails: Toward a New Western History.* Lawrence: UP of Kansas, 1991.

McGrath, Roger D. *Gunfighters, Highwaymen and Vigilantes: Violence on the Frontier.* Berkeley: U of California P, 1984.

Marx, Leo. *The Machine in the Garden: Technology and the Pastoral Ideal in America.* New York: Oxford UP, 1964.

Nash, Gerald. *Creating the West: Historical Interpretations, 1890–1990.* Albuquerque: U of New Mexico P, 1991.

Nash, Roderick. *Wilderness and the American Mind.* New Haven: Yale UP, 1967.

Noble, David. *Historians Against History: The Frontier Thesis and the National Covenant in American Historical Writing Since 1830.* Minneapolis: U of Minnesota P, 1965.

Pascoe, Peggy. *Relations of Rescue: The Search for Female Moral Authority in the American West, 1874–1939.* New York: Oxford UP, 1990.

Pearce, Roy Harvey. *The Savages of America: A Study of the Indian and the Idea of Civilization.* Rev. ed. Baltimore: Johns Hopkins UP, 1965.

Rogin, Michael. *Ronald Reagan, the Movie, and Other Episodes in Political Demonology.* Berkeley: U of California P, 1987.

Roosevelt, Theodore. *The Winning of the West: Selections.* Ed. Harvey Wish. Magnolia (MA): Peter Smith, 1990.

Settle, William A., Jr. *Jesse James Was His Name; or, Fact and Fiction Concerning the Careers of the Notorious James Brothers of Missouri.* Columbia: U of Missouri P, 1966.

Smith-Rosenberg, Carroll. *Disorderly Conduct: Visions of Gender in Victorian America.* New York: Oxford UP, 1985.

Turner, Frederick Jackson. *Rereading Frederick Jackson Turner: "The Significance of the Frontier in American History" and Other Essays.* Ed. John Mack Faragher. New York: Holt, 1994.

Utley, Robert M., and Wilcomb E. Washburn. *Indian Wars.* Boston: Houghton, 1977.

Weber, David J. *The Spanish Frontier in North America.* New Haven: Yale UP, 1992.

White, Richard. *"It's Your Misfortune and None of My Own": A New History of the American West.* Norman: U of Oklahoma P, 1991.

Worster, Donald. *Under Western Skies: Nature and History in the American West.* New York: Oxford UP, 1992.

The West and the Western

Aquila, Richard, ed. *Wanted Dead or Alive: The American West in Popular Culture.* Champaign: U of Illinois P, 1996.

Bishop, W. H. "Story-Paper Literature." *Atlantic Monthly* 44 (Sept. 1879): 383–93.

Bold, Christine. *Selling the Wild West: Popular Fiction, 1860–1960.* Bloomington: Indiana UP, 1987.

Cawelti, John G. *The Six-Gun Mystique.* Bowling Green: Bowling Green U Popular P, 1971.

Comstock, Anthony. *Traps for the Young*. 1883. Rpt., ed. Robert Bremmer. Cambridge: Belknap-Harvard UP, 1967.

Curti, Merle. "Dime Novels and the American Tradition." *Yale Review* 26 (Summer 1937): 761–78.

Everett, William. "Dime Books." *North American Review* 99 (July 1864): 303–9.

Fiedler, Leslie. *Return of the Vanishing American*. New York: Stein and Day, 1968.

Grant, Barry Keith. *Film Genre Reader*. Austin: U of Texas P, 1986.

Harvey, Charles M. "The Dime Novel in American Life." *Atlantic Monthly* 100 (July 1907): 37–45.

Jones, Daryl. *The Dime Novel Western*. Bowling Green: Bowling Green U Popular P, 1978.

MacDonald, J. Fred. *Who Shot the Sheriff? The Rise and Fall of the Television Western*. New York: Praeger, 1987.

Noel, Mary. *Villains Galore . . . The Heyday of the Popular Story Weekly*. New York: Macmillan, 1954.

Pearson, Edmund. *Dime Novels; or, Following an Old Trail in Popular Literature*. 1929. Port Washington, NY: Kennikat P, 1968.

Reynolds, Quentin. *The Fiction Factory; or, From Pulp Row to Quality Street*. New York: Random House, 1955.

Slotkin, Richard. *The Fatal Environment: The Myth of the Frontier in the Age of Industrialization, 1800–1890*. Middletown: Wesleyan UP, 1985.

———. *Gunfighter Nation: The Myth of the Frontier in Twentieth-Century America*. New York: Harper, 1992.

Smith, Henry Nash. *Virgin Land: The American West as Symbol and Myth*. Cambridge: Harvard UP, 1950.

Stern, Madeleine B. "Ann B. Stephens: Author of the First Beadle Dime Novel, 1860." *Bulletin of the New York Public Library* (1960): 303–22.

Tompkins, Jane. *West of Everything: The Inner Life of Westerns*. New York: Oxford UP, 1992.

White, Edward G. *The Eastern Establishment and the Western Experience: The West of Frederic Remington, Theodore Roosevelt, and Owen Wister*. New Haven: Yale UP, 1968.

Wright, Will. *Six-Guns and Society: A Structural Study of the Western*. Berkeley: U of California P, 1975.

Popular Culture and Mass Culture: Theory and History

Barthes, Roland. *Mythologies*. Trans. Annette Lavers. New York: Hill & Wang, 1972.

Benjamin, Walter. "The Work of Art in the Age of Mechanical Reproduction." *Illuminations*. Trans. Harry Zohn. New York: Schocken, 1969.

Bennett, Tony, ed. *Popular Fiction: Technology, Ideology, Production, Reading*. New York: Routledge, 1990.

Bordwell, David, Janet Staiger, and Kristin Thompson. *The Classical Hollywood Cinema: Film Style and Mode of Production*. New York: Routledge, 1985.

Cawelti, John G. *Adventure, Mystery, and Romance: Formula Stories as Art and Popular Culture*. Chicago: U of Chicago P, 1976.

Davis, Cathy, ed. *Reading in America: Literature and Social History*. Baltimore: Johns Hopkins UP, 1989.

Davis, Kenneth C. *Two Bit Culture: The Paperbacking of America*. Boston: Houghton, 1984.

Denning, Michael. *Mechanic Accents: Dime Novels and Working-Class Culture in America*. New York: Verso, 1987.

Grossberg, Lawrence, Cary Nelson, and Paul Treichler, eds. *Cultural Studies*. New York: Routledge, 1992.

Haltunnen, Karen. *Confidence Men and Painted Women: A Study of Middle-Class Culture in America, 1830–1870*. New Haven: Yale UP, 1982.

Harris, Neil. *Humbug! The Art of P. T. Barnum*. Boston: Little, 1973.

Hobsbawm, Eric. *Bandits*. New York: Pantheon, 1981.

Horkheimer, Max, and Theodor Adorno. *Dialectic of Enlightenment*. 1944. New York: Seabury Press, 1972.

Jameson, Frederic. "Reification and Utopia in Mass Culture." *Signatures of the Visible*. New York: Routledge, 1990, 9–34.

Kasson, John F. *Amusing the Million: Coney Island at the Turn of the Century*. New York: Hill, 1978.

Lowenthal, Leo. *Literature, Popular Culture and Society*. Englewood Cliffs: Prentice, 1961.

Marx, Karl. "The Eighteenth Brumaire of Louis Bonaparte." 1852. *Karl Marx and Frederick Engels, Selected Works*. New York: International, 1968, 95–179.

Modleski, Tania, ed. *Studies in Entertainment: Critical Approaches to Mass Culture*. Bloomington: Indiana UP, 1986.

Moretti, Franco. *Signs Taken for Wonders: Essays in the Sociology of Forms*. London: Verso, 1983.

Nye, Russel B. *The Unembarrassed Muse: The Popular Arts in America*. New York: The Dial Press, 1970.

Propp, Vladimir. *Morphology of the Folktale*. Austin: U of Texas P, 1970.

Radway, Janice. *Reading the Romance: Women, Patriarchy and Popular Literature*. Chapel Hill: U of North Carolina P, 1984.

Ross, Andrew. *No Respect: Intellectuals and Popular Culture.* New York: Routledge, 1989.

Smith, Henry Nash, ed. *Popular Culture and Industrialism.* Garden City: Doubleday-Anchor, 1967.

Williams, Raymond. *The Sociology of Culture.* New York: Schocken, 1982.